NIGERIA:
Modernization and the Politics of Communalism

NIGERIA:

Modernization and the Politics

of Communalism

EDITED BY

ROBERT MELSON and *HOWARD WOLPE*

Michigan State University Press

1971

Copyright © *1971*
Michigan State University Press
Library of Congress Catalog Card Number: 72–168377
Standard Book Number: 87013–161–3
MANUFACTURED IN THE UNITED STATES OF AMERICA

TO

Gail AND *Nina*

PREFACE

The Nigerian/Biafran war was not unique. It was only too representative of countless similar conflicts which have led to massacres in Turkish Armenia, Eastern Europe, India/Pakistan, Indonesia, and other parts of Africa, and which today pose no less a threat to the existence of peoples everywhere. Intergroup conflicts within culturally plural nation-states are endemic to modern times. Whether our focus be the Western hemisphere or the Eastern, industrialized nations such as Canada and the United States or developing nations such as Kenya and India, the most pressing political question is the same: how to reconcile the demands of communal groups for security and autonomy with the requirements of the nation-state for order and unity. Probably no conflicts are more emotionally laden or carry greater destructive potential than those between communal antagonists, for communal conflicts raise to the fore the fundamental issues of identity and survival. This volume attempts to come to terms with the problem of communal conflict by exploring the political experience of Nigeria, one country in which the destructive potentialities inherent in all communal confrontations were tragically realized.

Our argument, spelled out more fully in Chapter 1, is that much contemporary communal conflict is being waged not by traditional entities, but by communities formed in the crucible of mobilization and competition. Moreover, political conflict associated with cultural pluralism is due not to the nature of pluralism or diversity in itself, but to a process of inhumane and uncontrolled modernization which pits one communal group against another in a frantic search for wealth, status, power and security. In short, as we state in the introduction, it is probably more accurate to suggest that conflict produces "tribalism" than to argue that "tribalism" is the cause of conflict.

The twenty-five papers of this volume, eight of which are

original contributions, are organized into five sections. The introductory section consists of two chapters. The first of these elaborates our theoretical framework, while the second, by Richard L. Sklar, places the Nigerian/biafran conflict into a historical and political perspective. The next three sections— Competitive Communalism, Institutional Communalism, and Communal Transformation and Compartmentalization— group several contributions in terms of the theoretical themes identified in Chapter 1. Finally, the concluding chapters by James O'Connell and the editors address themselves to certain of the policy implications of the Nigerian/Biafran struggle.

The contributions to this volume stand on their own and do not fall neatly into any set of imposed categories. In selecting and arranging these papers, we have attempted to highlight three analytically distinguishable factors which underpin communalism: the competition for scarce goods, the institutional framework, and the changing nature of cultural identity. We felt this theoretical approach to be preferable to a chronologically ordered presentation or to one organized in terms of disciplinary contributions, in that it helps to identify and clarify more precisely the key dimensions of communal conflict. It is only by understanding the fundamental causes of communalism that we can hope to control its destructive force.

In preparing this volume we received support from a number of institutions, and help and suggestions from many individuals for which we are grateful. Thanks are due the Midwest Universities Consortium for International Activities, the Departments of Political Science at Michigan State University and Western Michigan University, the African Studies Center at Michigan State University, the College of Arts and Sciences at Western Michigan University, and the Center for Advanced Study at the University of Illinois. Among our friends and fellow scholars, we would like to express our appreciation, first of all, to our contributors. In addition, we are especially indebted to David B. Abernethy, Cathy Czanowski, Carl K. Eicher, Carl Liedholm, David Myers, Richard Niehoff, John Paden, Lucian W. Pye, Platon Rigos, Richard L. Sklar, Ronald Stockton, and Crawford Young. Finally, we are most appreciative of the assistance extended us by Robert Solo, organizer of the interdisciplinary workshops held at Michigan State University during the period 1968–70.

CONTENTS

NIGERIA:
Modernization and the Politics of Communalism

CHAPTER 1

Modernization and the Politics of Communalism: A Theoretical Perspective[1]

ROBERT MELSON *and* HOWARD WOLPE

It has been said that technological and economic development lead ultimately to the decline of communal conflict, and that the emergence of new kinds of socio-economic roles and identities undercuts the organizational bases upon which communal (that is, "racial," "ethnic," "religious," or "tribal") politics rests. In the past decade, several scholars working in culturally plural societies have challenged this conventional view. They have suggested that communalism may in fact be a persistent feature of social change, and that the dichotomous tradition-modernity models which have often guided our empirical investigations have obscured this theoretical alternative and thereby produced false expectations concerning the direction of change.[2] This paper attempts to synthesize the various elements of this emerging theoretical perspective through the formulation of several propositions which link modernization to communalism. While our discussion will draw primarily upon the Nigerian experience for illustrative material, the propositions are intended to be applicable across societies.

"Communalism," in this paper, refers to the political assertiveness of groups which have three distinguishing character-

Reprinted with minor revisions from *The American Political Science Review, LXIV,* 4 (December 1970), pp. 1112–1130. Copyright © 1970 by *The American Political Science Review.* Reprinted by permission of the publisher.

istics: first, their membership is comprised of persons who share in a common culture and identity and, to use Karl Deutsch's term, a "complementarity of communication;"[3] second, they encompass the full range of demographic (age and sex) divisions within the wider society and provide "for a network of groups and institutions extending throughout the individual's entire life cycle;"[4] and, third, like the wider society in which they exist, they tend to be differentiated by wealth, status, and power. Communal demands and conflict are politically distinctive in that they may reflect a desire for separation and may threaten to alter the political boundaries of the wider society.[5] The Nigerian experience, it will be contended, runs counter to the view that communal "particularism" or "communalism" is an historical anachronism, ultimately destined to be submerged by the "universalistic" tidal wave of modernity. An analysis of the Nigerian case suggests, rather, that modernization, far from destroying communalism, in time both reinforces communal conflict and creates the conditions for the formation of entirely new communal groups.

In these respects, the Nigerian case is by no means unique. The Nagas have not become Indians indistinguishable from other Indians, any more than Ibos and Yorubas and Tivs have become interchangeable Nigerians. Overseas Chinese and Javanese have not become Indonesians. Nor have French Canadians and Black Americans "melted" into their respective wider societies. In each of these cases, the contemporary pattern of communal formation and conflict may be seen as an immediate by-product of the modernization process.

The Nigerian case is a particularly appropriate illustration of the relationship between communal conflict and modernization, in that on most social and economic indices, Nigeria showed signs of relatively rapid growth in comparison to other developing nations subject to comparable ecological and historical conditions.[6] Accompanying these developments was a high rate of social mobilization and a significant expansion of the traditional frameworks of empathy and social identification. It was precisely Nigeria's success in these economic and social spheres which produced the constantly optimistic appraisals of the course of Nigerian development. But economic and social success were not matched in the political sphere and, in retrospect, it is clear that Nigeria's very economic and social progress sowed the seeds of the nation's political crisis. That crisis, it will be argued, is traceable neither to poverty nor, as some popular accounts would have it, to the simple fact of cultural diversity and the reassertion of traditional tribal antagonisms. On the one hand, the group frustrations which underlie communal antagonisms are as much a reflection of change and the blocking of new aspirations as they are of impoverishment. On the other hand, inter-group conflict is seldom a product of simple cultural diversity and, in the Nigerian case, there is little that is "traditional" about the contemporary pattern of political divisions. On the contrary, Nigeria's political crisis is traceable directly to the widening of social horizons and to the process of modernization at work within the national boundaries.

Social Mobilization and Communal Conflict

The propositions discussed in this chapter attempt to unravel the complicated web of factors which link communalism with modernization. The fourteen propositions listed below focus upon four themes: (1) competitive communalism; (2) institutional communalism; (3) communal transformation; and (4) communal compartmentalization. Following their listing, we turn to a more detailed analysis of each of these themes.

I.   *Competitive Communalism*
    1.   In a culturally plural society, the competition engendered by social mobilization will tend to be defined in communal terms.
    2.   Differential rates of mobilization among communal groups exacerbate communal conflict by multiplying coincident social cleavages.
    3.   In the short term, the reduction of communal imbalances in wealth, status or power may serve to intensify communal antagonisms.
II. *Institutional Communalism*
    4.   Social or geographical segregation of communal groups may lessen communal conflict if it reflects a mutually agreed upon reduction or elimi-

nation of competitive communal interaction; however, if mobilized and competitive communal groups desire, or are forced, to interact within the same system of social stratification, segregation may intensify communal conflict.

5. The formation of communal associations, in response to inter-communal contact and competition, furthers communal conflict.

6. The subordination of political institutions to the interests of particular communal groups tends to reinforce and politicize communal conflict.

7. The greater the number of equally powerful communal groups, the greater the likelihood that political institutions will be able to retain their coherence and impartiality vis-à-vis communal competitors.

8. Political institutions which encourage the participation of the masses in the recruitment of leaders tend to further politicize and intensify communal conflict.

III. *Communal Transformation*

9. In an environment of social mobilization and communal competition, communal groups will tend to fuse or to expand their traditional boundaries to include groups and individuals with whom they can identify and who might prove useful allies during inter-group conflict.

10. Mobilization and competition lead also to the increasing internal differentiation of communal categories along socio-economic and ideological lines.

11. Accompanying communal fusion and expansion is the deparochialization of traditional group ties and perspectives.

12. Communal transformation entails the multiplication rather than the substitution of social identities.

IV. *Communal Compartmentalization*

13. Since politically salient identities are situationally specific, communal and non-communal polit-

            ical orientations may well co-exist within the same person.

14.   Since communal and non-communal political orientations may co-exist within individuals, each activated in different social contexts, modernization need not eliminate communal differentiation and conflict.

I. Competitive Communalism

Proposition 1. In a culturally plural society, the competition engendered by social mobilization will tend to be defined in communal terms.

A convenient starting point of this analysis of modernization and communal conflict is the concept of "social mobilization," defined by Karl Deutsch as "the process in which major clusters of old social, economic and psychological commitments are eroded or broken and people become available for new patterns of socialization and behavior."[7] Social mobilization, in our view, generates the new kinds of social competition and new kinds of scarcity which underlie contemporary communal antagonisms.

The linked processes of change subsumed within the concept of social mobilization—such as urbanization, the introduction of mass education, the diffusion of the mass media, the development of increasingly efficient and productive commercial networks—alter the human landscape in two significant respects. First, "social mobilization" means the reorientation of a large number of citizens to a new system of rewards and paths to rewards in all spheres of society. People's aspirations and expectations change as they are mobilized into the modernizing economy and polity. They come to want, and to demand, more—more goods, more recognition, more power. Significantly, too, the orientation of the mobilized to a common set of rewards and paths to rewards means, in effect, that many people come to desire precisely the same things. Men enter into conflict not because they are different but because they are essentially the same. It is by making men "more alike," in the sense of possessing the same wants, that modernization tends to promote conflict.

Second, "social mobilization" means not only the emergence of a new set of motivating values and career paths but also that the demand for scarce resources cannot keep up with their supply. Nowhere is the reality of "modern scarcity" experienced more intensely than in the cities, wherein the rate of population growth almost invariably exceeds the rate of economic development and the availability of new jobs. It is here that the various elements of the mobilized population are thrown into direct, and very personal, competition with one another—for positions within governmental agencies and commercial concerns, for the control of local markets, for admission to crowded schools, for induction into the army and for control of political parties. It is not surprising, therefore, that many of the competitors perceive themselves as involved in a "zero-sum game," in which one man's failure is attributable to another man's success. While this perception may or may not be accurate in any given instance, the perception itself leads to the increasing competitiveness of the modern sector.

It is against this backdrop of social mobilization and a highly competitive modern sector that communal conflict in culturally plural societies must be understood.[8] On the one hand, it is the competitor within the modern sphere who feels the insecurities of change most strongly and who seeks the communal shelter of "tribalism."[9] The tradition-bound rural villager, though he may indeed be caught up in the competitive struggle of his urban-based kinsman, by contrast experiences contemporary tribalism only vicariously and at second hand. On the other hand, men become tribalists not only out of insecurity but also out of the many opportunities created by social mobilization in a communal milieu. In culturally plural societies, citizens tend to perceive their competitive world through a communal prism and to be responsive to communal appeals. Communalism therefore becomes a matter of opportunism. It matters not that, in any given competition, communal criteria are inappropriate to the determination of the outcome and may not in fact have been operative. What is important is that the personal fortunes of individuals are generally believed to depend on their communal origins and connections. This being the case, individuals plan and organize accordingly. Thus, the aspirant Nigerian politician seeks to mobilize his "tribal un-ion" behind his candidacy; at the same time, his townspeople—those resident in their home community as well as those resident in the alien city—view his candidacy as an expression of their group aspirations and his election as an indicator of group recognition and power. (Conversely, the members of other communal groups view his candidacy as a threat to their own group aspirations and vested interests.) Similarly, the job applicant or prospective schoolboy turns to his kinsmen for assistance, while his benefactors view the job or financial assistance they extend as a communal investment to be reciprocated by the beneficiary. In short, the common expectation of the primacy of communal criteria produces the self-fulfilling prophecy of communally-oriented competitive strategies in virtually all walks of life.

> *Proposition 2.* Differential rates of mobilization among communal groups exacerbate communal conflict by multi-plying coincident social cleavages.

The various communal groups which comprise a culturally plural nation-state are seldom mobilized at the same rate, with the consequence that the members of the more slowly mobil-ized communities are placed at a disadvantage in the competi-tion for the national rewards of wealth, status and power. This section explores, first, the factors underlying differential mobilization and second, the implications of differential mobil-ization for the character of communal conflict.

There are at least three analytically distinguishable factors which work to create inter-group differentials in the develop-mental process—the nature of Western contact, environmental opportunities and cultural predispositions. While it is difficult to assign weights denoting the relative significance of each, it is apparent that all are involved in determining the timing and pace of social mobilization. First, variations in the timing, in-tensity and character of Western contact yield group variations in the rate of urbanization, the spread of literacy, the diffusion of the mass media, the acculturation of Western norms and techniques. In Nigeria, for example, accidents of history and geographical location have been especially important in pro-

ducing very different kinds of contact experiences and resultant rates of social change as between North and South. Thus,
the exclusion of missionaries and hence Western schools from
the Islamic north was a crucial factor accounting for the subsequent domination by Southerners of both administrative and
technical occupations. Similarly, coastal and riverain communities, which were relatively more accessible to the coloniz-
ing agents, tended to have contact with the West at an earlier
date than communities situated in rural hinterlands, and
tended often to be subject to a relatively more intensive and
qualitatively quite different acculturative experience.

Second, variations in the kinds of environmental opportunities available to different communities have also contributed to
variations in the rates of social mobilization. Such variables as
the availability of mineral resources, the fertility of the soils,
the export value of indigenous agricultural commodities, the
proximity of a transportation crossroads—all condition the
pace of social change and the economic potentialities of a given
community. Just as Western Nigerian economic growth in the
post-war period was at least partially attributable to the profitability of the indigenous cash crop of cocoa, so Northern
Nigeria's relative poverty and lower developmental rates were
partially attributable to the harsh economic reality that
groundnuts were a less valuable agricultural commodity.[10]
More recently, the discovery of significant petroleum deposits
in Eastern and Mid-Western Nigeria has meant that the developmental potential of this sector has become very large indeed.
Yet another example of environmental influences on social
mobilization is that of land shortage in densely populated Iboland contributing to the high out-migration of Ibos to Nigeria's
urban centers. As a result of this out-migration, Ibos came
to constitute the principal stranger populations of Northern
and Western cities, with many individual Ibos performing
highly visible commercial, administrative and technical functions.

Finally, variations in the cultural predispositions of different
groups produce variations in their response to Western contact
and to existing environmental opportunities. As the work of
McClelland, Hagen, LeVine, Young and Ottenberg suggests,
some cultural groups appear to be more predisposed than oth-

ers to compete successfully for the rewards of modernization.[11] Thus, in the Nigerian case, it has been suggested that relatively rapid rates of mobilization and development in Eastern Nigeria are traceable, in part, to the receptivity to change on the part of the Ibos and to the relatively high incidence of "need achievers" to be found within this cultural group.[12]

The consequence of communal groups being mobilized at different rates is that some peoples gain a head start in the competition for the scarce rewards of modernity. New socio-economic categories therefore tend to coincide with, rather than intersect, communal boundaries with the consequence that the modern status system comes to be organized along communal lines. There is, consequently, little to ameliorate the intensity of communal confrontations. The fewer the cross-cutting socio-economic linkages, the more naked such confrontations and the greater the likelihood of secessionist and other movements of communal nationalism.

Thus, in the Nigerian case, a Northern Hausa—because of differential mobilization—came to be not only culturally dissimilar from an Eastern Ibo; he came also to be distinguished by his Islamic religion (as contrasted with the Christianity of the Ibo), his relative poverty, and his relative educational backwardness. In short, the lines of cleavage as between Hausa and Ibo all coincided. As a result, conflict of any sort—whether over jobs, markets or political office—threatened an all-out communal struggle.

Differential mobilization in Nigeria widened the socio-political cleavages not only between the country's major nationality groups but also between majority and minority communal groups within each administrative region and even between sub-groups of a single nationality. Thus, differential rates of educational expansion and economic growth in Eastern Nigeria heightened the previously latent cleavage between the landlocked Owerri Ibo interior, on the one hand, and the more advantaged marginal Ibo (Onitsha, Oguta, Aro) riverain groups and non-Ibo (Ijaw, Ibibio, Efik) coastal communities, on the other.[13] In similar fashion, the commercially prosperous Lagos and Ijebu Yoruba came to be set off from the less advantaged Yoruba interior. Likewise, within Northern Nigeria, the non-Hausa speaking Middle Belt developed economically and educationally more rapidly than the upper North; and, within the upper North, those Emirates which played a significant role in the colonial administrative and commercial systems—such as Kano and Katsina—assumed preeminent positions in the modern stratification system.[14] In short, differential mobilization had the effect of creating sets of coinciding cleavages within as well as between the three dominant cultural core areas.[15]

> *Proposition 3.* In the short term, the reduction of communal imbalances in wealth, status or power may serve to intensify communal antagonisms.

While it seems clear that, given an environment of social mobilization, communal imbalances in wealth, status and power exacerbate communal tensions, it does not follow that progress toward the elimination of such imbalances will be accompanied by communal accommodation. It is true that inter-group equalization is a necessary condition for the emergence of cross-cutting socio-economic linkages. That does not mean, however, that the members of different communal groups will in fact perceive the commonality of their socio-economic interests or that, if they do perceive this commonality, they will act upon it. In the short term, at least, there are two factors which may link progress toward inter-group equalization with the intensification rather than the amelioration of communal antagonisms.

First, upward communal mobility normally leads to the alteration of reference groups on the part of the communal participants and, hence, to the alteration of their perceptions of their relative status vis-à-vis their communal competitors.[16] This is what appears to have been involved in the determination of the late-starting Ibos to "catch up" with—indeed, to surpass—Western Nigeria's Yorubas, a group with which the Ibos did not even interact in the pre-colonial period. In a very real sense, it is their equality rather than their inequality which is at the heart of contemporary Ibo/Yoruba communal conflict. In short, communal mobility, rather than producing a sense of competitive gain and satisfaction, may lead to a deepening sense of relative deprivation and communal insecurity. The actual intensity of these feelings of communal deprivation and insecurity will depend very largely upon the responsiveness of the wider society to the new communal assertiveness. The blocking of new communal aspirations to wealth, status and power will tend to intensify group frustrations and to radicalize political response.

Second, communal mobility may intensify communal dissatisfaction by producing increased impatience with the remaining imbalances. The closer the members of a formerly deprived group approach equality on one of the dimensions of wealth, status and power, the more intolerable becomes inequality on the other two dimensions. It is to this phenomenon that the "revolution of rising aspirations and frustrations" refers. This notion seems to fit more closely the American race experience, for example, than the simple observation that Black deprivation leads to Black militancy. It is seldom the very poorest who are the most militant.[17]

II. Institutional Communalism

To this point in our discussion, we have considered the relationship between social mobilization and communal conflict without reference to the institutional context in which these processes unfold. But this context is itself directly related to the nature and intensity of communal conflict. Institutions which divide groups from each other *at the same time as they encourage political competition and participation* can only exacerbate communal conflict. Of course, these separatist institutions (such as residential segregation and communal associations) are themselves a reflection of existing patterns of communal conflict. This reciprocity between institution and conflict comprises the subject matter of the next set of propositions.

Proposition 4. Social or geographical segregation of communal groups may lessen communal conflict if it reflects a mutually agreed upon reduction or elimination of competitive communal interaction; however, if mobilized and competitive communal groups desire, or are forced, to interact within the same system of social stratification, segregation may intensify communal conflict.

Some scholars have been tempted to conclude that social mobilization and, in particular, urbanization, entailing as they normally do complex functional inter-relationships between culturally diverse populations, would significantly contribute to the destruction of communal barriers and the creation of integrated and socially cohesive national communities. This view closely parallels the popular "melting pot" hypothesis of American folklore and sociology which asserts that inter-group contact in the United States has led to the "fusion" of these groups so as to produce a distinctive American national stock.

Such a view—whether applied to the developing African continent or to the economically prosperous United States—lacks secure empirical foundation. In the United States, for example, inter-group interaction, while producing a fairly high degree of *cultural* assimilation, has produced far less *structural* assimilation than is conventionally assumed. While most white Americans have been assimilated within the secondary institutions of the society, their primary group relationships remain highly segregated by nationality or religion, and ethnicity remains a persistent fact of political life. Insofar as race relations are concerned, structural assimilation has been almost non-existent—Blacks merely abandoning the segregation of the rural South for the segregation of the urban North—and in some cases even the trend toward cultural assimilation seems to have been reversed. In short, most Americans, despite their adherence to a common set of national norms, live out their private lives in fairly tight and often segregated communal compartments.[18]

Much the same may be said of the citizens of other culturally plural nation-states. In Nigeria, for example, while isolated instances of cultural and/or structural assimilation may be cited, most urban communities evolved segregated residential patterns, especially with regard to the "strangers" vis-à-vis the indigenous host population. The isolation of Ibos in the *Sabon Garis* of Northern Nigeria is the most dramatic example of this pattern of urban segregation. Segregated Hausa quarters were similarly to be found in the major towns of Eastern and Western Nigeria, and urban life was invariably compartmentalized according to communal categories.[19]

The relationship between communal segregation and communal conflict is more complicated than conventionally assumed. Segregation *per se* does not create or intensify communal conflict. On the contrary, to the extent that communal segregation reflects a mutually agreed upon reduction or elimination of competitive communal interaction, segregation means the reduction or elimination of sources of potential communal conflict. Indeed, history yields several examples of segregated communities living in peace. Whether in the *ante bellum* southern United States, in the religiously pluralistic Ottoman Empire, or in Nigeria's feudal North, segregation maintained inter-group peace while perserving mutually accepted notions of group privilege and status. Similarly, there are examples in which the separation of groups in conflict has led—as a result of a decline in competitive interaction—to a decline in the level of communal conflict. This would appear to be one implication, for example, of the fragmentation of the Austro-Hungarian Empire and of the partition of India into Moslem and Hindu states.

If, however, mobilized and competitive communal groups desire, or are forced, to interact within the same system of social stratification—as in the contemporary United States—segregation may intensify communal conflict. First, under these circumstances the effect of communal segregation is to preserve communal inequalities in wealth, status and power. In the abstract, segregation need not mean inequality; it can be, rather, a means of allowing communities a modicum of autonomy in their cultural and social life. In the modern world, however, segregation has meant more than just cultural and social autonomy; it has meant also unequal access to education, to the economy and to political power. It is by maintaining and promoting such inequalities that segregation has promoted communal conflict.

Second, in a competitive political system (see Proposition 8), the social and physical separation of communal groups encourages the development of communally-based political institutions and strategies. Thus, it is the geographical concentration —and separation—of Black Americans in urban areas which makes the drive for urban "Black Power" politically viable. It may be that, in the long run, separatist forms of "Black Power," which are themselves a product of segregation, will be able to achieve a breakthrough in the relative wealth, status and power of Blacks. But it should be noted that segregation also permits the political and economic isolation of the Black minority by the dominant white community, an isolation which might well have the effect of preserving communal inequalities.

Third, the geographical separation of communal groups means that territorial or residential interests come to coincide with communal interests. Consequently, the range of political issues which activate communal identities and hence communal conflict is widened. Thus, the siting of an industry or the allocation of social amenities (e.g., paved roads, medical centers, schools) may become the occasion for communal confrontation. This, in effect, is but a corollary of the proposition that coincident social cleavages operate to exacerbate communal conflict (Proposition 2).

Fourth, as Gordon Allport has observed, "Segregation markedly enhances the visibility of a group; it makes it seem larger and more menacing than it is."[20] So it was in the case of the Ibo strangers resident in Northern Nigeria. The conspicuousness Ibos possessed by virtue of their economic, technical and administrative pre-eminence was enlarged by their physical separation from the indigenous community. This segregation was partly self-imposed and partly the result of Northern exclusionary policies. Laws were passed, for example, specifically forbidding non-indigenes from acquiring local land. In some instances restrictions were placed upon Ibo commercial activity. The important point, however, is that whatever the causes of Ibo segregation might have been, their physical separation from the host community furthered the out-group stereotype of the Ibos as "clannish" and "concerned only with their own." In short, communal segregation was an essential ingredient of urban tensions and violence in Northern Nigeria.

Proposition 5. The formation of communal associations in response to inter-communal contact and competition tends to further communal conflict.

Throughout the developing world, scholars have noted the rise of what have come to be known as "communal associations" or "para-communities" in Asia, "improvement associations" or "tribal unions" in Africa. Such unions, associations and para-communities are a blend of both the cosmopolitan and the parochial. In much the same manner as the immigrant political machines of America's urban communities, the communal organizations of Asia and Africa provide certain badly needed social services. They tend to be future-oriented and concerned with achievement and social welfare not only in the cities, where most of their members live, but also in the rural hinterland, which remains an important reference point for many urban dwellers. By helping to promote loyalty to communal groups, communal associations reduce the discontinuities inherent in migration and rapid social change.[21]

The important point, however, is that as communal associations serve their respective constituents, increasingly large numbers of urban residents develop a vested interest in their communal identities and organizational affiliations. Moreover, it has become clear that some communal groups have more of what it takes to organize than do others, with the result that whole occupational categories come to be monopolized by particular associations and their members. For these reasons, communal associations tend to stoke the engine of differential social mobilization and its attendant communal conflict.

The examples of communal organization in Nigeria are legion. The Ibos and Ibibios of Eastern Nigeria assumed the initial organizational initiative during the 1920's and 1930's, and their success inspired similar initiatives among Nigeria's other communal groups. Although in their inception these organizations served mainly social and economic functions, they soon became politicized, acting as communal pressure groups both with regard to the party and to the government. Thus, local improvement associations would attempt to influence the selection of party nominees to stand election in local electoral constituencies or would make demands upon government officials with respect to the allocation of amenities to their home communities. Similarly, at higher levels of communal structure, such organizations as the Ibo State Union and the Egbe Omo Oduduwa (the Yoruba-speaking Sons of the Descendants of Oduduwa) furthered the development of nationality-wide communal consciousness, and advanced the interests of their respective nationalities within party and governmental circles.[22] Significantly, however, as communally-oriented single-party systems became established within each region, and national politics became a matter of competition between the three communally-based regional parties, the nationality-wide organizations found their political functions usurped. The parties, in effect, became the defenders of majority communal interests. However, at the sub-nationality level of town and clan, "improvement unions" continued to play a significant role in intra-party political conflict.[23]

> *Proposition 6.* The subordination of political institutions
> to the interests of particular communal groups tends to
> reinforce and politicize communal conflict.

The degree of intensity of communal conflict will be determined very largely by what Huntington has termed the "autonomy" of the society's political institutions. To quote Huntington,

> Political institutionalization, in the sense of autonomy,
> means the development of political organizations and
> procedures that are not simply expressions of the interests
> of particular social groups. A political organization that is
> the instrument of a social group—family, clan, class—
> lacks autonomy and institutionalization.[24]

If political institutions do not possess institutional integrity and appear to be in the control of particular communal interests, those communal groups lacking power and position will tend to question the legitimacy of the institutional order and will be encouraged politically to "go it alone." It should be noted that it is not the nature of primary institutions and primary group interaction which are at issue: people may in fact live their private lives within their communal compartments without jeopardizing the political viability or stability of the wider society. What *is* at issue is the character of those secondary institutions of the society through which the members of communally discrete sub-societies may relate to one another in a systematic and orderly fashion.

This analysis may be illustrated by reference to both the

American and Nigerian cases. Thus, in the United States, communal separatism at the primary group level—that is, with respect to marriage, friendship cliques, etc.—has characterized intra-white as well as Black/white relationships. However, in the case of white Americans, the secondary institutions of the national society were sufficiently flexible and autonomous as to be relevant and legitimate for virtually all communal elements. Only in the case of non-whites—most notably, of course, of Black Americans—were the secondary institutions unresponsive and exclusionary. In effect, from the perspective of the wider society inclusive of both Blacks and whites, the political institutions of the society have never possessed autonomy but, rather, have been historically subordinated to the interests of the majority racial group. It is not surprising therefore that the most determined separatist sentiment in the United States has been voiced by the members of that group which has been least participant—in the sense of sharing in responsible decision-making power—in the secondary institutions of the society.[25]

Similarly, in Nigeria, both national and regional political institutions came to be identified with the interests of particular communal groups, thereby impairing their legitimacy in the eyes of minority communal interests at both national and regional levels.[26] More concretely, with the creation of Nigeria's Federal constitutional system and, in particular, with the creation of regional sources of wealth and power, it became clear that political parties which controlled the machinery of government could control the political and economic fate of the region.[27] Since Nigeria's administrative boundaries were so drawn as to give clear numerical superiority to a single nationality within each region, political parties on appealing to majority communal interests quickly came to dominate the regions. Much the same dynamics were operative at the national level, wherein the major communal groups competed for marginal advantages and sought to form opportune communal coalitions. It became evident, however, that no coalition was stable and that no group could feel secure in the Federal system.

In the course of this communal competition for control of regional and national governmental institutions, communal minorities rapidly became disenchanted with the prevailing institutional structures. Significantly, in the light of the Biafran secession, even communal groups which were dominant at the Regional level (i.e., the Ibos, Yorubas and Hausas) were in a minority position with respect to the national institutions and hence shared the same sense of communal insecurity as was characteristic of the regional minority groups. The important point is that at both the federal and the regional levels, governmental institutions became identified with the interests of particular communal groups, thereby losing their legitimacy and institutional effectiveness for crucial elements of the wider society.

Proposition 7. The greater the number of equally powerful communal groups, the greater the likelihood that political institutions will be able to retain their coherence and impartiality vis-à-vis communal competitors.

As in the case of non-political institutions, in the political realm there is a significant reciprocity between institution and conflict. While the political institutions of any society directly affect the nature and intensity of communal conflict, so will institutional development itself be influenced by the pattern of communal formation and conflict characteristic of that society. In particular, it would appear that the greater the number of equally powerful communal groups, the greater the likelihood that institutional coherence and impartiality will be retained.

On the one hand, the dispersion of power among a number of communal competitors makes less likely the identification of political institutions with a particular communal group or a coalition of such groups. On the other hand, the dispersion of power among a number of communal competitors helps not only to maintain a stable communal balance but also to encourage the development of a system of shifting communal coalitions which, in turn, lessens the intensity of communal conflict. In a society in which no communal group is sufficiently large or powerful to stand alone, it becomes necessary to form communal alliances. The greater the number of communal competitors, the less likelihood that the same communal groups will join together on all issues. As issues change, so do communal alliances. The resulting pattern of shifting and intersecting communal alliances will tend to mitigate the intensity of communal conflict on any particular issue.

Thus, in the Nigerian case, though there have always been enough communal groups potentially to create an ongoing pluralistic political system, the constitutional compromises of the early 1950's had the effect of excluding communal minorities from the national political system and of creating a three-person zero-sum game among the three major nationalities. As a result, there were enough states to insure conflict along communal dimensions, and too few states to ensure competitive stability. This was the tragic structural flaw of the Nigerian federal system. Although leaders such as Dr. Nnamdi Azikiwe and Chief Obafemi Awolowo well understood this point, their advice to create a greater number of states went unheeded. By the time enough states were created to ensure the minorities a modicum of self-determination and to prevent any single communal group from wielding inordinate power, civil war had engulfed Nigeria.

Proposition 8. Political institutions which encourage the participation of the masses in the recruitment of leaders tend to further politicize and intensify communal conflict.

The greater the dependence of political leaders upon the support of their communities of origin, the greater the likelihood that the political process will itself become "communalized." In a culturally plural society, the participation of the masses in the political process encourages aspirant politicians to make appeals to the most easily mobilized communal loyalties, and to define themselves primarily as the representatives of communal interests. In the process, the political order comes to be organized along communal lines.

The stimulating effect of mass participation on communal conflict can readily be seen in the Nigerian case. With the introduction of the franchise at Federal and regional levels of the governmental system, there emerged political parties such as the Yoruba-based Action Group and the Hausa-centered Northern Peoples' Congress which made very explicit communal appeals to the pride and self-interest of the Yoruba and Hausa peoples respectively. This appeal found an immediate response and led to the rapid rise of communally based regional parties. In turn, the development of communal parties among majority nationality groups stimulated the emergence of communal parties among the minority groups in each region. Parties such as the Northern Elements Progressive Union, the Bornu Youth Movement, the United Middle Belt Congress, and the Nigeria Delta Congress translated communal minority dissidence within each region into political terms. Still a further illustration of this politicization of communal conflict was the attempt made by the major communal parties to increase their strength at the Federal level by appealing to dissident minorities in each of the other regions. Thus, the Yoruba-dominated Action Group, based in Western Nigeria, became in time an important minority party in the Eastern Region and in the Middle Belt of the Northern Region.

It should be noted that at the same time that mass participation in the recruitment of political elites acts to stimulate communal appeals and hence communal conflict, so does the resulting conflict itself further the communalization of the elites. In effect, a vicious circle insures perpetuation of communal conflict in a participant political system: aspirant politicians make communal appeals and communal demands which exacerbate communal tensions; these tensions, in turn, encourage the recruitment of leaders who will make communal appeals and demands. Examples of this cyclical process are plentiful in the political experience of nationalist movements. Thus, the B.R. Ambedkars and Rajagopalacharis challenge the leadership of the Nehrus, the Suhartos that of the Sukarnos, and the Carmichaels and Browns that of the Rustins and Wilkins.

Such a challenge was notably successful in Nigeria, wherein democratization and mass involvement in the political process led to the gradual displacement of moderate and universalistic political elites by more militant and more communally parochial leaders.

At its inception, the leadership of Nigeria's first nationalist party, the National Council of Nigeria and the Cameroons (NCNC), though drawing primarily on Ibo and Yoruba sources, encompassed all of the country's major communal groupings and espoused a pan-Nigerian nationalist ideology. But this "nationalist" period was short-lived. With the introduction of the franchise and the gradual transfer of power to Nigerian hands, communal slogans and communally-oriented political elites acquired increasing appeal. With Regionalization, in the early 1950's, the communalization of the political system was complete. The original nationalist leadership began to sound a more parochial line, and the radical pan-Nigerian nationalists were displaced by champions of communal groups. Thus, by 1963 most of the NCNC's Yoruba contingent had broken away to found a new Yoruba-based political party and, by 1964, the NCNC had to all intents and purposes become the party of the Ibos.

Thus, democratic regimes which encourage mass participation and competitive political parties appear to be especially subject to the communalization of political competition. Indeed, judging from the experience of post-colonial regimes, it would seem that it is communal conflict and not class conflict which is most likely to undermine fledgling democracies.

III. Communal Transformation

Frequently it is said that communal categories and identities are the givens of social life. One can change one's occupation, but one cannot change one's communal group as readily. Recently, however, scholars have pointed out that under conditions of social mobilization and inter-group conflict, communal boundaries are indeed transformable. In fact, much contemporary communal conflict—whether in Nigeria, India or the United States—is being waged not by traditional entities, but by communities which were formed in the crucible of mobilization and competition.[28] Thus, it is probably more accurate to suggest that conflict produces "tribalism" than to argue, as the conventional wisdom would have it, that "tribalism" is the cause of conflict.

In the discussion of competitive and institutional communalism we made the tacit assumption that the culture, identity and boundaries of communal groups are formed independently of environmental forces. This clearly is an oversimplification which we now wish to drop. This section considers the various ways in which communal identities and boundaries are transformed in response to changing social and political exigencies.

> *Proposition 9.* In an environment of social mobilization and communal competition, communal groups will tend to fuse or to expand their traditional boundaries to include groups and individuals with whom they can identify and who might prove useful allies during inter-group conflict.[29]

A number of observers have noted the emergence within urban areas of communal identities and groupings which are considerably wider in their embrace than the communities of the traditional order. This comment on the case of African urbanization is illustrative:

> A reductive process takes place in the town: the intricate mosaic of the countryside becomes simplified to a manageable number of ethnic categories. A sense of membership in a group significantly expanded in scale from the clan and lineage system of the very localized rural 'tribal' community develops.[30]

Similarly, addressing themselves to the Indian case, the Rudolphs use the term, "fusion," to describe the process whereby Indian *Jatis* (popularly known as "castes") of unequal status join to form political and economic alliances against their competitors. It is the exigencies of modern competition which provide the impetus to alliance formation: "The higher castes need numerical strength to sustain their power and status; the lower need access to resources and opportunities that support of the higher can yield."[31] As the Rudolphs note, such alliances raise the ritual status of the lower castes and thus transform their traditional identities.

Exemplifying the process of communal expansion in Nigeria is the emergence in this century of new, affectually laden identities of "nationality", identities which reflect a modern consciousness of cultural and linguistic unities of which traditional man was largely unaware. The evolution of "Ibo" national identity illustrates the newness of contemporary identities of nationality especially well, for in the predominantly Ibo-speaking East, pre-colonial societal fragmentation was particularly pronounced. As Simon Ottenberg has observed,

> No political superstructure, such as a federation, a confederacy, or a state existed. The Ibo units remained a relatively balanced grouping of independent political structures which never developed into a large formal organization, though some units absorbed or conquered others, some died out, some fragmented, and some changed their characteristics through immigration and emigration.[32]

But the general pattern of pre-colonial fragmentation and post-colonial expansion or fusion was characteristic not only of the Ibo but also of many other loosely knit linguistic groups which today possess a new social and political cohesiveness and self-consciousness. It was only when these groups were brought together within a new administrative framework and forced to interact—and to compete—that nationality-wide organizations and ideologies emerged. Of course, the recency of these developments notwithstanding, few will be surprised if "revisionist" Ibo (or, for that matter, Ijaw or Yoruba or Hausa) historians of the future find many more "historical" ties that explain contemporary communal cohesiveness.

The process of communal expansion in Nigeria is manifested not only in the emergence of identities of nationality but also in the emergence of new, politically salient administrative identities. Again, this process is most clearly seen in the traditionally most fragmented area, Eastern Nigeria. There, the new administrative units of Native Court Area, Division and Province incorporated traditionally autonomous communities within a common structural framework and, in the process, generated new political interests and identities which were related to, but transcended, the village and village-group boundaries of the traditional system. Thus, in the 1960's, Ibo-speaking urban dwellers typically identified themselves to new acquaintances by reference not to their traditional community of origin, but to the administrative division and province in which that community was located. It was these "geo-ethnic" identities around which intra-Ibo political conflict normally revolved, for it was only at these wide, non-traditional levels of social grouping that Ibos were sufficiently numerous to make a political impact upon the regional political system.[33]

While this pattern of administrative fusion was especially pronounced in Eastern Nigeria, it was also evident in Western and Ncrthern Nigeria. In the latter cases, the traditional units were considerably larger and more populous, so that the new administrative boundaries tended to correspond more closely to the existing communal boundaries. Even here, however, the creation of new administrative structures had an effect analagous to "fusion", in that competition for governmental patronage—both in colonial and in independent Nigeria—placed a premium upon communal cohesiveness. In Western Nigeria, for example, Oyos were in competition with Ekitis and Ijebus for the scarce rewards of the administrative system, and the very competitive process furthered the development of Oyo unity. Inasmuch as Oyo, Ekiti and Ijebu constituted traditional entities as well as modern administrative units, intra-Yoruba competition had an especially volatile character. By contrast, the politically relevant administrative units of Iboland were essentially artificial creations commanding relatively little affect on the part of their members. Consequently, intra-Ibo political competition acquired a distinctively pragmatic and pacific character, political success being a function of coalition development among traditionally autonomous communities.

The process of fusion also operated at the level of the *regional* governments. As will be detailed below, the tri-partite administrative system developed by the British and by Nigerian leaders led to a considerable concentration of power in regional institutions. Therefore, those who lived within a given region had a direct stake in identifying themselves with those who controlled the regional apparatus of government. In particular, minority ethnic groups stood to be penalized—for example, through the denial of government patronage to their members or the non-allocation of government amenities—if they opposed the government of the day. Thus it was that some influential members of the Tiv community sought to ally themselves with the Northern Peoples' Congress, despite Tiv antipathies toward the Muslim Hausa.[34] Moreover, this tendency toward intra-regional fusion was furthered by the regional competition for control of the federal government and for federal revenues which was built into the national political system.

Proposition 10. Mobilization and competition lead also to the increasing internal differentiation of communal categories along socio-economic and ideological lines.

Under social mobilization, individuals move into new kinds of occupational and other social roles, and become differentiated by socio-economic and ideological criteria. New kinds of social identities and conflicts emerge—based upon such reference points as occupation, class, and political party. These new identities may or may not crosscut the lines of communal cleavage. When they do, they may produce political divisions which—in given situations—over-ride communal loyalties.

The Nigerian experience offers two major illustrations of politically significant intra-communal differentiation based on social class and ideology. The first illustration refers back to the immediate aftermath of World War II and the emergence, on the one hand, of a national trade union movement and, on the other, of the radical Zikist Movement. The second refers to the emergence of what Richard L. Sklar has called, the "political class."

In 1945 and again in 1964, successful general strikes demonstrated conclusively that the Nigerian labor movement had come of age and was capable of united and effective action. In both instances, communal divisions were cast aside and an united labor front was able to win significant concessions from both governmental and private employers. Somewhat less successful was the short-lived radical Zikist Movement, organized in the late 1940's by militant trade unionists and intellectuals, most of whom were Ibo, to rejuvenate the NCNC and to force the pace of the independence movement.

With the administrative regionalization of the country in the 1950's, a nationalist party like the NCNC, which until then had been unitarist in its constitutional outlook, had to take part in elections on the regional level. This meant that within the NCNC the fortunes of politicians and groups which were communally well connected via the tribal unions stood to rise, while the fortunes of labor activists and radical intellectuals were destined to fall. Believing constitutional advances to be a subterfuge for the protection of communal interest and convinced that independence would come only by way of revolution, the more radical wing of the unitarists responded to the dilemmas of regionalism with a call to direct action. Revolution would put an end to constitutional subterfuge, weaken the hand of the communal faction in the NCNC and accelerate the pace of independence.

However, the revolutionary aspirations of the labor activists and Zikists were thwarted. Moreover, unable to rely upon the personal support of Azikiwe, the Zikists were cut off from the main body of the NCNC. Many subsequently turned away from the party to Marxism, some out of conviction and some out of friendship for those who were convinced. Not until the strike of 1964 did the Zikists' isolation from Nigerian politics come to an end. From what they considered to be the NCNC's earlier betrayal and from their own obvious decline in power during the regionalist phase, the activists had learned to distrust the communal parties and their leaders and to be unalterably opposed to regionalism. Regionalism, in their view, was the structural cause underlying their political demise of the 1950's and early '60's.

The second manifestation of intra-communal diversification was the emergence of a privileged Nigerian political class whose security was tied to the maintenance of regional bases of power. As Sklar has noted, the accelerating political crises which led up to the military coup of January 1966—indeed, the coup iself—can all be viewed as phases of a continuing confrontation between this political establishment and a collection of anti-regionalist dissident groups, the latter including increasingly disaffected communal minorities and the long-alienated radical trade unionists and intellectuals.[36]

Developments such as these—the appearance of ideologically toned political manifestoes and organizations, and the formation of a privileged political class—have been cited by some students of non-Western societies as evidence of the deterioration of communal identities and institutions. Indeed, implicit in many of the dichotomous models which have been employed in studies of non-Western development is the notion that communally "particularistic" and socio-economically "universalistic" roles and identities lie at the opposite end of a single social continuum, the emergence of the latter heralding the disappearance of the former. As Propositions 11–14 below suggest, this view of social development possesses neither theoretical nor empirical foundation.

> *Proposition 11.* Accompanying communal fusion and expansion is the deparochialization of traditional group ties and perspectives.

As traditional communal entities are fused to form new and more organizationally effective groupings, the content and significance of traditional identities are substantially changed. Changes of particular importance are the generally reduced affect associated with the traditional order and the widening of social and political horizons. The Rudolphs' description of these developments in India is applicable also to Nigeria:

> .... As the block and district headquarters, the extravillage enterprise and the market town, the local school, cinema, and radio set, have become increasingly relevant for village lives, they have created alternative environments for profit, prestige, and self-esteem. By enlarging the reach of empathy, broadening horizons, and multiplying reference groups, they have helped to deparochialize the intimate and closed world of the village. New opportunities, sentiments, and ideas have reduced and dispersed the concentration of affect, power, and economic dependence at the local level.[37]

In short, social mobilization leads to the widening of social horizons and the loosening of traditional bonds. Urbanization, for example, removes individuals from constraints of traditional authority and leads them to participate in numerous social roles which not only have no traditional sanction but also which often involve interaction across the communal boundaries of the traditional order. As a result, new interests and loyalties and authorities come to have a claim upon the individual's time and attention. This does not mean that traditional identities and institutions disintegrate; to the contrary, they may well persist and retain both social and political significance. It does mean, however, that such identities and institutions, if they persist, will acquire new functions and new meaning.

From the standpoint of conventional theory, it would seem paradoxical that deparochialization has been associated with intensified rather than diminished communal conflict. Too frequently, political development has been seen in terms of a struggle between "nationalism" and "traditionalism", the fall of the latter thereby signalling the rise of the former. In fact, the passing of traditionalism does not mean the passing of communalism. Indeed, the developmental process yields many new and competitive communal groupings, of which the nation-state is but one variant, and one moreover which is relatively remote. Yet, to note the tenuousness of nation-state loyalties is not to denigrate the significant integrative processes at work at regional and sub-regional levels of many polities. It might well be argued in the Nigerian case that the very success of lower-level communal integration has made more difficult the task of national integration.

Proposition 12. Communal transformation entails the multiplication rather than the substitution of social identities.

The emergence of new patterns of communal identity through expansion, fusion and deparochialization does not necessarily mean the destruction of old communal loyalties. It means, more commonly, the superimposition upon the traditional reference points of wider concentric circles of communalism. The old identities, in effect, coexist with the new, with the consequence that citizens come to hold multiple communal identities (for example, to their family, village, region, nationality, church and nation-state). By the same token, the internal differentiation of communal categories by socio-economic and ideological criteria signals the proliferation of additional social reference points rather than the substitution of the new for the old. An individual may be an Ibo and also a factory worker. His acquisition of a new socio-economic identity need not mean the elimination of his prior communal point of reference. This point is crucial, for it explains, in part, the paradoxical persistence of communal sentiments and communal conflict within modernizing and modernized societies. The precise relationship between communal and non-communal identities is the subject of the next set of propositions.

IV. Communal Compartmentalization

Proposition 13. Since politically salient identities are situationally specific, communal and non-communal political orientations may well co-exist within the same person.

The individual's perception of the social situation determines which of his multiple identities will be most politically salient at any given moment. The relative political salience of an individual's multiple social identities is not fixed. It is, rather, in a constant state of flux. As Anderson, von der Mehden and Young state, "Every actor in the political community, no matter how unimportant has a multiplicity of potential foci of social solidarity. The appropriate role is prescribed by the nature of the situation—or more precisely, by the actor's perception of the situation."[38] This formulation highlights the element of contingency which underpins the always-shifting lines of political cleavage. In some situations, men join together in defense of their common religious commitment. In others, they organize to protect their economic interests or, at election time, to promote the interests and prestige of their communities of origin. The crucial point is that political response is inexplicable without reference to the actor's social context and to his perceptions of that context.

This theoretical position relies heavily on the work of scholars associated with the Rhodes-Livingston Institute, in particular, Max Gluckman, A.L. Epstein and J. Clyde Mitchell.[39] Thus Gluckman has pointed out that "though developments in urban and in rural areas affect one another . . . the specific associations of each may exist independently . . . the Africans' lives are partly dichotomized, and they live in separate compartments like other men."[40] Though in this context, Gluckman emphasizes the urban-rural dichotomy, in principle it can be argued without doing violence to his major point that men "compartmentalize" their identities *within* urban and rural areas as well as between them.

Since the various identities of any given individual are each "triggered" by different social situations, seemingly incompatible or conflicting identities may well co-exist within the same person. Social roles may, in effect, be "compartmentalized," thereby permitting the individual to respond flexibly to changing social and political circumstances. Thus, it is possible for the same person to join a trade union to advance his occupational interests, a communal association to promote his social or electoral objectives, and a religious interest group to lobby for educational reforms. In short, it is possible for an individual to be both a communal and a non-communal political actor.

Returning to the Nigerian case, we are now in a position to explain both the success of the 1945 and 1964 general strikes and the failure of the trade union leaders, in 1964, to convert their labor following into votes for labor candidates at election time.[41] When it came to questions of the pocketbook—to questions of salary and conditions of service—Nigerian workers held much in common irrespective of their diverse communal attachments. During the strike actions in both 1945 and 1964 it was the socio-economic identities of these men which were in the foreground; in the confrontation with employers, their communal points of reference held little salience and labor unity was possible. But when it came to the election of parliamentary candidates in 1964, their communal identities were "triggered" once again and the trade unionists voted their communal loyalties. As a result, the same trade union leaders who had enjoyed the support of a communally heterogeneous rank-and-file during the 1964 general strike were deserted when they subsequently transformed themselves from leaders of a socio-economic protest into parliamentary candidates in opposition to the communally-based regional parties. The moment the strike was concluded, the lines of political cleavage within the nation were redrawn, socio-economic identities once again being subordinated to the communal identities of region and nationality.

Proposition 14. Since communal and non-communal political orientations may co-exist within individuals, each activated in different social contexts, modernization need not eliminate communal differentiation and conflict.

A clear implication of the argument advanced above is that there is no necessary incompatibility between functioning as a modern economic man, on the one hand, and performing as a communal political actor, on the other. We have suggested, in brief, that one can participate effectively in a communally heterogeneous industrial occupation and trade union five days a week, and still vote his communal loyalties at election time. If this is so, it would appear to follow that communal differentiation and conflict may well persist in the midst of economic modernization. Not only may communal particularism be compatible with a modern industrial order, the foregoing suggests that it may well be an essential component of that order. For, by the multiplication and compartmentalization of both communal and non-communal identities, individuals are able to respond more flexibly to changing social and political circumstances. In effect, the retention of communal points of reference enables industrial man to receive the best of two worlds —the collectivism inherent in the functionally diffuse ties of language and culture, and the individuation requisite to effective performance in the modern commercial and industrial milieu. We are suggesting, in short, that the essence of modernity may lie not in the transition from particularistic to universalistic forms, but rather in their compartmentalization.[42]

How well individuals and groups do in fact compartmentalize their many identities is of course an empirical question. It can be expected that the extent to which co-existing social identities will be compartmentalized will vary with how individuals and groups perceive and interpret particular situations. There arise situations, for example, in which individuals may experience "role conflict" or "cross-pressures," which reflect a difficulty in choosing among conflicting loyalties or in determining which set of loyalties is most appropriate to a particular situation.[43]

An illustration of this problem can be gleaned from the experience of Nigerian workers after the June General Strike of

1964 and before the December Federal elections. Two kinds of politicians began to compete for the labor vote. On the one hand, there were politically oriented labor leaders who wanted to take the opportunity of the strike and of the elections to form a labor party. They made their appeals to the class interests of Nigerian workers. On the other hand, there were the politicians of the major political parties who made their appeals to their communal loyalties. Thus between June and December 1964, workers were cross-pressured between their class and their ethnic loyalties. As it turns out the cross-pressure was weak and a majority of workers supported their communal parties.

How the workers responded to the cross-pressure was clearly related both to the objective situation of growing communal conflict during the election and to their perception of the incompatibility between choosing a labor party and choosing a communal party. With regard to the first point it should be noted that the Federal election of 1964, coming as it did on the heels of the many political crises of Federation, raised the salience of communal security and survival. Therefore, we should not be surprised that at first, in June, almost nine out of ten workers indicated support for a labor party, but that as the election progressed a growing number of workers indicated support for regional parties and diminishing support for labor parties. With regard to the second point we should not be surprised that almost a fifth indicated their allegiance to *both* parties throughout the election period. Such inconsistency may have been based on a shortage of political information, and on the confusing situation which existed during the election. It is significant, for example, that the more educated the trade unionist and the longer his involvement in the trade union—that is, the more information the worker had at his disposal—the less likely was he to be inconsistent and to support both parties.[44]

In order to understand the political behavior of actors who are cross-pressured between their communal and non-communal identities it becomes necessary to specify to what extent roles are compartmentalized and to what extent cross-pressures are actually felt. This empirical variance among individuals and between situations does not detract, however, from the basic point that there need not be an inherent incompatibility among co-existing communal and non-communal identities.

Conclusions

In concluding this analysis of the relationship between modernization and communal conflict, three themes require emphasis. The first concerns the political distinctiveness and significance of communal conflict, as contrasted with other types of inter-group conflict. Clifford Geertz has noted that communal groups differ from groups formed on the basis of economic interest or "class consciousness" in that the latter are seldom ". . . considered as possible self-standing, maximal social units, as candidates for nationhood."[45] Since communal groups may in fact be considered as "candidates for nationhood," communal conflict—unlike, for example, class conflict—may bring into question the very boundaries of the nation-state.[46] This is not to suggest that class conflict may not possess the same intensity as communal conflict: the Russian and French revolutions testify as to the potential intensity of class conflict. Nor is it to suggest that communal conflict may not be significantly motivated by socio-economic issues: on the contrary, to the extent that communal conflict touches on problems of redistribution of wealth, status, and power it tends to resemble class conflict. The important point, however, is that conflict between social classes which are not also communal groups does not threaten the integrity of national political boundaries, whereas the very nature of communal conflict involves the potentiality of secession and boundary revision. Of course, to the extent that modernization uproots communal groups from particular geographical areas and distributes their members according to the exigencies of the market place, the probability of actual secession is greatly reduced. Thus, secession did not prove a viable strategy for pre-war European Jews, despite the fact that intense communal conflict produced minority demands for geographical and political separation. Indeed, it was from such roots that there sprang the Zionist movement.[47] For similar reasons, the chances for secession by Black Americans in the contemporary United States are slim indeed, though the Nation of Isalm and Republic of Africa movements are eloquent testimony to the intensity of separatist sentiment within some segments of the Black American community.[48] It should be noted that the foreclosure of the secessionist option is one of the factors underlying the sense of powerlessness of communal minorities in modern societies.

The second critical theme which bears elaboration is the persistence of communalism in transitional and modern as well as traditional societies. This is so because communal formation and conflict are not merely the reflection of cultural "givens" and "primordial sentiments."[49] Social change leads to the formation of entirely new communal groupings which crystallize around new foci of culture and identity. Communalism, in short, is an inherent aspect of social change in all culturally heterogeneous societies. This suggests that the disappearance of those groups which comprise a culturally heterogeneous society at any particular point in time herald neither the disappearance of all communal formations nor the amelioration of communal conflict. Thus, in the United States, the weakening of traditional Italian, Irish, and Polish identities and institutions has signalled not the disappearance of communal politics, but the emergence of a more inclusive communalism based upon religious denominationalism and ethnic solidarity.[50] Similarly, in Nigeria, the weakening of traditional authority and cohesiveness has been accompanied not by the disappearance of communal identities but by their transformation and expansion.

Finally, the potentially disintegrative implications of intense communal conflict, together with the likelihood of its persistence, suggest that policy makers must begin to come to terms with communalism. If we are correct in our analysis of the relationship between modernization and communalism, communal categories might well become more rather than less politically salient. Intense communal conflict poses an especially trying dilemma for fragile democratic regimes. To the extent that such regimes encourage social mobilization and participation, they may be undermining the very basis of their legitimacy and stability. Political arrangements must be found which accord to all communal groups a meaningful role in national life and which are able to keep communal conflict within manageable bounds. The stability of culturally plural societies is threatened not by communalism, *per se,* but by the failure of national institutions explicitly to recognize and accommodate existing communal divisions and interests.

Notes

1. Research was supported by the Departments of Political Science at Michigan State University and Western Michigan University, and by the African Studies Center at Michigan State University. We both greatly benefited by association with faculty and students in a workshop on the Nigerian experience sponsored by the Midwest Universities Consortium for International Activity. We also wish to acknowledge, with gratitude, the helpful comments of the following colleagues who read this paper in manuscript form: Karl W. Deutsch, S. N. Eisenstadt, Justin Green, Daniel Lerner, James O'Connell, Simon Ottenberg, Lucian W. Pye, Lloyd I. and Susanne Hoeber Rudolph, Richard L. Sklar, Saadia Touval, Crawford Young and Aristide Zolberg. An earlier version of this paper was presented at the meetings of the American Political Science Association in New York, September 1969.

2. In particular, see the following works: Charles W. Anderson, Fred R. von der Mehden, Crawford Young, *Issues of Political Development* (Englewood Cliffs: Prentice-Hall, Inc., 1967), pp. 15–83; James S. Coleman, *Nigeria: Background to Nationalism* (Berkeley and Los Angeles: University of California Press, 1960), excerpt reprinted in this volume, pp. 69–92; S. N. Eisenstadt, "Reflections on a Theory of Modernization," in Arnold Rivkin (ed.), *Nations by Design* (Garden City: Doubleday and Co., 1968), pp. 35–61; Clifford Geertz, "The Integrative Revolution," in Clifford Geertz (ed.), *Old Societies and New States* (Glencoe: The Free Press, 1963), pp. 105–57; Martin Kilson, *Political Change in a West African State: A Study of the Modernization Process in Sierra Leone* (Boston: Harvard University Press, 1966); Lloyd I. and Susanne Hoeber Rudolph, *The Modernity of Tradition: Political Development in India* (Chicago: Chicago University Press, 1967); Richard L. Sklar, "The Contribution of Tribalism to Nationalism in Western Nigeria," *Journal of Human Relations,* VIII (Spring-Summer, 1960), pp. 407–415, reprinted in this volume, pp. 463–476; Myron Weiner, *The Politics of Scarcity: Public Pressure and Political Response in India* (Chicago: University of Chicago Press, 1962); C. S. Whitaker, Jr. "A Dysrhythmic Process of Political Change," *World Politics,* XIX, No. 2 (January 1967), pp. 190–217; W. Howard Wriggins, "Impediments to Unity in New Nations: The Case of Ceylon," *American Political Science Review,* 55 (June 1961), pp. 313–320; Crawford Young, *Politics in the Congo* (Princeton: Princeton University Press,

1965); Aristide Zolberg, *One-Party Government in the Ivory Coast* (Princeton: Princeton University Press, 1964).

3. According to Deutsch, complementarity of communication in a group "consists in the ability to communicate more effectively and over a wider range of subjects with members of one large group than with outsiders." See his pathbreaking *Nationalism and Social Communication* (Cambridge: M.I.T. Press, 1953), p. 71.

4. Milton Gordon, *Assimilation in American Life* (New York: Oxford University Press, 1964), p. 39.

5. It should be noted that communal groups are not alone in sharing culture, identity and complementarity. An age-grade among the Masai, for example, does in fact share in these characteristics. So does the upper class in Britain. But age grades and social classes are not to be thought of as communal groups, because they do not encompass the full range of demographic divisions within a society and they are not socio-economically heterogeneous. It is these latter characteristics which give to communal groups their distinctive political significance in that they are, to use Clifford Geertz' term, "candidates for nationhood." See Geertz, *op. cit.,* p. 111. The term, "communalism," is not to be confused with the concept of "communal participation" developed by Richard L. Sklar, in his *Nigerian Political Parties: Power in an Emergent African Nation* (Princeton: Princeton University Press, 1963), pp. 474–480.

6. Carl K. Eicher, for example, has written, "Nigeria's rate of economic growth of approximately 5 percent per annum since 1960 is impressive and second only to that of the Ivory Coast among West African nations. Nigeria became the world's tenth largest exporter of petroleum in 1966 and its petroleum reserves are estimated to match those of Libya." See his "The Dynamics of Long-Term Agricultural Development in Nigeria," *Journal of Farm Economics,* 49, 5 (December 1967), pp. 1158–1170. According to an estimate of Carl Liedholm, Eastern Nigeria in the early sixties possessed the fastest growing industrial sector in the world. See Carl Liedholm, "Preliminary Estimates of an Index of Industrial Production for Eastern Nigeria, from 1961–66," Enugu: Economic Development Institute, March 1967. For a more extensive discussion of Nigerian economic development, see Gerald K. Helleiner, *Peasant Agriculture, Government, and Economic Growth in Nigeria* (Homewood: Richard Irwin, Inc., 1966). For lucid discussions of the political consequences of Nigeria's rapid rates of educational expansion and urbanization, see James S. Coleman, *op. cit.,* and David Abernethy, *The Political Dilemma of Popular Education: An African Case* (Stanford: Stanford University Press, 1969), excerpt reprinted in this volume, pp. 400–432.

7. Karl W. Deutsch, "Social Mobilization and Political Development," *American Political Science Review,* 55 (September 1961), pp. 493–514; reprinted in Jason L. Finkle and Richard W. Gable (eds.), *Political Development and Social Change* (New York: John Wiley and Sons, Inc.), pp. 205–226.

8. Following Anderson, von der Mehden and Young, "cultural pluralism" refers to "the existence within a state of solidarity patterns, based upon shared religion, language, ethnic identity, race, caste, or region, which command a loyalty rivaling, at least in some situations, that which the state itself is able to generate." Charles W. Anderson, Fred R. von der Mehden, Crawford Young, *op. cit.,* p. 17.

9. For an insightful discussion of the psychological dimension of social change, see Lucian W. Pye, *Politics, Personality and Nation-Building* (New Haven: Yale University Press, 1962).

10. Concerning the goundnut industry, see J. S. Hoggendorn, "The Origins of the Groundnut Trade in Northern Nigeria," in Carl Eicher and Carl Liedholm (eds.), *Growth and Development of the Nigerian Economy* (East Lansing: Michigan State University Press, 1970).

11. See David C. McClelland, *The Achieving Society* (Princeton: Van Nostrand, 1961); Everett E. Hagen, *On the Theory of Social Change* (Homewood: Dorsey Press, 1962); Crawford Young, *op. cit.,* especially pp. 256–265; Robert A. LeVine, *Dreams and Deeds: Achievement Motivation in Nigeria* (Chicago and London: University of Chicago Press, 1965), excerpts reprinted in this volume, pp. 170–214; Simon Ottenberg, "Ibo Receptivity to Change," in William R. Bascom and Melville J. Herskovits (eds.), *Continuity and Change in African Cultures* (Chicago and London: University of Chicago Press, 1962), pp. 130–143.

12. The precise role and significance of such cultural predispositions in the development process is as yet uncertain. For a criticism of the McClelland thesis, see S. N. Eisenstadt, "The Need for Achievement," *Economic Development and Cultural Change,* Vol. II, No. 2 (January 1963), pp. 420–431. For a critical analysis of the Ibo "receptivity to change" hypothesis, see Richard Henderson, " 'Generalized Cultures' and 'Evolutionary Adaptability': The Comparison of Urban Efik and Ibo in Nigeria," *Ethnology,* Vol. 5, No. 4 (October 1966), pp. 365–391, reprinted in this volume, pp. 215–253.

13. See Howard Wolpe, "Port Harcourt: Ibo Politics in Microcosm," *Journal of Modern African Studies,* Vol. VII, No. 3 (October 1969), pp. 469–493, reprinted in this volume, pp. 483–513.

14. For an excellent analysis of communal conflict and violence within Nigeria's upper north, see John Paden, "Communal Competition, Conflict and Violence in Kano," this volume pp. 113–144.

15. For a parallel analysis of Ivory Coast inter-group relationships, see Aristide R. Zolberg, *op. cit.*

16. Daniel Lerner, for example, has suggested that "A person with high achievement may still be dissatisfied if his aspirations far exceed his accomplishments. Relative deprivation . . . is the effective measure of satisfaction among individuals and groups." See his "Toward a Communication Theory of Modernization," in Lucian W. Pye (ed.), *Communications and Political Development* (Princeton: Princeton University Press, 1963), p. 333. For a parallel treatment of the problem of relative deprivation, see Ulf Himmelstrand's application of rank-equilibration theory to Yoruba-Ibo competition in "Tribalism and Nationalism in Nigeria," this volume pp. 254–283.

17. For an extensive discussion of how "deprivation" enters into civil strife, see Ted Gurr, "A Causal Model of Civil Strife: A Comparative Analysis Using New Indices," *American Political Science Review,* LXXII, No. 4 (December 1968), pp. 1104–1124.

18. The terminology is Milton Gordon's. See *op. cit.,* pp. 60–83. "Cultural assimilation" implies that a group has changed its cultural patterns to those of the host society. "Structural assimilation" refers to the group's membership actually entering into the cliques, clubs, and institutions of the host society, on the primary group level.

19. For an incisive analysis of Yoruba/Hausa segregation and the communalization of commercial activity in the city of Ibadan, see Abner Cohen, "The Social Organization of Credit in a West African Cattle Market," *Africa,* XXXV, No. 1 (1965), pp. 8–19, reprinted in this volume, pp. 93–112. For related discussions of inter-communal trade, see E. Wayne Nafziger, "Inter-Regional Economic Relations in the Nigerian Footwear Industry," *The Journal of Modern African Studies,* 6, 4 (1968), pp. 531–542, and John Harris and Mary Rowe, "Entrepreneurial Attitudes and National Integration," this volume, pp. 145–169. See also the forthcoming studies by Barbara Callaway on Aba urban politics and by George Jenkins and K.W.J. Post on the political history of the important Ibadan political leader, the late Adelabu.

20. Gordon W. Allport, *The Nature of Prejudice* (Garden City: Doubleday and Company, Inc., 1958), p. 256.

21. See for example, Kenneth Little, *West African Urbanization: A Study of Voluntary Associations in Social Change* (Cambridge: Cam-

bridge University Press, 1963); Immanuel Wallerstein, "Ethnicity and National Integration in West Africa," in Pierre L. Van Den Berghe (ed.), *Africa: Social Problems of Change and Conflict* (San Francisco: Chandler Publishing Company, 1965) pp. 472–482. For careful analyses of this phenomenon in India see Lloyd I. and Susaane Hoeber Rudolph, *op. cit.* and Myron Weiner, *op. cit.*

22. Oduduwa is a culture hero and mythical progenitor of the Yoruba people. See Sklar, *op. cit.,* p. 67.

23. Interesting discussions of the relationship between improvement unions and political parties are to be found in Audrey Smock, "The Political Role of Ibo Ethnic Unions," this volume, pp. 320–341, and Alvin Magid, "The Idoma State Union: Minority Politics in Northern Nigeria," this volume, pp. 342–366.

24. Samuel P. Huntington, *Political Order in Changing Societies* (New Haven: Yale University Press, 1968), p. 20.

25. See Stokely Carmichael and Charles V. Hamilton, *Black Power: The Politics of Liberation in America* (New York: Vintage, 1967).

26. This discussion of the Nigerian experience draws heavily upon the following studies: James S. Coleman, *op. cit.;* Richard L. Sklar, *Nigerian Political Parties, op. cit.;* K.W.J. Post, *The Nigerian Federal Election of 1959* (London: Oxford University Press, 1963) and John P. Mackintosh (ed.), *Nigerian Government and Politics* (Evanston: Northwestern University Press, 1966).

27. See Richard L. Sklar, "The Ordeal of Chief Awolowo," in Gwendolen M. Carter (ed.), *Politics in Africa: 7 Cases* (New York: Harcourt, Brace and World, Inc.), pp. 119–166.

28. See Crawford Young's discussion of the Congolese "Bangala," an example of "artificial ethnicity" produced by inter-group competition, in his *Politics in the Congo, op. cit.,* pp. 242–246. It should be noted that contemporary "Ibo-ness" and "Yoruba-ness," like contemporary American "Black-ness," are also new forms of communalism engendered by mobilization and competition.

29. For a parallel analysis of the relationship between conflict and group formation, see Lewis A. Coser, *The Functions of Social Conflict* (New York: The Free Press, 1956).

30. Anderson, von der Mehden, and Young, *op. cit.,* p. 30.

31. Rudolphs, *op. cit.,* p. 100.

32. Simon Ottenberg, "Ibo Oracles and Intergroup Relations," *Southwestern Journal of Anthropology,* 14, 3 (Autumn 1958), p. 296. For an incisive discussion of the political implications of communal transformation among the Ibo, see Paul Anber, "Modernization and Political Disintegration: Nigeria and the Ibos," *The Journal of Modern African Studies,* 5, 2 (1967), pp. 163–179.

33. The concept of "geo-ethnicity" has much the same meaning as Immanuel Wallerstein's concept of "ethnicity," in Wallerstein, *op. cit.* The former term is preferred here for two reasons. First, it offers a sharper conceptual tool than that of "ethnicity" to describe the new kinds of urban groupings which are based upon non-traditional or neo-traditional communities of origin. Second, the use of the "geo-ethnicity" concept to describe urban groupings based upon new, artificial entities enables us to reserve the concept of "ethnicity" for urban groupings based more strictly on kinship, cultural and linguistic ties. See Wolpe, *op. cit.* and Wolpe, "Port Harcourt: A Community of Strangers—The Politics of Urban Development in Eastern Nigeria" (unpublished Ph. D. dissertation, Massachusetts Institute of Technology, 1965).

34. See Martin J. Dent, "A Minority Party—the UMBC," in John F. Mackintosh (ed.), *Nigerian Government and Politics* (Evanston: Northwestern University Press, 1966), pp. 461–507.

35. On the Zikist Movement, see Sklar, *Nigerian Political Parties, op. cit.,* pp. 72–82. For a discussion of the emergence of Nigeria's political class, see Sklar, "Contradictions in the Nigerian Political System," *The Journal of Modern African Studies,* 3, 2 (1965), pp. 201–213, reprinted in this volume, pp. 514–529.

36. See Sklar, "Nigerian Politics in Perspective," *Government and Opposition,* Vol. 2, No. 4 (July-October 1967), pp. 524–539, reprinted in this volume, pp. 43–62.

37. Rudolphs, *op. cit.,* p. 101.

38. Anderson, von der Mehden and Young, *op. cit.,* p. 60.

39. See Max Gluckman, "Tribalism in Modern British Central Africa," in Van Den Berghe, *op. cit.,* pp. 346–360. This article first appeared in *Cahiers D'Etudes Africaines,* 1 (January, 1960), pp. 55–70. Also, A. L. Epstein, *Politics in an Urban African Community* (Manchester: Manchester University Press, 1958); and Clyde Mitchell, *The Kalela Dance* (Manchester: Manchester University Press, 1956). For a recent application of the situational mode of analysis developed by the Rhodes-Livingstone group to the Nigerian scene, see Leonard Plotnicov, *Strangers to the City; Urban Man in Jos, Nigeria* (Pittsburgh:

University of Pittsburgh Press, 1967), excerpt reprinted in this volume, pp. 606–625.

40. See Gluckman, *op. cit.,* p. 359. For a critical discussion of Gluckman's views, see Michael Banton, *Race Relations* (New York: Basic Books, 1967), pp. 239–240.

41. See Robert Melson, "Politics and the Nigerian General Strike of 1964," in Robert Rotberg and Ali Mazrui (eds.), *Protest and Power in Black Africa* (New York and London: Oxford University Press, 1970), pp. 771–787, and Wolpe, "Port Harcourt: A Community of Strangers," *op. cit.,* pp. 423–454.

42. As the Rudolphs note, "Compartmentalization not only physically separates . . . home and family from work place and colleagues, but also prevents the different norms of behavior and belief appropriate to modernity and tradition from colliding and causing conflict in the lives of those who live by both." *Op. cit.,* pp. 121–122.

43. "Cross-pressures are combinations of characteristics which in a given context would tend to lead the individual to vote on both sides of a contest." See Bernard Berelson, Paul F. Lazarsfeld, *et. al., Voting* (Chicago: University of Chicago Press, 1954), p. 283.

44. See Robert Melson, "Ideology and Inconsistency: The Politics of the 'Cross-pressured' Nigerian Worker," this volume, pp. 581–605.

45. Geertz, *op. cit.,* p. 111. See also Deutsch, *Nationalism and Social Communication, op. cit.,* p. 78: "In an age of nationalism, a nationality is a people pressing to acquire a measure of effective control over the behavior of its members. It is a people striving to equip itself with power, with some machinery of compulsion strong enough to make the enforcement of its commands sufficiently probable . . ." For Deutsch, what differentiates a people from a nationality is precisely the attempt by a communal group to gain power in order to discipline itself and to have its demands met by others. In that sense, Nigerian political parties, to the extent that they became representatives of a particular communal group served the function of transforming a people into a nationality. Thus, by 1965, Nigerian politics had come to resemble the politics of the multinational nation-states of Europe before the First World War. See also Anderson, von der Mehden and Young, *op. cit.,* p. 17: "By 'nationalism' we mean the assertion of the will to constitute an autonomous political community by a self-conscious group whether or not the group coincides with a recognized state."

46. It is interesting that many scholars have tended to discount the significance of communal conflict. Ralf Dahrendorf, for example,

while distinguishing between communal and class conflict, dismisses consideration of the former in favor of an analysis of the latter. In formulating a theory of class conflict, he asserts, ". . . we are by no means considering a general theory of social conflict, although I would undertake to defend the assertion that we are dealing here with one of the most important, if not the most important type of social conflict. However important as problems of social conflict St. Bartholomew's Night, Crystal Night, and Little Rock may be [these are all examples of communal conflict], the French Revolution, the British General Strike of 1926, and the events in East Berlin on June 17, 1953, seem to me more germane for structural analysis . . . the sociological theory of conflict would do well to confine itself for the time being to an explanation of the frictions between the rulers and the ruled in given organizations." See Dahrendorf, "Toward a Theory of Social Conflict," in A. Etzioni (ed.), *Social Change* (New York: Basic Books, 1964), p. 101.

47. On the Zionist movement, see Ben Halpern, *The Idea of the Jewish State* (Cambridge: Harvard University Press, 1961).

48. On the Nation of Islam movement, see E. U. Essien-Udom, *Black Nationalism. A Search for Identity in America* (Chicago: University of Chicago Press, 1962).

49. Geertz' term, "primordial sentiments," may be an unfortunate label, if it suggests that the bonds which define the cohesiveness of a communal group are in some sense pre-historical, given, or unchangeable. *Op. cit.,* p. 109.

50. Michael Parenti, "Ethnic Politics and the Persistence of Ethnic Identification," *The American Political Science Review,* LXI, 3 (September, 1967), pp. 717–726.

CHAPTER 2

Nigerian Politics in Perspective

RICHARD L. SKLAR

On 15 January 1966, a crisis-bound Nigerian government was overthrown by a swift military *coup d'etat.* The Prime Minister of the Federal Republic and his powerful associate, the Federal Minister of Finance, were seized by soldiers in Lagos. Neither survived, although the death of the Prime Minister, who was not personally unpopular, may not have been premeditated. His political chief, the premier of the vast Northern Region, was killed in Kaduna, and the latter's ally, the premier of the Western Region, died violently in Ibadan. Their major opponents among Nigerian office holders, namely the President of the Republic and the premiers of the Eastern and Midwestern Regions, escaped death. The President was on leave outside the country; it is not clear whether the two surviving premiers were spared by design or mistake. In any case, the tendency in Nigerian politics with which the survivors had been identified did appear to have triumphed despite their personal losses of power.

After the *coup,* two somewhat contradictory explanations of the event were widely entertained. Neither does justice to the

Reprinted from *Government and Opposition,* 2, 4 (July-October 1967), pp. 524–538. Copyright © 1967 by *Government and Opposition.* Reprinted by permission of the publisher and Richard L. Sklar.

complexity of Nigerian politics. One comforting explanation attributes the *coup* and its popular acceptance to widespread revulsion against the sins of the politicians—corruption, maladministration, tribalism, waste, drift and electoral fraud. This indictment is easy to document in detail; every item was cited to justify the event. But an enumeration of sins will not add up to an historical explanation. Governments are rarely if ever overthrown because they are abusive or incompetent. Revolutions are not automatic; they are *made* by men who believe in themselves and feel frustrated by the political order.

A second unsatisfactory explanation of the January *coup* panders to the conventional stereotype of African politics as a struggle between antagonistic tribes. It is true enough that conflicts and violence in Africa are commonly channelled along tribal divisions. What does that prove? It tells us little about the actual causes of inter-group conflict and violence. Will any sociologist or psychologist assert that Negroes fight Puerto Ricans in New York because of their diverse ethnic backgrounds? Nor, in fairness, do many scholars tell us that Hausas fight Ibos in Kano because of their diverse ethnic or religious backgrounds. The debatable explanation at point here is a cut or so above common journalese.

To elaborate. There are an estimated 8–9 million Ibos in Nigeria, 6–7 million of whom live in the overcrowded Eastern Region—overcrowded, that is, for an industrially underdeveloped country and by African standards. The others are scattered throughout Nigeria, employed in the provision of many crucial economic and social services. The industrious qualities of the Ibo people are proverbial and widely respected throughout West Africa. In the Eastern Region itself, traditional Iboland, comprising half of the region's area, sustains a majority of its population. The East is also a petroleum-rich region. However, most of the known oil deposits are located in territories that are either at the margin or outside of Iboland. These facts are crucial to many political developments.

Under the old regime, Ibo disaffection had been a growing source of political instability. The independence government of 1960 had been formed by a coalition of the Northern Peoples' Congress (NPC) and the National Convention of Nigerian Citizens (NCNC), with Sir Abubakar Tafawa Balewa, vice-president of the NPC, as Prime Minister of the Federation. At first, Sir Abubakar's party held a strong plurality in the federal House of Representatives; eventually, his party acquired an absolute majority in the House as opposition Members of Parliament from the Northern Region crossed over to the NPC. We need to remark that more than half of the federal parliamentary constituencies were located in the Northern Region, since constituencies were apportioned among regions in accordance with their populations, and the 1953 census had given the North some 56 per cent of the national total.

The NCNC, oldest of the nationalist organizations in Nigeria, was both trans-regional in operation and trans-tribal in composition. But the party's main strength was in the Eastern Region and Ibos have supported it to the virtual exclusion of all national competitors. Certainly, Ibo solidarity under one party banner is unrivalled by the other major ethnic groups. Within the federal government coalition, severe tensions developed between the NPC and the NCNC. These were symptomatic of a deeper conflict between the Northern and Eastern regional governments. Leaders of those two regions vied for the fruits of national power. Their conflict was liable to facile articulation in tribalist language as a struggle between the Ibos and the Hausas, who constitute a majority in the North. As always, rival politicians were able to muster mass support by appealing to tribal sentiments. On that ground, the explanation of political conflict based on tribal rivalry is realistic. But it reveals little about the underlying causes and nature of the inter-regional conflict itself. These may be comprehended by a social and historical analysis that delves deeper than tribalism.

An explanation of the first coup d'état

Few "laws" in political science have stood the test of time as well as James Harrington's "law" of the "balance".[1] Succinctly, this law propounds that the divorce of property from political power will produce instability and civil war. True to his discovery, Harrington perceived that the English civil wars would result in a transfer of power from the King to the landed gentry, where it remained in fact until after 1832.

In modern times, the critical forms of property are linked to industrial technology. With the breakup of communal and quasi-feudal social systems in Africa, new classes have emerged to demand power. Elsewhere, I have suggested that the political system of the first Nigerian Republic was undermined by an acute contradiction between the constitutional allocation of power and the real distribution of power in society.[2] The constitution gave dominant power to the numerical majority—i.e., to the dominant party of the Northern Region— while the real distribution of power is determined by technological and educational development, in which respect the southern regions are far superior. Since the dominant party of the North was determined to hold power at all costs, a political upheaval was likely to occur.

In this light, the issue may appear to have been North versus South rather than North versus East (although the balance of technological power in the South is probably in the Eastern Region). However, an explanation of the upheaval in terms of North versus South is hardly less superficial than an explanation in terms of tribal rivalry. It simply overlooks the very real possibility of redressing the imbalance by means of negotiation and agreement among the power groups of the several regions.

Here we encounter the elements of chance and choice in social change. As in the English civil wars, there were at least two possible solutions to the imbalance between legal and real power—one conservative, the other radical. Nigerian conservatives, like the "silken gentlemen" of Cromwell's army, who finally won out, had a formula for peaceful development. I have termed it the "principle of regional security."[3] It prescribed the full regionalization of all political organizations capped by an agreement among regional leaders to respect the political *status quo* and share the fruits thereof on an equitable basis. That conservative tendency was as strong among leaders in the South as among leaders in the North. In fact, it was ardently espoused by the government of the Western Region and it had powerful advocates in the Midwestern and Eastern Regions.

It might be objected that the regional power system was bound to fail in the end because the politicians in power were too deficient both in ideas and in organizational ability to cope with the great economic problems of unemployment and wasteful expenditure. That, however, cannot be proved, and a few hard-headed economists did have faith in the political structure of the first republic. In any case, the failures of governments alone do not make revolutions, and the driving force of revolution in January 1966 can only be appreciated in the fullness of recent Nigerian history.

For twenty years, the question of regional power has been a critical issue in Nigerian politics. In 1946, governmental regions were created in the North, East and West, leading to the adoption of a federal constitution in 1954. For about ten years, from 1952–62, the system of regional power was relatively stable. There were three major political parties, each dominant in a region and rooted in its main cultural-linguistic group— Hausa in the North, Ibo in the East and Yoruba in the West. Each party was the organizational core of a political class, defined to include those who control the dominant institutions of society.[4] The regional party leaders operated highly effective systems of patronage, dispensing jobs, contracts, commercial loans, traditional titles and scholarships. Young people in all parts of the country were pressured in various ways to support the regional government parties. Many of them regretted this necessity; others became cynical. Opinion follows interest, and many young adults furthered their careers by adopting regionalist principles and tribalist ideologies. According to this analysis, tribalism followed regionalism as an attitude of the political class.

However, regionalism in Nigeria never fully triumphed. Originally, it was a colonial policy, while anti-regionalism was the main authentic tradition of the Nigerian nationalist movement. The high point of anti-regionalist assertion was, perhaps, 1951, when the leading nationalist party of that time—the NCNC—repudiated a regionalist constitution and affirmed its belief in unitary government. That stance, however, was shortly thereafter revised.

The anti-regionalist cause in Nigeria was similar to the anti-provincialist cause of the nationalist movement in India. A great difference between the course of nationalism in Nigeria and that in India may be perceived in Gandhi's dictum that no national leader should hold a provincial government office under the 1935 scheme of provincial autonomy. In Nigeria, the decisive decision to the contrary may have been Nnamdi

Azikiwe's decision to become Premier of the Eastern Region in 1954. The rationale of his action lies in the complex nature of the Nigerian nationalist struggle, involving intense competition for economic as well as political power.[5] The strategies adopted by Azikiwe and other nationalists, in particular the decision to compromise with regionalism, were strongly opposed by radical members of Azikiwe's own party, the NCNC. The radical movement as a whole never abandoned its anti-regionalist cause. That tendency has persisted among radicals in all sections of the country, notably in the major urban centres and among the radical intelligentsia of the universities and the trade union movement.

After independence, the anti-regionalist cause was espoused by Obafemi Awolowo, leader of the Action Group—the dominant political party of the Western Region—who had become leader of the opposition in the Federal House of Representatives. Awolowo's attempt to transform the Action Group into an explicitly socialistic party, aiming to divide the existing regions into smaller states, was resisted by his principal associates in the Western Region itself. Increasingly isolated from conservative and moderate opinion within his party, Awolowo became embroiled in clandestine activities, leading to his imprisonment and conviction upon a charge of treasonable felony. In the course of these events, his party split and lost control of the Western Regional government. Then the anti-regionalist cause merged (some would say that it became confused) with the political cause of the Eastern Region. The NCNC, the battered Action Group, and their radical allies in the North combined to form the United Progressive Grand Alliance, while their opponents, in control of the Northern, Western and federal governments, formed the Nigerian National Alliance.

The officers intervene

Meanwhile, in 1963, the NCNC had counted on a new census to reveal a population shift from North to South that might enable it and its allies to gain control of the federal government by electoral means.[6] To its dismay, the disputed census enumerated 30 million people in the Northern Region to 26 million in the south. In December 1964, UPGA leaders decided to boycott the federal election, alleging that it had been rigged against them, mainly in Northern constituencies. After a brief crisis, featuring a sharp dispute between President Azikiwe and the Prime Minister, Sir Abubakar Tafawa Balewa, over the validity of the election, an agreement was reached that left the Northern-dominated NNA in control of the federal government.[7]

It has since been alleged that "as far back as August 1965, a small group of army officers of a certain ethnic group [obviously Ibo] dissatisfied with political development within the Federation, began to plot, in collaboration with some civilians, the overthrow of what was then the Government of the Federation of Nigeria and the eventual assumption of power in the country".[8] The existence of a military plot became a virtual certainty after the blatantly rigged Western Regional election of October 1965, followed by a general breakdown of law and order in wide areas of that region. Local district meetings were reported to have declared their "independence" of the regional government at Ibadan. Behind the warring factions in the Western Region stood the Northern and Eastern regional governments. It has been reported that the Premiers of Northern and Western Nigeria had been informed of the military threat and had taken a firm decision to crush their military and political opponents. In these circumstances, the lightning *coup* of January 15 may have averted a civil war.

All but a few of the fourteen *coup* leaders who have been identified[9] were Ibo junior officers, although their men belonged to various tribes. The victims, with one known exception, were non-Ibo officers and politicians who were identified (rightly or wrongly) with the old regime. It should not be forgotten that the Yoruba people of the Western Region had been in a state of insurrection for three months. From a radical Yoruba, i.e., Action Group, viewpoint, it was up to the Ibo officers to deliver the *coup de grâce.* Typologically, the Ibo junior officers, personified by the young major C. K. Nzeogwu, who killed the Northern Premier, reincarnated the radical Zikists of the later 1940s who had been frustrated by the growth of regionalism and the conditions of bourgeois nationalism.[10]

On 17 January Nzeogwu surrendered to Major-General Aguiyi-Ironsi, who had taken over in Lagos as supreme commander of the military government at the request of the federal council of ministers. It was reported that the insurgents had intended to kill the general, but decided to capitulate to him when their way to power was blocked by the bulk of the army. General Aguiyi-Ironsi, an Ibo, was acclaimed throughout Nigeria as the saviour of the nation. It was not until a year later, after the general had been assassinated, that his successors accused him of complicity in the coup, hinting, with scant evidence, that he had been in the picture from the beginning.[11]

The advent of Aguiyi-Ironsi was approved by Nigerians of diverse ideological persuasions. Radicals revelled in the fall of the old regime; the southern bourgeoisie, especially its Eastern component, was glad to be rid of 'northern domination'; conservative elements, like official western commentators, were obviously relieved by the figure of a politically moderate supreme commander, who appeared to have thwarted the perilous designs of his rebellious subordinates. The general acted with delicacy to establish the non-tribalist nature and ideal of the new regime. A new deal was promised by the military government and joyfully anticipated by the country. Tribalism would be suppressed, corruption would be rooted out, wasteful drains on the treasury would be stopped, and the discredited politicians would not be allowed to return. Symbolically, the four regions were redesignated as groups of provinces under military governors who were tactfully chosen from the main respective ethnic groups. It was announced that a new territorial framework would be designed to replace the old regional system.

Apparently, political power had shifted away from the Northern rulers and their allies to a more progressive section of the population. The dangerous imbalance between legal and technological power had been corrected. What had been socially necessary had been accomplished by political forces rooted in the specific historical conditions of Nigeria. The conflict between nationalism and regionalism, engendered by colonial rule, appeared to have been resolved by a decisive victory for the anti-regionalist side.

Why the military government failed

The overthrow of regional power in Nigeria was not in itself a social revolution. To be sure, the ruling class of the North had been deprived of federal power and a slothful section of the Southern ruling class had been severely chastened. Anything more would depend upon the uncertain character of the military government.

In keeping with its popular mandate and posture of public morality, the military government initiated a number of investigations into corruption and maladministration under the old regime. It also commissioned an expert review of constitutional alternatives. However, the basic problems of the country were neither moral, administrative, nor constitutional; they were political, and the military government was lacking in political acumen. It relied too heavily upon the advice of senior civil servants, many of whom have contempt for the vocation of politics and harbour ingrained technocratic sentiments. The new regime heaped scorn upon all the old politicians, almost without exception, and failed to appreciate political realities that should not have been ignored.

In May, the military government decreed both the abolition of the regions as legal entities and the unification of the several public service establishments. Political parties and tribal associations were banned and General Aguiyi-Ironsi declared that the military government would hold power for three years, unless its aims could be accomplished sooner. There was a sharp reaction in several Northern towns, where mobs attacked Ibos over a two day period, causing some hundreds of deaths. Subsequently, a meeting of Northern chiefs and Emirs, convened by the Northern military governor, accepted assurances from the military government that no permanent constitution would be imposed on the country without a democratic referendum. But the situation continued to deteriorate. Many of the old politicians were back in the field and Nigerian politics was about to revive in an ugly mood. Because the military government had neglected to create a political basis for its new administrative structure and grand design, the political revival was destined to be chaotic.

On 29 July an army mutiny broke out in the West. General

Aguiyi-Ironsi was killed along with the Western military governor and many Ibo officers. It emerged that Northern soldiers had the upper hand and the Supreme Military Council asked Lt-Colonel Yakubu Gowon, a Northerner, who held the position of army chief of staff, to assume command. On 1 August, he addressed the nation, deploring the 'sad and unfortunate incidents' of 15 January and declaring that unitary government was unworkable in Nigeria. He acted immediately to release that staunch advocate of a strong federal government based on many states, Chief Awolowo, from prison. Shortly thereafter, Awolowo was chosen "leader of the Yoruba" by a conference of "leaders of thought" in the West.

Soon it appeared that the long-cherished hope of many antiregionalists—a federal state of small regions, no one of which could dominate the rest, while each would have a sufficient degree of autonomy to feel secure in its identity—might actually be in the offing. Promising a rapid return to civilian rule, the new military government repealed the 'unification decree' of 24 May, restored the legal identities of the four regions, and took steps to convene a conference of regional representatives to formulate new constitutional principles. Colonel Gowon asked the conference, known as the *ad hoc* constitutional committee, to rule out the extreme ideas of unitary government on the one hand and dissolution of the country into its component parts on the other.

Among the members and advisers of the several delegations were men of outstanding political skill, notably politicians who had been identified with the UPGA cause in the Northern, Western and Midwestern Regions: Awolowo from the West, Anthony Enahoro, who had been imprisoned with Awolowo, from the Midwest, and two radical opposition leaders in the Northern Region, Aminu Kano and J.S. Tarka. Eventually, all delegations, save the Eastern, accepted the idea of a strong federal government based on small states. Ironically, the Easterners, long-time partisans of centralization, now favoured a loose association (or confederation) of strong regions. So long as the NCNC had existed, independently or as part of a greater political alliance, the leaders of Eastern Nigeria had never espoused regional separatism to the detriment of Nigerian unity. Now the party was gone, abolished by decree, and the East, smarting under the blows of the July mutiny and continued organized violence against Ibos in many areas of the North, had given way to a regionalist tendency. While the East is an overcrowded area, it is also the centre of a vast and growing petroleum industry. Sorely provoked, the Ibos were in a mood to break away with the precious oil, *a la* Katanga. But non-Ibo elements in the East, in whose land the oil reserves are largely located, were adamantly opposed to secession. Soon, hopes for a reversal of the uncharacteristic Eastern position began to rise. They were dashed brutally in late September by a wave of systematic violence against Ibos throughout the Northern Region that lasted for several days, dealing the cause of Nigerian unity a seemingly irreparable blow. Some thirty thousand persons were killed and more than a million refugees, mainly from the North, fled to the East. When the constitutional talks resumed in late October, Eastern delegates did not attend.

Many reports from Nigeria confirm that the "pogrom" (a term used in official statements and publications of the Eastern regional government) in the North had been carefully planned and ruthlessly executed. In many towns, killings began in the evening of 30 September. Earlier that day the federal military government had disclosed the contents of an interim report by the constitutional committee, including "substantial but not as yet unanimous agreement that more States should be created in Nigeria" in accordance with "the wishes of the people" as determined by plebiscite. The Northern delegation is reported to have concurred in this recommendation and it was hoped that the Easterners would be persuaded to reconsider their objections. In this light, the "pogrom" might be seen as an attempt by die-hard Northern politicians to destroy the hope of an anti-regionalist settlement. But another disquieting fact indicated that such a Machiavellian explanation was not the whole story. Some of the worst crimes were committed by soldiers of Northern origin, most of whom, however, were neither Hausa nor Muslim.[12] Moreover, Ibos were assulted ferociously by non-Hausa Northerners in the southerly portion of the Northern Region, where the inhabitants are presumed to favour the creation of a Middle Belt state. Non-Hausa Middle Belters are predominant among Northern soldiers; indeed, Colonel Gowon, himself a Christian, hails from a small Middle Belt tribe.

Why did non-Muslim Middle Belt soldiers join with Muslim Hausas to massacre non-Muslim Ibos? Surely it was not in defense of the existing regional pattern, since the Middle Belters have long wanted their own state and it was Middle Belt pressure that forced the Northern delegation to the constitutional conference to support the creation of new states. When the conference convened in September, both the Northern and the Eastern delegations had favoured a loose federation of the existing regions. The Western delegation seemed ready to conform until Middle Belt pressures produced a change in the Northern position.[13] At this juncture, J.S. Tarka, leader of the Middle Belt state movement, emerged as the most formidable of the Northern delegation members. In short, the Middle Belters, like minority elements in the Eastern Region, were both anti-Ibo and anti-regionalist. Can their position be interpreted in terms other than plain tribalism? An historical view is once again required.

Regionalism and Tribes

We have argued that regionalism was the chief political characteristic of the first republic, its underlying political issue, and the cause of its great crisis. Closely related to regionalism, but analytically distinct from it, was another prime characteristic of the old system, namely the political predominance in every region of a major tribal group—Hausa in the North, Ibo in the East, and Yoruba in the West. The political structure of the first republic had been based on a tripartite agreement between leaders of the big tribes, and big tribe chauvinism was a legacy of the tripartite system. The so-called minority tribes had never been satisfied with the political structure of pre-*coup* Nigeria. Repelled by big tribe chauvinism within the major political parties, ambitious and gifted activists of minority tribe origin found scope for their talents in the trade union movement, in small radical parties, and in subregional separatist parties.[14] Statistically, the chances of serious disaffection from the system were relatively great, since the combined minorities comprise over one third—possible forty per cent—of the total population. There is a paradox in much writing on Nigeria that has often been overlooked. There are said to be over 400 ethnic groups in the country, but most commentaries dwell mainly on conditions within and relations among the big three tribes. We have very few detailed studies of political behaviour among the other forty per cent.[15] In fact, it has been generally assumed that the minorities were too fragmented to act together as a political force, and they have been overlooked in the distribution of economic goods, political power, and psychological consideration.

Since 1957, Awolowo, as leader of the Action Group, has been a champion of the minority group demand for more states. He has held this view sincerely on intellectual grounds, but it is also true that so long as his party, based mainly on the Yoruba, was in opposition to the federal government coalition, his principle was also good politics for the Yoruba. At the constitutional conference convened by Colonel Gowon in September 1966, only the small Midwestern Region, which had been excised from the West in 1963, did not waver in its espousal of a strong federal government based on small states. When the chips were down, the minorities could not rely on any big region support, but they were now supreme in the army, and Tarka, the unquestioned leader of a million Middle Belt Tiv, pressed his point to the hilt, while the leaders of minority tribes in the East stoutly resisted the secession of that region.

If the January *coup* tolled the overthrow of regionalism, the July mutiny and its cruel aftermath spelled revenge against big tribe chauvinism. The neglected and ever-disparaged "pagans" of the Middle Belt joined forces with beaten regionalists to advance their own cause and assert their presence in Nigerian politics. Their victims were their natural competitors in a world of scarcity—industrious Ibos from the East, who did everything they would like to have done themselves. This is more than "tribalism." It is the deeper, chaotic agressiveness of depressed people who resent the mean conditions of their lives. Tribal persecution, like racial and religious persecution, is a consequence of poverty, insecurity, and the lack of opportunity for satisfying employment.[16]

Why the issues persist

Looking back on the course of Nigerian politics since the second world war, we may perceive a continuing oscillation between national and regional values. This may be attributed to the following causes among others. First, an inner contradiction of British colonial policy: "There was always a hidden conflict, a constitutional tug-of-war, between Indirect Rule—which tended to accentuate differences within and between Regions—and the developing system of Crown Colony Government—which, in the reforms of 1922–54, had to reconcile such conflicts at the centre."[17] Secondly, the growth of culturally particularistic forms of nationalism within the nationalist movement;[18] thirdly, the identification of privileged class interests with regional power, so that regionalism itself became an ideological posture in Nigerian politics.

An extreme assertion of regionalism by the conservative rulers of the first republic engendered an equally extreme thrust in the opposite direction by their centralizing successors. Particularism struck back vengefully, and the current oscillation may yet culminate in a complete breakaway of one or more regions. After the September massacres, Eastern delegates did not return to meetings of the *ad hoc* constitutional committee. At length, in January 1967, the Supreme Military Council met at Aburi, Ghana. Lt-Col. C. Odumegwu-Ojukwu, Military Governor of Eastern Nigeria, presented the views of his dissident region.[19] For the time being, he said, the regions would have to 'move slightly apart' for the country to survive. His region did not even recognize the existence of a central government or supreme commander. The Military Council, he suggested, should be headed by a 'titular' commander-in-chief, who would function as a 'chairman' and 'constitutional' (non-executive) head of state. All decisions affecting the regions would require their concurrence, and all decrees in force to the contrary should be repealed forthwith. In short, the East demanded regional autonomy and an effective veto over measures that it might not accept. The meeting went a long way towards acceptance of the Eastern view. It was agreed that the chairman of the Supreme Military Council would be titled Commander-in-Chief of the Armed Forces and Head of the Federal Military

Government; that all decisions affecting 'the whole country' would be determined by the Supreme Military Council (although the need for unanimity in the taking of decisions and the question of whether the council could be convened in the absence of one or more of the military governors were left vague); that such matters would be referred to the regional military governors for 'comment and concurrence' whenever the Military Council could not meet; that all decrees of the national and federal military governments that were contrary to these agreements would be repealed within a few weeks; that senior appointments in the armed forces, police, federal government, and diplomatic service would be made by the Supreme Military Council; that the army would be organized into regional commands, subject to the control of regional military governors in matters of internal security.

Special committees were created to deal with fiscal, legal, and military problems, and with the rehabilitation, employment, and property of displaced persons. The Eastern Military Governor reported that his region had absorbed 1.5 million refugees. For security reasons, he did not feel able, as yet, to permit the return of non-Easterners who had been expelled from that region. He did, however, accept that the Midwestern and Western Regions might have to send Easterners back to the East to ease the acute unemployment problems of those regions. Finally, it was agreed to reconvene the Supreme Military Council in Nigeria.

Soon thereafter, the Eastern Military Governor voiced his dissatisfaction with the implementation of the agreements reached in Ghana. Inevitably, there were problems of interpretation. When the military leaders met in March, at the midwestern capital of Benin City, the Eastern Military Governor did not attend. Disavowing secessionist aims, he declared that his region would move, unilaterally if need be, towards greater 'decentralization' and autonomy.

The secession of one or more regions will not settle the issue of territorial separatism. Non-Ibo separatism is a powerful force within the Eastern Region, and any number of separatist movements are either active or latent in the rest of the country. Nonetheless, we should not assume that this process of fragmentation is irreversible in our time. At bottom, the nationalist tradition is not narrowly nationalistic; it is inspired by supra-national goals of the African renaissance. If Nigeria splits apart, the nationalist vanguard may yet regroup on a greater regional, e.g., West African, basis. The state system of post-colonial West Africa as a whole is bankrupt and the time for a revival of West African nationalism may be ripe.

If Nigeria does stay together as one sovereign state, its viability would seem to depend upon the discovery of a political formula that will satisfy local aspirations for self-government, while it permits the national government to grow in stature through the promotion of economic development and the provision of social welfare services.[20] It is unlikely that a confederation of regions would be equal to that task. Truly national institutions would be too few in number, too limited in their binding effects, and too distant from the people to offset the divisive forces of regional self-interest. Any serious disagreement between the regions, e.g., over revenue allocation or matters of foreign policy, could result in a final division of the country.

On the other hand, a constitutional settlement that provides for an effective national government on paper seems unlikely to work in practice unless it is underpinned by a viable political settlement. There is need for a nation-wide party, front, congress, or whatever it may be called, to avert ethnic and sectional separatism in political organization. Heretofore, entire sections of the population have been alienated from the national government. The West was an 'odd region out' during the first republic. The East was 'out' after the abortive 1964 election. The North was 'out' during the first military regime. The East was 'out' after the July mutiny. Middle Belters, midwesterners, peoples of the Cross River, and Niger Deltans have been 'out' most of the time. It is, perhaps, to Nigeria's credit that partial regimes do not survive.

It has been suggested that a constitution might be devised to ensure that no section of the country will be excluded from its fair share in the central government. Doubtless, something can be done in that direction. But constitutional provisions alone are not likely to prevent the political isolation or neglect of ethno-sectional groups. That is a political task, best undertaken by a nation-wide party of national purpose, within which there could be a beneficial exchange of ideas and a creative development of doctrine. This does not imply the legal institution of a one-party state. It is always dangerous to proscribe opposition in a politically vibrant society of people who want to be free.

A Postscript*

The causes of conflict in post-colonial Nigeria are complex and controversial. What cannot be doubted now is the desire of the great mass of the Ibo-speaking people to secede from Nigeria. Few peoples or nations in modern times have been as resolute and united in the face of death as have the Ibo. If the principle of self-determination means much today, it should apply in this case.

Biafra's right to be independent of Nigeria has been contested on various grounds. First, it is alleged that the non-Ibo people of Biafra do not desire to secede with the Ibos. This, surely, is a negotiable and soluble issue. The right to self-determination of all peoples who suffer in this tragedy should be upheld. Biafra's government has offered to abide by the principle of free choice. This principle should also be extended to the hapless Ibos of the neighboring Midwestern State.

Secondly, many Nigerians, especially among the intelligentsia, have a strong emotional commitment to the preservation of Nigerian unity. Many of those who feel this way are deeply patriotic. My criticism of their stand is tempered with respect for their idealism. Yet, I think it is wrong to put the value and interest of the state—Nigeria—over and above the clearly asserted interest of the people. It seems irrational for an African government to decimate an African people merely to maintain the unity of a recently inherited state. What price such unity? Here it is the reduction of a proud and prosperous people to the bare bones of existence.

A third argument against Biafran independence is rational in terms of the self-interest of other Nigerian groups. They fear that if one section goes, others too may go. If the Ibos can be independent, why not the Yorubas, the Kanuris, or the Kano

*"A Postscript" is an addendum to the original publication, and was written for inclusion in this volume. It has appeared in *Africa Today,* Vol. 16, No. 1 (February—March 1969), pp. 3–4.

State? Minority groups in the Middle Belt, especially, dread the breakup of the country into three or four parts, in which case they might revert to their previous condition of appendages to the emirate system of Northern Nigeria. It is not surprising that these elements, now so prominent in the army, are among the most vehement campaigners to keep Nigeria one.

Their views are reasonable, and therein lies the tragic core of this dispute. It is not right for the Ibos to be punished and denied their freedom; yet the Federal Government has a cogent case. The war goes on mainly because there is no logical solution to be found within the context of the existing pattern of petty statehoods. The way out is via a truly pan-African solution—one that would transcend both the parochial nationalism of Nigeria and the parochial nationalism of Biafra. We should sympathize with the values of the best of the Nigerian patriots. With them, we should say "unity." But unity need not be predicated on the preservation of states created during the colonial era. Local boundary adjustments, when they are desired by the people concerned, need not be inconsistent with the promotion of African unity and may even facilitate that purpose. Is this visionary? Perhaps; but the pan-African vision is a better guide to action than the destructive *realpolitik* of parochial nationalism.

From the pan-African perspective, Biafran nationalism and Nigerian nationalism are equally parochial and inadequate. Certainly the Nigerian nationalist position is not superior to the Biafran. Neither one should be maintained as a political fetish.

NOTES

1. *The Commonwealth of Oceana,* 1656.

2. "Contradictions in the Nigerian Political System", *The Journal of Modern African Studies,* 3, 2, 1965, pp. 201-13.

3. "Nigerian Politics: The Ordeal of Chief Awolowo, 1960-65", in Gwendolen M. Carter, ed., *Politics in Africa: 7 Cases.* New York, 1966, p. 156.

4. Gaetano Mosca, *The Ruling Class* (1896); republished by the McGraw-Hill Book Company, New York, 1939.

5. See my analysis in *Nigerian Political Parties,* Princeton, N. J., 1963, pp. 143-89.

6. In January 1966, prior to the *coup d'etat,* Dr. Chukuka Okonjo, director of the Centre for Population Studies of the University of Ibadan, read a paper to the First Annual Population Conference held at the University of Ibadan, bravely asserting that "the best available estimate of the 1962 mid-year population" was some 45 million—22 million in the north and 23 million in the southern regions. "A Preliminary Medium Estimate of the 1962 Mid-Year Population of Nigeria." See also S. A. Aluko, "How Many Nigerians?", *The Journal of Modern African Studies,* 3, 3, 1965, pp. 371-92.

7. The most complete account of this crisis is by John P. Mackintosh, *Nigerian Government and Politics,* London, 1966, pp. 545-609, who asserts that President Azikiwe tried to take over the government during the crisis, an assertion that has also been made on several occasions by the London weekly, *West Africa.* I see Azikiwe's actions as an attempt to prevent a dangerously unfair electoral *coup* by the NNA. See also Oluwole I. Odumosu, *Constitutional Crisis: Legality and the President's Conscience* (n.d.).

8. Document published by the Federal Military Government, quoted in the *Daily Times,* Lagos, 21 October 1966, p. 2. A subsequent publication by the Federal Military Government revised this statement to allege that Ibo army officers planned to seize power as far back as December 1964. *Nigeria 1966,* Lagos, 1967, pp. 5-6.

9. *Ibid.,* p. 5.

10. The Zikists derived their inspiration from the nationalist doctrines of Nnamdi Azikiwe.

11. *Nigeria 1966,* p. 6.

12. See Colin Legum's report in *The Observer,* London, 23 October 1966.

13. *West Africa,* 24 September 1966, p. 1079.

14. I am indebted for this observation on the contribution of persons of minority tribe origin to the trade union and organized radical movements to Robert Melson, whose political study of socialists in the Nigerian labour movement is in preparation.

15. An outstanding exception is Martin J. Dent's study of politics in Tivland in J. P. Mackintosh, *op. cit.,* pp. 461-507.

16. See the sophisticated interpretation of tribal violence in Nigeria by Colin Legum in *The Observer* (London), 16 October 1966, and my comment in "Political Science and National Integration—A Radical Approach," *The Journal of Modern African Studies,* 5, 1, 1967, pp. 6-7.

17. Dennis Austin, *West Africa and the Commonwealth,* London, 1957, p. 82.

18. James S. Coleman, *Nigeria: Background to Nationalism,* Berkeley and Los Angeles, 1958.

19. Federal Republic of Nigeria, *Meeting of the Nigerian Military Leaders held at Peduase Lodge, Aburi, Ghana 4th and 5th January, 1967,* Lagos, 1967.

20. See Obafemi Awolowo, *Thoughts on the Nigerian Constitution,* Ibadan, 1966; Nnamdi Azikiwe, "Essentials for Nigerian Survival", *Foreign Affairs,* XLIII, No. 3, April, 1965, pp. 447-61; W. Arthur Lewis, *Politics in West Africa,* London, 1965.

Part I

COMPETITIVE COMMUNALISM

Competitive Communalism

Editorial Introduction

By reorienting formerly separated peoples to a common system of increasingly scarce rewards and paths to rewards, modernization tends to promote competition among the newly mobilized elements of the society. In a context of cultural pluralism, in which men perceive their competitive world through a communal prism, appeals to communal loyalty are an effective vehicle for personal advancement. Moreover, communalism provides a comfortable and a convenient shelter for those experiencing the trauma of rapid social change. As the first five papers in this section make clear, with mobilization the competitive life of the modern sector rapidly becomes communalized (See Proposition 1 of the Introduction).

In the opening selection, James Coleman describes the communalization of competition in Nigeria as between Ibos and Yorubas. The "Ibo awakening," Coleman suggests, was largely motivated by Ibo perceptions of their backwardness vis-à-vis the better-educated and occupationally dominant Yorubas. Just as the drive for pan-Ibo unity was, in part, a reaction to discrimination against Ibos resident in the cosmopolitan center of Lagos, so the Ibo predominance within both the leadership and mass membership of the Nigerian nationalist movement may be viewed as the extension of the Ibos' competitive struggle to overcome their technological underdevelopment. By the same token, later Yoruba chauvinism was in large measure a defensive reaction of educated Yorubas to the pre-eminence of Ibo-speaking Nnamdi Azikiwe and to the Ibo domination of the ranks of the NCNC. With the emergence of Yoruba communal nationalism, the competitive communalism cycle had, in effect, come full circle. Coleman's discussion highlights the manipulative aspects of communal politics—" . . . during the three-year period 1948–51, tribalism and regional nationalism became not only the most legitimate but the most effective means for educated nationalists to secure power"—and shows how constitutional developments in the early 1950's provided fuel to the communalization of the political system.

The papers by Abner Cohen and John Paden detail the communalization of competition in Nigeria, both as between Yorubas and Hausas and as between Ibos and Hausas, in the two urban centers of Ibadan and Kano. Thus, in Ibadan, the division of labor within the cattle market follows communal lines, Hausas serving as sellers and Yorubas as the buyers and butchers. As a result, Cohen indicates,

> . . . the cleavage in the market between buyer and seller, debtor and creditor, is also a cleavage between Yoruba and Hausa and, indeed, both sides describe their mutual relationships in tribalistic terms.

Cohen's analysis of the cattle trade in Ibadan serves as an important reminder that economic integration is, in itself, an insufficient condition for political integration. Indeed, the Ibadan case suggests that economic intercourse may actually encourage the communalization of political relationships.

The paper by Paden is concerned more specifically with those factors underlying communal violence. Paden distinguishes between three types of communal violence: first, violence induced by value incompatibility; second, violence resulting from competition between groups valuing the same things; third, violence which constitutes the displacement of communal frustrations upon a scapegoat-minority. He argues that the communal violence between Ibos and Hausas in Kano (in 1953 and again in 1966) was far more the result of competition stemming from the sameness of values than of conflict generated by divergent value-systems.

The paper by John Harris and Mary Rowe on the impact of entrepreneurial attitudes upon Nigerian integration adds still a further dimension to the communalization of competition in Nigeria. Of particular importance are their observations that the Nigerian pre-war economy was far less integrated than has been popularly believed—interregional trade in locally produced goods for domestic consumption constituted only 5% of GDP and less than one-third the value of merchandise imports in 1963. Challenging the notion that business interests are politically integrative they note that the Yorubas and Hausas had gained a competitive advantage by the exodus of the Ibos from their regions.

Not only does competition in culturally plural societies tend to be defined in communal terms, but generally the competition involves groups which are differentially mobilized into the modern sector of the economy. As a consequence, competitive interaction multiplies coincident social cleavages and thereby exacerbates communal conflict (Proposition 2). The chapters by Robert A. LeVine and Richard Henderson are concerned with those factors in the Nigerian context which have contributed to the differential mobilization of populations.

LeVine and Henderson take quite different approaches to this question. In the excerpts from *Dreams and Deeds* which are presented, LeVine relates his empirical finding that Ibo, Yoruba and Hausa student populations contain varying proportions of individuals with high "need achievement" to the nineteenth century (pre-colonial) status-mobility systems of the three cultures. It is suggested that the relatively high incidence of "need achievers" among Ibos, and to a lesser extent among Yorubas, accounts in part for the relatively high levels of economic development and entrepreneurial activity in Southern Nigeria. In an important postscript to his original study, LeVine suggests that n-achievement of a cultural group may vary over time. "Hence," he concludes, "group differences such as the ones reported in *Dreams and Deeds* might reflect the different phases in socioeconomic development that the group happened to be in at the time of assessment. . . ."

Henderson, by contrast, draws attention to the difficulty in linking contemporary behavioral patterns to antecedent cultural variables. If cultural predispositions were in fact crucial

determinants of "adaptability," Onitsha Town Ibo would manifest patterns similar to the Ibo strangers in their midst. But
occupationally and in terms of organizational innovativeness,
the Onitsha Town Ibo who have remained resident within their
home community are more like the seemingly less adaptable
Calabar Efik than they are like the immigrant Ibo. Consequently, Henderson concludes,

> . . . it is clearly too facile to infer directly from general
> structural differences in precolonial systems to differ-
> ences in modern urban adjustments. An assessment of a
> community's adaptation to modern conditions must take
> account of (1) the complexity of the wider ecological, eco-
> nomic, and governmental settings within which adapting
> traditional systems operate, and (2) the multiple possible
> directions in which successful modernizing adaptations
> may occur. Only when the determining effects of settings
> and opportunities are fully understood can the importance
> of traditional structures be adequately assessed.

In the final paper in this section, Ulf Himmelstrand explores
some of the socio-psychological implications of criss-crossing
social ranks in a culturally plural society. While conventional
theorizing has indicated that the emergence of socio-economic
linkages cross-cutting communal boundaries helps to prevent
the emergence of potentially disintegrative political conflict,
recent work on rank-equilibration processes suggests that
criss-crossing lines of social division may, under certain conditions, intensify rather than soften conflict (Proposition 3).
Focusing upon Ibo-Yoruba relationships within Western Nigeria, Himmelstrand shows how both "tribalism" and supra-
tribal "nationalism" can be understood in terms of rank-
equilibration theory. Sounding a theme which runs through
this entire volume, Himmelstrand observes,

> . . . The Nigerian 'tribalism' of recent years is mainly a
> *political* tribalism stemming not from primordial ethnic
> loyalties as such, but from politically exploited and rein-
> forced reactions to strains in the emerging stratification
> system.

It is with the theoretical analysis of Ibo-Yoruba structural
strain and social reaction that this paper is concerned.

CHAPTER 3

The Ibo and Yoruba Strands in Nigerian Nationalism

JAMES S. COLEMAN

The Ibo Awakening

Iboland is one of the most densely populated rural areas in the world. In some places the density is more than 1,000 persons to the square mile. Moreover, the soil is comparatively poor. As a result, in the past the Ibo expanded territorially and exported to other areas large numbers of seasonal laborers and even semi-permanent residents. In fact, the Ibo were expanding territorially in many directions at the time of the British intrusion. Since then this outward thrust has continued and has been the source of anti-Ibo feeling among the tribes bordering Iboland (for example, the Igala, the Idoma, the Tiv, and even the Ibibio). The Nigerian historian Dike argues that "perhaps the most important factor conditioning Ibo history in the nineteenth century and in our own time is land hunger. . . . The Ibos pressing against limited land resources had, of necessity, to seek other avenues of livelihood outside the tribal boundaries."[1] British policy has been, in effect, one of containment,

Excerpted from James S. Coleman, *Nigeria: Background to Nationalism* (Berkeley and Los Angeles: University of California Press, 1958), pp. 332–352. Copyright © 1958 by University of California Press. Reprinted by permission of the publisher and James S. Coleman. The notes are presented in slightly revised form.

mainly by supporting the peripheral tribes through land regulations designed to halt Ibo expansion. But this policy did not prevent Ibos from migrating to other areas, particularly Yorubaland, to work as farm laborers or as servants and unskilled workers.

After British pacification, individual Ibo colonizers steadily drifted to other areas. During the forty-year period 1911–1951, the number of Ibos in Lagos increased from 264 to 26,000.[2] In the Northern Provinces there were less than 3,000 Ibos in 1921, and nearly 12,000 by 1931; by 1951 the number had increased to more than 120,000, excluding settled Ibo minorities along the boundary between the Eastern and Western regions. These figures become more meaningful when it is realized that most of the Ibo immigrants gravitated to the urban centers where wage employment could be obtained. By the end of World War II Ibo clerks, artisans, traders, and laborers constituted a sizable minority group in every urban center of Nigeria and the Cameroons, as indicated in Table 21.

As a consequence of the comparative lack of opportunity in their homeland, and other factors to be noted subsequently, the Ibo embraced Western education with great enthusiasm and determination. Christian missions were welcomed, and were encouraged to set up schools in Iboland. Village improvement unions sponsored scholarships, and Ibo students flocked to secondary schools in what is now the Western Region. By the late 1930's the Ibo were more heavily represented than any other tribe or nationality in Yaba Higher College and in most Nigerian secondary schools. Thenceforward the number of Ibos appointed to the African civil service and as clerks in business firms increased at a faster rate than that of any other group. By 1945 the gap between Yorubas and Ibos was virtually closed. Increasing numbers of Ibo barristers and doctors began to arrive from England. By 1952 the number of Ibos (115) enrolled at University College, Ibadan, was nearly equal to the number of Yorubas (118). The influx of Ibos into the towns of the west and the north and their rapid educational development, which made them competitors for jobs and professional positions, were two indicators of their emergence as an active group in Nigerian affairs.

Another factor of indeterminate significance in the Ibo

TABLE 21

ETHNIC COMPOSITION OF POPULATIONS OF SELECTED URBAN CENTERS IN NIGERIA

Region and center	Indigenous group	Northern groups		Western groups		Eastern groups		Total other	Non-Nigerian Africans	Total population	Per cent nonindigenous
		Hausa	Nupe	Yoruba	Edo	Ibo	Ibibio-Efik				
Western Region											
Ibadan	Yoruba	5,538	2,177	434,732	3,500	7,335	943	4,541	430	459,196	5.4
Lagos	Yoruba	4,132	444	195,974	5,708	31,887	1,921	18,518	8,823	267,407	26.7
Abeokuta	Yoruba	1,499	75	80,648	300	1,119	83	572	155	84,451	4.0
Ilesha	Yoruba	850	132	69,833	183	398	10	603	20	72,029	2.0
Benin City	Edo	306	19	2,124	43,676	5,411	66	2,024	127	53,753	18.7
Sapele	Mixed	635	78	2,428	3,335	11,974	333	14,681	174	33,638	77.2
Eastern Region											
Onitsha	Ibo	3,339	1,813	2,693	799	66,119	314	1,688	156	76,921	14.0
Enugu	Ibo	1,557	71	1,574	862	54,465	1,331	2,427	477	62,764	13.3
Port Harcourt	Ibo	624	64	1,935	889	45,503	2,022	6,733	1,076	58,846	22.6
Aba	Ibo	259	14	590	162	52,888	1,947	1,695	232	57,787	8.4
Calabar	Efik	384	a	665	219	15,613	15,952	13,386	486	46,705	65.8
Northern Region											
Kano	Hausa	100,834	1,103	5,783	839	11,135	564	8,437	1,478	130,173	22.5
Zaria	Hausa	73,435	1,169	4,346	529	7,385	a	4,885	459	92,208	23.5
Sokoto	Hausa	42,863	1,202	476	a	1,151	a	6,226	68	51,986	17.5
Ilorin	Yoruba	4,561	1,147	34,573	a	342	a	360	11	40,994	15.6
Kaduna	Mixed	24,482	1,707	4,888	571	10,645	a	7,799	543	50,635	51.6
Jos	Birom	14,097	259	5,061	243	8,889	a	2,472	561	31,582	99.1
Minna	Gwari	3,056	1,659	2,182	a	2,988	a	2,819	106	12,810	98.1

a Exact number not known.

Sources: *Population Census of the Western Region of Nigeria, 1952* (Lagos: Government Statistician, 1953–1954); *Population Census of the Northern Region of Nigeria, 1952* (Lagos: Government Statistician, 1952), pp. 26–28; *Population Census of the Eastern Region of Nigeria, 1953* (Lagos: Government Statistician, 1953–1954).

awakening was certain characteristic personality and behavioral traits attributed to the group. Some observers have sought to relate such traits to distinctive patterns of Ibo culture. M. M. Green points out that it is the "go-getter" who is admired, "the man who has wives and children and bestirs himself and makes money. . . . A man who just sits quiet is not respected."[3] Life in some traditional Ibo societies tends to be highly competitive, and great stress is placed upon achieved status. Some of these traits are particularly characteristic of the Aro, a subgroup within Ibo society. Fanning out from Arochuku, their homeland, the Aro, by shrewdness, strong familial bonds, and hard work, acquired substantial influence in many Ibo towns where Aro colonies were formed.[4] These facts are, of course, very suggestive, but generalizations about "national character" and culturally determined behavioral traits must be treated with great caution. Competitiveness, materialism, and emphasis upon achieved status are not unique with the Ibo, nor necessarily common to all Ibo. At the very highest level of generalization and comparison, however, they are traits that gave birth to certain national stereotypes and provided a basis for distinguishing the attitudes and behavior of the typical Ibo from those of the typical Yoruba or Hausa. But even here a distinction would have to be made between generations, as second- and third-generation Yoruba and Hausa youths have been less affected by traditional cultural determinants.

One of the most provocative features of the emergence of the Ibo has been their role in political activity and in the nationalist movement. At the outset it should be noted that Ibos overwhelmingly predominated in both the leadership and the mass membership of the NCNC, the Zikist Movement, and the National Church.[5] Postwar radical and militant nationalism, which emphasized the national unity of Nigeria as a transcendent imperative, was largely, but not exclusively, an Ibo endeavor. The important and relevant questions here are: (1) Why did politically conscious Ibos tend to gravitate toward radical and militant nationalism? (2) Why did they incline toward a Pan-Nigerian ideal as the nationalist objective? (3) What was the effect of these orientations upon the development of nationalism among other nationalities?

There are several possible answers to the first question. In the first place, certain aspects of traditional Ibo culture might predispose an Ibo toward nationalist activity. Three such aspects—expansiveness, competitiveness, and emphasis upon acquired status—have been discussed in preceding paragraphs. In addition to these, the traditional pattern of Ibo political organization is of decided significance. As one observer has written:

> The fact . . . that they possessed traditionally a form of political organization within which power was widely distributed, and were not encumbered with chiefs or held back by excessive respect for authority, made them naturally inclined, once they turned their attention to national politics, to question the principles on which colonial rule was based.[6]

The Ibo attitude toward authority and Ibo individualism in political affairs were partly the outgrowth of the conciliar and "democratic" character of Ibo political processes. Moreover, the Ibo political system gave great latitude to youth. An enterprising, talented young man who acquired wealth could attain political power, even over his elders.[7] Ibo youths were organized into age-grade associations which not only had disciplinary power over their members but also played important political and judicial roles within the community.[8] In these features, Ibo culture differed rather markedly from both Yoruba and Hausa cultures, which placed a great value on age and ascribed status.

Nnamdi Azikiwe's leadership provides another explanation for the inclination of many Ibos toward a more emphatic nationalism. His special role in the awakening of the Ibo peoples, and the charisma with which he was endowed in their eyes, have already been mentioned. Azikiwe's own nationalist orientation helped to shape the attitudes of his large Ibo following. As we have seen, however, Azikiwe's attitude cannot be dissociated from his American experience; nor can one ignore the fact that a substantial number of postwar Ibo political leaders had had a similar experience. This suggests that politically conscious Ibos were unusually assertive in their nationalism because their leaders, more than the leaders of any other nationality in Nigeria, were strongly influenced by America and, more particularly, by the American color problem.

Finally, of the three major groups in Nigeria, the Ibo had historical and environmental justification for a militant protest against the existing order. In a sense their anti-British nationalism was but an extension of their competitive struggle within Nigeria to overcome their technological underdevelopment. The powerful urge for progress and self-transformation which drove them to assert themselves in the affairs of Nigeria was in effect the same that drove them on to take the lead in early postwar nationalism.

The special predisposition of the Ibo for assertive nationalism is thus partly explainable in terms of certain unique traits of their traditional culture, the influence of Azikiwe and the American Negro, and their reaction against their status in Nigeria. But what about the second question we have asked? In contrast to most educated Hausas and Yorubas, why, in the immediate postwar period, was the educated Ibo nationalist more attracted to Pan-Nigerian objectives? This question is not meant to suggest that non-Ibo nationalists had a lesser objective, but rather that those from other dominant groups (Hausa and Yoruba) placed greater emphasis upon their own cultural heritage, even though they too believed a Nigerian federation was desirable. The difference is one of emphasis and degree, but it is an important difference. A partial answer to the question is provided by the same factors that inclined the Ibo to a more emphatic nationalism. Azikiwe's own tendency to define nationalism in Pan-Nigerian or Pan-African terms was undoubtedly communicated to his large Ibo following. Azikiwe's mission was to free Africa, to free the African wherever he lived. He affirmed that "an African is an African no matter where he was born, whether at Kibi or at Zungeru . . . Bathurst or Accra, Patagonia . . . or Tuscaloosa . . . Nairobi or Amedica [sic]. . . ."[9] It was the force of circumstances and the obvious need to work within a particular political framework which forced Azikiwe to localize his nationalism in the core area of Nigeria and the Cameroons.

A student of Ibo culture has suggested that the scale and form of their traditional political organization made it easier for the Ibo, as distinguished from the Hausa or the Yoruba, to be attracted to Pan-Nigerian or Pan-African ideals. The argument runs as follows:

One of the most striking features of present nationalist agitation is the conspicuous role of leaders and spokesmen originating in the region of Nigeria which was completely uninvolved in any of the former large-scale states. . . . There actually seems to be an inverse relation between the passion for modern [territorial] nationhood and the long-standing indigenous experience of large-scale organization. Thus the Ibos have carried a minimum of excess baggage so to speak, in the way of tribal or quasi-national organization crystallized around symbols which inhibit broader, trans-tribal identification of indefinitely broader scope.[10]

This is certainly a suggestive hypothesis, yet, as Professor Dike has pointed out, "beneath the apparent fragmentation of authority [in Iboland] lay deep fundamental unities not only in the religious and cultural sphere, but also . . . in matters of politics and economics."[11] The crux of the distinction, which would lend some validity to the hypothesis, is not that strong unifying forces were absent in Iboland (Dike has shown that there were many), but that for environmental and historical reasons the Ibo did not develop a highly centralized, monolithic Pan-Ibo state structure, whereas the Hausa, for the same reasons, did develop such a structure. Once this is noted, it is not unreasonable to suggest that differences in the scale and form of traditional political organization might well have contributed toward different perspectives regarding larger-scale modern political systems.

Educated Ibo leaders have been particularly resentful over the cliché that Africans have no culture and no history. It is axiomatic that all societies have a culture (that is, a way of life) as well as a history (even though it be oral history, as in large areas of Africa). What uninformed and ethnocentric critics probably had in mind, however, was a culture and a history which they themselves found attractive either because of its quaintness or because of its functional virtues, or which the advanced and educated members of the group concerned found meaningful and worthy of development. In this sense, many early European observers glorified the cultures, traditions, and histories of the Hausa states, and, to a lesser extent, of the Yoruba kingdoms, to which the Ibo, and other groups similarly placed, were invidiously contrasted.[12]

Another possible explanation for the Ibo gravitation toward a Pan-Nigerian objective lies in cruel economic realities. As described above, a mixture of poor soil and extreme overpopulation made Iboland in particular, and the Eastern Provinces in general, the "depressed areas" of Nigeria. Moreover, the poverty, lack of opportunity, and overcrowding would, in the absence of rapid industrialization or drastic and compulsory resettlement, continue indefinitely. The wide dispersion of educated Ibo clerks, artisans, and traders throughout Nigeria and the Cameroons has resulted not only in increased tension between Ibo colonizers and the non-Ibo populations among whom they live, but it has fostered among the Ibos abroad a consciousness of the potentialities of Nigerian unity and a more universalist frame of mind. The Ibo, as well as the Ibibio, had strong personal economic reasons for wanting Nigeria to be a nation with freedom of movement and enterprise. The existence of this sentiment was well demonstrated by a minority report submitted by representatives from the Eastern Region (six Ibos, four Ibibio-Efiks, one Cameroonian, and one Ijaw) as part of the recommendations of the General Conference on the review of the Nigerian constitution in January, 1950. They protested against the majority recommendation whereby southerners resident in the north would be rendered ineligible for election to the Northern House of Assembly:

> It is in our view invidious that any Nigerian could under a Nigerian constitution be deprived of the right of election to the House of Assembly in any region in which he for the time being—or permanently—has his abode merely by reason of the accident of birth or ancestry. . . . In the last analysis the unity of Nigeria is the unity of the individuals in it. The individuals are bound together by political ties of nationality. Identical nationality of any country must surely carry with it identical political rights. . . .[13]

It is significant to note that of the twelve eastern signatories to this report, only three were supporters of Azikiwe and members of the NCNC; indeed, the remaining nine opposed Azikiwe in varying degrees, and some were definitely pro-British. It is equally important to emphasize that the discriminatory provision opposed by the easterners was supported by all representatives from the Northern and Western regions. In short, the Pan-Nigerian ideal was a more emphatic objective of the Ibo and of others from the Eastern Region because the growth and the institutionalization of regional separatism might well have affected the careers and future opportunities of large numbers of easterners resident abroad.

These, then, are some of the historical, cultural, and economic factors that help to explain why the Ibo were predisposed toward an emphatic assertion of nationalism, as well as toward a Pan-Nigerian focus of that nationalism. This predisposition was only part of what can be termed the "Ibo challenge"; other aspects of the challenge were (1) the growth of a Pan-Ibo movement, and (2) the political and journalistic activities of Nnamdi Azikiwe.

The Ibo drive for rapid educational advance began in the early 1930's. Educated Ibos, domiciled in Lagos and other urban centers throughout Nigeria, organized village, town, and clan "improvement" and "progress" unions. The admirable activities of these unions in furthering the progress of rural areas have been discussed elsewhere. In 1935, when Sir Francis Ibiam, the first Ibo doctor, returned from Europe, a few energetic Ibos in Lagos urged the formation of a federation of all the small Ibo village and clan unions organized during the previous decade, to be called the Ibo Union (Lagos). This was the beginning of a Pan-Ibo movement, the main purpose of which was to advance the Ibo peoples, principally in the field of education. As one of the leaders argued in 1933:

> ... education is the only real agent that will give rebirth to the dying embers of the Ibo national zeal.... It will be the means to free the Ibos from the throes of both mental and moral thraldom and I see no better place to start the work of reunion than Lagos.[14]

At the inaugural meeting of the Ibo Union (Lagos), held in June, 1936, the leader of the movement stated:

> Brethren, this is the day and the hour when the Ibos of Nigeria should rally together ... [and] sink all differences —geographical, lingual, intellectual, moral and religious,

and unite under the banner of our great objective—the tribal unity, co-operation and progress of all the Ibos.[15]

Since most non-Yorubas resident in Lagos suffered varying forms of discrimination, particularly in regard to housing, it is not unlikely that this Ibo drive to unity stemmed in part from a real common grievance. In 1943 the general secretary of the Ibo Union (Lagos) launched a campaign to federate all Ibo unions throughout Nigeria. The following year the Ibo Federal Union, a Pan-Ibo organization, was inaugurated with headquarters in Lagos. Its specific objective was to raise money to build and maintain five secondary schools in Iboland. One of the leaders affirmed: "Give a boy a good secondary education and he can rise to any height in the world without being dragged down by the dead weight of inferiority complex." Since that time Ibo leaders have insisted that "there is nothing tribal in the affair," pointing out that the fund would be open to all subscribers and the schools to all tribes. The sincerity of this pledge cannot be questioned, particularly in view of the nondiscriminatory policy of the Ibo secondary school in Kano, an institution which became a center of enlightenment for the children of all Nigerian groups in that education-starved northern city.

During the period 1944–1947 the Ibo Federal Union, under the leadership of the Lagos branch, made great strides toward the realization of an Ibo educational plan. At one Lagos mass meeting Azikiwe donated £100 to the scheme. The meeting ended with the singing of the Ibo "national anthem."[16] A decision was made later to found a national bank of Iboland.[17] During this same period the Ibo Union (Lagos) was one of the most active member organizations supporting the NCNC; and the provincial branches of the Ibo Federal Union often took the initiative in organizing the reception of the NCNC delegation during its famous tour of the country in 1946. It was this apparently close alliance between the Pan-Ibo movement and the NCNC Pan-Nigeria movement which alarmed the leaders of other nationalities, who saw what they suspected to be a growing threat of Ibo domination. In actual fact, the Ibo Federal Union devoted its attention solely to the problems of education and of the material improvement of Iboland. It was not until 1948, after the outbreak of Yoruba-Ibo conflict in Lagos, that Ibo leaders converted the Pan-Ibo federation into a quasi-political organization.

Perhaps the most provocative features of the Ibo entrance into Nigerian politics were the political activities and journalistic enterprise of Nnamdi Azikiwe. Some Yoruba and Hausa leaders resented Azikiwe and his associates because they felt he threatened their positions and challenged their own aspirations for leadership. The Ibo as a group tended to be the victims of this resentment either because Azikiwe was an Ibo or because they were among his principal supporters. A not uncommon sentiment expressed by non-Ibo leaders was that, if Azikiwe had never intruded himself upon the Nigerian political scene, tribal tension and separatism would not have developed in the nationalist movement.

The animosity toward Azikiwe might have been linked to two characteristic themes in Azikiwe's political thought. Azikiwe firmly believed that there could be no compromise on the question of imperialism. In his view imperialism was based upon the ethics of force and could be liquidated only by a radical alteration of the power structure. His belief on the priority of power was cast in these terms:

> After having studied the history of man through the ages, I have come to the conclusion that control of political power is the only key which can open the door of happiness and contentment to a man as a political animal. Without political power no country can live a full life.[18]

Azikiwe's critics accused him of being power-mad, of being intolerant of any political competition, of shunning any political movement unless he could dominate it, and of having a consuming passion to be Nigeria's first president. Besides the emphasis upon power, Azikiwe believed that in a renascent Africa the young must displace the old:

> If the New Africa must be realized, then the Old Africa must be destroyed because it is at death-grips with the New Africa. . . . Renascent Africans must be equal to the task and must salvage the débris of Old Africa through the supreme efforts' of Youth.[19]

Statements of this sort, and frequent press criticisms of traditional rulers, tended to antagonize some of the Yorubas and chiefs of the west, and some of the emirs in the north.

Guided by these imperatives—the priority of power and the reformation of African society by youth—Azikiwe carried out a frontal attack upon what he called "Uncle Tom Mis-leadership": ". . . these mis-leaders developed a psychosis which had emasculated them so that they had to cringe and to curry for favours, making dolts of themselves and their posterity."[20] As the chiefs, emirs, and educated Yorubas were the Nigerian leaders at the time Azikiwe wrote these lines, it is understandable that they interpreted his remarks as a direct attack upon themselves.

Azikiwe's critics further allege that through his *West African Pilot* he exercised a tyranny based on fear—fear that anyone who dared to oppose or criticize Azikiwe would have his career or reputation shattered by being branded as an "Uncle Tom" or an "imperialist stooge." They also point out that from the beginning Azikiwe's newspapers glorified the achievements of individual Ibos at home and abroad, but seldom gave publicity to the activities of prominent Yorubas; they claim, on the contrary, that Azikiwe carried on a sustained program of character assassination against them.[21]

In his public statements and in many of his activities, Azikiwe consistently opposed tribalism. As he points out in *Renascent Africa,* his newspaper office in Accra was a "miniature West Africa, . . . a laboratory of intertribal fellowship" in which most of the major West Coast tribes and nationalities were represented.[22] There is, in fact, little evidence to support the charge that Azikiwe deliberately favored Ibos in the employment policy of his newspaper enterprises. He made an effort to present a multitribal front in the NCNC. In his newspapers, and later in the Legislative Council, he consistently denounced tribalism and separatism. Yet, even though he was not a conscious tribalist, his objectives, his methods, and his ambitions, and the predominance of Ibos among his political supporters, provoked strong opposition among the leaders of other groups, particularly the Yoruba.

The Growth of Yoruba Nationalism

Modern associational activity among the Yoruba has a rich history. In 1918 the Egba Society was founded in Lagos to promote the interests of Egbaland. Throughout the interwar period similar associations were formed, first in Lagos, and subsequently in urban centers of Yorubaland and elsewhere (for example, the Union of Ijebu Youngmen in 1923, the Yoruba Union in 1924, the Egbado Union, the Ekiti National Union, the Ife Union, the Ijaiye National Society, the Offa Descendants' Union, the Ogbomoso Progressive Union, the Owo Progressive Union, and the Oyo Progressive Union). In the late 1930's these associations formed a federation. In 1942 the Yoruba Language Society was organized (a) to awaken and foster among the Yoruba people a pride in their mother tongue, (b) to encourage the study of Yoruba, (c) to raise funds to train eligible Yorubas in scientific studies, (d) to encourage the formation of societies and groups of students, and (e) to give financial and moral support to the publication of works written in Yoruba.[23] Thus, by the end of World War II there existed a wide network of Yoruba associations which undertook to act collectively for certain purposes. There were also Pan-Yoruba associations devoted to the study and development of Yoruba culture. This associational development paralleled, but was independent of and in no respect competitive with, the similar development among the Ibo people.

In London, in 1945, a small group of Yoruba students founded a Pan-Yoruba cultural organization called the Egbe Omo Oduduwa, which translated means the Society of the Descendants of Oduduwa, who was the mythical founder of the Yoruba peoples.[24] One of the founders of this organization was Obafemi Awolowo, who had endeavored to reorganize and rejuvenate the Nigerian Youth Movement during the period 1941-1944. Until 1948 the Egbe functioned only in London. Meanwhile, certain Yoruba circles in Nigeria had become agitated about the activities of the NCNC and the more general problems of Nigerian political development. Several of the leading Yoruba chiefs, in particular, were apprehensive over the political orientation of Yoruba youth. Prominent Yorubas in

Lagos were also concerned over Azikiwe's assumption of a commanding position in the nationalist movement. Upon Awolowo's return to Nigeria in 1948 these elements joined together to found the Egbe Omo Oduduwa as a Yoruba cultural organization in Nigeria. At the time of its founding in 1948 it had the following objectives, among others:[25]

1) *Cultural development:* ". . . to foster the study of the Yoruba language, culture and history."

2) *Educational advancement:* ". . . to plan for the improvement of educational facilities . . . especially by means of Scholarship awards by the Society . . . [for] the pursuit of Secondary and university education by Yoruba boys and girls."

3) *Yoruba nationalism:* ". . . to accelerate the emergence of a virile modernised and efficient Yoruba state with its own individuality within the Federal State of Nigeria . . . [and] to unite the various clans and tribes in Yorubaland and generally create and actively foster the idea of a single nationalism throughout Yorubaland."

4) *Protection of chiefs:* ". . . to recognise and maintain the monarchical and other similar institutions of Yorubaland, to plan for their complete enlightenment and democratisation, to acknowledge the leadership of Yoruba Obas."

5) *Nigerian federation:* ". . . to strive earnestly to cooperate with existing ethnical and regional associations and such as may exist hereafter, in matters of common interest to all Nigerians, so as thereby to attain to unity in federation."

That one of the Egbe's objectives was inculcation of the "idea of a single nationalism throughout Yorubaland" did not necessarily mean that Yoruba leaders wished to minimize or detract from any movement for Nigerian independence. Yet it might well have had that effect. But the concept of Yoruba nationalism was nothing new; indeed, as has been shown, there were early efforts in that direction. As early as 1908, a member of the Legislative Council spoke in favor of reconstructing the boundaries of Yorubaland so as to have all Yorubas together. During 1911–1912 E. D. Morel, a strong Afrophile, argued repeatedly for an official policy of creating a united Yoruba state: "It is from Oyo that Yoruba nationalism could be revived if the Yorubas could be brought to appreciate all that they have lost from its

decay, all that they might gain from its re-birth."[26] The Conference of Yoruba Chiefs, the United Kingdom visit of the Alake
of Abeokuta as a representative of the Yoruba obas, the founding of the Yoruba Literary Society in 1942—all these were developments logically preceding the formation of a Pan-Yoruba
cultural organization. Moreover, most Yoruba leaders thought
in terms of a federal Nigeria in which cultural diversities
would be explicitly recognized. The previous quotations from
Awolowo's *Path to Nigerian Freedom* make this abundantly
clear.

The original founders of the Egbe realized that the inauguration of the organization might be misinterpreted. As one of
them subsequently remarked:

> When at the end of 1945 a handful of us in London
> came together to form the Egbe . . . we foresaw that the
> allegation would be made that the aim of the Egbe was
> anti-Ibo . . . and decided that not only must we not be anti-
> Ibo but we must not make it appear that we were anti-
> Ibo.[27]

Apprehension on this point was the primary motivation for
including among the Egbe's objectives the encouragement of
similar organizations among other ethnic groups in Nigeria.
When advocating such an organization in 1944, the editor of the
Daily Service remarked: ". . . we anticipate . . . an era of whole-
some rivalry among the principal tribes of Nigeria . . . [and]
while they must guard against chauvinism and rabid tribalism
the great Yoruba people must strive to preserve their individuality."[28]

Despite such efforts to avoid provocation, leading Yorubas
did make statements both before and after the organization of
the Egbe which were interpreted as tribalistic. Thus, when the
Egbe held its inaugural conference at Ile Ife in the early part
of June, 1948, Sir Adeyemo Alakija, the president, stated: "This
Big Tomorrow . . . [for the Yoruba] is the future of our children.
. . . How they will hold their own among other tribes of Nigeria.
. . . How the Yorubas will not be relegated to the background in
the future."[29] As Ibo-Yoruba tension mounted during the summer of 1948, remarks like the following, made by a member of
the Egbe, became more common:

> We were bunched together by the British who named us Nigeria. We never knew the Ibos, but since we came to know them we have tried to be friendly and neighbourly. Then came the Arch Devil to sow the seeds of distrust and hatred. . . . We have tolerated enough from a class of Ibos and addle-brained Yorubas who have mortgaged their thinking caps to Azikiwe and his hirelings.[30]

Statements of this type, and intemperate retaliatory remarks made by prominent Ibos, resulted in a press war of unprecedented violence, in which the *West African Pilot* and the *Daily Service* were the principal contestants.

From July to September, 1948, Yoruba-Ibo animosity boarded on the verge of violence. At the height of the tension, radicals on both sides descended upon the local markets and bought up all available machetes. At a mass meeting the Ibos of Lagos decided that all personal attacks on Azikiwe would be considered attacks upon the "Ibo nation," because "if a hen were killed, the chickens would be exposed to danger."[31] Azikiwe's *Pilot* declared:

> Henceforth, the cry must be one of battle against Egbe Omo Oduduwa, its leaders at home and abroad, up hill and down dale in the streets of Nigeria and in the residences of its advocates. . . . It is the enemy of Nigeria; it must be crushed to the earth. . . . There is no going back, until the Fascist Organization of Sir Adeyemo has been dismembered.[32]

The most significant outcome of the "cold war" of 1948 was the politicization of the Pan-Ibo (Ibo Federal Union) and Pan-Yoruba (Egbe Omo Oduduwa) nationality federations. In December, 1948, at a Pan-Ibo conference at Aba, the Ibo Federal Union was converted into the Ibo State Union, ostensibly to organize the "Ibo linguistic group into a political unit in accordance with the NCNC Freedom Charter."[33] Nnamdi Azikiwe was elected Ibo state president, and other prominent Ibos—both NCNC and anti-NCNC—joined to form the Provisional Committee. At the first Ibo State Conference in 1949, Azikiwe, doubtless hoping to foster self-respect among the Ibo, made certain statements in his presidential address which his critics ultimately turned against him:

... it would appear that the God of Africa has specially created the Ibo nation to lead the children of Africa from the bondage of the ages. ... The martial prowess of the Ibo nation at all stages of human history has enabled them not only to conquer others but also to adapt themselves to the role of preserver. ... The Ibo nation cannot shirk its responsibility. ...[34]

Such statements, coupled with Azikiwe's position as president of both the Ibo State Union and the Pan-Nigerian NCNC, were interpreted to mean that the NCNC was determined to impose Ibo dominion over Nigeria. These fears were not assuaged by such statements as the following, which appeared in the *West African Pilot:*

Nigerian nationalists, in this year of destiny, are not only struggling for freedom. They are seeking to impose freedom upon all worshippers of servitude and "pakistan." And relying on the NCNC we shall build the nucleus of a Socialist Commonwealth of Africa.[35]

As previously noted, between 1943 and 1948 Azikiwe had advocated a federal system for Nigeria, with eight protectorates, some of which would roughly coincide with tribal boundaries. At the Kaduna National Assembly of the NCNC, held in 1948 after the inauguration of the Egbe Omo Oduduwa, the NCNC further defined its stand in its Freedom Charter, advocating a federal system based strictly upon tribal units. Thus, its federalistic aims were quite similar to those which the Egbe supported. Indeed, it would seem that the NCNC was nudged into such a position by the action of the Egbe. In any event, as noted above, the Ibo organized the Ibo State Union and other groups followed suit; for example, the Edo National Union, the Ibibio State Union (a new name for the oldest all-tribal federation in Nigeria), and the Warri National Union were organized. Finally, at the NCNC convention held at Kano in September, 1951, the NCNC leaders suddenly decided to abandon federalism and switch to a unitarian position, because of their belief that the government and anti-NCNC Nigerians were using federalism as a cloak for dismembering Nigeria.[36]

In addition to the reasons previously given for this dramatic about-face on the part of the NCNC, two others should be noted:

(1) the emergence of a strong and well-organized political party in the Western Region; and (2) the structure and organization of power under the new Macpherson Constitution of 1951. The first point cannot be fully understood without a brief description of the new constitution and the manner in which it evolved. It will be recalled that in 1948 the new governor, Sir John Macpherson, proposed that the hated Richards Constitution be revised as soon as possible and that such revision be carried out in full consultation with the peoples of Nigeria. Throughout 1949, village, provincial, and regional conferences were held, and in January, 1950, a general conference of representatives from all sections of Nigeria assembled to reconcile the regional recommendations. At that conference the majority voted to retain the existing regions as the political units into which Nigeria was to be divided, although the question of the status of Lagos was held over for consideration by a select committee of the Legislative Council. This committee, composed of all unofficials of the old council (including Azikiwe), recommended that Lagos be abolished as a colony and be incorporated into the Western Region. In a well-documented minority report, Azikiwe recorded his dissent (and that of the NCNC) from both regionalization and the inclusion of Lagos in the Western Region. He objected to the tripartite division of the country on the grounds that "it is an artificial creation and must inevitably tend towards Balkanization"; he recommended instead "the division of the country along the main ethnic and /or linguistic groups [i.e., ten] in order to enable each group to exercise local and cultural autonomy." In the course of his argument he stressed the desire of the non-Yoruba peoples of the Western Region to "remain masters of [their] own destiny in a separate region." His critics allege that the position assumed by Azikiwe and the NCNC during the period 1948–1951 is proof positive that in his quest for power Azikiwe was the foremost tribalist, playing upon tribal sentiment, especially among the non-Yoruba tribes in the Western Region and the Middle Belt tribes in the Northern Region, in order to dissociate them from the Yoruba and the Hausa in a regionalized Nigeria.

On the incorporation of Lagos into the Western Region, which the select committee approved, Azikiwe and three other dissenting members argued that "Lagos representation in the

Central Legislature should be direct and unfettered—and not through the Western House of Assembly which must, in turn, select the same Lagos Representatives in that House of the Central Legislature." Azikiwe's Yoruba critics argue that he opposed the merger of Lagos with the Western Region because he feared that an anti-Azikiwe, Yoruba-dominated, Western House of Assembly would not only freeze him out of the central House of Representatives (for which it was the electoral college), but would also legislate for Lagos, the main center of his political power and his business enterprises. Actually, in 1952 Azikiwe was excluded from the central House in this manner.

These constitutional provisions regarding regionalization and the status of Lagos would not have been consequential had it not been for the emergence of a new Western Regional political party, the Action Group. By the beginning of 1950 it had become evident that the new constitution would not only preserve the regions, but would also greatly increase their powers. At that time Awolowo called a secret meeting of several of his Yoruba followers, as well as of selected individuals from other groups in the west, such as the Edo, the Ishan, and the Jekri. In March, 1951, this small group, after some months of planning, publicly inaugurated the Action Group.

The new organization received its strongest support from the old Yoruba families and the Yoruba professional class of Lagos, from the growing Yoruba middle class based upon the cocoa trade, from Yoruba chiefs (who were patrons of the Egbe Omo Oduduwa, of which Awolowo was general secretary), from Yoruba intellectuals opposed to the NCNC on grounds of principle, and from selected leaders of minority groups (the Jekri and the Edo) in the Western Region. Awolowo and the other leaders made special efforts to prevent the organization from being stigmatized as Yoruba-dominated. This was difficult because Yorubas constituted the majority of the population of the Western Region.

The Action Group aimed at one specific objective: the capture of power in the Western Region under the electoral system of the new constitution. It differed from all previous Nigerian political organizations in several respects: (1) its leadership was collegial—and this at Awolowo's insistence; (2) it developed a definite program in a series of policy papers dealing with all aspects of governmental activity (for example, education, agriculture, health, and local government), and pledged reforms if elected; (3) it developed a permanent organizational structure and utilized modern techniques of mass persuasion and electoral campaigning; and (4) it shunned Lagos, partly because of Awolowo's emphatic belief that the capital city was a cesspool of intrigue, petty bickering, and confusion.

The aims of the Action Group included the following: (1) "to encourage and strengthen most sedulously all the ethnical organizations in the Western Region"; and (2) "to explore all possibilities for and to co-operate wholeheartedly with other nationalists in the formation of a Nigeria-wide organization which shall work as a united team towards the realization of immediate self-government for Nigeria." Awolowo consciously sought and largely succeeded in obtaining the coöperation of prominent leaders of some of the non-Yoruba tribes in the Western Region.

The dominant theory of the Action Group leaders was that under the circumstances then prevailing in Nigeria the only certain avenue to power was a regional political party.[37] Accordingly, one of the main themes in the group's electoral campaign was common opposition to Azikiwe and to the threat of Ibo domination under a unitary scheme. In response, the NCNC felt compelled to use tribalism among the non-Yoruba and quasi-Yoruba tribes of the west as an instrument to undermine the Yoruba-dominated Action Group. Thus, during the three-year period 1948–1951, tribalism and regional nationalism became not only the most legitimate but the most effective means for educated nationalists to secure power. The victory of the Action Group over the NCNC by a sizable margin in the 1951 elections in the Western Region was the triumph of regional nationalism.

These, then, were the steps in the evolution of subgroup nationalisms from a vague awareness of differentiation to a sentiment employed as a conscious instrument in politics. Certain basic underlying differences in history, culture, temperament, and levels of development and acculturation provided the classical setting for intergroup friction. The net effect of British policy was to aggravate these differences. The decisive determinants, however, were educated Nigerian nationalists, and among this group Azikiwe and Awolowo were the most influential. Azikiwe had a burning passion to liberate Africa, but circumstances limited his field of operation to Nigeria and the British Cameroons. An important ingredient in his zeal was his great desire to elevate his own people—the Ibo—who were behind other major groups in the race toward modernity. Although he publicly eschewed tribalism, most Ibos looked upon him as the leader not only of the Ibo nationality but also of the Nigerian nation of their dreams, and Ibos were in the front ranks in his Pan-Nigerian crusade. These circumstances aroused apprehensions that Azikiwe's crusade was in reality a Pan-Ibo affair. On the other hand, more in the tradition of Burke, Awolowo had always been a Yoruba nationalist first and a Pan-Nigeria nationalist second. From the beginning, therefore, there was a fundamental difference in attitude regarding the ends toward which the nationalist movement should be directed.

The cleavage and tensions produced by this difference were further aggravated by an equally basic difference in attitude regarding the tempo at which nationalists should pursue their common objective of a self-governing Nigeria. The crucial point is that all these differences fell roughly along nationality or regional lines. From our discussion it is clear that in the early postwar period Azikiwe and his Ibo followers tended to be more militant in their nationalist demands and more emphatic in their desire for and expectation of early self-government than were Awolowo and most educated Yorubas, as well as most northerners. Yet there can be no doubt that this very difference compelled the Yorubas to assume a more radical position. In order to compete for leadership with Azikiwe and the NCNC in the 1951 electoral campaign in the Western Region, the Action Group took an uncompromising stand on the question of self-government. This change in tempo is brought out most vividly by a comparison of the political thought of Awolowo as set forth in his book in 1947, with the views he propagated in his Ibadan daily, the *Nigerian Tribune,* during the period 1950–1952.

There can be little doubt that the implementation of the Constitution of 1951 accelerated the drift toward subgroup nationalism and tribalism. Educated Nigerians who aspired to fill the new positions of power and status opened up to Nigerians by that constitution realized that their most secure base of support would be the people of their own groups. The indirect electoral system strengthened this realization. They also recognized that the disagreement among themselves regarding nationalist objectives, and the tempo with which those objectives were to be pursued, would be fairly well settled by the outcome of the constitutional elections. In the struggle that ensued, tribalism was the dominant note; but when appealing to the people for support, the competing parties strove to outdo each other in the use of nationalist slogans . . .

NOTES

1. K. Onwuka Dike, *Trade and Politics in the Niger Delta, 1830–1885* (Oxford: Clarendon Press, 1956), p. 28.

2. P. Amaury Talbot, *The Peoples of Southern Nigeria* (London: Oxford University Press, 1926), Vol. IV; *Population Census of the Western Region of Nigeria, 1952,* Bulletin no. 5 (Lagos: 1953).

3. M. M. Green, *Ibo Village Affairs* (London: Sidgwick and Jackson, 1947), p. 255.

4. On the role of the Aro in the history of Iboland see Dike, *op. cit.,* pp. 39 ff.

5. With few exceptions, the Freedom Movement which succeeded the Zikist Movement was an Ibo group. The National Church membership was almost wholly Ibo.

6. Linville Watson, "Some Cultural Aspects of Nigerian Nationalism" (unpublished manuscript), p. 17. See also Thomas Hodgkin, "Background to Nigerian Nationalism," *West Africa,* Sept. 1, 1951.

7. C. K. Meek, *Law and Authority in a Nigerian Tribe* (London: Oxford University Press, 1937), pp. 197 ff.

8. Talbot, *op. cit.,* IV, 191.

9. Nnamdi Azikiwe, *Renascent Africa* (Accra: 1937), p. 24.

10. Watson, *op. cit.,* p. 12.

11. *Op. cit.,* p. 44.

12. See, for example, F. D. Lugard, *The Dual Mandate in British Tropical Africa* (4th ed.; London: William Blackwood, 1929) pp. 64 ff.

13. *Proceedings of the General Conference on Review of the Constitution, January, 1950* (Lagos: 1950), p. 246.

14. *Nigerian Daily Telegraph,* Feb. 3, 1933.

15. *Comet,* June 27, 1936.

16. *Daily Times,* Sept. 24, 1944.

17. *West African Pilot,* March 7, 1946.

18. Nnamdi Azikiwe, *Political Blueprint of Nigeria* (Lagos: 1943), p. 54.

19. *Renascent Africa,* pp. 18, 21.

20. *Political Blueprint of Nigeria,* p. 7.

21. The main criticisms of Azikiwe and the NCNC have been published in a pamphlet entitled *NCNC: Their Black Record* (London: n.d.).

22. Azikiwe, *Renascent Africa,* p. 29.

23. *Daily Times,* Oct. 7, 1942.

24. See J. O. Lucas, *Oduduwa* (Lagos: 1949).

25. *Constitution of the Egbe Omo Oduduwa* (Ijebu-Ode: 1948), pp. 5–6.

26. African Mail, Aug. 29, 1912.

27. Ayotunde Rosiji, "The Egbe and Nigerian Unity," *Egbe Omo Oduduwa Monthly Bulletin,* I (Dec., 1948), 7.

28. *Daily Service,* Oct. 17, 1944.

29. Minutes of the First Inaugural Conference of the Egbe Omo Oduduwa, June 1948 (typed copy).

30. Oluwole Alakija in *Egbe Omo Oduduwa Monthly Bulletin,* I (Dec., 1948), 4.

31. *West African Pilot,* Aug. 30, 1948.

32. *Ibid.,* Sept. 9, 1948.

33. Minutes of First Pan-Ibo Conference, Aba, 1948 (typed copy).

34. *West African Pilot,* July 6, 1949.

35. *Ibid.,* May 25, 1951.

36. *Daily Times,* Sept. 8, 1951.

37. For Chief Bode Thomas' suggestion that regional political parties be formed, see Nnamdi Azikiwe, *The Development of Political Parties in Nigeria* (London: 1957), p. 16. In a speech made at the time of the laying of the foundation stone of the Action Group headquarters building, on September 14, 1954, Premier Obafemi Awolowo recounted the early history of the Action Group. The first meeting, called by Awolowo, was held in his Ibadan home on March 26, 1950. Although fifty persons had been invited, only eight attended. The purpose of the meeting, as explained by Awolowo, was "to try and devise some means whereby it would be possible to have an organised body of people in the New House of Assembly who would be capable of representing the Western Region." It was decided to organize a new association for this purpose because the existing associations were considered to be poorly organized, lacking in popular support, or otherwise unsuitable for the new situation.

CHAPTER 4

The Social Organization of Credit in a West African Cattle Market[1]

ABNER COHEN

Credit is a vital economic institution without which trade becomes very limited. In the industrial Western societies, where it is highly developed, it operates through formal, standardized arrangements and procedures by which the solvency of the debtor is closely assessed, securities against possible default are provided, and the conditions of the agreement are documented and endorsed by the parties concerned. Ultimately, these arrangements and procedures are upheld by legislated rules and sanctions administered by central, bureaucratized, fairly impartial, efficient, and effective courts and police. In West Africa, on the other hand, where long-distance trade has been fostered by varying ecological circumstances, such organization has not yet evolved, particularly for long-distance trade. Nevertheless extensive systems of credit have been developed.

I discuss in this paper the organization and operation of credit in one Nigerian market which I studied intensively. After a preliminary description of the formal organization of the market and of the credit by which it functions, I discuss some non-economic social relations which, while formally ex-

Reprinted from *Africa,* Vol. 35 (1965), pp. 8–19. Copyright © 1965 by *Africa.* Reprinted by permission of the publisher and Abner Cohen.

terior to the market situation, are in practice built into the structure of the credit system in such a way that they make its functioning as a going concern possible.

Nearly 75,000[2] head of cattle are sold every year in the cattle market of Ibadan, capital of the Western Region of the Federation of Nigeria. The forest belt of West Africa, of which Ibadan is part, is infested with the disease-carrying tse-tse fly which is fatal to cattle. The inhabitants depend for their beef supplies on herds of cattle brought from the savannah country, hundreds of miles to the north. These herds are collected mainly from the semi-nomadic Fulani by Hausa dealers from Northern Nigeria and are then brought south to be sold with the help of local Hausa middlemen. In the Ibadan market, which is locally known as 'Zango', the buyers are Yoruba butchers and are total strangers to the Hausa dealers. Nevertheless, all sales are on credit and there is always an outstanding total amount of about a hundred thousand pounds current debt.[4] No documents are signed and no resort is made to the services of banks or to the official civil courts, and the whole organization, which has developed over the past sixty years, is entirely indigenous.

The cattle are brought to Ibadan either on foot or by train. In the market there is a sharp distinction between the two categories of cattle, not only in price but also in the organization and the scale of the business. After about five weeks of continuous travel, the foot cattle[5] arrive at the market thin, weak, and already having been exposed, for many days, to the disease[6] as they penetrated the forest area. The manoeuvrability in selling them is therefore limited in both time and place and dealers are always eager to sell. This eagerness is further enhanced by the need of the dealers to release, as soon as possible, the capital invested in the herd in order to have a quicker business turn-over. In recent years, cattle have increasingly been brought south by train, but between 30 and 40 per cent, still come on foot, either because they are brought from districts which are remote from a railway line, or because no train wagons happen to be available at the time. The principal advantage of bringing cattle on foot is that part of the herd can be sold on the way to small towns and villages which are not served by the railways or which are not large enough to have cattle markets.[7]

Foot cattle are brought by smaller-scale Hausa dealers, each dealer making an average of four journeys to Ibadan in a year, bringing to the market each journey an average of seventy head of cattle.[8] The herd is driven by hired Fulani drovers, an average of one drover[9] for every twenty-five head. The herd owner walks with his cattle as far as Ilorin, where he usually parts with the caravan and starts a reconnaissance trip, by lorries and mammy wagons along the ninety-five-mile route to Ibadan stopping at the cattle markets in Ogbomosho and Oyo, and also at other smaller towns, choosing the most advantageous place to sell. The more southerly the place, the higher the price, but the greater the hazards to the health of the cattle and the longer the period in which the capital is engaged.

The train cattle[10] are either brought by smaller-scale dealers, who travel with the herd, or are sent by relatively larger-scale dealers to their permanent agents in Ibadan. The cattle are transported in special wagons, each wagon accommodating between twenty and thirty head.[11] The herd in each wagon is looked after by an attendant[12] whose main task is to guard the beasts against theft. The journey to Ibadan takes two to three days and the few cattle who show signs of sickness in the meantime are slaughtered and sold in the several intervening stations, where local butchers are always waiting for such opportunities.

According to men in the business, the life expectancy of cattle after arriving in Ibadan is about two weeks for those brought on foot and about two and a half months for those brought by train. Train cattle therefore fetch a higher price than foot cattle of the same size and quality, particularly because they are demanded by butchers, not only from Ibadan, but also from neighbouring towns and villages. Also, when prices in Ibadan are unfavourable train cattle can be taken south as far as Lagos.

Despite the sharp distinction in the market between the two categories of cattle the organization of credit is essentially similar in both cases.

When the cattle dealer,[13] whether he is the owner of the herd or only an agent of the owner, is in Ibadan he lodges with his usual 'landlord' in the Hausa Quarter. The word 'landlord' is a literal translation of the Hausa term *mai gida,* but the *mai gida* plays several kinds of roles in the cattle business which are not denoted by the English translation and need to be analytically separated. In the first place, the *mai gida* is a house owner, having, besides that in which he and his family live, at least one more house for the accommodation of his dealers from the north. Of the twelve cattle landlords who operated in Zango in 1963, one had six such houses, a second had four, two others had two houses each, and the rest had one each. The landlords usually own additional houses in which their assistants, clerks, servants, malams, and other men of their entourage are accommodated, free of charge. The landlord also provides three meals a day for his dealers and entertains them in the evenings, but this function as inn-keeper is by no means the most fundamental of his roles.

The landlord is also a middleman[14] who mediates between his dealers and the local butchers in the market. Each landlord has for this purpose a number of middlemen[15] working under him, but responsibility for their business conduct remains always with him. Thus, when the herd of the dealer arrives at the market, the landlord entrusts its sale to one of his middlemen. The dealer then accompanies the middleman in the market and remains with him until the whole herd is sold. But no transaction can be finally concluded without the approval of the landlord.

Here we come to the role of the landlord as insurer or risk-taker, which is the most crucial factor in the operation of the whole market. As sale is on credit, the landlord is the guarantor that the money will eventually be paid, and that if the buyer should default, he would pay the full amount to the dealer himself. This obligation means that he must be very well acquainted with the buyers, and it is only through long experience in the business that he comes to acquire the necessary knowledge. He has to know not only where a buyer slaughters the cattle, or where he has his shop or market stall, but also where he lives, who are his relatives and associates, what is the size of his business, and how honest and trustworthy he has proved himself to be in his dealings so far. In this way, every butcher in the market is informally graded by the landlords and their middlemen on a scale of credit worthiness from nil up to about £1,000 of credit, for a period of up to four weeks. No sane landlord would give a butcher credit in excess of the latter's 'quota.'

Misjudgement in this respect can ruin the business house of the landlord. This actually happened early in 1963 to one of the landlords, when a number of butchers who had bought cattle through him defaulted, and he eventually failed to pay the money himself to the dealers. These stopped lodging with him and complained to the Chief of the Cattle Market. He finally sold his only house of strangers to meet his obligations and became an ordinary middleman.

Thus landlords need to have not only a precise assessment of the buyer's social background and of his business conduct in the past, but must also be continuously vigilant as to his day-to-day purchases in the market. For while a dealer is attached to one landlord at a time, the butcher is free to buy through any landlord, and he usually makes his purchases through many landlords. It is conceivable, therefore, that he may succeed in buying, within a short period of time, from several unsuspecting landlords in excess of the limits of his credit-worthiness. The only way in which the landlords can meet this potential danger is by the continuous exchange of business information. No formally institutionalized channels for such an exchange exist in the market, but the objective is nevertheless achieved through informal relations.

Landlords interact very intensively among themselves, since it is in the nature of their business both to compete and to co-operate. They compete fiercely over business, and countless disputes arise among them over what they describe as "stealing of dealers". Generally speaking, a dealer has one landlord to whom he is accustomed to entrust the sale of his cattle whenever he comes to Ibadan. This attachment of a dealer to one landlord usually holds for years and sometimes continues to hold between their sons when they die. Landlords do much to keep their dealers attached to them, offering them various services, some of which have little to do with the cattle business. When a dealer finally goes back to the North, after selling his cattle, his landlord gives him a present; the minimum standard being a bottle of French perfume costing (as in 1963) 18 shillings.[16] But some dealers, particularly those of foot cattle who come to Ibadan only occasionally, *do* change their landlords, for one reason or other, and sometimes landlords send emissaries as far as Ilorin to meet such dealers, offer them presents, and direct them to lodge with their masters.

Disputes between landlords over dealers have often led to political crises within the Hausa Quarter. The basic principle of political grouping among the 5,000 Hausa of the Quarter is that of the client-patron relationship, which is essentially diadic, holding between the patron and each client separately, without leading to the formation of corporate groups. A man's clients are his employees, attendants, and tenants. The patrons of the Quarter are the thirty landlords, in the various economic fields, who control much of the employment and of the housing of the rest of the population. Each one of them is the head of what may be described as a 'house of power'. Clients often 'change house', i.e. change their allegiance from one landlord to another, which often means literally moving from one house to another. Generally speaking, landlords are old residents in Ibadan while most of their clients are new migrants.[17]

The landlords and their clients pay allegiance to the Hausa Chief of the Quarter,[18] who mediates between them and the authorities, adjudicates—with the help of his advisers—in cases of disputes within the Quarter, and appoints men to titled positions who regulate communal affairs. One of these positions is that of the 'Chief of the Cattle Market',[19] who is responsible for keeping order in the market and who arbitrates in cases of disputes within it.

Of all the patrons, the cattle landlords are the most powerful as they have dominated the Quarter politically ever since its foundation in 1916. The Chief of the Quarter has always been a cattle landlord and, since 1930, he has also been the Chief of the Cattle Market.[20]

The cattle business is thus directly involved in the politics of the Quarter. The same men who meet in the cattle market as landlords confront each other in the Quarter as political leaders, and their behaviour in the one role affects their behaviour in the other. For example, one of the duties of the Chief of the Quarter is to give accommodation to any Hausa stranger who comes to him, and the Chief runs many houses for this specific purpose. When a new cattle dealer comes for the first time to Ibadan and lodges in one of these houses, as a stranger, it is only natural that he should eventually sell his cattle through the Chief, in the latter's role as cattle landlord.

Within the context of the Quarter, one major source of dispute between the landlords has been the struggle for the control over houses, since from the early 1930's these have become relatively scarce because of overcrowding. A man needs housing in the Quarter to secure membership of the community, to establish himself in business, to gather clients around him, to enlarge his family by marrying more wives, to foster the sons and daughters of his kin, and to accommodate malams whose services in the mystical world are indispensable to his success and well-being. Thus, command over housing is in no small measure command over economic and political power. When the Quarter was first established, the land, which had been allotted for the purpose by the city's native authority, was distributed in equal plots among the first settlers. But since then many changes have taken place in the ownership and distribution of houses and land. In 1963 only five of the many hundreds of houses of the Quarter were registered as deeds. There were no documents of any kind to establish ownership over the rest of the houses. Most of the original houses and plots have changed hands many times through sale or the death of their owners. The houses of persons who died without leaving heirs have been 'inherited' by the Chief of the Quarter, who is presumed to use them for the general welfare of the community. In this way the Chief has come to control scores of houses in which he accommodates, rent free, several hundreds of people who have in this way automatically become his clients. Landlords thus struggle over the ownership of houses in the Quarter because these are the means to political and economic power.

In the cattle market the landlords also compete over the buyers and each landlord has a number of young men who act as 'advertisers', trying to draw the attention of the butchers to the herds marketed through their employers. But landlords are at the same time forced to co-operate in the market in several respects, the most important being to present a united front *vis-à-vis* the butchers. These are very powerfully organized through an association which has played an important role within the Ibadan polity and only a strong landlords' front can keep the necessary balance in the market.

The market is held twice a day, once in the morning, between 9 and 10, and again in the afternoon, between 5 and 7. These official hours are enforced by the Chief of the Market.[21] But landlords come to the market about an hour before each session to sit informally together and 'joke', often very clumsily, and it is in the course of this joking that much of the vital information on the buyers is exchanged.

Another informal channel through which business information is exchanged is the interaction between the clerks. Every landlord has a clerk[22] whose main duty is the registration of sales and the collection of money from the debtors. As soon as a transaction is concluded, the middleman involved calls the clerk of his landlord to note down the details. These include the date of the transaction, name of dealer, name of middleman, name and address of buyer, the number of cattle sold, the price and total amount as well as the exact time and place of payment.[23] The clerk occupies a central position within the structure of the 'business house' because, while the middlemen and the other assistants are individually related to the landlord and are not formally related to each other, the clerk is formally related to everyone within the house, and thus knows about all the transactions concluded through the house. Being also the collector of substantial amounts of money, he is always a man who is fully trusted by the landlord. Of the twelve landlords in the Ibadan market, three have their own sons as clerks, two their 'fostered'[24] sons, and three perform the task themselves. The clerks are young, educated 'in Arabic',[25] and are Ibadan-born. They speak Yoruba as well as Hausa and belong to the same age-group. Sharing the same background, they belong to the same group whose members pray, eat, learn, and seek entertainment together.[26] They thus meet in various social situations every day and in the course of their interaction they exchange information about the solvency of the butchers, which they eventually pass on to their respective masters.

These exchanges of information, however, relate only to the behaviour of the butchers in the past and it is conceivable that a butcher may in one hour buy from several landlords who, in the pressure of business, may not realize that he is exceeding his limits. A protection against such a possibility is obtained through the informal activities of, and interaction among, the 'boys',[27] who perform various jobs in helping their landlord and his middleman in the market. These 'boys' can be seen everywhere in the market, and indeed the literal meaning of the Hausa word *kankamba* is 'going hither and thither'. Their tasks take them to many parts of the market and they mingle with the 'boys' of other landlords. When, in the course of their activities, they notice a butcher who, having already bought cattle in other corners of the market, comes to buy also from the landlord, then they alert the middlemen to the impending danger.[28]

Thus, joking and gossiping between the landlords, informal meetings among the clerks, and the activities of the 'boys' serve as means of disseminating business information and help to guard against the hazards of credit.

But the conflicting interests of the landlords are implicit even in this very fundamental issue of exchanging information about the butchers' purchases and it sometimes happens, though not often, that a landlord tries to suppress information. I witnessed in 1963 a case of a butcher who failed to pay, on time, a debt of a few hundred pounds to a landlord, but promised to do so as soon as his business improved. The landlord withheld this news from the other landlords, since otherwise these would have refrained from selling cattle to the butcher, who would thus have been without business and would have failed to settle his original debt. An unsuspecting landlord eventually sold cattle to the butcher in question, who duly settled his debt to the first landlord but defaulted in payment to the second. When the first landlord was later blamed for his unethical conduct he replied that no one had asked him to give the information which he had withheld. The landlord who suffered in this case had himself acted as his own clerk and had therefore no means of knowing of the default of the butcher except from the first landlord. Landlords are thus sometimes in an invidious position about revealing information concerning their sales.

The credit is given for a period of two to four weeks.[29] Dealers in foot cattle usually remain during this period accommodated and fed by the landlord, and when the money is finally collected it is kept by the landlord until the dealer arranges transport for himself to go back to the North.[30] Dealers in train cattle often go back to the North as soon as their cattle are sold and collect the proceeds when they come back with the next herd.

The landlord receives no direct reward whatsoever from the dealer for accommodation, food, mediation, banking, or risk-taking. On the contrary he gives the dealer not only presents but also part of his own earning from the sale of the cattle. The landlord's remuneration is a fixed commission, known by the Hausa term *kudin lada* or simply *lada,* which he collects from the buyer in cash, on the conclusion of the sale. During 1963 the commission in Ibadan was 13 shillings on each head of cattle, irrespective of the price. From this amount the landlord pays 3 shillings to the middleman who arranged the transaction, about a shilling to the clerk and the 'boys', 2 shillings to the dealer himself, and retains the rest to cover his expenses and to remunerate himself for the financial risks he has taken in assuring the credit.[31]

This credit arrangement is not fool-proof and cases of default occur, but, barring political or economic upheavals, the risks are greatly reduced by a variety of factors.

In the first place a loss is always distributed among several individuals because a butcher is usually indebted not to one landlord but to many, and a dealer's herd is sold, not to one butcher but to many butchers. Thus, if a butcher defaulted the loss would be shared by the several landlords who gave him credit. The incidence of the loss is spread still wider when the case is eventually arbitrated, and in nearly all the cases I have recorded the dealer was made to share in the loss even though the formal principle is that the whole loss should be borne by the landlord.[32] I am talking here of loss, but it nearly always happens that an arrangement is reached as a result of arbitration, by which the butcher undertakes to pay his debt by instalments over several months. During these months he is allowed to buy from the market but must pay in cash.

Unless a butcher is prepared to go out of the business altogether he is forced to abide by such an arrangement, since according to municipal rules he would forfeit his license as a butcher if he did not slaughter at least one beast every week. This is a very important source of pressure on him because a license is very difficult to obtain and is also very expensive. He cannot evade payment by buying cattle elsewhere. The Hausa throughout the region, indeed throughout southern Nigeria, monopolize the sale of cattle and control all cattle markets.

These markets, together with the Hausa Quarters to which they are attached, constitute a widespread network of highly interrelated communities. In each of the three large cattle markets which are within a radius of sixty miles of Ibadan (Ogbomosho, Oyo and Abeokuta) the Chief of the Cattle Market is himself the Chief of the Hausa Quarter, as well as being a cattle landlord. Thus, when the landlords in the Ibadan market decide not to sell to a defaulting butcher, they usually send a word to the neighbouring cattle markets about him and if he ever appeared there no one would sell to him even if he paid cash.

An equally important form of pressure on individual defaulters comes from the butchers themselves, who are organized in eight slaughter-houses, as well as within the overall occupational association. When one butcher defaults, the landlords are often forced to retaliate by declaring a temporary boycott of all the butchers within his slaughter-house. I witnessed one such case in 1963 when a butcher failed to pay a debt of about £700 which he owed to many landlords. In their gossiping time one day the landlords decided to refuse selling any cattle to the whole slaughter-house of the defaulting butcher in order to mobilize the pressure of his colleagues on him. This action was so effective that the butchers involved, together with the chief of the whole Association,[33] as well as the defaulting butcher, came to the Chief of the Hausa Quarter in his capacity as Chief of the Cattle Market, on the same evening and an arrangement was made there and then to settle the matter. Indeed it happens sometimes that when a butcher shows signs of financial difficulties, some of his colleagues within the same slaughter-house will caution some of their trustworthy middlemen not to sell to him. Thus, the butchers on their part watch each other's conduct in business and can exert a great deal of pressure on potential defaulters.

The market is therefore not seriously disturbed by the occasional default of individual butchers. Indeed, from the study of cases seen against the background of the history of the market organization, it appears that occasional default (as crime in Durkheim's analysis)[34] has led to continual re-examination and retightening of the control mechanisms in the market and thus made the continuity of the credit system possible. The cattle landlords' main worry is not the individual defaulter but the sudden collapse of the market as a result of a concerted hostile action on the part of the butchers .[35] The position of the land-lords is particularly vulnerable, since the pressure which they can exert on the butchers is limited in degree and is not without its dangers. This is because the cleavage in the market between buyer and seller, debtor and creditor, is also a cleavage between Yoruba and Hausa and, indeed, both sides describe their mutual relationships in tribalistic terms. The landlords often talk of the 'machinations' and the 'treachery' of the Yoruba and the butchers of the 'exploitation' and 'greed' of the Hausa. When the Ibadan cattle landlords appeal for support and solidarity from the cattle landlords in other markets in the region they actually do so not in the name of the profession but in the name of Hausa-ism, and the communication between the markets is effected through the respective Hausa chiefs, acting *as* Hausa chiefs, and not as chiefs of the cattle markets.

In the same way, the butchers confront the landlords as a tribal group and rely on the support of various other Yoruba groupings in this confrontation. The butchers resent the fact that it is they, and not the Hausa sellers, who are made to pay the commission to the landlords, and for years they have been agitating against it. In this agitation they have often succeeded in mobilizing support from the press and from the city's tradi-tional chiefs, who on several occasions in the past reminded the Hausa that they were strangers, that the Quarter stood on the Olubadan's land, that if they did not behave they would be made to leave, and so on. The landlords are always afraid that the city council or the regional government may impose on them new taxes or new restrictions on the movement and sale of cattle, or that they will decide to remove the Hausa Quarter or to 'scrap' it altogether.

The cattle landlords have not been passive in the face of such threats. When during the 1950's the butchers affiliated them-selves within the predominantly Yoruba Action Group Party, which was until 1962 in power in the Western Region, the Hausa landlords reacted not only by joining the same party themselves, but also by dragging almost the whole Hausa Quar-ter with them in joining it, and in successive elections the Iba-dan Hausa gave their votes to it.[36] In the 1961 election for the

Ibadan local council, 93 per cent of the votes in the Quarter went to the Action Group candidate. Within the party, the Hausa eventually formed a strong pressure group. According to the 1952 Census of Nigeria there were in the Western Region nearly 41,000 Hausa residents and even then it was realized that there were many more Hausa who for a variety of reasons had not registered themselves. In 1953 the chiefs of all Hausa communities in the Region formed a joint Hausa association[37] and unanimously elected the Ibadan Hausa Chief as their chairman. This occurred on the eve of the 1954 Federal Election and there is little doubt that the association played an important role in mobilizing Hausa support for the party chosen by their chiefs. At that time the Action Group was struggling to establish itself, not as a regional, but as a national, party which was to gain the support of the masses from the other tribes of the Federation of Nigeria. For that purpose the party fought particularly hard to gain a foothold in Hausaland in the North, as that region contained more than half the population of the Federation. A party with such objectives could not allow the persecution of a Hausa minority in its own capital. Thus, the party not only prevented hostile action being taken against the cattle landlords, but even tried to prevent individual butchers from defaulting, by exerting pressure on these to honour their obligations, and sometimes by granting loans to those among them who did not have the cash to pay.

The risks of the credit system have thus made it necessary for the cattle landlords to act politically within the Hausa network of communities, as well as within the Ibadan, the regional, and the national polities. To do so, they have had to act not on occupational but on tribal lines, and it has therefore been essential for them to control the Chieftaincy of the Hausa Quarter. Under the prevailing conditions it is only through the Chieftaincy that political interaction with other Hausa communities, on the one hand, and with the Yoruba, on the other, can be effected.

The cattle landlords are few in number and, together with all their middlemen, clerks, and assistants, constitute only 6 per cent of the working Hausa male population of the Quarter.[38] Yet, they have always been so dominant that the history of the Quarter is to a great extent the history of the cattle trade in

Ibadan. From the very beginning of Hausa settlement in Ibadan, at the beginning of the present century until today, the Chief of the Quarter has always been a cattle landlord. And this is the case not only in Ibadan but also in the other Hausa communities in those Yoruba towns where a cattle market exists. Indeed it was initially this sociological problem, i.e. 'How is it that a handful of cattle landlords have come to dominate the whole Quarter politically?', which led me to study the organization of the cattle market.

There are various factors involved in this phenomenon, but it is beyond the limits of this paper to discuss them in detail. It is sufficient to point out that the landlords not only 'need' the Chieftaincy because of its role in the organization of credit, but also have the power and the organization to dominate the Quarter. They interact among themselves most intensively, as they meet in a relatively small place (the market) twice a day, seven days a week. In contrast, the kola landlords, for example, who run business on similar lines and who, as an occupational group, constitute nearly 18 per cent[39] of the working Hausa males in the Quarter, and certainly command greater wealth, do not have opportunities to interact so frequently and so intensively, since they have to leave the Quarter every morning and disperse in all directions within a radius of about forty miles in quest of supplies. They also operate mainly with cash and, since they are dealing in a local product for export from the area, whenever credit is involved, they are the debtors, not the creditors, and hence are not impelled to political action to the same degree as are the cattle landlords, who seem to be always beset by great anxieties over the thousands of pounds of credit which continuously weigh on their conscience. Another factor which should be taken into account is that of continuities from the past. The cattle landlords and middlemen were among the very first of the Hausa migrants to Ibadan. In a census taken in the Quarter in 1916, a few months after its establishment, 56 out of 261 (20 per cent.) Hausa males were described as cattle traders, which means that men working in the cattle trade constituted a much higher proportion of the working population in the past than today. On the other hand, the kola men came to the Quarter mainly during the past generation, since kola has been grown in the Western Region of

Nigeria only in recent decades. For the cattle landlords, seniority in the Quarter has meant greater opportunities for acquiring houses, for rallying clients, and for establishing connexions with local sources of power and authority. These are advantages which help the cattle landlords, within the contemporary situation, to control the Quarter.

I am not arguing here that the majority of the Quarter blindly align themselves for political action behind the cattle landlords, to the latter's private interests. I am suggesting that, because of their role in the cattle market, the cattle landlords are more politically active and better organized for political action than any other group within the Quarter. They are also the group most sensitive to any changes in Hausa-Yoruba relations. When the 1962 emergency situation in the Western Region of Nigeria came to an end, in January 1963, and the former Premier, Chief Akintola, returned to his previous position in Ibadan, the cattle landlords and middlemen, who had been ardent Action Groupers until the emergency, went *en masse,* taking with them any Hausa they could mobilize, to greet the returning Premier and to express allegiance to him and to his party (at the time the UPP), which had emerged in opposition to the Action Group. They did this not as cattle men but as Hausa, representing the whole Hausa Quarter. It is significant, incidentally, that at the doors of the Premier they came face to face with another delegation who had also come to express their allegiance—it was the delegation of the Yoruba butchers.

The cattle landlords have very serious reservations about submitting their disputes with the butchers to the civil courts. There are many reasons for this attitude. When a butcher defaults he is usually indebted to many dealers from whom he has bought cattle. As these dealers are the legal creditors, it is they, not the landlords, who should apply to the courts for adjudication, which means that a number of dealers should act jointly in order to pursue their case against the defaulting butcher. But this is highly impracticable. The amount due to each dealer from the defaulting butcher is relatively small, while the expenses of adjudication are high. Furthermore, court procedure is long and the dealers, whose residence is usually far in the North, cannot wait in Ibadan indefinitely. There is also the problem of language and cultural differences. Furthermore, the landlords believe that court rulings in cases of this nature are not effective, since a butcher who pleads that he has no money can be asked to pay only a few pounds a month to his creditors until an amount of hundreds of pounds could be finally settled.[40]

Arbitration by the Chief of the Market, on the other hand, is prompt, convenient, and effective. It is performed by a Hausa, but in nearly all cases of dispute, the Chief of the Butchers, a Yoruba, participates in the arbitratory process. The ruling of the Chief of the Market is final and is nearly always honoured.[41]

Thus the organization of credit in the market is ultimately upheld, not by the civil courts, but by what may be labelled as 'tribal politics'. In the market, debtors and creditors face each other as tribesmen as well as business men. This double cleavage is basic to the operation of the credit system. It is the product of a number of processes which have driven the Hausa out of the butchering business, on the one hand, and prevented the Yoruba from performing the functions of the cattle landlords, on the other. Until the early 1930's many of the butchers of Ibadan were Hausa, and the Quarter's Hausa 'Chief of the Butchers' was a very powerful man. But today there is only one Hausa butcher[42] in the city, and the title 'Chief of the Butchers' within the Quarter has sunk into insignificance.[43] On the other hand, all the attempts that have been made every now and then by some ambitious Yoruba to act as cattle landlords or even as cattle dealers have completely failed.

I have attempted to show that in order to understand the operation of credit in the cattle market in Ibadan we need to consider such phenomena as informal gossiping and joking, age-grouping, and inter-tribal politics. These are essentially non-economic factors which seem to be exterior to the market situation. In considering credit in Western society, it is equally essential to take into account some non-economic factors, but because of the highly developed centralization, communication, and bureaucratization, these factors are fundamentally the same throughout the society and there is therefore one unitary system of credit. In his analysis, the economist can thus regard these factors as constant, take them for granted, and never mention them. In a pre-industrial society, on the other hand, there are many systems of credit, each having its own structure which consists of both formal and informal relations. This is why, in order to explain such a system, the economist has to rely much on anthropologists or become one himself.

NOTES

1. The material on which this paper is based was collected in the course of field study among Hausa migrants in the Western Region of Nigeria between September 1962 and November 1963. I am grateful to the School of Oriental and African Studies, University of London, for financing the project and to the Nigerian Institute of Social and Economic Research and the University of Ibadan for their invaluable help in carrying it out.

2. This is an approximate figure which is higher by about 12 per cent, that that obtained from the records of the veterinary service offices.

3. Throughout the Western Region of Nigeria the cattle markets are locally known by the Hausa word *Zango* (literally meaning a camping place of caravan or lodging place of travellers), while the local Hausa quarter is known as *Sabo,* short for *Sabon Gari.* In Ghana, on the other hand, the word *Zango,* which is usually pronounced as *Zongo,* is used for the native strangers' quarter which is often predominantly Hausa.

4. This again, is an approximate figure derived from the number of cattle sold in the market, the average price per head and the average length of the period of credit.

5. *Shanun Kasa.*

6. Trypanosomiasis.

7. According to figures from the veterinary service offices, for the years 1959 to 1962, 20 per cent of all the cattle which started the journey from the North towards Ibadan as the final destination did not actually reach Ibadan, which means that they were sold on the way. As nearly all the cattle brought by train eventually arrived at Ibadan, this percentage represents the foot cattle which are sold on the way. This means that about 50 per cent of the foot cattle originally destined for Ibadan are sold on the way.

8. These figures are from a survey covering 118 dealers in foot cattle.

9. *Dan Kore.*

10. *Shanun Jirgi.*

11. Depending on the size of the animals. Usually the horns of the cattle are cut short before the journey so that more cattle can be accommodated in a wagon, and in the market, train cattle can usually be easily identified by their shorter horns.

12. *Dan taragu,* literally "son of the wagon".

13. *Mai shanu.*

14. *Dilali.*

15. Between them, the twelve cattle landlords operating in Ibadan in 1963 had fifty-two middlemen working for them. The senior among these middlemen had assistants under them, as they were usually given more cattle to sell than were the junior middlemen. Some of these senior middlemen provided food cooked by their own wives to the dealers who were "allotted" to them and they therefore received a greater proportion of the commission. There were a few middlemen in the market who were not attached to any particular landlord but who worked on a temporary basis for landlords who had more business on their hands than could be dealt with by their permanent middlemen.

16. It is customary for Hausa *men* to wear perfume.

17. According to census material which I collected in 1963, only 12 per cent of the Hausa migrants in the Quarter had been in Ibadan for twenty years or more.

18. Known as *Sarkin Hausawa* and sometimes as *Sarkin Sabo.*

19. *Sarkin Zango.*

20. These two positions, the *Sarkin Sabo* and the *Sarkin Zango,* have become so involved in each other that in some situations it is difficult to separate them, even analytically.

21. The beginning and the ending of a session are announced by a whistle blown by one of the "boys" of the Chief of the Market.

22. Known as *malam,* in the sense of "literate", not of "religious functionary".

23. The register in which these details are written down serves as a reminder, not a document. The details are neither checked nor ratified by the buyers.

24. Child fostering is very widespread among the Hausa.

25. All education in the Hausa Quarter is "Arabic" education which consists mainly in learning to read the Kor'an and to write in Arabic.

26. The overwhelming majority of the Hausa in Sabo adhere to the Tijaniyya order which enjoins intensive collective ritualism and ties initiates to a ritual leader known as *mukaddam*. Groupings emerging in the course of ritual performance tend to become fraternities whose members co-operate in many social fields.

27. *Kankamba.*

28. The butchers are always under constant observation by the landlords and their subordinates. The absence of a butcher for three or four days in succession is always marked with suspicion in the market.

29. As the Hausa are Muslims, the dealers do not in principle charge interest for the credit they give to the butchers. But cash price is always lower than credit price by £1 to £3 for a head of cattle which is usually sold at £20 to £40.

30. Landlords often keep in their houses several thousands of pounds, in cash for their dealers. The money is kept in simple wooden chests which are protected from thieves by amulets prepared by the malams and are also watched night and day by trusted attendants.

31. There are slight variations in the distribution of the commission between foot cattle and train cattle.

32. A landlord would run the risk of losing all his dealers if he did not meet his obligations. The payment of compensation to the dealers is always by monthly instalments, in accordance with the ruling of the Chief of the Market in the case.

33. The *Sarkin Pawa.* The incumbent of the office is of course a Yoruba man.

34. See E. Durkheim, *The Rules of Sociological Method,* pp. 64-75, translated by S. A. Solovay and J. H. Mueller, and edited by G. E. G. Catlin, The Free Press, Glencoe, Illinois (1950).

35. Such an action is not unlikely to happen. It happened in 1963 in the Abeokuta cattle market, when the butchers stopped paying their debts to the dealers and completely paralysed the market for about five weeks, until the two sides accepted arbitration by the Ibadan Hausa Chief. The dispute arose when some of the Hausa cattle landlords attempted to enter the butchering business by slaughtering a number of cattle and selling the meat to local retailers. The arbitrator eventually ruled that no slaughtering should be done by the landlords.

36. Men in the Quarter do not conceal the fact that in their political behaviour they follow the instructions of their patrons unquestionably.

37. The association was formally called "The Federal Union of the Western Sarkis Hausawa".

38. Ninety-seven out of a total of 1,570. The figures are from a general census which I took in Sabo with the help of local assistants.

39. 285 out of a total of 1,570.

40. The landlords often skip over most of these factors and dismiss the case for submitting disputes to the courts by saying: "After all these are *Yoruba* courts."

41. One of the most striking phenomena I witnessed in this respect was the obedience which the Yoruba butchers showed towards the Hausa Chief, whose authority was so strong that he could send his messenger and summon any butcher to his office.

42. Besides this licensed butcher there are a few Hausa men who work as "meat cutters", buying wholesale from Yoruba butchers and selling within the Quarter or in the neighbouring Mokola Quarter.

43. The case of dispute between the local Yoruba butchers and the Hausa cattle landlords mentioned in footnote 35 points in the same direction.

CHAPTER 5

Communal Competition, Conflict and Violence in Kano

JOHN N. PADEN

I would like to begin this essay with a personal statement. My academic research in Kano[1] did not focus on relationships between the Hausa and Ibo communities but rather on other aspects of northern society. Now, out of a sense of necessity I am trying to assess in retrospect the major elements of Hausa-Ibo relations in Kano. My assessment is prompted not only by the recent termination of the Nigerian civil war, but by the less noticeable but equally dramatic efforts in Kano and other parts in Nigeria to construct a future which does not repeat the mistakes of the past. The problem of communal identity and competition will be at the core of efforts to avoid future conflict.

I CONCEPTS OF ANALYSIS

In this essay, five concepts will be of special importance: communalism, competition, conflict, violence and value congruence. It will be asserted that communal violence in Kano has stemmed more from competition, based on a similarity of values, than from a conflict in cultural values. This essay will not try to develop measurements of psychological predisposition or general cultural orientation,[2] but to infer from the inter-group behavior of specific communal groups certain areas of value congruence or incongruence.

In the introduction to this volume, the editors have discussed in detail the concept of communalism. To summarize, communalism refers to ascriptive types of identities, adherence to cultural norms and values, and loyalties or obligations towards members of an identity group which tend to be relatively diffuse rather than specific or contractual. There are probably four major categories of communal groups: racial, religious, linguistic and ethnic. Ethnicity usually entails some notion of kinship or common origin. It is clear, of course, that some groups (such as linguistic or religious groups) may be either communal or associational. It is also clear that communal identities may change according to situation.[3]

The concept of competition in this essay will refer to the active but regulated pursuit of goods, resources or goals, in which two or more units strive with each other for maximization of benefits. Competition may lead to cooperation between the competitive units, in which both sides maximize benefits through regulated interaction. However, a breakdown in the "regulation" of competition may lead to violence.

Conflict will be regarded in the narrow sense of dissonance based on an incompatibility of values. Values are regarded as "preferences," rather than as abstract goals. Conflict may lead to violence, which is defined simply as physical damage to persons or property.

The question as to whether communal conflict will lead to violence may depend on several factors. Perhaps of prime importance are the degree to which particular values are central (rather than peripheral) to coordinated interaction between units, and the degree to which institutions are available to help resolve matters of value conflict. For example, the values of modernization may be central to the economic interaction between two ethnic units. It has been argued[4] that the dissolution of the Swedish-Norwegian union in the late nineteenth century, and the Irish split with Great Britain in the twentieth century were due in some measure to different attitudes toward modernization. By the same token, in cases where a legitimate legislative body and legal system do not exist to mediate between units on matters of competition or minor conflict, the probability of violence increases.

On the other hand, it is clear that communal violence may occur when values are similar. If two groups are actively pursuing modernization, it may be that competition for scarce goods will result in violence. The conflagration of World War I may be explained partly in terms of competition between England, Germany, Russia and France for the same types of scarce goods. All were modernizing and needed raw material, markets and allies.

In addition to value conflict and unregulated competition, it is clear that other factors may lead to communal violence. Violence may stem from a variety of individual or social frustrations which have nothing to do with the conflict or competition of the units engaged in violence. Theories of frustration and displacement would suggest that a group may do violence to a "scapegoat" as a substitute or release for internal or third-party directed tensions. Thus, the anti-semitic pogroms of Eastern Europe and Russia in the nineteenth century may have been reflections of the tensions between the peasant class and the aristocracy. The characteristics of the "scapegoat" group usually include the following: clear-cut minority status in terms of population; proximity to dominant group; clearly established communal identity; identity characteristics most nearly opposite those of the dominant group, by local standards; relatively recent immigration.

In short, three things may lead to violence: value conflict, unregulated competition and frustration displacement. The definitions and examples mentioned above are important to an assessment of violence and conflict between communal groups —notably Hausa and Ibo—in Kano, Nigeria. It is clear that no single explanation will be sufficient since many types of violence have been evident. It will be a major contention of this essay, however, that violence in Kano has resulted more from the excesses of competition, than from incompatibility of values between the Hausa and Ibo. Thus, in reply to the publicized analogy of Ibos as being "the Jews of Africa," one Hausa trader from Kano commented: "*We* are the Jews of Africa. There is no city in West Africa where the Hausa trader has not gone in pursuit of material gain." To a certain extent the "outside world" has misinterpreted the Hausa-Ibo relations by focusing on the alleged difference of modernization values. While there may be a difference on preferred means or behavioral norms, it is clear that much of the trouble in Kano has resulted from the fact that both Hausa and Ibo communities have very similar values with regard to achievement, materialism, and modernization. It seems necessary at this time to stress the importance of the two types of violence which are not based on value conflict: that which may stem from competition and similarity of values, and that which may stem from the displacement of frustration resultant from the internal tensions of the Hausa/Fulani stratification system and the stresses of urbanization.[5]

The purpose of this essay will not be to prove or disprove a particular set of propositions, but rather to explore the configuration of factors which may have led to communal competition, conflict and violence in Kano. In particular, the essay will examine the impact of communal migration and urbanization in Kano, the institutional framework for resolving conflict, and the varieties of economic competition (for markets, jobs and land) in which Ibos and Hausas were engaged. Some conclusions will be drawn regarding the nature of communalism and violence in Kano.

II URBANIZATION AND ETHNIC PLURALISM IN KANO

Since the beginning of the Fulani era (1806), Kano City has been the major commercial center of the central Sudan. During the colonial period (1903–60), it increased in economic importance, although with independence the northern capital (Kaduna) emerged as a economic competitor to Kano. Still, as late as 1965, Kano accounted for half of all trade in the Northern Region of Nigeria and 50% of all cash turn-over in the north.

With regard to population, in 1952 Kano was three times larger than the next largest northern city. At present, Kano has increased to about one-quarter million persons. Throughout the twentieth century, the rate of urbanization in Kano has been dramatic. There was a 26.8% increase in population from 1911 (39,368) to 1921 (49,938). By 1952, the population had increased to 130,173, and this figure more than doubled (260,687) during the next ten years.

Residential Sectors in Kano

This population increase has been distributed in six separate residential sectors within the Kano urban area. Each of these sectors has been distinctive in terms of ethnicity, standard of living, and recency and rate of immigration. The characteristics of the sectors are summarized in Figure 1.

Several patterns emerge from Figure 1. First, Kano City is the dominant sector in the urban area and consists mainly of Hausa/Fulani families who have a considerable sense of establishment and tradition. The city also reflects the full range of social stratification in Hausa/Fulani society. Second, Fagge is the "new" Hausa sector, consisting of merchants, traders, and young men who settled just outside the "old" city because of their apparent need for a more modern style of life. Third, Tudun Wada and Gwagwarwa are new locations, where many of the northern (Hausa/Fulani/Kanuri) migrants settled during the period 1950–1965. They are physically separated from the Fagge (Hausa) and City (Hausa) sectors by the Sabon Gari (Ibo). To some extent there was a spill-over from the Sabon Gari into Gwagwarwa in the early 1960's, making this sector the only Hausa/Ibo mixed area. Fourth, Sabon Gari has consisted of Ibo and other southern Nigerian ethnic groups in a densely populated area. The Sabon Gari was established in the early colonial period as a residential area for non-indigenous, semi-skilled labor attracted to meet the needs of the colonial administration in Kano. Fifth, the Township was originally the area where colonial administrators and expatriate businessmen lived. During the independence period, many of the Nigerian civil servants have chosen to live in the modern and affluent sector, along with the Lebanese and British commercial elite.

Because of the special importance of the relationship between Kano City and the Sabon Gari, it may be useful to further

FIGURE 1

CHARACTERISTICS OF RESIDENTIAL SECTORS IN KANO URBAN AREA

Variable	Name of residential sector					
	Kano City	Fagge	Tudun Wada	Gwagwarwa	Sabon Gari	Township
1. Population/ 1964	165,455	21,190	7,980	10,800	40,000	9,250
2. Ethnic identity	Hausa/ Fulani	Hausa/ Arab	Hausa	Hausa/ Ibo	Ibo and Southern	European/ Lebanese/ Nigerian Civil Ser.
3. Income level	Mixed	Mixed	Low	Low	Mixed	High
4. Date of founding	Pre-10th Century	Late 19th Century	Post WW II	Post WW II	Early 20th Century	Early 20th Century
5. Population growth p.a. 1958–62	11.5%	14.5%	28.9%	33.0%	5.6%	11.5%
6. Number of houses 1964	27,000	3,325	1,160	920	1,700	1,550
7. Persons per room 1964	1.4	3.0	1.8	2.0	7.0	1.4

Source for Figures: Trevallion, *op. cit.*

elaborate some of the ethnic characteristics of each sector. In both cases, during the period 1930–60, these sectors came to be identified with their respective dominant ethnic groups: Hausa and Ibo.

Kano City Ethnicity

At present, it would be difficult to distinguish the composite ethnic groups in Kano City, because of the processes of amalgamation and assimilation which have occurred in the past thirty years. In the census of 1931, however, a delineation was made of distinct ethnic groups in Kano City. There were six major groups in the City, as indicated in Figure 2.

FIGURE 2

KANO CITY ETHNIC COMPOSITION (1931)

Ethnic Group	Population	Percent Total
1. Hausa	68,515	77.15
2. Fulani	10,014	11.67
3. Kanuri	6,168	6.61
4. Tuareg	1,741	1.62
5. Nupe	1,190	1.43
6. Yoruba	854	.76
7. Arab	399	.49
8. Shuwa Arab	281	.27

Source: N.J. Brooke, *Census of Nigeria, 1931* (London, Government Printer, 1933, Vol. II, p. 45).

As was noted above, "Hausa" became the prevailing identity for the City. In one sense, northern groups such as the Kanuri and Fulani were assimilated into Hausa culture and identity, but in another sense a new communal amalgamation emerged in which people became identified with the City itself. This amalgamated identity has been more noticeable in areas outside of Kano Emirate, in other parts of Nigeria and along the Coast of West Africa where people from Kano City are known as *Kanawa*. The factors[6] which have contributed to this Hausa-Kano identity have included common religious identity (Islam of a distinctive nature), common language (Hausa, with a distinctive accent), and the external ascriptions of southern Nigerians and expatriates.

Sabon Gari Ethnicity

In 1954 the Sabon Gari was approximately 60% Ibo. This percentage probably increased to 80% by 1965. Yet, in an administrative survey in 1954/55, at least sixteen groups were regarded as distinctive. These are indicated in Figure 3.

FIGURE 3

SABON GARI ETHNIC COMPOSITION (1954–55)

Ethnic *Classification*	Men	Women	Boys	Girls	Total	Per cent
1. Ibo	3,670	3,758	2,844	2,496	12,770	59.05
2. Yoruba	1,484	1,710	928	1,046	5,174	23.92
3. Urhobo & Itsekiri	360	400	108	67	935	4.32
4. Efik & Ibibio	279	530	48	49	906	4.18
5. Benin, Ishan & Kukuruku (Edo)	168	144	74	60	446	2.06
6. Ijaw (Okirika & Kalabari)	195	101	33	20	349	1.61
7. Nupe & Igala	105	210	40	24	379	1.75
8. Idoma & allies	80	131	16	8	235	1.08
9. Gold Coast, Togo & Dahomean	48	34	20	15	117	.54
10. Hausa & Fulani	16	74	8	6	104	.48
11. Cameroonian	20	30	15	8	73	.37
12. Sierra Leonean	10	20	10	8	48	.22
13. Tripolitanian & Sudanese Arab	12	3	21	5	41	.18
14. Tchadian	18	10	6	4	38	.17
15. Kanuri	3	4			7	.03
16. West Indian	2				2	.01
Total	6,470	7,165	4,171	3.814	21,624	100.00

Source: N. A. K. 1954–1955, Kano Province #5908, (Tribal Population Statistics).

In terms of out-group perceptions, the Sabon Gari came to be regarded as including three ethnic groups: Ibo, Yoruba, and "other". The factors of language and religion were, as in the City, important reinforcements to communal identities. The Ibo and Yoruba languages were recognizable and distinct, but of perhaps more importance, English came to be the lingua franca in the Sabon Gari, just as Hausa was in the City. With regard to religion, again the Ibos were distinctive in their adherence to Roman Catholicism and "Nigerian national churches," while the Yoruba tended to be identified with the orthodox Protestant and the evangelical Aladura-type churches. (Many Yoruba families were Muslim, although of the Ansar-udeen and Ahmadiyya types which are uncommon in the north.) Yet, despite the association of persons in the Sabon Gari with Christian religious identities, the northern perception of the religious identity of the Ibo community was that they were only nominal Christians (or perhaps associational Christians rather than communal), and in reality "pagans".

In all time periods the northern community has made a distinction between Ibos and others in the Sabon Gari, although in some situations the Sabon Gari as a whole was regarded as a distinctive communal unit.

Sabon Gari Development

In 1912, the railway linked Kano to Southern Nigeria. The amalgamation of Northern and Southern Nigeria in 1914 had the effect of encouraging immigration to the north. During the period 1913–18, approximately 320 plots were established in the Kano Sabon Gari area to accommodate southern migrants, many of whom were associated with the railroad. By 1936 there was a total of 560 plots in Sabon Gari. With the outbreak of World War II, the number of plots increased to 1,472.

In terms of ethnic distribution of population growth, the 1921 census indicated less than 2,000 immigrants in the Sabon Gari of which 1,478 were Yoruba. At that time, Ibos were so few that they were not mentioned in the census. (In 1921, there were only 3,000 Ibos in the whole of Northern Nigeria, although this figure rose to 12,000 by 1931.) Not until after World War II did Ibos begin to outnumber the Yoruba in the Kano Sabon Gari. This same period witnessed the dramatic growth of the Sabon Gari, reaching a peak in the period 1954–64, when the population doubled from 21,000 to 40,000.

The timing of this development will be considered later in assessing ethnic competition and conflict in Kano. Two points should be noted however: the immigrants who came to Kano after World War II were born outside of Kano and hence had a different legal and social status from those in the Sabon Gari (mainly Yoruba) who had been born in Kano; the continued increase in immigrants during the 1950's coincided with the growth of political parties in Northern Nigeria, and was interpreted by many northerners as an attempt to "take over" Northern Nigeria through political means.

Sabon Gari Administration

The colonial policy of indirect rule required the local emirate system to serve as "Native Authority" and handle all matters of law, taxation, and land use within the Emirate. Yet, the colonial administration did not feel it possible to attract southern migrant labor to Kano under conditions whereby migrants would be subject to Islamic law and authority. Commercial enterprise could not be attracted for precisely the same reasons. Also, in 1912, when non-Muslims were prohibited by the Emir from living inside Kano City it was clear that other residential arrangements were necessary. Thus, a reserved area called the Township was set up, (outside of the walled city), which was not subject to Native Authority jurisdiction.

In 1918 a regulation was enacted which made it possible for southern Nigerians to hold title to plots in the Township area. Legal affairs were handled by a Kano Station Magistrate, subordinate to the High Court. Thus, Sabon Gari residents were directly under the European Local Authority. In 1925, the Sabon Gari plots were reordered into their present grid-like pattern. In 1934, the Sabon Gari area was enlarged.

Meanwhile, the Sabon Gari was still part of the Township area. An unofficial Township Advisory Board, which did not have official status, was set up and by 1936 two Africans (from Sabon Gari) were serving on the Advisory Board. In 1940, however, an administrative decision was made to excise the Sabon Gari from Township administration and to "return" it to Native Authority jurisdiction. This was done in 1941, and the Sabon Gari became part of a larger area known as "Waje". Then, in 1956, constitutions were introduced establishing two urban Councils; one in Waje and one in Kano City. Elected members had certain real control over financial expenditures in each of these councils.

According to the 1957 annual report:

> The newly elected Waje Council has proved itself to be a live and active body with a fair sense of its responsibilities and duties. It has tackled many problems which have daunted its predecessors . . .[7]

In 1958, the Waje Council was dealing with a budget of £41,267. A portion of this budget was directed to improving the "Waje Market," which began a series of long disputes with the Native Authority over matters of jurisdiction. At this time, the market had an annual revenue of only £12,000. In 1959, the three-year term of office for members to the Waje Council expired, but new elections were postponed so as not to conflict with the Nigerian Federal Elections. Although the Waje Council budget was increased to £60,000, the colonial administration began to fear that the Council committees might "tend to overstep the limits of their powers and usurp functions which are the prerogative of the Native Authority."[8]

In October 1960, Nigeria became independent. In May of that year elections to the Waje Council were held with a resultant reversal in the political composition of the council. The controversial elections produced a majority for the Northern Peoples Congress. (Previously the National Council of Nigeria and the Cameroons, and its allies, the Northern Elements Progressive Union had held a majority.) It is perhaps symbolic that the year of Nigerian independence marked also the transfer of power over the Sabon Gari to the Kano Emirate power structure. In retrospect, however, it is perhaps most important that at the time of Nigerian independence there was no truly integrated decision-making institution, and no central mechanism for conflict resolution within the Kano urban area. This dualism may have resulted from colonial "necessity" but was hardly a portent for cooperation between the Sabon Gari and the City.

III ECONOMIC COMPETITION BETWEEN KANO CITY AND THE SABON GARI

The Kano urban area fits the classic Furnivall model of a plural society. The three major communities—Northern Nigerian, (Hausa-Fulani), southern Nigerian (Ibo/Yoruba) and expatriate (British/Lebanese)—have been linked together through the central commercial zone, but have not been integrated in social and political spheres. The commercial area served as a physical buffer zone between the three communities. It should be noted that the expatriate community has commercially dominated the urban area. However, it will be the purpose of this paper to concentrate more on the economic competition between the northern and southern communities in Kano. The three major types of competition to be discussed will be market competition, employment competition and land competition.

Market Competition

The Kano City market once stood as the greatest emporium of the Central Sudan. In the early post-independence period, however, the Kano Sabon Gari market began to surpass the City market in terms of volume and value of business. To a certain extent the two markets served their respective communities in terms of staples, yet there was competition on prices, and the Sabon Gari market increasingly came to dominate the total market on "modern" types of consumer items. In 1965, the two markets consisted of almost parallel types of stock, but with the Sabon Gari dominating the field of imported textiles, canned food, footwear and other modern sector items. This is apparent from Figure 4.

By 1965, the Sabon Gari market had surpassed the City market in terms of number of traders, in value of turn-over, and in average profit per trader. This reversal of status, which is illustrated in Figure 5, did not contribute to better relations between the two markets. Among the types of criticism voiced by the City traders were that profits from the Sabon Gari were sent to the Eastern Region, rather than remaining in Kano. It should be noted, however, that many of the larger Hausa merchants were no longer doing business through the petty market system, but were establishing wholesale businesses in competition with the expatriate community. Thus, the relative decline of the City market had more impact on the average and lower class Hausa traders than on wealthy Hausa families.

FIGURE 4

DISTRIBUTION OF STALLS IN CITY AND SABON GARI MARKETS: 1965

Type of Stock	Sabon Gari Market Stalls	City Market Stalls	Total Stalls
1. Food (local)	443	535	978
2. Food (canned)	1,457	592	2,049
3. Meat	548	249	797
4. Drugs/medicine (including traditional)	68	105	173
5. Textiles	517	397	914
6. Blankets	76	58	134
7. Clothing	508	438	946
8. Footwear	527	64	591
9. Secondhand	233	129	362
10. Ornaments	297	160	457
11. Crafts	281	427	708
12. Enamelware	195	147	342
13. Electrical	20	16	36
14. Spare parts	219	44	263
15. Tires/tubes	121	17	138
16. Furniture	139	63	202
17. Timber	77	45	122
18. Unclassified	1,074	664	1,738
Total	6,800	4,150	10,950

Source: Trevallion, *op. cit.*, p. 85.

FIGURE 5

COMPARISON OF KANO CITY AND SABON GARI MARKETS: 1965

Variable	Sabon Gari Market	City Market
1. Total Number of Traders	3,571	1,902
2. Total Stock (£1,000)	794.5	212.7
3. Average Stock per trader per month (£)	222	112
4. Monthly sales (£1,000)	519.7	160.2
5. Average sales per trader per month (£)	145	84
6. Average profit per trader per month (£)	28	15

Source: Trevallion, *op. cit.*, p. 136–37.

The physical destruction of the Sabon Gari market in 1966 will be described later. As an epilogue to the issue of market competition, it is possible to report[9] that during 1967–68, the market was rebuilt, using cement and other permanent materials, and that throughout the war the Sabon Gari Market was flourishing (despite war shortages), with Yoruba traders who had remained, plus a large number of Hausa traders who had moved in from the City and Fagge. Rent on Ibo-owned property was collected by the Kano Local Government Authority and held in trust until the end of the war. Whether Ibo merchants will ever return to Kano is impossible to predict. The fact remains, however, that in 1966 a social upheaval occurred in which the Hausa community in Kano regained control over the urban market system.

Employment Competition

Economic competition in the area of employment was no less acute than in the markets. The two main arenas came to be white-collar jobs and semi-skilled work in light industries. In both cases, southern Nigerian dominance in these areas was reversed in the late 1950's through the political policy of northernization, to be described later.

The original demand for southern labor focused on the category of clerks literate in English. Employers included the railroad, the banks, the post office, the colonial administration, and the expatriate companies. During the 1930's however, Lebanese businessmen came to Kano, settled in Fagge and engaged in light industry and wholesale merchandising. During World War II, many new industries were initiated in Kano.[10] By the end of the war, Kano had the largest "modern" sector in Northern Nigeria. The manpower for this sector was drawn largely from Southern Nigerian immigrants who settled in the Sabon Gari.

In 1949, a Kano Native Authority Five-Year Plan was instituted, the first such development plan in Northern Nigeria. In 1950 this was transformed into a Kano Ten-Year Plan.[11] Colonial policy had selected Kano as the main urban area in Northern Nigeria for economic modernization.

From 1954 to 1962 a considerable number of new industries were established in Kano. Yet by examination of the Kano labor exchange reports(which indicate the number of persons who were actively looking for jobs) it is clear that by the end of the

1950's, the overwhelming majority of persons seeking semi-skilled work in the "modern" sector were northerners. The high rate of northern rural immigration into the Kano urban Hausa sectors placed a premium on employment and thus increased competition for jobs, despite the general expansion of the light industry sector.

Tension regarding job competition was heightened during this period (1954–62) by two additional factors: the political leverage of the northernization policy which gave employment preference to persons born in the north, and the near monopoly by Ibos of clerical and semi-skilled jobs in the postal service, banks and railway. The maintenance of this latter pattern, despite the policy of northernization, was felt by northerners to be due to nepotistic hiring practices.

These tensions were offset to some extent by the fact that the Kano economy was growing rapidly during this period. However, in 1963, this process began to slow down. During 1963–65 virtually no new industries were established in Kano. This was partly due to the regional government policy of encouraging industrial location in Kaduna, and partly due to the fact that in the late 1950's Kano had received a disproportionate share of industrial establishment in Northern Nigeria. The relocation of industry from Jos to Kano had been dramatic during the period 1956–1960. In 1956, Jos had 233 industrial establishments (21% of the northern total), each employing over 10 persons, while Kano had 170 such establishments (15% of the northern total). In 1960, the number in Jos had decreased to 192 (13% of the northern total), while the number in Kano had risen to 231 (22% of the northern total).

The tensions which occurred in Kano after 1963 as a result of this stand-still in industrial development provoked anger in the Kano Hausa community both regarding Ibo domination of semi-skilled work, and the policy of the regional government in Kaduna. It was partly out of this latter frustration that the Kano State Movement was established in the summer of 1965, incorporating all elements in the Kano community and demanding separation from the Northern Region.

In retrospect, the types of light industries which had been established in the Kano urban area had three effects in terms of ethnic division of labor. (1) Non-indigenous ethnic groups (from Southern Nigeria) came to dominate skilled and semi-skilled positions in the modern sector. (2) The traditional administrative class in Kano (Fulani) came to hold lucrative advisory positions in the management structures of the new industries which tended to exacerbate relations with the Hausa lower class. (3) Northern ethnic groups became associated with unskilled labor but increasingly came to compete for semi-skilled occupations in the modern sector.

Again as an epilogue to the Ibo exodus in 1966, most semi-skilled positions held by Ibos were filled with little transitional difficulty by northerners. This included clerical employment in the post office, the banks and the commercial firms, plus technical employment in the transportation industry. In short, the Ibo semi-skilled worker was not ousted by people who did not want to modernize, but by people who were in direct competition for his job.

Language and Education

At the core of all these employment patterns was the language and education issue. The author has described elsewhere how government-sponsored education in Northern Nigeria was largely conducted in Hausa until the 1950's.[12] A large number of traders were literate in Hausa, using Arabic script. Also, Christian mission education was prohibited in Kano, except in the Sabon Gari. It is not surprising that as late as 1952, the total number of persons literate in English in Kano Province was 23,000 (out of 3.4 million) of whom approximately half were non-northerners. According to an official report in 1953:

> In consequence, both in terms of Government Departments and of Commerce, the Region has been very largely dependent for its clerical staff and for technicians and artisans on the Southern Region.[13]

The disparity between Kano City and the Sabon Gari on western education/English facility is illustrated by the official figures for percentage of children (of appropriate age groups) attending western schools in 1965: Kano City, 5%; Sabon Gari 98%.

The matter of western education almost became a symbol of ethnic identity in Kano. The major social organization of the Sabon Gari, the Ibo Union, sustained as a matter of highest priority private educational facilities which, because of their quality, gave access into the employment structure of Kano. According to the Kano Twenty-Year Plan:

> The Ibo people of Sabon Gari and elsewhere in Kano identify themselves primarily with the Ibo Union. This organization makes provision for a variety of activities including well-run and staffed primary schools and one secondary school. The establishment of schools which cater almost exclusively for Ibo children was probably forced upon the community through lack of educational facilities provided by the local education authority. However, while the Ibo Union performs a valuable function, its existence, as with any other organisation catering solely for a significantly large ethnic group, is disadvantageous. It indirectly stands in the way of the identification of the people with their town.[14]

The policy of "northernization", which was initiated in the late 1950's by the Premier of the Northern Region, attempted to balance the commercial importance of English language with incentives for increased use of Hausa language. It also set restrictions on employment of persons who were not born in the north. Thus, in situations where there was a northerner available for a job, he would take precedence over a southerner. At the same time efforts were made by the government to increase the amount of western education available to the northern community. The class of northerners graduating from secondary school in 1966 was sufficiently large and trained that it could be utilized by the government to keep most vital services (especially postal services) functioning after the crisis in 1966. At the same time, the attempt by General Ironsi to unify the civil service in Nigeria in the spring of 1966 was interpreted in the north as giving preference to those with more English-language skills (i.e., Ibos), and was clearly a major factor in the failure of his regime. It is important to note that at present the restrictions on job opportunities for Southerners have been removed. In August, 1970,the Kano State government reported that approximately 800 Ibos had returned to Kano State.

The distinction remains, however, between English language skills (and hence employment opportunities) and attitudes toward modernization. What is of central importance in understanding ethnic economic competition in Kano prior to 1966 is that use of English-language was not a crucial indicator of attitudes toward modernization. Many Ibos in Sabon Gari were "traditional" in the sense of adherence to ethnic cultural values, and many Hausa traders in Kano City (most of whom were literate in Hausa and many in Arabic as well) were modern in their aspirations and organization. It is also clear in retrospect that many of the Hausa/Fulani elite, impeccable in their use of English, were among the most traditional elements in the north. The question of tri-lingualism in Kano (Hausa/English/Arabic) will continue to pose difficult problems with regard to modernization; it no longer appears to be a major symbol of ethnic differentiation.

Land Competition

The final category of ethnic economic competition in Kano concerns land rights and use. Traditionally, all land in Kano Emirate was "crown land" and the Emir granted rights of usufruct. As noted earlier, the original purpose of establishing the Kano Township was to remove control of certain land from the Native Authority. The land outside Sabon Gari could not be alienated to persons not "originally" resident in the north. According to the 1946 Commission on Land Tenure in Kano:

> It is . . . doubtful whether . . . any persons not of Northern
> Nigerian origin who live in the Emirate but outside the
> Sabon Gari have any title [to land] the Ordinance recog-
> nizes.[15]

During the period of "northernization", this ordinance was interpreted to exclude all persons not born in the north from land ownership. This policy was resented by southerners living in Kano (as was the policy of restrictions on jobs), but the result was an over-crowding of the available land in the Sabon Gari. The average number of persons per room in Sabon Gari was seven, compared to an average of 1.9 for the other five urban sectors. The Kano Twenty-Year Plan described the Sabon Gari in 1965 as "overcrowded" and "uniformly dirty and untidy".[16] The report further interpreted the organization of the Sabon Gari as dysfunctional to family and community stability.

> The vast majority of people [in the Sabon Gari] are Ibo. There is no evidence of sub-divisions which are socially meaningful, such as the Ungwa in the City. Similarly the family is less of a unit and of less social importance. The Ibo people appear to feel as strangers to Kano despite the duration of their stay, often a lifetime ... Excessive over-crowding and the relatively large numbers of families in one house, the numerous 'stranger' lodgers, and the separation of the real family between Kano and the home town in Eastern Nigeria, act disadvantageously against close family life.[17]

In retrospect, the *lack* of ethnic competition for land in Kano, that is, a restrictive residential system, had the effect of reinforcing ethnic tensions in other areas. Again as an epilogue, all restrictions on land ownership by southerners have now been removed by the Kano State Government.

IV. COMMUNAL CONFLICT AND VIOLENCE IN KANO

Despite the degree of economic competition and social tension in Kano, there have been relatively few instances of overt violence in modern times. The three major instances of such violence occured in May 1953, May 1966, and October 1966. In the latter case, which was by far the most massive in terms of deaths, the participants were situationally identified less in terms of the Kano system, than as actors within a national context. This was especially true since many of those who inflicted death were federal soldiers stationed in Kano, who used automatic weapons to prevent Ibos from throughout the north (who had come to Kano to use the air and rail facilities) from returning to the Eastern Region. According to firsthand reports, the group of soldiers who disobeyed orders at the Kano airport and set off the chain of events were not men from Kano Province. In any case, the violence of October 1966 is difficult to assess even though the civil war is over. It clearly constituted a preliminary volley in the war.

Conflict and Violence in May 1953

The situation in May 1953, when rioting occurred between the City and Sabon Gari, is somewhat more amenable to analysis. A commission of inquiry report was published[18] as well as a confidential addenda which is now available. In addition the Nigerian Archives at Kaduna have good records of this period.[19]

The preceived impetus to the riots occurred in Lagos (April, 1953) when the Northern delegates to the Federal Budget session felt themselves harrassed by street mobs. In retaliation, when Mr. Akintola of the Action Group proposed a speaking tour of Kano, several Northern Peoples Congress officials prepared a procession of protest. In the events that followed it is of some significance that although the occasion was one of Yoruba politicians visiting Kano, the violence which developed focused almost exclusively on the Ibo community. Of the 21 Southerners killed, none were Yoruba, and of the 71 Southerners injured only two were Yoruba.

It is clear that both the Sabon Gari and the City/ Fagge areas expected trouble at the time of the impending Action Group tour. According to the official report:

> . . . there were signs of growing tension in the City . . . Messrs Leventis had sold 172 matchets to Southerners on Friday afternoon and there had been a considerable theft of scrap iron, and the U. A. C. Motor Department had reported that their grind-stone had been worn right down overnight by being used for sharpening matchets and scrap iron. The Senior District Officer, Kano also reported that the Ibo Union had asked for protection against Northerners who were stated to be coming into the town from nearby villages, many carrying weapons. . . .[20]

The actual fighting began on Saturday evening. According to the report:

> More and more Northerners in small groups now began to concentrate in Sabon Gari and by 15:30 there was an estimated crowd of about 2,000, many mounted and the majority armed in some way or other. . . . At about 16:00 hours the crowd started to get out of hand and the first act of violence took place: an Ibo who was riding by on his bicycle being assaulted and his bicycle smashed. There-

after any Southerner seen in the area between Fagge and Sabon Gari was attacked.[21]

The fighting continued sporadically until Tuesday, when police reinforcements, many of them southerners, established order, and a "Reconciliation Committee" was established consisting of leading members of the Sabon Gari, Fagge and the City.

The events of the May 1953 riots parallel closely those of May 1966. Although, the 1953 commission report focused primary attention on immediate causes of trouble or on individual responsibility for the trouble rather than on the structural aspects of communal competition. It was perhaps predictable that in May 1966, when the structure of communal relationships was almost identical to that of 1953, a second riot would occur in Kano so parallel in detail to its predecessor that the same report might have been used to describe and explain it. One technical difference was that "economic development" has brought a number of petrol stations to major roads surrounding the Sabon Gari, which meant literally, that conflagration was less difficult than before.

Conflict and Violence in May 1966

For various reasons it is not possible to attempt a full assessment of the riots of May, 1966. Reliable data do not exist at present. A commission of inquiry was appointed by the military government to produce details on the Kano riot, but this commission, which was to have reported on August 2, 1966, did not report because of the counter-coup at the end of July.

The first military coup of January 1966 was greeted with relief and expectation in Kano, for the political tension with Kaduna had reached a near-breaking point. None of the Kano leaders and politicians had been killed in the coup, although the commanding officer of the Nigerian Army in Kano, Lieutenant Colonal Odumegwu Ojukwu (later, leader of the Biafran forces) did arrest and hold in detention temporarily the Emir of Kano, Ado Bayero. It was not until April and May that disillusionment with the military regime of General Ironsi began to be noticeable in Kano. Public posters were circulated in Kano of the executive advisers to Ironsi, and it was apparent that most of these advisers were Ibo. At the same time, the prevailing interpretation of the new military regime by the Kano Sabon Gari was that it represented an "Ibo" victory over the Hausa. The relief and pride felt by the Ibos at this status reversal was evident. Also with the "unification of the civil service" decrees issued by Ironsi on May 24th, it was clear to the Hausa/Fulani elite in Kano that their administrative future both in the north and in Nigeria was seriously jeopardized. This may have accounted for the important role played by students in "peaceful" demonstrations which preceded the riots of May 29th.

On Saturday afternoon (May 29th) come students from Abdullahi Bayero College, the Provincial Secondary School, the School for Arabic Studies, and the Technical Training College peacefully demonstrated against Ibo domination of the national government. This included an orderly visit to the Emir's palace. The demonstrators passed out through one of the gates of the City (Kofar Mata) leading to the Sabon Gari. The next day, lower-class and unemployed Hausa young men in the Kofar Mata area threw stones at some Ibo workers who were going to work in the City. Tensions were high in both the City and the Sabon Gari on Sunday and that evening the *yan banga* (hooligans), *yan iska* (uprooted young men) and *yan haya* (bicycle renters) streamed out from the City toward the Sabon Gari (down Ibo Road and Airport Road). An incident occurred and fighting began. Apart from the Sabon Gari, the locations where violence developed in the next three or four days were places where Ibos were known to dominate the employment structure: the post office, the railway station, and certain commercial areas. The exact number killed during this period is hard to estimate, but in Kano it was probably between 100 and 200 persons. (The *New York Times* estimate for the entire North was 600 killed.) This Kano figure includes Hausa and rural Fulani who were killed while caught inside the Sabon Gari market when the trouble began. The figures given unofficially by the authorities in Kano State are as follows: seventy-two persons killed in Kano, of whom forty-six were northerners, mostly women. The police arrested twenty-nine persons; fifteen were convicted, and fourteen were released for lack of evidence. Order was restored within three to four days.

During June and July, tension developed in both the Sabon Gari and the City. With the northern military coup against General Ironsi, on July 29th, full-scale Ibo emigrations from Kano began. The disengagement of the Ibo community from Kano, which occurred in August, September and October, was paralleled by the division of the Nigerian army by region of origin (including the departure of Ibo troops from Kano, and the return of Hausa troops). The disruption and tension of this period culminated in massive killings throughout the North in October 1966. The official Nigerian estimate was that a total of 5,000 persons (of both northern and southern origin) were killed in the north as a whole. Ibo leaders originally estimated that 10,000 persons were killed, but later revised this figure to 30,000. Some European observers put the figure at about 7,500. The author of this essay has no way of assessing the accuracy of these estimates.

Comparative Aspects of Conflict and Violence

The details of the May 1966 troubles in Kano may be of less importance than some of the broader systemic aspects. It is possible to isolate at least six major dimensions of urban communal violence which might be appropriate to the study of any particular instance. These include: duration of violence, intensity, characteristics of participants, apparent causes, role of authorities, and timing. Some indicator/variables for each of these dimensions are suggested below in Figure 6, along with some preliminary coding of Kano data from the May 1953 and May 1966 periods.

V. CONCLUSIONS

There are several conclusions which may be drawn from the Kano experience with regard to communalism, competition, conflict, violence and value congruence in an urban context. I have categorized these conclusions according to a rough sequence of factors which seem to build on each other: immigration and urban pluralism, institutional linkages, economic competition, identity and communalism, and immediate causes of violence.

Communal Immigration and Urban Pluralism

There are at least three effects on potential violence stemming from communal immigration and urbanization in Kano:
the effect of high urbanization on the potential for violence, the
effect of residential segregation on propensity for violence, and
the effect of colonial-sponsored immigration on post-colonial
propensity for violence.

The general rate of urbanization in Kano was projected by
the Kano Twenty-Year plan as follows: 1962, 150,000; 1967,
390,000; 1972, 650,000; 1977, 1,100,000; 1982, 1,200,000 or possibly
1,800,00.[22] This doubling or tripling of size every ten years
would have continued the pattern of the past twenty years. The
cost of accommodating such urbanization in terms of providing
an infrastructure of services (police, water, electricity, etc.)
and of housing, would clearly have been prohibitive. The dramatic increase in population over the past twenty years, which
was restricted in no way by either the colonial government or
the Nigerian government, was not accompanied by proportional increases in facilities. One safety valve in the past was
the fact that since migration to Kano City involved no major
adjustment in life style, an individual Hausa could return to the
rural area if he could not find work or accommodation. Still
there appears to have been a high degree of social tension resulting from this rate of urbanization, and such social tension
carried with it the potential for violence.

The pattern of urbanization based on segregated residential
sectors did provide a choice to the Hausa immigrant, who could
settle in the City, in Fagge, in Tudun Wada or Gwagwarwa. Yet
the option of migrating into a "new" Hausa sector or an "old"
Hausa sector was not accompanied by an adjustment in balance of power between new and old Hausa sectors, since all
power resided in the hands of the old sector. This may have
reinforced some tensions within the Hausa community, especially since power in the old sector was clearly identified with
elite elements of the Fulani community.

With regard to government encouragement of communal migration (e.g. the colonial creation of the Sabon Gari and demand for manpower) it is hard to imagine this situation
repeating itself, although the present policy of protecting re-

FIGURE 6

DIMENSIONS OF URBAN COMMUNAL VIOLENCE IN KANO

Dimension:	Variable	May 1953	May 1966
I. Duration	1. Number of days of violence	3–4	3–4
II. Intensity	2. Number killed	36	100–200
	3. Number injured/treated in hospital	241	?
	4. Amount of property damage	£10,418	extensive burning
	5. Instruments of violence	Machetes/guns/stones	machetes/guns/fire/stones
III. Participants	6. Social characteristics of host community participants	Hausa	Hausa
		Lower class	Lower class
	7. Social characteristics of immigrant community participants	Ibo (few Yoruba) all classes	Ibo (not Yoruba) all classes
	8. Ratio of host to gretto participants killed (approximate)	1:1 (no Yoruba killed)	1.2
IV. Apparent Causes	9. Initial impetus within urban context	"Peaceful" demonstration by northerners against southern domination at national level.	"Peaceful" demonstration by northern students against Ibo domination at national level.

Dimension:	Variable	May 1953	May 1966
	10. National political context	Extreme tension between north and south over constitutional future of Nigeria. Northern leaders "insulted" in Lagos and feared southern domination.	Extreme tension due to northern fear of Ibo domination in Ironsi military regime.
	11. Economic situation	Not critical, many new economic developments and change.	Inflationary prices/shortages due to dislocations of military takeover.
	12. Degree of social tension between sectors of host community	Considerable rivalry between NEPU and NPC parties, representing social divisions in Hausa/Fulani society.	Relative solidarity after coup, although pre-coup tension extremely high, especially vis-a-vis Kaduma
V. Role of Authorities	13. Role of local authorities	Emir old and ill. Some councillors tried to stop riots by riding in cars with Sabon Gari leaders. Others ambivalent.	Young emir, broadcast to people instrumental in regaining order. Many officials ambivalent.
	14. Role of Police	Total of 365 police, using tear gas, smoke grenades, baton charges but seldom direct fire-power. Many police southern. Well disciplined.	Combination of Native Authority and Nigerian police, many of latter Ibo. Well disciplined, effective.

Dimension:	Variable	May 1953	May 1966
	15. Means by which control regained	Police set up barbed wire along road between Fagge and Sabon Gari. Arrested provocateurs.	Combined police effort.
VI. Timing	16. Season/month	May: Last month of dry season. Food supplies low. Extremely hot (110°–120°) and uncomfortable by local standards.	May: last month of dry season. Food supplies low. Extremely hot (110° – 120° and uncomfortable by local standards.
	17. Day riots began	Friday: half day holiday because of Friday prayers at Central Mosque. Many shops also closed Saturday and Sunday for long weekend.	Sunday: Many shops closed Saturday and Sunday for long weekend.
	18. Contagion effect from other areas.	Rumors of potential trouble in other northern cities.	Rumors of potential troubles in other northern cities, which in fact, did materialize. Bukuru, near Jos, actually rioted prior to Kano.

turning Ibos may be a step in this direction. Persons who migrate without the protection of a colonial/military regime may be more careful in establishing workable relations with their host community. Kano has been a cosmopolitan city for several hundred years. In the past immigration has included major groups such as Arabs, Kanuri, Nupe, Yoruba, Tuareg, plus a host of smaller ethnic groups. In most cases, these ethnic groups have worked out some accommodation with the host community. Colonial authority removed the necessity for accommodation with the host community, and it is not surprising that removal of colonial power would create a potential for violence between Kano City and the Sabon Gari.

Institutional Linkage

In the plural society model, as described by M. G. Smith, ethnic communities of a given location share a common economic system, yet maintain separate social and political institutions. This was clearly the case in Kano during the colonial era. The Sabon Gari had its own legal institutions, decision-making institutions, and educational institutions.

A community may be regarded as integrated when it has common institutions for decision-making and conflict resolution. The potential for violence and the probability of conflict is increased in a situation where the colonial supra-structure is about to be removed (i.e. mid-1950's) or has recently been removed (mid-1960's), without the substitution of a political structure which links the major communal components in the plural society.

Economic Competition

Some regulation of competition, whether through self-imposed rules of the game or through some external arbitrator, is particularly necessary when economic interaction has a strong communal base. Such rules-of-the-game are normally established through political means. In the case of Kano, the transition from colonial rule to northern rule meant that substantial modifications could be made through political means in the rules-of-the-game. The policy of northernization was an attempt to affect the competitive economic position of ethnic groups in northern Nigeria. While this policy was resented by non-northerners, it was clear that some effort was politically necessary to redress the imbalance of access to modern economic power. Yet, northernization established clear sub-ordination of economics to politics, which made political competition at the highest level a matter of primary concern. In both 1953 and 1966, it appeared to northerners that their national political power was in jeopardy.

Distribution of economic resources within a community is normally arbitrated through political structures. In cases where competition involves ethnic groups as well as individuals, it may be necessary to have some proportional ethnic representation in the political process. In Kano this was not the case.

Identity and Communalism

The competition which stemmed from economic modernization added a further dimension to the patterns of multiple ethnicity found in Kano. The development of identities such as "northerner" and "southerner" were, in both cases, supplemental to other types of identity. This ethnicity was reinforced by the factors of language and religion, but was basically a result of the expansion of relevant socio-political context and the development of immigration patterns which established new "we-they" boundaries. This does not imply that other types of ethnicity were abandoned. It meant an increase in the scope of multiple identities. Once this new identity became established it became associated with an ethnic stratification system which was reinforced by patterns of economic competition.

The crystallization of interethnic competition between the Hausa and Ibo resulted in part from the demographic importance of these groups. Yet it would appear in retrospect, that certain culture traits of Ibo and Hausa, namely propensity for trade and commerce, resulted in particularly intense competition. In addition, certain Ibo cultural traits seemed to take on special importance within a Hausa context, especially those traits which resisted assimilation: endogamy, maintenance of obligations in the Eastern Region, and persistence of certain traditional religious customs among lower classes. These characteristics did not pertain to the same extent in the Yoruba community, many of whose members shared the cultural propensities of the Hausa, and were partially assimilated with Hausa society through intermarriage and religion.

The Immediate Causes of Communal Violence

The intention of this essay has been to suggest that on matters of economic well-being, the values of the Hausa and Ibo community in Kano were very similar. The Hausa community in Kano was the center of a trade network which extended from Algeria to Congo, and from Senegal to Sudan. The development of an Ibo trading network was seen as a direct threat to Hausa dominance in the field of commerce. Partly because of Ibo social networks in the port areas of southern Nigeria, Ibos emerged as stronger competitors for markets in the north than even the Hausa traders. This status reversal was difficult to accept in the Hausa community.

Of equal importance was the competition which began to emerge in the field of semi-skilled industrial and clerical occupations. When economic development in Kano began to level off, competition for jobs became acute. The Ibo semi-skilled worker was perhaps the equivalent of the migrant Indian in East Africa, and was the first to feel the pressure from beneath.

It is not intended to underestimate the differences in cultural style between the Hausa and Ibos in Kano. This cultural style involved differences in dress, speech, and religious affiliation. None of these stylistic factors, however, seems sufficient in itself to have caused the degree of violence which developed.

Finally, I would like to suggest that the highly stratified structure of the Hausa/Fulani community in Kano, particularly the growth of a class of unemployed Hausa youth in the City and Fagge may have resulted in a "frustration displacement" on the part of this lower class. This was "allowed" to materialize in those situations where the Hausa/Fulani political elites felt threatened by the southern community on the national level. In this respect, a satisfactory settlement of national political issues (at least with regard to establishing acceptable decision-making processes and institutions of conflict resolution) would seem to be a prerequisite for order and non-violence in the multi-ethnic urban centers of Nigeria.

NOTES

1. My field research was conducted in 1964–65, under a grant from the Foreign Area Fellowship Program. Unless otherwise stated, the statistical data in this paper is from B. A. W. Trevallion, *Metropolitan Kano: Report on the Twenty Year Development Plan, 1963–1983* (New York: Pergamon Press, 1966).

2. As has been done by Robert LeVine, *Dreams and Deeds: Achievement Motivation in Nigeria,* (Chicago: University of Chicago Press, 1966).

3. See John N. Paden, "Situational Ethnicity in Urban Africa, with Special Reference to the Hausa." Paper presented to the African Studies Association, November 2, 1967, New York City. Also, John N. Paden, "Urban Pluralism, Integration, and Adaptation of Communal Identity in Kano, Nigeria," in Ronald Cohen and John Middleton (eds.) *From Tribe to Nation in Africa* (San Francisco: Chandler Press, 1970).

4. Karl Deutsch, seminar lecture, Northwestern University, Jan. 8, 1969.

5. The concept of urbanization is directly related to the concept of communalism, for urbanization entails a process of differentiation which may affect the diffuseness of communal loyalties and produce new forms of communalism. It may also produce new types of communal violence insofar as rapid urbanization may entail social frustrations and tensions.

6. For an evaluation of religious factors in the integration of Hausa/Fulani/Kanuri/Arab communities inside Kano City, see John N. Paden, *Religion and Political Culture in Kano* (Berkeley and Los Angeles: University of California Press, forthcoming).

7. Northern Region of Nigeria, *Provincial Annual Reports, 1957* (Kaduna: Government Printer, 1959), p. 82.

8. Northern Nigeria, *Provincial Annual Reports, 1959* (Kaduna: Government Printer, 1962), p. 94.

9. BThe author had an opportunity to visit the Sabon Gari area in December 1968 and again in 1970.

10. See Nigerian Archives Kaduna, SNP, 5/1: 3338 (Wheat mills at Kano, 1940–42); 3182 (Beeswax Industry, 1939–48); 4183 (Soap Industry, 1937–52); 4530 (Kapok Industry, 1939–53); 4737 (Hides and skins, 1942–44).

11. Administered by a Kano Provincial Development Committee. See Sharwood-Smith, *Kano Survey, 1950* (Zaria Gaskiya), p. 39, for complete survey of Kano. For background to this survey, see Nigerian Archives Kaduna, SNP, 5: 6991 (Kano Economic Survey, Minutes, 1950); 7014 (Kano Native Treasury Five Year Plan, 1949–54); 7173 (Kano Province Economic Survey, 1951–54).

12. John N. Paden, "Language Problems of National Integration in Nigeria: The Special Position of Hausa," in J. A. Fishman, C. A. Ferguson, and J. Das Gupta, (eds.), *Language Problems of Developing Nations* (New York: John Wiley & Sons, 1968), pp. 199–213.

13. Northern Regional Government, *Report on the Kano Disturbances: 16th, 17th, 18th, and 19th, May 1953* (Kaduna: Government Printer, 1953), p. 2.

14. Trevallion, *op. cit.,* p. 38.

15. C. W. Rowling, *Report on Land Tenure, Kano Province* (Kaduna: Government Printer, 1949), p. 25.

16. Trevallion, *op. cit.,* p. 48.

17. *Ibid.,* pp. 37–38.

18. *Report on Kano Disturbances* (Kaduna: Government Printer, 1953).

19. For examples of materials in the Nigerian Archives, Kaduna, see Kano Provincial Files: #6630 "Relations between the Tribes of Nigeria, 1954"; #6661 s.20 "Election complaints and petitions, 1951–52"; #8133 sl. "Kano Riots Victims: Ex gratia payment, 1953–56". Also see Secretariat Northern Provinces Files 12 and 16: Gen. #1100/s.6 "Kano Riots: Atrocities Human and Animal, 1953"; Gen. #1100/s.10 "Kano Riots: Diaries, 1953."

20. *Report on Kano Disturbances: op. cit.,* p. 9.

21. *Ibid.*

22. Trevallion, *op. cit.* p. 8.

CHAPTER 6

Entrepreneurial Attitudes and National Integration: The Nigerian Case

JOHN R. HARRIS *and* MARY P. ROWE

This paper will examine the impact of entrepreneurial attitudes in Nigeria on national integration.[1] We define "entrepreneurs" broadly as those who respond to economic opportunity by taking business risks and who organize and manage (or exercise great influence over the organization and management) of business enterprise. This definition includes both Nigerians and expatriates in the private sector as well as those government personnel whose decisions strongly influence private and public enterprise. By Nigerian "integration" we are taking the word in its simplest sense: *de facto* preservation of Nigeria as a national unit with common citizenship and without extensive internal customs or other economic barriers. For purposes of analysis, the alternative to integration will be assumed to be independent units based on pre-war regional boundaries, even though there may be other reasonable alternatives.

I. Entrepreneurs and Integration

Students of political integration for the most part consider economic development to be an integrative force.[2] Since such development usually includes increased specialization of economic activity, a widening of the area (both geographic and demographic) of economic interdependence occurs. Of course, there is also a converse relationship: political integration, by creating larger units within which productive factors can be mobile, fosters increased specialization, hence increased productivity and economic development.[3]

Our point of departure is the notion that entrepreneurial groups will contribute to integration or disintegration according to the extent that either state will provide profitable opportunities to be exploited. This is not meant to imply that entrepreneurs seek only profits—undoubtedly non-economic factors such as ethnicity and political affiliation weigh even more heavily than economic considerations in individuals' attitudes towards national unity. Furthermore, individuals frequently fail to perceive their "true" economic interests. Nevertheless, we feel that it is useful to concentrate on this single aspect of behavior and to draw some implications in the form of *ceteris paribus* statements. Thus, we will concentrate on the relationships between national unity and economic opportunities, and on the effectiveness with which entrepreneurial groups articulate their own interests.

The effect of entrepreneurial activity is not unambiguously favorable to political integration. That it can work in either direction is made clear by Coleman when he states that:

> . . . the processes of urbanization, commercialization, and Western education have furthered the widening of perspectives, accelerated social mobility, created new reference groups, as well as a nationally minded educated class. In some instances, however, these processes have operated to sharpen previous lines of cleavage or to create new ones, thereby obstructing the process of national unification around new territorial symbols and institutions. This differential development of groups or areas within territories has been malintegrative in two ways: the less-developed groups fear domination in the new territorial systems, and the more highly developed groups do not want either their affluence diluted, or their traditional status lowered, through merger with economically depressed and lower status groups.[4]

Furthermore, integrative/disintegrative effects may vary, dependent on whether entrepreneurial groups are indigenous, expatriate, or governmental, at regional or federal levels.[5]

II. Integration of the Nigerian Economy

Although Nigeria presents a potentially large market with its almost 50 million people[6] and relatively abundant resources, it would take an immense stretch of the imagination to claim that it was an integrated economy by 1966. The latest (questionably reliable) statistics available are for 1962 and they indicate manufacturing accounting for less than 4% of Gross Domestic Product.[7] Preliminary estimates of interregional trade in locally produced goods for domestic consumption made by Hay and Smith of the Nigerian Institute of Social and Economic Research indicate a value of about £60 million in 1964—approximately five percent of GDP and less than one-third the value of merchandise imports in 1963.[8]

The events of 1966 disrupting interregional trade, have caused some shortages of foodstuffs—particularly in Lagos. Commenting on these events, Mr. A. A. Ayida, the Permanent Secretary of the National Ministry of Economic Development, has said:

> Nigerians must also recognize the economic interdependence of various regions. . . .It is unrealistic to imagine that any one Region can maintain its existing or potential level of economic prosperity in isolation. . . .
>
> The pattern of food production and distribution in Nigeria shows that though Nigeria as a whole could be, relatively speaking, self-sufficient in food production, each of the Regions cannot easily be self-sufficient in local food production and at the same time, maintain its agricultural export production at a reasonable level.[9]

Nevertheless, the quantitative importance of interregional trade remains surprisingly small, and we can conclude only that the regions for the most part are exporters of agricultural products and raw materials and importers of finished goods (both consumer and producer goods) from outside Nigeria. The major portion of output is consumed within the region of origin.

These observations are buttressed by our own study of industrial entrepreneurship in Nigeria. Table 1 indicates that the vast majority of the 264 indigenous industrialists in our study were operating businesses in their region of birth.[10] In fact, a further breakdown of these data by province indicates that the majority are operating businesses in their province of birth; almost all of the others are operating in a province adjacent to the one of their birth.

TABLE 1

REGION IN WHICH BUSINESS IS LOCATED

Region of Birth	Greater Lagos	Western	Mid-West	Eastern	Northern	Total
Greater Lagos	34	0	0	0	0	34
Western	92	35	0	1	2	130
Mid-West	12	0	16	0	0	28
Eastern	22	0	0	38	2	62
Northern	3	0	0	0	7	10
Total	163	35	16	39	11	264

Although the evident lack of geographic mobility on the part of indigenous industrialists is not conclusive in itself since industrial investment, being of a fixed nature, may require the kind of security afforded by location in one's home area, Table 2 indicates that these firms are producing primarily for geographically limited markets.

TABLE 2

MARKETING AREAS OF NIGERIAN INDUSTRIAL FIRMS

Marketing Area	No. of Responses	% of Responses
Local vicinity	132	49.3
Regional	72	26.9
Multi-regional	40	14.9
Overseas	24	9.0
Total	268	100.00

It must be borne in mind that this sample represents only indigenous firms employing more than 10. Kilby's study of industry in Eastern Nigeria indicates over 10,000 establishments in that region along in 1962, almost all of which are engaged in production for local markets only.[11] Important industries include baking, sawmilling, furniture making, rubber processing, printing, garment making, and shoemaking. None of these industries exhibit significant economies of scale. Hence, the natural protection of transportation costs favors the replication of relatively small units serving compact market areas.[12]

Expatriate-controlled industries are for the most part of larger scale than those controlled by indigenous entrepreneurs. Nevertheless, brewing, tobacco manufacture, textile manufacture, cement production, metal fabrication, stationery manufacture, motor vehicle assembly and glass manufacture, each of which involve some scale economies, are undertaken in more than one region by expatriate firms. This is due in part to the promotional efforts of the respective regional governments prior to 1966 which included special concessions and financing arrangements. Much of the duplication of plants was undoubtedly uneconomic from a national standpoint, although some of it can be justified by the protection afforded by transportation charges. Other industries involving economies of scale such as tin smelting, plywood manufacture and vegetable oil extraction are undertaken near sources of raw materials in large plants. National integration plays no important role in the determination of plant size in these industries since they are engaged exclusively in export from Nigeria. The only industries now contemplated for which a national market is required to justify production on an economic scale are petroleum refining, petro-chemicals, and steel making; only a few others depend on other-regional sources of raw materials (e.g., textiles in the south).

Interregional integration is more important in activities other than manufacturing in Nigeria. Transportation and trade necessarily involve a sizeable number of entrepreneurs in interregional trade. It has been estimated that the departure of Ibos from the Northern Region following the riots of October 1966 resulted in a transfer of almost half of the trucking capacity from the North to the East. Sharp rises in the rates for foodstuff transport in the North were subsequently reported.[13]

Although transport of foodstuffs between the North and West was entirely in Northern and Western hands in 1964, the departure of Ibos from the North caused disruption in the flow of yams from the North to Lagos. While the general shortage of transport and the ensuing high rates may explain part of the disruption, the more important explanation appears to be that collection of food stuffs from the village level and assembling them in quantity for shipment to Lagos was largely in the hands of Ibos.[14] The departure of Ibo traders from Lagos also gave evidence that a large proportion of wholesale and retail trade there had been in Ibo hands.

It has been reliably reported that the exodus of Easterners from the North also caused grave disruption of public services in that region. The postal and tele-communications systems almost came to a halt. The same was true for the railroad. Commerical firms and banks were hard hit by the loss of their key personnel. This provides some evidence for the importance of interregional migration of skilled manpower. Crash programs were quickly instituted for the training of Northerners to fill the vacancies, and while reliable information remains scanty, it appears that the Northern economy is beginning to mend.[15]

The burden of this argument has been to indicate that the Nigerian economy had been, at best, minimally integrated. Although we cannot give any precise estimate, it appears that the short-run costs of disintegration would be small. The longer-run costs would undoubtedly be greater. We would expect the benefits to be heavily discounted because of uncertainty by entrepreneurial units which, for the most part, would realize the benefits only indirectly. [16]

III. The Strength of Entrepreneurial Motivation in Nigeria

Entrepreneurial responses in "modern activities" have been most important in manufacturing, mining, transportation, construction and trading sectors of the Nigerian economy. Table 3 indicates the relative importance of these sectors in 1962.[17]

TABLE 3

RELATIVE IMPORTANCE OF SELECTED ECONOMIC SECTORS
NIGERIA 1962

Sector	% G.D.P
Manufacturing & public utilities	4
Mining (including oil exploration)	2
Transportation	4
Construction	3
Distribution	12

The *1963 Industrial Survey* estimates the amount of paid-up capital in manufacturing contributed by Nigerian private interests, expatriates, regional and Federal Governments. These figures (in percentages) are presented in Table 4.[18]

TABLE 4

SOURCES OF PAID-UP CAPITAL IN MANUFACTURING (PERCENTAGES)
NIGERIA 1963

	Region					
Source	Lagos	West	Mid-West	East	North	Total
Nigerian private	8	15	15	8	7	10
Expatriate	84	67	73	52	67	68
Regional governments	1	18	12	36	26	19
Federal government	7	—	—	4	—	3
Total	100	100	100	100	100	100
% of Total Paid-Up Capital in Mfg.	29	27	4	22	18	100

These data point out the relative smallness of the manufacturing sector and the dominant position of expatriates within it. Paid-up capital data are available only from incorporated enterprises; since a smaller proportion of indigenous firms are incorporated, and the vast majority of such firms employ less than 10 workers (hence, were excluded from this survey), there is probably a systematic bias towards understating the proportion of industrial assets owned by private Nigerians. However, it is extremely unlikely that this proportion exceeds fifteen per cent.

The important role played by the Eastern and Northern regional governments (and the insignificant one of the federal government) in industrial development is apparent from Table 4. Although the Lagos complex accounts for some forty per cent of total industrial assets (almost one-half of the assets recorded for the West were located in Mushin and Ikeja which are part of greater Lagos) there is reason to believe that the East gained relatively between 1963 and 1965 from expansion in the Port Harcourt area.

No comparable data are available for the mining, transportation, construction and distribution sectors. However, it is clear that mining (including oil production) is more than ninety per cent controlled by expatriates. Construction has a pattern of ownership quite similar to manufacturing, while transportation is probably controlled to a larger extent by private Nigerians. It is not at all clear what the proportions in distribution may be, although on the basis of casual empiricism, private Nigerians play at least as important a role in trade as in transport.[19] Expatriates are involved in distribution activities such as department stores, motor agencies, and warehousing operations which would make a comparison of assets meaningless if data were available.

Private Nigerians have been quite responsive to industrial opportunities within their technological and managerial capacity to exploit. They control significant portions of the following industries: sawmilling, furniture, rubber processing, tyre retreading, printing, garment making, baking and shoe manufacture. Each of these industries are marked by relatively simple technology, and can be entered with relatively little capital since economies of scale are not of overriding importance. We found little evidence that capital shortage has been a serious deterrent to development of these industries. Many firms started on a small scale; the more profitable firms have been able to expand rapidly through reinvested earnings. However, current standards of financial management and production control in these firms are woefully low. Most of them are potentially vulnerable to entry by efficiently managed competitors.

Within these industries, capacity has been expanded much faster than demand (at current prices) during the past five years. As soon as new processes or products have been seen to be profitable under Nigerian conditions, they have been imitated with great rapidity. Tyre retreading, sawmilling and printing industries are good cases in point. This rapid emulation has resulted in the majority of firms in these industries working at very low levels of capacity utilization. Prices of output have remained quite "sticky." Profits have been reduced by lowering rates of utilization. Our data indicate median rates of return on industrial investment by Nigerians in the range of eight-twelve per cent. Why, under conditions of free entry approximating perfect competition profits are driven down by overcapacity rather than by lowered prices of output with full utilization of a smaller productive capacity requires further investigation.[20]

The important point to be made is that Nigerians are extremely responsive to economic opportunities which lie within their capacity to exploit. This has been nicely stated by Kilby:[21]

> We have identified the dominant favorable characteristics exhibited by the majority of Nigerian bakers as a keen perception of and response to economic opportunity, willingness to adapt to changing market conditions, and marked competitive abilities. To their debit, most of these Nigerian entrepreneurs showed less skill in carrying out the organization functions of a business enterprise, a lack of persistence in everyday supervision, and little effective interest in improving the quality of their product . . . Indeed, it is the veritable surfeit of such perception of economic opportunity which threatens the established entrepreneur—in the employment of his skilled journeymen he is but training his soon-to-be competitors. Where he is not protected by a high investment threshold for entry into the industry, the entrepreneur's prime defense must lie in the extent of his own technical mastery and the quality of his product.

Industry represents a relatively new outlet for Nigerian entrepreneurial activity. Trade, transport and construction have been widely engaged in for longer. Many Nigerians in these fields have been notably successful.[22] The large expatriate companies have largely withdrawn from transport and much of wholesale and retail trade because of increased competition from Nigerians.[23] Many Nigerians have also found outlets for their entrepreneurial drive in such diverse activities as insurance, hospitals, real estate development, labor contracting, chartered accountancy and school ownership. Although it represents in many ways a "backward sector," there also has been marked response to changing opportunities in agriculture. The spread of cocoa production, poultry farming and the adoption of new cotton varieties each represent important changes.[24] Large scale piggeries and irrigated fruit farming have recently been taken up by a few Nigerians—modern agriculture is just starting to appeal to educated Nigerians.[25]

Marked differences in entrepreneurial responsiveness between different ethnic groups of Nigeria are popularly believed to exist. Ibos are generally considered to be more aggressive in business dealings than other groups, although Yoruba and Hausa traders have long been important throughout West Africa. LeVine's recent study of achievement motivation among secondary school students in Nigeria indicates that Ibos score higher on n-Achievement tests than do Yorubas (although not statistically significant, the differences were consistently in that direction), while both Yorubas and Ibos have significantly higher n-Achievement scores than Hausas.[26] On the basis of both achievement testing and analysis of traditional social structures, we were led to predict the following ordering of entrepreneurial responsiveness by ethnic grouping: Ibo, Ibibio, Yoruba, Edo and Hausa.

In our study of 269 industrial entrepreneurs, we correlated ethnic grouping with size of business, growth and profitability of the firm, innovation and changes made since establishment. Although our data do not seriously contradict the predicted ordering, the correlations are weak and lend little support to it. In any event, an alternative hypothesis that ethnic differences in entrepreneurial performance are attributable to the differences in economic structure of the regions, exposure to Western education and "modern" occupational experience cannot be rejected.[27]

Although our evidence seems to indicate that the motivation or desire to respond to economic opportunities is widespread in Nigeria, the lack of technical and managerial skills presents a great impediment to expansion of the entrepreneurial group.[28] The popular belief that there are marked regional disparities (particularly between North and South) in entrepreneurial resources is justified. However, we remain agnostic with respect to the causation of these differences. The available data do not permit us to state unambiguously whether motivational factors or "objective" factors (such as economic structures, education, experience, alternative opportunities and presence of expatriates) are more important.

IV. Attitudes of Eastern Entrepreneurs.

Attitudes of Nigerian entrepreneurs toward integration vary greatly depending especially on origin and size of their operation. For most Ibo entrepreneurs, the initial reaction to pre-July (1966) "unity" was very favorable. It is impossible to separate later Eastern responses to disintegration from Eastern responses to violence, but Eastern newspapers made clear that Ibo entrepreneurs outside of their home region were deeply shocked and unhappy over the loss of their businesses and property. Easterners were least disrupted in Lagos, but in December 1966 it was popularly estimated that at least fifty per cent of the Easterners had gone home, some going only with their inventories (and families), some leaving permanently.

Ibos were well known for their mobility and responsiveness to business opportunities. In Lagos, Ibo industrialists were, according to our study, likelier than others to be running modern industries; their plans for future enterprises were in general more grandiose. As the largest group of non-Northern Nigerian entrepreneurs in the North, and the only large group of non-Yoruba, Lagos-based indigenous industrialists, they plainly had more to lose than others from disintegration. There were only a few major Eastern-based Ibos, such as textile producers and those who were paying heavy federal import duties, who might have expected an increase in profits from Eastern secession. Those leaving Lagos were bitterly unhappy at leaving, although all felt warmly patriotic toward their homes.[29]

Many who stayed (cloth traders in Lagos who returned, having safeguarded their inventories and families at home; a large industrialist; some Ministry of Industry officials) felt the keenest pain at Nigeria's threatened breakup. They felt careers and fortunes threatened and enjoyed none of the sympathy of neighbors available to those who returned East. Indeed the reverse was true. Such was the extreme pressure from the East on all Ibos to return home, that a businessman resisting this pressure and remaining elsewhere was made to feel disloyal, extremely ill-advised and irresponsible—in short, deeply guilty for "forsaking" his home.[30]

As long as the opportunity remained for moving freely throughout the Federation to conduct business, a large number of Ibo entrepreneurs actively favored integration. However, after the October massacres, these opportunities were seen to be largely denied, regardless of the institutional framework. The number who nevertheless remained in—or returned to—

homes outside the East prior to the declaration of secession attests to the strong economic pressures felt by Ibos toward maintenance of the nation.[31]

As for eastern government decision makers, publicly expressed feelings were entirely bent toward regional independence: the pulling home of Ibo economists to work on the Eastern Plan, rejection of Kainji-grid power, "Buy Eastern" programs and subsidies, illustrate this position. Possibly these men were persuaded than an autonomous East could keep oil flowing and oil revenues for the East alone which would, if true, provide a powerful incentive. They undoubtedly had an important influence on the East's decision to declare itself independent at the end of May, 1967.

The few Eastern government decision makers left in Lagos continued to work hard and influentially for Federation. Their motivations, at least partly economic, were based on a different view of the facts.

V. Attitudes of Western Entrepreneurs

Yoruba businessmen in the West were engaged in serving small markets with goods and services obtainable locally. Many found their competition reduced when Ibos departed. However, nearly all business declined sharply during the initial period of violence and unrest. Disintegration has, therefore, been felt by Yoruba entrepreneurs to have reduced profits; this has been true even for Yoruba cloth traders who sell primarily to Yorubas. The overall decline in business has harmed almost everyone. What all desire is peace.

Some Yoruba professionals in Lagos (e.g., lawyers) had their practices grow sharply as competition declined; banks, accountants and insurance men, on the other hand, lost more business through the general dislocation. A few businessmen worked hard for integration—a prominent Chartered Accountant, for instance, tried hard to bring the East to the conference table.[32] Depression of the housing market and difficulties in raising capital have harmed Yoruba contractors. Exact statistics on disruption of the food trade are not available; nevertheless, it has been clear that food-producing Westerners have felt keenly the loss of internal agricultural markets.[33]

VI. Attitudes of Northern Entrepreneurs

In the North, relief at the Ibos' departure, chauvinism, bitterness toward their more economically agressive neighbors, and public disregard of business losses were the norm expressed in one author's hearing in December 1966. There may have been Northern Nigerian businessmen who deplored the loss of skilled labor, transport facilities and Ibo consumers, but the only deep regret one author heard was "that the events of the summer of 1966 had caused the Southerners unfairly to raise the price of petrol." Probably most Northern businessmen felt on balance that the North should be "economically independent," and that the departure of Ibos was a great opportunity. Furthermore, there were now a few powerful Northerners with sufficient expertise to take over business opportunities from the departed Ibos—this included transporters, wholesale traders and 50-100 small industrialists: grain millers, garage people and the like.[34]

VII. Expatriate Entrepreneurs

Foreigners in Southern Nigeria tend to be relatively big businessmen for whom greater markets, internal stability, resource mobility and protection of Federal Government contracts are very important. Many of course are not directly involved with Nigerian markets (e.g., U. S. Plywood in the East), though even for these companies, stability is of course vital.[35] In the North, medium and small-sized expatriates publicly support the regionalism philosophy: some also stand to gain from reduced competition or enhanced prestige with Ibos gone.[36] In private, however, expatriates, especially the Lebanese, deplore the loss of skilled labor and management; commercial people feel keenly the loss of wholesale markets; many, seeing the handwriting on the wall, realize the Northerners may push out all non-Northerners as soon as they feel able. The manager of one very large British firm was very concerned about loss of his Ibo (wholesale trader) market.

Certain expatriate entrepreneurs exercised great influence in Nigeria during 1966. Some British interests in the North are said in diplomatic circles to have applied considerable pressure on Governor Katsina for peace. The oil companies, while maintaining public "neutrality" and whatever their private views, steadfastly refused in 1966 to deal openly with the East on renegotiation of production rights, thus stymying one powerful Eastern reason to secede, and raising the apparent costs of secession.

Constant allegations of disintegrative interference by resident foreigners in the stability of the Federation have yet to be publicly proven; it seems clear that at least on balance, expatriate entrepreneurs did much to hold the Federation together in 1966.

VIII. The Articulation of Entrepreneurial Interests

Private Nigerian entrepreneurs as a group or "class" have not been particularly successful in articulating their interests so as to influence policy. This is not to deny close ties between business and politics; nevertheless, where businessmen have had important influence over policy, this has stemmed more from political or social position than from business affiliations *per se.* There is little evidence that entrepreneurs have formed a coherent interest group. Interest grouping appears to coalesce on communal or ethnic bases, rather than along lines of economic class.

Sklar has argued the contrary case. His analysis of occupational backgrounds of major political party leaders indicates that 26.8% of the NCNC, 21.2% of the Action Group, and 25.7% of the NPC leaders were previously (or presently) businessmen.[37] In a later article, he interprets conflict between regional and national interests in terms of class interests.

> Who are the masters of the regional governments? High ranking politicians, senior administrators, major chiefs, lords of the economy, distinguished members of the learned professions—in short, members of the emergent and dominant class. This class is an actual social aggregate, engaged in class action and characterized by the growing sense of class consciousness . . . Political power is the primary force that creates economic opportunity and determines the pattern of social stratification . . . While regionalism is a characteristic attitude of the political

class, anti-regionalism is the logical posture of the ideological opponents of that class.[38]

The 1962 crisis in the Western Region is interpreted by Sklar as arising from a fundamental conflict between the regional orientation of this dominant class and Awolowo's concept of a national party. "The Action Group had come to an ideological breaking point, with the class content of power in question."[39]

We question this interpretation of the crisis. Among the Yoruba, the Ijebus are noted for entrepreneurial drive. They frequently liken themselves to the Ibo, and have been resented by other Yorubas in much the same way that Ibos have been resented in the North. Conflict between Ijebus and other Yorubas has been particularly important in Ibadan where Ijebus control much of trade, industry, and valuable urban property. Within our study of industrialists, Ijebus accounted for almost 40% of the Yorubas, and controlled larger than average firms. If Sklar's hypothesis were correct, we would expect Ijebu industrialists (and other businessmen) to have strongly supported the NNDP in the 1965 election. Yet, according to our interviews, Ijebus were almost unanimously in support of the Action Group. Ijebu province was the center of opposition to the NNDP; violence broke out earlier and persisted longer in that province than in any other following the events of October 1966. It appears that ethnic loyalty to Awolowo (an Ijebu) overrode loyalty based on class interest. The point to be drawn is that political activity of entrepreneurs has not been based primarily on considerations of entrepreneurial interest. This, of course, does not mean that entrepreneurs have not sought to advance their own economic position through political activity —merely that they have not acted as a separate interest group.

Of the 269 industrialists in our study, less than twenty-five per cent were actively engaged in politics. The majority contributed to political parties (usually to both, if there were competing parties) and attended public meetings of governing parties. This activity was, for the most part, defensive. Even when contributors could not demand special favors from political parties, they tried to avoid being victimized. Following the 1962 crisis in the Western Region, entrepreneurs who had actively been connected with the Awolowo wing of the Action

Group suffered greatly. Contracts with government, licenses, loans and other aids evaporated. In some instances, machines were destroyed and factories burned by gangs of hired thugs. This lesson was widely heeded by other businessmen.

Henry Bretton has made the following observations.[40]

> Previous research . . . had led to the conclusion that control over the means of production and allocation of wealth was crucial in the political influence structure. Accordingly it was assumed that certain leaders of business, finance, and industry, both indigenous and expatriate, occupied key positions in the influence structure. It was noted, however, that indigenous leaders frequently had gained access to wealth through acquisition of political power, largely derived from association with nationalist movements and drives. Present research indicates that both expatriate and nonparty indigenous business interests have experienced a marked decline in power and influence since independence, and that indigenous political leaders, basing their power primarily on party association, are now dominating business, finance, and industry as well. . . .
>
> The principal channels of communication of relevance to the exercise of influence over the outcome of critical socio-economic issues appear to be firmly in the control of political party leaders whose major concerns are management of political power, retention of office and continuous acquisition of additional means of power and influence.

Chambers of Commerce have been formed in most of the major commercial centers, and the Nigerian Employers' Consultative Association was formed to negotiate with organized labor. However, none of these organizations has exerted an important influence on policy formation. Most have suffered from expatriate-indigenous cleavages.

Expatriate entrepreneurs have probably made their voices heard with more success. Policy makers have been sensitive to the impact of their decisions on expatriate entrepreneurs. Furthermore, many expatriate businessmen are in a position to make their opinions known to the diplomatic delegations of their countries, providing an additional channel of communication.

IX. An Assessment

One is drawn to conclude that, on balance, entrepreneurial attitudes have been distintegrative but not of overriding importance. It is quite clear that the market, income and resource advantages of a unified Nigeria are relatively unimportant in the short run for most indigenous entrepreneurs. Exploitation of opportunities for which integration is necessary requires organization and capital on a scale which is beyond the capability of most (if not all) indigenous entrepreneurs. Indeed, exploitation of such opportunities would likely by undertaken by expatriate or governmental units to the detriment of existing indigenous private units oriented to limited markets.

Integrative forces should have been strongest among Eastern entrepreneurs. They had migrated from their homeland to take advantage of opportunities elsewhere, and had engaged in interregional trade and transport to a greater degree than had entrepreneurs from other regions. It is interesting to note that the Eastern Government, in a pre-secession *New York Times* advertisement, stressed the mobility of Easterners and the importance of every Nigerian being free to take advantage of opportunities anywhere in the nation.[41]

Since disintegration would mean protection from outside competitors, it was to be expected that Northern entrepreneurs, desiring elimination of their Ibo competitors, would favor disintegration.

The balance of forces in the West was less obvious. However, since most Western businesses were small scale, oriented to regional (or sub-regional) markets and since there was some fear of Ibo competition, entrepreneurial attitudes were probably somewhat disintegrative.

The attitudes of expatriate entrepreneurs have probably been more integrative. If anything, they might have preferred a unitary state to continued federalism since they would then have had to deal only with one level of government instead of two. Expatriates have been in a better position to benefit from larger markets and more mobile resources; they possess the requisite technical and managerial skills to exploit scale economies. We have pointed out, however, that these considerations apply mainly to expatriate corporations; there was a sizeable number of private expatriate businessmen who were oriented toward regional markets and who relied heavily on favors from regional governments.

Economic decision makers in government at the federal level have played an important integrative role; those at the regional level have probably favored greater regional autonomy or independence.

Finally, the weak articulation of entrepreneurial interests indicates that their importance has been quite limited.

X. Conclusions and Implications for Policy

1. Indigenous entrepreneurs were probably in sum a disintegrative force in Nigeria during 1966.

2. Large expatriate corporations probably provided an integrative force in Nigeria; private expatriate businessmen were probably disintegrative.

3. The Nigerian economy in 1965 was not highly integrated. It is not clear that the short-run economic cost of regional independence would be great.

4. Because private entrepreneurial interests were poorly articulated, they probably had little influence on the course of events.

5. It would be a great mistake to try to interpret the apparent disintegration of Nigeria primarily in economic terms. Although there were economic aspects (primarily governmental) of this process, it appears that political and ethnic factors were far more important.

If the Eastern secession is successful, the question of entrepreneurial influence will again arise. Will a change of government be accompanied by further disorder? The only common desire of most private entrepreneurs is for stability and for peace, whether in one nation or several. If federation can be maintained, or if some common market arrangement can be negotiated, economic benefits of unity may become clearer. Although economic theory predicts (and most economists believe) that unity would, *ceteris paribus,* make the entire country better off, it is far from certain that all constituent parts of the country would be better off.

A slow rebuilding of the nation built on the net integrative desires (some of them economically motivated) of hundreds of influential Nigerians could take place. If entrepreneurs came to feel more secure throughout Nigeria, presumably the economic benefits of unity would become clearer. Nevertheless, it is likely that protectionistic sentiments of entrepreneurs will dominate their thinking. There is little evidence that entrepreneurs have been an important driving force behind other common market agreements. If unity is to be preserved, the impetus is unlikely to come from entrepreneurial groups.

NOTES

1. This is a revised version of a paper presented to the conference on "Problems of Integration and Disintegration in Nigeria," at Northwestern University, March 31, 1967. It is part of a broader study of Nigerian industrial entrepreneurs. One part of this study has been published as "Entrepreneurial Patterns in the Nigerian Sawmilling Industry," *Nigerian Journal of Economic and Social-Studies,* Vol. 8, No. 1 (March 1966). pp. 67–98. Another part is J. R. Harris, "Nigerian Entrepreneurship in Industry," in Carl Eicher and Carl Liedholm (eds.), *Growth and Development of the Nigerian Economy* (East Lansing: Michigan State University Press, 1969), pp. 299–324.

We are grateful for financial support from the SSRC/ACLS Foreign Area Fellowship Program, the Nigerian Institute of Social and Economic Research, Northwestern University Council for Intersocietal Research, and the M.I.T. Department of Economics which made this research possible.

Professor H. F. Williamson and Mr. Geoffrey Gowen gave particular help. Our other debts are too numerous to list. Although they cannot be named, we would like to thank the numerous Nigerians—both governmental and private—who gave their time so graciously during very difficult times. Obviously, we alone are responsible for remaining errors and infelicities.

2. Notable contributions to this literature have been made by Karl Deutsch, Philip E. Jacob, and Henry Teune. See Philip E. Jacob and James V. Toscano (eds.), *The Integration of Political Communities* (Philadelphia: J. B. Lippincott Co., 1964).

3. For example, see W. W. Rostow, *The Stages of Economic Growth* (Cambridge: Cambridge University Press, 1962), pp. 26–30; or W. A. Lewis, *Theory of Economic Growth* (London: George Allen & Unwin, 1955), Ch. III. Dankwart Rustow, "The Vanishing Dream of Stability," *AID Digest* (U.S. Department of State), August, 1962, pp. 13–16, points out that the direction of causation between political stability and economic development is far from clear. In fact, doubt is cast on the proposition that economic development will lead to political stability.

4. James S. Coleman, "The Politics of Sub-Saharan Africa," in Gabriel Almond and J. S. Coleman (eds.) *The Politics of the Developing Areas* (Princeton: Princeton University Press, 1960), p. 367. Coleman also refers to his "Current Political Movements in Africa," *The Annals,* No. 298 (March, 1955), p. 106 which contains a further discussion of this point.

5. J. S. Coleman in Almond and Coleman, *op. cit.,* p. 537, states: "The processes of commercialization and industrialization of the economies of these [developing] societies have not everywhere contributed to social or political integration, or to the emergence of a politically relevant entrepreneurial or middle class. One reason is that in the initial stages at least, commercial activity has been in the hands of alien groups."

6. The 1963 Census reported a population of 55.7 million; this has been the subject of internal political strife. I.I.U. Eke, in his article "Population of Nigeria: 1952–1965," *Nigerian Journal of Economic and Social Studies,* July 1966, pp. 289–310, estimates that the actual population in July 1963 was somewhere between 40.46 and 46.82 million. We believe his estimates to be as good (or probably much better) than any others.

7. *Annual Abstract of Statistics: Nigeria 1964* (Lagos: Federal Office of Statistics, 1965) p. 144.

8. A.M. Hay and R.H.T. Smith, "Preliminary Estimates of Nigeria's Interregional Trade and Associated Money Flows," *NJESS,* March 1966, pp. 9–36. Merchandise imports are estimated to be £207.5 million in 1963, *Annual Abstract of Statistics: Nigeria 1964, op. cit.,* p. 67. Note that Professor Smith, in a paper presented at the Northwestern conference, has revised his estimate of interregional trade upwards to £64 million. Our conclusions remain unaffected.

9. "Prospects for the Nigerian Economy," *Nigerian Opinion,* (Vol. 2, No. 11) (November 1966), p. 126.

10. Our sample contained 269 indigenous industrialists with more than 10 employees. Of these, 143 have more than 20 employees; we estimate that we have included more than 85% of such firms. In Table 1, we were unable to identify regions of birth of 5 respondents.

11. Peter Kilby, *The Development of Small Industry in Eastern Nigeria* (Washington: U. S. Agency for Industrial Development, March 1962).

12. Carl E. Liedholm, "Production Functions for Eastern Nigerian Industry," *Nigerian Journal of Economic and Social Studies* (November 1966), presents some evidence for scale economies in several lines of Nigerian industry. Given the limited range of firm size and the quality of the data (particularly for capital inputs), great reliance on this evidence is unwarranted. Our data, based on profitability, fails to confirm important scale economies in these industries, which conforms to the observed pattern of continued replication of small units. We believe that this finding reflects managerial limitations of Nigerian entrepreneurs. The inclusion of large expatriate firms in Liedholm's data probably accounts for his findings of scale economies. Even so, there is little evidence that economies of scale are of sufficient importance in these industries that there would not continue to be replication of firms under any political management.

13. "The Crisis and Interregional Trade," *Nigerian Opinion, op. cit.,* p. 125. (Signed by "R.G.").

14. "The Crisis and Interregional Trade," *op. cit.* Smith's paper presented at the Northwestern conference documents the fact that most interregional trade was in the hands of "strangers"—predominantly Ibos.

15. Part of the gap has been filled by hiring expatriates. For instance, it is reported that Englishmen have been hired to run the railroad in the North.

16. Harvey Leibenstein, "Allocative Efficiency V. 'X-Efficiency,'" *American Economic Review,* June 1966, summarizes some recent studies of potential gains from proposed tariff reductions in common market agreements. His Table 1, p. 393, is reproduced below in part:

CALCULATED "WELFARE LOSS" AS PERCENTAGE OF GROSS OR NET
NATIONAL PRODUCT ATTRIBUTED TO MISALLOCATION OF RESOURCES

Study	Source	Country	Cause	Loss
T. Scitovsky	(1)	Common Market 1952	Tariffs	.05%
J. Wemelsfelder	E. J. 1960	Germany 1958	Tariffs	.18%
L. H. Janssen	(2)	Italy 1960	Tariffs	max .1%
H. G. Johnson	Manchester School 1958	U.K. 1970	Tariffs	max 1.0%
A. Singh	(3)	Montevideo Treaty Countries	Tariffs	max .0075%

(1) *Economic Theory and Western European Integration*, Stanford, 1958.
(2) *Free Trade, Protection and Customs Union*, Leiden, 1961, p. 132.
(3) Unpublished calculation made by A. Singh based on data found in
A. A. Faraq, *Economic Integration: A Theoretical Empirical Study*, University of Michigan, Ph. D. Thesis, 1963.

The point to be made is that gains from tariff reduction (or losses from tariff imposition) based on resource allocation are of insignificant orders of magnitude. This reasoning would imply that the economic costs of Nigeria's breakup into independent regions enjoying normal trade relationships within a structure of tariff barriers would be quite small. Given the relatively small volume of present interregional trade, this conclusion is reinforced.

Of course, this is an excessively narrow approach based primarily on static analysis. The real losses that would ensue when dynamic elements are taken into consideration may be substantially greater. Even though the East, West, and North would each constitute a large and viable economic unit by African standards, they still would represent small markets when aggregate purchasing power is considered. Furthermore, it is far from clear that units based on present regional boundaries represent a realistic alternative to continued federation— significant pressures for further disintegration to provincial level units might well ensue.

G. K. Helleiner, *Peasant Agriculture, Government, and Economic Growth in Nigeria* (Homewood, Illinois: Richard D. Irwin Inc., 1966) pp. 294–99 contains an excellent discussion of economic advantages of the Federation. He points out that "common markets in underdeveloped areas are generally more important for the potential which they represent, in terms of larger markets for those new industries benefiting from scale economies, than for any current measurable benefits," (p. 295). Advantages relating to centralized management of foreign exchange reserves, centralization of public sector activity, and coordination of economic planning are also discussed. The conclusion still stands that the short-run costs of disintegration would be small.

17. Calculated from *Annual Abstract of Statistics,* 1964, *Op. Cit.,* p. 144. The figure for trade is estimated as a residual sector and is probably overstated.

18. Calculated from *Industrial Survey, Op. Cit.,* Tables 8, 23, 38, 53, 68, and 83. The reliability of these data leave much to be desired. However, they serve to indicate orders of magnitude.

19. E. K. Hawkins, *Road Transport in Nigeria: A Study of African Enterprise,* (New York: Oxford University Press, 1958) is an excellent study of indigenous participation in the transport sector. Unfortunately, little is known about the trading sector, although O. Olakanpo is currently undertaking research in this important area in association with the Nigerian Institute of Social and Economic Research.

20. These issues are dealt with at length in J. R. Harris, *Op. Cit.* Corroborating evidence can be found in Peter Kilby, *African Enterprise: The Nigerian Bread Industry* (Stanford University: The Hoover Institution, 1965) and Sayre P. Schatz, *Development Bank Lending in Nigeria: The Federal Loans Board* (Ibadan: Oxford University Press, 1964).

21. Kilby, *Op. Cit.,* pp. 111–112.

22. Margaret Katzin, "The Role of the Small Entrepreneur," in M. J. Herskovits and M. Harwitz (eds.) *Economic Transition in Africa* (Evanston: Northwestern University Press, 1964) presents an interesting study of traders in Onitsha. E. K. Hawkins, *Op. Cit.,* documents the rapid response of Nigerians to opportunities in Road Transport. K. O. Dike, *Trade and Politics in the Niger Delta 1830–1885* (Oxford: Clarendon Press, 1956) contains a fascinating account of the rapid and flexible responses of Nigerians to changes in the slave and palm-oil trades. A classic in the field is P. T. Bauer, *West African Trade* (New York: Cambridge University Press, 1954) which describes the West African trader in the following terms: "Exceptional effort, foresight, resourcefulness, thrift and ability to perceive economic opportunity."

23. See United Africa Company, *Statistical and Economic Review,* No. 28, April 1963, on "Redeployment."

24. See R. Galetti, K. D. S. Baldwin, and I. O. Dina, *Nigerian Cocoa Farmers: An Economic Survey of Yoruba Cocoa-Farming Families* (London: Oxford University Press, 1956) shows the responsiveness of Nigerian farmers to changed opportunities. Polly Hill, *Migrant Cocoa Farmers of Southern Ghana* (Cambridge: Cambridge University Press, 1963) and R. H. Green and S. Hymer, "Cocoa in the Gold Coast: A Study in the Relation Between African Farmers and Agricultural

Experts." *Journal of Economic History* (September 1966), show conclusively that Ghanaians have responded with great vigour to new opportunities in cocoa farming. We have good reason to believe that responses in Nigeria have been quite similar. G. K. Helleiner, *Op. Cit.*, also contains evidence of responsiveness by farmers.

25. S. A. Aluko, "The Educated in Business: The Calabar Home Farm —A Case Study," *NJESS,* July, 1966, describes a Nigerian woman who, after receiving agricultural training in England, has attempted to undertake modern farming near Calabar. Several educated Nigerians have started poultry farming on a fairly large scale.

26. R. LeVine, *Dreams and Deeds* (Chicago: University of Chicago Press, 1966).

27. J. R. Harris, *Op. Cit.,* pp. 12–22 deals with this issue in detail.

28. See Footnote 34, *infra,* for evidence of latent Northern entrepreneurship.

29. One author witnessed the distress of many Ibos who were reluctantly leaving Lagos after July 1966.

30. A *West Africa* (No. 2584, 10 December 1966, p. 1411) correspondent writes of the "peculiarly monolithic" nature of Eastern opinion on the future of the country.

31. See the letter to the editors by Sam Aluko, "The Displaced Nigerians," *West Africa* (No. 2610, June 10, 1967).

32. *West Africa* (No. 2579, November 5, 1966), p. 1278.

33. See footnote 12, *Supra.*

34. This figure is drawn from the number of new applications for small industry loans made to the Northern Ministry of Trade and Industry during 1966. These Northerners will be taking over established markets, using already tested methods; their chances for success are greatly enhanced. It is clear that their present outlook is one of taking advantage of opportunities now existing. From the outsider's point of view, it also appears as if economic advantages may be sought by Northerners who fail to see concomitant disadvantages from Ibo departure.

35. Patterson-Zachonis announced substantial profits for the unsettled financial year 1965–1966 (*West Africa,* No. 2584, December 10, 1966, p. 1427), indicating that expatriate trade was still very profitable through May 1966.

36. Industrialists in a potentially overcrowded market, such as textiles, will probably benefit in the short and medium-run, from protection and the possibility of diversification. British businessmen, in particular, in conversation with one another, spoke casually: "The Ibos brought it on themselves." It is interesting to note that the International Finance Corporation (A World Bank affiliate) agreed in February 1967 to participate in financing a $5 million expansion of Arewa Textile Mills in the North (Washington D.C.: IFC Press Release, 67/1, February 24, 1967). By the end of 1965, economists in the Federal Ministry of Industry were concerned that textile capacity was being expanded more rapidly than market conditions would justify. Each of the regional Governments had participated in organizing new textile mills during that year and four additional mills were begun in 1966. The proposed expansion of Arewa would probably not be justified in a unified Nigeria—it may be profitable in a North which discriminates against goods from the South.

37. Richard L. Sklar, *Nigerian Political Parties* (Princeton: Princeton University Press, 1963), pp. 480–94 and R. L. Sklar and C. S. Whitaker, Jr., "Nigeria," in J. S. Coleman and C. G. Rosberg, Jr. (eds.) *Political Parties and National Integration in Tropical Africa* (Berkeley and Los Angeles: University of California Press, 1964), p. 614. The latter article also refers to J. S. Coleman, *Nigeria: Background to Nationalism* (Berkeley and Los Angeles: University of California Press, 1958), pp. 378–83, which analyzed educational backgrounds of political leaders.

38. R. L. Sklar, "Contradictions in the Nigerian Political System," *The Journal of Modern African Studies,* Vol. 3, No. 2, 1964, pp. 204–5.

39. *Ibid.,* p. 208. Although we are arguing here that entrepreneurial groups have not effectively articulated their interests as a class, nevertheless it is interesting to note that Sklar evidently believes their class interest to lie in the exercise of regional rather than national power. This confirms our previous finding that national unity is not of particular importance for most indigenous entrepreneurs.

40. Henry L. Bretton, "Political Influence in Southern Nigeria," in Hubert J. Spiro (ed.), *Africa: The Primacy of Politics* (New York: Random House, 1966), pp. 81–82. The earlier research referred to in the passage quoted appeared in Bretton's own *Power and Stability in Nigeria* (New York: Frederick A. Praeger, Inc., 1962).

41. *New York Times,* Friday, March 10, 1967, p. 12.

CHAPTER 7

Dreams and Deeds:
Achievement Motivation in Nigeria

ROBERT A. LEVINE

When the three large ethnic groups of Nigeria came under
British rule in the late nineteenth and early twentieth centuries, they differed drastically from one another in their systems
of social stratification. In this chapter we attempt brief reconstructions of these systems, with particular reference to status
mobility, on the basis of available ethnographic evidence. It
must be stated at the outset that the pre-colonial Hausa, Ibo,
and Yoruba had in common a number of relevant socioeconomic attributes which they shared with other West African
societies. First of all, the three societies exhibited a relatively
high degree of occupational differentiation on a base of subsistence agriculture. In each group, although men were tillers of
the soil, there were many craft specialists as well as professional traders: for example, workers of metal, wood and
leather, musicians, butchers, dyers and weavers, professional
hunters, although not all were found in all three groups. Most
of these occupational specialties were hereditary, being concentrated in particular lineages or compounds and passed on

This selection is excerpted from Robert A. LeVine, *Dreams and Deeds:
Achievement Motivation in Nigeria* (Chicago: Chicago University Press,
1966), "Status Mobility in Nineteenth-Century Nigeria," Chapter 3, pp. 23–41,
and "Conclusions," Chapter 8, pp. 78–94. Copyright © 1966 by University of
Chicago Press. Reprinted by permission of the publisher and Robert A. LeVine.

from father or uncle to son. Second, the Hausa, Ibo, and Yoruba all practiced slavery and engaged in active slave trading during the nineteenth century. Although slavery took different forms, slaves formed a significant segment of the population of each group. Third, in spite of slavery, none of these groups was a rigidly stratified society; in each there were some opportunities for freemen, and usually for slaves as well, to better themselves economically, socially, and politically. Status mobility was a characteristic of the Hausa, Ibo, and Yoruba societies in the nineteenth century, and some positions at or near the top of the locally recognized status hierarchy were often filled by men of obscure origins who had begun life with few resources besides their own skills and energies. Thus the variations in status systems among the three societies were not discrete differences in kind but major differences in degree and emphasis. The common characteristics formed a background against which we can contrast the divergence.

Several caveats and qualifications must be made concerning the reconstructions which follow. Wherever the term "traditional" is used, it is equivalent to "nineteenth-century" or "immediately pre-colonial." Both Hausa and Yoruba societies underwent great upheavals in the early nineteenth century, resulting in profound changes in status mobility patterns from the eighteenth-century base. It is clearly incorrect to assume that at the beginning of British administration any of the social structures was in its traditional form, if by "traditional" is implied an unaltered archaic residue of several centuries earlier. To dispel the possibility of confusion on this point, it must be understood that for the purpose of this study the late-nineteenth-century condition of these societies—on which we in any event have the most accurate ethnographic material and which is most likely to have an influence on contemporary behavior—is taken as the ethnographic present in preference to earlier periods.

Two other problems are posed for the comparison contained in this chapter. One is that the ethnographic materials on which it is based are uneven in their coverage of the points essential to the comparison. Numerous anthropologists have worked among and written about the Hausa, Ibo, and Yoruba; but few of them have been specifically interested in status mobility as such, and some have presented relevant data concerning topics on which others are silent. The comparison is necessarily blunted by this lack of comparable evidence. Furthermore, each of the ethnic groups is extraordinarily large for Africa and contains considerable internal variation in social stratification, not all of which is equally well described in the literature. Even where the internal variants are adequately documented, the predictive nature of this study has required that they be overlooked in favor of a generalized picture of each group's status system, and has meant making arbitrary decisions in order to capture the central tendencies of each system at the points of divergence from the other groups. The decisions were to concentrate on the characteristics of the central, dominant, or culturally purest subgroup for which most ethnographic evidence was available. The result is for each group a composite but selected description at a fairly abstract level of generalization, which does not hold true for a number of marginal or culturally mixed subgroups. Although subject to valid criticisms by experts on each of the three societies, the descriptions are able to serve adequately for the present comparative purposes because of the great magnitude of difference in central tendencies among the traditional status systems of the Hausa, Ibo, and Yoruba. It should be noted that errors of ethnographic characterization, whether they consist of overestimating the differences between groups or of other misinterpretation, increase the probability of failure in predicting the results of psychological testing. The greater the extent to which the following characterizations represent an excessive generalization of patterns drawn from a subgroup to the whole ethnic group, the less likely is a sample of individuals drawn from several varying subgroups to manifest the psychological dispositions hypothetically connected with the ethnographic description. The more the descriptions represent exaggerations of the actual differences between the three groups and underestimations of the internal diversity of each group (the "uniformitarian fallacy" of A. F. C. Wallace),[1] the less likely are the heterogeneous (with reference to subgroup) subjects to exhibit the ethnic group differences predicted on the basis of the ethnographic characterizations. Thus faultiness of ethnographic description in this chapter, although by no means desirable, leads to a more severe test of the hypothesis, rather than biases the results in favor of confirmation. In other words, if the differences among the three ethnic groups are so strong as to show themselves even when their prediction has been based on crude judgments that ignore sources of overlapping distributions between the groups, we can conclude that the differences are at least as potent as they seem to be.

The Hausa

The Hausa are a predominantly Islamic people, with a population of more than eight million in Nigeria alone, who inhabit north-western Nigeria and adjacent areas of the Niger Republic. Although Islam was introduced among them more than five hundred years ago, its effect on the population was greatly intensified after 1804. At that time Fulani religious leaders in the town of Sokoto began a holy war that resulted in the rapid conquest of most of the Hausa territory and its reorganization as a series of semi-independent kingdoms under the orthodox Islamic and political leadership of the sultan of Sokoto. The most important kingdoms were Kano, Katsina, Sokoto, Zaria and Daura, each of which had its own capital city which was also a market center. At the time of British intervention in 1900, these kingdoms were autocratic monarchies ruled by dynasties of Fulani origin who had intermarried with and adopted the language as well as many of the customs of the Hausa. The ethnic complexity of Hausa society was further increased in the nineteenth century by their massive capture and enslavement of the pagan peoples of Northern Nigeria. The Hausa language, Islamic religion, and slavery itself provided a framework for the rapid assimilation of large numbers of alien persons into the traditional Hausa culture as modified by the Fulani conquerors.

Nineteenth-century Hausa social structure is known exclusively from the publications of M. G. Smith,[2] who has written primarily on the Hausa of Zaria. Accordingly, our presentation is based on Zaria materials, but is followed by a discussion of the extent to which the characterization of that kingdom applies to the other Hausa states.

After the Fulani conquest in 1804, the Hausa political system (in Zaria) developed into what Smith calls a "short-term autocracy." Zaria was a vassal state in the Sokoto empire, and its king was appointed by the sultan of Sokoto from one of three dynastic lines among whom the kingship rotated. A new king had the power to discharge a large number of political officeholders and to appoint in their places his own followers, who were thus rewarded for their loyalty to him. Most offices carried with them fiefs—that is, territorial segments which the officeholder administered and in which he collected tax or tribute, keeping a part for himself and sending the rest to the king. The higher officials lived in the capital and had agents who managed their fiefs; there were local officials who replicated their rights and responsibilities at the village level. Although the king had advisers, there were no councils of any governmental importance; government was conducted through a vertical hierarchy of ranked officeholders. Commands flowed from the top down, and disobedience could be punished by removal from office (even the king could be, and was, deposed by the sultan of Sokoto); tax and tribute from fiefs and vassal chiefdoms flowed from the bottom up, with each officeholder deducting his part. In the frequent wars and slave raids, officeholders raised troops in their fiefs for the king and were handsomely rewarded with booty and captive slaves. So long as an officeholder retained the favor of the king through demonstrations of loyalty and obedience, he was allowed to overtax and keep the surplus himself as well as to exceed his formal authority in a number of other ways. Thus the system had a despotic character, turning on relations of dependence and power between subordinates and their superiors. The rotation of the kingship among the dynastic lines, however, made the domination by any single group of state officials finite; when the king died, many of the officials were deposed as the new king brought his own followers into office.

The social status system in nineteenth-century Zaria was complex, but its basic outlines and its relationship with the political system are clear. At the top were those of Fulani ancestry (at least in their father's line), who were favored for office, especially those who were members of the dynastic lines and the hereditary nobility. At the bottom were slaves (about half the population of Zaria) and those of slave ancestry, who retained positions of subordination to their free masters and were eligible only for offices reserved for slaves. In the middle were the Hausa freemen, who were for the most part ranked according to hereditary occupation (mallams and wealthy traders at the top; cloth workers, silversmiths, commission agents, and farmers in the middle; butchers, tanners, eulogists, hunters, blacksmiths at the bottom; merchants varying according to wealth and other criteria) and who were eligible to all offices except those reserved for members of the royal lineages and those that were hereditary. Despite the largely ascriptive nature of this system of social placement, a man's fate was not entirely determined at birth. The principal means of rising socially, for those of both Fulani and Hausa ancestry, was by becoming the client or follower of someone of higher status (sometimes a kinsman, sometimes not) who would reward his loyal client with appointment to office if he himself was successful in obtaining an official position. In the early days of Fulani rule, many Hausa attained high office, but as the Fulani patrilineages expanded through numerous marriages with Hausa women, high-status Fulani competitors for office became numerous and began forcing out the Hausa. Nevertheless, most Fulani were not officeholders and were the political inferiors of those Hausa who were. High office led to personal enrichment, but many factors prevented the development of hard and fast social classes: the dynastic succession, which dismissed many officeholders when a new king came to power; the proliferation of Fulani lineages, which in Islamic inheritance distributed wealth equally among large numbers of heirs; and the general dependence of a man's fortunes on the favor and fortunes of his patron, which fluctuated. Thus falling socially was as common as rising; with each official who fell, so fell his numerous clients and his clients' clients, and so on.

Having sketched the outlines of the system, we must emphasize three points: political office was the most important means of acquiring wealth and social position, overshadowing other alternatives; clientage was the primary means of acquiring political office; clientage was widely practiced in the population and was an attribute of social organization at all levels. These points are amplified as follows in Smith's account:

Office provided its holders with opportunities for the accumulation of wealth, booty and slaves, and slaves were the main sources of farm labor. . . . An owner having sufficient slaves usually established his own settlement. This was called a *rinji* (slave-village or hamlet, plural, *rumada* . . .). The number and size of the *rumada* which a person or family controlled was evidence of the owner's wealth and power. Merchants and many other non-officials had slaves, but permission was necessary in order to build separate settlements for *rumada,* and this was generally given only to the nobility. In Zaria, the majority of the larger *rumada* were the principal forms of capital investment in Zaria, and thus political status was closely related to the distribution of wealth; conversely, the distribution of wealth was related to the distribution of political office.[3]

The king was at once the wealthiest and most powerful man in the kingdom.[4]

The extensive participation of Habe (non-Fulani Hausa) and Fulani in slave-raiding and war was achieved by mobilizing contingents from the fiefs; and military action offered such troops rewards in the form of booty, appointments and promotion. The frequency and success of these military adventures may have persuaded many people to support the system of government. Since political and administrative office provided the principal means of enrichment and social mobility together, and had clear military committments, the recruitment of officials for these expeditions presented no problem.[5]

These quotations serve to indicate that the greatest economic rewards in Hausa society went to the occupants of the highest governmental positions, from the king downward. It should be noted particularly that merchants in this highly developed mercantile economy were prevented from building slave villages, "the principal forms of capital investment," which were allowed to high officeholders. In addition to tax, tribute, and slave holding, the economic rewards of military action augmented the economic position of the official as compared with that of the nonofficial. Thus in nineteenth-century Hausa society (in Zaria), political advancement led to wealth rather than the reverse. But what lead to political advancement?

Competition for office took a variety of forms. Of these clientage was perhaps the most important. Individuals might become clients of particular persons, such as office-holders eligible for promotion to the throne; or they might enter into a looser association with an important family or branch of a family; or one family or descent-line could be clients of another or of an office.[6]

Within the system of competing patrilineages, client-ship served to bring Fulani and Habe (non-Fulani Hausa) into close political association thereby reducing the separateness and unity of these conquered groups. Solidary political relations of clientage were the usual bases of Habe appointments to office; and although offices allocated to Habe were generally subordinate to those filled by Fulani of noble lineage or royal descent, they provided their holders with opportunities for the accumulation of wealth, for upward social mobility, and for the exercise of power.[7]

Persons appointed to fief-holding office would normally have received some training in this political and administrative organization as subordinates or clients of senior officials. Dynastic personnel who were acquainted from youth with political competition and administration had less need for such training than others, and were occasionally given office at an early age. . . .[8]

The rule was for a new king to dismiss his predecessor's kin and supporters from important office, and to appoint people of his own. . . . Thus office circulated rapidly among an expanding population of competitors and this circulation of official position carried with it increased prospects of appointment for the numerous competing candidates. It thereby stimulated the development of clientage by the hopes of political competition, as the sole alternative to political impotence and loss of status.[9]

In distributing office among his clients, the king sought to elicit the widest possible support for his regime among the aristocratic Fulani and subject Hausa.[10]

In discussing the government of contemporary (1950) Zaria, Smith indicates that clientage is still the principal path to political advancement. Social status, he says, is based on occupation, income, kinship and marriage relations, age, slave or free ancestry, and conformity to Islamic prescriptions of wife seclusion and pilgrimage to Mecca, but:

An even more important type of relation which affects a person's status and prestige is clientage. . . . The client whose patron is successful in the quest for office, often has clients of his own, on whose behalf he seeks to exercise influence with his powerful patron. By fortunate relations of clientage, an individual may himself obtain political office, and thereby social mobility. Personal power corresponds with an individual's position in the structure of clientage relations which hold between and within the official and non-official sectors of the society as a political system. Although clientage is an exclusive relation, it may be changed or renewed as occasion warrants; and the client's capacity for independent political action and upward mobility alike may be a result of his ability to change patrons opportunely.[11]

From these statements we conclude that clientage—that is, being a loyal and obedient follower of a man's patron in his own struggle for office—was essential to the political advancement of all in the society except those who had hereditary claim to the very highest offices, and probably to them as well. The rapid circulation of incumbents in offices provided a strong incentive for ambitious clients, and the widespread distribution of clientage among subgroups whose allegiance was desired by the king, gave grounds for hope to those of humble birth. Successful clientage involved early training in habits of subordination and political intrigue and opportunistic choice of patrons. Once in office,

> Its holder had two major committments: the first was loyalty to the king, and this allegiance was demonstrated by gifts and obedience; secondly, the official had to execute the king's instructions effectively and promptly, to collect the required tax, tribute, supplies or military detachments, and to discharge the various routine tasks already described. Throughout this system the great administrative sin was the sin of omission, the failure to execute promptly the order of one's immediate superior. Unless political disaffection was thereby expressed, actions beyond the strict authority of an individual's office were quite irrelevant. . . .[12]

Clearly, this system of status mobility placed a premium on loyalty, obedience, and sensitivity to the demands of those in authority over a man; excellent performance in an independent occupational role, self-instigated action towards goals that did not benefit the competitive chances of a man's patron, did not yield the man access to the major status rewards of the society and might conceivably damage his career. Furthermore, as suggested above, and shown below, there were no significant alternatives to clientage and its authoritarian habits for a man of ambition.

Smith has described the ubiquity of clientage in Hausa social relationships: between top officials and their subordinate titleholders, between ordinary officeholders and their agents and community chiefs, between ordinary non-office-holding men, between wealthy merchants and their clients, and between women.[13] The single term *barantaka* refers to political, domestic, and commercial clientage, and denotes a relationship of unequal status in which the superior rewards the loyalty of his subordinate with office, title, wives, cash, or goods. The pervasiveness of clientage is well conveyed by Smith's remarks concerning its persistence in contemporary Zaria.

Differences of political maturity and minority are assumed and expressed in the structure of clientage relation. Among the Hausa a compound head is politically mature in the sense that he deals directly with his local ward or village chief, but normally he is also a client or dependent of some more powerful person, through whom he deals indirectly with the local chief of the latter's superiors. The compound head's patron is equally likely to be a client of some yet more powerful person through whom he seeks to deal with his rivals of comparable status, and with those officials whose activities bear on his immediate interests. At the top of this pyramid is the Emir.... *"L'etat, c'est moi,"* is the constitutive principal of the emirate; and this being the case, its official hierarchic administrative structure is paralleled and combined with a hierarchy of unofficial clientage. . . . The competing leaders of groups of clients carry with them the political fortunes of their supporters, as well as those of their own kin. The client whose patron fails to secure office is at a disadvantage compared with him whose patron succeeds; and the more important the office secured by the patron, the higher the political status of the client. In such a system the commoner without a patron is not merely a deviant but also a rebel, since he admits of no personal allegiance; and such an individual occupies a disadvantageous position in this society. *The fact that some people nowadays avoid entering into clientage is frequently mentioned by Hausa and*

Fulani as an indication of overambition, disloyalty and
of social disorganization through change. But these so-
cial isolates are few in number, and are especially likely
to emigrate.[14] (Italics ours.)

This indicates that clientage and its attendant patterns of
subservience and obedience were inescapable aspects of social
life in traditional and contemporary Zaria. Success in trading
or acts of religious devotion might somewhat raise a man's
prestige, but major social rewards beyond those to which he
was born were achieveable only through clientage. Furthermore, refusal to enter into clientage was socially punished in
the sense that it put a man at a serious disadvantage compared
to others and was also disapproved on moral grounds. This was
a status system which strongly favored qualities of servility,
respect for authority, allegiance to the powerful, and rejected
qualities of independent achievement, self-reliant action, and
initiative. The selective effect of this status mobility system
was felt not only by the free Hausa and slaves, who were inferior by birth and could only hope to rise through affiliation
with those of higher birth, but also by the high-born Fulani,
whether commoners, noble, or royal, because their greater access to political office in the autocracy made their allegiances
of great importance in the struggle for political power.

This description applies to Zaria, but what of the other Hausa
kingdoms? Smith says that, in contrast to the administration of
Zaria, the Fulani administrations of Daura, Katsina, Kano, and
Sokoto were based on hereditary offices; favored clients of commoner birth could not occupy high office, although there were
numerous offices reserved for slaves. Status mobility was altogether less common. In such situations the rewards of successful clientship were much less than in Zaria, but most
evidence indicates that clientship and slavery were important
forms of social relationship there too, and that independent
achievement and self-reliant action were no more favored than
in Zaria. In other words, a man of ambition with no hereditary
claim to office had less chance of bettering his status dramatically through clientage in the other Hausa kingdoms, but that
is not to say that he had a greater chance of bettering his status
by any other means. On the basis of available evidence, then,

we have no reason to conclude that the other Hausa kingdoms constituted more favorable environments for the man of self-reliant achievement than did the well-described Zaria kingdom.

The Ibo

The Ibo are a southeastern Nigerian people, with a population of more than seven million, who lacked political centralization, urban organization, and Islamic influence in the pre-colonial period. Dwelling mainly in the tropical rain forests, they practiced agriculture, trading, and crafts, and were importantly involved in the European slave trade from the seventeenth century to the middle of the nineteenth century. Actual contacts with Europeans in this period and until the twentieth century were confined to small numbers of mobile traders who visited or lived at the non-Ibo coastal areas; most Ibo operated in the hinterland as suppliers of slaves, other goods, and services to the coastal peoples. Although speaking related dialects and with many cultural similarities, the people whom we now call Ibo were traditionally more than two hundred politically independent territorial groups with their own local customs and social systems who conducted intermittent warfare against one another. Each autonomous group consisted of one or more villages or a community of dispersed settlement, organized along the lines of patrilineal descent groups. With few exceptions, internal decision making was performed not by a single leader but by councils of elders which, although some men were more influential than others, were highly responsive to the popular will. There were, varying from one area to another, age grades, title societies, individual title systems, or secret men's societies, which, together with the descent groups, served as organs for the differential allocation of social status and as channels for the flow of influence in the community.

Ibo social structure is known largely through the original work of C. K. Meek,[15] G. I. Jones,[16] M. M. Green,[17] and Simon and Phoebe Ottenberg,[18] although many other persons have written on various groups of Ibo. Few of the published works contain as much detail on social status as Smith's Hausa material, and those that do, deal with a single village or cluster of villages, which cannot be taken as representative of more than one local area. In consequence, we rely in this presentation primarily on summaries made by Ibo specialists whose acquaintance with the range of Ibo social structures is more intimate than our own. Despite the large number of regional variations and the lack of adequate detail, the basic outlines of the Ibo status system, and its striking contrasts with Hausa and Yoruba patterns, are so clear as to be easily presented in general form.

The most characteristic feature of Ibo status systems, although not found everywhere, was the title society. This consisted in its most developed form of a series of ranked titles, the entry to which was contingent upon acceptance by existing titleholders, payment of a set entrance fee, and providing a feast for members of the society. Membership was open to anyone of free birth, but the fees and feasts effectively limited titleholding to those of some wealth. This was increasingly true as a man progressed to higher titles. Membership in the society entitled a man to share in the entrance fees paid by new members and to enjoy the prestige of titleholding. In many areas the title society also constituted a political oligarchy in the village or village-group, controlling the making of decisions even at public meetings at which all men had a right to speak and in which decisions were formally imposed by the heads of descent groups. The most important titles were not inherited, but fell vacant upon the death of a titleholder.

The title society was thus a means by which the wealth of a man could be translated into social and political status, ultimately the highest status which the local social system had to confer. In some areas the societies involved only a single title rather than a series of graded ranks; in others there were simply individual titles without a title society; in still others there were "secret societies." All shared the characteristic of providing individuals of exceptional wealth with exceptional authority and status. Furthermore, as Forde and Jones say, "Even where there was no title taking a man of wealth could attain to considerable political power, apart from any authority derived from his place in a kinship system, because he could provide the gunpowder and firearms needed for raiding and protection, and could build up a considerable following."[19]

The evidence indicates that although the wealth necessary for acquiring high status could be inherited, it could also be accumulated through a man's own efforts; in either instance it needed to be accompanied by specific personal qualities. Ottenberg is quite definite on this point.

> The Ibo are a highly individualistic people. While a man is dependent on his family, lineage, and residential grouping for support and backing, strong emphasis is placed on his ability to make his own way in the world. The son of a prominent politician has a head start over other men in the community, but he must validate this by his own abilities. While seniority in age is an asset in secular leadership, personal qualities are also important. A secular leader must be aggressive, skilled in oratory, and able to cite past history and precedent. A man gains prestige by accumulating the capital (formerly foodstuffs, now largely money) required to join title societies and perform other ceremonies. Much of the capital necessary for these activities is acquired through skill in farming and ability to acquire loans. Successful farming is a matter not merely of diligently using the proper agricultural techniques but often of a person's ability to obtain the use of the land resources of his friends, conjugal relatives, and his own unilineal groups. The ability to secure loans readily is a reflection of a person's prestige, the respect granted him, and the effectiveness of his social contacts. . . .
>
> The possibilities of enhancing status and prestige are open to virtually all individuals except descendents of certain types of slaves and are not restricted to members of particular lineages, clans or other social units. Ibo society is thus, in a sense, an "open" society in which positions of prestige, authority and leadership are largely achieved.[20]

Farming was not the only means of acquiring wealth. As Ottenberg says, "A number of alternative paths lead to success and prestige. A successful man may be a wealthy farmer or trader, in some cases a fisherman, an influential priest, or an important secular leader. He may—though he need not—combine two or more of these social positions."[21] He points out that there are similar choices in religion (which is highly individualistic), the selection of associational groups, and the settlement of disputes, concluding: "Ibo culture thus provides alternatives which the individual must decide upon in terms of his own skill and knowledge. Their significance for the individual is that he rapidly develops experience in making decisions in which he must estimate his own position and opportunities for success."[22]

The over-all picture which emerges of the traditional Ibo status system is not only of an open system in which any freeman could attain high status but of one that placed a premium on occupational skill, enterprise, and initiative. The man more likely to rise socially is the one who was sufficiently self-motivated to work hard and cleverly marshal available resources in the cause of increasing his wealth. He must have had social skills, but these involved manipulating others to allow him use of their resources without becoming bound in subservience to them. His career was basically dependent on what he made of himself rather than (as among the Hausa) what he helped make of someone else. Higher social status was granted by the title societies and other agencies as subsequent recognition of a man's having already amassed wealth through occupational achievement and of his possessing capacities for leadership. The occupational performance was the primary locus of social evaluation, and performing well enough as a farmer, trader or fisherman to obtain a title or provide firearms for followers required the continual application of his own efforts in the service of his individual goals. Thus the Ibo man who rose socially could correctly think of himself as a self-made man whose status mobility was a recognition of his own individual achievements.

The nineteenth-century Hausa and Ibo status systems differed in the following ways: As a large, centralized, and highly differentiated hierarchy of ranks, the Hausa status system entailed much greater differences in wealth, power, and prestige between top and bottom statuses than the Ibo system. Social position was much more determined by hereditary criteria (for example, Fulani versus Hausa ancestry) among the Hausa than among the Ibo. Mobility of social status was connected primarily with the competition for political office among the Hausa and with economic role performance among the Ibo. Individual status mobility (upward) was primarily attainable among the Hausa through the success of a man's high-status patron, whereas among the Ibo it was through the man's own success. The personal qualities most rewarded by higher social status were obedience, loyalty, and submissiveness to superiors among the Hausa, and dedication to occupational achievement among the Ibo.

The question of which system offered greater incentives for status mobility is not easily resolved. On the one hand, it could be argued that the incentives were greater among the Hausa, since the top statuses among them carried much more relative wealth, power, and prestige than their nearest Ibo counterparts and since the rotation of dynasties afforded opportunities of advancement for many groups of patrons and clients. On the other hand, an equally cogent argument is that the high statuses of the Ibo, although less richly endowed with dramatic status-transforming qualities, constituted greater incentives for mobility because they were more attainable by the average man, being less hedged by restrictions of birth and more numerous in each local area. It is a question of whether the magnitude of the goal or the chance of attaining it is more important in determining its strength as an incentive.

One point which is entirely clear, however, is that the Hausa status system was politically oriented, whereas the Ibo one was occupationally oriented. Among the Hausa, political office led to wealth; among the Ibo, the acquisition of wealth led to political power. Thus status mobility was achieved in one instance through demonstrating capability of playing a role in an authoritarian political system, and in the other instance through the demonstration of economic skills of an entrepreneurial sort. The ideal successful Hausa man seems to have been the officeholder who faithfully supported his superior and rewarded his followers; the Ibo ideal appears to have been the energetic and industrious farmer or trader who aggrandized himself personally through productive or distributive activity. By Ibo standards, the Hausa ideal was overdependent and confining to the individual; by Hausa standards, the Ibo ideal was dangerously selfish and anarchic. A Hausa man who conformed to the Ibo ideal might amass some wealth, but would be prevented by his excessively independent spirit from winning the favor of the officeholders who control access to the major social resources. An Ibo man who conformed to the Hausa ideal might gain some friends by his inoffensive manner, but would lose in the individualistic struggle for wealth. Each set of status mobility values favored a man with different personality characteristics, and although it is by no means inconceivable that one man could combine both or change himself according to what was required, we propose that the relative frequencies of certain personality characteristics varied systematically between the Hausa and Ibo. The Ibo system was a more favorable environment for the man with n Achievement and is therefore likely to have produced a higher incidence of it in the male population.

The Yoruba

The Yoruba inhabit southwestern Nigeria and adjacent sections of Dahomey, with a population of about six million in Nigeria alone. They have an ancient tradition of kingship, going back perhaps a thousand years, and dominated a large part of the West African coastal region and its hinterlands, under the Oyo Empire, until early in the nineteenth century. At that point the northern part of the empire came under the sway of Fulani invaders from the north, and the rest of it, which had been weak and divisive for some time, disintegrated into a number of warring kingdoms. The wars and consequent migrations and resettlements continued intermittently until British domination in 1890.

A Yoruba kingdom consisted of an urban center, in which the political, economic, and social affairs of the kingdom as well as a large part of its population were centralized, and some satellite towns whose rulers paid fealty to the king. Despite considerable variations in political structure from one kingdom to another, it can be generally said of these Yoruba states that their rulers were divine kings whose prestige and ritual status far exceeded their political power, and that one or more councils of state, consisting of hereditary chiefs and representatives of major territorial and associational groups in the town, were the main decision-making organs. Unlike the active Hausa kings, Yoruba monarchs were restricted by their divinity to their palaces, from which they rarely ventured. Although a

Hausa king could be deposed only by his overlord, the sultan of Sokoto, Yoruba kings could be (and were) deposed and ordered to commit suicide by their councils, which selected the successor. Yoruba monarchy was far from autocratic, being rather lightly superimposed on a social structure which contained strong and independent groupings organized on the basis of lineage, territory, and associational (that is, age, religious, occupational) ties. For the most part these groupings selected their own leaders, who acted as a check on the central authority of the king and as a means for the development of a popular consensus on issues before decision making. Thus the Yoruba political system, despite its hierarchical form, was not an authoritarian one in which commands flowed from the king down the ranks of obedient officeholders; instead, power was dispersed among partly self-governing segments, with relatively little concentration at the center.

There are many excellent publications on Yoruba social organization by P. C. Lloyd, William Schwab, W. R. Bascom, and a number of others,[23] but the status system has not been described and analyzed as such. Like many other aspects of Yoruba society, the allocation of social status was complicated by the occurrence of many variations and alternatives and by an often misleading deviation of social reality from outward appearance. Concerning the disparity between appearance and reality, for example, the hereditary principle seems to have been strongly emphasized in Yoruba leadership, but on closer inspection it is revealed that from a large pool of possible heirs to a chieftaincy title a man would be selected who was wealthier, had demonstrated greater leadership capacity, and so on. There is no single principle of recruitment into high social positions that would adequately represent the complexity of nineteenth century Yoruba society.

At the most general level, we can distinguish the following ascriptive statuses: members of the several royal lineages, who could inherit the throne; members of non-royal lineages in which chieftaincy titles were invested and inherited; commoners whose lineages had no hereditary claims to title; slaves. Among the commoners there were also hereditary craft occupations of varying status, but these were not as strictly ranked as among the Hausa. Birth into one of the four ascriptive status groups was only roughly correlated with ultimate social status, because institutions existed by which an individual could rise very high despite his birth. For example, in several Yoruba kingdoms there was the Ogboni society, sometimes called a secret society, sometimes a religious cult. It was in effect a kind of title association; although any adult male could join it, its higher ranks were open only to those who could pay the expensive fees. Its highest officers constituted a politically influential council in the central government, in some places the most important council surrounding the king. This, then, was a way of translating wealth, which might be amassed through occupational activity, into political power and status, in a manner resembling that of the Ibo title societies. On the other hand, however, there was the royal court, in which an individual could rise simply by gaining favor with the king. The king's favorite slaves and eunuchs were raised by him to positions of great importance and affluence, far exceeding most titled men in status. This status mobility pattern resembles Hausa clientage. Thus the Yoruba status system contained within it drastically different legitimate means of rising socially.

A critical difference between the Yoruba and Hausa systems is that the Yoruba kings and their officials did not have the control over the wealth of the society which characterized the Hausa governing elite. Chieftaincy did not involve fief holding, and did not thereby give access to vast sources of wealth. Even the king himself, although his court was lavishly provided for, was not permitted to enrich himself personally or his heirs through the permanent acquisition of property. Yoruba political officeholders, having much less control over their subjects than their Hausa counterparts, were in no position to exploit the kingdom's resources for their own benefit. There were, then, in trade especially, means outside and independent of the political system by which a man might make himself as wealthy as or wealthier than many chiefs of note. Furthermore, the Ogboni society and the appointment of wealthy men to council membership and even chieftaincy titles provided political recognition for men whose rise had been based on occupational achievement rather than political activity.

The anarchic state of nineteenth-century Yorubaland and the large-scale slave-trading activities provided unusual opportunities for, entrepreneurial activity of a kind that was not possible in the more tightly centralized Hausa system. A dissident member of the royal family would raise a band of followers, migrate to a different place to found a separate town or join one of the new military centers such as Ibadan, and engage in slave-raiding and other military activities as well as establish a civil settlement. The loyal warriors of such a prince would be rewarded with land, slaves, booty, and even newly devised hereditary titles. This kind of pioneering and military adventurism occurred so frequently that it must have constituted a major outlet for the energies of the more individualistic Yoruba men throughout the mid-nineteenth century, and could have provided a substantial incentive for the development of achievement strivings. It should be noted, however, that it took the form of an authoritarian military organization with a patron-client relationship operating within it, so that the independence and self-reliance were likely to be limited to the founder of the new settlement, and he was likely to be of high birth. Moreover, such new settlements replicated the hereditary structure of the kingdoms from which they sprang. As in other Yoruba social behavior patterns, their pioneering too represented an amalgam of hereditary privileges and restrictions with opportunities for individual achievement.

On the basis of available evidence, we surmise that the status mobility system of the nineteenth-century Yoruba constituted an environment rewarding to both the independent occupational achievement of the Ibo ideal and the loyal clientage of the Hausa ideal. It is clear that there were many more status mobility opportunities for the independent man of occupational skill and industry who could not endure subservience than were afforded in Hausa society. It is equally clear that there were more hereditary restrictions, particularly on reaching the highest status positions, and more scope for success through sycophancy, then existed in Ibo society. The only possible conclusion is that Yoruba society was intermediate between Ibo and Hausa as an environment favorable to the development of n-Achievement.

Predicted Differences in Personality

The foregoing analyses of the nineteenth-century status mobility systems of the Hausa, Ibo, and Yoruba can be summarized briefly as follows:

Hereditary restrictions on status mobility were greatest among the Hausa, but the rewards of wealth and power were also greatest in the centralized feudal autocracy that prevailed. The mobility system was politically oriented, and a man could rise only through clientage—that is, a relation of loyal and obedient support to a high-born person who was or might become a powerful officeholder in the authoritarian political system. Social incentives thus favored the subservient follower who could perform well in the political system over the independent entrepreneur or occupational achiever.

Hereditary restrictions were few among the Ibo; in the small-scale local status systems that prevailed, there were many opportunities for the average man to rise to the top. The Ibo status mobility system was occupationally oriented—that is, rising was dependent on individual achievement in pecuniary activity, with the resultant wealth being used to purchase social prestige and political influence in a ranked title society. Social incentives favored enterprise, diligence, and independent effort on a man's own behalf.

Yoruba society provided alternative paths of status mobility through occupational achievement in trading which could be politically recognized, as well as through political clientage in the royal court and in military adventures. It thus combined the Ibo and Hausa systems. Hereditary restrictions were, however, much greater than among the Ibo, and opportunities for mobility generally, and mobility through occupational performance specifically, were much greater than among the Hausa. Social incentives favored both the authoritarian political virtues of subservience and obedience (but less so than the Hausa) and the occupational virtues of enterprise and independent effort (but less so than the Ibo). If we assume that incentives provided by a status mobility system for some personality characteristics affect the actual distribution of such characteristics in the population for several generations, . . . then we are led to predict that in comparable groups of Hausa, Ibo, and Yoruba males, the Ibo will contain the largest proportion of individuals with n-Achievement, the Yoruba the next highest, and the Hausa the least. . . .

The most significant empirical findings reported . . . are summarized in the following paragraphs.

In a study of Nigerian male secondary school students:

1. The frequency of achievement imagery in dream reports was greatest for the Ibo, followed by the Southern Yoruba, Northern Yoruba and Hausa, in that order, as predicted by the status mobility hypothesis. The Ibo-Hausa and Southern Yoruba-Hausa differences are statistically significant. The order of the groups does not correspond to their ranking on frequency of educated parents. Differences between groups comprised on the basis of mothers' education are extremely small in the sample as a whole and in the Ibo and Southern Yoruba subsamples. Moslem-Christian differences are highly significant but almost entirely confounded with ethnic group membership. Among the Northern Yoruba, the only group with enough adherents of both religions, there is no difference in frequency between Moslems and Christians.

2. The frequency of obedience and social compliance value themes in essays on success written by the students was greatest for the Hausa, followed by the Southern Yoruba and Ibo, in that order. The Ibo-Hausa and Yoruba-Hausa differences are statistically significant.

In a nation-wide public opinion survey of Nigerian adults:

1. The proportion of persons mentioning self-development or improvement as a leading personal aspiration was greatest for the Ibo, followed by the Southern Yoruba and Fulani-Hausa, in that order. Ibo-Fulani-Hausa and Southern Yoruba-Fulani-Hausa differences were highly significant statistically.

2. The proportion of persons mentioning improvement of standard of living or national prosperity through technological advance as a leading aspiration for Nigeria was greatest for the Ibo, followed by the Southern Yoruba and Fulani-Hausa, in that order. Ibo-Fulani-Hausa and Southern Yoruba-Fulani-Hausa differences were highly significant statistically.

The Ibo have moved into higher education and professional occupations, formerly dominated by the Yoruba, very rapidly and in large numbers since 1920.

In the rest of this chapter we shall discuss these findings in relation to . . . three questions fundamental to psychological anthropology . . . We shall attempt to draw conclusions regarding the reality of the group differences revealed in this study, their sociocultural causes or determinants, and their consequences for the functioning of the Nigerian social and political systems.

The Validity of the Findings

Do the data presented above demonstrate a real psychological difference between the populations studied? We raise this question in its most extreme form because we believe it has been too often overlooked by culture-personality investigators, who have not paid enough attention to the validity of their measures of group differences. We have attempted to solve this problem by methods of cross-validation—that is, by developing independent lines of evidence that can be checked against one another in the way a historian checks several documentary sources or an ethnographer checks informant's accounts of the same events. Correspondence between facts independently arrived at makes it more likely that they represent an objective reality and less likely that they are derived from a bias of the instrument used to collect them. In this study, three methods of cross-validation were used: checking different measues of the same factor against one another, checking theoretically opposite factors against one another, and comparing contradictory predictions concerning group differences on one factor.

Identical group differences in achievement motivation were found in the analysis of the dream reports and in the public opinion data. These two measures were alike in giving the individual a relatively free opportunity to express his needs and wishes, but they were unlike in most other ways. The request for a dream report elicited an elaborate personal fantasy in narrative form without asking directly about personal desires; the survey questions asked directly about personal aspirations focused specifically on self and nation. The two different methods were employed by different administrators with different samples of the ethnic groups under different conditions. Thus their concordant results cannot be attributed to similarity in method of approach, investigators, samples, or conditions of administration. Their independence and diversity make the identical group differences less likely to be due to errors of measurement in either.

The differences between the Hausa and the two other groups are supported by statistical tests in both bodies of evidence. The Ibo-Yoruba differences are so consistent in these data and in the information on achieving behavior that we are inclined to accept them as real (although of lesser magnitude) despite their consistent lack of statistical significance. The likelihood of such differences being due to chance is lessened by their replication in diverse sets of data.

The validity of the findings in this study can also be assessed by examining the relation of achievement motivation to a behavioral disposition that is theoretically opposed to it, authoritarianism. In theory n-Achievement is closely linked to self-reliance and individualism as personal attributes; hence, individuals and groups high on n-Achievement should be low on submission to, and dependence on, authority. The more a man is disposed to yield to the commands of others, the less he is likely to set his own goals and strive to achieve them. It is logical, then, to predict that n-Achievement should be inversely related to a measure of authoritarianism. The failure of our measure of achievent values in the schoolboys' essays prevented our running this correlation across individuals, but we did find the order of groups on obedience and social compliance values to be the reverse of their order on n-Achievement. Furthermore, the same group differences were statistically significant on both variables. This predicted reversal on an independently defined and scored factor confirms the concept of n-Achievement as antagonistic to authoritarianism as a personality dimension; it also indicates that our methods of assessing achievement motivation were measuring what they purported to measure, a dimension inconsistent with strong obedience values. This is another independent line of evidence supporting the likelihood that our group differences in n-Achievement were not due to chance.

Finally, we can examine the validity of the findings by comparing the results predicted by the status mobility hypothesis, which involves real differences between ethnic groups, with those predicted by rival hypothesis, stating that apparent ethnic differences are masking underlying differences in acculturation, religion, examination anxiety or temporary conditions of administration. These findings are presented in detail for the dream report data . . . they show that none of these factors accounts as adequately for the variations in achievement imagery as the assumption of genuine ethnic differences. The acculturation factor (as measured by parents' education) is most effectively examined by multiple comparisons: across groups, across individuals for the sample as a whole, and within two subsamples. None of these comparisons yielded results predicted on that basis. The hypothesis that factors of examination anxiety or other temporary conditions of the schoolboys accounted for the group differences are made less likely by the convergent data of the public opinion survey, conducted with adult respondents in normal community settings. The religious factor cannot be ruled out, although subsample comparison among the Northern Yoruba did not support it. Thus the testing of hypotheses that cast doubt on the reality of ethnic group differences did not support the idea that non-ethnic factors could better account for the revealed differences in achievement motivation.

On the basis of the convergent support for the ethnic group differences from several independent and diversely varying bodies of evidence, and with the additional knowledge that data casting serious doubt on the ethnic nature of these differences have been sought and not found, we conclude that a strong likelihood has been established for the reality of the differences between Hausa, Ibo, and Yoruba reported above. This means that we find the evidence convincing enough to say that the differences found between the samples studied are probably characteristic of the populations and would manifest themselves in further studies using other samples and other instruments of measurement.

Explanations of the Group Differences

Assuming that the differences in n-Achievement among Hausa, Ibo, and Yoruba are real, what caused them? Since we predicted these differences from the status mobility hypothesis, we tend to see proof of them as confirmation of that hypothesis. But do the findings constitute an adequate demonstration of the validity of that hypothesis, or are they susceptible to explanation on other theoretical grounds?

We are convinced that the results of the predictive study support the status mobility hypothesis but leave some relevant questions unanswered. The full theory assumes that a system of status mobility affects parental values (concerning the ideal successful man), which in turn affect their child-rearing practices, which in turn produce a certain level of n-Achievement and other personality characteristics relevant to successful mobility. The findings presented in this study do not include data on parental values as such or on child-rearing practices, thus leaving open the question of whether these factors are necessary to explain the ethnic group differences. A more conclusive study would show correlations of n-Achievement with child rearing, and parental values, both within and between groups. Furthermore, although we had hundreds of individual instances of n-Achievement, there were only three instances of status mobility systems, and the Hausa, Ibo, and Yoruba differ in many other ways apart from status mobility: religion, population density, colonial history, and so forth. We cannot at present be certain that it is not one or more of these latter group differences that might account for the variation in achievement motivation. With a set of fifty diverse ethnic groups varying in both status mobility patterns and n-Achievement scores, we could make comparisons that did not confound status mobility with other cultural or structural properties of groups. In such a sample it would be possible to examine the relation of religion and population density to n-Achievement independently of status system, and to discover which of these group characteristics was the best predictor of n-Achievement and what proportion of the variance in n-Achievement each accounted for. Until this larger scale comparison is undertaken, our conclusions concerning the relation of status mobility to achievement motivation will remain tentative.

In the absence of a more conclusive study confirming the status mobility hypothesis, we can nevertheless compare that hypothesis with alternative explanations of the present findings. If we find these alternatives less plausible, we might retain our original hypothesis as the best explanation in light of the available facts; if we find one or more of them equal or superior in plausibility, we might reject or modify the status mobility hypothesis. Our examination of alternative explanations has as its aim not only the decision of which to accept but also a deepening insight into the problem of accounting for achievement differences between ethnic groups. The only determinant of these differences mentioned so far as has been the degree of conduciveness of the traditional status mobility system to the self-made man. We now review three other possible determinants of n-Achievement in groups: population pressure; withdrawal of group status respect; contemporary status mobility patterns. The discussion of each determinant separately is followed by a consideration of complex interactions of factors and of possible research designs for answering the empirical questions which have been raised.

Population pressure. The basic point here is that the Ibo homeland in Eastern Nigeria is one of the most densely populated regions in Africa, and overpopulation has been held responsible for Ibo activity in non-agricultural occupations. We are fortunate in having the case for this determinant stated by Horton as part of a theoretical argument concerning psychological explanation in anthropology and as applied knowledgeably to the Ibo.

> Perhaps the most prevalent form of naiveté is the psychologist's readiness to accept certain obvious purposes and attitudes as ultimate, and to search at once for their causes. The social anthropologist, in many cases, would point out that these purposes and attitudes had "reasons." That is, he would show that they were not really ultimate, but on the contrary, were rationally justified by other purposes and attitudes lying beyond them.
>
> The Ibo people of Eastern Nigeria have become renowned in recent years for the value they set on aggressive competition, the struggle for achievement, and the willingness to explore new avenues of power and status. A culture-and-personality theorist, whom I talked to about them, took this value as an obvious "ultimate," to be interpreted as the effects of certain causes—possibly in the realm of child training. As a social anthropologist, I was suspicious of this. I pointed to the fact that over much of Iboland there is acute land shortage, that anxious parents

quite "reasonably" encourage their children to struggle for a school success that will fit them for some career other than farming, and that when the children grow up, their own "reason" tells them that their only hope of a comfortable existence lies in continuing the struggle in outside trade, or in jobs in government or the big commercial firms. To back up this interpretation, I pointed to the fact that in pockets of adequate land supply like Nike and Abakiliki, where everyone can still get along comfortably in a farming career, this syndrome of aggressive competition and readiness to exploit new avenues of advancement is not at all obvious.[1]

This position deserves serious consideration not only because the population pressure argument has a great deal of face validity for anyone acquainted with Nigeria but also because it presents a familiar and important challenge to psychological anthropology. Horton's hypothesis is that Ibo achievement behavior is a conscious, rational adaptation to an obviously difficult economic situation. The implication is that the Ibo response is that of any rational man in a coercive environment, and therefore needs no more complex psychological assumptions about the Ibo than that they can perceive their environment and are reasonable enough to want "a comfortable existence." We believe this rationalistic view does not help explain the most important aspects of the Ibo "syndrome of aggressive competition."

The first important aspect of Ibo achievement behavior overlooked by Horton is that it was not the only "reasonable" course of action open to them. When a rural family is faced with a decline in income such as that caused by overcrowding on the land, there is a choice between lowering standards of consumption and finding new sources of income. The former alternative, which involves becoming accustomed to increasing poverty, is in fact adopted by families in economically depressed areas all over the world. Such families operate on a principle of least effort in which the comfort of remaining in familiar surroundings and doing familiar things, even when faced with starvation, outweighs the future economic benefits that might be gained from drastically changing their way of life. So long as their impoverishment is gradual, they will put up with it, for it affords known and immediate gratifications that would be missing were they to seek new productive activities. Their behavior is by no means totally irrational; it is based on a short-run hedonistic calculus into which long-range considerations do not enter. To persons predisposed to adopt this course of action (or inaction), the Ibo willingness to uproot themselves and give up accustomed if reduced rewards, seems unreasonable and unnatural.

Another path available to the Ibo was that followed by the Hausa. The latter have not been reluctant to leave their land in search of nonagricultural income; Hausa traders are everywhere in West Africa. Their pattern of trade, however, is traditional, and no matter how long they stay in modern cities like Accra and Lagos, they remain conservative with regard to education, religion, and politics, and aloof from modern bureaucratic and industrial occupations. This does not seem to be an unreasonable adaptation, but it is very unlike that of the Ibo migrants to the same cities. There were, then, at least three possible courses of action open to the Ibo in response to their acute land shortage: to accept impoverishment at home, to extend traditional trading patterns while remaining as un-Westernized as possible, and to pursue Western-type economic activity with the changes in ways of life that were required for it. Other peoples have adopted the first two alternatives in response to economic adversity; although some Ibo undoubtedly did too, many chose the third course. The difference is not one of rationality but of energy and effort.

In simplest terms, the successful pursuit of a novel occupation involving a high degree of enterprise or education is not for a lazy man, no matter how hard pressed he is financially. To be as successful as so many Ibo have been they had to have adopted long-range goals of self-improvement, renounced immediate comfort and consumption in order to pursue these goals, applied themselves mentally and physically to this pursuit over a long period of time. Such efforts require extraordinary energy, of which many men are not possessed, no matter how poor they are initially; it is this energy factor that we call achievement drive or motivation.

Even if it be granted that population pressure caused the Ibo to seek employment in the cities, this would not explain why they strove to excel when they gained these opportunities. Every evidence we have indicates that Ibo, unlike many others, have not been content with "a comfortable existence"; they have restlessly worked toward the top in their new fields of endeavor. This crucial difference between simply making a living and persistent striving for long-range success is another point overlooked by Horton and unaccounted for in his rational adaptation hypothesis.

In our opinion, then, this hypothesis is unconvincing because it fails to explain those aspects of Ibo economic behavior that indicate a consistent pattern of success strivings above and beyond the need for subsistence. We do not reject as implausible a relationship between population pressure and economic achievement, but only Horton's account of the mediating psychological factors involved. Achievement-oriented responses to overpopulation seem to be more common in Africa than in many other parts of the world, since a number of the apparently most enterprising African peoples, for example, the Kikuyu, are also among the most overcrowded in their rural homeland. This is a subject worthy of comparative research. If measures of n-Achievement and achieving behavior could be obtained for a sample of African ethnic groups varying widely in population density or in capacity to subsist by agriculture, we could determine whether population pressure is related to achievement. Following Horton's suggestion of local differences in overcrowding and achieving behavior in Iboland, we could compare more and less crowded Ibo rural populations on n-Achievement. Finally, we could carry such study one step further by comparing highly achieving Ibo individuals with their less enterprising fellows from the same areas on the amount of land to which they or their families had access. Until such investigations are carried out, we cannot be certain about the relationship of population pressure to economic achievement. Such a relationship would not be incompatible with our general formulation. It seems to us quite plausible that population pressure is translated into economic achievement in Africa through the child training practices of anxious parents which produce higher levels of n-Achievement in their children. Investigation of the amount of time elasped between the onset of severe land shortage and the rise in achieving behavior would be crucial to the testing of this hypothesis.

This brings us to Horton's argument about "ultimates," by which he presumably means enduring behavioral dispositions which have a driving force of their own, as opposed to adjustable perceptions of the changing environment. Although mentioning Ibo encouragement of children's academic achievement, Horton clearly does not believe that this encouragement produces in the individual a disposition to achieve that is later applied to economic behavior; the economic achievement is seen as based independently on a perception made in adulthood concerning available occupational opportunities. This implies that the adult achieving behavior is a specific economic response to an economic challenge or incentive; there is no reason or pressure for Ibo to manifest achievement strivings outside the economic sphere. There is evidence, however, that Ibo manifest such strivings in a variety of non-pecuniary activities. Mrs. Ottenberg, discussing the values of the rural villages of Afikpo, mentions achievement in connection with athletic contests, a feature of traditional Ibo village life that has remained important.[2] The efforts and accomplishments of many individual Ibo in art, literature, science, and nationalist politics have been conspicuous and cannot be reduced to pecuniary motives. Their tendency to achieve seems as strong in athletic, cultural, and political activities as in business, civil service, and the professions. The generality of this disposition can be seen also in the data of this study, in which samples of their behavior ranging from dream reports to hopes for the future of Nigeria showed the Ibo ahead of other groups on achievement. This consistent performance suggests an internal drive that seizes the opportunity for expression in any type of situation rather than a specific adjustment to economic necessity. As Horton's hypothesis fails to account for the suprarational energy involved in Ibo achieving behavior, so it cannot explain the generality of that behavior, particularly in non-pecuniary spheres of activity.

To return to our original consideration, does population pressure vary concomitantly with n-Achievement in the three ethnic groups of our study? There can be no question that population pressure among the Ibo is more severe than in the other two groups. With rural densities ranging above one thousand per square mile,[3] the Ibo home country is one of the most overcrowded in Africa. The Southern Yoruba have an average density of three hundred to four hundred per square mile,[4] and their rural homeland has been one of the most prosperous agricultural areas in West Africa. Cocoa cultivation in particular has provided a high income yield from land, and there is arable land available that has not been farmed. The situation among the Hausa is not strictly comparable to that of the other two, since they inhabit a different vegetation zone with less rainfall; the densities vary greatly from one local area to another. It is clear, however, that the Hausa have not experienced the severe population pressure that the Ibo have. Thus the difference in n-Achievement between the Ibo and Hausa might be accounted for in terms of population pressure, but the consistently significant differences between Yoruba and Hausa cannot be explained in this way. The Yoruba and Hausa are closer to one another in their ability to subsist adequately through agriculture, but the Yoruba are much closer to the Ibo in achievement motivation. The effect of rural population pressure on n-Achievement cannot be ruled out, but does not account for the results obtained herein. It is to be hoped that the questions raised by the population hypothesis receive the systematic research attention they deserve.

Withdrawal of status respect. Hagen[5] has raised the question of why a "traditional society" or some group within it will suddenly abandon traditional ways and turn its "energies to the tasks of technological advance." His theoretical answer is that "the basic cause of such change is the perception on the part of the members of some social group that their purposes and values in life are not respected by groups in the society whom they respect and whose esteem they value."[6] The group so affected by "withdrawal of status respect" is first demoralized and then prompted to find alternative means of righting itself with the disparaging wider society. In so doing—a process which Hagen believes to inolve changes in child rearing and personality development—the group assumes a role as technological and economic innovator, thus promoting economic growth in a hitherto stagnant society. Can this concept of withdrawal of status respect account for the differences in n-Achievement among our three Nigerian groups? We must examine their history under colonial administration to find out. The Ibo could certainly be considered to have suffered a withdrawal of status respect during the early colonial period. Before British administration they constituted a relatively isolated cluster of societies, although they traded with coastal groups and some of their other neighbors. Once they came under British rule, however, various factors—their traditional entrepreneurial energies and/or population pressures—induced many of them to move to coastal towns like Lagos and Calabar and other centers of population. In those places they found peoples, like the Yoruba and Efik, who had had much more Western contact and education and were firmly entrenched in the best civil service jobs and professional positions. These sophisticated peoples despised the Ibo not only as bush people lacking in Westernization but as savages whose traditional culture lacked cloth and clothing, urbanism, and political centralization, and allegedly involved cannibalism. Being regarded as naked savages from the forest with an inferior culture must have hurt many Ibos profoundly. Coleman has mentioned both the resentment and the ethnocentric Western scale of values which gave rise to the disparagement:

> Educated Ibo leaders have been particularly resentful over the cliché that Africans have no culture and no history. . . . Many early European observers glorified the cultures, traditions, and histories of the Hausa states, and, to a lesser extent, of the Yoruba kingdoms, to which the Ibo, and other groups similarly placed, were invidiously contrasted.[7]

Out of their resentment at being despised as a backward people, and also at being discriminated against in jobs and housing in towns dominated by other ethnic groups, may have come the tremendous Ibo determination to get ahead, to be more modern than anyone else, to favor technological advance, and to succeed in every field individually and as a group.

It can be argued with equal cogency that the events since 1900 have afforded the Hausa maximal protection from the withdrawal of status respect which often accompanies colonialism. In the system of indirect rule they were allowed to retain their own rulers and continue the traditional life fostered by those rulers. Lord Lugard's agreement insulated them from Christian missionaries and Western education,[8] so that they never suffered the jolts to cultural self-esteem which are inflicted on a non-Western people by mission Christianity, by knowledge of the outside world, and by a new scale of educational values. In other words, they could continue to see as undiminished in splendor their traditional culture with its monarchy, orthodox Islam, orientation toward Mecca, and Koranic schooling. They did not suffer the invidious comparison with European culture or Europeanized Africans which southern Nigerians did. Furthermore, they maintained their autonomy until they were able to enter into a federation with the southern regions with themselves as the dominant leaders, having a majority of the voting population under their control. Hence, when the Hausa-Fulani political leaders came to Lagos, they came as the rulers of the Federation of Nigeria, without having to bow their heads to the Nigerians who had acquired European sophistication. Although the history of the Ibo indicates they were maximally exposed to disparagement in terms of the European scale of values introduced by colonialism, Hausa history indicates that they were maximally insulated from it.

The Yoruba were intermediate on withdrawal of status respect; although they were not insulated from the inevitable disparagement involved in intensive missionization and Western schooling, they received these blows to their cultural self-esteem so early, relative to the other groups, that they were able to view themselves as superior to the less Westernized peoples. Furthermore, although their traditional culture did not receive the respect paid by the British to Hausa culture, its monarchical tradition and associated cultural complexity protected the Yoruba from a low evaluation of their own group as contrasted with Europeans.

If, then, we view the three ethnic groups in terms of the hypothesis derived from Hagen that withdrawal of status respect leads to something like n Achievement, we can indeed find support for such a hypothesis. The Ibo, leading in n Achievement, certainly suffered the most complete group loss of respect during the colonial period; the Hausa, lowest on n Achievement, were most insulated from the conditions producing social disparagement in a colonial society; and the Yoruba, in a sense, had it both ways. On the basis of our Nigerian comparison, we cannot reject the theory which views achievement striving as a reaction to group disparagement, and we must admit it as a plausible explanation of our findings. The only fact it cannot explain is the greater achievement orientation of the precolonial Ibo as compared with the Hausa and Yoruba.

Contemporary status mobility patterns. A final alternative hypothesis arising in the course of analyzing the data is that the ethnic group differences in *n* Achievement are due to variation in the *contemporary* situations in status mobility in the three groups. Since the contemporary status mobility system of the group is a complex precipitate of the traditional system, its modification under colonial administration, and the present state of economic opportunities, this hypothesis is an eclectic one in which there is room for several of the factors hitherto considered.

The basic idea in this hypothesis is that the frequency of *n* Achievement in the group is determined primarily by the more or less accurate perception of the growing male child as to: the chances of his rising socially, and the behavior which leads to success in the status system. His perception is determined by the information concerning the state of the system which he receives from various individuals and institutions, including older members of the family, school teachers, religious instructors, books, and mass media. Let us assume that he forms a fairly stable image from these diverse sources of information by the time he is fourteen years old. If his image is that the chances of his rising socially are good and that individual competition with a standard of excellence is what leads to success, then he will manifest the achievement motive. If his image is that he has little chance of rising socially and that obedience and social compliance lead to what success is available, then he will not manifest the achievement motive. Intermediate examples will vary between these extremes, according to the amount of the perceived opportunities and the strength of the perception of achievement behavior as instrumental in success. Thus the frequency of *n* Achievement in a population will co-vary with the strength of the incentives for achievement behavior perceived by the men as being offered by the status mobility system during the years in which they were growing up. In this theory there is little time lapse between changes in status mobility system and changes in n Achievement, at least in the younger generation, and neither parental values nor child-training practices are involved as mediating variables—only the transmission of information to the child.

How does such a theory explain the findings of this study? Beginning with the Hausa, we can say, following Smith, that both the hereditary privilege of the Fulani and the institution of clientage have strongly survived into the present (at least as of 1950, when he did his study), and determine the magnitude and nature of opportunities in the contemporary Hausa status mobility system. This is, of course, because the colonial policies of indirect rule, prohibition on Christian missions, and slow development of Western education had enabled the traditional system to survive almost intact into the present. Thus a Hausa boy who was nineteen in 1962 would have grown up with an image of the possible in status mobility which was not drastically different from that of a boy growing up in 1865, the date for which Smith provides a picture of the traditional system. Our analysis of that latter system, then, holds good for the present, uncontaminated by notions of local democracy, the individual Christian conscience, and achievement of high status through successful education, and reinforced by Islamic injunctions of obedience as the highest virtue. The conclusion is that our sample of Hausa students, and the Fulani-Hausa adults surveyed in the national poll, had their level of achievement motivation formed by a status system which, now as in the past, does not offer strong incentives for independent achieving behavior.

Making the same assumption about the perceptual relationship between contemporary status mobility patterns and level of n Achievement, we have to consider rather different social factors in the Ibo case. Let us assume that the traditional Ibo system at very least predisposed Ibo children to be unusually sensitive to information about opportunities for alternative paths of rising socially and, specifically, opportunities for rising through occupational performance. The overpopulation and consequent decline in local agricultural opportunities forced adults to seek increasing amounts of information about outside opportunities in a variety of types of work information which in the normal course of events was passed on to children.

The flow of this type of information was vastly increased by the work of Christian missions and Western schools, which furthermore operated—along with the development of Western bureaucratic institutions in government and commerce—to create new institutional settings for the advancement of achievement oriented persons through the acquisition of education and modern technical skills. The current generation of Ibo (including those whose behavior was sampled in 1962) reached maturity with a high level of n Achievement aroused and reinforced by the strong incentives for achieving behavior which they perceived by being exposed to an extraordinary amount of information concerning opportunities outside their local and traditional horizons. Thus the status mobility system which incites their achievement motivation is that of all modern Nigeria, not that of their local environment.

The Yoruba occupy the intermediate position, according to this theory, because, although they were exposed even earlier than the Ibo to a great deal of information about modern occupational opportunities and advancement through schooling (because of Christian missions, widespread Western education and the introduction of Western bureaucratic institutions), the other side of the picture was balanced by local agricultural prosperity (primarily through cocoa farming) which reinforced not only the traditional occupation of farming but also many segments of the traditional sociopolitical status system. Since opportunities for wealth and status enhancement existed in agriculture, and land tenure was traditional, it was possible for ascriptive aspects of the traditional status system to be bolstered directly or indirectly through agriculture. A Yoruba youth would reach maturity with the perception that opportunities existed locally and in old-fashioned institutions as well as in the translocal world of modern achievement. Although he would perceive many incentives in the latter—hence his much greater level of n Achievement than that of his Hausa contemporaries—he would be more likely than his Ibo counterpart to be attracted to reliance on modified forms of local clientage, which have managed to survive in the contemporary Yoruba social structure.

This theory of contemporary status mobility and achievement motivation does plausibly account for the ethnic differences in n Achievement which form the core of findings in the study. Its central difference from the theory of traditional status mobility presented in chapters 2 and 3 is that the latter involves parental values of individualism and specific training of the child in independence and achievement to develop the achievement motive, whereas the former assumes that a status mobility system can communicate its incentives to the child fairly directly and cognitively, without the familial manipulation of his motives. It is possible to devise research designs which would pit these theories against one another in contradictory predictions. The theory originally proposed predicts that, regardless of the contemporary system and its incentives, only those individuals who have been subjected to certain routines of independence and achievement training will manifest n Achievement; the other theory predicts that n Achievement will vary from one group to another concomitantly with the contemporary state of opportunities and incentives, independently of specific training routines in the individual life history. The next step is to conduct comparative studies of n Achievement with measures of child rearing and the perception of opportunities as part of the data collection procedures.

We believe that our discussion has illuminated the problem of finding determinants for the ethnic group differences in n Achievement, but it has not led us to reject as implausible all of the alternatives to our traditional status mobility hypothesis. More definite conclusions must await further research.

Social and Political Consequences of the Group Differences

Whatever their origins, the motives, attitudes, and behaviors reported on here seem to have some clear implications for the directions of social change in Nigeria. This investigation indicates that associated with well-known regional variations in levels of economic development and Westernization in Nigeria are individual behavioral dispositions of a deep-seated nature which are probably resistant to change. If this is true, they will continue to influence Nigerian social life, at least in the foreseeable future.

The behavioral dispositions studied are not randomly or uniformly distributed among the three major ethnic groups of Nigeria; they vary significantly, and form a distinctive cluster. The cluster consists of achievement motivation, concern with self-improvement, non-authoritarian ideology (here measured through obedience and social compliance values), a favorable attitude toward technological innovation, and rapid advancement in Western education and the Western type of occupational hierarchy. The Ibo and, to a lesser extent, the Yoruba are high on all of these dimensions; the Hausa are low. This should not be interpreted as a simple absence in the Hausa instance, but rather as an attachment to an authoritarian ideology probably strongly reinforced by continued training in Islamic orthodoxy, a personal fatalism (probably also reinforced by the Hausa version of Islamic doctrine), and a conservatism in educational and economic affairs.

One effect of this clustering of dispositions is that those individuals most prepared to occupy the positions of professional, technical, and bureaucratic leadership in the newly formed Nigerian nation are persons favoring the modern advance symbolized by technological innovation and antagonistic to traditional authoritarian government and doctrines of passive obedience. As the southern Nigerians (Ibo and Yoruba) race forward in preparing themselves for these positions, the inevitable conflicts between them and the Hausa leaders of the North (who dominated the federation politically until 1966) have assumed an ideological as well as a sectional flavor. It is not simply Hausa versus the ethnic groups of southern Nigeria, but conservatism versus modernism, authoritarian versus democratic ideology, and Islamic obedience versus Christian individualism. For example, post-independence measures to exclude job-hungry educated southern Nigerians from civil service and teachings posts in the North for which few Hausa are qualified, were based not only on a desire not to be dominated by other regions but also on a rejection of the values which the educated southerners represent and might propagate. The overproduction of achieving individuals in southern Nigeria and their underproduction in the North thus result not simply in a problem of ethnic allocation of jobs but in a confrontation of contradictory ideologies of modernization and authority. This confrontation played an important part in the Ibo officers' revolt of 1966. . . .

The Yoruba, in their intermediate position on these dimensions of individual disposition, have been pulled in both directions. The Yoruba ethnic group contains within it individuals who are among the most Westernized and attitudinally modern in tropical Africa, but it also includes a large rural population which has had to change little in order to survive effectively in the contemporary period and which is still strongly oriented toward traditional patterns of leadership as represented by the *obas* (kings) and chiefs. For a while the Yoruba were able to operate as something of a political unit, but since early 1962 they have been torn by a severe political schism. What is notable from the viewpoint of this study is that the schism increasingly took on the flavor of a fundamental ideological conflict. Despite numerous countertrends, the main thrust of the split involved one faction appealing to traditional and less educated elements in the population, whereas the other gained support from modernizing intellectuals, professionals, and urban militants. Significantly, in 1964 the former became allied with the Hausa-dominated Northern Peoples' Congress, and the latter with the Ibo-dominated National Council of Nigerian Citizens. Thus the contemporary political behavior of the Yoruba, like their responses as measured in this study, shows them torn between the ideological poles represented by the more extreme Ibo and Hausa.

None of this will come as a surprise to the student of Nigerian politics. We present it in order to suggest that there is a consistent pattern of group differences revealed in unconscious imagery, explicit value-attitude formulations, educational achievement, and economic and political behavior. Although there are other ways of viewing it, we propose that the latter behaviors are the outcomes of culturally determined differences in the incidence of personality characteristics such as n Achievement and authoritarianism among the three ethnic groups. If this view is correct, then personality differences between ethnic groups are factors deserving more attention in the analysis of contemporary African social behavior than they have heretofore received.

Postscript 1970

The research for *Dreams and Deeds* was done in 1962, little more than a year after Nigerian independence, and the book was written in 1964 except for a few comments on the current political situation added just before it went to press in January 1966. In retrospect, it seems to me that my analysis incorrectly presumed that the relative position of Nigerian ethnic groups with respect to education and modern occupations in 1962 represented a stable adjustment to the modernizing institutional environment. It now seems more reasonable to assume that the 1962 situation represented for each of the three ethnic groups studied its particular phase in an ethnic trajectory that should be viewed in historical perspective.

During the colonial period and early years of independence in Nigeria and some other African countries, there was a typical sequence of socioeconomic adjustment through which many ethnic groups and subgroups passed as their participation in modern educational and occupational institutions widened. There was (1) an early phase in which participation and the values accompanying it were confined to a few and expanded slowly, (2) a rapid expansion phase in which participation became a reality for a large number and the aspiration of the vast majority, (3) a stabilization phase, in which participation expanded at a slower rate as the group consolidated its position within a particular ecological niche specialized by occupation, trading commodity, or locality. As the groups who started early because of geographic position reached phase 3, groups starting later expanded first into ecological niches not already occupied and those offering the best opportunities at the time they reached phase 2. Some ecological niches became obsolete, giving advantages to late arrivals over early starters, and others became arenas for intense competition. The late starters also used the climate of ethnic competition to generate an ideology of "catching up" which moved them through phase 2 at a more rapid rate than their predecessors.

This uneven pattern of ethnic development in a changing institutional environment gave rise to a phenomenon that might be thought of as "leap-frogging", in which later groups succeed earlier ones in dominating the most rapidly expanding sectors of the economy or bureaucracy and gaining control over property, political power, and other crucial resources. Thus early-starting Nigerian groups such as the Egba (Yoruba) of Lagos and Abeokuta, the Efik, and the Onitsha Ibo became locally dominant early in the twentieth century but were later succeeded or superseded by the Ijebu (Yoruba) and the Ibo of Owerri (and adjacent areas); still later the people of Ondo and Ekiti in Yorubaland and many others elsewhere began "catching up." Hausa subgroups are also characterized by differential participation in trade and schooling, and it remains to be seen whether the established differences among them will be reinforced or changed by the current expansion of industry and education in the northern states. One point is clear: a comparison of Nigerian ethnic groups with respect to achievement behavior must take account of the pace of ongoing change in educational and occupational mobility within each ethnic group or subgroup.

Each group can be seen as beginning its participation slowly, accelerating it to a peak or asymptote, and then levelling off. The acceleration phase requires psychological mobilization of the population, and it is during this phase that we might expect the members of a group to be more preoccupied with success and achievement in modern terms. If this is true, then the same population tested before or after the acceleration phase should show less achievement motivation and values than during it. Hence group differences such as the ones reported in *Dreams and Deeds* might reflect the different phases in socioeconomic development that the groups happened to be in at the time of assessment, and assessing the same groups at an earlier or later period of history might have produced a different pattern of results. According to this theory, assessment thirty years earlier might have shown the Yoruba more preoccupied with achievement than the Ibo, and investigation thirty years later might show the Hausa more so than the groups in the south.

This historical theory, which I favor without any strong evidence to support my belief, is not necessarily inconsistent with the status-mobility hypothesis advanced in the book. The chronological period at which a group embarks on its trajectory of participation is obviously due to a variety of geographical and institutional factors determining access to modern schools and jobs, but the *rate* at which it moves through the phases outlined above, may be partly determined by the motives and values favored by the status-mobility system with which it begins the trajectory and enters the phase of acceleration. A group with an occupationally oriented status mobility system is, I would argue, likely to move more rapidly into and through the phase of acceleration, than one with a politically oriented system—other things being equal. Nigerian history suggests that other things have not been equal for its ethnic groups; beginning the sequences of phases in different places and at different periods in the development of Nigeria, they have encountered differing opportunity structures with different potentials for rapid expansion of educational and occupational participation. Precolonial status-mobility variations are thus confounded with other between-group variations, thwarting any attempt to detect their separate effects with certainty. Although a final conclusion may be impossible, it is at least possible to read the findings of my 1962 study as historical data, and that is what I recommend.

Note: The research and writing represented by the material published in this volume (both excerpts from the original book and the postscript) were supported by a National Institute of Mental Health Research Scientist Development Award (K02–MH–18, 444–08).

NOTES

1. Anthony F. C. Wallace, *Culture and Personality* (New York: Random House, 1962).

2. M. G. Smith, "The Hausa of Northern Nigeria," in *People of Africa*, ed. J. L. Gibbs (New York: Holt, Rinehart & Winston, 1965); "Introduction" in *Baba of Karo: A Woman of the Muslim Hausa* by Mary F. Smith (London: Faber & Faber, 1954); *The Economy of Hausa Communities of Zaria* (London: H.M.S.O., 1955); "The Hausa System of Social Status," *Africa, XXIX,* (1959), pp. 239–52; *Government in Zazzau* (London: Oxford University Press, 1960).

3. Smith, *Government in Zazzau,* p. 81.

4. *Ibid.,* p. 93.

5. *Ibid.,* p. 100.

6. *Ibid.,* p. 83.

7. *Ibid.,* p. 88.

8. *Ibid.,* p. 100.

9. *Ibid.,* p. 104.

10. *Ibid.,* p. 121.

11. *Ibid.,* pp. 252–53.

12. *Ibid.,* p. 106.

13. Smith, "Introduction," in *Baba of Karo,* pp. 31–33, and "The Hausa System of Social Status."

14. Smith, *Government in Zazzau,* pp. 244–45.

15. C. K. Meek, *Law and Authority in a Nigerian Tribe* (London: Oxford University Press, 1937).

16. G. I. Jones, "Ibo Land Tenure," *Africa, XIX* (1949), pp. 309–23; "Ibo Age Organization with Special Reference to the Cross River and Northeastern Ibo," *Journal of the Royal Anthropological Institute, XCII* (1962), pp. 191–211. Cf. also Daryll Forde and G. I. Jones, *The Ibo and Ibibio-Speaking Peoples of Southeastern Nigeria* (London: International African Institute, 1950).

17. M. M. Green, *Ibo Village Affairs* (London: Sidgwick and Jackson, 1948).

18. Simon Ottenberg, "Improvement Associations among the Afikpo Ibo," *Africa, XXV* (1955), pp. 1–28; "Double Descent in an Ibo Village-Group," *Proceedings of the Fifth International Congress of Anthropological and Ethnological Sciences* (1956), pp. 473–81; "Ibo Oracles and Intergroup Relations," *Southwestern Journal of Anthropology, XIV* (1958); "Ibo Receptivity to Change," *Continuity and Change in African Cultures,* ed. W. R. Bascom and M. J. Herskovits (Chicago: University of Chicago Press, 1958), pp. 130–43. Phoebe V. Ottenberg, "The Changing Economic Position of Women among the Afikpo Ibo," *Continuity and Change in African Cultures.* "The Afikpo Ibo of Eastern Nigeria," *Peoples of Africa,* ed. J. L. Gibbs.

19. Daryll Forde and G. I. Jones, *op. cit.,* p. 20.

20. Simon Ottenberg, "Ibo Receptivity to Change," pp. 136–37.

21. *Ibid.,* p. 138.

22. *Ibid.*

23. P. C. Lloyd, "The Yoruba of Nigeria," *Peoples of Africa,* ed. J. L. Gibbs; "The Yoruba Lineage," *Africa, XXV* (1955), pp. 235–251; "The Traditional Political System of the Yoruba," *Southwestern Journal of Anthropoloty, X* (1954), pp. 366–84; "Sacred Kingship and Government Among the Yoruba," *Africa, XXX* (1960), pp. 221–37; *Yoruba Land Law* (London: Oxford University Press, 1962). W. R. Bascom, "The Principle of Seniority in the Social Structure of the Yoruba," *American Anthropologist, XLIV* (1942), pp. 44–46; "Urbanization among the Yoruba," *American Journal of Sociology, LX* (1955), pp. 446–54; W. B. Schwab, "Kinship and Lineage Among the Yoruba," *Africa, XXV* (1955), pp. 352–74. Cf. also S. O. Biobaku, *The Egba and Their Neighbors 1842–1872* (London: Oxford University Press, 1957); Daryll Forde, *The Yoruba-Speaking Peoples of Western Nigeria* (London: International African Institute, 1950); J. F. A. Ajayi and Robert Smith, *Yoruba Warfare in the Nineteenth Century* (Ibadan, Nigeria: Cambridge University Press, 1964).

24. W. R. G. Horton, "The Boundaries of Explanation in Social Anthropology," *Man, XLIII* (1963), pp. 10–11.

25. Phoebe Ottenberg, "The Afikpo Ibo of Eastern Nigeria," *Peoples of Africa,* ed. J. L. Gibbs (New York: Holt, Rinehart & Winston, 1965), p. 6.

26. Cf. Simon Ottenberg, "Ibo Receptivity to Change," *Continuity and Change in African Cultures,* ed. W. R. Bascom and M. J. Herskovits (Chicago: University of Chicago Press, 1958), pp. 130–43.

27. Galletti, Baldwin et. al. *Nigerian Cocoa Farmers* (London: Oxford University Press, 1956).

28. Everett E. Hagen, *On the Theory of Social Change* (Homewood, Ill.: Dorsey Press, 1962).

29. *Ibid.,* p. 185.

30. James S. Coleman, *Nigeria: Background to Nationalism* (Berkeley and Los Angeles: University of California Press, 1958), p. 338.

31. *Ibid.,* pp. 133–40.

CHAPTER 8

Generalized Cultures and Evolutionary Adaptability: A Comparison of Urban Efik and Ibo in Nigeria[1]

RICHARD N. HENDERSON

Current anthropological concern about problems of modernization in the underdeveloped countries has attracted attention to the Ibo speaking peoples of Eastern Nigeria because of their apparent eagerness to accept Western patterns of life. Ottenberg explains this "receptivity to change" partly in terms of traditional Ibo culture, particularly their egalitarian individualism and achievement emphasis operating in a flexible system based on a multiplicity of social forms.[2] More recently, this notion of a "flexible system" has been extended by Morrill. Comparing urbanization processes among immigrant Ibo and the indigenous Ibibio-speaking Efik residing in the Nigerian city of Calabar, Morrill attributes a greater urbanizing "adaptability" among the Ibo to their "generalized" cultural tradition and argues that the Efik, in contrast, are culturally more "specialized" and therefore less adaptable to modern urbanism.[3] Analyses of this sort, which attempt to explain change in terms of concepts derived from evolutionary biology, have been gaining currency in recent years.[4] They deserve careful criticism

Reprinted from *Ethnology*, Vol. V, No. 4 (October 1966), pp. 365–391. Copyright © 1966 by *Ethnology*. Reprinted by permission of the publisher and Richard N. Henderson. The notes are presented in slightly revised form.

because upon their validity hinges the assessment of evolutionary concepts in the social sciences.

Building a defensible case for the differential "adaptability" of two cultures or societies requires several analytical steps. First, models of the two "traditional systems" must be constructed which concisely delimit a set of contrasting structural features within a framework of more general similarity. Second, differing structural changes in the two systems must be identified. Finally, these changes must be traced through time as processes of transformation in the traditional systems—transformations rendered intelligible in terms of both changing objective conditions and the changing subjective orientations of the actors and groups involved.[5] Only through analyses which combine systematic categorization of structural features with longitudinal tracing of change can we be certain that specific "adaptive" changes are related on the one hand to the presence of particular antecedent structures and on the other to given new conditions.

This paper applies a systematic comparative analysis to problems of Ibo and Efik responses to contemporary Nigerian urbanism. It begins with a critique of Morrill's model of Ibo and Efik adaptations in the Nigerian city of Calabar, redraws the model with greater precision, and then broadens the comparative perspective by introducing data from the Nigerian city of Onitsha. Finally, a historical analysis is made of the Onitsha case, in order to facilitate the assessment of the evolutionary concepts used by Morrill and to further illuminate the processes and problems of organizational innovation in contemporary Nigerian cities.

A MODEL OF CALABAR URBANISM

Calabar was an early settlement of Ibibio-speaking people, the Efik, located by the Cross River estuary in what is now Eastern Nigeria. Owing to its strategic location by the sea and its access to the Ibibio- and Ibo-speaking peoples inland, it became an urban center of the slave trade in the eighteenth century, and its people acted as middlemen trading Ibibio and Ibo slaves to the European slavers. In the latter part of the nineteenth century, it became a nucleus from which the British began their expansion of imperial control over Southern Nigeria, and thereby an important administrative, commercial, and educational center. Since the development of rail communications elsewhere in Nigeria, it has declined in significance but remains an important city with a population around 50,000. The numerically preponderant tribal groups are the indigenous Efik and the immigrant Ibo, the objects of Morrill's comparative study.

Paraphrasing Morrill's analysis, two base-line models are presented. The cultural background of the Ibo immigrants to Calabar is characterized as one of hard-working farmers on poor soil, who were also engaged in numerous specialized occupations and whose societies rested on ascriptive bases of descent which nevertheless had to be validated by achievement. There was diversity of political structure in different areas, but the village was consistently the widest political unit, and within it those who achieved could gain wide influence.[6] In contrast, the indigenous Efik of Calabar are described as people accustomed to an "easy life." During the slave trade, their wealth became concentrated in the hands of the ascriptively defined heads (*etubom*) of patrilineage "houses" (*ufok*), who became an emulated managerial and leisure class, so that working occupations other than farming came to be regarded as un-Efik. The Calabar Efik were tribally or multi-village organized and were controlled centrally by a "king" (*obong*) who operated in and through a secret society which cross-cut village divisions and was dominated by the patrilineage heads. Leadership was thereby fundamentally ascriptive.[7]

Morrill argues that these base-line cultural differences determined the emergence of a series of differences observable among the Ibo and Efik in Calabar today. It is especially notable that, although the Calabar Efik were among the first people of Eastern Nigeria to gain mission education, and although they early became favored administrators under the British, a recent sample of Efik and Ibo in Calabar reveals the apparent decline of a formerly more prominent people.

The Ibo first came to Calabar as slaves of the Efik, and later as laborers and traders. But today Ibo, and not Efik, dominate the enrollment in Calabar schools. According to Morrill's occupational data, about 30 per cent of the urban Efik call themselves farmers, suggesting a trend back toward emphasis on traditional subsistence activities, while about 15 per cent of Efik are unemployed, and almost none are willing to class themselves as unskilled laborers, for they prefer unemployment to work they consider demeaning. Commerce has been appropriated by the Ibo to the exclusion of the Efik, who instead seek clerical work. In this latter occupation the Efik percentage is somewhat higher than that of the Ibo, but the Ibo immigrants work not only as clerks and traders but at every other kind of job as well, and hardly any Ibo are willingly unemployed. The contrasting relevant statistics as provided by Morrill[8] are listed in Table I. In brief, the Ibo are reported as willing to do anything and to work hard in a great variety of occupations, whereas the Efik prefer to sit back and wait for prestige jobs or else to gain subsistence from traditional tasks.

TABLE 1

SOME PERCENTAGES OF OCCUPATIONS FOR EFIK AND IBO IN CALABAR

Occupation	Indigenous Efik (percentage)	Immigrant Ibo (percentage)
Farming	31	1
Unemployed	10–20	(few)
Commerce	(few)	32
Skilled trades	29	30
Unskilled labor	(few)	10
Clerical	16	15

Furthermore, the Ibo in Calabar have formed new voluntary associations to meet the urban situation. They have developed a series of interrelated "improvement unions," from the family or village unions which provide basic urban welfare services to the pan-Ibo Federal Union which has fought for Ibo rights in the city and has come to dominate urban politics. The very absence of traditional tribal unity above the village level, it is argued,[9] has made possible experimentation and innovation in tribal organization; in contrast, the indigenous Efik, whose orientations remain too ascriptive, have formed few new organizations (even these have proven ineffective), and they seem to be unable to develop organizational unity on new bases.

Morrill's explanation for these differences in occupational variety and success, and in the formation and effectiveness of urban tribal associations, is that the increased complexity of the urban environment demands increased occupational and organizational specialization. However, he argues, only "generalized" cultural backgrounds can foster such specializations, and Ibo culture was generalized in that it allowed a range of occupational and political alternatives in which men could gain influence by achievement. In contrast, Efik culture in adapting to the slave trade had become too specialized too early —occupationally, to the ideal of an easy life as a leisure and managerial class, and politically, to an ascriptively ordered system centralized at the tribal level. As expressed by Morrill.

> Efik were unable to maintain their dominance in the face of increasing complexity of the environment. Their social specialization confined them to a niche of increasingly less importance because they could not compete with the illiterate immigrants. The latter adapted to the new environment because they came from cultures which were generalized and therefore had potentiality for specializations to meet environmental shifts.[10]

This suggestive and challenging interpretation offers the evolutionary notion of "cultural specialization" versus "cultural generalization" as contrasting determinants of differential tribal adaptability to a highly complex urban situation. Before it can be assessed or elaborated, the cultural contrast must be recast, for both ethnographically and conceptually Morrill's presentation is inaccurate and somewhat misleading.

The predictive utility of the notion of a "generalized culture," capable of making a number of possible "adaptive specializations" to new environments, cannot be assessed unless the concept of "cultural generalization" is clearly defined. However, Morrill nowhere makes clear what he means by this term. On the one hand, it appears that he derives his picture of Ibo "generalized culture" by abstracting organizational patterns from a wide variety of village groups in the Ibo language area, and then he compares this overview of many communities with a single community of Ibibio-speaking Efik."[11] These are not comparable units. On the other hand, just what features are to be compared is also unclear. In several contexts Morrill[12] attempts to draw contrasts between the clearly symbolic (i.e., "cultural") features of Efik "ascription" and Ibo "achievement," but elsewhere he concentrates upon features of social organization such as the "wide variety of occupations" in "traditional Ibo culture," and on the "wide variety of alternatives" which it allowed to individuals within the single community.[13]

The confusion in this use of the idea of "generalized culture" results from a failure systematically to distinguish culture from social system.[14] If this important analytical distinction is drawn, it becomes evident that one may deal with either a "generalized culture" or a "generalized social system." Since Morrill's analysis pertains primarily to Ibo and Efik groups adapting to an urban environment in their social roles, it is the social system which is the primary object of comparison here.

However, strategic to the structuring of social systems are their cultural patterns of value orientation, especially the variables of universalism *versus* particularism and ascription *versus* achievement.[15] In social systems, universalism is associated with role relationships based on general rules defining abstract class membership criteria, while particularism is associated with role relationships based on a social object's particular relationships to Ego. Universalistic criteria are therefore symbolically generalized definitions of roles. Achievement defines role relationships in terms of an actor's performances, while ascription defines them in terms of an actor's "given" attributes and is therefore a less "flexible" criterion.

Although all societies utilize all of these criteria in defining various roles and groups, they vary in their degree of emphasis on different alternatives and in the extent to which the alternatives are structurally separated from one another. "Modern" societies emphasize univeralism and achievement while isolating and limiting the scope of particularism and ascription. "Primitive" societies, especially tribal systems organized around descent groups, strongly emphasize ascription and particularism. Since the problem under consideration here concerns members of tribal societies "adapting" to the conditions of "modern" urbanism, it may be argued that a tribal system which includes some distinct achieved and universalistic institutions is more "generalized" than one which does not, in the sense that the former is more capable of generating new solutions to social problems requiring flexible criteria of membership and new kinds of performance.

These distinctions are in fact crucial to the contrast which Morrill is trying to make between Ibo and Efik. As regards universalism *versus* particularism, he argues that the Efik had developed a particular multi-village tribal system possessing a definite structure of authority, while the Ibo had not developed beyond the level of autonomous villages within which there were no structured foci of leadership. In terms of the potential formation of new multi-village associations, then, the Ibo lacked a defined particularistic structuring of their "tribal" groupings and authority roles and were therefore open to new and more universalistically ordered experiments in a way in which the Efik were not. As regards ascription *versus* achievement, he argues that Ibo individuals were oriented toward seeking both new occupations and new positions of leadership, while the Efik were trained to rely on "given" seniority relationships and were therefore less capable of mobilizing initiative.

The difficulty with these contrasts, however, is not merely that they were not formulated clearly; they are also ethnographically inaccurate. Although it is clear enough that Ibo societies stressed achievement, it is less evident that the Calabar Efik were traditionally dominated by ascription, since some of the major accounts[16] suggest considerable achievement emphasis. Moreover, Morrill's view that Ibo societies were not organized above the village level is simply incorrect.

Adequate comparison of Ibo and Efik societies requires careful analysis of roles and subgroups in order to permit assessment of these variables of value orientation. An overall characterization of Ibo systems must be phrased initially in terms of their structural complexity, for, as Ottenberg has observed, the Ibo differ sharply from flexible but "loosely structured" social systems

> in that they have clearly defined, well-organized, and effective social groupings, particularly unilineal organizations but also age-grades, village societies, and other as-

sociations. The "flexibility" in Ibo [social systems] does not lie in any structural weakness in these groupings but in individuals' ability to work through and across them to achieve desired goals and in their freedom to select alternative activities.[17]

An Ibo social system might, then, be considered "generalized" in the sense that it possesses a considerable extent of role differentiation but that no one role or role-set is overwhelmingly dominant in terms of prestige or control over the activities of the others. In such a system there are alternative models of organization and role definition.

The following discussion develops a base-line model of the social structure of the indigenous Onitsha Ibo community in Eastern Nigeria. This provides a departure for recasting the comparison between the Efik and Ibo in line with what has been said above and for broadening the terms of that comparison. The Onitsha community, unlike an abstracted "Ibo culture," constitutes a unit directly comparable to the Calabar Efik and to various similar Ibo communities as well.

PRE-COLONIAL ONITSHA IBO SOCIETY

Onitsha today, like Calabar, has become a major commercial, administrative, and educational center of Eastern Nigeria, but, in contrast to Calabar, both the indigenous and the major immigrant populations are Ibo-speaking. Analysis will focus upon the indigenous group, the Onitsha, as opposed to the immigrants or non-Onitsha Ibo, who will be referred to simply as Ibo.

Prior to the period of European domination, Onitsha was one of many independent northern Ibo "village-groups," as these multi-village communities are called, but was distinctive in that it was located at the only point on the lower Niger where the uplands of Eastern Nigeria extend westward to the river. It thereby became an early focus of market exchange and later a center for European penetration of the eastern interior. The traditional Onitsha "town" (*obodo*), estimated in 1857 to have a population of about 13,000,[18] was divided into a number of villages. In the traditional system, each Onitsha village was normatively also a patrilineage, but the two kinds of units were distinguished from one anther. The village (*ogbe*) emerged as a residential unit which had possessed at one time a representative chief (*ndičie*) selected from amongst its members by achievement criteria (in theory, for valor in war), and it possessed the organizational features of a masquerade society and an age-grade system. The patrilineage (*umunna*), however, was organized through a hierarchy of priests (*ɔkpala*) who succeeded by strict sibling seniority[19] and who controlled by ascribed right the lineage estate of houseland, farmland, dwellings, women, and shrines. The chiefs had no special rights in these lineage estates, although they represented villages and subvillages which were usually also segments of patrilineages.

Both patrilineage and village were relativistic conceptions for the Onitsha in that they were applied on a sliding scale. The *umunna* ranged in application from its primary meaning, "children of father," to the widest range of recognized patrilineal kinsmen, and many segmentary levels of such groupings might hold significant common estates. More remarkably, *ogbe* might likewise be applied to several nested levels of residential groupings or "villages," and, as there were three status levels of chiefs in Onitsha, it was possible for three residential levels simultaneously to be represented by chiefs, just as there was a hierarchy of patrilineage priests.[20] One must inquire, then, about the interrelations between chief and patrilineage priest.

There were important differences between these two roles. The patrilineage priesthood was an ascribed role—a "given" following from legitimate birth order—and it was diffusely defined, involving pervasive "patrifilial" relations which applied to any social context. The chiefly role, in contrast, was by definition achieved, and it was less diffusely defined, involving decision-making prerogatives in disputes and in war as well as rights in certain prestigeful ceremonies. The two roles were regarded as incompatible in that high-level chiefs and major or maximal lineage priests could not be the same person; however, chiefs might be patrilineage priests at low levels of lineage segmentation.

While there was a strong pressure for separation of these two roles, both were grounded in a common religious matrix. Both lineage priests and persons seeking to attain chieftaincy first had to undergo a ritual purification involving achievement through wealth expenditure, which made them titled men (*ndi-ɔzɔ*) of quasi-ancestral status. In eight of the nine major descent groups of Onitsha, this purification was bestowed upon their own members by the exceptionally "purified" maximal lineage priest (*eze idi*) of each group. In the ninth (and largest) descent group, however, a change had occurred; the sacred person who bestowed purification was not the purified maximal lineage priest but rather a son of a junior lineage segment, who was selected not only by his own senior lineage priests but by all the chiefs and descent groups of the town. This person was the inchoate Onitsha "king" (*eze oniča*).

The king had the right to bestow chieftaincy upon titled men of the community,[21] presided over plenary councils of his chiefs, and in theory made the ultimate decisions on all community issues. However, he lacked an independent means of administration, for the chiefs ritually validated their positions and could not be dismissed. Because of the spiritual bases of his greatness, both he and his wives had to be secluded and hedged in by a variety of other ritual restrictions. These were important limitations, for the women of Onitsha possessed a title system reflecting that of the men and involving their roles as traders, and chiefs through their trading wives and sisters traditionally directed partnerships active in community marketing. The king had little control over these independent chiefs, the seniors of whom emulated some of the symbolic trappings of the King's own greatness and whose strivings for power were limited mainly by their competitive multiple numbers.

Consideration of these roles suggests that Onitsha society had important elements of prestige stratification and hierarchy. However, it was not a fully "stratified" society, for in important senses all descent groups and/or villages were segmentarily "equal." First, although there was a "royal" lineage, this was highly segmented and comprised the major portion of the population, and the non-royal groups oriented to their own "hidden" or "silent" kings (*eze idi*), who in some senses were equal or superior to the king in traditional prestige. Second, the senior chieftaincies, which approached the status of the king so that in a sense he was *primus inter pares,* were distributed to the major residential units of the community partly in accordance with their numerical strength. Third, all major lineage segments were exogamous, and, since this exogamy comprised the only prescriptive rule in the marriage system, all descent groups were intertwined as equals in a web of affinal relations.

Age-grades (*ɔgbɔ*) organized men in Onitsha by the universalistic, ascriptive criterion of age at the village level, while age-sets and senior level age-grades crosscut villages and their members might emerge at the community (*obodo*) level of social control. They would do this by escorting sacred masquerades, which were owned by masquerade "secret societies" composed of village members but whose leadership was partly distinct from lineage priesthood and chieftaincy and was sharply separated from the kingship. In the context of age-set and masquerade activities, leadership was open to men who had not won formal titles or reached ascriptive seniority but who could influence others through oratory which exalted traditional values. At crises the orator-spokesman (*ɔnu-ekwulu-ɔra*), by appealing at public assemblies to the relatively universalistic values of age-sets and simultaneously to the ascriptive, tradition-oriented values of the masquerade, could mobilize these units into a massed organization which might oppose any other leadership roles and thus exercise decisive power. The role of orator, then, was relatively universalistic in the sense that it crosscut village and descent-group loyalties, whereas the other leadership roles were particularistically defined in that they related to particular memberships in village or descent groups. It was achieved, and it tended to be defined with reference to specific situations, giving the orator no general status prerogatives.

To summarize and interpret this material, four points are relevant. First, the Onitsha polity was not limited to the village (*ogbe*) level but included a higher level of village-group or "town" (*obodo*) integration. In this regard it was similar not only to the Calabar Efik but to most other Ibo communities. Ibo multi-village systems might unite a population comparable in numbers to that of the Calabar Efik tribe, and, contrary to Morrill, these communities were likely to be crosscut by unified age-set systems which in some cases attained multi-town levels of integration.[22] Therefore the level of political organization *per se* is not a point of contrast between Efik and Ibo.

Second, Onitsha concepts of village and patrilineage were relativistic, sliding, generalized scales of group definition, again typically Ibo, but the association of the "town" level of integration with a priest-king role was not universal among Ibo though it did occur among Northern and Western Ibo. There is no consistent evidence that the Calabar Efik contrasted very sharply with the Onitsha or many other Ibo in this regard.[23]

Third, the Onitsha community possessed not one set of leadership roles but several differentiated ones, interrelated in a complex manner merely hinted at here. The most remarkable of these was the universalistic, achieved role of the orator-spokesman which, in its dynamic relationship to the age-sets, possessed a structural similarity to modern "mass" democratic organizations. Besides these various roles (some of which had counterparts among women), there were a number of recognized occupational specialties (*omenka*). In their general development of role differentiation, the Onitsha were typically Ibo but contrasted with the Calabar Efik, who by all accounts were less differentiated and appear to have emphasized one major role set.

Fourth, the Onitsha possessed the beginnings of a system of status stratification by prestige in the form of several sets of high-prestige roles. It also had an incipient centralization of co-ordinating control, consisting in the insitutionalized requirement that the king should legitimize any community-binding decision, however made. However, his effective powers were so slight that he could neither halt feuds between villages nor mobilize all of them against an external threat. There was a high degree of devolution of authority, so that various actors, including women, might on occasion take political initiative. In prestige terms, although the king was laden with awesome spiritual qualities, there were other roles (senior chiefs and "hidden" kings) which were considered in some senses equal to his.

These patterns of stratification and decision-making were (with the exception of the Onitsha king's right to select chiefs and to "legitimize" decisions) typical for many Ibo groups, and to some extent they contrast with those of the Calabar Efik. It appears that in pre-colonial Calabar a single major role complex, that of the *etubom* representing the lineage "house," dominated the social system, and that these roles were partly "ascriptively defined"; but the *etubom* have always been chosen partly for demonstrated ability, and active leadership in Calabar traditionally could be attained only by advancing in the many-graded secret society ranks through ritual distribution of wealth to grade members.[24]

It would seem, therefore, that the differences between the Efik and Ibo involved role differentiation more than ascription and achievement. The Calabar Efik may have been rather more "centralized" than the Ibo in that the king as a member of the highest grade in the secret society was in a position to mobilize the lower grades to do his bidding, but the embedding of his decision-making powers within the heavily ritualized company of his high-grade peers indicates strong balances against his powers and authority.[25] This secret society was also the sole structure involving universalistic membership criteria in Calabar, but being bound up with the *etubom* and with kingship it lacked the organizational independence of the Ibo age-set and orator-spokesman complex and was therefore of less structural significance. Finally, while the secret-society grade system and the societal prominence of the *etubom* and king suggest a hierarchy of prestige, all accounts indicate that the exogamous "houses" of Calabar were relatively equal in status,[26] so that the system remained "segmentary" in this sense.

To summarize, the Onitsha and other Ibo may be characterized as differentiated and "balanced" role systems in contrast to the less differentiated and "ritual-centralized" Calabar Efik system; both groups exhibit some trend towards prestige hierarchy, but the two Ibo systems institutionalize more elaborately the criteria of achievement and possess independent universalistic structures. It could be predicted in line with Morrill's thesis, then, that the indigenous Onitsha Ibo would contrast sharply with the Efik of Calabar in their adaptation as indigenes to the forces of modernizing urbanism in greater Onitsha and would instead manifest patterns similar to Ibo immigrants. At this point it will be illuminating to examine the occupational and associational structure of the modern community of greater Onitsha, bearing in mind the data for Calabar summarized above in Table 1.

THE MODERN URBAN ONITSHA COMMUNITY

Today the traditional Onitsha village-group has been encapsulated by a massive immigration of hinterland Ibos, as greater Onitsha has become one of modern Nigeria's largest and most important commercial, educational, and administrative centers. Nevertheless, the traditional village-group community has maintained its residential and cultural integrity as the Onitsha "Inland Town," while the immigrant Ibos have gradually settled in the "Waterside" or commercial area as individuals, and not in tribal enclaves. During 1961 the author conducted an anthropological census in several villages of the traditional community and in selected areas of the "Waterside." Occupational data derived from this research bear comparison with Morrill's data for Calabar, and are herewith summarized in Table 2.

TABLE 2

A SAMPLE OF OCCUPATIONS IN ONITSHA TOWN[27]

Occupation	Indigenous Onitsha (percentage)	Immigrant Ibo (percentage)
Farming	13	3
"Pensioners"	5	1
"Householders"	9	0
"Applicants" and other unemployed	16	0
Commerce	3	40
Skilled trades	15	31
Unskilled labor	3	11
Clerical	21	10
Supervisory	7	1

Comparison of the distribution of these percentages with those of Table 1 shows that occupationally the home-village-resident Onitsha indigenes are very similar to the Efik of Calabar but are strikingly different from the immigrant Ibo of both Calabar and greater Onitsha, who in turn are closely similar to one another. If the unemployed "pensioners," "householders," and "applicants" are grouped together with subsistence farmers as a category of persons standing outside the modern occupational structure, more than 40 per cent of the indigenous adult males have been accounted for. Over 21 per cent are clerks (or teachers), but very few call themselves traders or unskilled laborers, for these occupations are regarded as beneath the dignity of a "real Onitsha man." As in Calabar, the immigrant Ibo engage in a great variety of occupations, with commerce and skilled trades predominant, but almost none are willingly idle.

Furthermore, turning to organizational innovation, the local indigenous Onitsha Improvement Union has proved an ineffective social unit and is today moribund, while the immigrant Ibo have organized flourishing improvement unions in Onitsha and have combined these to further their political interests in an organization called significantly the "Non-Onitsha Ibos Association," which has enabled them to gain political dominance in local civic affairs. Again the Onitsha indigenes parallel the Calabar Efik in their responses.

At this stage of analysis, then, these contrasts in modern urban ecology and social structure cannot be understood directly in terms of the structural diversity, role differentiation, or value orientations of the traditional systems. Although an alternative explanation might be advanced involving the common traditional Onitsha and Efik characteristic of a centralized focus of decision-making, it is clearly too facile to infer directly from general structural differences in precolonial systems to differences in modern urban adjustments. The necessary next step is a careful time-depth analysis of the urbanization process in Onitsha, an analysis which takes into account the introduction of major organizational developments associated with "modernization": rational-legal bureaucracies, market systems based on money, generalized universalistic legal norms, democratic associations, and the Western educational facilities which serve to inculcate knowledgeable orientations to these institutions.[28]

ANALYSIS OF ONITSHA HISTORY

The Mission Impact

Like Calabar, Onitsha was early settled by European and Sierra Leonean traders and missionaries, who in 1857 occupied a portion of the "Waterside" and began the effort to halt the slave trade by substituting Christian humanitarian ethics and legitimate trade. For a quarter of a century thereafter, foreign traders and missionaries lived within the political orbit of the Onitsha king and his chiefs. The secluded king merely received periodic tribute, but the Onitsha chiefs and titled men, free to engage openly in secular activities, used their wives, sisters, and female slaves to manipulate trade relationships with the local foreign Christians. Traditional history and early historical records indicate a progressive increase in the scope of achieved status and a trend towards political decentralization during this period, particularly through a rise in the powers of wealthy chiefs at the expense of the king.

Meanwhile, the elders of Onitsha grudgingly sent their lesser sons or young slaves to the Christians for mission education; these youths were educated, then trained as clerks in the local "factories" and as teachers and emissaries of the gospel. Some of these converts began using their new Christian contacts to develop roles as local traders, breaking a traditional ban on direct male trading activities and in some cases overshadowing the Onitsha women traders. Such men gained positions as intermediaries between the foreign trading and mission community and the chiefs and king. Other converts began going out with the missionaries among the continguous Ibo communities, which had been sporadically at war with Onitsha but which began accepting "enlightened" Onitsha Ibo missionaries as esteemed carriers of the new and powerful culture. Thus in two spheres of activity, neither of which was traditional in any sense, new occupational roles emerged for the Onitsha people.

Inevitably converts occupied contradictory statuses. As their wealth and influence expanded, they were tempted to emulate the chiefs in keeping many wives and slaves, and were expected to validate their enhanced status by the expensive rituals of title-taking. As Christians, however, they were expected by the missionaries to abhor polygyny, slavery, and pagan ritual, and to press for radical community reforms. In order to gain stable status positions such men had either to change their reference orientations entirely, or defect from the mission.

Both alternatives began to be followed in the early period. The first solution drew catechists (and their families) away from Onitsha status references toward living as honored missionaries among the hinterland tribes; this encouraged an interlocal orientation. The second led active traders away from the church, so that they allied themselves with the traditional chiefs and sought to gain influence in the traditional community by taking titles. This infused some educated leadership into chiefly roles but simultaneously generated socially disruptive processes, which in 1879 brought conspiring Onitsha chiefs and their defected-convert cohorts under fire from British guns and caused a temporary evacuation of the mission and trading establishments.[29]

From this time into the 1880s, these changes accelerated. The missions at Onitsha became competitive as the Anglican Church Missionary Society (CMS) was joined at the Waterside by an ambitious Roman Catholic Mission (RCM), and it became fashionable for the Onitsha indigenes to defect from one to the other. Competition forced both CMS and RCM into more actively evangelizing the continguous Ibo hinterland. Meanwhile, the various trading companies which had settled on the river joined together to defend themselves against the unsurpations of chiefs and their semi-educated cohorts. This amalgamated firm made treaties with the chiefs of the various communities on the Niger bringing them under the protection and jurisdiction of the company, and gained a royal charter from the British to act as Government along the river under the name of Royal Niger Company. The company hired some of the local Onitsha converts as police, and some of them gained great wealth from their positions of power, turned aside from church affairs, and stabilized their positions in the community by taking traditional titles and becoming chiefs.

Therefore, when in 1905 the British Government set up a District base at Onitsha, from which to open and stablize the Ibo hinterland to the east, three new trends had been established in traditional Onitsha society. First, some Christian Onitsha men had become active, successful traders, thus ending a traditional proscription on direct trading by men. Second, the competing churches were educating others to leave the community and to live as catechists and teachers among the contiguous Ibo peoples. Third, some semi-educated personnel had been infused into the stratum of chiefs, and even the king was mission-trained. This limited the opposition between the old order and the new and ensured a continuing level of prestige for traditional chiefly leadership.

British Rule and Its Occupational Consequences

The British had encouraged the development of this situation in Onitsha, and when they became the colonial power they took full advantage of it. Importing their rational-legal bureaucracy, the colonial officials began recruiting local Onitsha convert teachers into their administrative staff for the purpose of expanding orderly control over the vast, heavily populated, and socially disrupted Ibo interior regions. Subsequently government, competing missions, and trading firms moved out together into the hinterland, and all three organizations used educated Onitsha men as intermediaries because, as Ibo-speakers, they could quickly grasp the dialects of the peoples living to the east. In the new bureaucratic role of Court Clerk, some Onitsha men attained levels of wealth never before realized in the Onitsha community.

By the 1920s, more than half of the non-European administrative staff of Onitsha Province was composed of Onitsha men (the remainder were mainly Sierra Leoneans and men from the Gold Coast), although the Onitsha community comprised only a tiny fraction of the population of the province.[30] This continuous, perennially expanding occupational demand drew Onitsha people out of their home community in large numbers and scattered them as administrators, company clerks, and educators in the Local Authority Headquarters and burgeoning cities all over Nigeria. By 1931, for example, the population of the "Inland Town" had dropped from the 13,000 estimated in 1857 to an estimated 3,271.[31] By the 1930s, educated Onitsha men had become a part of a permanent urban elite scattered all over Nigeria, and today they retain this elite status on the national level. The number of Onitsha men who have attained great prominence in Nigerian affairs is remarkable in proportion to their total population, and since they provided one of the first truly interlocally oriented elite strata of Nigerians, it is perhaps not surprising that some of the most active nationalistic Nigerian politics have been natives of Onitsha.

But even as new colonial developments were orienting many

Onitsha people interlocally, the British administrators were also following policies which provided legal support to some aspects of the traditional Onitsha society but undermined others. They had intervened in an interregnum dispute in 1900 and bestowed kingship upon a semi-educated former cook trained under the RCM, who belonged to a long-dispossessed segment of the "royal" patrilineage. This generated a major split in the community, but by giving the king a seat on the District Native Court the Government supported his role. They also placed certain sophisticated Onitsha men in positions of jurisdiction over the affairs of the "Waterside" and gave them seats on the Native Court, and these men followed the established pattern of achieving traditional titles and chieftaincy.

For a time, some of these Onitsha chiefs were also vested with the right to call out men from various age-sets in their Inland Town villages to do communal labor for the administration. This resulted in a rapid decline of age-set solidarity, which, along with Government's strict suppression of the violent traditional sanctions of the masquerade society, weakened the old structural limitations on the ambitions of powerful men.

However, the British administrators also applied their universalistic legal standards to the support of native land law and thereby strengthened the traditional role of patrilineage priest. As lineage-owned Onitsha farm lands became valuable urban property, a renaissance of ancestor worship and title-taking occurred in the community, and there developed a struggle amongst chiefs, king, and others to ally themselves to important land-controlling priests. The community split into a welter of factions expressing their conflicts through land litigation and disputes over rights to chieftaincy and to lineage priesthood succession, but simultaneously the centrifugal force of interlocal movement had been counterbalanced by permanent local interests in land.

Finally, the Pax Britannica also made it possible for the first time for Ibos from the hinterlands to enter Onitsha town freely in search of work. They were recruited by the Government as laborers, because as hungry men from the overpopulated bush they were more tractable and willing to work for lower wages than were the urbanized local Onitsha indigenes. Immigrant

Ibos also attached themselves to Onitsha converts living in the Waterside and to non-native traders; and, calling their kinsmen into the city after them, they proceeded to develop trading networks with their home towns which began to by-pass the indigenous Onitsha middlemen. When the Administration introduced changes to develop a market system based on money and modern modes of exchange, Onitsha women opposed them while the immigrants responded positively. When the Onitsha Main Market was moved to permit rationalization and greater expansion, Onitsha women lost their traditional advantages of market location and control, while the immigrant Ibos constructed a *pasar* type of marketing system which swamped Onitsha traders. The first independent African trade association in Nigeria had been represented on the national Legislative Council by an Onitsha man who was a prominent trader; but he was one of the last, and today most Onitsha men deny they would engage in such an occupation, which they derogate as a woman's role. Instead, Onitsha people concentrated on controlling rents in market stalls, urban houses, and land.

Interpretation of Occupational Trends

The discussion thus far provides a basis for understanding the occupational structure of the modern Onitsha community (cf. Table 2). The high rate of unemployment among the local Onitsha indigenes and their unwillingness to engage in commerce or unskilled labor must be viewed, not primarily as a result of old ascriptive orientations or cultural or social "specializations" *per se,* but rather as reflections of a highly selected population whose orientations are the result of a long-range structuring of opportunities within and without the city.

The most prominent cluster of indigenous occupations— farmers, pensioners, unemployed householders, and applicants —represents two social categories. The first comprises retired elders, some of whom now occupy roles of patrilineage priest or chief, while others are simply beyond working age and indigent. The better-off are living on small pensions, rents from patrilineage lands and houses, fees received as chiefs, or in some cases aid from their more successful nonresident kins-men. The elderly poor augment their subsistence by small-scale farming on nearby patrilineage lands. The second category comprises younger Onitsha men who have failed in striving for education and/or for senior civil service jobs. These "youths," if uneducated, attach themselves to local Inland Town politicians and lawyers as thugs, messengers, or touts. If they have some education they attempt to become "cultural experts" within the traditional community by attaching them-selves to a prominent elder and by occupying posts as secretar-ies of such varied local organizations as the patrilineage, the age-set, the local political movement. They may be hired as teachers within the urban community, but they do not care for teaching as a career; instead they seek greater wealth and op-portunity through political activity. The stratum of "alienated youth" in greater Onitsha is dominated by Onitsha indigenes. In short, the Onitsha Inland Town has become in part a welfare home for the underprivileged and the retired.

There is a small proportion of Onitsha indigenes who hold supervisory occupations (cf. Table 2), including some wealthy contractors and senior civil service personnel. These are the few educated men who have managed to find their occupa-tional niches within the city and who furthermore have inter-ests which draw them to reside within the traditional section of town. They are men who may seek to dominate the politics of the indigenous community and who are likely to aspire to positions of high title.

Development of Tribal Unions in Onitsha

The indigenes of Onitsha were early leaders of the "improve-ment union" movement in Nigeria, and like other initiators they began their union during the 1920s in urban centers away from home where they were free from traditional constraints. However, their Onitsha Improvement Union developed rather differently from those of more rural-based Ibo, for shortly after successful "branch organizations" had been established in Lagos, Jos, Enugu, and other more advanced urban centers, a "mother" or "home" branch was also inaugurated in Onitsha by a small core of local educated elite.

During the late 1920s and early 1930s the British administration in Onitsha sought to introduce indirect rule in Ibo country based on the traditional authorities, and to build a model Onitsha Town Native Authority utilizing the most "advanced" Ibo rulers, namely the Onitsha king and his chiefs. By this time, two indigenous strata of self-styled elite had emerged in the traditional town. The first was an established semi-educated (or at least semi-cosmopolitan) elite represented by the king, his chiefs, and some aspiring titled men—a "neo-traditional" group which recognized the expanding importance of chieftaincy in the coming new order of local government. The second was a small local "new elite" of strongly Anglicized and Christianized school teachers and clerks, who aspired to introduce a fully British pattern of life into local affairs but who had no organization or traditional positions. It was evident to these young educated men that "progress" toward these ends would be attained at a very slow rate if initiative were left to the king and his chiefs, since almost every modernizing innovation proposed by the British and accepted by the king was automatically opposed by a bloc of senior chiefs, and the community was thereby immobilized by factionalism.[32]

As the Government held out the promise of a new order of chiefly rule, the Onitsha king died in 1931, and the indigenous community fragmented in political struggle. At the same time, the immigrant Ibo of the Waterside were beginning to organize their tribal groupings. A new development then took place in the Inland Town, which restored some of the checks and balances on conflict formerly operative in the traditional system. A self-educated Onitsha man of low birth, who had been a leader in several kinds of local enterprises, assumed the traditional role of orator-spokesman and called upon the Onitsha indigenes to forget their conflicts and to reconcile the glories of their tradition with modern requirements of education and unity. He remobilized the moribund age-sets into a mass organization which gave decisive support to the most educated of the king candidates, and the revitalized age-sets then re-established orderly relations among the neo-traditional elite.

It was in this tradition-renascent context among the indigenes that the educated "new elite" began their "home" branch of the OIU. These men were in contact with friends in the more advanced centers and were therefore aware of the new tribal associations developing elsewhere, as well as among the local Ibo Waterside residents. They had gained positions of relative prestige in local European-controlled organizations (the United African Company, the provincial administration, the missions), and they sought to exploit their new opportunities by forming this organization.

In 1935 the Home Branch of OIU initiated its program of activities. First, its charter members defined themselves as an English-emulating, Christian-enlightened elite, and they therefore screened Home Union membership very carefully to exclude uneducated, unemployed, and parasitical "natives" or "boys," as they referred to the lower strata of the traditional community, and they also discouraged active participation by the traditional heads of the community by refusing to take part in the important pagan funeral ceremonies of traditional life. They made Westernization the criterion for membership, and they courted the goodwill of the British administrators by opening a tennis court to which European guests were invited and by sending delegations to the District Officer with constructive suggestions for civic improvement. By these activities they gained the respect of the administration, so that when, in 1938, the Onitsha Town Native Authority Council of the king and his chiefs was expanded to include members of the "educated class," most of the untitled men appointed by the Government were members of the Home Branch of OIU.

Second, the Home Union attempted to amalgamate the various branch unions located "abroad" into a Federal Union under their control, and in 1936 they succeeded in registering the union under government ordinance as a unitary body, overriding the initial objections of the larger and better established Lagos branch. They thereby gained the right to screen and direct all "federal" projects.

Third, they sought to establish themselves under the aegis of the Onitsha king. Toward this end, they arranged for the king to act as "patron" of the Home Union, and offered their services in arranging the non-ritual aspects of his annual public festival. With these efforts and with the prestige conferred upon them by the local authorities, they seem to have obtained an advantageous position in community affairs, and they began pressuring the king and his councillors to recognize them as the official agents of modernization in the indigenous community.

After reaching this initial peak of prestige and accomplishment, however, the OIU Home Union faltered, lost its initiative first on the local and then on the Federal level, and progressively lost membership until by 1961 it was moribund and the branch unions also showed drops in membership from the levels attained in the thirties. The causes of this general decline were many, but the course of events can be briefly summarized.

First, when the Home Union as an elitist group pressured the traditional authorities to accept them as a new and prominent component of the community, a reaction developed. Two men whose educational attainments had been barely sufficient to gain them membership in the union, but who were regarded as orator-spokesmen in the indigenous society, began to demand that a mass movement with universal democratic membership should be organized to direct town improvement. Rebuffed on the grounds that the "quality" of the Home Union must be protected, they resigned from it and mobilized the renascent age-set organization, forming a "Committee of Forty-nine" drawn equally from the seven most active sets. This Committee began agitating for a plenary meeting of the Inland Town to decide which local organization would direct its progress.

At this meeting, attended by the king, his chiefs in council, and all interested persons of the Inland Town, the orator-spokesmen of the Committee argued that, as a mass organization catering not to special elite interests but to the interests of all, the age-sets should control the directing of change, while the Home Branch of OIU maintained that the age-sets could be represented in their centrally and efficiently organized, interlocally attuned, and literate body. Since the king and his chiefs were supported in their own positions by the progress-oriented British Government, they could not oppose "progress" by rejecting both organizations. They selected the orator-led age sets, which were most responsive to their own directives and which had mobilized mass consensual support in a traditional way, as the official agent to direct civic improvement.

This strategic failure of the Home OIU to establish an institutionalized relation to the traditional social structures greatly weakened its position. While the age-sets (whose victory had in effect strengthened and stabilized the positions of the senior age-grades, the chiefs, king, and lineage priests) turned their new legislative powers to the task of making small modifications of traditional practices, the Home Union was forced to cast about for some independent project which would re-establish their superiority. They shifted their policy toward universal democratic membership, but now had difficulty in attracting desirable new members, for they had no program which immediately appealed to the local people. Meanwhile, the branch unions abroad were demanding some evidence of accomplishment that would validate the Home Union's continuing central position in the Federal network.

A situation peculiar to the indigenous groups living within modernizing urban centers in Nigeria is that many of the needed welfare projects most amenable to mobilization by improvement unions (schools, dispensaries, etc.) were early undertaken by the government or the missions. It was not accidental that the Home OIU had begun its career by constructing a tennis court for the use of an anglophile elite rather than, for instance, building a maternity home of benefit to everyone.

To regain its initiative, the Home Union therefore sought to build an impressive town hall for the use of Onitsha indigenes, and to start a modest scholarship program. From the beginning, however, there was a lack of cooperation between the home and branch unions. The Lagos Branch, for example, which had been established before 1920, and which already had an active scholarship program when the Home Union became prominent, refused to forego their own projects in the interest of centralizing funds. Although the annual Federal Meetings (dominated by the Home Union, which consistently had the most delegates on the scene) continually voted levies from each branch toward building the hall, the Home Branch was unable actually to collect the funds. Begun in 1939, construction of the hall tottered along into the 1950s, and the ramshackle building which ultimately resulted became a disgrace for the OIU.

During and after World War II, when the Home Branch sought to widen its local support by admitting all educated indigenous youths, a number of the "cultural experts"—the educated but marginally employed who seek opportunistically to make their livings off various local organizations—became active in the Home Union, and one popular view of the town-hall debacle holds that "many thousands of pounds" contributed by the branches were simply embezzled by these persons. Although there is no evidence beyond hearsay that more than £500 was ever allocated to the project, its failure greatly diminished the stature of the Home Union. Without an accepted headquarters providing central direction, the branch unions themselves have lacked foci of common interest and have tended to split internally over matters of social status.

Underlying these developments has been a common denominator involving the orientations of Onitsha men as Nigerians. In contrast to the unified and active Ibo "town" and divisional unions, the OIU never established any approximation to compulsory universal membership; in fact, the initial definitions of their groupings appear to have been generally class-based and exclusive. However, even after World War II when a concerted effort was made everywhere to woo maximum membership, OIU branches frequently reported widespread lack of interest and outright refusal to join. The basis for this contrast lies in the fact that Onitsha men "abroad" are more thoroughly urbanized and more individualistic in their social orientations than are their Ibo counterparts, because their education, manifold urban experience, and general occupational security (whether directly through salaries or indirectly through "welfare aid" from wealthy kinsmen) have given them greater independence from the collective constraints of Union demands. One of the most common contrasts drawn by Onitsha men between themselves and other Ibo concerns this compulsory aspect of many Ibo unions, which they ridicule as indicative of sheeplike mentality and as offensive to the Onitsha man's concept of his individuality. Those indigenes living outside of Onitsha tend to regard themselves as Nigerians first and Onitsha men secondarily.

The Ibo immigrants to Onitsha contrast with this overall pattern of organizational development in almost every way. As immigrants they faced serious problems of residence and occupation and lacked the economic independence of those who had education and could obtain bureaucratic posts; they were therefore initially dependent upon their fellow tribesmen for welfare aid and were readily committed to compulsory union membership. The implications of such universal compulsion for organizational solidarity and for effectiveness in mobilizing communal effort should be evident to anyone versed in the character of social systems. Moreover, the immigrants came mostly from rural areas sorely lacking in even rudimentary amenities of modernization, and therefore, wherever such urban unions became effective in mobilizing even small donations from large numbers of people, they became able, by turning some of these funds back into the rural areas, to exert strong influence and even domination over their less effectively organized natal communities.

Although the Ibo immigrants possessed traditional social knowledge and orientations not dissimilar to those of local Onitsha indigenes, by immigrating they found the scope of their traditional commitments sharply limited, and their context of operation and innovation was thereby simplified. In the city, some traditional value orientations might remain relevant, but traditional role foci did not, and within the framework of compulsory union membership the committed group was able to tailor their organization to meet the requirements at hand, without finding it necessary to come immediately to terms with recalcitrant traditional authorities. Under these circumstances, some unions built federated organizations so radically different and more effective than traditional ones that these unions came to overshadow the traditional rural authorities. This was a sharply different situation from that faced by the Onitsha new elite, who found that the very "flexibility" of their traditional Ibo social structure, the very multiplicity of its social forms, and the diversity of its role types facilitated the continual revision and revitalization of traditional role structures, so that these limited and even overwhelmed new forms of modernizing organization.

Finally, the Home Branch of OIU failed in yet another way to make their organization significant in urban development, namely, by participation in an active local Ibo State (or Federal) Union. The Home Branch of OIU was unable to integrate in this structure, although the ISU was present in Onitsha just as in Calabar, simply because a part of the indigenes' self-definition was their contraposition to the increasingly vocal community of immigrant Ibo living in the commercial Water-side town. Although frequent attempts were made to join, under a common ISU banner, the Home OIU with the local branches of immigrant Ibo unions, these efforts never brought the OIU actively into the local "pyramidal" structure. The Home Union was, moreover, incapable of mobilizing opposition to the ISU among its branches abroad, because these branches —particularly the Lagos branch—had joined hands with the ISU at its inception during the rising political activism of the late 1940s in Lagos. It proved impossible for the ISU to operate as an effective pyramidal structure in Onitsha, in contrast to Calabar, because the indigenous Onitsha people were able to bring some Riverain Ibo groups living in the town to support them and thereby vitiated the unity of ISU in Onitsha. However, the more numerous and prominent immigrant Ibo groups then proceeded to form an *ad hoc* organization, the "Non-Onitsha Ibos Association," which was able (in spite of its lack of a high degree of formalization) to tap sufficient support from the immigrant Ibo town unions and the local organization of Ibo market traders to mobilize an immigrant Ibo vote which in 1955 gave them control of the Onitsha Urban council. Once this had been accomplished, this association ceased to function.

ONITSHA AND CALABAR: SIMILARITIES AND DIFFERENCES

If all these differences in occupation and association building between Onitsha indigenes and their Ibo immigrant neighbors can be explained with so little reference to contrasts in the nature of their traditional societies *per se,* to what extent may the Calabar case be similarly analyzed? This cannot be definitely answered here, but some guideline suggestions can be made.

In both Onitsha and Calabar, missions, trading firms, and the government provided the indigenes with early access to education and salaried employment. In both cases, immigrant Ibo comprised a lower prestige population with whom the indigenes contrasted themselves, but who developed an undercutting competition in commerce and crafts because of the conditions analyzed above. In both cases, moreover, through the institutions of indirect rule, major elements of the traditional indigenous social systems remained intact as part of the urban social matrix with which innovating "new elite" indigenes had to come directly to terms. Finally, in both cases salaried occupations among the indigenes produced an independence of orientation which precluded compelling them to participate in tribal associations. These common factors clarify the responses of the Calabar Efik to the modern urban situation. It is likely that the two indigenous communities are ecologically similar in a variety of ways; there is, for example, definite evidence for the kind of "associational individualism" among the Efik which likewise characterizes Onitsha men today.[33]

However, there have also been significant differences in the urban development of the two cities, particularly in the geographic relation of the city to its hinterland. The location of Onitsha on relatively infertile land, at the edge of an extensive region heavily populated with a culturally related people, favored the outward-looking expansion of social dominance by its people once its locational advantages were supplemented by those of education and occupation. Calabar, in contrast, lies on relatively fertile and under-populated land. Being situated geographically to the east of the extensive Cross River estuary, it is isolated from the hinterland of Ibibio peoples to the west, who are culturally and linguistically related to the Efik. The major mission established at Calabar did not expand its educational services into this densely populated hinterland, but instead, as Jones has observed,

> . . . followed the line up the Cross River [into a region of low population and socially fragmented groups—RNH] while the Ibibio hinterland was developed by other missions; the Efiks did not maintain their lead in education and Old Calabar failed to expand its educational activities and become the Ibibio cultural centre.[34]

As railway development west of the Cross River drew the Ibibio into such centers as Port Harcourt and Aba, Calabar declined in economic, educational, and administrative importance (in contrast to Onitsha, which became a focal center of Ibo life), while its fertile and underpopulated hinterlands provided an easy means for indigenous Calabarese to take up an alternative occupation in farming. These contrasts in the situations of Onitsha and Calabar may explain some apparent differences in the long-run occupational success of the two indigenous groups.

At this point the relevance of differences in base-line social structure to directions of change remains unassessed, although these have been reduced here to residua of less than strategic significance. Some concluding remarks about the relevance of the traditional social patterns to system "adaptability" are now in order.

DISCUSSION AND CONCLUSIONS

This paper began by reconsidering a suggestion that two different Nigerian peoples, the Efik and Ibo, have varied in their "adaptability" to modern urbanism in the city of Calabar, and that this variation has been caused by differences in their traditional cultures. This evolutionary interpretation attributed to the indigenous Efik of Calabar a "specialized" culture lacking potentialities for further change, and to the immigrant Ibo a "generalized" culture capable of more complex occupational and organizational innovations. Since the utility of such concepts depends upon their precise formulation, the argument was recast in terms of social systems, and the elements of comparison were more rigorously isolated. The frame of comparison was then broadened to include the Nigerian city of Onitsha, where both the indigenous and major immigrant tribes are Ibo-speaking.

The traditional tribal groups compared formed two contrasting categories: (1) the Onitsha Ibo indigenes and the Ibo groups immigrant to Onitsha and Calabar towns, having relatively differentiated and balanced role structures with some individualism and emergent universalism associated with general achievement emphases, and (2) the Calabar Efik, possessing less differentiated, rather "centralized" traditional role structures with achievement patterns which were more "contained" within a single major organization. Since modern societies are highly differentiated and tend to stress universalism and achievement, it was predicted that the tribesmen of the Ibo systems would in all cases be more effective in their occupational and organizational adaptations than those of the Efik.

An overview of these conditions in Onitsha showed that, contrary to expectation, the indigenous Onitsha Ibo manifest occupational and organizational responses similar to those of the Calabar Efik but contrasting with the immigrant Ibo of both Onitsha and Calabar. This suggested that a primary determinant of differential response was the immigrant *versus* indigene variable, and that direct prediction from the traditional culture to the current situation short-circuited necessary analysis. A time-depth study of trends in Onitsha urbanism was presented to fill this analytical gap.

A series of developments in Onitsha were traced, involving differential impacts of British colonial activities upon indigenes and immigrants, through which the indigenes were driven into salaried or rentier occupations, and the Inland Town became something of a "welfare home," while the immigrants gained predominance in Onitsha commercial affairs. These developments explain the occupational patterns of greater Onitsha today without recourse to differences in "traditional social structure." Moreover, these patterns cannot be validly interpreted in terms of immigrant Ibo "success" and indigenous Onitsha "failure" within the city, for the major direction of the Onitsha occupational "adaptation" has been a response to the requirements of nation building rather than to the interests of their home community.

Similar considerations apply concerning innovation of urban associations. The slow emergence of the urban center facilitated the adaptation of certain traditional Onitsha leadership roles to more cosmopolitan conditions. By converting Onitsha chiefs and king into salaried civic councillors and by supporting the patrilineage priests' control of local lands, the government preserved the importance of these roles for the indigenes and also maintained a factional balance between them which sharply limited the ability of anyone to innovate.

The home-centered Onitsha Improvement Union which attempted to remedy this situation failed, in the first place, because its organization and institutionalization as part of the indigenous Onitsha community were blocked. It is remarkable that the counterattack against the OIU was led by men playing the traditional role of "orator-spokesmen" who simultaneously set forth the modern ideal of universalistic mass democratic association and swayed the indigenous community to support the tradition-oriented age-sets as local "leaders of progress." In this case the most "modern" of traditional Onitsha social roles, achieved and rather universalistically defined ones, operated to secure the status quo against modernizing change. The very diversity and flexibility of the traditional system was a block to innovation, because chiefs, orators, and others could also claim certain of the qualifications of Westernization in advancing their rights to lead.

Second, the union could not develop sufficient unity and effectiveness at the interlocal level to override these disadvantages at home because there were no genuinely essential home projects amenable to improvement union activity, and because the occupational and social independence of Onitsha men precluded their compulsory membership and coordination. The Home Union and the branch unions tended also to find themselves at cross-purposes on crucial issues, the Home leaders defining themselves as "anti-Ibo" in order to retain local indigenous prerogatives but the leaders elsewhere orienting to more broadly defined problems on the national level. This latter point makes clear a salient feature of the value orientations of the indigenes when residing in their "home city." In this situation their particularistic relationship to an entrenched collectivity regarding themselves as "rightful owners" of that city inevitably tends to be foremost in their minds, but this particularism may diminish when they reside in other cities.

It has been pointed out that the situation of Ibo immigrants to Onitsha contrasted with that of the indigenes in many ways. Readily committed to union membership, they could evolve effective organizations independent of traditional constraints, and therefore on the basis of more universalistically defined interests. However, even where such organizations did find it necessary to come to terms with their rural communities, these communities were so devoid of needed amenities, and their traditional leaders so lacking in the rudiments of Westernized sophistication, that leaders of new organizations could often establish themselves even against opposition.

It has been shown, finally, that the distinctive ecological situation of the Calabar indigenes may likewise help explain the similarities and differences in their contemporary social patterns *vis-à-vis* those of the Ibo groups without resort to "tradition" as a determinant. However, there remains some probability that differences in traditional systems may have exerted an influence on these differential responses. To what extent can this probability now be assessed?

Although there are a number of traditional differences between the Onitsha Ibo, Calabar Efik, and various Ibo groups, all share many similarities of social structure, for all were traditionally achievement-emphasizing "segmentary" or "tribal" systems; governmental activities were embedded in ritual institutions organized about graded "title" societies, leadership was multiple, and kinship groups remained relatively equal in societal status. In each there was some trend to hierarchic stratification, but in none had this developed into a systemic societal differentiation of upper and lower kinship classes consistently differing in prestige and control of important facilities but linked together by clientage relations.[35] The Efik case appears to have been somewhat more "centralized" than the others, while the greater structural differentiation of the Ibo systems appears to have limited the elaboration of societal status hierarchy. However, it is doubtful that these differences were crucial determinants of the patterns of change observed.

There are three salient common features of Onitsha Ibo and Calabar Efik which do contrast with many Ibo groups: their initial prestige as indigenous urbanites, their preservation of traditional forms of control over valuable urban lands, and their possession of one central leadership role ("kingship") around which the British built native administration. It is difficult to find test cases among the Ibo in which the effects of these variables could be sorted out by further comparison, for in most of Iboland important urban centers were established rapidly by colonial fiat so that urban land became crown land and indigenous groups were deprived of important bases of prestige support. However, I do know of a Northern Ibo community which traditionally lacked kingship but which has held a position analogous to that of Onitsha in an early slowly commercializing center, and which has also held traditional controls over increasingly valuable floodplain farmlands. This community, the indigenous "village-group" of Umerum on the

Anambra, has proven strongly resistant not only to new associations but also to new occupations among its indigenes.[36]

It is clear from the results of this study that the distinction between "generalized" and "specialized" cultural traditions, as applied to comparable tribal groups presumed to be "adapting" to a "complex urban situation," is too gross to be of any wide utility, for an assessment of a community's adaptation to modern conditions must take account of (1) the complexity of the wider ecological, economic, and governmental settings within which adapting traditional systems operate, and (2) the multiple possible directions in which successful modernizing adaptations may occur. Only when the determining effects of settings and opportunities are fully understood can the importance of traditional structures be adequately assessed. It has been suggested above that such assessment can then be made most definitively in terms of social systems possessing various role structures viewed as operating within the frameworks of varying value systems. However, in the cases here considered neither the traditional value system nor role differentiation appears to have been a crucial determinant of the differing patterns of adaptation observed.

Some positive conclusions also emerge. It is clearly difficult to create and develop effective new forms of "tribal" organization in the presence of one's own urban-based tribal community when that community has preserved the prerogatives of its traditional roles (however diversified these may be), because this inevitably forces the innovator into situations which are particularistically, defined in terms of those roles and prerogatives. It is much easier to do so when the urbanites' tribal community is rural, remote, and lacking in educational advantages, for in this situation a "simplification" of the frame of reference occurs for the urban immigrants which makes possible a more universalistic approach to the organizational problems of city life.

However, it is also clear that development of such tribal organizations is not the sole direction in which successful urban adaptation may occur. For the Onitsha indigenes, the reference orientation in terms of which their adaptations should be assessed has shifted to the national more than the local level, and nationally they have adapted with great success. Viewed in this light, the somewhat conservative, "welfare home" character of the urban indigenous community is comparable to that which may be observed in the rural homes of the Ibo immigrants, while the ineffectiveness of the Onitsha Improvement Union may be regarded less as an adaptive failure of the traditional society than as an index of the extent to which Onitsha men in general have successfully pursued their interests in an interlocally oriented style of life. The same may be partly true for the Calabar Efik.

NOTES

1. An earlier draft of this paper was read at the annual meetings of the American Anthropological Association in November, 1964. Research was carried out in England and Nigeria during 1960–1962 under a Ford Foundation Foreign Area Training Fellowship. I am indebted to H. Scheffler, H. Henderson, B. Denton, and G. Herschberger for helpful comments and suggestions.

2. Simon Ottenberg, "Ibo Receptivity to Change," in W. R. Bascom and M. J. Hershovits (eds.), *Continuity and Change in African Cultures* (Chicago: University of Chicago Press, 1959), pp. 141–143.

3. W. T. Morrill, "Immigrants and Associations: The Ibo in Twentieth Century Calabar," *Comparative Studies in Society and History,* 5 (1963), p. 448.

4. For an anthropological example which surveys some of the literature, see M. Sahlins and E. Service (eds.) *Evolution and Culture* (Ann Arbor: The University of Michigan Press, 1960). For evidence of current developments among sociologists, see T. Parsons, "Evolutionary Universals in Society," *American Sociological Review,* 29 (1964), pp. 339–357, and S. N. Eisenstadt, "Social Change, Differentiation and Evolution," *American Sociological Review,* 29 (1964), pp. 235–247.

5. This statement of the problems of adequate explanatory interpretation derives from Max Weber, *The Theory of Social and Economic Organization,* (Glencoe: The Free Press, 1947).

6. W. T. Morrill, *op. cit.,* pp. 425–428.

7. *Ibid.,* pp. 428–430.

8. *Ibid.,* pp. 435–438. There are certain problems of interpreting Morrill's presentation of this evidence in terms of its comparability with material from Onitsha introduced below. The percentages included women, but their proportion is unstated. Morrill's dissertation ("Two Urban Cultures of Calabar" [unpublished Ph. D. dissertation, University of Chicago, 1961], Appendix) gives a listing of occupations which differs somewhat from that summarized here. The question of comparability is further discussed in note 27.

9. Morrill, "Immigrants and Associations: The Ibo in Twentieth Century Calabar," *op. cit.,* pp. 438–443.

10. *Ibid.,* p. 448.

11. *Ibid.,* p. 447.

12. *Ibid.,* pp. 427–430.

13. *Ibid.,* p. 447.

14. For the theoretical foundations of this distinction, see T. Parsons, *The Social System* (Glencoe: The Free Press, 1951).

15. For a systematic treatment of these and other "pattern-variables" of value orientation, see *Ibid,* and T. Parsons, "Pattern Variables Revisited," *American Sociological Review,* 25 (1960) pp. 467–483.

16. For example, see G. I. Jones, "The Political Organization of Old Calabar," in C. D. Forde (ed.), *Efik Traders of Old Calabar* (London: Oxford University Press, 1956), pp. 124, 131–132; G. I. Jones, *Report of the Position, Status, and Influence of Chiefs and Natural Rulers in the Eastern Region of Nigeria* (Enugu, 1958), p. 34; and H. M. Wadell, *Twenty-nine Years in the West Indies and Central Africa: A Review of Missionary Work and Adventure 1829–1858* (London, 1863).

17. Simon Ottenberg, *op. cit.,* p. 141.

18. S. Crowther and J. C. Taylor, *The Gospel on the Banks of the Niger* (London, 1859).

19. There were exceptions to this rule, reflecting the implicit emergence of achievement criteria in defining succession, but the statement suffices for present purposes.

20. The complex unit comprising a venerated maximal lineage which had long held the status of a major village was called *ebo.*

21. Important restrictions were placed upon the king's rights of selection. Major villagers were always able to assert their corporate rights to representation by senior chiefs, and candidates for chieftaincy had to validate their selection by obtaining the consent of incumbent chiefs through a series of ritual payments made to them as well as to the king.

22. G. I. Jones, "Ibo Age Organization, with Special Reference to the Cross River and North-Eastern Ibo," *Journal of the Royal Anthropological Institute,* 92 (1962), p. 195.

23. Morrill, "Immigrants and Associations: The Ibo in Twentieth Century Calabar," *op. cit.,* p. 429, suggests there were eight or nine co-ordinate patrilineage "houses" in Calabar, thus implying a "fixed" level of group definition, and treats the king as a single "paramount chief;" Jones, "The Political Organization of Old Calabar," *op. cit.,* pp. 121, 127, suggests there were several levels of patrilineage segmentation and observes that there were traditionally two or more kings in the Calabar community at any given time. My own assessment is that the degree to which Ibo and Efik communities have developed single foci of unity was rather similar, although the variation in Ibo systems is considerable and some Southern Ibo groups notably lack such foci.

24. The importance of achievement in gaining the position of headman in the Efik "house," and in attaining the highest position in Yampy Egbo (the top secret-society grade associated with the role of *obong* or king) is documented by Waddell, *op. cit.,* pp. 310–313. Competition for this position formerly sometimes involved killing members of rival segment units (*ibid.,* pp. 496–497).

25. Waddell, *ibid.,* p. 310, recounts the case of an envied wealthy ruler of Creek Town in Calabar who was "chopped to nothing" economically after a trumped-up charge was successfully brought against him in the secret society. There are other indications of the extent to which community power was vested collectively in this society (*ibid.*, p. 314), in which the king was but a peer among equals (*ibid.*, p. 504; cf. Jones, "The Political Organization of Old Calabar," *op. cit.*, pp. 139-140), and in which his own canoe men might openly resist his will (Waddell, *op. cit.*, p. 379).

26. The equality among houses is documented by Waddell, *op. cit.,* pp. 313, 507. Jones, "The Political Organization of Old Calabar," *op. cit.,* pp. 122–123, 132–135, suggests that status differences between houses and house segments correlate highly with relative numbers.

27. This table deals with adult males only, and hence only the trends and not exact percentages can be compared with Morrill's material,

which includes an unspecified proportion of females. The addition of females here would not change the pattern contrasts but would introduce complications of classification. A major proportion of indigenous Onitsha women are engaged in part-time petty trade supplemented by part-time gardening, a pattern which Morrill ("Immigrants and Associations: The Ibo in Twentieth Century Calabar," *op. cit.,* p. 437) apparently classes as "farmer," while others class themselves merely as "housewives" as do the majority of immigrant Ibo women.

28. For an illuminating account of the significance of these elements from an evolutionary point of view, see Parsons, "Evolutionary Universals in Society," *op. cit.*

29. See Great Britain, Foreign Office, "Slave Trade," 1880, No. 2; Correspondence Relating to the Bombardment of Onitsha (Parliamentary Papers, 1889, V. 74), London, 1888, for an account which attempts to explain the causes of these disruptive processes.

30. Nigerian National Archives, *Onitsha Province Annual Report (1926)* (Enugu, 1926).

31. Nigerian National Archives, *Onitsha Province Annual Report (1931)* (Enugu, 1931). Since this figure was probably extrapolated from the counted resident population of taxable adult males, it was probably considerably underestimated. Today there is a higher percentage of women than men in the Inland Town, particularly in the 20–50 age range, and this has probably been the case since the bureaucratic exodus began.

32. See Nigerian National Archives, *Onitsha Province Annual Report (1926)* (Enugu, 1926), for an official report illustrating this chronic problem.

33. The extent to which Calabar Efik occupational and associational patterns parallel those of the Onitsha indigenes appears to be much greater than can be substantively shown here. Morrill, "Immigrants and Associations: The Ibo in Twentieth Century Calabar," *op. cit.,* suggests that Efik church affiliations are casual, individualistic, and inconstant, differing from the compulsive and collectivity oriented affiliations of the immigrant Ibo. Onitsha indigenes are well known for displaying similar trends. W. T. Morrill, "Two Vibar Cultures of Calabar," *op. cit.,* also indicates patterns of Efik elite emigration from the home community, a skewing of age distributions and a "retirement-home:" character of the resident Efik population, all of which are features closely paralleling the Onitsha indigenes.

34. G. I. Jones, *Report of the Position, Status, and Influence of Chiefs and Natural Rulers in the Eastern Region of Nigeria, op. cit.*

35. The societal cleavage between freeman and slaves which obtained in Calabar is not considered here to have produced a distinctively hierarchical stratified system. Although Ibo societies likewise had such social cleavages, even in Onitsha, where there was a very active slave trade, no large social stratum of slaves arose comparable to that of Calabar. However, although socially the Calabar slaves had greater impact on their society, they were incorporated into the system as members of "houses," and the system as a whole remained a "segmentary" one.

36. The development of Umerum is more analogous to Calabar—on a much smaller scale—than to Onitsha, for its importance as a commercial center has declined gradually over the years. The traditional "power elite" of elders in this Ibo community has been consistently reactionary to "progressive" efforts by its younger citizens.

CHAPTER 9

Rank Equilibration, Tribalism and Nationalism in Nigeria[1]

ULF HIMMELSTRAND

This paper attempts to apply rank-equilibration theory to the problem of Nigerian political integration, with special reference to Ibo-Yoruba relations. This restricted focus is prompted by two considerations. Firstly, there are obvious theoretical advantages in avoiding too much complexity: taking too many ethnic groups into account in launching a study of tribalism and nationalism would distract attention from the identification of the basic processes involved. Secondly, the present writer happened to have more access to information about Yoruba-Ibo relationships than about other facets of Nigeria's multi-ethnic social structure.

Obviously our limited focus will restrict the validity of any conclusions one might be tempted to draw from our argument as regards the *causes* of the war between Nigeria and Biafra. But to the extent that our argument is sound within the historical and geographical limits we impose, and theoretically convincing, it can still serve a useful purpose in drawing attention to factors that should be controlled in order to prevent *future* escalations of civil strife into war. As we will have occasion to re-emphasize, the "causes" on which we will focus attention can only be considered contributing causes—but as such they may still be of crucial importance.

On this point it is well to recall that civil unrest in the Western Region in 1965 played a major role in triggering the sequence of events which finally led to the civil war; and intermittently Yoruba-Ibo relationships had a significant influence on these events in the Western Region. It has even been said that the secession of Eastern Nigeria and the formation of Biafra was a response not only to the May and September riots in Northern Nigeria, but equally to the frustrations springing from the increasingly strained Ibo-Yoruba relationships at the University of Ibadan in Western Nigeria and earlier at the University of Lagos.[2] If that is so, we are justified from a larger historical perspective in paying special attention to Yoruba-Ibo relationships, in spite of the fact that other ethnic group relations have recently come to occupy a more prominent position in the Nigerian crisis.

The substantive discussion falls into three parts. The first indicates the central theoretical issues with which we will be concerned, and outlines briefly the basic concepts, assumptions and predications of rank-equilibration theory. The second section then attempts to apply the insights of rank-equilibration theory to the Nigerian experience. Part three closes with a summary of the argument and considers its principal theoretical implications.

A THEORETICAL PERSPECTIVE

The Criss-Cross of 'Gemeinschaft' and Social Class

While the concept of 'class' is pivotal to several theories of societal dynamics, its significance tends to be belittled in studies of the societies which today seem to be the most involved in the dynamics of social change.[3] For instance, it has been said about African society that it is classless, that kinship and other kinds of *Gemeinschaft*-relationships are predominant while social class has little meaning. Even in modernizing African society where strata become increasingly differentiated we do not have classes in the strict sense, it is maintained, because people do not think and feel in such terms. Kinship, clanship, tribe or other communal relationships provide emotional bonds tying together top and bottom of the stratification pyramid, thus eliminating the most important criterion of a "class for itself"—the definition it is given by various strata of people involved in inter-strata conflict.[4] Furthermore, modernization is said to strengthen rather than to reduce the potency of some communal ties; people can now better afford to fulfill their traditional obligations. The wealthy businessman or politican who derives his origin from a poor and traditional village is not considered as belonging to another class but is considered as a successful native son who symbolically as well as materially gives a measure of grandeur to his village. To the wealthy man himself it may be more attractive (or perhaps opportune) to define himself as a son of his village and his clan than to consider himself as belonging to an upper class as distinct from the class of his poor relatives and clansmen.

But even though a distinctive class-consciousness and exclusive styles of life have not yet developed in most contemporary African stratification systems, because of the peculiar social rewards that still flow from crosscutting kinship and communal bonds, one can rather safely assert that social classes in Weber's sense, that is categories of people who because of their power and market position share the same typical chances with respect to the good things of life,[5] are fast emerging in Nigeria. Perhaps the first visible product of such class formation is the post-colonial "political class"—visible not because of any outwardly manifested identification with well-defined class symbols but because of the accumulation of conspicuous power, wealth and, sometimes, intellectual resources in the same hands. In Dahrendorf's language we may here speak of extensive "superimposed cleavages";[6] in the terminology of Lenski we may talk of a high degree of "status crystallization."[7] Status crystallization may of course differ in degree at various levels of the stratification system. In modernizing West African society there often seems to be more status crystallization in the higher strata of professionals, businessmen and civil servants than in the lower strata of craftsmen, petty-traders and farmers.[8] Industrial workers still are relatively few—in Nigeria about two percent of the total population—and are sometimes relatively well-off compared with the rest of the population in the lower strata.

It is thus clear that the various strata of African incipient stratification systems often criss-cross tribal and other communal affiliations. According to some sociologists, such "criss-cross" should help to prevent the emergence of sharp social cleavages.[9] More recent research and theorizing, however, have thrown some doubt on the straightforward and unconditional predictions often made from criss-cross theory and related notions. The work on rank-equilibration theory by Galtung, Anderson and Zelditch is particularly pertinent in this regard.[10] Their analyses point up the complexity of responses to the "imbalanced," "inequivalent" or "inconsistent" sets of social ranks which become more common among individuals the more pronounced the criss-cross of rank dimensions is in society as a whole. The attempts made by these authors to specify what responses will be made under what conditions do not claim to be more than tentative, and are more convincing on the microsociological level of dyadic analysis than on the macrosociological level, but they do suggest something about those conditions which determine whether criss-crossing lines of social division help to soften social conflict or to supply social conflict with additional dynamics. We turn, now, to a brief outline of the central features of rank-equilibration theory.[11]

Rank-Equilibration Theory

Basic to rank-equilibration theory are the concepts, "status-set" and "rank inconsistency." All of a person's statuses (i.e., distinct social positions) taken together, at a given time, are called his status-set.[12] Statuses have several characteristics: one of them is *rank*. The ranks occupied by a person in the various positions of his status-set may differ or may be approximately equal. One may also find more or less difference or similarity between the rank profiles exhibited by any one individual in his status-set and the corresponding rank-profiles of his significant others. As a generic term for the degree of similarity of ranks in individual status-sets or of rank profiles between individual status-sets we may speak of degree of "rank consistency." Galtung has suggested the term, *rank equilibrium*, for complete similarity of individual ranks in a status-set, and the term, *rank equivalence*, for complete similarity of rank profiles between persons.

The basic assumption in rank equilibration theory is that rank-inequilibrium as well as rank-inequivalence gives rise to a need for rank-equilibration. The individual wishes to set things straight so that rank-inequilibrium and possibly rank-equivalence is attained. For example, given rank-inequilibrium, he may become involved in activities which eventually raise his lower ranks. Or, in the case of rank-inequivalence, he may try to isolate himself from invidious comparisons with significant others who exhibit a more attractive rank profile than himself. Rank-equilibration theory, in short, attempts to specify different types of rank inconsistencies and to explain and predict the rank-equilibrating responses elicited, under various attendant circumstances, by such inconsistencies. It is to the analysis of rank inconsistencies and rank-equilibrating responses characteristic of Yoruba-Ibo inter-relationships in Nigeria that we now shift.

RANK EQUILIBRATION AMONG THE IBO AND YORUBA

Some Aspects of the Nigerian Social Structure

In some multi-ethnic societies we find a coincidence of social stratification and ethnic differentiation, the members of one tribe occupying mainly unskilled and less well-paid jobs with the members of other tribes occupying a wider range of positions including some high-ranking professions. In these cases, different ethnic affiliations confer different ranks to the members of the ethnic groups concerned. Thus, in Nigeria, Ibos in the past were ranked lower than Yorubas. This is said to have been the view of the British to whom a tribe without kings and chiefs was relatively less-developed. This down-grading attitude was readily taken over by non-Ibo Nigerians who had been in touch with Western influences earlier than the Ibos and who felt threatened as modernization helped to push members of the low-ranking Ibo group into more high-ranking positions.[13] To despise the Ibo as some kind of "bushman" until recently seemed to be part of a sometimes suppressed and sometimes flourishing folklore among other ethnic groups in Nigeria.[14]

By his receptivity to modernization the Ibo has himself contributed significantly to alter his image as seen by others, but we still must give due attention to the relatively low ethnic rank historically ascribed to him. This low ethnic rank may now perhaps be considered a cultural lag but, as such, seems to have been the basis for devaluation of the Ibo in contexts where he has been seen, at one and the same time, as threatening and vulnerable. It should not be forgotten that the Ibo in the kind of situation where we will be studying him most closely—that is, in interaction with other ethnic groups such as the Yoruba far away from his home region—always is an outsider, a "stranger." In a society still largely characterized by some degree of communalism the position of "stranger" in the community is a very significant status. Whether this status is ranked high or low will partly depend not only on the kind of cultural lag mentioned previously, but also on the position of the stranger element in the given political structure. It has been observed, for instance, that the "stranger-Ibos" (as well as some "stranger-non-Ibos") in Port Harcourt, Eastern Nigeria, defined themselves as of higher status than the Ibo-speaking Diobu indigenes, and the Diobus in some instances held corresponding views.[15] But Eastern Nigeria was the "political home" of the Ibos who were strangers in Port Harcourt, and they wielded a dominant influence both in the Region and in Port Harcourt as a result of their majority status. In Western Nigeria, however, they were a minority element and strangers from outside the region. In such a case, to the extent that the community is still dominated by communal sentiments, "strangers," by definition, are more low-ranking than those who belong to the community. In the eyes of crucial segments of the Western population, Ibos in Western Nigeria were not seen as entitled to the rights and privileges of indigenes. This meant that an Ibo, even when he was no longer likened to a "bushman" or viewed as an inferior being, still could receive a lower ascriptive rank by virtue of his being Ibo.

Rank-Inequivalence and Rank-Equilibration

As various factors relating to social structure, population pressures and modernization push members of previously low-ranking ethnic groups into more high-ranking socio-economic strata,[16] we may easily obtain the kind of rank-inequivalence in individual status-sets which has been discussed by Anderson and Zelditch. One of the cases they consider has the following structure:

FIGURE I

	Rank I	Rank II
	ETHNICITY	INCOME
Ego (Ibo)	Low	High
Alter (Yoruba)	High	High

It should be said at the outset that the Ibo and Yoruba in this paradigm are "theoretical" actors occupying only the particular pattern of statuses and ranks associated with Ego and Alter, respectively. What is said below applies only to those who fulfill the theoretical conditions specified in Figure I. It should also be noted that there are several other constellations of ranks applying to one ethnic group or another that are not represented in our discussion, because they do not pose the same behavioral dilemma. For instance, the Hausa trader in Yorubaland ranks rather low in ascriptive terms simply because he is a Hausa trader, but he also tends to be rather low on the socio-economic scale. At least in these two respects, and probably also in others, he exhibits rank-equivalence and thereby becomes less interesting from the point of view of studying rank equilibration. The same is true to some extent of Ibos who until recently carried out menial jobs in Ibadan. One further case, that of the poor Yoruba carrying out menial jobs in places where Ibos occupy top positions, does have interest for rank equilibration theory, but such cases appear to be empirically rare. In short, this paper—for both theoretical and empirical reasons—concentrates on the relationship between the economically successful Ibo and the equally wealthy Yoruba.

In considering processes of rank equilibration among the Ibo and Yoruba, we follow the reasoning of Anderson and Zelditch very closely. However, two of their basic assumptions, in our opinion, are unnecessarily restrictive. These assumptions are that Ego and Alter share the same evaluations of relevant ranks and, secondly, that they at the outset agree on the weights to be given the criteria by which they evaluate each other. If this sharing of evaluations and weights means that both must equally accept those evaluations, this is an unnecessary assumption. What is required is that both Ego and Alter *operate* from the same evaluations and weights of relevant ranks, and this they can do without accepting them. They need only have a common understanding of what, for instance, the most influential and powerful interaction partner thinks of the relative ranking of Ego and Alter. If Ego is in a "stranger" position in a community where Alter represents a powerful majority, Ego may consider it wise to *operate* on the basis of the evaluation he is given by the majority of significant others in the community—without necessarily accepting and internalizing this evaluation. One can take the role of the other without taking his standpoint. This is important to emphasize in the case of the Ibo: he did not generally seem to accept the ascriptive reduction of rank that his ethnic status underwent outside his home region, but to some extent he had to operate on the basis of the evaluations of significant and powerful others.

Returning, then, to the paradigm presented in Figure I, if Ego were an Ibo who compared himself with Alter, a Yoruba, and if Ego anchored his judgment in his economic rank as related to his ethnic rank, he may have argued that "for an Ibo I'm doing quite well, since I make as much money as Alter." But if Ego focussed more attention on his ethnic rank in relation to his income rank he might have reasoned: "I make as much money as Alter but Alter still won't accept me as an equal because I'm an Ibo." In the first case, the result would be relative *satisfaction;* in the latter case, relative *deprivation.* It is the case producing relative deprivation which holds particular interest for the present analysis.

Anderson and Zelditch point out that the relative deprivation in the second case may produce at least three different rank equilibration responses: (1) isolation, (2) ethnic atrophy and (3) stratum mobility. It is to be noted that since those factors which affect the choice of rank-equilibrating responses may vary between situations, the same individual can exhibit quite different and even somewhat contradictory rank-equilibrating responses in different situations, even when the rank inequivalence to which he is exposed is constant. By the same token, different subcategories of individuals, possessing different behavioral predispositions, may react differently to the same type of rank inequivalence. In what follows, the situational and predispositional variables are held constant; we are interested merely in considering the range of most probable responses.

First, Ego may segregate or isolate himself with Alter. This is like saying, "I do not want to know about Alter's evaluation, nor am I going to depend upon Alter; I don't care what Alter thinks of me."

Second, Ego may try to conceal or deemphasize his ethnic status. At least two types of ethnic concealment or "atrophy" can be distinguished. One type has been called, *passing,* and is a form of individual mobility. A member of a low-ranking ethnic group attempts to take over and incorporate the cultural attributes of another more high-ranking and dominant ethnic group in a way that implies compliance or even over-compliance with the cultural norms of the latter group. "Passing" in the American setting, which Anderson and Zelditch use for their examples, is illustrated by the American Negro or Jew who tries to atrophy his ethnic status and to pass as a "true American" by embracing the traditionally conservative Republican's political views, and generally by attempting to appear "respectable." In the Western Nigerian setting in which we are viewing our "theoretical Ibo," what is generally called "passing" would imply attempts on his part to dress like a Yoruba, talk like a Yoruba, embrace the views of the *Action Group* or even the *NNDP* and generally to make every attempt to assimilate Yoruba culture, as tempered by modern times, perhaps.

The second type of ethnic atrophy is that of nationalist assimilation, wherein Ego looks for some overriding principle or substitute status under which he and Alter would have the same rank. Such a status, for instance, is the status of a Nigerian citizen. In terms of Abelson's "modes of resolution of belief dilemmas," this is a "transcendent" resolution of the original rank inequivalence: Ego tells himself (and perhaps Alter), "Both of us are Nigerians."[18] In fact, it is well-known that Ibo supra-tribal Nigerian nationalism in the past made important contributions to nation-building in Nigeria.

Finally, Ego may engage in activites designed to *change the social evaluation given his ethnic group.* This can be done in various ways, for example, by the preaching of egalitarianism or by trying to improve the living conditions and the accessibility to higher positions of one's own ethnic group. Here we have *group* or *stratum* rather than *individual* social mobility.

In addition to these three categories of rank-equilibrating responses which, with some slight modification, have been borrowed from Anderson and Zelditch, one more type of rank-equilibration, aggressive behavior, may occur when other ways of achieving equilibrium fail. When Ego combines one low ascriptive rank with a high achieved rank, as in the case of our "theoretical Ibo," aggression will be directed toward Alter.[20] Rather than conceiving aggression as a separate kind of rank-equilibrating response, we will here consider it an element of other types of responses such as isolation and stratum mobility. Certain types of aggression against Alter might be considered as extremely active types of isolating response or, in cases of collective aggression, as an element of extreme or revolutionary stratum mobility.

Rank Equilibration: An Assessment of Costs

Before discussing Ibo and Yoruba responses to rank inconsistency, a few remarks are in order about the conditions which determine, firstly, the *strength* of the drive toward rank-equilibration and, secondly, the *type* of rank-equilibration. Generally speaking, the drive toward rank-equilibration should be stronger the larger the economic or psychological *investment* made in acquiring the higher status which brought about the rank-inequilibrium in the first place. The *type* of rank-equilibration utilized would seem to be determined by the relative *cost* of the potential responses.[21]

To begin with, the higher the division of labour in a given society, and the more pronounced the interdependence of functional roles, the more costly it would be for people occupying closely-related roles on the same level of organization to attempt isolation as a response. No doubt this did apply to a large number of Ibos in Lagos and in Western Nigeria during the years before 1966.

The ecological factor of housing is also releveant in this context. It is less costly for Ego to apply isolation as a means of rank-equilibrium if he lives in completely separate quarters from Alter. In Nigerian government housing, civil servants of different ethnic affiliation often lived wall to wall. The psychological cost of isolation in this case definitely would be less than in the kind of work context previously mentioned, but could still be significant.

"Passing" probably was very costly to many or most Ibos who lived as "strangers" in regions other than their own. Cultural differences, and the sacrifice of particularistic relationships with one's own kin and tribe would imply this. In contrast, many Yorubas, because of their Muslim religion, and/or their affinity with hierarchical social structures containing elements of aristocracy seem to have found it easier to assimilate among the northern Hausa.

As regards stratum mobility as a means of rank-equilibration, this is a time consuming, uncertain and therefore costly process to embark upon.

Finally, it would seem that the "transcendent" type of rank-equilibration which we have called "nationalist assimilation" might be the least costly type of rank-equilibration (particularly during the period when Nigeria fought for its independence), with various forms of isolation and insulation occupying the second place. When the macro-context of rank-equilibration is discussed below, we will pay attention to conditions under which this particular ordering of costs might be reversed. In micro-terms the relative cost to Ego of nationalist assimilation vs. insulation or isolation seems to be a joint function of the amount of rebuff or outright rejection that Ego receives from Alter, and the degree of functional interdependence of the rules of Ego and Alter.

The Ibo Response to Rank Inconsistency

We will now consider the extent to which Ibo responses to rank inconsistency fall within the three categories described above. It should be kept in mind that the potential responses are not mutually exclusive. On the one hand, rank-equilibrating responses of the same individual will vary across situations. On the other, drives other than the rank-equilibrating drive will also affect behavioral response. We should not be surprised, therefore, to find an Ibo man appearing as a staunch Nigerian nationalist in some contexts while being an active member of the Ibo State Union in others. Indeed, to the extent that such situational variations in responses to rank inconsistency and to other relevant circumstances are intra-individual they may contribute to the kind of "fusion" of "traditional" and "modern" elements of a mixed political culture which, according to Gabriel Almond, is such an important condition of political stability.[22]

The only possible exception to the lack of mutual exclusivity of response categories is that of "isolation." It would appear to be a contradiction in terms to talk of isolation as a rank-equilibrating response when responses which are the opposite of isolation are exhibited by the same individual in other situations. I would tend to think that the term "isolation" should be defined so as to exclude the possibility of "non-isolation" responses by the same individual in different situations. Thus, while it is true that the wide-ranging and intensive activities of the Ibo State Union, and of other Ibo ethnic or clan associations, to some extent "isolated" Ibos from their fellow Nigerians,[23] membership in such organizations was nevertheless compatible with participation in nationalist or various integrationist activities in other situations. Hence, membership in an Ibo union in itself would not constitute "isolation" in terms of the response categories defined above.

Turning, then, to the analysis of Ibo response patterns, it is evident that at different points in time Ibos have reacted to their wider social environment in quite different ways. Thus, as long as Ibo elements felt that they could participate fully in the politics and economy of Nigeria, the response of nationalist assimilation was especially pronounced. Indeed, in the postwar decade, Ibos more than any other tribal group emphasized the nationalistic content of the movement toward Nigerian independence. Nnamdi Azikiwe, more than any other political leader in pre-independence. and early post-independence Nigeria preached the credo of de-tribalization, national unity and a strong central government, while most of his political opponents at that time favoured a regionalistic brand of federalism.[24] To interpret those tendencies *only* in terms of the ethnic atrophying response of "nationalist assimilation" would of course constitute an excessive and ridiculous form of simplification. But the historical facts in this case at least do not contradict rank-equilibration theory: a need for rank-equivalence or, more precisely, a wish to atrophy a low ethnic or "stranger" rank, quite possibly could have been one important factor providing motivation or the preponderant participation of the Ibo in Nigerian nationalist politics.

In recent years, the dominant Ibo response pattern has been transformed from one of "assimilation" to one of "isolation." This clearly is the meaning of the Ibo withdrawal into their own region and the subsequent declaration of the Biafran secession. One's evaluation of the righteousness of the Biafran cause obviously must take many other factors into account (such as, the position of ethnic minorities within Biafra). But regardless of this one must acknowledge that the Ibo withdrawal essentially was a response to their rejection in other regions, and a reflection of the complete breakdown of the trust in some Ibo circles as regards the willingness of leading politicians in the other camps to allow Ibo elements to participate on equal terms with them in Nigerian politics.[25]

Still further aspects of the Ibo experience may be interpreted in terms of the response pattern of "stratum mobility." Thus, Ibo tribal cohesion may be seen as a partial result of a need for rank-equivalence, that is, as an attempt to improve the conditions and the positions of one's own tribesmen through upward "group" mobility.

There is only one type of rank-equilibration which we have not mentioned as being common among those who fit the description of our "theoretical Ibo." The Ibos appear to have resisted the kind of rank-equilibration implied by "passing," in the strict sense of assimilation to, or even over-compliance with, the cultural norms of a more high-ranking and dominant ethnic group. However, the individual mobility implied by Ibo success in many modern sectors of Nigerian society may itself be viewed as a kind of "passing". A drive to compensate for low ethnic or "stranger" rank through "careerism" may be as important a factor in explaining Ibo success as the uncentralized, segmental character of Ibo social structure and the individualistic and flexible type of personality presumably generated by it.[26]

The Yoruba Response to Rank Inconsistency

How would Alter, the Yoruba, react to the behaviour of Ego, the Ibo? Again there are essentially two ways in which he could react, according to rank-equilibration theory, one giving rise to relative *satisfaction,* the other to relative *deprivation.* The second type of reaction is more interesting: "How come this Ibo man makes as much money as I do?" "How come these Ibos increasingly occupy high positions?" An obvious reaction to this kind of relative deprivation is what Anderson and Zelditch call "rank reassertion". Alter, the Yoruba man, will try to increase the *weight* with which his already high ethnic rank enters into his total rank in the community. Yoruba chauvinism and nativism, and xenophobic reactions toward the Ibo are possible manifestations of such rank reassertion. The period after Nigerian Independence in 1960 and particularly after the Action Group crisis in 1962–63 did indeed generate many manifestations of Yoruba ethnic rank reassertion.

A word of caution is in order once again when we speak of phenomena like "Ibo tribal cohesion," "Ibo nepotism and favouritism," "Yoruba xenophobic tribalism," "Yoruba ethnic reassertion," etc. Any such general labels tend to give the naive reader a blanket impression that every Yoruba or every Ibo has the characteristics indicated. But we have already strongly emphasized that these expressions here have a much more limited scope relating to a particular but still very important constellation of ranks.

The Macro-Context of Rank-Inequivalence and Rank-Equilibration

Karl Deutsch has formulated a number of propositions about the appeals of nationalism, one of which seems to mesh neatly with what we have had to say about Nigerian nationalism among the Ibos up till about 1965. Furthermore, this proposition helps to link our micro-sociological conceptualization of rank-inequivalence with macro-sociological theory. Says Deutsch: "The intensity and appeal of nationalsim in a world of sharply differentiated income and living standards perhaps may tend to be *inversely proportional to the barriers to mobility be-*

tween regions and classes, and *directly proportional to the barriers against cultural assimilation, and to the extent of the economic and prestige differences between classes, cultures and region".* [27]

Disregarding for the moment the problems of commensurable scale units, the mathematical relationships between the variables in Deutsch's propostion can be assumed to be of the following general kind:

$$\begin{array}{ccccc} \text{APPEAL OF} & = & \text{RATE OF INTER-} & \times & \left(\begin{array}{cc} \text{ASSIMILATION} & + & \text{RANK DIFFERENCES} \\ \text{BARRIERS} & & \text{BETWEEN SEGMENTS} \end{array} \right) \\ \text{NATIONALISM} & & \text{SEGMENT MOBILITY} \end{array}$$

The mobility variable is here made to have a "gate-keeper" function; only if the gate for mobility is open will it matter what kind of cultural assimilation barriers and rank differences exist between various segments of the population; if mobility is zero (or below some threshold parameter which can be built into the equation) then "appeal of nationalism" will also be zero regardless of variations in "assimilation barriers" and "rank differences". Our main reason for combining the two latter variables by way of addition rather than multiplication is our belief that barriers to assimilation and rank differences more or less act as functional equivalents in the context of nationalistic appeals. If the magnitude of assimilation barriers is practically zero, this can be compensated in the equation by a greater rank difference between the population segments involved.

Let us try to link Deutsch's proposition to Nigerian reality. It is our contention (1) that Ibos have met with relatively few barriers to inter-regional mobility within Nigeria, as evidenced by the fact that they could be found in relatively large numbers in all the other regions of the country up till recently, while at the same time (2) they confronted rather sharp cultural differences which made assimilation with other ethnic groups rather difficult[28] and (3) experienced a relatively low ascriptive prestige ranking of themselves as an ethnic or "stranger" category. Furthermore, we have pointed out the early and strong appeal of Nigerian nationalism to the Ibos of Nigeria. Our previous argument, then, on "nationalist assimilation" and "ethnic atrophy" as one type of rank-equilibration, adds to Deutsch's proposition mainly by providing intervening variables linking the independent macro-variables appearing in that proposition, with the dependent variable, "appeal of nationalism."

To supplement this picture we should now look for other less mobile, and culturally more integrated and more highly ranked, Nigerian ethnic groups, and determine their reaction to the immigration and upward social mobility of Ibos. We suggest the following general proposition as a kind of dialectical supplement to Deutsch: When there are large cultural, social and/or economic differences between segments of a population, and one previously handicapped segment, X, is overcoming or throwing off its handicaps, the previously more privileged segment, Y, will tend to look with suspicion on X's rising rate of upward social mobility. Y will interpret the statistical catching up implied by this mobility as a result of sinister and corrupt infiltration or as attempts at domination on the part of X. Privileged groups, such as Y, will as a rule have quite exaggerated views as regards the frequency and long-range importance of corrupt practices among groups rising from their handicaps.

Now, as it stands, this may seem rather too unspecified a proposition. One could no doubt mention a number of variables that would account for variations in the degree to which this proposition would hold true.[29] But even in such a general form, this supplementary proposition would seem to fit the Nigerian situation sufficiently well to justify further examination.

If we combine the two macro-propositions just introduced with our previous micro-thesis about rank-inequivalence and rank-equilibration, we arrive at some rather disheartening conclusions. If X, our "theoretical Ibo," originally accomplished rank-equilibration through "nationalistic assimilation," it seems likely that some other type of response will become more dominant following the type of rejection of X by Y which has just been predicted in our last proposition. X will then most likely try to equilibrate his ranks by seeking to *isolate* himself from Y—particularly if X continues to be rebuffed and rejected. Isolation, in its turn, relates to the first of the independent variables in Deutsch's proposition—that is, inter-regional mobility—so as to further reverse the process of nation-building, and turn it into a vicious circle ending in a complete breakdown of relationships between X and Y. Factors such as relative power and economic viability will then determine the final outcome.

However, it is possible to stop such disintegration if there are some other, preferably non-ascriptive, lines of cleavage cutting across X and Y. If, for instance, some degree of consciousness of class-cleavage had been allowed to develop in Nigeria—and we have maintained that the objective bases for such a consciousness were not entirely absent in the early sixties—such a class cleavage could have been an integrative force in the process of nation-building since it would cut across divisive ethnic lines of demarcation. The forces of nation-wide class struggle were too weak, however, and the only leading politician who in the beginning of the 1960's started to build a party allegiance which to some extent was designed to follow class divisions, Chief Awolowo, was imprisoned in 1963.[30] The only political party which from its very inception in the early '50's emphasized the theme of class struggle, the Northern Elements Progressive Union (NEPU), was too weak even in the overall Northern setting to contribute to the restructuring of the Nigerian cleavage system.[31]

But even if the forces of *nation-wide* class struggle were too weak, the upheavals that took place in the *Western Region* of Nigeria after the blatantly rigged regional election in 1965, could well be interpreted as an expression of "incipient class conflict"—or, more precisely, as a conflict between a tacit and not very well organized alliance of various popular forces on one side, and a corrupt and coercive regional political class, as represented by the tribalist leadership of the NNDP, on the other. This is an important part of the interpretation given by Richard Sklar[32] and in a more orthodox Marxist fashion by a Nigerian, Ola Oni.[33]

In this perspective, the lightning military coup of January 1966 can be seen as an initially successful attempt by an important section of the top functionary stratum—Nigerian army officers trained to serve universalistic national values, and knowledgeable in the ugly aspects of particularistic civil strife from their participation in the U. N. Congo forces—to take the side of the people in overthrowing the coercive rule of the tribalist political class. From this standpoint, then, the coup amplified on a nation-wide scale the outcome of an incipient class conflict which had found its most violent expression in the Western Region, and put an end temporarily to the disintegrative forces set in motion by the power-seeking political exploitation of tribalist themes. There is no question about the widespread and even euphoric support initially rendered by the peoples of the southern regions to the new military leaders. At the time, the January coup was hailed as the beginning of a new, less tribalist, and more nationalist Nigeria. Whether this was a realistic interpretation is of less concern to us, in the present context, than the fact that this interpretation was itself a significant reality to a majority of the peoples of the south.

The Integrative Potential of the Macro-Context

Rank-equilibration processes take place within a rather narrow intra-personal and inter-personal context. But this context is inevitably linked, in a variety of ways, to a wider macrostructure of culture and social structure. As indicated in the previous section, some linkages operate to encourage rank-equilibration processes. Others, however, tend to eliminate rank-equilibration process completely and to replace them with other processes. For example, existing social organizations may prescribe, in a normative way, that emphasis be placed on certain status ranks common to all present or potential organizational members, to the neglect of other differentiating and possibly rank-disequilibrating statuses. It is true that such organizations in their formative stage may have derived some impetus from rank-equilibrating processes. We have already mentioned nationalist movements, in this connection, and much the same argument possibly can be made with regard to working class movements which seem to emerge, initially, not among those who are thoroughly deprived but among those who have been uplifted in some respects so that rank-inequilibrium is created. But once such organizations have been established, they become social facts (in Durkheim's sense) which may completely eliminate the need for rank-equilibration by drastically redefining the weights of the different ranking dimensions involved in the original rank-inequivalence. Another set of social facts of a macro-nature which may intervene to prevent rank-equilibrating processes from taking place in situations where we otherwise might expect them to occur, are some of the facts of *modern, bureaucratic, commercial and industrial culture.* We include here both formal and informal aspects of such culture, insofar as the informal aspects derive, not from particularistic and competitive affiliations brought into the bureaucratic or industrial setting from outside, but from the network of interaction necessitated by the nature of the bureaucratic or industrial work process itself.[34] It would seem that bureaucratic and industrial culture, even when defined not in ideal-type terms, but in the very broad sense I have suggested, always is more universalistic and performance oriented in the Parsonian sense than most of the norms of affiliation and loyalty which, in a developing country, exist outside the bureaucratic and industrial setting.[35] Within this setting, however, members of different ethnic groups who individually exhibit more or less rank-inequilibrium, presumably come to see themselves increasingly not in terms of relative inter-individual or intra-individual rank dimensions, but in the perspective of the *social exchange* of services and goods, demands and decisions characteristic of industrial and bureaucratic social systems. In such systems, certain universalistic rules of exchange emerge, and the individual now tends to evaluate himself and others more from the vantage points of these relatively universalistic standards and rules as they apply to his "exchange status", and less from the point of view of rank-inequivalence.

Springing from these more universalistic criteria of evaluation of exchange which probably become shared by many of those employed in modern settings, a new type of conflict is likely to emerge with those segments of society which are based on the particularism of privilege and patronage, and on the political exploitation of particularistic sentiments. It is our contention that—in addition to the class conflict already mentioned—the conflict between emerging universalistic orientations in the modernizing sector of Nigerian society *and* the coercive particularism which was manifest among the most influential segments of the regional political classes, was a central factor contributing to the popular military coup in January 1966.

There are several quite reasonable reservations which could be made about the relative universalism of the "modern, bureaucratic, commercial, and industrial culture." The most serious reservation stems from the frequently made observation that the more highly placed and more educated Nigerians have generally exhibited more "tribalism" than people less educated and lower down on the salary scale.[37] This phenomenon can be accounted for by the larger stakes and the tougher competition for higher posts, and also by the more "politicized" nature of the competition for these positions. Even if such positions are not strictly political, they wield more power than lower placed jobs, and thus tend to become relevant in the political struggle of a developing nation. And, in Nigeria, as we have already indicated, this struggle increasingly became infused with tribalist particularism.

The tribalism of some more educated and highly placed persons in modern settings can thus be seen as injected into the modern system from "outside" in the shape of "particularistic and competitive affiliations". We have already made a reservation about the possibility of such "outside" interference with the regular processes of social exchange in modern systems. From our own observation, and from some as yet unpublished data, it would seem that the reduction of ethnic particularism which we expect in modern bureaucratic and industrial settings is most clearly seen among salaried employees somewhat lower down on the scale who have had an opportunity to work together with members of other ethnic groups.

The significance of the macro-structure, then, is that it might help to dampen the disintegrative implications of rank-equilibration by replacing rank-equilibrating processes with processes of social organization, social exchange and universalism. These latter processes would appear to be more profoundly integrative than the "transcendent," compensatory kind of nationalism deriving from one kind of rank-equilibration. But our rather complex macro-micro model, of which only a very broad outline has been presented, does not therefore predict increasing integration or stability. *At any point the process can be reversed by the destruction of some of the social facts of emerging social organization and universalistic culture; and then the society may be thrown back to the stage where the individually rank-equilibrating but socially disruptive forces of isolation and ethnic reassertion once again become predominant, as predicted by our dialectical supplement to Deutsch's proposition on the appeal of nationalism.*

The crucial factors determining the likelihood of destruction of integrative social facts fall outside the compass of the present paper. The distribution of power and authority within the given economic-political-military structure obviously is one such crucial factor.

Summary and Conclusions

The increasing salience of the "tribalism" issue in Nigerian politics after independence did not mean that class or stratum were unimportant categories of social differentiation in Nigerian society. The Nigerian "tribalism" of recent years is mainly a *political* tribalism stemming not from primordial ethnic loyalties as such, but from politically exploited and reinforced reactions to strains in the emerging stratification system. Our analysis has focused upon one kind of "structural strain" involved in the development of "political" tribalism, namely, the kind of strain which emerges:

    (a) when most individual status-sets in a society are based on widely understood distinctions of *ascribed* as well as *achieved* statuses;

    (b) when ascribed statuses at one time were very differently evaluated or ranked—some high, some low;

    (c) when rank-orders of achieved and ascribed statuses in individual status-sets at one time were rather highly correlated so that a low rank in an ascribed status was likely to be accompanied by low-ranking achieved statuses; and

    (d) when social change or modernization results in a reduction of this rank-correlation so that rank-orders of achieved statuses now come to cut across the rank-orders of ascribed statuses to a larger extent, thus increasing the frequency of rank inconsistencies in individual and dyadic status-sets.

Secondly, we have discussed various types of "rank-equili-brating" responses to structural strain as reflected in individ-ual or dyadic status-sets. Those who experience the kind of strain mentioned above try to reduce it in ways which seem rather inconsistent. A close-up view of the matter seems to reveal the following general pattern:

(a) People who combine low rank in an ascriptive status and high rank in an achieved status will try to reduce this rank-inconsistency either (1) by a trophy of their ascribed status ("passing" and "nationalist assimilation"), or (2) by attempts to improve the rank, of their own ascriptive category as a whole (group mobility), or (3) by segregating or isolating themselves from people in more high-ranking ascriptive statuses.

What has often been referred to as Ibo tribal cohesion may be partly explained in terms of the two last types of response (group mobility and insulation); the Nigerian nationalism and centralism found among several leading Ibo politicians in the Federal context could be partly explained in terms of the first type of response (ethnic atrophy and nationalistic assimila-tion). The rather curious mixture of Ibo tribal cohesion and supra-tribal nationalism, however, inconsistent it may seem at first glance, is not too puzzling, then, in the context of rank-equilibration theory.

(b) Those who combine high rank in an ascriptive status with an equally high achieved status, and confront significant others with equally high achieved statuses but a lower ascrip-tive status will try to improve their total community rank by giving more weight to their own *high* ascriptive rank as well as to the *low* ascriptive rank of their achieved status equals. We suggested that Yoruba ethnic reassertion and the rather xeno-phobic tribalism that characterized the last phase of the NNDP Government in the Western Region of Nigeria before the mili-tary takeover on January 15, 1966, and which found some reso-nance among well educated and well situated Yorubas but failed to impress the rank-and-file, could be *partly* explained in these terms.

It is evident that the NNDP leadership in the last phase of its reign in Western Nigeria was forced by the tensions created by its own illegitimate rule to try to redirect internal hostilities toward outside targets, and here again the Ibos were found to be suitable scapegoats. In our terms this can be described as a last desperate attempt to crosscut the sharp cleavage that had developed between the "political class" and the people of Western Nigeria—a clear case of class conflict—by emphasizing particularistic ties of Yoruba unity and loyalty, and slogans of Ibo infiltration and domination.

(c) The size of the economic or psychological *investment* made in the more high-ranking status which brought about the rank-inequivalence in the first place will probably determine the strength of pressures toward rank-equilibration. The relative *cost* of different types of rank-equilibration will probably determine the type of rank-equilibration actually taking place. To a large number of highly placed Ibos the least costly type of rank-equilibration probably was the one brought about by "transcendent" nationalist assimilation, with isolationist rank-equilibration in second place. Of course, the rebuff and rejection which many Ibos met in various parts of Nigeria in the mid-sixties naturally led to a strengthening of the *isolationist* response at the expense of those types involving ethnic atrophy. More generally, structural variables such as the division of labour, functional interdependence and closeness of roles, degree of ecological segregation of living quarters, and cultural variables making assimilation difficult, tentatively have been related to the cost of various types of rank-equilibration.

Thirdly, we have considered the ways in which macro-sociological processes may help create rank-inequivalence in individual status-sets. Karl Deutsch has analyzed the extent to which nationalist appeals are influenced by regional and class mobility, by barriers to cultural assimilation, and by existing rank-differences, and his propositions fit our argument very well. We have devloped them a little further to take account of the dialectical opposition of tribalistic and nationalistic appeals.

Fourthly, we have discussed the integrative potential of the macro-context. Modernization, at the same time that it generates the structural strain which, to some extent, underlies both tribalism and supra-tribal nationalism, also creates an institutional framework of organizations, modern cultural values and class loyalties which can help to eliminate rank-equilibration processes. Commercial, industrial and administrative modern-

ization and class conflict seem to imply a continuing sup-
plementation of particularistic forms of exchange, such as
mutual aid and patronage between kinsmen and tribesmen,
with a more universalistic exchange of goods and services in
terms of power bargaining, contract or legally defined rights
and obligations as well as emerging class organizations cutting
across and deemphasizing particularistic ethnic loyalties. We
have suggested that increased participation in such universalistic exchange and organization could do away with tribalism
as a political phenomenon.

It is as a political phenomenon on the elite level and in the
emerging middle class that ethnic loyalties easily become disruptive and dangerous. As a means for collective support and
self-help, for instance among poor urban immigrants, ethnic or
clan loyalties may instead have beneficial and integrative
effects—as long as they are not exploited by powerful tribalist
politicans. Whether such a tribalist political exploitation will
occur depends largely on factors beyond the explanatory power
of rank-equilibration and criss-cross theory.

Whatever the merits of the micro- as well as macro-sociological theorizing advanced in this paper, we should be aware of its
limitations and the need to supplement it with other approaches. What will become of the various impulses to tribalism or nationalism stemming from the sociological micro- and
macro-conditions mentioned depends largely on various aspects of *political* and *military* power structure which we have
not discussed here in any detail. To predict the direction of the
rank-equilibrating and dialectical processes of particularistic
tribalism and universalistic nationalism we must take account
of whether the given power structure is an expression of a
system of "regional security and consolidation,"[38] such as illustrated by the previous regional set up in Nigeria and by the
withdrawal and secession of Eastern Nigeria, or whether it is
characterized by a more differentiated and interdependent set
of smaller, less powerful, and more numerous political units
such as in the present multi-state Nigerian federation.

In Nigeria today, where as a result of the creation of more
states within the federal structure the political power of the
majority ethnic groups (Hausa, Ibo and Yoruba) is more effectively balanced by the power of numerous minority ethnic

groups, one can of course still find many traces of a political exploitation of tribalist themes. But it is now much less likely that this will lead to sharply polarized and disastrous clashes because of the proliferation of power centers.

But that is the topic of another paper.[39]

NOTES

1. This is part of a more comprehensive working paper originally presented to the Sixth World Congress of Sociology at Evian, France, 4–11 September 1966. I am indebted to Dr. Albert Imohiosen and Dr. Ukpabi Asika of the University of Ibadan, Nigeria, and to Professor Philip Foster, University of Chicago, who was Visiting Professor in Ibadan, 1966–1967, for both substantive and analytic comments on various drafts of this paper. I have also benefited from the criticism of Dr. Howard Wolpe and Dr. Robert Melson. I am solely responsible for the use I have made of all the suggestions received.

The Bank of Sweden Tercentenary Fund by a grant enabled me to spend time on revising a second draft of the paper. I am indebted to the Center for Advanced Study in the Behavorial Sciences, Stanford, California, for making their facilities available to me in the final revision, and to my co-Fellow at the Center, Hayward Alker, for several useful suggestions as regards the final editing of the paper.

A somewhat more elaborate and differently organized version of the present paper has been presented as "Tribalism, Nationalism, Rank-Equilibration and Social Structure," *Journal of Peace Research*, Vol. 6, No. 2 (1969).

2. James O'Connell, "The Scope of the Tragedy," *Africa Report*, Vol. 13 (February 1968), pp. 9–10.

3. Until recently the literature about "the new societies in tropical Africa" rarely contained references to social class or stratification in their subject indexes. *Social Change in Modern Africa,* edited by Aidan Southall (London: Oxford Univ. Press, 1961), contains a few chapters where the matter is touched on briefly, and played down. Lloyd Faller's chapter in C. Geertz (ed.), *Old Societies and the New States* (Glencoe, Ill.: The Free Press, 1963), probably remains the most thorough treatment of the subject from a theoretical point of view but does not give much detail. More recent elite studies have put a stronger emphasis on class and stratification. Peter C. Lloyd (ed.), *The New Elites of Tropical Africa* (London: Oxford Univ. Press, 1966), has

admirably summarized arguments about class and elite in tropical Africa (*ibid.,* pp. 49–62), and has some interesting but noncommittal remarks to make about the "ideology of classlessness" which members of some African elites find it opportune to maintain in the face of the internal exploitation developing in some post-colonial African societies (*ibid.,* pp. 59 ff.). The works of social anthropologists may have helped to bolster such ideologies. See also Peter C. Lloyd, *Africa in Social Change* (Harmondsworth: Pengiun Books, 1967), pp. 313–317, on "the non-consciousness of class."

4. For a discussion of the distinction made by Karl Marx between "class in itself" and "class for itself," see Ralp Dahrendorf, *Class and Class Conflict in Industrial Society* (Stanford: Stanford University Press, 1959), Chapter I.

5. H. H. Gerth and C. Wright Mills, *From Max Weber: Essays in Sociology* (New York: Oxford University Press, 1947), pp. 181–182.

6. Ralf Dahrendorf, *op. cit.,* pp. 213–216.

7. Gerhard Lenski, "Status Crystallization: A Non-Vertical Dimension of Social Status," *American Sociological Review,* Vol. 19 (1954), pp. 405–413.

8. Peter C. Lloyd, *op. cit.,* p. 58: " . . . it is probably easier to define limits to the elite."

9. Lewis A. Coser, *The Functions of Social Conflict* (Glencoe, Ill.: The Free Press, 1956).

10. Bo Anderson and Morris Zelditch, Jr., "Rank Equilibration and Political Behavior," in *Archiv. Europ. Sociol.,* Vol. V (1964), pp. 112–125. A more formal treatment of the same kinds of problems can be found in M. Zelditch, Jr., and Bo Anderson, "On the Balance of a Set of Ranks," in Berger, Zelditch, and Anderson (editors), *Sociological Theories in Progress,* Vol. One (Boston: Houghton Mifflin Company, 1966), Chapter II. Johan Galtung's contribution to the same volume, "Rank and Social Integration: A Multidimensional Approach,"—is also relevant to the present analysis, particularly pp. 168–179. See also Johan Galtung, "International Relations and International Conflicts: A Sociological Approach," *Transactions of the Sixth World Congress of Sociology* (Geneva: International Sociological Association, 1966), pp. 121–161.

11. Galtung has made the quantitatively most refined exploration of multidimensional and multi-unit rank inconsistencies; but Zelditch and Anderson are more detailed in their exploration of various types

of response to such inconsistency. For our purposes it seems more important to take account of the larger repertory of rank-equilibrating responses discussed by Anderson and Zelditch, and we will therefore rather closely follow their line of argument without neglecting to benefit from some aspects of Galtung's discussion. On the whole, Galtung and Zelitch and Anderson arrive at very similar conclusions.

12. See Robert K. Merton, *Social Theory and Social Structure,* /rev. and enl. ed./ (New York: The Free Press, 1957), pp. 370, 380.

13. James S. Coleman, *Nigeria: Background to Nationalism* (Los Angeles and Berkeley: University of California Press, 1958), pp. 338 ff.

14. The present writer has personally witnessed many educated Yorubas and Hausas report on or express this "bushman" stereotype. Its saliency seems to be related to the political climate of the day, which suggests a very delicate cognitive balance in inter-ethnic perception.

15. I owe this example as well as the remark that "strangers" are not always more low-ranking than indigenes to Howard Wolpe. See his "Port Harcourt: Ibo Politics in Microcosm," *The Journal of Modern African Studies,* 7, 3 (1969), pp. 469–93, reprinted in this volume, pp. 483–513.

16. For a vivid description of the "Ibo awakening," see Coleman, *op. cit.,* pp. 332–43; reprinted in this volume, pp. 69–92.

17. This, probably, is the mechanism that led to the formation of the Black Muslims in the U. S. A. See E. U. Essien-Udom, *Black Nationalism. A Search for an Identity in America* (Chicago: University of Chicago Press, 1962).

18. Robert P. Abelson, "Modes of Resolution of Belief Dilemmas," *Journal of Conflict Resolution,* Vol. 3 (1959), pp. 346 ff.

19. J. S. Coleman, *op. cit.,* pp. 335 ff. Coleman also gives a much fuller description of Ibo participation in Nigerian nationalism than we can give with our narrow theoretical concern.

20. Galtung, "International Relations and International Conflicts: A Sociological Approach," pp. 142 ff.

21. Compare Berger, Zelditch and Anderson, *op. cit.,* pp. 251 ff. Certain portions of the argument in Abelson, *op. cit.,* pp. 346–351 are also relevant to our discussion. Galtung's propositions that aggression will be directed to self if ascribed ranks are higher than achieved ranks,

and directed to others if ascribed ranks are lower than achieved ranks could be derived from the principle of relative *cost* of different types of rank-equilibrating responses. See Galtung, "Rank and Social Integration: A Multidimensional Approach," pp. 168 ff., and Galtung, "International Relations and International Conflicts: A Sociological Approach," pp. 142 ff.

22. Gabriel Almond, "Introduction," in G. Almond and J. S. Coleman (eds.), *The Politics of the Developing Areas* (Princeton: Princeton University Press, 1960), pp. 24 ff.

23. The relative cohesiveness of Ibo unions has been commented upon by a number of writers. See, for example, Richard E. Sklar, *Nigerian Political Parties* (Princeton: Princeton University Press, 1964), pp. 460 ff.

24. Sklar, *ibid.,* Chapters V and VI.

25. For accounts and interpretations of recent Nigerian events, and their background, see for instance Richard L. Sklar, "Nigerian Politics in Perspective", *Government and Opposition,* Vol. 2 (1967), pp. 524–39, and James O'Connell, *op. cit.,* and by the same author, "The Political Class and Economic Growth", *The Nigerian Journal of Economic and Social Studies,* Vol. 8 (1966), pp. 129–140.

26. See Simon Ottenberg, "Ibo Receptivity to Change," in W. R. Bascom and M. J. Herskovits (eds.), *Continuity and Change in African Cultures* (Chicago: University of Chicago Press, 1959), pp. 130–143.

27. Karl W. Deutsch, "The Growth of Nations: Some Recurrent Patterns of Political and Social Integration", *World Politics,* Vol. V (1953), p. 180.

28. Robert A. LeVine, *Dreams and Deeds: Achievement Motivation in Nigeria* (Chicago: Univ. of Chicago Press, 1966), summarizes some evidence about differences between main ethnic groups in Nigeria with regard to culture and social structure. See Chapter 3 and pp. 92–94, portions of which are reproduced in this volume, pp. 170–214.

29. We interpret Deutsch's proposition as introducing, "barriers to inter-segmental mobility" and "barriers against cultural assimilation" as cross-country averages, or as averages in any smaller unit whose overall nationalism is measured as a dependent variable. It would seem possible to further specify our supplementary proposition by taking off from the independent variables in Deutsch's proposition but formulating the first two of them in terms of *differences* rather than

in terms of *averages* or *overall totals.* Stripping off all parameters (which must be empirically estimated anyway) we thus arrive at the following two equations of which the first one is Deutsch's proposition (slightly rewritten), and the second one our "dialectical" supplement:

(1) $+N_u = M_u \times (\text{Basmu} + \text{ascrRdiff}_u)$

(2) $-N_y = (M_x - M_y) \times [(\text{Asmy} - \text{Asmx}) + (\text{ascrR}_y \text{ in } u - \text{ascrR}_{x \text{ in } u})]$

(3) $u = x + y$

where N is "appeal of nationalism"; $-N$ is "rejecting nationalism"; M is inter-habitat mobility, where habitat is defined as any geographical *or* sociological location with which a given segment of the population is customarily identified; *Basm* is "barriers against cultural assimilation"; *Asm* is "degree of assimilation of a given population segment with the culture dominant in its place of domicile" which may not be the same as the habitat; *ascrR* is "ascriptive rank"; u is a given unit of analysis, and x and y are sub-units of u.

This is not the place to explicate the mathematical properties even of such a highly simplified system of equations. Let it be said, however, that the differences between inter-habitat mobilities of various population segments in equation (2) plays the same "gatekeeper" role as the overall or average mobility in equation (1).

30. Richard L. Sklar, "The Ordeal of Chief Awolowo", in Gwendolen M. Carter (ed.), *Politics in Africa: 7 Cases* (New York: Harcourt, Brace & World, Inc., 1966), pp. 126–131, particularly p. 129."

31. K. W. J. Post, *The Nigerian Federal Election of 1959* (London: Oxford University Press, 1963), p. 76 footnote and pp. 425 ff.

32. Richard L. Sklar, "Contradictions in the Nigerian Political System," *The Journal of Modern African Studies,* Vol. 3 (1965), pp. 201–213: reprinted in this volume, pp. 00–000.

33. Ola Oni, "The Root of the Crisis, "*Nigerian Socialist,* Vol. 1 (January 1967), pp. 5 ff. For a somewhat different emphasis by another Nigerian Marxist, see Eskor-Toyo, *The Working Class and the Nigerian Crisis* (Ibadan: The Sketch Publishing Co., Ltd., not dated).

34. See, for instance, Geroge C. Homans, *The Human Group* (New York: Harcourt-Brace, 1950), and Peter Blau, *The Dynamics of Bureaucracy* (Chicago: University of Chicago Press, 1955).

35. See, for instance, Talcott Parsons, *Essays in Sociological Theory,* rev. ed. (Glencoe, Ill.: The Free Press, 1954), pp. 41 ff.

36. In a forthcoming publication this theory of "social differentiation and exchange" as applied to the Nigerian setting will be explicated more fully.

37. The evidence on this point is scattered, and largely impressionistic. See footnote 2 and Peter Lloyd (1966), *op. cit.,* pp. 58 ff.

38. The expression, "system of regional security," has been coined by Richard L. Sklar in "For National Reconciliation and a United Front," *Nigerian Opinion,* Vol. I, no. 1 (January 1965), p. 5.

39. A tentative and condensed discussion of some of these problems is contained in the version of the present paper appearing in the *Journal of Peace Research,* Vol. 6, No. 2, 1969. See also Ulf Himmelstrand, "Har Nigeria en framtid?" (Is there a future for Nigeria?), *Utrikespolitiska Institutets Informationshaften,* No. 3, 1969.

Part II

INSTITUTIONAL COMMUNALISM

Institutional Communalism

Editorial Introduction

The papers in this section are concerned with the institutional context in which the processes of social mobilization and communal conflict have unfolded in Nigeria. This context has both reflected and influenced developing patterns of communal conflict, and the reciprocity between institution and conflict is a recurrent theme in the analyses which follow. Though the emphases of these eight papers overlap considerably, they each tend to focus upon one or another of the five dimensions of institutional communalism summarized in our propositions (Chapter 1).

Abner Cohen's opening essay on the "Politics of the Kola Trade" highlights the complex reciprocity which exists between residential and social segregation of communal groups, on the one hand, and the communalization of economic competition, on the other. Cohen describes the evolution of a cohesive and highly autonomous Hausa community within Ibadan, in response to the requirements of the Hausa long distance trade in kola nuts. As Cohen notes, the development of an efficient commercial network depends, in large measure, upon the existence of trust between the parties to a transaction. Relationships of trust are most likely to exist among those who share what Cohen terms a "moral community," of which the segregated Hausa Quarter is both a cause and an effect. Moreover, Cohen argues, Hausas have been required to organize themselves politically in order to maintain their monopoly in the kola trade, and this segregation has contributed to their political cohesiveness. At the same time, their Yoruba hosts have also furthered the residential and social segregation of the Hausa community by reacting defensively against Hausa incursions and assigning to Hausas a special residential area. The end product of these developments is communally specialized commercial networks and the transformation of commercial competition into communal conflict. In Cohen's words,

> . . . a great deal of the control exercised by the Hausa over the kola trade is interconnected with Hausa political autonomy and Hausa social organization in Yorubaland. The Yoruba kola traders and farmers, as well as their political supporters, must have realized this, since it is evident from the records that whenever a dispute with the Hausa kola landlords flared up there was an almost instantaneous attack by Yoruba political groupings on the autonomy of Sabo and on its political institutions.

The succeeding papers by Audrey Smock and Alvin Magid on Ibo ethnic unions and the Idoma State Union, respectively, focus on the political significance of tribal unions, institutions which, like segregated communal neighborhoods, both reflect and perpetuate existing patterns of communal division. Smock's principal focus is upon the role Ibo ethnic unions played vis-à-vis the dominant Eastern political party, the NCNC. She observes that the colonial regional administration left the structure and parochial ethos of local communities pretty much intact and that the NCNC, while subsuming within its embrace the melange of parochial groups, made little attempt to dissolve local allegiances or communal boundaries. Smock draws attention to the political functions performed by many local ethnic unions, and to the considerable variation which existed in the relationship of these unions to the party. She illustrates how the dynamics of modern political competition "accentuated the importance of village and clan identities, and ethnicity as the structuring principle of political competition." The ethnic unions, however, were merely "convenient organizational appendages" to this communalization of political competition and did not themselves inspire the "politics of ethnic confrontation and compromise."

Alvin Magid's chapter on the Idoma Hope Rising Union offers an intensive case study of a single tribal union within the Middle Belt sector of Nigeria's Northern Region. The history of the I.H.R.U. illustrates the extent to which "tribalism" is often far more a reflection of modernization than it is of traditional forces. Indeed, in this instance, the traditionalists within Idoma successfully opposed the separatist efforts of the "young Turks" within the I.H.R.U. to press for the creation of a Middle Belt Region. The traditionalists were also successful in withstanding the I.H.R.U.—inspired pressures for the democratization of the Native Authority system within Idoma Division. Magid's discussion of these internal conflicts sheds light not only on the dynamics of Idoma politics but also on the relationship between the I.H.R.U. and the Nigerian political party system.

The next three papers on the Nigerian military and the Nigerian educational system are each concerned with the integrative significance of these important national institutions. They indicate the extent to which the institutions of the military and the educational system, despite their pretensions to supra-tribal status, both reflected and reinforced the politicization of communal conflict (Proposition 6). Thus, as Martin Dent indicates in his chapter on "The Military and Politics," the tribal composition of the different levels of Nigeria's army hierarchy, with the better-educated Southerners (especially Easterners) dominating the officer corps, reflected the socioeconomic inequalities of the wider society and made the military very susceptible to political pressures from without. Once elements of the military intervened in the civil political process, the communal divisions latent within the army quickly came to the fore and communal conflict was rapidly escalated: " . . . the medium of conflict is no longer political manoeuvre, manifestoes, votes, and speeches but rather violence, with an immense advantage to the side which strikes first." Dent's paper offers the most detailed analysis of the military coups of January and July 1966 yet to appear, and contains many penetrating observations on the political failure of military rule in Nigeria.

The papers by David Abernethy and Alan Peshkin concerning the relationship between education and integration in Nigeria parallel Dent's discussion of the military. Not only did the educational system overproduce unemployable school leavers, Abernethy points out, but it also increased the disparity between the North and the South. On the whole, Abernethy suggests, "the disintegrative effects of educational expansion seem to outweigh the integrative ones." Turning to the political socialization function of education, Peshkin indicates that schools were seldom used to foster a sense of common nationality or a sense of communal tolerance.

In "Tarka and the Tiv: A Perspective on Nigerian Federation," Martin Dent offers a political profile of one of Nigeria's most prominent leaders. His focus is upon the ways in which Tarka's background as a Tiv and a member of a communal minority has conditioned his outlook on Nigerian federation and his style of leadership. Tarka's advocacy of the Federal cause, together with his advocacy of the creation of new states, may both be understood in terms of his minority background. The Tiv, together with other minority groups, have long felt their security hinged upon the protection of the Federal "umbrella"; by the same token, they have long urged the creation of new states as a means of countering "big-tribe chauvinism". As noted in the theoretical introduction to this volume (Proposition 7), the organizational tragedy of the Nigerian experience was that the constitutional compromises of the early 1950's had the effect of excluding communal minorities from the national political system and of creating a three-person zero-sum game among the three major nationalities. Tarka's own political initiatives have been directed at ensuring a modicum of self-determination to minority groups and at preventing any single communal group from wielding inordinate power. As Dent indicates, Tarka may well play a crucial role in the Nigeria of the future.

The last chapter in this section on institutional communalism, "The Contribution of Tribalism to Nationalism in Western Nigeria," by Richard L. Sklar, illustrates the extent to which the democratization of the Nigerian constitutional system, by encouraging the participation of the masses in the political process, tended further to politicize and intensify communal conflict (Proposition 8). Sklar, however, suggests that in several respects the tribalism induced by modernization and democratization makes a positive contribution to nation-state nationalism. On the one hand, the "pan-tribalism" implicit in notions of "Ibo-ness" and "Yoruba-ness," has been promoted by the "rising class" elements in each nationality group as a way of overcoming the particularism of the traditional order; hence, movements which appeal to the unity of nationality groups may be viewed as integrative in their effect. On the other hand, appeals to "communal partisanship" provided a vehicle for linking the mass of the people with the nationalist drive for Nigerian independence. "Communal partisanship," Sklar asserts, "based on psychological commitments to the traditional values of tribal groups, was utilized by nationalist leaders to mobilize mass support in rural areas and old towns." That there were significant disintegrative potentials inherent in this political strategy should be self-evident, and it would appear that it is these which have recently carried the day. But Sklar's analysis points up a side of the "tribalism" coin which is too frequently ignored. Sklar's discussion is also distinctive in its emphasis upon the factor of class as affecting competitive relationships and political strategies. While the editors would quarrel with the assertion that "By and large, ethnic affinities are outweighed by class interests. . . ," Sklar's conclusions reinforce the theme of modernity-induced communalism: to all intents and purposes, "tribalism" became the organizational vehicle for the personal and political advancement of the members of Nigeria's Westernized elite.

CHAPTER 10

Politics of the Kola Trade[1]

ABNER COHEN

Introduction

In his important pioneering study of migrations into Ghana,
Rouch makes the observation that different tribal groups of
migrants organize themselves differently in the foreign towns
to which they migrate.[2] The forms of their organization fall
into a continuum between two extremes. At the one end are
migrants who form only segmental, temporary, tribal groupings. At the other end are migrants who form autonomous,
multi-purposive, tribal communities. Banton makes a similar
observation in his study of migrants in Freetown.[3] Neither
Rouch nor Banton analyses this difference in detail, though
both tend to explain it in terms of differences in tribal tradition
culture.[4]

It is obvious, however, that this is a complex problem in
which other variables are involved, some of which can be, under certain circumstances, more crucial than the cultural variable and both Rouch and Banton are fully aware of this. To
isolate these variables and to analyse the nature of their interconnexions will require a great many comparative, cross-cul-
tural studies. It is particularly necessary to analyse situations
in which some of the variables can be held constant so that the

Reprinted from *Africa,* Vol. 36 (1966), pp. 18-35. Copyright © 1966 by *Africa.*
Reprinted by permission of the publisher and Abner Cohen. The notes are
presented in slightly revised form.

operation of other variables may be examined under more controlled conditions. One variable which can be easily controlled is that of cultural tradition. This can be done by the intensive study of the social organization of different categories of migrants from one ethnic group.

For a period of about fifteen months between 1962 and 1963 I carried out field study among Hausa migrants in Yorubaland, in the Western Region of the Federation of Nigeria. Rouch rates the Hausa high among the community-forming type of migrants in Ghana.[5] Indeed, discrete Hausa migrant communities are ubiquitous, not only in Ghana and Southern Nigeria, but throughout the rest of the forest belt of West Africa. A community of this type usually occupies a special quarter within the foreign town and is headed by a Hausa chief, the *Sarkin Hausawa*, who is recognized as such by both the community and the local authorities. Members of such Hausa communities in Yorubaland often explain their ethnic exclusiveness within the host towns, in cultural terms, repeatedly offering the simple, cliché-ridden, motto: 'Our customs are different'. But the culture and the system of social relations in these communities are far from being reproductions of the culture and the social system in Hausaland in the North. What is more important for this discussion is that not all Hausa migrants into Yorubaland find it necessary to live within these autonomous Hausa communities. There are tens of thousands of Hausa who migrate annually to southern Nigeria to seek seasonal employment,[6] who live in small, scattered, loosely knit worker gangs, without forming or joining organized communities.[7] Hausa cultural tradition is thus not the crucial factor in the formation of these Hausa communities in Yoruba towns, even though this cultural tradition is in many ways the basis on which these communities have been established.

The study of a few of these communities has shown that their development and their structure are closely interconnected with the development and organizational requirements of long-distance trade in which most of their members are directly or indirectly engaged. By long-distance trade in this context I mean the purchase or sale, and the transfer of goods, usually of perishable nature, between the forest zone and the savanna in Nigeria, across a distance of several hundred miles by the use of indigenous methods of business organization, without regular resort to such modern institutions as banking, insurance companies, police, civil courts, or the exchange of documents, even though very large sums of money are involved.

Under the pre-industrial conditions prevailing in Nigeria, long-distance trade involves difficult technical problems which can be efficiently overcome when men from one tribe control all or most of the stages of the trade in specific commodities. Such a tribal control, or monopoly, can usually be achieved only in the course of continual and bitter rivalry with competitors from other tribes. In the process, the monopolizing tribal community is forced to organize for political action in order to deal effectively with increasing external pressure, to co-ordinate the co-operation of its members in the common cause, and to mobilize the support of communities from the same tribe in neighbouring towns. In this way a closely knit network of well-organized Hausa communities developed during the past few decades, covering nearly all Yoruba towns, and enabled Hausa traders and commission agents to establish monopoly over the trade in a number of important commodities.

The trade in each one of these commodities has a different history which is differently interconnected with the different processes of the formation of these communities. Some communities have developed in connexion with the trade in a single commodity; others in connexion with two or more commodities. The trade in every commodity has its own social organization and its own politics. In order to simplify the sociological issues which are the subject of this discussion and to reduce further the number of variables, I focus in this paper on the social organization of a single commodity—the kola.[8]

The Kola

The kola is a nut, the size of a Brazilian nut, with a colour ranging from dark-red to cream-white. It is consumed very widely among the savanna peoples of West Africa by men, women, and sometimes even children, is exchanged as a gift, used as a drug for certain illnesses, and is offered to guests in ceremonies. It is sustaining as food, but people derive satisfaction mainly from chewing it and from its stimulating effects. Men become addicted to it, carry it in their pockets and, in company, offer it to each other like cigarettes. The nuts are usually retailed by relatively large numbers of boys and girls, aged 7 to 14. The kola has been consumed in the Sudan for many centuries but its massive consumption is, according to the available evidence, only recent and is due partly to improved, quicker, and cheaper transport and partly to the spread of Islamic orders which strictly forbid smoking, as well as drinking alcohol.

While its major centres of consumption are in the savanna, the kola is grown only in the forest zone, where the necessary humid climatic conditions prevail. Until the end of the nineteenth century, the peoples of Northern Nigeria depended for their supplies on imports brought in very expensively operated caravans from the Gold Coast, Sierra Leone, and some other neighbouring countries. With pacification and the opening up of the Lagos-Kano railway line, an ever-increasing volume of imports from those same producing countries came by sea to Lagos and was then dispatched by train to the North. These imports, however, dwindled very rapidly as farmers in Southern Nigeria, principally those in the Western Region, with much guidance and encouragement by the authorities, greatly expanded kola cultivation along with their cocoa plants. A dramatic turning-point came with the world-wide economic crisis during the late twenties and the early thirties, when imports rapidly dwindled to a negligible quantity.[9] The importers tried hard to persuade the Nigerian Administration to cut down the customs duties and also to reduce the railway freight charges, but were not successful. Their allegations that large quantities of the nut were being smuggled into the North by land routes through French territories were investigated and found untrue. Officials who carried out the investigation in both North and South reported that the imported nut was everywhere being ousted by the Nigerian nut, whose special flavour rapidly made it more popular with the northern consumers. Today Northern Nigeria depends heavily for its supplies on the South.

During the 1930's and 1940's most of the trade was carried out by small-scale Hausa dealers and by what may be called Hausa amateurs. The kola offered, and still does, much scope and excitement to the enterprising 'wandering Hausa'. One can start business with almost any size of capital, even with as little as £5, while, in comparison, in the cattle trade one needs hundreds of pounds in order to make a start. Furthermore, the kola is comparatively easy to transport and so widely in demand that it can serve as an article of exchange for which a buyer can immediately be found nearly everywhere. Thus, almost every Hausa who was on the move between the South and the North —migrant labourers, cattle dealers, malams, beggars, porters, and petty traders of all sorts—bought kola with the money he had and took it back to the North.

That phase of adventure, however, is now over. Today one can still find non-professionals buying small quantities of kola to take back to the North, but they usually do so either for the private consumption of their families or for sale in the small immediate locality of the traders' homes. The trade has gradually fallen under the control of relatively few specialized professionals and entrepreneurs. Intense competition between traders, quicker and cheaper transport, and increasing economies resulting from widening the scale of business, have narrowed the margins of profit and the amateurs have slowly been driven out. Today almost everyone who has any connexion with the kola trade—such as a carrier, packer, middleman, watchman—describes himself as a 'kola trader', but this is done mainly to claim social prestige. The number of actual traders is very small in relation to the total number of the men connected with the business.

Technical Problems of the Trade

The trade has always been risky and full of technical pitfalls, and even with the professionals of today it is attended by a great many uncertainties which call for the continual consultation of divining malams, since many of the ups and downs of the business are attributed to mystical forces. At almost every stage the entrepreneur is faced with the task of making decisions because the factors involved and the alternatives open for action are numerous.

To begin with, there are different types of kola. The nuts vary in size and in shade and, generally, the larger the size and the lighter the shade the higher the price. They differ also in flavour. In the major producing areas of the Western Region of Nigeria, different areas produce different types with different flavours of nut. Also, different areas have different kola seasons. Thus, in the Shagamu area the season is October to January while in the Ibadan area, which is only about fifty miles further north, the season is January to March. Continuity of supplies for the off-season period is secured by storing the nut under special conditions. The kola is a very delicate nut and can be highly perishable, and the stored supplies have to be examined continually and tended in special ways. The storing has to be arranged in the producing areas in the South because the dry climate of the North is unfavourable to the nut. According to men in the business, stored kola greatly improves in flavour. Because of the scarcity of fresh supplies, of the expenses of storage, of the cost of expert care, and of the risks of speculation, off-season stored kola fetches nearly twice the price of fresh kola.

The business is further complicated by the fact that in the North, too, conditions vary. Different consuming areas favour different types of kola. Also, some areas can be supplied by rail and road, others only by road. Retail prices fluctuate all the time with changes in the forces of supply and demand.

It is thus essential that traders should have day-to-day knowledge about the changing conditions of supply and demand. Decisions must be taken by the trader almost every day as to what kind of kola he should buy, in which areas he can buy it, and which of these areas offer supplies at the lowest price. At the same time the trader should also know which consuming area in the North will offer him the widest margin of profit.

A second technical problem in the trade is that it is fundamental that the trader should have immediate packing services and prompt transport facilities. These require the services of a large number of men in different specialized occupations.

A third problem is the necessity of securing credit and trust, without which the flow of the trade cannot be maintained. At almost every stage in the trade total strangers have to trust one another with large sums of money or quantities of goods.

Under pre-industrial conditions in West Africa, the difficulties in meeting these problems are numerous. Literacy is low, and the means of rapid communication of information not well developed. This is made the more difficult and complicated by the differences in language and cultural tradition between the centres of consumption in the North and the centres of production in the South—more specifically between Hausa and Yoruba respectively. Also, because of the lack of a high degree of effective centralization, contractual relations cannot be easily maintained or enforced by official central institutions, and modern methods of insuring goods in the various stages of transit between suppliers and retailers are not developed, though security of property is not yet very high.

The Social Organization of a Tribal Monopoly

In the course of evolving ways to meet these technical difficulties, the Hausa have managed to develop an extensive, intricate, business organization which covers every stage of the trade. A network of Hausa centres for the purchase, storing, packing, and transporting of the kola to the North sprang up all over the producing areas in Yorubaland. Hausa communities already established in connexion with long-distance trade in cattle and some other commodities served as bases from which men of the kola trade operated. Those communities consequently expanded and their organization became more complex. In areas where no such Hausa communities had been in existence new communities were founded. From all these communities branched smaller Hausa communities and Hausa collecting-stations interspersed between the Yoruba farms.

The most crucial role within the structure of the organization of the kola trade, as well as within the polities of the respective local Hausa communities, is that of the kola landlord, known to all, Hausa and non-Hausa alike, by the Hausa term *mai gida*. As in the cattle trade,[10] so in that of the kola, the landlord is a Hausa migrant who is permanently settled in Yorubaland. He plays several important roles. He runs at least one house for the accommodation of kola dealers who come on business from the North. The nine kola landlords in the Ibadan Hausa Quarter, known as Sabo,[11] which serves as basis for the subsequent analysis and description, run fourteen such houses. Attached to these houses they also run stores and packing yards.

The kola landlord is also the head of a commission agency which is served by several 'commission buyers' who go out daily to the outlying centres in the bush or directly to the farms, to buy supplies. Four of the nine kola landlords in Sabo act also as dealers, buying supplies regularly with their own money and sending it to agents of their own in the North. The remaining five landlords also act as dealers but do so only occasionally. For clarity of the analysis, however, it is important to separate the role of the landlord as dealer in his own right from his other roles.

Within the local Hausa community the kola landlords are usually among the biggest employers. In Sabo they have about 18 per cent of the working males of the Quarter directly under them. Apart from these employees, the kola landlords provide work for men in other occupational categories like carriers, transport commission-agents, and traders in material used in packing the nut. They also provide, in indirect ways, work for a large number of men and women who provide services of various sorts, such as cooked-food sellers, barbers, tailors, malams, and washermen.

The kola landlords are permanent settlers in the local community, while most of their clients are recent migrants. In those Hausa communities which have developed directly as a result of the development of the kola trade, like that in Shagamu, they run the Quarter politically, and the chief of the quarter is always recruited from amongst themselves. In those communities which had been in existence before the kola business in the region developed, they share political power with the landlords of other trades. Together with the other landlords, they maintain the various institutions which give the community the social stability and cultural continuity which keep it running, despite the continual mobility and change of some of its personnel.

The principal task of the landlord in the kola business is to buy kola for northern dealers. A few of these dealers come down to Ibadan themselves, bring their money with them, and lodge with a landlord. They will then go in the company of a commission-buyer, who is attached to that landlord, to the sources of supply, buy the quantity they need, return back to the Quarter with the goods, supervise the packing, and then dispatch the bundles or actually accompany them on the journey to the North. But these are relatively small-scale dealers. A few other dealers send a permanent representative, who is usually a relative, to lodge with the landlord and conduct the dealer's business with the help of the landlord.

The majority of the dealers, however, trust the local landlord to act as their agent, sending him orders and money, and leaving the conduct of the business at the supplying end to his honesty and discretion. The dealer will merely send an amount of money with a simple request to 'buy good kola' of a certain type. There is no question of specifying the exact quantity of the consignment or the price at which it should be bought. Conditions change from day to day and it is not possible to exchange correspondence and quote exact prices. The whole job is left entirely in the hands of the landlord and it is he who decides on the spot what to buy with the money, where to buy it, and at what price.

This means that the landlord must enjoy the full confidence of the dealer. Such a high degree of trust is achieved by the landlord after many years of business during which he proves his honesty and his wisdom in buying. His position, reputation, and connexions within the local community are equally important in building up his business trustworthiness. Sometimes he sends to the dealer, along with the dealer's order, a consignment of his own, which he buys with his own money, and entrusts its sale to the northern dealer. He does so only partly for profit, his main purpose being to gain the confidence of the dealer by showing mutual trust. The landlord's commission is not fixed. He is in fact at liberty to fix his own, but in order to retain the dealer's confidence he usually cuts that commission to a minimum. The landlord's commission is nearly always in the form of a lump sum, deducted from the amount sent to him, and not a percentage.

In addition to his roles as chief commission-buyer, innkeeper, and dealer, the landlord also runs a packing service. The kola is packed in a special way, in basketlike bundles, about four feet in height and two feet in diameter. The main packing material is rope imported from the North and special fresh green leaves brought from the forest. The packing is done by skilled workers. Usually three men work as a team on each package. One of them is the chief packer, the second his assistant, and the third is a 'measurer' who ascertains the exact quantity of kola in the package by bringing the nut to the packers from a large heap in a special standard-sized basket. A bundle will usually take about twenty minutes to finish. The chief packer gets two shillings for each bundle and out of this he pays sixpence to his assistant. The measurer is paid separately by the landlord. Usually there are, in each packing yard, several teams of packers. In addition to packers and measurers, the yard is also served by several carriers whose sole job is to carry the nut from the lorries to the yard and to carry bundles from the yard to the lorries.

The transport of the goods to the North is arranged by the landlord, who maintains for this purpose connexions with transport commission agents who are Hausa living within the Quarter. If the consignment is to be sent by rail, it is taken by lorry to the railway station where it is immediately entrusted to a "porters' supervisor" under whom work a number of porters. In the Ibadan railway station there are between 200 and 300 (depending on the season) Hausa porters, who are organized within four business houses under four landlords in the Quarter. Under each landlord work a number of supervisors whose task is to receive the goods from the lorries and to make all the paper arrangements with the railway authorities and, finally, to supervise the loading on the wagons.

If the consignment is to be sent by lorry, then the arrangements are made in one of the two lorry parks[12] of the Quarter. Business in these lorry parks is dominated by two transport landlords who have under them several commission agents, each of whom is aided by a number of 'boys'. One of these two landlords bears the title 'Chief of the Transporters', after nomination by the men in the business and after official installation[13] by the Chief of the Quarter. The transporters of the Quarter are commission agents who negotiate business for lorry owners and lorry drivers who regularly call at the Quarter's two lorry parks. The transport landlords also run houses for the accommodation of lorry drivers and lorry owners as well as of passengers in transit.

In recent years more kola has been sent by lorry than by train. The railway authorities are trying to lure back the traffic by

offering cheaper freight charges and by providing lorry services between kola yards and stations. But the advantages of
the lorries are still numerous. Lorry service is more personal
than that of the railway; the trader entrusts his goods to a
responsible transport landlord who is permanently settled
within the Quarter, and is a reputedly trustworthy person who
undertakes to compensate the owner of the dispatched goods
for any loss incurred in transit. The transport landlord and his
agents, in their turn, are personally acquainted with the lorry
owners and drivers. Lorry transport is also faster than rail
transport and more convenient, in that the goods are taken
straight from the yard in the South to the dealer's place in the
North. Those northern kola dealers who travel south themselves to supervise the purchase of a consignment usually
travel back to the North in the same lorry that carries their
kola. Some of these dealers even manage to sell all or some of
their consignment on the way, towards the end of the journey.
Sometimes, the consignment is redirected at the last moment
to another destination, still in the North, where sale conditions
are known to have become more favourable.[14]

Contract and the Moral Community

One significant aspect of all these arrangements for the purchase, packing, and dispatching of the kola is that they involve
a large number of men in different occupational specializations which are functionally interdependent. A second aspect
is that these men live in spatial proximity, within the same
Quarter, and can thus co-operate promptly and efficiently.
Thirdly, all these men are Hausa who share the same language
and the same cultural tradition. Among other things, these conditions contribute greatly towards solving the problem of speed
which is so crucial in the long-distance trade in a perishable
commodity.

A more important aspect, however, is that these men share
membership in a Hausa moral community, under a Hausa chief
and Hausa social and cultural institutions. By a moral community in this context I am referring to the multiplicity of informal, face-to-face, essentially non-contractual relations which
link and cross link members of the community and which im-

pel men to act in accordance with intrinsic values and norms, without much consideration for specific gain. In Sabo every man is at the centre of a network of such primary relations which condition a great deal of his social conduct. Although these are non-contractual relations, they are often created in the course of the development of contractual or of other types of formal relations. Thus, men who are brought together in the conduct of business, in the performance of religious ceremonies, in learning Arabic, or in political action, soon develop such relations since they partake in small informal, mostly dyadic, groupings. These relations develop an autonomy of their own and in their turn affect in many ways the formal relations which initially occasioned their formation.

In Sabo, primary relations are nearly always described in terms of the few kinds of specific primary relations within the nuclear family; father, mother, brother, and sister. The Hausa of Sabo are bilateral and many men do not know even the names of their grandparents on either side. Men and women divorce or separate a number of times and children remain in the custody of either parent in accordance with circumstances, even though the Islamic family law is formally in force. Furthermore, child fostering is very extensively practised. The Hausa also observe inter-generational avoidance as well as age grouping. Classificatory terms of the primary family relations are used to cover a wide range of social relations. Under these conditions it can take the foreign observer in Sabo a long time to sort out, for example, which of the men who call each other by the term 'brother' are real brothers and which are not.

There are no corporate political groupings in Sabo and the major principle of political alignment is that of the patron-client relationship. This relationship is nearly always described in terms of the 'father-son' relation. The 'Chief-subject' relation is described in the same terms. Early in my field-work in Sabo, a fairly young cattle landlord was instructed by the Chief of the Quarter to take a certain action which involved paying the Chief a substantial amount of money. The landlord obeyed unquestionably although the order seemed to me to have been very arbitrary. When I questioned the landlord what made him obey the order, he replied in astonishment: 'But the

Chief is my father.' He then explained to me that his own father had been an intimate 'brother' of the Chief for a long time and that the Chief had always treated him as a son. He cited a series of incidents in his life to substantiate this statement. I was most surprised at the time as he told me that when his own father had died, he himself, in the company of two of his intimate age mates (whom he described as 'brothers'), had gone to the Chief to convey to him their condolences over the loss of the Chief's 'brother'.

It is obvious that these primary relations require time to develop and that therefore the longer the period a man has been living in the Quarter, the stronger and the more numerous these relations become. On the basis mainly of seniority of residence in the Quarter, but also considering other, usually highly overlapping, criteria, the people of Sabo can be classified into three major categories which I call 'the permanent core', 'the new migrants', and 'the transient population'.[15] By virtue of their length of residence and of the numerous enduring primary, as well as contractual, ties holding between them, men of the permanent core constitute the nucleus of what I have called here 'the moral community'. And it is these men who maintain and support the relations of credit and of trust not only within the Quarter but also between men from the Quarter and outsiders who conduct business with them. Among these men are those who own the houses of the Quarter and control the employment of most of the rest of the community. They are also the men who operate the various institutions which ensure social stability in the Quarter despite a great deal of mobility on the part of its members. To the northern dealer a man from this category has a fixed 'address', and a well-defined status, within the intricate context of Sabo society, which exercises continual moral and political pressure on the man and make him honour his financial obligations. Often, it is sufficient that the dealer should have the man recommended by the Chief of the Quarter for the dealer to trust the man financially even without having had business with him before.

The intimate relations which make up the texture of such a moral community can arise only between men who can easily and effectively communicate with each other, by using the same language and sharing the same cultural symbols, customs, and traditional values. Within a multi-tribal society they can arise mainly between members of the same tribe. Thus, tribal specialization in the trade in specific commodities contributes towards the solution of the problem of credit and trust which is so crucial for the trade.

The community is also organized as a polity and when the need arises its members are capable of acting corporately against external pressure. This capacity for political action has been important in the kola trade, as well as in the cattle trade, because the business organization has been evolved in the course of continuous competition and dispute with Yoruba kola traders and farmers who, in their struggle with the Hausa, have had the support of Yoruba political groupings and moral support.

Inter-Tribal Politics

The development of the community as a polity has been interconnected in a variety of ways with the development of the trade. The nature of this interconnexion can be best examined through the analysis of a chain of events, extended through time, which exhibit the arrangement of alignments. Events of this kind can be taken from the history of the kola trade, in the Ibadan District, over the last three decades.[16]

In 1934, after the steady increase in the volume of kola exported to the North during the preceding few years, the Ibadan Native Authority Council decided to establish a kola market on a plot adjacent to the Hausa Quarter, Sabo, in order to facilitate the trade, assuming that supplies would be brought to the market by enterprising Yoruba traders who would buy the kola from the farmers and sell it to the Hausa. The all-Yoruba Council were enthusiastic and hopeful. They decided that the market, which was to be called 'Aleshinloye', would be opened by an official ceremony and that notices about its opening should be put in railway stations 'as far as Kano and in all the principal towns'. They instructed the Chief of Sabo to send his messengers to the northern provinces in order to announce the establishment of the market to the great merchants in the major towns and to see to it that those merchants should attend the opening ceremony.

From the records of a few years later one learns that the market was a complete failure. The Hausa kola traders were not in attendance there. Fighting shy of the Yoruba kola traders, they continued to go to the sources of the kola, penetrating deeply into the forest, and buying their supplies straight from the farmers. When export from this area had begun, the Hausa traders had operated from the already existing Hausa communities as bases, leaving these communities in the morning and returning to them later in the day with the purchased supplies. But within a short period they had established Hausa stations, within Yoruba settlements near the farms, which served as outposts from which Hausa commission buyers operated, with the help of locally stationed Hausa guides and brokers. In a few years time these outposts turned into fully fledged and well-organized Hausa communities.

The process, as manifested in the histories of the few communities which have been studied, seems to have been similar everywhere. A number of Hausa brokers would lodge temporarily with Yoruba house-owners, and then, as their number increased, and as they were joined by men from related occupations, they constituted a social problem within the polity of the settlement. The Yoruba population would complain that the Hausa were harbouring burglars, pick-pockets, and other categories of 'undesirables' who endangered law and order in the community. To meet this danger, and also to meet the simultaneous clamour of the Hausa to live on their own—'because our customs are different'—the local chiefs would decide to allot to the Hausa a special Quarter within the settlement and would recognize one of the Hausa men of influence (always one of the important business landlords) as chief, who would be held responsible to them for the conduct of his people, inform the authorities about the undesirables in his community, and help in the collection of taxes. More men would then join the community: tailors, barbers, malams, petty traders, and beggars.

At the same time women would come in and consolidate the community in other respects. The prostitutes[17] would have been there from the first stages and many of them would eventually be married by some of the men and slip into the respectability of family life. Men who were already married would bring their wives to settle with them. The women would bear children and also foster other children and would soon establish a trade, usually preparing cooked food for the large number of bachelors and strangers in the community. In the process, the community organized itself in ways which would make it possible to accommodate and serve a large number of Hausa men who would come for business during the kola season. With its development and consolidation and with the development of its business, the community became the basis from which further ramification of the Hausa network became possible and Hausa business penetrated deeper into the forest.

Thus, in the course of the 1930's and 1940's, scores of such communities sprang up in the Ibadan, Shagamu, Abeokuta, Agege, Ifo, Ijebu, and other districts, each community serving as a centre of Hausa trade and Hausa culture. Each community has a core of permanently settled Hausa population who maintain an institutional framework which makes it possible for other parts of the population to be on the move. In the course of each year these mobile men circulate in various communities, following the different seasons.[18]

By means of these processes the Hausa have established an elaborate, large-scale, complex organization by which they have managed to control the kola trade, to overcome the difficulties involved in achieving this control, and even to dictate prices to the farmers.

As Hausa monopoly over the trade tightened up, the Yoruba kola traders organized their efforts for counter-action. As from the early 1930's they began to submit one petition after another to the Administration and to the local Yoruba chiefs demanding that the Hausa 'strangers' should be prevented from going direct to the farms and should be forced to buy their supplies from the formally established markets. In 1940 the Council of the Chiefs of Ibadan discussed the matter in a number of its meetings and resolved that a rule should be officially laid down 'that no one other than a native of Ibadan and its villages should buy kola in the Ibadan District except in the kola markets'. But the Resident vetoed the decision on the ground that it would be a direct interference with the freedom of trade.

The matter was again discussed in several meetings during

1943 and the Chiefs suggested the establishment of rural kola markets from which the Hausa were to be forced to buy. But here again the District Officer objected, ruling that no one should be forced to buy or sell anywhere. Representatives of the Yoruba kola traders, who were also present in the discussion objected to the idea of rural markets, maintaining that there was no need for such markets and that all they wanted was a ruling prohibiting the Hausa from going to the farms. The representative of the kola farmers, who was also present in the discussion, declared, on the other hand, that the farmers were quite satisfied with the current arrangements by which the Hausa buyers came straight to their farms, as these arrangements solved for the farmers the problem of labour shortage. He pointed out that large numbers of men were needed to act as carriers to convey the kola from the farms to the markets; the Hausa buyers brought with them their own carriers, together with the lorries which carried the kola away.

The traders' representatives were shocked at what they later described as tribal treachery. They stated to the local authorities that the attitude of the farmers' representative was detrimental to the interests and progress of 'his own kith and kin' and only helped the Hausa strangers to thrive. They claimed, furthermore, that in Hausa-land the authorities prevented southern strangers from going to the villages to sell kola unless those strangers were accompanied by local Hausa brokers who extracted their commission from the strangers on the spot. In Yorubaland, on the other hand, they went on, the Hausa went to the villages, bought the kola, packed and loaded it on their lorries, and went straight to the North, evading the payment of taxes and cheating the helpless farmers.

The dispute continued for years and has been recently carried over to the post-independence period. The restraining influence of the former Administration has been replaced by that of the Federal Government and federal party politics. The Hausa kola landlords continue to manoeuvre their way by repeatedly accommodating their tactics to changes in party politics on the local, regional, and federal levels.

Today some kola is sold in a number of markets in the Region. In Ibadan there is a special section for the sale of kola in the King's Market (oja-Oba). Also, some Yoruba farmers and traders occasionally load lorries with kola and go direct to the Hausa Quarter to offer the nut for sale to the kola landlords. But the quantity of kola involved in all this is only a small fraction of the total volume of export to the North. The bulk is still bought by the Hausa straight from the farms.

Struggle Over the Commission

The dispute between Hausa and Yoruba was not confined to the question of the collection of supplies. At some stages, both Yoruba farmers and Yoruba kola traders joined forces against the Hausa over the payment of commission, known by the Hausa term *lada.* From the beginning the Hausa claimed that it was only proper and 'in accordance with the accepted custom' that the Yoruba sellers should pay the commission, amounting to 10 per cent of the purchase price, to the Hausa commission buyers. When a Yoruba seller refused to comply with this demand, the Hausa boycotted him until he was forced to pay. What has angered the Yoruba most is that while the commission in the case of the kola is taken from the seller, it is taken from the buyer in the case of cattle—the payer in both cases being Yoruba.

The Yoruba have not stopped agitating against this apparent "injustice" and at some stages they tried to hit back. In 1950 the Hausa kola landlords throughout the region declared a boycott of the kola farmers from Agege who had refused, *en masse,* to pay the commission to the Hausa agents. The Nigerian *Daily Times* wrote (on 13 May 1950) that Kola planters from Remo, Ijebo-Ode, Ifo, Attan, Otta, Abeokuta, Ojokoro, and other centres, had resolved to give the Hausa kola traders a one and a half month ultimatum to reconsider their decision of boycotting the Agege sellers, and to stop the collection of *lada* in all kola-producing areas. At the expiration of the period of the ultimatum, if the Hausa traders remained unyielding, the planters would start direct dealings with consumers in the North. The paper mentioned that the decision had been taken at a meeting held at the 'Headquarters Store of the Nigerian Farmers' Union', Agege, at which representatives were present. In their speeches the delegates were reported to have urged all Kola planters to stand firm and to endeavour to put an end to what they called 'bad practice' of the Hausa traders.

But the odds against the farmers' stand have been many. They are numerous and are scattered over a wide region with few occasions on which they can interact. They have made many attempts to organize effectively, but their associations have been mainly local and ephemeral. These associations have come into being only during a particular, immediate crisis, at the end of which they have disintegrated.

In contrast, the kola landlords are much fewer in number, possibly not exceeding 200 (in 1963) over the whole Region. Although they are based in particular localities, they regularly and frequently meet together. As different areas have different types and different seasons of kola, a landlord buys supplies from different areas. His business interests are thus not confined to his local settlement but cover a very large part of the Region. They often meet at the kola sheds of the railway stations and in the lorry parks. In addition to this interaction between the landlords, thousands of Hausa commission buyers, carriers, packers, and porters circulate, in accordance with the seasons, between the various centres and are also followed in this movement by men and women from different occupational categories to provide the necessary services for them. For all these the kola is a fundamental vested interest and their moral and political support of the stand of their patrons, the landlords, is unquestionably given. For these Hausa men, kola is their life, and is a tribal political issue of the first order.

The Politics of Ethnic Exclusiveness

This does not mean that the Hausa have always been in perfect harmony among themselves in the conduct of the trade. In Ibadan, when Sabo became congested, some Hausa began to settle as tenants in Yoruba houses near the King's Market (*oja-Oba*), where kola was being sold. At first these Hausa were agents and employees of the kola landlords of Sabo, but towards the end of the 1930's some of them began to work as agents or landlords on their own.

In Sabo this development was viewed with alarm. During 1939 and 1940 the Chief and the leading business landlords of the Quarter submitted a number of petitions to the Native Authority demanding that the individual Hausa who were living in the centre of the town should be compelled to move their residence to Sabo. In justification of this demand, the petitioners claimed that what they called 'the floating Hausa population' had been harbouring thieves and other undesirables and evading the payment of taxes, and were able to do so only because they lived out of the control of the Chief and of the rest of the community. At the same time, the petitioners did not hide the fact that they were demanding the withdrawal of these Hausa from the town for economic reasons. The "floating Hausa", the petitioners maintained, were going to the railway station to meet Hausa strangers coming from the North, and then taking these strangers straight to *Oja-Oba* and thus depriving the Sabo landlords of their source of livelihood. The problem was discussed at length by the Ibadan Native Authority but the Resident was opposed to any official measure which aimed at forcing people to reside where they did not want to, though he suggested that indirect measures could be taken, such as persuading Yoruba landlords not to let accommodation to Hausa. He also suggested that the Council should forbid men from sleeping in mosques, sheds, streets, or any other public places.

What actually disturbed Sabo landlords was not just the competition which those Hausa presented to them in their business, for they themselves were in competition with each other all the time. They were disturbed rather by the fact that those Hausa were out of the control of the moral and political pressure of the community and were thus a threat to the interests of the whole Hausa network of communities in their control of the business. The dissident Hausa could offer the Yoruba farmers or traders higher prices and exact lower commission from the northern dealers and sooner or later this would have been a serious breach in the united stand of the Hausa *vis-à-vis* the Yoruba.

A similar kind of 'loophole' in the Hausa organization of the trade appeared when some of the Hausa outposts which served the main Hausa trading communities developed their own landlords, became autonomous, and started to compete with the older communities. Thus, for example, there arose lengthy disputes between the Ibadan Hausa community and the rising

Hausa community at Akanran. The disputes went on for years and were further complicated, during the 1950's, by the intrusion of party politics.

In nearly all these cases a compromise solution was duly found. In the case of the Hausa 'floating population' in the centre of Ibadan, as well as in the case of Akanran, a junior chief was nominated by the local Hausa and officially 'turbanned' by the Chief of Sabo, the junior chief thus acknowledging allegiance to the Sabo community. In recent years the Akanran community has developed further and become an autonomous community, within the Hausa network of communities in the Region, even though much of its business is still in connexion with Sabo.

In 1953 the Hausa communities in the Western Region expressed their tribal solidarity when their chiefs officially formed a joint association which they called 'The Federal Union of the Western Hausa Chiefs'. The Chief of Sabo (Ibadan) was elected as Chairman.

The point which I want to emphasize here is that there is a close interconnexion between Hausa organization of trade and Hausa political organization. This political organization is based as much on the economic interdependence between individuals and groups within the community and between the community and other Hausa communities in the Region, as on ethnic exclusiveness.[19] Even though Ibadan is predominantly Islamic, Sabo constitutes a separate, localized, ritual community centred around its own Central Mosque under its own chief Imam. The community is also an autonomous polity organized around the chieftaincy and the various political institutions connected with it. Apart from his wealth, invested in both business and housing, by which he commands the services and allegiance of a large number of people, the Chief also derives much power and authority from his role as arbitrator in cases of business disputes and from his role as a *kadi,* a Shari's judge, to whom all matters relating to the family are submitted. He is also mediator between his people and the local Yoruba authorities and his word with these authorities is usually effective. He also has important connexions with sources of power outside the Quarter which greatly enhance his position among his people. He is helped to maintain his authority by a relatively large number of retainers, advisers, messengers, praise-singers, announcers, and malams. Through his office he can exert a great deal of pressure on individuals and make them act in conformity with the general interests. Within the Ibadan polity the community expresses its identity in the idiom of Hausa culture and Hausa ethnic exclusiveness.

From this it can be seen that a great deal of the control exercised by the Hausa over the kola trade is interconnected with Hausa political autonomy and Hausa social organization in Yorubaland.

The Yoruba kola traders and farmers, as well as their political supporters, must have realized this, since it is evident from the records that whenever a dispute with the Hausa kola landlords flared up there was an almost instantaneous attack by Yoruba political groupings on the autonomy of Sabo and on its political institutions. Thus when during the early 1940's the dispute was particularly intense, there was a great deal of agitation in Ibadan against Hausa religious separatism from Yoruba Islam, against the messengers of the Hausa chief wearing special uniforms and against alleged insulting behaviour on the part of the Hausa chief towards some eminent Yoruba chiefs. In 1941 the chiefs of Ibadan seemed to be alarmed at Hausa expansion in their town because they insisted that the D.O. should make the Hausa realize that however long they might remain in Ibadan they would always be regarded as strangers and that on no account would they be allowed in the future 'to express self-determination' of any kind. In 1942 one Yoruba political association officially demanded that the man occupying the position of Chief of Sabo at the time should be immediately dismissed from his office because he had been found guilty by a civil court of buying stolen property. The Administration had, on principle, to comply with this demand. The Chief was subsequently dismissed against the protest and bitter opposition of almost the whole Quarter. And because the Hausa would not accept for the position a candidate nominated by the Yoruba chiefs and supported only by a few individuals within Sabo, the Quarter remained for about a year in a state of continual disorder.[20]

Conclusion

Migrants in West African towns, as everywhere else, seek the companionship of men from their own ethnic group, with whom they can communicate intimately through the use of the same language and other cultural symbols. Men from the same tribe tend to help each other in finding jobs and accommodation and to participate in common ceremonial. Spontaneous groupings of this type often serve as a basis for the formation of more or less formal tribal associations.[21] As Gluckman states of similar groupings in the industrial Central African towns, this kind of 'tribalism' is the 'tribalism' of all migrants in all towns the world over. It is based on a limited number of interests and does not involve, as in rural tribalism, participation in a living, highly organized, system of political, economic, and other social relations.[22]

In contrast, the Hausa communities in Yoruba towns which I have been discussing, *do* involve the participation of their members in such a living system. Sabo is a highly autonomous, multi-purposive, integrated community. Its men are engaged in occupations which are functionally interdependent and which bring them into intensive interaction with each other. These men not only live, but also work, worship, and seek entertainment and companionship, within the Quarter. The Quarter is a highly enduring, on-going system of roles, maintained principally by the landlords in their manifold activities.

The people of Sabo express their autonomy by greatly emphasizing their cultural identity and exclusiveness. But the Hausa generally are far from being a chauvinistic people and it is widely known, even among themselves, that they descend from different ethnic stocks and that the assimilation of strangers into their society and culture is a process which goes on all the time. What is even more significant about this emphasis is that Sabo is very far from being a social or cultural "extension" of Hausaland. Sabo culture and system of social relations differ radically from their counterparts in Hausaland in such important respects as stratification, pattern of marriage, occupational structure, nature of the chieftaincy, the composition and organization of the domestic units, and so on. Sabo culture, and that of the rest of the network of Hausa communities in Yorubaland, is thus distinct from northern Hausa culture. Rouch makes a similar statement about the culture of the Hausa migrant communities in Ghana which he studied. This is not the original Hausa culture changing slowly in a process of the so-called 'detribalization' of the new migrants, but a highly stable culture existing in its own right and maintained principally by men of the permanent core, many of whom have been living in Yorubaland for two or three generations.

Culture is a way of life, but for the people of Sabo it is also a political ideology which stresses identity as well as exclusiveness and which can be explained by reference, not to northern Hausa culture, but to the roles these people play in the conduct of long-distance trade. It is important for the business landlords and for those working under them to emphasize in every way that they are Hausa, because under the circumstances Hausa northern dealers will entrust their goods and money only into the hands of Hausa 'brothers abroad',[23] who live within a highly stable Hausa moral community. Also, it is essential for this community to organize politically in order to maintain Hausa monopoly in trade, by preventing foreigners from infiltrating into the organization and by preventing Hausa 'black legs' from disrupting it, and this political organization is achieved under the banner: 'Our customs are different; we are Hausa.'

I have left out of this discussion many demographic, political, and historical processes involved in the formation and functioning of these communities. An integrated analysis of these and some other processes would require a detailed monograph. What I have been attempting here is only to indicate that there seem to be some significant systematic interconnexions between the organizational requirements of long-distance trade and the tendency of migrants from tribal groups which are engaged in this kind of trade, to form autonomous tribal communities in the foreign towns in which they operate.

It is hard to find detailed systematic data on the development and organization of tribal migrant communities of this type for other parts of West Africa. But the partial, often fragmentary, information which abounds in the literature suggests that such communities are widespread in the towns of the forest belt. This is because the broad conditions for the formation of such communities prevail over the larger part of the sub-continent. Firstly, ecological conditions vary widely, with the sharp division into forest and savanna cutting right across and thus giving rise to wide economic variations which tend to stimulate exchange and economic interdependence.[24] It is only in recent years that scholars have become aware of the importance of internal trade in West African economies and of the large volumes of goods and money involved in it.[25] Secondly, ecological divisions, particularly those between forest and savanna, often overlap with tribal divisions.[26] In Nigeria alone which, as Forde states, represents a cross-section of the various physical conditions in the Guinea lands,[27] there are approximately 248 distinct languages.[28] Thus, trade between different ecological areas often involves interaction between individuals and groups from different tribes. Thirdly, what have been called 'pre-industrial conditions' prevail over the whole area, and the new states of West Africa are still grappling with the problems of economic development, communication, and the establishment of efficient, centralized administration. Many of the towns of the area can still be described as pre-industrial. Ibadan, which is the largest city in tropical Africa, has often been described as a 'city-village', because over 70 per cent of its Yoruba adult males are farmers.[29] The structure of such towns is in sharp contrast to that of the highly integrated industrial urban centres discussed for Central Africa by Epstein, Gluckman, and Mitchell.[30] Fourthly, the organization of long-distance trade is an indigenous tradition which has been evolved in the course of many centuries and has been widely practised throughout the area.[31] The landlord system which is a crucial part of this organization has existed in many parts of West Africa for a long time now.[32]

These conditions have tended to foster tribal specializations in long-distance trade and have led in many parts of West Africa to the development of tribal networks of migrant communities, in the formation of which culture has followed the trade.

NOTES

1. I am grateful to Professor Daryll Forde and to Dr. David Arnott for reading an earlier draft of this paper and commenting on it. For convenience of presentation, the term "tribe" will be used in this discussion for "ethnic group".

2. J. Rouch, "Migration au Ghana," *Journal de la Société des Africanistes,* XXVI (1956).

3. M. Banton, *West African City* (London: Oxford University Press, 1957).

4. Rouch expressed his position on this point more explicitly at the 1964 conference on "Tropical African Studies" when he stated that the traditional culture patterns and social institutions of migrants were among the most crucial factors in the variations of response to the modern situation; see D. Forde, "Tropical African Studies," (Report), *Africa,* XXXV, No. 1 (1965), p. 38. Banton suggests as a working hypothesis that "other things being equal, the more devolution of authority there is in tribal societies the more rapidly contractual associations like companies emerge (in towns)"; see Banton, *op. cit.,* p. 195.

5. Rouch, *op. cit.*

6. See R. M. Prothero, *Migrant Labour from Sokoto Province Northern Nigeria* (Northern Region of Nigeria: Government Printer, 1959).

7. R. Galletti, K.D.S. Baldwin, and F. O. Dina, *Nigerian Cocoa Farmers* (London: Oxford University Press, 1956), write: "It is stated that in some places, especially in the Abeokuta and Ilesha areas, the Hausa labourers recognize a local head, who may bargain about wage rates on their behalf with the farmers and help them to obtain lodging. But such a head of the Hausa community does not recruit labour or hold himself responsible for the conduct and welfare of the labourers" (p. 209). However, no such arrangements were found in the Ibadan district between the thousands of Hausa migrant labourers working in the surrounding farms and the chief of the local Hausa community, though many of these labourers occasionally pay short visits to the Hausa quarter. When one of these labourers dies, his body is brought to Sabo for the arrangement of his burial and if he did not leave money or had no relatives, the Sabo chief would then pay the expenses of the burial.

8. In a previous paper I discussed some aspects of the social organization of the trade in cattle, though this was in connexion with a differ-

ent sociological problem. See A. Cohen, "The Social Organization of Credit in a West African Cattle Market," *Africa,* XXXV, No. 1 (1965).

9. P. T. Bauer, *West African Trade* (London: Routledge & Kegan Paul, Ltd., 1963), quotes figures indicating trends in this respect for the period 1920–48 (pp. 381–2).

10. See Cohen, *op. cit.*

11. Short for *Sabon Gari.*

12. One is known as the Kano Lorry Park and the other, a much smaller one, as the Sokoto Lorry Park.

13. The official ceremony is referred to as "turbanning", as it involves putting a white turban by the Chief of the Quarter on the head of the man on whom the title is conferred.

14. The discussion in this paper covers the organization of the trade only at the exporting end in the South. Information on business organization at the receiving end in the North can be found in Forde, "The Native Economies," in M. Perham (ed.), *The Native Economies of Nigeria,* pp. 22–215; M. G. Smith, "Exchange and Marketing Among the Hausa," in P. Bohannan and G. Dalton (eds.), *Markets in Africa* (Evanston; Northwestern University Press, 1962), pp. 299–334; and Bauer, *op. cit.,* pp. 379–392.

15. More details on this categorization are given in A. Cohen, "Stranger Communities: The Hausa," in P. C. Lloyd, A. L. Mabogunje, B. Awe (eds.), *The City of Ibadan* (forthcoming).

16. Unless otherwise stated, all the historical data contained in this discussion are from written records.

17. Known as *Karuwai.*

18. During the few off season months some of them engage in petty trading while others go to the North to do some agricultural work.

19. Bauer, *op. cit.,* draws attention to this relation between the political organization of these Hausa communities and Hausa control over trade (see pp. 389–92). He also makes the penetrating observation that "Effective price rings seem to be most easily organized where there are few traders and where these are of the same race or tribe; the activities of the Hausa cattle traders are an example of this" (p. 392).

20. Later, as business began to suffer, the people of the Quarter decided that it was better for them to have an unpopular man in the

position of Chief of the Quarter than to have no chief at all, and so they finally accepted the proposed candidate. After a few years of continual disturbance and agitation the dismissed candidate was returned to his position.

21. In Nigeria they are often known as "tribal unions". See J. Coleman, *Nigeria: Background to Nationalism* (Los Angeles and Berkeley: University of California Press, 1958), pp. 213–214.

22. See M. Gluckman, "Anthropological Problems Arising From the African Industrial Revolution," in A. Southall (ed.), *Social Change in Modern Africa* (London: Oxford University Press, 1961).

23. As Coleman puts it, *op. cit.,* p. 214.

24. See D. Forde, "The Cultural Map of West Africa: Successive Adaptations to Tropical Forests and Grasslands," in S. and P. Ottenberg (eds.), *Cultures and Societies of Africa* (New York: Random House, 1960), pp. 116–138.

25. See Bauer, *op. cit.,* pp. 379–92; Forde, "The Native Economies," *op. cit;* P. Hill, "Some Characteristics of Indigenous West African Enterprise," in Nigerian Institute of Social and Economic Research, *Conference Proceedings March 1962* (Ibadan: N.I.S.E.R., 1963).

26. See Forde, "The Cultural Map of West Africa: Successive Adaptations to Tropical Forests and Grasslands," *op. cit.*

27. Forde, "The Native Economics," *op. cit.*

28. Coleman, *op. cit.,* p. 15.

29. See P. C. Lloyd, *Yoruba Land Law* (London: Oxford University Press, 1962).

30. Respectively: A. L. Epstein, Politics in *An Urban African Community* (Manchester: Manchester University Press, 1958); Gluckman, *op. cit.;* J. C. Mitchell, *Tribalism and the Plural Society* (An Inaugural Lecture) (London: Oxford University Press, 1960).

31. See R. Oliver and J. D. Fage, *A Short History of Nigeria* (London: Pengiun African Library, 1962), pp. 107–11; E. W. Bovill, *The Golden Trade of the Moors* (London: Oxford University Press, 1961); Smith, *op. cit.*

32. See V. R. Dorjahn and C. Fyfe, "Landlord and Stranger," *The Journal of African History,* III, 3 (1962); and Hill, op. cit., p. 447.

CHAPTER 11

The Political Role of Ibo Ethnic Unions

AUDREY C. SMOCK

Ethnic unions constituted the most widespread type of semi-modern organization among the Ibo-speaking people in the former Eastern Region of Nigeria. These Ibo ethnic unions resembled similar ethnic associations in other transitional political systems that combine a modern structure and functions with an ascriptively defined membership base. In contrast with the sporadic formation of such ethnic associations in India and other African countries, a very high percentage of the Ibo villages, clans, divisions and provinces established ethnic-improvement unions. By 1951, when the colonial administration began to initiate substantial political reforms, ethnic unions existed at various levels of the political system in Ibo-speaking areas, representing both traditional communities and colonial administrative units.

Ethnic unions, like the political parties which followed them, were a reaction to the forces of social change unleashed by the western impact. In Nigeria immigrants to urban centers began to form ethnic unions in the late 1920's in their attempt to provide for security in the alien and sometimes hostile environment. Gradually Ibo ethnic unions transformed themselves from mutual aid societies with an ethnic base into multi-purpose agencies with both urban aid and rural community development functions. Many Ibo unions managed to collect a portion of the salaries of their members in the urban branches to finance community development projects in their home villages, particularly the building of schools and the endowment of scholarships. Consequently Ibo ethnic unions, unlike the urban based ethnic associations of some other groups, organizationally linked immigrants in the cities with their home communities. Ethnic unions therefore played a significant role in the rapid Ibo educational advance beginning in the 1930's and in the development of modern facilities in the countryside.

The establishment of this network of Ibo ethnic unions in most places preceded the efforts of the leaders of the National Convention of Nigerian Citizens (NCNC), the dominant party in the Eastern Region, to organize local branches based on individual membership. Hence while the NCNC never encountered serious opposition by another political party in its home territory, it did have to reach some kind of accomodation with the ethnic unions. The general willingness of the ethnic unions to cooperate with the NCNC and to assume a supportive role reduced the possibility that structural weaknesses would injure the NCNC's electoral prospects. Instead of expending the requisite time and resources for building an effective, coordinated, mass party, the NCNC could depend on the ethnic unions to perform many political functions. Thus the accomodation of the NCNC with the ethnic unions seemed to diminish the incentive for the NCNC to develop a strong organization of its own. According to some observers the NCNC as a party never transcended the sum total of such supporting organizations. John Mackintosh, for example, described the NCNC as "a gathering of clan and town unions rather than a party based on individual membership."[1]

When this author studied the relationship between the NCNC and some ethnic unions, the political role of the ethnic unions proved to be far more complex than previous analyses had suggested. Ethnic unions varied considerably in the political functions they performed depending on three factors: first, their organizational structure; second, the community they represented; and third, the political environment in which they operated. Moreover, there was no direct correlation between the political role assumed by the relevant ethnic unions and the strength of the local NCNC organization. Weaknesses in the NCNC structure and operation, and there were many, resulted from factors other than the existence and effectiveness of ethnic unions.

The extraordinary number of Ibo ethnic unions and the range in the functions they performed preclude any generalizations as to what constituted a "typical" Ibo union. For this reason, this paper will examine the relationship between the NCNC and four groups of ethnic unions which differed in respect to the three aforementioned variables. These ethnic unions also represented a wide spectrum in terms of the functions they executed in their communities. The following ethnic unions will be analyzed: the ethnic unions representing some of the small village groups in Abaja Ngwo County; the Abiriba Communal Improvement Union, which was based on a large clan in Bende Division; the clan and county ethnic unions in Mbaise, a county council area in Owerri Division; and the urban branches of the ethnic unions constituted by the immigrants from Abiriba and Mbaise in Port Harcourt, the industrial center of the Eastern Region.[2]

All of the ethnic unions discussed in this paper operated on the micro-political rather than on the regional level. There was a more inclusive Ibo union, the Ibo State Union, which claimed to be the agent of "all the Ibos." The Ibo State Union did not, however, operate as an effective political force on any level of the political system. While the Ibo State Union theoretically included every branch of all Ibo unions, only a small fraction of the existing Ibo unions ever registered, sent delegates to conferences, or communicated with the central chapter. Furthermore, the officers and the executive committee of the Ibo State Union never exerted any kind of control over those unions which did affiliate. Ethnic unions, which had formed in response to local needs and goals, resisted the occasional and superficial efforts of the Ibo State Union to divert them from their parochial orientation.

Moreover, the traditional, colonial, and post-colonial Eastern political systems all were relatively decentralized. Prior to the imposition of colonial rule, Ibo-speaking people lived in autonomous village groups without any centralized authority within or above the local community. While the colonial system did for the first time establish a regional government and county councils, the predisposition for indirect rule precluded the evolution of a regional administration with extensive control over and penetration of local communities. In the Eastern Regional political system the formulation of demands, recruitment of political leaders, communication between the politicans and the populace and competition for amenities took place primarily on a local level. Regional politics subsumed the melange of parochial groups without subordinating their conflicting interests to some higher principle like loyalty to the NCNC or Ibo unity. With Ibos constituting approximately two-thirds of the population, cleavages within the Ibo community on geographical (or subnational) and religious lines energized the political system. Due to its inclusiveness, the Ibo identity did not constitute a salient political referent. On a regional level generally an alliance of several Ibo subgroups would confront a similar coalition with minority (non Ibo) groups joining one or both sides.

To comprehend the political role of Ibo ethnic unions and their relationship with the NCNC it is therefore necessary to study political configurations in subregional entities. Local councils operated at the village and county levels. Municipalities, like Port Harcourt, constituted another important political arena. The organization of the NCNC reflected the existing administrative divisions, which coincided with elected bodies.[3]

Abaja-Ngwo County

Before the war the Abaja-Ngwo County, which was part of Udi Division, had a population of approximately 125,000 people. Each of the 27 village groups constituting Abaja-Ngwo County had its own local council, as well as representation on the Abaja-Ngwo County Council. Village groups tended to be small in size with their population ranging from about 1,700 to 6,000. During the colonial period administrative officers recognized sixteen clans in Udi Division. These clan divisions did not, however, reflect traditional identities in the Udi area, any more than similar clan designations did in other Ibo-speaking areas. Unlike the Mbaise area, where colonial clan designations gradually became accepted identities, in Abaja-Ngwo villagers adhered to the more primary and traditional village group as their frame of reference. Consequently ethnic unions in Abaja-Ngwo represented the interests of village groups rather than clans. Residents from Abaja-Ngwo in Enugu, the nearby regional capital, once tried to form an Udi Union, but the more inclusive union ceased operating due to a lack of support.

Ethnic unions in Abaja-Ngwo did not develop a complex organizational structure comparable to the ones in Abiriba, Mbaise and other more developed Ibo areas. In contrast with the other Ibo ethnic unions discussed in this paper, the village unions in Abaja-Ngwo had a much smaller membership base, almost all of which was located either at home or in Enugu. Hence there was no need for an organizational structure linking together representatives of urban branches with the community at home. The relatively low level of educational development in this part of the Eastern Region, when combined with the small size of the village groups, meant that, unlike in other areas, there was a scarcity of educated men to lead the ethnic unions. Moreover, few ethnic unions in Abaja-Ngwo achieved the central position in the life of the community that the Abiriba Communal Improvement Union and the Mbaise clan unions did. In most of the village groups in Abaja-Ngwo the existence of a number of organizations, some traditional and some modern, resulted in a fragmentation of power and the inability of any one association to make binding decisions. Under these circumstances few of the village unions managed to undertake community development activities or to become strong political vehicles.

Almost every village group in Abaja-Ngwo had a branch organization of the NCNC at some time. Like some of the other organizations there, many of the NCNC branches had a somewhat tenuous existence. The low level of political consciousness and the consequent irrelevance of party activities for village affairs and for the operation of the county council made it difficult to sustain NCNC branches. Even when an effort was made to resuscitate village branches in 1962 and 1963, only a very few people attended meetings.

Despite the general lack of interest in politics, some people came to resent the inability of any of their NCNC representatives in the Eastern House of Assembly to become members of the cabinet. Without a spokesman in the cabinet, Udi Division could not receive assistance for special development projects. Before the 1961 regional election people from most village groups in Abaja formed a new organization, the Oha-Ode-N'ozo Union, which sponsored an independent candidate for the local seat in the Eastern House of Assembly. Since the NCNC candidate was supported only by his own village group and a few others, the independent candidate was elected. The Ona-Odo N'ozo Union did not remain a significant political force after the election. By 1964 the Abaja people once more supported the NCNC.

Abiriba

Abiriba was before the war a town or village group of approximately 40,000 people. Like many other Ibo communities, the Abiribans considered themselves to be a kinship group descended from a common ancestor, as well as a geographical unit. The Abiribans had a long heritage of trading in various parts of what is now Biafra and in other areas of Nigeria and the Camerouns. As a consequence of their traditional commercial activities, they had become one of the wealthiest communities in Eastern Nigeria. Since more men were traders than farmers, up to three-fourths of the adult males could be absent from Abiriba at any given time. By World War II, a considerable number of traders had emigrated to urban centers in search of better economic opportunities.

Abiribans formed an ethnic union in 1941, which became the instrument through which the community maintained its cohesion and tapped the financial resources of wealthy traders for the development of Abiriba. The Abiriba Communal Improvement Union (ACIU) had branches in some twenty urban centers and towns throughout Nigeria and the Camerouns in 1966. Three times a year, the various branches sent delegates to a central conference in Abiriba to discuss policy and to coordinate activities. Each year the delegates elected officers, who, along with an appointed, full-time, paid administrative secretary, directed the ACIU and managed its projects. By 1966 these projects included two secondary schools, one primary school, a hospital and a rubber tree plantation.

The establishment of the ACIU preceded the decision of the colonial administration to constitute local government councils in Eastern Nigeria. Hence the ACIU preempted the role the local council might have played. As an Abiriban stated, "the ACIU is the government of Abiriba." The local government council rarely met, and its members, generally illiterate, old farmers, accepted its subordination to the ACIU. In contrast with the local council members, the officers of the ACIU included many of the best educated and most widely experienced Abiribans. Consequently, the ACIU, rather than the local government council or the county council, made the decisions and undertook the projects most relevant to Abiriba. The Owuwa Anyanwu County Council, whose jurisdiction encompassed three other clans and one small provincial city besides Abiriba, provided few services for Abiriba. Consequently Abiribans, unlike most other Eastern Nigerians, did not concern themselves with the activities of their county council.

The NCNC did not have a functioning chapter in Abiriba. Yet Abiribans considered themselves faithful and loyal members of the party and frequently reminded their political representatives of this. From the inauguration of the Eastern Legislative Assembly in 1953 until its dissolution in 1966, an Abiriban barrister represented the constituency including Abiriba. After his initial election to the House of Assembly, he joined the NCNC and became a minister in the government. As he grew in influence within the party, leaders of the ACIU found it increasingly to their advantage to stress their loyalty to the ruling party by voting for him.

Although Abiribans elected representatives for the local council and the county council, the ACIU was not seriously involved in these lesser political contests and the NCNC did not determine recruitment at these levels. The lack of prestige and influence accorded by membership on the local council, along with the stipulation that members be permanent residents of Abiriba, discouraged most Abiribans, with the exception of the older, illiterate farmers, from seeking election to the local council. Furthermore, the ACIU passed a resolution making the teachers in the Abiriban schools, many of whom otherwise fulfilled the requirements for council membership, ineligible. Few Abiribans sought election to the Owuwa Anyanwu County

Council for similar reasons. At times the ACIU did, however, recruit Abiribans for membership: in 1948 the ACIU decided to elect its president to represent Abiriba in the Bende Native Authority, the predecessor of the Owuwa Anyanwu County Council. Again in 1951 the ACIU directed its president to submit his name as a candidate and then reimbursed him for his campaign expenses. Subsequently, though, neither the ACIU nor the NCNC influenced the selection of candidates for the county council.

Originally the ACIU rather than the NCNC determined the selection of the Abiriban barrister for the regional constituency including Abiriba. When the barrister returned from England in 1952 he sent a letter to all ACIU branches indicating his availability for political office. The ACIU endorsed his candidacy and then persuaded the other candidate to withdraw. The ACIU's continuing endorsement in subsequent elections probably discouraged other Abiribans from attempting to oppose him. Hence, while the NCNC formally designated him as their nominee for the constituency, the party did not play a significant role in the process of political recruitment.

The officers of the ACIU held their political representative accountable to the community through themselves. Consequently the relationship between the representative and the community was mediated through the ethnic union. The regional representative did regularly enact a ritual of accountability by reporting the services he performed for Abiriba at ACIU conferences. When it was not possible for the ACIU to satisfy certain needs of the community, like the construction of paved roads or the installation of water pipes, branches of the ACIU would petition the Abiriban minister to remind him of his obligations to his constituency.

Mbaise

In contrast with Abiriba, Mbaise was a larger and more ethnically heterogeneous community. During the Eastern administrative reorganization in the 1930's, colonial officers designated five clans in the Mbaise area, only one of which coincided with a traditional clan unit. Several years later in 1941, when the administration was encouraging the formation of larger native authority units, these five clan court areas agreed to federate and took the name Mbaise, which means five towns in Ibo. All but one of the original five clan court areas gradually became accepted as a relevant identity for its members. While a Mbaise identity also evolved, it did not eradicate the more primary village and clan identities, but instead became superimposed on them. The existence of a relatively effective unit of government, the Mbaise County Council, helped to weld together the approximately 225,000 people in the county.

The pattern of ethnic unions in Mbaise reflected the ethnic complexity of the county council area. Clan unions were introduced into Mbaise beginning in 1937 by educated men, who had urban experience. In 1944, three years after Mbaise was formed, this same group of educated men began a Mbaise union. Later, some villages within Mbaise launched their own unions. Hence, a Mbaisan could potentially have belonged to three levels of unions: those of his village, his clan and Mbaise. However, none of the Mbaise unions attained the organizational complexity or the assured resource base of the ACIU. Their inability to collect dues regularly from their members discouraged most unions from undertaking development schemes of their own. Those that did raise some funds invariably spent the money for political purposes.

The NCNC did have a party apparatus in the Mbaise County Council area. Branches of the NCNC were established in each of the nine local council jurisdictions constituting the Mbaise County Council, and representatives of these branches formed a Mbaise district executive. NCNC branches, however, rarely met except before and during electoral campaigns. Hence the party never translated its support in Mbaise into a corps of active members. Due to the ineffectiveness of the local organization and its lack of relevance, leading politicians in Mbaise did not bother to assume office in it.

As in Abiriba, the NCNC never faced a serious threat from an opposition party in Mbaise. But unlike the situation in Abiriba, NCNC candidates in Mbaise often found themselves opposed by independents, who had bolted the party after failing in their efforts to be nominated by the NCNC. The threat posed by the independents haunted the NCNC in the Eastern Region, especially in the 1961 regional election when multi-member constituencies were divided into single-member electoral units. As the electoral results in Mbaise demonstrated, an independent candidate sponsored by a large, relatively well-organized union could have a decisive advantage in some constituencies over the regular party nominee. The NCNC, which did not impose lasting penalties on independents, failed to counteract the temptation to oppose the official nominee. Threats of expulsion had little effect since the NCNC felt it necessary to reincorporate the independents into the party after elections.

Most of the improvement projects completed in Mbaise and the amenities distributed were sponsored and at least partially financed by the county council. The local councils and most of the ethnic unions lacked the resources with which to undertake ambitious schemes since Mbaise was a relatively poor area with a very high population density. As a consequence, groups directed their demands for improvement projects at the county council. The campaign to secure as large a slice of the development pie as possible devolved upon the clan unions as the most important organized subunits in the Mbaise system.[4] Although councilors were elected by and officially represented village groups, as in Abaja and Owuwa Anyanwu counties, the councilors considered themselves representatives of their clans. Since all participants in the competition for development resources belonged to the same political party, membership in the NCNC was irrelevant as a basis for contending for scarce funds. Hence the clan unions, and not the NCNC, were the most important formulators of demands in Mbaise.

Mbaisans vigorously contested elections to the Mbaise County Council, the House of Assembly and the House of Representatives. Two factors intensified the attractiveness of these political offices: first, political office conferred more prestige in Mbaise than office in a clan union, educational achievements or wealth; second, the demand for political office derived from the perception in Mbaise of a link between political influence and both communal and personal economic gains. Village unions or informal groups of villagers generally recruited prominent members of their community for candidacy to the county council. Sometimes would-be politicians themselves approached kinsmen to inform them of their availability.

The reapportionment of the constituencies for the Eastern

House of Assembly before the 1961 election precipitated a marked increase in the involvement of the ethnic unions in the process of political recruitment. Problems in Mbaise arose from the new grouping of local government areas into constituencies which either split clans or included two groups which refused to accept the other's control over the seat. In their drive for political recognition, clans first approached the NCNC nominating committee for the relevant constituency. Often the clan would hold a kind of primary to choose its candidate before petitioning the nominating committee. Since membership on the nominating committees did not reflect the exact ethnic distribution of the constituency, the candidates selected did not necessarily come from the largest clan group.[5] When the NCNC nominating committee rejected candidates of the clan unions for the 1961 regional election, the unions decided to sponsor their independent candidacies by donating money and having officers canvass clan members to remind them of their ethnic obligations. Both of these independent candidates won. The official nominees in the two other Mbaise regional constituencies, who were returned successfully in the election, were ministers in the Eastern Government and incumbent or past officers of the numerically dominant clan unit in their respective constituencies.

In Mbaise, ethnic bonds could be loosened by political stresses. Because of a split in one clan over the siting of certain development projects, the clan union did not meet for a prolonged period of time during which one clan member, who was a Regional minister, joined forces with a rival clan union to protect his own position, at the expense of a fellow clansman who was an incumbent member of the Federal House of Representatives. A similar conflict within another clan over the allocation of amenities and the alleged responsibility of a representative in the Federal House for the new regional constituency boundaries cost that representative his renomination when one section of his clan refused to support him.

Most political representatives in high office in Mbaise held more than one important position. Frequently they were officers of their clan unions and also sat on the Mbaise County Council. Communication, as in Abiriba, was rarely through the NCNC apparatus. Unlike Abiriba, however, ethnic unions did not monopolize the channels of political communication in Mbaise. Since ethnic unions in Mbaise were less institutionalized than in Abiriba, contacts with political representatives tended to be more informal. The link between the representative and his constituency, however, continued to be largely on the basis of ethnic obligation.

Port Harcourt

Port Harcourt, the largest city and the industrial center of Eastern Nigeria before the war, was a city of rural immigrants, virtually all of whom retained strong ties with their village of origin.[6] While Port Harcourt marked the dividing line between the Ibo and Ijaw areas, the population of Port Harcourt consisted predominantly of Ibos, approximately eighty per cent of the total. Most came from Owerri and Bende Divisions with significant representation from Orlu and Onitsha Divisions. The largest and most important communities of emigrants from Abiriba and Mbaise resided in Port Harcourt, which was within a day's drive of their home villages. In Port Harcourt, unlike in many other African cities, these emigrants found themselves living in ethnically heterogeneous and integrated neighborhoods.

In addition to the village and clan unions commonly found in the countryside, divisional associations based on divisional administrative boundaries of the colonial period proliferated in Port Harcourt. The lower-level village and clan unions provided a crucial physical link and communications network between the immigrants in Port Harcourt and the community at home, thus sustaining identity with the more parochial community, and also lent assistance, money, and support to members to facilitate their adjustment to urban life. Most divisional associations did not meet on a regular basis and performed few concrete functions for members. The key function of the more inclusive divisional and provincial unions was to mobilize support behind members running for political office.

Despite the long tenure of some of the residents in Port Harcourt, the immigrants from Abiriba and Mbaise concerned themselves more with developing their home communities than with securing improvements to the city. Even the most

educated and anglicized participated in the activities of their
ethnic unions, returned home frequently, and expressed a
desire to retire to their villages. While members of both communities actively pursued economic and political goals in Port
Harcourt, they still identified themselves with their home villages. Their membership in the various ethnic unions, at whose
meetings they discussed home affairs rather than conditions in
Port Harcourt, signified their preoccupation with rural development. The politicians whom they invited to address them at
ethnic union meetings invariably represented their home constituencies rather than Port Harcourt, unless the Port Harcourt
representative happened to be a member of their community.
Even when an officer of the ethnic union was a member of the
Port Harcourt Municipal Council, members of the union usually refrained from discussing anything relevant to Port Harcourt. Many immigrants in Port Harcourt belonged only to one
or two ethnic unions and did not participate in any Port Har-
court-oriented association. Hence Port Harcourt before 1968
was a city of immigrants, most of whom had lived there less
than ten years and still considered themselves only temporary
residents.

The NCNC was organized on the basis of wards in Port Harcourt. Representatives of each ward constituted the Port Harcourt divisional executive. Before major elections each of the
wards in the township chose a member for the NCNC divisional executive, which then served as the nominating committee. In Port Harcourt, unlike in the rural constituencies,
nomination by the NCNC divisional executive usually ensured
the election of the candidate.[7] Since Port Harcourt was more
populous than rural constituencies and since no ethnic community predominated in any area of the city, ethnic unions refrained from sponsoring independent candidates. Divisional
unions operated within the NCNC to attempt to place a sufficient number of supporters of their candidates on the NCNC
divisional executive. Within the large and complex Port Harcourt political arena, even sponsorship by one or two divisional
unions did not guarantee the nomination for regional or federal
parliamentary seats.[8] A would-be politician had to have also
the skills of the American party boss at the turn of the century,
who welded together coalitions of supporters from diverse eth-

nic groups by performing services and favors for them. Hence
political success in Port Harcourt depended on the ability to
generate support beyond narrow ethnic boundaries.

As residents of a particular urban neighborhood, the immigrants in Port Harcourt had needs and demands relating to
living conditions in Port Harcourt: more schools, better roads,
improved sewage disposal and more police protection. To secure these amenities, they had to work through their representatives on the Port Harcourt municipal council. But many
people were disenfranchised in Port Harcourt because they
maintained voting registration at home. Since municipal councilors represented constituencies in which their kinsmen constituted only a small portion of the population, ethnic unions
could not function as the communications link between the
politician and his electors, as they did in rural areas. Under
such circumstances it would seem likely that residents would
turn to the NCNC for an organizational forum in which they
could easily communicate with one another to formulate demands or to petition their representatives. However, the NCNC
atrophied between elections, especially at the ward level, because politicians conceived of the NCNC primarily as a periodically functioning electoral machine rather than as an
ongoing political vehicle to resocialize the population. The
heterogeneous ethnic composition of the constituencies and
the absence of an organization able to hold the municipal councilor accountable for his conduct probably reduced the incentives for the councilor to bargain in the municipal council for
improvements for his neighborhood. Most councilors were
probably more interested in utilizing whatever influence they
could muster to gain access to patronage, which they could
dispense to their kinsmen.

Political Role of Ethnic Unions

Having detailed the operation of Ibo ethnic unions in four
different areas, we are now in a position to assess the impact
of the variables of organizational structure, community context and political environment upon their political role and
significance. This section attempts such an assessment through
a comparative analysis of the effectiveness with which each of

the ethnic unions performed five political functions: (1) general community leadership, (2) the organization of community development projects, (3) the recruitment of candidates for political office, (4) the securing of patronage and community amenities, and (5) the channelling of communications between political representatives and constituents.

Of the ethnic unions discussed in this paper, the ACIU and the clan unions in Mbaise most successfully performed the first function. The ACIU sponsored more community development activities than the other ethnic unions, but when need arose to obtain contributing funds for the installation of water pipes by the Government throughout the Eastern Region even the village unions in Abaja-Ngwo and the clan unions in Mbaise began collecting money for this purpose. Clan unions in Abiriba and Mbaise and divisional unions in Port Harcourt participated in the recruitment of candidates to regional and federal assemblies. In Abaja-Ngwo a temporary association, somewhat resembling ethnic unions, sponsored an independent candidate in the 1961 election. Clan unions in Abiriba and Mbaise regularly petitioned their political representatives to remind them of the need to secure patronage for their communities, and since both communities were influential in regional politics, their ministers often did obtain special amenities for them. In Port Harcourt patronage often was dispensed on an ethnic basis but rarely involved ethnic unions. The ethnic unions in Abiriba and Mbaise operated regularly as a communications link between politicians and constituents.

The organizational structures of the various ethnic unions differed considerably, ranging from the complex and highly institutionalized ACIU with its paid administrative secretary, to the village unions in Abaja-Ngwo, most of which lacked any regularized procedures and branches. Since the organizational tentacles of the highly centralized ACIU were able to reach and to rally the Abiribans living throughout Nigeria and the Camerouns, the ACIU could maintain its eminent position in that community. The somewhat less ordered and regularized management of the clan unions in Mbaise still allowed them to perform several significant political functions. In Port Harcourt branches of the ACIU met weekly and most other village and clan unions held monthly meetings. Most divisional unions met only a few times a year. Moreover, the divisional unions consisted of delegates of other village and clan unions rather than of direct individual members. The weak institutional structure of the village unions in Abaja-Ngwo prevented them from asserting themselves vis-à-vis the other organizations in their community.

The communities with ethnic unions varied in their size, their homogeneity, and their wealth. At one end of the spectrum, the village unions in Abaja-Ngwo were too small to be effective as political vehicles. At the other end, the Mbaise Federal Union performed no vital political functions in Mbaise, because the Mbaise unit was too inclusive for the distribution of amenities and subsumed several regional and federal constituencies. The large population and geographical size of Mbaise county limited use of a particular school, water facility, medical dispensary, or maternity center—the kinds of amenities the people were interested in receiving—to only one clan or local government area. Political constituencies in Mbaise reflected and reinforced the clan divisions. In Port Harcourt the village and clan unions had too few members to compete in Port Harcourt politics, while the divisional unions incorporated too many and diverse people to serve as patronage-oriented pressure groups. Divisional unions operated periodically as recruitment blocs within the Port Harcourt NCNC apparatus, but they did not attempt to pressure municipal councilors in order to influence the distribution of amenities by the Port Harcourt Municipal Council. To a great extent, this was because the available forms of patronage that political actors competed for in Port Harcourt, like market stalls, jobs, and contracts, could be allocated to only a limited group. Hence municipal councilors favored fellow clansmen rather than divisional members. On the other hand, the ACIU and several of the clans in Mbaise represented sufficiently large communities as to constitute strong blocs within regional and federal constituencies and at the same time were units within which amenities could be shared.

Another factor which contributed to the effectiveness of the ACIU was the unity and cohesiveness of Abiriba. Unlike the clans in Mbaise, most of which originated as artificial native court areas designated by the colonial administration, Abiriba constituted a traditional kinship unit. In Mbaise two of the largest native court-clans had a tendency to divide on the basis of village groups or of local government areas and by so doing to impair the ability of the clan union to function. The largely ceremonial and symbolic role of the Mbaise Federal Union in Mbaise derived in part from the salience of clan identities as compared with the more inclusive Mbaise identity. However, in Port Harcourt the Mbaise Federal Union displaced the clan unions as the primary political vehicle for the community since immigrants found it more advantageous to compete with the divisional unions on the basis of the more inclusive identity. As a consequence of the considerable ethnic diversity of Port Harcourt, the city abounded with ethnic unions, thus limiting the independent political role of any one of them.

Along with the advantages of size and homogeneity, the ACIU benefited from the relative affluence of its traders, whom it was able to tax to pay for its projects. Since Mbaise was a fairly impoverished area, the ethnic unions there relied on contributions from its residents in urban centers. A far smaller proportion of Mbaisans lived in urban centers, and many of those who did were laborers rather than traders or contractors. Furthermore, when ethnic unions did raise money they usually spent it on political campaigns in Mbaise rather than on development projects. The ethnic unions in Port Harcourt were limited in their activities because of their financial positions. Village and clan unions there were obliged to remit virtually all of their dues collections to the parent union, and divisional unions received very little funding from their constituent village and clan unions. In addition to all of their other problems, the village unions in Abaja-Ngwo suffered from a very low financial base because of their size and because most of the emigrants from there worked in the coal mines.

The environment in which the ethnic union operated, its political arena, also affected how it functioned. Branches of unions in Port Harcourt obviously could not duplicate the roles assumed by the parent union in the rural home area. Furthermore, the ethnic fragmentation characteristic of all sections of Port Harcourt contrasted with the homogeneity of the parts viewed individually of even a complex ethnic unit like Mbaise.

The ACIU could undertake a series of political functions because it was able to achieve its goals by operating within an Abiriban context. If the ACIU had to petition the Owuwa Anyanwu County Council, as the clan unions in Mbaise did, to accomplish its objectives, it would not have been as successful. In contrast with Abiriba, the limited frame of reference of the village unions in Abaja-Ngwo reduced the incentives for the unions to become more effective. Village unions in Abaja-Ngwo operated only within their own village group and thus could survive despite their irregular and disordered institutional state. Had these ethnic unions cast their net into a wider political arena in a sustained manner, it would have encouraged the formation of more inclusive unions, like the one which came into being in 1961 to sponsor the electoral campaign of an independent for a seat in the Eastern House of Assembly.

The NCNC and The Ethnic Unions

There was no direct correlation between the political roles assumed by an ethnic union and the strength of local branches of the NCNC. As we have seen, ethnic unions sometimes undertook several of the functions generally associated with political parties. In Abiriba and Mbaise ethnic unions provided forums for the formulation of demands for securing patronage and amenities and for the recruitment of candidates to political office. Also the communication between a political representative and his constituents usually occurred there through the ethnic unions' apparatus or on the basis of ethnic bonds rather than through the NCNC. However, in areas where ethnic unions did not perform political functions as effectively, as in Abaja-Ngwo and Port Harcourt, the NCNC was not any stronger than in Abiriba and Mbaise. Although the size of Port Harcourt and the ethnic heterogeneity of its constituencies deterred even the divisional unions from assuming the paramount position ethnic unions sometimes had in rural politics, the NCNC party apparatus atrophied between elections in much the same manner as in the rural areas. In Abaja-Ngwo County the NCNC suffered from the same organizational deficiencies as the ethnic unions. Moreover, when a strong ethnic union, like the ACIU, cooperated with the NCNC, the party benefited from the ability of the union to assume certain political roles. Hence a strong ethnic union could either enhance the status of the NCNC in a community or weaken it, as in Mbaise when clan unions sponsored independent candidates.

With certain qualifications, the decisive factor limiting the NCNC's capabilities seemed to be its inadequate institutional structure at the local level of the political system rather than the activities of ethnic unions. The NCNC institutional apparatus was geared for only one political function at the local level, the nomination of candidates before elections. Other aspects of the process of political recruitment, as well as the formulation of demands and communication, required a more permanent organization than the NCNC had in most places. Apparently NCNC leaders envisioned a limited role for the party and were content to allow the ethnic unions to undertake other political functions. The NCNC and the ethnic unions rarely competed to perform a specific function in the same political arena. The major exception to this generalization was the conflict over political recruitment in the rural areas. Yet even then, if the NCNC had a more effective organization, it would have prevailed over the ethnic unions more frequently. Ethnic unions confronted the NCNC with their candidates and sometimes bolted the party with impunity. If the NCNC had imposed some kind of meaningful penalty instead of gradually reincorporating defectors after elections, it would have discouraged the ethnic unions from departing on their independent course. After the NCNC waited three years to readmit most of the independent elected in 1961 and inaugurated new nomination procedures, only fifteen independents contested the 1964 election.

The NCNC never expended resources on fostering a stronger party machinery, particularly in the Eastern Region, because it was irrelevant to its needs. A shoddy party apparatus did not jeopardize its electoral prospects, since independents petitioned to rejoin the NCNC after elections and opposition parties campaigned primarily in a few non-Ibo constituencies. The NCNC, like several other African parties, was a victim of its own success. NCNC party teams generated so much support on their initial forays into the East that the party did not have to form local branches in order to win large electoral majorities.

Despite several attempts to organize the NCNC more effectively, party leaders were unable to centralize power in party headquarters and to exert control over local communities. In part this reflected the limitations of party headquarters, which operated without sufficient professional staff and adequate sums of money for party organizational work. Most party leaders apparently also lacked the interest or the aptitude for the day to day drudgery of party building. Hence the NCNC neither had the head to direct nor the arms to reach down and penetrate society.

Another factor limiting the NCNC's capabilities was its inclusiveness which led more particularistic interest groupings to compete within the party. As a political umbrella for the vast majority of politically active groups, in the Eastern Region the NCNC incorporated various political antagonists and opponents within it. Given the ardent desire for amenities and the scarcity of resources at all levels of the political system, the competition between groups within the NCNC became the salient dimension of politics in the Eastern Region. Political affiliation could not provide a basis for the formulation of demands, because virtually everyone belonged to the NCNC. Somewhat ironically, just as exposure to aspects of modernity reduced the significance of some traditional cultural distinctions, the dynamics of politics accentuated the importance of village and clan identities and ethnicity as the structuring principle of political competition. Ethnic unions served as convenient organizational appendages but did not themselves inspire this politics of ethnic confrontation and compromise.

NOTES

1. John P. Mackintosh, "Electoral Trends," in John P. Mackintosh, ed., *Nigerian Government and Politics* (London: George Allen and Unwin, Ltd., 1966), p. 522.

2. The data for the ethnic unions in Abiriba, Mbaise, and Port Harcourt was gathered during the first half of 1966 in Eastern Nigeria from minute books, correspondence files, records, publications of the relevant communities, and interviews. For the conceptualization of

Port Harcourt politics, this author is also indebted to Howard Wolpe. The material on the Abaja-Ngwo County is taken from David R. Smock, "From Village to Trade Union in Africa: A Study of Power and Decision-Making in the Nigerian Coal Miners Union and in the Villages from which the Coal Miners Migrated" (unpublished Ph. D. dissertation, Cornell University, 1964).

3. The NCNC was theoretically organized on the village level and on the divisional level. In addition there were intermediary nominating bodies in the rural areas corresponding with the constituencies for the regional and federal parliaments.

4. There were six clan unions in Mbaise. A clan union never encompassed all of the constituent parts of one of the native court areas. Instead two clan unions, each representing a traditional clan within that native court area, formed and the third section was invited to join another clan with which it had some traditional links.

5. The NCNC was often plagued by the composition of its nominating committees since they were not directly proportional to the population in the area. In one Mbaise constituency for the Eastern House of Assembly, for example, the three ethnic components had equal representation, although one of them constituted a majority of the population.

6. The 1963 census estimated the size of Port Harcourt at 180,000, but many of the residents from Abiriba and Mbaise, as well as other Ibo communities, either failed to register or went home to be counted in their villages. Some administrators and long time expatriate residents there estimated the population as being at least 300,000 and perhaps significantly higher.

7. One constituency for which the Port Harcourt NCNC executive nominated a candidate, the Ahoada Central seat for the Federal House, was predominantly rural. Hence politics within that constituency more closely resembled those of rural areas. In the 1964 federal election an independent candidate running with the support of rural-based ethnic unions won.

8. In Port Harcourt's main township, urban immigrants from Eastern Nigeria's old Owerri Province (old, in that administrative boundaries were revised in 1959) usually were allied against immigrants from the old Onitsha Province. However, ethnic political groupings were highly unstable, and political alliances were often formed across provincial boundaries.

9. For models of types of African political parties see James S. Coleman and Carl G. Rosberg, Jr., "Introduction," in their *Political Parties*

and National Integration in Tropical Africa (Berkeley and Los Angeles: University of California Press, 1964), p. 5: Thomas Hodgkin, *African Political Parties* (Baltimore: Penguin Press, 1961), pp. 68–75; Ruth Schacter, "Single Party Systems in West Africa," *American Political Science Review,* LV (June, 1961), pp. 294–307. For a reevaluation of this typology see Aristide A. Zolberg, *Creating Political Order* (Chicago: Rand McNally, 1966).

CHAPTER 12

Minority Politics in Northern Nigeria: The Case of the Idoma Hope Rising Union

ALVIN MAGID

In the aftermath of the Second World War, educated elements throughout English-speaking Africa were agitating for a greater share in the political and administrative life of their territories.[1] Nationalists were especially vehement in demanding greater participation in government and administration as a prelude to independence. In Nigeria, many who sympathized with those aspirations were at the same time strongly committed to a gradual approach. According to Margery Perham, for example, democratization of the Native Authority (or local administrative) system was preferable to either (1) the rapid entrance of Nigerians into upper levels of the civil service, or (2) the rapid expansion of powers in the Legislative Council at Lagos.[2]

Official acceptance of a gradual approach was reflected in post-war constitutional developments. Thus, in March 1945, Governor Sir Arthur Richards presented the Legislative Council with his plan for constitutional reform; its nucleus was subsequently incorporated into the so-called "Richards Constitution" that governed Nigeria until 1951.[3] The most important sections dealt with the organization of a Nigerian state and the place within it of a Native Authority system. A series of compromises between contentious separatists and federalists produced a state comprising three Regions: East, West, and North. Each Region had an administrative establishment and a House of Assembly. The latter was authorized to formulate the regional budget and discuss legislation. Native Authorities in each Region appointed members of the House of Assembly. Each House, in turn, appointed five delegates to the Legislative Council at Lagos. By establishing a hierarchy of indirectly-elected councils connecting apex and base, the colonial power perpetuated the Native Authority system as the foundation for local administration. Not surprisingly, many Nigerians opposed the conservative orientation of government and constitution.

Opposition to official conservatism penetrated all sectors of the Nigerian political system. Even as Nnamdi Azikiwe, Obafemi Awolowo, Anthony Enahoro, and others worked at the center for change, lesser lights engaged in complementary activities nearer the periphery. For example, members of minority groups in the Middle Belt[4] organized tribal unions which pressured government to accelerate Native Authority reform along democratic lines.

Many of these tribal unions were eventually drawn into a tug-of-war between the three major political parties. While the Northern Peoples' Congress (NPC) encouraged integration of the Middle Belt with the Moslem North, both the Action Group (AG) and the National Council of Nigeria and the Cameroons (NCNC) promoted the creation of a separate Middle Belt Region; the two southern parties favored Middle Belt regional autonomy as a means of preventing the political domination of Nigeria by traditionalists in the Northern Region. During the 1950's, it was clear that both the organization of an independent Nigerian state and the relative power of the political parties within it would depend, in large measure, on developments in the Middle Belt.

Among the Middle Belt elements who participated in both the agitation for local administrative reform and the conflict between the major political parties were young men in Idoma Division, Benue Province.[5] At the close of the Second World War, literate youths organized as the Idoma Hope Rising Union (IHRU) began to press for democratic reform of, and a policy role in, the Idoma Native Authority. In time, the IHRU was drawn into the tug-of-war over the future of the Middle Belt.

It is the object of this paper to examine (1) the activities of the Idoma Hope Rising Union as a reformist tribal union, and (2) the relationship between the IHRU and the Nigerian political party system. The examination of reformist activities focuses on the tribal union's unsuccessful attempt to secure a major policy role in a democratized Native Authority apparatus. The relationship between the IHRU and the party system is examined with particular reference to the regional minorities or Middle Belt issue during the period 1952–1958.

Both the attempt by the Idoma Hope Rising Union to secure a major policy role and its relationship with the party system were set against the background of official conservatism in post-war Nigeria. The organization's views on two crucial issues—local reform and the future of the Middle Belt—were generally at odds with the official commitment to gradual change. Government responded to IHRU demands by instituting ostensibly democratic reforms in the Idoma Native Authority. Concomitantly, government reaffirmed its commitment to gradual change (1) by helping to lay the groundwork for the demise of the reformist tribal union and (2) by encouraging close ties between the IHRU's increasingly powerful adversary, the Native Authority, and the governing party in the Region, the conservative Northern Peoples' Congress. We shall subsequently examine these developments in greater detail. It is first necessary, however, to identify those elements in the organizational character of the IHRU which influenced its performance in divisional and Middle Belt politics.

THE IDOMA HOPE RISING UNION AS A REFORMIST TRIBAL UNION

The Idoma Hope Rising Union: Origin, Organization, and Outlook

A. Origin and Organization

The Idoma Hope Rising Union was founded in 1942 by a group of youths meeting at Oturkpo Town, the administrative center for Idoma Division. From 1942 until its demise in 1959, the organization tended to recruit members and supporters[6] from the growing body of primary school leavers in the Division. Idoma school leavers were generally oriented to careers in the administrative establishment. As a result, the IHRU tended to attract both employees and former employees of government or the Idoma Native Authority. The latter group comprised two elements: (1) those who had been dismissed from positions in government or the Native Authority, and (2) those who had been led by feelings of frustration and disillusionment to resign their positions. Predictably, the former employees emerged as the most militant members of the IHRU.

The Idoma Hope Rising Union was organized in accordance with the branch principle. By 1957, eighteen branches were theoretically in operation throughout Nigeria.[7] In fact, only the units at Igumale (in southern Idoma Division), Ilorin, Jos, Kaduna, Kano, Keffi, Lagos, Minna, Oturkpo Town and Zaria were more-or-less active. Few branches held regular meetings. In most units, the decision-making process was controlled by an informal committee which consisted of elected branch officials —the unsalaried president, secretary and treasurer—and several of their most ardent followers. Since the IHRU did not have many dues-paying members, the branches were chronically short of funds. Periodic attempts by the informal committees to collect special subscriptions generally met with little success.

From 1942 until 1955, the founding branch at Oturkpo Town served as headquarters for the Idoma Hope Rising Union. According to the organization's constitution, representatives of the various branches were to meet annually at Oturkpo Town for two purposes: (1) to formulate general policy and (2) to elect the nine-member Executive Committee. The Committee, operating out of headquarters, was formally responsible for the day-to-day activities of the IHRU. In fact, the Annual Conference was held on only nine occasions during the seventeen-year history of the organization. Moreover, individual branches— especially those at Kaduna, Kano, Lagos, and Zaria—persistently challenged both the authority of the headquarters branch and the competence and integrity of the elected IHRU officials who staffed it; some units even refused to remit funds to headquarters. In time, intense competition for power and prestige between Oturkpo Town and the other branches threatened to destroy the IHRU. Finally, in 1955, the Annual Conference voted (1) to dissolve the positions of several controversial officials at Oturkpo Town, (2) to eliminate the salaries of all elected officials in the organization and (3) to transfer the headquarters to Kaduna.[8] Despite these drastic measures, tension between the virtually autonomous branches continued unabated until the demise of the IHRU four years later.[9]

B. Outlook

Throughout its history, the Idoma Hope Rising Union displayed a curious ambivalence toward organized political activity. On the one hand, the IHRU employed conventional political methods (e.g., electioneering and lobbying) in the pursuit of political objectives; on the other, it consistently denied that it was a political organization. The members generally preferred to view the organization as a reformist tribal or cultural union.[10] Many reasoned as follows: organized political activity in general and political party activity in particular are bad because they "spoil the Land"; that is, they inevitably engender friction, bitterness, and disunity. The IHRU sought to unite the people of Idoma Division by promoting their social, economic, and cultural development. Therefore, they concluded, the organization was essentially non-political.[11] As we shall see, the ambivalence of the IHRU toward organized political activity affected its relationship with the Nigerian political party system.

In an effort to accelerate social and economic development in Idoma Division, the Idoma Hope Rising Union lobbied government and the Native Authority for the following amenities: better roads, pipe-borne water systems, postal facilities in rural districts, agricultural co-operatives, and more Native Authority schools and scholarships.[12] Its interest in cultural matters was reflected in several activities. First, the IHRU appealed to the Native Authority for assistance in sponsoring traditional art, music and dance.[13] Second, the organization petitioned various Native Authorities throughout Nigeria to repatriate Idoma prostitutes who were allegedly damaging the reputation of the Idoma people.[14] Finally, alarmed by the alienation of ancestral land to stranger elements—especially Ibos—the IHRU lobbied both government and the Native Authority to restrict immigration into the Division.[15]

According to the Idoma Hope Rising Union, the lethargic pace of social, economic and cultural development resulted largely from the inefficient, corrupt and undemocratic practices of the Idoma Native Authority.[16] It is to the political confrontation between the reformist tribal union and the local administrative apparatus that we now turn.

The Idoma Hope Rising Union: Official Conservatism and Reform of the Native Authority

An acephalous people, the Idoma traditionally vested political authority in (1) elders, (2) Clan Heads or "Land" chiefs[17] and (3) the *ojira,* which was a mass meeting of adult men for the purpose of dealing with daily affairs. A consensual democratic principle governed the Idoma decision-making process. Significantly, the occasional emergence of an autocratic Clan Head did not permanently challenge the legitimacy of the constitutional system. Rather, it signaled a temporary disruption of the constitutional equilibrium rooted in principles of gerontocracy, chieftaincy and democracy in the *ojira.*

Unable to reconcile administrative needs with the democratic and gerontocratic principles, the colonial power turned instead to the third principle of Idoma constitutionalism: chieftaincy. During the inter-war period, it attempted to establish an efficient Native Authority apparatus by strengthening chieftaincy at the district level. District Headships were created and filled by both Clan Heads and persons without traditional title or office. In the process, the legitimacy of the constitutional system was subverted, thereby encouraging autocratic chieftaincy in the Native Authority.

At the close of the Second World War, government undertook to reform the Idoma Native Authority, ostensibly along democratic lines. The reforms, which in fact reflected the official commitment to gradual, controlled change, precipitated a political confrontation between the Idoma Hope Rising Union and the Native Authority.

The decentralized Native Authority system of the inter-war period was replaced by a central administration and judiciary designed to promote unity and efficiency in Idoma Division.[18] At the apex of the reorganized apparatus was an Idoma Chieftaincy created in 1947.[19] In that year, Ogiri Oko, combined Clan Head-District Head of Adoka, was designated *Och'Idoma* ("Chief of Idoma") for life. Shortly thereafter, four administrative departments—Finance, Local Government, Police-Judiciary, and Works—were organized at Oturkpo Town to manage the day-to-day affairs of the Native Authority.

In 1948, an Advisory Council was established to assist the *Och'Idoma* in administering the Division. Its five members were recruited in the following manner: Each District Council elected a representative to one of four Intermediate Area Councils in Idoma Division. Members of each Intermediate Area Council, in turn, elected one representative to the central administration of the Native Authority. The *Och'Idoma*'s Advisory Council consisted of the four representatives elected by the Intermediate Area Councils, plus a co-opted scribe. Later that year, the *Och'Idoma* and his council were gazetted as the Idoma Central Court. That body was authorized to hear appeals passing from District Courts through four Intermediate Area Courts.

As early as 1942, the Idoma Hope Rising Union had supported the notion of Native Authority centralization under an Idoma Chieftaincy.[20] Somewhat naively, it had assumed that such a reform would (1) break the political strangle-hold of traditionalist District Heads and Clan Heads, (2) stimulate progressive development in the Division and (3) secure the IHRU a major policy role in the local administrative apparatus. IHRU members were, therefore, understandably outraged when a District Head and three elderly Clan Heads, all four illiterate, were elected to the first Advisory Council in 1948. By 1949, many in the organization strongly opposed the formal inauguration of a conservative and allegedly corrupt *Och'Idoma*.[21] The inauguration of Ogiri Oko provoked even more vehement demands for change.

Government responded by granting limited recognition to the dissidents in the Idoma Hope Rising Union. Thus, in 1950, the organization was invited to attend the Provincial Conference which had been called to discuss such matters as local government reform and electoral procedures under the constitution.[22] Still dissatisfied, the IHRU proceeded to agitate for immediate doubling of Intermediate Area Council representation on the *Och'Idoma*'s Advisory Council.[23] Government countered by merely acknowledging the possibility of IHRU elements (1) sitting on the Intermediate Area Councils as unofficials and (2) participating as an advisory committee in the central administration of the Idoma Native Authority.[24] Not surprisingly, the organization rejected a proposal which appeared to legitimize control of the intermediate and central levels of the Native Authority by illiterates and traditionalists.

The Idoma Hope Rising Union proceeded to force the issue. Preparing for indirect elections to the Northern Region House of Assembly in 1951, it managed to gain control of electoral colleges at the district and divisional levels. Whatever factors accounted for the electoral *coup*—genuine popularity, organizational ability, or, as government contended, popular apathy in the districts[25]—it was abundantly clear that the IHRU had maneuvered into a position from which its demands for administrative reform could be more effectively articulated. The organization continued to agitate for change. The appointment of two literates to combined Clan Head-District Head positions in Boju and Orokram districts provoked demands for even more radical change.

Finally, in 1952, both government and the Native Authority granted several concessions. First, the Advisory Council was enlarged to include a scribe and two members elected to three-year terms by each Intermediate Area Council. The new nine-member Advisory Council included six literates averaging 35–40 years in age;[26] three IHRU men were members of the literate majority. Second, each District Council was empowered to appoint one person to sit with the District Head on the Intermediate Area Council. Third, the District Court system was reorganized to include court members elected from officially-recognized, kindred-based constituencies.

The Idoma Hope Rising Union greeted the three reforms with self-congratulation. The response was unjustified on two grounds. First, the reforms did not ensure that the organization would secure a major policy role in the local administrative apparatus. In fact, the IHRU subsequently failed to establish a stable foothold at the district, intermediate, and central levels of the Native Authority. Second, in retrospect it appears that government was influenced only in part by IHRU pressures for reform. Of even greater significance were developments taking place at the regional level. In 1950, the Northern House of Assembly had called for an inquiry into the state of local administration.[27] By the end of the following year, a commission of inquiry had prepared a detailed report on the Native Authority system. The report noted the existence of a wide variety of generally ineffective councils, conferences and committees. It also confirmed a trend toward conciliar administration in the Native Authorities of the Region.[28]

The House of Assembly, perhaps sensitive to local reform in the Western and Eastern Regions, moved that the Native Authority councils be strengthened forthwith.[29] A program of local administrative reform was adopted. It included (1) the replacement of all Sole Native Authorities (i.e., emirships and chieftaincies without legal responsibility to councils) by statutory "Chief-in-Council" or "Chief-and-Council" organs,[30] and (2) the enactment of the Native Authority Law of 1954.[31] The Law codified existing legislation relevant to local administration, granted legal status to existing local councils, and empowered the Native Authorities to establish new councils. Moreover, it underscored a *formal* commitment to democratic local administration by stipulating that all councils were to include elected majorities.[32]

Thus, Native Authority reforms in Idoma Division resulted from a convergence of forces: (1) persistent agitation by a reformist tribal union, and (2) government's post-war commitment to gradual change. A gradual approach, forming the thread with which the "Richards Constitution" and the Native Authority Law were woven, guided future developments in the Division.

The influence of the Idoma Hope Rising Union in divisional affairs had reached its zenith with the Native Authority reforms of 1952. In the ensuing years, the IHRU continued to press for both an official policy role and the extirpation of corruption in the Native Authority. The organization failed to achieve the two objectives. Its strenuous efforts to expose corruption—including a virulent newspaper campaign against official venality[33]—were generally ignored by government[34] and resented by the Native Authority. The latter responded to IHRU attacks by instructing its employees to resign from the tribal union. In 1955, the Native Authority persuaded a group of IHRU defectors to organize the Idoma State Union (ISU). Native Authority sponsorship of the ISU was intended (1) to weaken the Idoma Hope Rising Union attack upon the local administrative apparatus, and (2) to isolate those militant elements in the IHRU who argued that a Middle Belt Region ought to be carved out of the Northern Region.[35] After two years of bitter wrangling, the two tribal unions merged under the name of the Idoma Hope Rising Union.[36] Despite the apparent restoration of unity, IHRU influence continued to decline.[37] By 1957, the President-General of the organization was prepared to concede that

> . . . [o]n the face of things, it . . . appear[s] that we have failed in achieving our aims in Idoma. We have little or no say in planning policies and in the affairs which affect the mass of the people in the Division for whom we fight to release them from their political and economic prison. (sic) We have struggled in vain to make our cries heard through one of the Legislatures of the country. . . .
>
> By standards which mortal beings assess successes and failures, we have seen no convincing signs of our achievement. . . .[38]

As the influence of the Idoma Hope Rising Union diminished, the power of the Idoma Native Authority increased. The increase in Native Authority power was accomplished by the *Och'Idoma*'s clever manipulation of the following administrative reforms: After lengthy experimentation, the local administrative apparatus was overhauled between 1957 and 1960. The four Intermediate Area Councils were replaced by a single Representative Council linking district and divisional levels. Councils of the six most populous districts each elected two persons to a three-year term on the Representative Council; sixteen District Councils each elected one Representative Councilor. Moreover, the *Och'Idoma*'s Advisory Council was supplanted by a General Purposes Committee. Its members were the *Och-'Idoma* (President), four Portfolio Councilors elected from the former Intermediate Areas, and Representative Councilors chosen in rotation.[39] Finally, administrative and judicial functions were separated, ostensibly to enhance Native Authority efficiency. The *Och'Idoma* and the District Heads were replaced as Presidents of the Central and District Courts, respectively; this was followed by abolition of the four Intermediate Area Courts.[40]

For several reasons, changes wrought in the Idoma Native Authority between 1957 and 1960 were most beneficial to the *Och'Idoma* himself. First, he was able to consolidate his position vis-à-vis the District Heads by appearing to support both government and the Idoma Hope Rising Union clamoring for democracy and efficiency. This was accomplished by excluding District Heads from the District Courts, the Representative Council, and the General Purposes Committee. Second, the *Och'Idoma* retained control of the upper judiciary by appointing a brother to the Presidency of the Central Court. The IHRU protested in vain.[41] Third, abolition of the Intermediate Area Courts eliminated points around which political opposition might crystallize. Fourth, as President of the General Purposes Committee, the *Och'Idoma* was able to control policymaking in the four administrative departments of the Native Authority.

By combining institutional change and political skill, the conservative Ogiri Oko had outmaneuvered his foes in both the Idoma Hope Rising Union and the Native Authority. Concomitantly, he had gained widespread support among the essentially conservative Idoma (1) by defending the institution of chieftaincy in the face of IHRU attacks upon traditionalist Clan Heads and District Heads, and (2) by appearing to favor both the elimination of autocratic District Headships and the restoration of a constitutional equilibrium rooted in principles of gerontocracy, chieftaincy, and democracy in the *ojira.*

The worst fears of the reformist Idoma Hope Rising Union had thus materialized by 1960. The post-war commitment to progressive, albeit gradual, change had provided Idoma Division with little more than unprecedented centralization—both political and administrative. In the process, the IHRU had been reduced to an isolated and largely ineffective gadfly in divisional affairs.

THE IDOMA HOPE RISING UNION, THE NIGERIAN POLITICAL PARTY SYSTEM, AND THE REGIONAL MINORITIES ISSUE

Minority Politics in the Middle Belt

The relationship between the Idoma Hope Rising Union and the political party system commenced as tribal groups in the Middle Belt were becoming deeply involved in nationalist politics. In order to examine the relationship between the IHRU and the party system, it is necessary that we first identify the political forces operating in the Middle Belt during the 1950's.[42]

In 1950, the Middle Zone League (MZL) was established for the purpose of organizing a separatist movement among tribal groups in the Middle Belt. Three years later, however, the organization reversed itself with a decision (1) to cooperate with the Northern Region Government, and (2) to enter into a working alliance with the governing party, the Northern Peoples' Congress (NPC). The decision produced a schism in the MZL. In July 1953, several MZL defectors established the Middle Belt Peoples' Party (MBPP). The new organization quickly affiliated with the National Council of Nigeria and the Cameroons (NCNC), a nationalist party, and its ally in the Northern Region, the Northern Elements Progressive Union (NEPU). The NCNC program, which supported Middle Belt regional autonomy and a strong central government, was anathema to the NPC.

After considerable wrangling, the Middle Zone League and the Middle Belt Peoples' Party merged in June 1955 under the name of the United Middle Belt Congress (UMBC). However, unity was destined to be short-lived; the merger was dissolved by the end of the year, whereupon the MZL and the MBPP renewed their alliances with the NPC and NCNC-NEPU, respectively. In January 1957, the UMBC was rehabilitated under the Presidency of Joseph Tarka, a Tiv. Later that year, the UMBC entered into a formal alliance with the Action Group (AG), another nationalist party committed to a separate Middle Belt Region.[43]

The Idoma Hope Rising Union, The Party System, And the Minorities Issue

On December 15, 1952, the Annual Conference of the Idoma Hope Rising Union rallied to the cause of a separate Middle Belt Region by voting to affiliate with the National Council of Nigeria and the Cameroons.[44] Rumors of impending affiliation had begun to circulate among the IHRU branches as early as October. While some units reacted favorably to the rumors, others were considerably less sanguine. For example, the Zaria branch was distressed to learn that the avowedly non-political tribal union was about to establish formal ties with a political party.[45] When the decision to affiliate with the NCNC was promulgated, many IHRU members throughout the country proceeded to resign from the organization. In an effort to stem the tide of resignations, the Kaduna branch requested that IHRU headquarters in Oturkpo Town reveal the full implications of affiliation with a political party.[46] The request was ignored.

Affiliation with the National Council of Nigeria and the Cameroons produced two cleavages in the Idoma Hope Rising Union. First, it engendered conflict between those members who preferred to view the IHRU as a non-political union and those who were prepared to acknowledge its essentially political character. Each faction accused the other of conspiring to "spoil the Land." The conflict underscored the ambivalence of the IHRU toward organized political activity. Second, the decision to affiliate with the NCNC exposed fundamental differences within the IHRU on the regional minorities issue. Some members had expressed their support for a separate Middle Belt Region by applauding affiliation with the NCNC. Others had expressed their support for integration of the Middle Belt with the Moslem portion of the Northern Region by rejecting affiliation with the NCNC.

Significantly, the two cleavages emerged when Idoma Hope Rising Union influence in divisional affairs had reached its zenith. Their intractability contributed to the subsequent decline of the organization. Persistent internecine conflict over the character of the IHRU and its position on the regional minorities issue seriously weakened the organization vis-à-vis the Idoma Native Authority. The local administrative apparatus—resentful of attacks upon its integrity and efficiency and strongly committed to both the Northern Peoples' Congress and Middle Belt affiliation with the Moslem North—stiffened its resistance to the IHRU. By sponsoring the Idoma State Union, the Native Authority was able to encourage defections from the IHRU; by supporting the merger of the contentious tribal unions in 1957, the Native Authority was able to perpetuate debilitating conflicts within the organization. In sum, IHRU influence declined in the period 1952–1959 as a result of internal erosion reinforced by external coercion.

The Idoma Hope Rising Union and the Minorities Commission

In 1955, the Idoma Hope Rising Union attempted to eliminate the two cleavages by withdrawing from the National Council of Nigeria and the Cameroons.[47] Thereafter, its relationship with the party system was limited to informal contacts by individual members with the NCNC, the Action Group, and the Northern Peoples' Congress. In turn, the three major parties and their allies appeared to limit cultivation of the IHRU to periodic proclamations of support for its objectives.[48] In the view of most IHRU members, the process of depoliticization was completed on September 1, 1957, when the Idoma State Union agreed to withdraw from membership in the NPC[49] and to merge with the IHRU.

In fact, neither depoliticization nor organizational stability was achieved. Withdrawal from the National Council of Nigeria and the Cameroons and the subsequent merger with a rival tribal union failed to insulate the Idoma Hope Rising Union from disruptive party currents. Individual members of the IHRU continued to operate within the organization as agents of one or another of the major political parties. By the end of 1957, party supporters in the IHRU divided over the regional minorities issue in general and the question of the Union's appearance before the Minorities Commission in particular. This division was destined to prove fatal.

At the constitutional conference of 1957, the decision was taken to appoint a commission of inquiry to investigate the fears of minority tribal groups throughout Nigeria and to propose means of allaying those fears. The commission held public and private meetings throughout the country between November 23, 1957 and June 12, 1958. Tribal unions and other groups were also invited to submit memoranda on the regional minorities issue.[50] In its final report, the commission affirmed that tribal minorities in the Middle Belt did have reason to fear domination by the Moslem majority in the Northern Region. At the same time, however, it observed that support for the creation of a separate Middle Belt Region was scattered and that the creation of such a Region would not allay the fears of minority groups. The commission concluded that political and legal reforms were more likely to allay those fears.[51]

Among the many organizations invited to present testimony to the commission of inquiry was the Idoma Hope Rising Union. On August 9, 1957, the IHRU Executive Committee met to consider the invitation. After lengthy discussion, it voted to send three IHRU officials—including the President-General, Wilson Onazi—to testify before the commission at Makurdi. The three representatives were instructed to communicate the IHRU's support for the creation of a Middle Belt Region.[52]

On February 15, 1958, the President-General of the organization summoned another meeting of the Executive Committee. At that meeting, Onazi observed that it would be inappropriate for the Idoma Hope Rising Union to testify before the commission of inquiry without a clear mandate from the branches. Thereupon, Onazi reported that he would not appear before the commission. When pressed to explain his *volte face*—Onazi had advocated regional autonomy as far back as 1952, when he voted for IHRU affiliation with the National Council of Nigeria and the Cameroons—the President-General merely conceded that he now opposed the creation of a Middle Belt Region. Several members of the Executive Committee then demanded that Onazi resign from office. At that point, the meeting broke up.[53]

Two days later, the President-General wrote to the commission of inquiry that he would not testify before it. He explained that his decision was based on the fact that a majority of the branches had not submitted a mandate on the regional minorities issue. Onazi also observed that he opposed the creation of a Middle Belt Region because it would weaken the well-run Northern Region.[54]

The response from the branches was rapid and widely critical. For example, the Igumale branch accused the President-General of subverting a legitimate Executive Committee mandate. Moreover, it vehemently denied that the North was a well-run Region. Finally, the Igumale branch demanded that Onazi withdraw his letter to the commission.[55]

From February 24 to 25, 1958, the other two representatives of the Executive Committee appeared before the commission of inquiry to argue for the creation of a Middle Belt Region. Discussion of the President-General's refusal to attend was renewed upon their return from Makurdi. Several members of the Executive Committee accused Onazi of having sold out to the Idoma Native Authority and the Northern Peoples' Congress.[56] The Igumale branch, among others, also accused the President-General of betraying the organization and demanded that he resign from office.[57] Onazi refused to accede to the demand. The President-General responded to the charges by reiterating his position on the regional minorities issue and by urging cooperation between the Idoma Hope Rising Union and the Native Authority.[58] The controversy finally subsided when the commission issued its report later that year.

Diminution of the controversy surrounding the President-General's refusal to testify before the Minorities Commission did not halt the organization's decline; the Idoma Hope Rising Union continued to lose members and influence. An indifferent membership permitted Onazi to remain in office but with little power or prestige. When the President-General designated Makurdi as the site for the 1959 Annual Conference—the 1958 Conference had been a dismal failure due to poor attendance—few branches expressed any interest. Onazi's final appeal for both unity in a non-political organization and branch financial support was largely ignored.[59]

By 1957, the Idoma Hope Rising Union had already been reduced to a state of lassitude. By 1959, the regional minorities controversy had combined with the inexorable increase in Native Authority power to sap the organization of its remaining strength. The once vigorous gadfly in divisional affairs passed from the political scene without ceremony in 1959, a year before Nigeria obtained its independence.

Conclusion

Born of the discontent of Idoma youth, and encouraged by post-war nationalist ferment, the Idoma Hope Rising Union sought a major policy role in a democratized Native Authority apparatus. It failed to achieve that objective. In conclusion, I would summarize the principal factors which contributed both to that failure and to the demise of the organization.

First, persistent internecine conflict prevented the Idoma Hope Rising Union from unifying against its leading adversary, the Idoma Native Authority. Rivalry between the branches combined with unresolved differences over the political character of the IHRU and its position on the regional minorities issue to limit organizational effectiveness. An increasingly powerful Native Authority, led by a politically astute *Och'Idoma,* managed to exacerbate those debilitating conflicts.

Second, the Idoma Hope Rising Union was weakened by its inability to produce a dynamic leader around whom the contentious factions might unite. Throughout its history, the organization was plagued by a coterie of generally inept and rivalrous officials. The situation in the IHRU contrasted sharply with that in the Tiv Progressive Union-United Middle Belt Congress-Action Group alliance; the alliance was dominated by an effective charismatic leader, Joseph Tarka.[60]

Third, the essentially conservative Idoma generally supported a Native Authority apparatus which was dominated by traditionalist elements; many in the Division viewed those elements—especially the *Och' Idoma*—as defenders of Idoma institutions and values. It is not surprising, therefore, that attacks by the Idoma Hope Rising Union upon traditionalist Clan Heads, District Heads, and the *Och'Idoma* were often bitterly resented by the populace. Other IHRU tactics also discouraged popular support. For example, a virulent newspaper campaign against official venality could hardly be expected to impress the illiterate masses in rural Idoma Division.

Fourth, the Idoma Hope Rising Union was weakened by government's post-war commitment to gradual, controlled change. The commitment encouraged an inexorable increase in Native Authority power at the expense of all opposition elements. By early 1959, that power had prepared the way for the demise of the IHRU. Later that year, the Idoma Native Authority was to demonstrate its political invincibility in the Division by leading three candidates of the Northern Peoples' Congress to easy victories in federal parliamentary elections.[61] By 1960, when Nigeria became independent, Idoma Division was firmly tied to the NPC, the political party which controlled governments in Kaduna and Lagos.

In sum, the failure of the Idoma Hope Rising Union to achieve a major policy role in divisional affairs may be attributed to the following principal factors: organizational instability, lack of widespread popular support, and the opposition of both government and the Native Authority. Beset by these problems, the organization managed to launch political offensives on only two occasions: (1) during the period 1949–1952, when it agitated for Native Authority reform along democratic lines, and (2) in early 1956, when it fueled a newspaper campaign against official corruption. While nationalist ferment in Nigeria did provide some encouragement to the IHRU in the period after 1952, it was not sufficient to sustain the organization. Operating in a politically inhospitable division and region, the IHRU eventually succumbed to the combined pressures of erosion from within and coercion from without.

This paper is based on field research undertaken in Idoma Division during 1962–1963. The research was facilitated by a Ford Foundation-Michigan State University International Programs Fellowship. I also wish to thank Mr. Ogwiji Ikongbeh (Oturkpo Town, Idoma Division) and my wife, Sally Joy Magid, for their valuable assistance during the research operation.

NOTES

1. See, for example, David Apter, *The Gold Coast in Transition* (Princeton: Princeton University Press, 1955), p. 131ff.; James Cole-

man, *Nigeria: Background to Nationalism* (Berkeley: University of California Press, 1958), p. 271ff.; David Apter, *The Political Kingdom in Uganda: A Study in Bureaucratic Nationalism* (Princeton: Princeton University Press, 1961), p. 216ff.

2. Margery Perham,*Native Administration in Nigeria* (London: Oxford University Press, 1962), p. 362; also Margery Perham, "Problems of Indirect Rule," *East Africa* (April 12, 1934), p. 622. [cited in Northern Nigeria, Benue Province, "Memorandum from Secretary, Northern Provinces, to Benue Province Resident and Idoma Senior District Officer" (unpublished, May 11, 1934).]

3. *Proposals for the Revision of the Constitution of Nigeria,* Cmd. 6599 (London: H.M. Stationery Office, 1945). [cited in Coleman, *op. cit.,* p. 271.]; also Kalu Ezera, *Constitutional Developments in Nigeria* (Cambridge: Cambridge University Press, 1964), pp. 64–81.

4. The Middle Belt sector of the Northern Region is generally assumed to include (1) the provinces of Adamawa, Benue, Ilorin, Kabba, Niger, and Plateau, and (2) the southern portions of Bauchi and Zaria Provinces.

5. Idoma Division is bordered by the Benue River (north), Tiv Division, Benue Province (east), Igala Division, Kabba Province (west), Enugu, Abakaliki, and Ogoja Provinces, Eastern Region of Nigeria (south). Approximately 225,000 Idoma inhabit sixteen of the twenty-two districts in Idoma Division. The provincial and Regional designations were altered in 1967, during the Nigeria-Biafra conflict.

6. Formally, membership in the Idoma Hope Rising Union was restricted to persons who paid dues; supporters were non-members who either expressed sympathy with IHRU goals or participated in its activities. Two former officers told the writer that there was no practical distinction in the organization between members (a minority) and those supporters who participated in its activities (a majority). For the purposes of this paper, I, too, shall ignore the formal distinction between members and supporters who were participants; both formal members and supporter/participants shall be referred to as members.

7. Idoma Hope Rising Union, *Minutes of the Annual Conference,* Oturkpo Town, Northern Region of Nigeria (unpublished, December 12, 1957).

8. Idoma Hope Rising Union, *Report of the Annual Conference,* Kaduna, Northern Region of Nigeria (unpublished, April 10, 1955).
The decision to eliminate the salaries of elected officials at the head-

quarters branch was based on two considerations. First, the Conference recognized that the headquarters treasury was nearly depleted. Second, the Conference wished to restore the confidence of those branches which were demoralized by the alleged corruption of salaried IHRU officials at Oturkpo Town.

9. Tension between the branches was undoubtedly exacerbated when several IHRU officials at Oturkpo Town refused to acknowledge the 1955 purge and the transfer of headquarters to Kaduna. As a result, some branches remained loyal to Oturkpo Town; others supported Kaduna as the headquarters unit.

The tension between the branches is reflected in the following correspondence: Idoma Hope Rising Union, *Letter from Secretary, Zaria Branch, to the Secretary-General at Oturkpo Town* (unpublished, February 11, 1957); Idoma Hope Rising Union, *Letter from Secretary, Lagos Branch, to the Secretary-General at Oturkpo Town* (unpublished, March 25, 1957); Idoma Hope Rising Union, *Letter from Secretary, Kano Branch, to the Secretary-General at Oturkpo Town* (unpublished, August 4, 1958); Idoma Hope Rising Union, *Letter from the President-General at Oturkpo Town to the Branch Secretaries* (unpublished, February 29, 1959).

10. Idoma Hope Rising Union, *Draft Convention and Rules* (unpublished, August 8, 1953); Idoma Hope Rising Union, *Letter from Secretary, Kano Branch, to Benue Province Resident* (unpublished, March 4, 1954); Idoma Hope Rising Union, *Report of the 1955 Annual Conference, op. cit.;* Idoma Hope Rising Union, *Letter from President-General and Acting Secretary-General to Premier, Northern Region of Nigeria* (unpublished, June 2, 1956); Idoma Hope Rising Union, *Letter from Secretary-General to Editor, Nigerian Citizen* (unpublished, September 20, 1957).

11. Many former members of the IHRU expressed this attitude in conversations with the writer.

12. Idoma Hope Rising Union, *Letter from Secretary-General to Editor, Nigerian Citizen, op. cit.;* Idoma Hope Rising Union, *Minutes of the Annual Conference* (unpublished, December 15, 1952); Idoma Hope Rising Union, *Letter from Secretary, Kano Branch, to Benue Province Resident, op. cit.;* Idoma Hope Rising Union, *Minutes of the Annual Conference* (unpublished, 1956).

13. Idoma Hope Rising Union, *Address of the President-General at Oturkpo Town* (unpublished, October 31, 1955).

14. Idoma Hope Rising Union, *Letter from Secretary, Kano Branch, to Kano Native Authority* (unpublished, October 4, 1955); Idoma Hope

Rising Union, *Minutes of the 1956 Annual Conference, op. cit.;* Idoma Hope Rising Union, *Letter from Secretary, Zaria Branch, to Zaria Native Authority* (unpublished, November 22, 1956); Idoma Hope Rising Union, *Letter from Secretary, Kano Branch, to Idoma Native Authority Council* (unpublished, March 28, 1957); Idoma Hope Rising Union, *Letter from Secretary, Lagos Branch, to Idoma Native Authority Council* (unpublished, June 24, 1959).

15. Idoma Hope Rising Union, *Letter from Secretary, Kano Branch, to Benue Province Resident, op. cit.;* Idoma Hope Rising Union, *Minutes of the Executive Meeting* (unpublished, July 19, 1958).

16. Idoma Hope Rising Union, *Minutes of the Annual Conference* (unpublished, December 15, 1952); Idoma Hope Rising Union, *Letter from Secretary, Kano Branch, to Benue Province Resident, op. cit.;* Idoma Hope Rising Union, *Letter from President-General and Acting Secretary-General to Premier, Northern Region of Nigeria, op. cit.;* Idoma Hope Rising Union, *Letter from Secretary-General to Editor, Nigerian Citizen, op. cit.;* Idoma Hope Rising Union, *Letter from Secretary-General to Premier, Northern Region of Nigeria* (unpublished, January 16, 1957); Idoma Hope Rising Union, *Minutes of the Executive Meeting* (unpublished, June 27, 1958).

17. The Clan Head in clans of central and northern Idoma traditionally combined secular and spiritual authority. In the clans of southern Idoma, the authority of the Clan Head was traditionally confined to the secular realm.

18. Northern Nigeria, Benue Province, *Annual Report for Idoma Division,* 1948 (unpublished). For an analysis of the pre-war Native Authority system, see my "British Rule and Indigenous Organization in Nigeria: A Case-Study in Normative-Institutional Change," *Journal of African History,* IX, 2 (1968) pp. 301–307.

19. As early as 1927 government had considered imposing a divisional chieftaincy on the acephalous Idoma. See Northern Nigeria, Benue Province, *Annual Report for Idoma Division,* 1927 (unpublished).

20. In that year, the Idoma Hope Rising Union petitioned Governor Sir Bernard Bourdillon to establish a divisional chieftaincy. See Idoma Hope Rising Union, *Letter from Secretary-General to Editor, Nigerian Citizen, op. cit.;* also f.n. 19.

21. Northern Nigeria, Benue Province, *Annual Report for Idoma Division,* 1949 (unpublished).

22. Northern Nigeria, Benue Province, *Annual Report for Idoma Division,* 1950 (unpublished).

23. *Ibid.*

24. *Ibid.*

25. Northern Nigeria, Benue Province, *Annual Report for Idoma Division,* 1951 (unpublished).

26. Northern Nigeria, Benue Province, *Annual Report for Idoma Division,* 1952 (unpublished).

27. L. Gray Cowan, *Local Government in West Africa* (New York: Columbia University Press, 1959), p. 79. I have drawn from Cowan (pp. 79–83) for the discussion of developments at the regional level.

28. K. P. Maddocks and D. A. Pott, *Local Government in the Northern Provinces of Nigeria* (Kaduna: Government Printer, 1951), pp. 1–35.

29. Cowan, *op. cit.,* p. 79.

30. *Ibid.,* p. 80.

31. Northern Nigeria, *Native Authority Law of 1954* (Kaduna: Government Printer, 1961).

32. See sections 55 and 59 of the Law.

33. Members of the Idoma Hope Rising Union fueled a serial on corruption in the Idoma Native Authority. See the *Nigerian Citizen,* January 19, 1956; January 25, 1956; January 28, 1956; February 4, 1956; February 15, 1956; February 22, 1956; February 25, 1956; March 3, 1956; March 17, 1956; March 28, 1956; March 31, 1956.

34. The Idoma Hope Rising Union frequently requested an independent commission of inquiry to investigate charges of Native Authority corruption. The IHRU request was supported by opposition political parties, including the Action Group and the United Middle Belt Congress. After a lengthy delay, government advised the Native Authority to appoint a board of inquiry to investigate the operations of its own Works Department. See Idoma Hope Rising Union, *Letter from President-General and Acting Secretary-General to Premier, Northern Region of Nigeria, op. cit.;* United Middle Belt Congress, *Letter from General Secretary to Minister for Local Government, Northern Re-*

gion of Nigeria (unpublished, May 12, 1956); Action Group, Idoma Branch, *Letter from Secretary to Premier, Northern Region of Nigeria* (unpublished, June 22, 1957); Northern Nigeria, Idoma Division, *Letter from District Officer to Benue Province Resident* (unpublished, August 6, 1957).

35. The position of the Idomá Hope Rising Union on the Middle Belt or regional minorities issue is examined on pp. 354–357.

36. Idoma Hope Rising Union and Idoma State Union, *Joint Press Release on the Merger of the Organizations* (unpublished, September 1, 1957).

37. Internecine conflict over the regional minorities issue further weakened the formally unified organization. See pp. 355–357.

38. Idoma Hope Rising Union, *Address of the President-General at the Annual Conference at Oturkpo Town* (unpublished, 1957).

39. Technically, the Portfolio Councilor is merely a consultant to one of the four administrative departments in the Idoma Native Authority. In fact, he is the chief executive officer of the department. Northern Nigeria, Ministry for Local Government, *Duties of Councilors* (unpublished circular No. MLG. 42/82, September 12, 1962).

40. Northern Nigeria, Benue Province, Idoma Native Authority, *Minutes of Executive Meetings* (unpublished, June 7, 1957); Northern Nigeria, Benue Province, Idoma Native Authority, *Minutes of Executive Meetings* (unpublished, January 22, 1958).

41. Idoma Hope Rising Union, *Letter from Secretary-General to Premier, Northern Region of Nigeria* (unpublished, January 16, 1957).

42. The discussion of developments in the Middle Belt during the 1950's draws from Coleman, *op. cit.,* pp. 366–367; also Richard L. Sklar, *Nigerian Political Parties: Power in an Emergent African Nation* (Princeton: Princeton University Press, 1963), pp. 344–347.

43. Action Group, *Address by the Honorable Chief Obafemi Awolowo, Federal President of the Action Group and Premier of the Western Region of Nigeria, 6th Action Group Conference* (Lagos, September 11, 1959), pp. 23–24.

44. Idoma Hope Rising Union, *Minutes of the Annual Conference* (unpublished, December 15, 1952).

45. Idoma Hope Rising Union, *Letter from Secretary, Zaria Branch, to Secretary, Kano Branch* (unpublished, October 4, 1952).

46. Idoma Hope Rising Union, *Letter from Secretary, Kaduna Branch, to the Secretary-General at Oturkpo Town* (unpublished, January 1, 1953).

47. Idoma Hope Rising Union, *Report of the Annual Conference, op. cit.*

48. See f.n. 34. Informal contacts between the Idoma Hope Rising Union and the Action Group increased after 1955 when Ogwiji Ikongbeh, Secretary-General of the tribal union, assumed the AG Secretaryship in Idoma Division. However, relations between Ikongbeh and Joseph Tarka, President of the United Middle Belt Congress and Vice-President of the AG, remained strained in that period; the strain was produced by tribal and political rivalry between the two men. See, for example, Action Group, Tiv Branch, *Letter from Joseph Tarka to Chief Obafemi Awolowo* (unpublished, February 25, 1961); Action Group, Idoma Branch, *Letter from Ogwiji Ikongbeh to Joseph Tarka* (unpublished, March 9, 1961).

49. Shortly after its founding in 1955, the Idoma State Union joined the Northern Peoples' Congress as a tribal union affiliate. See Sklar, *op. cit.*, p. 387.

50. The activities of the commission of inquiry are briefly examined in Ezera, *op. cit.*, pp. 251–252; also Sklar, *op. cit.*, pp. 138–140, 349, 354.

51. Great Britain, Colonial Office, *Report of the Commission Appointed to Inquire into the Fears of Minorities and the Means of Allaying Them* (London: H.M.S.O., 1958), pp. 71–73, 87.

52. Idoma Hope Rising Union, *Minutes of the Executive Meeting* (unpublished, August 9, 1957).

53. Idoma Hope Rising Union, *Minutes of the Executive Meeting* (unpublished, February 15, 1958).

54. Idoma Hope Rising Union, *Letter from President-General to the Secretary, Minorities Commission* (unpublished, February 17, 1958).

55. Idoma Hope Rising Union, *Letter from Secretary, Igumale Branch, to the President-General at Oturkpo Town* (unpublished, February 24, 1958).

56. Idoma Hope Rising Union, *Letter from Member of the Executive Committee to Secretary-General at Oturkpo Town* (unpublished, March 3, 1958). Some members of the IHRU even speculated that Onazi may have commenced his alleged betrayal in 1954, when he accepted a Northern Region Government scholarship for study in the United Kingdom.

57. Idoma Hope Rising Union, *Letter from Secretary, Igumale Branch, to Secretary-General at Oturkpo Town* (unpublished, March 17, 1958).

58. Idoma Hope Rising Union, *Minutes of the Executive Meeting* (unpublished, June 27, 1958).

59. Idoma Hope Rising Union, *Letter from President-General to the Branch Secretaries* (unpublished, February 2, 1959).

60. M. J. Dent, "A Minority Party—the UMBC," in *Nigerian Government and Politics: Prelude to the Revolution,* ed. John P. Mackintosh (Evanston: Northwestern University Press, 1966), p. 470.

61. K. W. J. Post, *The Nigerian Federal Election of 1959: Politics and Administration in a Developing Political System* (New York: Oxford University Press, 1963), p. 454.

CHAPTER 13

The Military and Politics:
A Study of the Relation Between the Army
and the Political Process in Nigeria

M. J. DENT

The Nigerian case history is exceptionally interesting for the study of the military in politics. In no other case have the tensions of the body politic reflected themselves in the military to such an extent that the army has turned upon itself in whole-sale slaughter. In no other country has the process of military disengagement revealed a country once, more or less united under civilian rule, not without tensions but with these tensions held in some sort of balance in the political process, brought by military rule to the point of break up. This is the kind of limiting case which is of peculiar interest in the study of tensions in the military, and of the escalation in the opposi-tional relationship that can happen in circumstances of law-less confrontation.

There have been valuable studies analysing the conduct of the military in politics and laying down categories to explain the circumstances in which they take power, the manner of their taking power, their conduct and values when in charge of Government and the difficulties in the process of disengage-

Reprinted, with minor revisions and the omission of appendices, from Kenneth Kirkwood, (ed.), *St. Anthony's Papers* (African Affairs, No. 3), No. 21 (1970), pp. 113–139. Copyright © 1970 by The Clarendon Press. Reprinted by permission of the publisher and Martin J. Dent.

ment. Professor Finer, for instance, in *The Man on Horseback,* has produced an analysis of these problems which illuminates the Nigerian case, but there are certain peculiar characteristics of the Nigerian experience which force us to broaden the assumptions that have previously been made.[1]

In three ways the behavior of the military in Nigeria has been different from the models created in *The Man on Horseback.* It is generally assumed in that book that the corporate sense of the military will always be so strong that they will act as a single corporation over and against the politicians, their rivals for governmental power. It does not seem to have been sufficiently realised that if the regional tensions in the body politic itself are very acute and if the means of the coming to power of the military increase those tensions and bring them into the army itself, then, far from the army uniting the body politic, the body politic may divide the army. We are then left with a situation where the officers of a certain tribal group become but the armed wing of a tribal political group, fighting against a similar combination of tribal group politicians and officers of the opposing tribe. The old political conflict is then fought out again, but the medium of conflict is no longer political manoeuvre, manifestos, votes, and speeches but rather violence, with an immense advantage to the side which strikes first. This is a situation of lawless confrontation, analogous to some models of international affairs; it has its own inherent logic towards pre-emptive strikes and treacherous violence.

Secondly, the model of *The Man on Horseback* assumes that the attitude of the military is to all intents and purposes that of its officer corps; the military hierarchy and the tradition of obedience is thought to be sufficient to ensure that the N.C.O.'s and other ranks take their attitudes from their superiors and act as an obedient instrument of their political purposes. In the Nigerian case, to some extent in the "loyal" recovery against the mutineers in January, and to a much greater extent in the events of July and of September, the attitudes of the N.C.O.'s and other ranks, the vast majority of whom come from the Northern Region, becomes of vital importance. It is from their outraged sense of loyalty and from their tribal fears that the impetus comes for the planning of the July coup. This effect came from the peculiarly asymmetrical structure of the Nigerian army.

A third peculiar characteristic of the Nigerian case is the breakdown of law and order during the process of attempted disengagement in September and in October, the evil combination of soldiers and thugs going out to fulfil a self-imposed task of driving every Ibo from the North.

The Nigerian disaster is the more remarkable because it occurred in a relatively developed society, one with a high sense of legality, a society which, with the exception of the Kano riots of 1953 (an incident of very limited spread and duration), the Tiv riots of 1960 and 1964 (a political situation aggravated by particular local phenomena), and the Western Region riots of 1965 (the result of particular quarrels among the Yoruba people and its aggravation by the polarities of the Nigerian political process), had been able to resolve its tensions without violence. That there were basic tensions between North and South, between Hausa and Yoruba and Ibo as well as between a hundred other smaller groups and sub-groups, goes without saying. These tensions were concerned largely with manoeuvering for positions in Government service, and attempts to get a larger share of government patronage and of the national economic pie.

This kind of conflict is contained in many political systems without breaking out into violence. In the North for instance, the economic tensions of Ibo and Hausa were not sufficient to cause any violence between them from 1953 to 1966, their relationships remaining sometimes competitive, sometimes symbiotic.[2] The Ibos did not seek political power at the local level; they were intent on making money and did not seek for trouble,[3] while the Northerners, whatever their feelings, are intensely law abiding,[4] obeying the dictates of the constituted authority not to take the law into their own hands. Only after the military coup did the idea begin to spread that there was a "licence to kill". The frail bonds of prohibition that protect the legality of the state were broken and wholesale violence began quite suddenly in the north in May, 1966. This was not the flash point of existing tensions raised to a level where they caused violence automatically (this is the wrong analogy) but was the result of a quite new situation in 1966, when it was discovered that murder could be successfully used as a means of changing the political process, and that there would be an exemption from the inexorable processes of criminal justice.

The intervention of the army in January, 1966 occurred as a result of a number of forces, and it is not easy to uncover the facts and to decide how much weight to give to each force.

Initially, the Nigerian army had a high flash point, that is to say unlike some Middle Eastern or South American armies, it required a strong incentive to make it abandon the traditional British attitude of aloofness from the political process and break its tie of loyalty to civilian authority. In 1964, the army was first used on a large scale in aid of the civil power in the Tiv riots.[5] Although these riots were partly the local reflection of the basic quarrel between North and South, and although there had been a considerable break-down of law and order with several hundred deaths, the army acted effectively and impartially. The Tiv people came to regard the army as a force which was irresistible but neither partial nor oppressive; a very few instances of punitive action were carried out by the army, but for the most part the Tiv rioters gave up their arms voluntarily and went home as the army advised them to do. The army proved conspicuously more successful and more acceptable than the police in this action: Anoforo of the East, Hassan and Pam of the North and many other officers from the East and North co-operated entirely successfully.

In the election crises of 1964/5 the army remained non-political, though its intervention was decisive in the conflict between the Prime Minister and the NNA, on the one side, and the President and the UPGA, on the other. The General Officer Commanding, Major General Welby-Everard, sought advice from the Chief Justice on his constitutional position, and circulated the reply to his senior officers, indicating that it was the Prime Minister and not the President who had the constitutional right to give instructions to the armed forces.[6] The commanders of the Army and Navy and the Police were sent for by Dr. Azikiwe, but it was clear they would take orders only from the Prime Minister. The army marched through Lagos with fixed bayonets, showing that they could counter any action of the Lagos crowds which were in favour of the President, and their intervention was probably the decisive element in influencing Dr. Azikiwe to come to a compromise and to ask Sir Abubakar to form a national Government. The recent Federal pamphlet, *Nigeria 1966,* has suggested that there was an abortive coup by some officers against the Government at this time, but that no punitive action was taken. I have found no evidence of any overt action at this time, though there may well have been a good deal of verbal expression of dissatisfaction.[7]

This dissatisfaction one would expect from the tribal structure of the Nigerian officer corps. The structure of the Nigerian army at this time was unusual; it was like a four-layer sandwich with different groups predominating in each layer. At the bottom the bulk of the riflemen were Northerners, mostly from the Middle Belt and Bornu—the Tiv, the Idoma, the Bachama, the men of Tangale Waja, the men of the tribes of the Plateau, the men of Bornu and some from Niger and Chad; the army did not publish tribal statistics, but it is clear that in the General Duty troops the proportion of Northerners was as high as 75% among N.C.O.s and men.[8] Among tradesmen, signaller's clerks and other ancilliary soldiers, the proportion of Southerners was much higher. Among the junior officers the representation of tribes was more or less equal, having been controlled by the quota of 50% Northern, 25% Eastern and 25% Western introduced by Alhaji Ribadu in 1961.[9] Finally, in the rank of Major and above, the composition of the Officer Corps was the result of the period of open competition and entry by academic qualifications introduced by the British in the mid-fifties and continuing until 1961. In this competition Southerners, and especially Easterners, predominated over Northerners in a ratio of some seven to one.

Of the 44 officers of the Nigerian army given in the 1960 army list (the last British list giving details of the Nigerian army), only six were Northern (of these, four were murdered in January, 1966 and a fifth, Gowon, escaped by good luck), twenty-three were Eastern and the remainder Western and Mid-Western.[10] Of the thirty lieutenants and second lieutenants, nineteen came from the East. Of the forty-four officers twenty-four were of Ibo origin. Whether this was the result of a surplus of educated people seeking jobs, or whether as has been suggested, there was tribal pressure on qualified young Ibos to join the army because of its strategic importance in the future balance of power in the Nigerian Government, is not clear. It was at this time that Ojukwu joined the army, having taken his degree at Oxford, and it has been suggested that he and others were advised to do so by Dr. Azikiwe. At the very top, the army had four brigadiers in 1965: Maimalari from the North, Ademelegun and Ogundipe from the West and Ironsi from the East. Ironsi was slightly the senior in length of service in that rank, and for this reason Abubakar overruled the professional advice of the departing General Officer Commanding,[11] Welby-Everard (who had recommended Ademelegun and Ogundipe as the first two choices and Ironsi as third choice), and the Sardauna (who supported the claims of Maimalari or Ademelegun). The fact that he was prepared to appoint an Ibo G.O.C. showed how clearly Sir Abubakar assumed that the army would remain loyal to the civil authority and would not attempt to seize power. The civilian control of the army was exercised first through Alhaji Ribadu and then, after his death, through Alhaji Inuwa Wada, both powerful NPC figures of a very conservative kind. Both appear at times to have exercised their powers to seek, where possible, to achieve balance in the officer corps by assisting in the more rapid promotion of Northerners and discouraging that of some Easterners. But on the whole the army was resistant to political pressures, although personal relations between Ironsi and Maimalari and Ademelegun had been bitter for many years.

The Nigerianisation of the army had started late and then proceeded at great speed. Nigeria, unlike the Sudan, entered Independence with an officer corps more than 70% British; by mid-1965 every single British officer had left the service, and Nigeria, unlike Ghana, declined to keep a Commonwealth training mission. This, it seems, was largely because of the personal attitude of Ribadu. The result of this very rapid Nigerianisation was that officers obtained extremely rapid promotion at a young age, but that at the end of the process the establishment was full and there was no room for further promotion, unless the Senior Officers at the top retired or died.[12] The army acquitted itself well in the Congo and had a high reputation; it was not without minor tribal tensions, but at this stage its corporate sense was more powerful than tribal divisions. None the less, at this time (1965) at least one Senior

Nigerian Officer foresaw the possibilities of future tribal division among officers and remarked on them to Major General Welby Everard.[13]

It can be seen from this analysis that the loyalty of the army was potentially vulnerable: Northern soldiers obeyed orders from Ibo officers, but there was a residual feeling in their minds that the Ibo were not really a martial race—they considered the Ibo people too articulate for warriors. "Mai fada ba zai yi surutu ba"—"The warrior is not talkative"—is a common Northern proverb; they regarded the martial qualities of the Easterners rather as the British other rank does those of the Italian, or the Punjabi does those of the Bengali or the man from Madras. This stereotype was as inaccurate as its opposite—the Ibo view of the North as backward, ignorant and inert. Northern and Eastern soldiers lived together in the same barracks, with no tribal separation, and as long as the divisions of the civilian political process could be kept out of the army there was no danger; but, once let the tribal struggle for power be introduced from the political process into the army itself and that corporation could be blown to pieces by an internal explosion.

The desire to intervene grows among the military as they see the progressive decline in the prestige of civilian rulers. Their corruption, their inability to run fair elections and the increasing divisions within Nigeria, made military intervention more likely. But the civilian authorities had not declined to the unpopularity of those in Ghana. Sir Abubakar remained a statesmanlike figure who used power with restraint and transcended his tribal origin; the N.P.C., the N.E.P.U. and the U.M.B.C. in the North, the A.G. in the West and elsewhere and, to a lesser extent, the N.C.N.C. in the East, continued to attract support as a focus of both political and tribal aspirations. A coup to remove these political cadres from power would not be as easy as was the removal of the C.P.P. in Ghana.[14] The reluctance of army officers to intervene in politics was, however, reduced by approaches from one of the contending political parties. It seems clear that certain officers were approached by members of the U.P.G.A. Some figures of the N.C.N.C. in Nigeria and of the A.G. in exile, despairing of ever redressing the tribal balance by constitutional means, decided to avail themselves of the preponderance of officers with U.P.G.A. sympathies to put an end by force to the dominant position of the N.P.C.[15]

The utter failure of the Government to do justice in the West after the rigged election, or to restore order there, provided a sense of urgency, a climate in which many people were looking to the army for deliverance. It is, however, easier to encourage the idea of making a coup than it is to control what happens when other people with guns begin to carry out that coup. The five Ibo majors who formed the nucleus of the officers preparing, from early in 1965, for a violent overthrow of the civilian Government soon decided that their corporate sense as army officers should take precedence over political allegiance. When they took power they would do so not in the name of politicians, whom they and most army officers considered to be corrupt and irresponsible, but rather in their own name. Initially, the plan seems to have been made not by Ibo officers only but by other officers from the South, and even perhaps radicals from the North. But, in execution, the plan was bent to a more tribal form. There took place a "coup within a coup".[16]

In Kaduna, operations were planned by Major Nzeogwu, an Ibo officer, born and brought up in Kaduna, speaking excellent Hausa, a man of cosmopolitan outlook. Nzeogwu was in a sense the "Brutus" of the coup. He neither drank nor smoked; he was unmarried and a daily communicant of the Catholic Church; he had a genuine hatred of corruption and a desire to maintain that "true Nigerianism" which he declared he found in the army. His political ideas were, however, simplistic: he considered it sufficient to "gun down all the bigwigs" to ensure a new Nigeria. The Commissioner of Police of the Northern Region, who saw a good deal of him both during his three days in power and after his detention, gave quite a sympathetic picture but described him as a man "whose feet were not on the ground".[17] This view is borne out by almost every officer who has known him, and prompted Gowon's tribute to Nzeogwu on his death as a "gallant but misguided officer". His broadcasts in Kaduna after the coup, pronouncing the death penalty for rape, homosexuality, sitting on the fence etc., were wild and disordered. In his appearance on television, Nzeogwu regarded the seriousness of killing the Sardauna and one of his wives somewhat lightly. In Kaduna the two senior officers, Brigadier Ademelegun, apparently a close friend of the Sardauna, and Colonel

Shodeinde, were murdered in their houses. Mrs. Ademelegun, a much respected hospital matron, was also killed.

In Ibadan, soldiers attacked and killed Akintola. In Lagos, they not only kidnapped the Prime Minister and the Minister of Finance but murdered four officers. All the senior officers of the 2nd Brigade had been summoned to Lagos for a Senior Officer's Conference. Fajuyi failed to arrive, and Nwawo, Ogundipe and Adebayo were absent from the country. The remaining officers arrived and during the conference, Brigadier Maimalari was asked to give a party to celebrate his new marriage. The many guests at the party included all five Northern Officers over the rank of Major—Brigadier Maimalari, Lieutenant Colonel Abogo Largema (Commander of the 4th Battalion), Lieutenant Colonel Pam (Adjutant General), Colonel Kuru Mohammed and Lieutenant Colonel Gowon (who was to take over Command of the 2nd Battalion from Lieutenant Colonel Njoku). Major General Ironsi was also present and the Ibo Majors Ifeajuna (Brigade Major to Maimalari), Okafor (Commander of the Federal Guard) and Anoforo. After the party the three Ibo Majors and other Ibo officers proceeded to murder their Northern colleagues. Maimalari was attacked in his house, escaped but was later killed near the golf course; Pam was taken from his house and despite promises made to his wife that he would be spared, was killed in a land rover outside (probably by Anoforo), Kuru Mohammed was shot by an Ibo officer when he answered the bell at his house in Lagos, Largema (who had been sent by the Sarduana to Lagos presumably to see Ironsi and to enquire about rumours of plots, which had reached Akintola and the Sardauna) was shot in his room in the Ikoyi Hotel. Gowon was undoubtedly an intended victim of the purge but managed to escape by concealing himself in Lagos for the night. The next morning he led in the troops of the 2nd Battalion to quell the mutiny and used the telephone to rally the loyal NCOs and Officers and to speak to Ojukwu in Kano warning him against disloyalty.[18] The much battered body of Okotie-Eboh was found on the road outside Lagos; the Prime Minister's body was found a week later. Most Southerners said that he had died of shock or suffocation; many Northerners maintained that he had been tortured and mutilated before death. Sir Abubakar was much respected within Nigeria and outside. He was regarded in the North as a gentle and God-fearing man, who had resisted pressure from within the North to push its advantage at the federal level. His murder by the Federal guard commander whose job it was to protect him was regarded as ungrateful and treacherous. Okafor had been almost a member of Abubakar's family.

One Ibo senior officer, Colonel Arthur Unegbe, the Quarter Master, was killed when he refused to give up the keys of the armoury in Lagos to the mutinous officers.[19] He died with great gallantry, defending his post of duty, but it is probable that he was not, like the other six senior officers, an objective of the coup, although he was the kind of tough and loyal officer who would have sought to revenge the death of Maimalari.

General Ironsi had a narrow and fortunate escape—too fortunate some Northerners thought—and when the rest of the army, led especially by the N.C.O.s and the soldiers of the Federal guard, rallied and began to take action against the mutineers, he put himself at the head of this action and took over Lagos nominally in the name of the Federal cabinet.[20] Within two days, however, he had induced the cabinet to hand over power to himself, in order to restore order, and he then dissolved the cabinet and parliament, appointed military governors, and vested all legislative and executive authority in the supreme military council.[21] The connection of Ironsi with the coup is likely to remain a matter of debate until historians have much fuller evidence than is available today. The Northern soldiers who killed Ironsi in July alleged that he had confessed some foreknowledge of the coup and that they had obtained written evidence to prove this; and certainly this was the general belief in the North, even before the July coup.[22] No hard evidence has yet been produced. This belief could, however, have been the result of bad publicity and political folly on Ironsi's part rather than of actual guilt. The deaths of the army officers were never published; there was no funeral service, an important element in the military mind, without which the injury done to the dead was made twice as great; there was no public eulogy. It was as though these officers had never existed; their killing had all the appearance of a "rubbing out" by the Mafia. So secret was their death kept that even a supposedly well informed publication like *Africa Confidential* wrote on

January 30 that the attitude of Northern soldiers to the coup would depend on the attitude of Maimalari: that officer had already been murdered two weeks before.[23] Among the private soldiers the rumours kept spreading that Maimalari was alive and was coming to rally them. To many of the Northern soldiers he was a kind of hero figure.

A senior officer has recently commented privately on the fatal effect produced by this fear and secrecy of the military rulers. By seeking to keep deaths secret, by refusing to set up inquests on Abubakar, the officers set a host of rumours in motion. They created a kind of cordite situation; material which might have raised no more than a fierce blaze if allowed to be discussed in the open, took on an incredibly explosive nature when contained in secrecy and prohibition.

Nzeogwu has accused Ibo Majors in charge of the coup in Lagos, not only of incompetence in failing to take over Lagos and control it but of tribalism in the one-sided way in which they carried out the coup.[24] It seems to me extremely probable that, faced with the brutal task of killing not only Northerners but their own compatriots, they warned Ironsi of what was about to happen and deliberately went through the motions of trying to kill him, rather than actually carrying out the deed. As soon as the coup failed to take power in Lagos, Ifeajuna fled to Ghana where he was welcomed as a hero by Dr. Nkrumah, but quickly became disillusioned with Nkrumah's intentions and managed, with the help of the Nigerian High Commissioner, to return to Nigeria where he was detained with the other plotters.[25]

Nzeogwu, in Kaduna, was genuinely angry at the failure of his co-plotters to take over Lagos or to kill Ironsi, and for a time thought of marching on Lagos and on Enugu to kill Okpara. After three days he was persuaded to surrender to Ironsi on favourable terms; had he not surrendered, there might have been civil war. The Federal Government had already made tentative approaches to the British military attaché for armed assistance in putting down the mutiny,[26] and at the same time Colonel Nasser, an old friend of the Sardauna, had telephoned threatening to send Egyptian paratroops to revenge the dead Premier.[27] There is a certain delightful irony in the prospect of British and Egyptian soldiers fighting side by side to overthrow a coup made by a Sandhurst Officer against supposedly "reactionary" politicians! When he went to Lagos, Nzeogwu expected to be executed; he was, in fact, left free for three days and was then detained. Ojukwu in Kano seems to have moved from an attitude of sympathy to the coup to one of support for the "loyalists". He detained an aeroplane sent to Kano from Kaduna by Nzeogwu to collect funds to pay his troops.

There were two reactions to the coup: a short-term one and a long-term one. Nigerian society is always ready to welcome a new beginning, and he who obtains political power has initially in his hands a kind of Aladdin's lamp giving him a claim upon popular support. In any case, the country as a whole was fed up with the politicians in power and with their corruption and greeted the coup as an act of liberation, but the reaction differed from region to region. In the East the coup was welcomed unreservedly. It represented at the same time ideological, tribal and national victory in its motivation. The coup of January is to be regarded neither as a purely "Ibo coup" nor yet as one free of tribalism. In the *abyssus profunda humani conscientiae*—the great depth of human personality—no clear distinction can be made between the personal, the tribal and the altruistic motive; they reinforce one another and occur in different combinations in the minds of different people in their reactions to these kinds of events.

The Yoruba people initially welcomed the coup wholeheartedly since it brought them deliverance from the unpopular regime of the N.N.D.P. The North was shocked into inactivity. Many people, including several leaders of the N.P.C., had become convinced that the Sardauna had so personalised the administration of the North that his removal was essential. In Tiv Division especially, the overthrowing of the Sardauna Government came as a great relief. But, as one Northern leader remarked, "We might have removed the Sardauna ourselves but we are not going to have an Ibo doing it". The attitude was, in general, one of "wait and see". The N.P.C., along with other political parties, issued a statement in favour of the military rule, but Dipcharima, the Senior Federal N.P.C. Minister, was clearly frightened. "The main task", he said, "is to survive". Later, as the North came to ponder the events of the coup in the light of the interpretation put upon them by certain less well-educated Ibos, they reflected in Hassan's words that the coup was one-sided since it was "more than a coincidence that of the nine figures deliberately killed by parties led by Ibo Officers not one was an Ibo".[28]

Political scientists sometimes underestimate the importance of the concept of justice in the popular mind in inducing people to obey authority. *Expella justitia it quid sunt regna nisi magna latrocinia*[29]—if you take away justice the kingdoms of the world are no better than great bands of brigands. In the minds of the Northerners justice was peculiarly connected with two elements—the element of proper procedure and the element of symmetry. By the procedures to which they had become accustomed during two generations of ordered British rule, a death involved an inquest and then, if it were found to be due to culpable homicide, a trial. Ironsi went so far as to set up, apparently under Gowon, a secret military enquiry into the coup.[30] He also detained about a hundred officers and men in connection with the coup. But he did not go to the extent of the judicial act—the trial of the accused.[31] Northerners begged him to do so, indicating that if those guilty were once tried and convicted he could commute the sentences without rousing opposition. Justice would have been done. The accused were, however, neither tried nor released but kept in prison under favourable conditions while they continued to receive their pay. Seven of them were promoted while in prison.

The murder of fellow officers at the time of the coup had a particularly bad effect on the morale of the Northern troops.[32] The killing smacked of treachery; it offended their sense of justice. It was from the private soldiers that pressure began to be put upon Northern officers to revenge their fallen comrades. Private soldiers openly abused Northern officers for their failure to take action.[33] It was because of these pressures that certain officers and men decided to take action against the Ironsi regime.[34]

The sense of symmetry was also outraged; taking the coup leaders at their own valuation, they had not followed up their principles. If the politicians were so corrupt that an example had to be made *pour encourager les autres,* why had the two Ibo Premiers been spared? If in Nzeogwu's plan it was necessary "to gun down all the bigwigs", why had no Ibo bigwigs been killed?

The gratuitous slaughter of northern officers in January sprang partly from a climate of opinion, both civil and military, that positively welcomed bloodshed as a means of building a new nation. The head of the political science department at Legon, who visited Ibadan in 1965, remarked to me on this unfortunate longing for bloodshed among certain radical Ibadan academics[35]—compensating perhaps for the uneventful nature of their University life by an academic cult of violence! A teacher and newspaper columnist wrote to a student of mine, rejoicing at the January coup and saying that if there was "any more filth about they would be only to delighted to take it to the morgue".[36] *Blut ist ein ganz besonders saft,*[37] and for the young Turks among the reforming and centralising nationalists it had a positively atavistic attraction.

The military regime took as its two professed objectives the removal of the corruption of the politicians and the unification of Nigeria from divisive tribalism. With a certain degree of naiveté, they assumed that the difficulties of the old regime were due to the faults of the politicians and not to the difficulties of the political process itself. They entirely overlooked the great difficulties of the task of conflict resolution, a task for which the military as a caste are entirely unfitted. Initially, Ironsi made little change in the political process beyond the removal of the whole political class from government. The civil service continued in its former functions, as did the chiefs, and they became the new intermediaries between government and people. The only group of more or less political origin allowed to remain in government were the old Governors, now retitled "advisers to the military governors".

The respect with which the "elder statemen" were regarded tends to reinforce the view that Ironsi would have done wisely to have inspanned more of the better politicians and civilian figures into the business of government. Some equivalent of the Ghanaian "political committee" would have provided an outlet for discontent and a means of the representation of civilian interests. Furthermore, by ignoring the more radical politicians of the North as well as the Action Group and the old opposition, Ironsi lost the chance of winning support from elements which had previously been in alliance with the South and could have made a bridge between the two opposed regions. To those who suggested that he should use political figures, Ironsi replied that "politician" had become a dirty word. The hopes of the minorities were likewise frustrated by Ironsi's refusal to consider the creation of new states, since he wished to abolish regions altogether.[38] This disappointment was particularly important in turning the Tiv people from a position of neutrality to one of hostility.

The army, which might have been well qualified to act as a kind of veto group to put an end to a particular period of civilian rule and make the civilians start again in a new way, was less qualified to undertake the business of government itself. This, however, it proceeded to do. For a time the corporate sense of the army was strong enough for them to put emphasis on their values and their unity over and against the former "corrupt" civilian rulers. The wound of January had not yet turned septic, though it was soon to do so. Increasingly, the army laid less emphasis on the temporary nature of its rule; it insisted that government was under military rule and that any civilians involved were either subordinates or advisers without power. Ironsi, however, had no political sense, and very soon proceeded to alienate all those elements whose support he might so easily have won. The Yoruba radicals turned against him; he failed to release Awolowo; he won the support of certain Northern Emirs and presented the Sultan of Sokoto with a silver coffee service, but failed to realise that Northern society was far more dynamic than the conservative society portrayed in the Southern stereotype of Northern behaviour. Northerners were not a people inert in the hands of their rulers, who could be led against their wishes. The Sultan of Sokoto, for instance, came to be referred to as *Garba mai Buta* — "Garba of the coffee pot"—and "Abubakar Abakaliki". When troubles came in the North the Emirs, who were as much the representatives of the people as their leaders, were unable to run counter to Northern discontent. Among the radicals, Ironsi rapidly made enemies where he might have made friends. Within three months of his coming to power, Tarka, Aminu Kano and Maitama Sule were meeting in Kano to consider how to meet what they regarded as a common threat to Nigeria.

Ironsi assumed the pomp of office, living in Government House and demoting the Regional Government houses to the title of "government lodges". He announced his intention to remain in power for three years; clearly the army had become more than a caretaker administration. In the actual formation of policy, however, Ironsi proved to be extremely pliable in the hands of certain Ibo advisers: Francis Nwokedi, Dr. Ikejiani, and Pius Okigbo were the most prominent. Decisions taken one way in the military council by day were altered after private discussion with his private advisers by night. Ironsi was not well-educated; he was affable and typified certain of the Sandhurst virtues, but these were ineffective in the political context; he had no ideas of the political state he was aiming to create. He had a strong personality, and up to the very end assumed that the Northerners gave him their loyalty and that he was in as much danger from the Ibo ginger group as from the Northerners. He was not personally a tribalist, and used jocularly to refer to his own people by their uncomplimentary nickname of "anyamari,"[39] but Ibo society was of such a kind that it was particularly difficult for him to resist certain tribal pressures requiring the fulfilment of their aspirations in the form of a greater share of the Federal jobs available. The shoes of the dead Northerners and Westerners were filled partly with Ibos in the first large scale promotions; seventeen of the twenty-three promoted were Ibo;[40] the vast majority of positions at the rank of Lieutenant Colonel were filled with Ibo officers. Even if they were those next in seniority, which is not clear, politically this was most unwise. From April onwards in the words of a Northern civil servant, "The Ibo Union took over State House," the early promise of the regime withered and Ironsi became more and more a confused figure manipulated by those cleverer than himself.

In May the unification decree was published on the advice of Nwokedi, and produced a violent outbreak over most of the North, partly organised by the old cadres of the N.P.C. and partly spontaneous.[41] From two to three thousand Ibos were set upon in the North and murdered. The Supreme Commander had misread the reactions of the North and was taken by surprise. His intermediaries, the civil servants, considered themselves threatened by the new decree and no longer exercised their restraining function on Northern anger.

From May to July the army itself became progressively involved in the division of the civilian society. The political class, deprived of their livelihood but not immobilised, became the focus for rapidly growing tribal animosity. The attitude of some Ibos at the local level made this animosity worse. They would stop Northerners in the market, show them pictures of Nzeogwu, and boast that he had killed the Northerners' father, the Sardauna, and that the Ibos' time had now come.[42] One of the curses of Nigerian politics is the concept of the false transferability of power to the local level so that the members of the group whose representative is in power at the centre assume that this gives them a right to ride roughshod over their neighbours at the local level.

When the N.P.C. were in power at the centre, the N.P.C. followers in Tiv Division used to chalk on the walls "N.P.C. Pawa" and assume that they could win any dispute with a non-N.P.C. man. When the military overthrew Ironsi in July, private soldiers at the local level assumed that they were above the law and could use force to get what they wanted and punish whoever they wanted.[43] Some of the Ibos in the North behaved also to some extent in this pattern from January to May, but their abuses were in word rather than in deed. The Northern authorities and civilians should have been quite able to chastise any offenders without bloodshed, since local power was in exactly the same hands as before January, but they failed to produce an intermediate response and stored up their anger until they were ready for wholesale violence.

The politicians now began to influence the army to their own point of view; the ties of common Regionalism proved stronger than those of the common *esprit de corps* of the officers. Inuwa Wada, Treasurer of the N.P.C. and Minister of Defence in the old regime, appears to have been particularly influential. He was supplied with the ample funds of the N.P.C. with which to make presents to those whose support he sought and he was also the close relative of Colonel Mohammed Murtala.

Northern Nigerian officers and men were not isolated from political and civilian opinion in the manner of the old German army. They were conscious of tribal and kinship ties, and under stress of the events from January to July began to think of themselves as threatened with an Ibo tribal domination. How far this was a real threat and how far an imagined one must be the subject for a deeper study, when there has been more time to sift the evidence. Once tribal attitudes and distrust began to grow in the army, the nature of the confrontation increased these tendencies towards violence. Each side was misinformed by gossip about the intentions of the other. The nature of the normal life of a battalion made it certain that there would be an immense advantage to whichever side struck first, for troops do not normally carry their arms about with them. The lesson of the events of January was that whoever struck and won would be able to assume power undeterred by a question of legality. (In the Aburi conversations in January 1967, Colonel Ojukwu laid great stress upon seniority and hierarchy as the necessary guide to rule in a military government;[44] in a situation of force, hierarchy might prove inadequate to counter the actual power of the men who carried the rifles.) Once they decided to obey the orders only of certain officers, those officers would assume power no matter what their seniority.

In the month of July, Ironsi began to apply pressure to the North and announced, without consulting the Governors concerned or even informing them in advance, that they intended to transfer them to other Regions. He also announced that the civil government in Provinces would be undertaken by Military Prefects as well as by the existing provincial secretaries. The North, which had previously been under the mere threat of Ibo interference in its actual process of government, now felt that that threat was likely to become an actuality. In this case, the army proceeded to a situation where officers of each group moved in mutual suspicion of those of the other group, and pre-emptive coups were prepared, probably on both sides. A Northern coup thought to be a pre-emptive one was planned probably with the knowledge of politicians; the policy which was at first put forward by its leaders was that which Sharwood Smith had first encouraged in 1953, namely Northern separatism. His influence was felt through the old Ministers of the N.P.C. A plan was finally made, though the date of execution was apparently put off several times.[45] There was apparently a plan to murder Ironsi during his visit to Kano, but this was not executed, owing to the strenuous efforts of the Emir of Kano.

Indeed, in Kano Ironsi was still cheered by the crowds. Finally, Ironsi called a conference of chiefs to Ibadan, and the plan was made to overthrow him there. One of Ironsi's last acts, it is said, was to gather the chiefs together to teach them to sing the national anthem, and apparently to indicate that he wished to post them around Nigeria in the same way as he was posting the governors—a suggestion so contrary to their ideas of the particular local ties of chieftainship that the Emir of Kano walked out of the meeting. On the night of July 29 a fight broke out at Abeokuta. The Ibo officers in this unit and many of the men were set upon and murdered. The troops in Ibadan did not take action until the next day. Whether this was because they were waiting for the troops from Abeokuta to come to help them, or whether, as was later said, they "refused to fight at night" as they said the Ibo officers had done in January, is not clear. Ironsi had heard rumours of the happening at Abeokuta, but was assured by his Northern hosts that there was nothing to fear. Next day he was arrested by Major A. and taken away. As he left, he thanked T., a Senior Northern Officer, for his hospitality, and this officer saluted and gave his last respects to Ironsi, saying that they had no option because "they had their orders". One must not think of this event as a kind of macabre charade, but rather as a desperate effort to retain the values and traditions of Sandhurst in a situation whose logic was driving these officers, despite their sense of honour, towards actions more reminiscent of Al Capone. As there had been treachery in January, so there was treachery in July, for this is the logic of lawless confrontation in a military regime once trust is lost. The officers concerned are men known to have a high sense of honour; that this kind of situation could arise between them is an indication of the appalling consequences of escalation in such a situation.

Ironsi was taken away and killed by other ranks, apparently after interrogation. They alleged that they had discovered evidence not only of complicity in the January coup but of a second and much more widespread "Ibo coup" planned for August. But no hard evidence has been produced as to this. In Ibadan and in the 2nd Battalion in Ikeja the other ranks took over and refused to let their officers interfere while they killed their Ibo comrades and officers. Part of the trouble was their memories of "shegantaka", abuse received from these Ibos in the past six months, partly it was a kind of beserk fury released by their attitude to January and to the supposed plots made against them by the Ibos. The men invented a strange language of their own: "take him to the Eastern House of Chiefs" meant kill him. They appointed an "executioner" from other ranks who killed those thus condemned. *Babu wasa sai wuta*—"Not a game but fire"—was their watch-word. Private soldiers killing Ibo officers assumed that they could take the rank of the officer thus killed. A soldier who shot the Provost Marshal of the army on Carter Bridge went around for almost a week saying that he was Provost Marshal himself, until he was persuaded that this was not the case.[46]

Northern Officers who tried to intervene were told that they would be shot. They were addressed respectfully but told to keep out of the way until the killing was over, and were compelled not to interfere.

Brigadier Ogundipe succeeded to the command but discovered that private soldiers would not obey him. Gowon telephoned to Ikeja to tell them that Ogundipe was sending him down to quell the mutiny. On his arrival he was put under guard and told by the men that he was their choice for Commander in Chief and must negotiate on their behalf. Meanwhile, Brigadier Ogundipe had sent a unit of Headquarters troops against the 2nd Battalion, but, far from finding a mutinous rabble, they were confronted by a fighting unit under Northern Officers who had prepared an ambush on the Lagos-Ikeja road. The H.Q. column was mown down and its remnants retreated in disorder. He decided to resign as Supreme Commander and change into civilian clothes and to depart post haste for London, where he was to take up the job of High Commissioner.

In the two Battalions stationed at Kaduna, the same actions took place, though on a smaller scale, and after a delay of twelve hours, some twenty to thirty people being killed in each Battalion.

In the third Battalion the Ibo troops had been disarmed and put under guard by the Northern Officers, but other ranks, on their own initiative, took out those "who had abused them in the past" and shot them. When the Northern Officers tried to interfere, they were held up by furious other ranks and told: "Put your hands up, sir." Only when they promised not to report the action were they allowed to resume command. Within three days every Ibo soldier serving outside the East was either dead or in flight, or in detention. Probably some two hundred to three hundred had been killed. Meanwhile, no action took place in Enugu where the 1st/6th Battalion was balanced by the force of the mobile police and where the splendid action of Colonel (Baba) Ogunewe, the Commanding Officer, dissuaded the Northern Officers from opening the armoury and prevented the Ibos from attacking the disarmed troops.[47]

Gowon was chosen as supreme commander by the decision of a majority of the surviving members of the Supreme Military Council, and proceeded to do his utmost to persuade the troops of the 2nd Battalion to go back to the barracks and to desist from their intention of killing civil servants in Lagos and of marching on the East. In the latter objectives he was successful. Soldiers from Ibadan, however, wreaked their fury on the leaders of the January coup by taking one of them (Okafor?) from prison and killing him by torture.

The East was, however, not under his control. In conversation with Ojukwu he agreed to repatriate the Ibo soldiers back to the East, while Ojukwu repatriated the six hundred Northerners of the 6th Battalion from Enugu, supplying them with arms for the journey "on loan". The coup of July, like that of January, was, as Ejoor said at Aburi, only half successful, and the army was now divided into two hostile sections with no possibility of soldiers from one section going into the areas under the control of the other section. It is clear that if Ojukwu had come to Lagos at this time he would have been murdered by Northern other ranks, despite any instructions from Colonel Gowon.[48]

Gowon, as supreme commander, although much respected by the soldiers, did not yet have full effective power. He was, at this time, much under the control of the officers and men of Ikeja. Colonel Mohammed Murtala of the Signals, whom some believed (probably erroneously) to have been the officer responsible for the planning of the July coup, was particularly influential. At first, Gowon had to reflect their political attitudes of doubt as to whether Nigeria could survive. In his broadcast Gowon said that Nigerians must "review their national standing", but within a few weeks of coming to power Gowon had begun to realise that he must keep Nigeria together under a Federal Government with an adequately strong centre. In this he was influenced by the advice of the British High Commission and the American Ambassador;[49] by his own natural inclinations as a man of a small tribe from the Middle Belt; by the pressure of the Middle Belt soldiers, especially the Tiv, to keep Nigeria together;[50] by the advice of Colonel Hassan from Kaduna;[51] and by the advice of senior federal civil servants who went out to meet the officers at Ikeja.

Gowon promised early disengagement by the military; he released all political prisoners and went to meet Chief Awolowo at the airport, saying that Nigeria needed Awolowo's constitutional wisdom and advice. Conferences of leaders of thought were called at the Regional level for an *ad hoc* constitutional conference in Lagos, to make recommendations for a new constitution for a return to civil rule.

Unfortunately, it was not possible to implement Gowon's other plan to appoint a body of day-to-day civilian advisers comparable to the Ghanaian political committee. There was still too much residual sentiment among the military against all politicians as a class.

The work of reconciliation and of consultation achieved a remarkable degree of success in August and early September, and it looked as though Gowon had been able to restore the situation and keep Nigeria together in peace.

In September, however, small units of the 4th Battalion began to go out in Kaduna, where they had been posted in August, and to make an evil combination with local thugs to fulfil a self-imposed task of driving every Ibo from the North. Small numbers of Ibos resident in Kaduna were robbed and sometimes beaten to death. A stern warning by Hassan had no effect, the soldiers saying that if the Governor did not shut up they would kill him as well.[52] The unit was later, on the 16th of September, by a piece of folly or perhaps by evil intent, posted to Gboko, to Makurdi and to Jos, to relieve the well-disciplined men of the 3rd Battalion. Everywhere they went they initiated pograms against Ibos in combination with thugs, organised in some cases by local branches of the N.P.C. The private soldiers were motivated, as Arikpo points out, by a kind of nihilism.

They were a new authority; they were experiencing the exhila-
ration of feeling that they could do what they liked because
they had their guns in their hands and because no questions
would be asked if they shot Ibos or those who were interfering
with their purposes; they had, in their view, a licence to kill.
Present in their attitude was also a kind of anarchic egalitarianism. Those soldiers in Gboko who arrested me and put me
into their land rover while waving knives and shouting "shegin
Bature" also commented that "you Europeans have had things
easy".[53] Yet, soldiers whom I knew from Tiv would behave in
a very friendly and respectful manner and do their best when
asked to stop killing and looting, but in the environment of
looting and murder there was no sufficient power of prohibition
to prevent some of the soldiers from regarding themselves
somehow as "the cock of the North" and continuing with these
actions. The 4th Battalion returned to Kaduna and carried out
even worse atrocities there. The contagion then spread to the
5th Battalion in Kano, which had hitherto remained well-disciplined. It mutinied on parade, shot some of its Northern Officers, and went out to shoot about one thousand Ibos in a few
hours, before being finally brought under control through the
courage of Colonel Hassan. Once he was able to punish the
soldiers responsible, the troops came back to discipline quickly,
but for the vast majority of acts in the North no punitive action
was taken. The soldiers were clearly encouraged in their action
by some civilian approval at the grass roots, and among some
of the old cadres of the N.P.C. In the West, where this approval
did not exist, and in Lagos, the troops killed very few civilians
indeed. Northerners were at this time assailed by rumours of
Ibo acts of sabotage. They came to believe that the Ibo civilians
in their midst were collecting arms to murder them, planting
bombs in their houses and poisoning their water supplies. The
vast majority of Ibos in the North were totally harmless and
law abiding and the rumours bore little relation to the facts.

There was, however, an act of sabotage in Lagos by an Ibo
University lecturer in mining and explosives. Mr. Agu, who
drove with a car load of explosives from the East, blew up a
bridge in the Mid-West and part of a hotel in Lagos before
demonstrating his incompetence by blowing himself up in his
own room. The murder of Ibos in the North provoked an an-

swering violence against Hausas in the East, equally horrible
but of far less extent, for the number of Northerners in the East
was scarcely a thirtieth of the number of Easterners in the
North. The killings of Easterners in the North did, however, set
off the massacre of Hausas in Port Harcourt and at the Imo
River on the 23rd of September. The report of this relayed from
Radio Dahomey on the 29th of September provoked large-scale
massacres of Ibos in the main towns of the North. In these
events it is hard to discern which side starts the killing and
which is merely retaliating. The killing, in fact, mounts from
small-scale murders to massacres by a process of mutual escalation.

The violence of September and October was so great that all
Ibos had to return from the North to the East, while the East
banished all non-Ibos, and the resulting bitterness swallowed
up the constitutional progress so far made. Contact between
Gowon and Ojukwu continued by telephone, but they were not
able to meet until January at Aburi. The unreal euphoria of this
meeting quickly gave way to mutual recrimination. Neither of
the two parties was able to make gestures of generosity without
running the risk of violent attacks from his own young Turks,
and it was also apparent that the military did not have the
necessary skill for the business of constitution-making. The
relations between the Federal Government and the East continued to deteriorate, and Gowon also became doubtful of how
far the West, now under the influence of Awolowo, would accompany him in maintaining Federal power against Eastern
secession. After the failure of his act of generosity in response
to the initiative of the National Reconciliation Committee, to
prevent the East from moving toward secession Gowon assumed emergency powers, decreed the division of Nigeria into
twelve states (six in the North and three in the East). This act
had been taken in the knowledge that the East was about to
secede. The secession duly took place on the 31st of May to be
followed shortly after by civil war which was to last two-and-a-
half years and to end only with the total defeat of the secessionists.

Military government, having demonstrated its inferiority to
civilian in the business of conflict resolution, retreats to its
ultimate logic:

"And for the last effect
still keep the sword erect

The same arts that did gain
a power must it maintain".[54]

NOTES

1. S. E. Finer, *The Man on Horseback* (London: Pall Mall Press, 1962).

2. It is significant that Alhaji Dan Tata, the great Kano trader and an important member of the N.P.C., employed many Ibos to man his petrol stations and in the clerical aspects of his business in preference to Northerners because they gave better value for money. Similarly, a great deal of the native authority contracting work was given to local Ibo traders, who remained on good terms with local native authorities in an association of mutual benefit. This was of course resented by Northern contractors, robbed of work in what they considered to be their legitimate private preserve.

3. The author can well remember the comment made to him by the Resident Benue in 1952, about the Ibo community in Makurdi, that in marked contrast to the Ibo community in the East, which was politically dynamic and ambitious, the four thousand Ibos in Makurdi had no political ambitions, were never any serious trouble to the administration and were only interested in preserving the peaceful political conditions, which would enable them to make a livelihood. When the Makurdi riots occurred in 1947 over the question of the chieftainship, it was the Tiv and the Hausa who fought each other for their rival claims. The Ibo community, though as large as the Hausa, would not have dreamed of making a claim to this sort of power at the local level. This was typical of Ibo attitudes in the North up to 1966. Whether there was a real change in Ibo attitudes in this respect after January 1966, remains to be investigated.

4. The intense emphasis placed on the word "biyeya" (willing obedience to constituted authority), in Northern thought, is indicative of this attitude. But when the establishment itself was threatened it could strike back with ruthless and deliberate violence, as for instance in the murder of two N.E.P.U. candidates in Sokoto in 1965, in the attack on Ibrahim Imam in Maiduguri in 1954, and in the murders of

A.G. supporters carried out by the N.P.C. leadership in Makurdi in 1965.

5. The settlement in Tiv was due to political reconciliation, following upon the report of the Coomassie Commission as much as to the advent of the army. But Tiv sources, European sources, and the comment of Colonel Hassan to the author all agree that whereas the army was able to restore order fairly quickly with a comparatively small amount of bloodshed, the police had opened fire indiscriminately and still had not been able to control the situation, several policemen being killed in ambushes by the Tiv. This is confirmed by Major General Sir Christopher Welby-Everard, to the author.

6. John Mackintosh, *Nigerian Government and Politics* (London: Allen & Unwin, 1965), p. 59. This is confirmed by the Major General Sir Christopher Welby-Everard to the author.

7. *Nigeria 1966* (Lagos: Nigerian National Press, January 1967), p. 5. "There had been a similar attempt during the 1964 Federal Election Constitutional crisis, which was foiled by prompt intervention of army officers who did not believe in the military seizure of power from civilians. On that and subsequent occasions, the army officers plotting to seize power were assisted by some civilians, including politicians. It is to the credit of the former civilian Federal Government that in the interests of peace no army officer or civilian was subsequently punished for the planned military coup of December 1964." General Gowon informed the author that Ojukwu and Banjo tried, at the time of the election, to persuade himself and Ejoor to join in a coup, but that he and Ejoor refused and warned Ojukwu to desist. He has also put a full account of these events on tape in an interview with a newspaper correspondent.

8. This is my own personal estimation based on observation and conversation with Nigerian soldiers and those in close contact with the army. It is corroborated by the Aburi discussions: "The Nigerian Army was a one army affair and right from the beginning people selected where they go for their training. Usually you find that most people from the South go in for the technical side and most people from the North go into the G. D. side." Col. Gowon, *Aburi Report* (Nigeria, 1967, p. 11, Meeting of Thursday, 5th January). See also, W. Guttridge, *The Military in African Politics* (London: Methuen and Co., 1969) p. 10. In 1950, almost 80% of all the soldiers came from the area north of the confluence of the Niger and Benue River.

The proportions of Northerners to Southerners seem to have been roughly equal in all units. In the 1st/6th Btn. the Northerners repatriated from Enugu comprised just over 600 out of 800 men.

9. I am indebted to Sir Christopher Welby-Everard for information on the introduction of the quota system.

10. The fate of these, the pioneers of the Nigerian military establishment and the cream of the Officer Corps, is indeed tragic, so large a proportion having been killed by each other in the coup of January and the counter-coup of July. Guttridge gives a figure of 80 for the Nigerian Officers on 1st Jan. 1961, out of a total officer force of 300. He suggests that of these 80, 60 were Ibo.

11. I am indebted to Sir Christopher Welby-Everard for details of his own recommendations and to various Senior Northern officials for the account of how bitterly the Sardauna quarrelled with Sir Abubakar on his choice of Ironsi as Commander in Chief.

12. I am indebted to Sir Christopher Welby-Everard for this information concerning the fatal effect on the morale of an army of knowing that the establishment is so full with young officers that there is no opportunity for further promotion. The possibility of young officers killing their Seniors for reasons of slow promotion has been shown by the confession of Lieutenant Arthur in Ghana. Operation "Guitar Boy" in Ghana was planned and the General in charge of the army was murdered as part of a coup whose mainspring seems to have been desire for more rapid promotion. One cannot imagine this motive being the main factor, influencing the young majors in January in Nigeria, but it could help to explain the gratuitous slaughter of Senior Northern and Western Officers during the execution of the coup.An intense bitterness with his status as a Major emerges from the manuscript which Ifeajuna wrote during his detention after the coup.

13. I am indebted to Major General Welby-Everard for his comment on this remark of a Senior Officer, who apparently indicated to him that he had thought of leaving the army, because he was sure that one day army officers of different tribes would turn upon one another.

14. After the coup the Ibo people were the most wholehearted in renouncing all allegiances to politicians. Dr. Azikiwe's prestige in the East had already suffered almost irreparable damage in the events of the 1964 election and its aftermath. In the West, however, the name of Awolowo was still one to conjure with among the masses. In the Mid-West, despite his original doubts about the creation of the state Enahoro had an important reputation, while in the North J. S. Tarka, Aminu Kano, Maitama Sule, Dipcharima, and others continued to have support. Of the more conservative politicians Inuwa Wada remained powerful, because of his power base in Kano.

When the regions were allowed to choose "leaders of thought" in

August 1966, it is significant that the delegations of both the West and Mid-West were led by politicians, while that of the North included J. S. Tarka, as well as the adviser to the Governor Sir Kasim Ibrahim.

15. No direct evidence has yet been made public. The first broadcast of Gowon on assuming power referred to: "A group of officers *in conjunction with certain civilians* decided to overthrow the legal government of the day but their efforts were thwarted by the inscrutable discipline and loyalty of the great majority of the army." (Author's italics.)

The Federal pamphlet, *Nigeria 1966,* speaks of a "small group of officers mainly from the Ibo ethnic groups of the Eastern Region, dissatisfied with political development beginning to plot in collaboration with some civilians, the overthrow of the Government of the Federation of Nigeria".

16. This was the verdict of a most distinguished Nigerian diplomat. It seems to be the only explanation to fit the facts of January. It would also explain the furious attempt of Col. Banjo, a Yoruba Officer, who was part of the original coup planning, to kill General Ironsi some two days after he had assumed power. According to this explanation he was furious at the way the coup had been executed, and felt that its purpose had been betrayed by tribal bias. See also note 28.

17. I am indebted to a distinguished police officer for this fascinating picture of Nzeogwu. At one time Major Nzeogwu threatened to shoot Alhaji Ali Akilu, the head of the Northern Civil Service, but was dissuaded from doing this. At another time he became furious with the failure of the Lagos plotters to kill Ironsi or Okpara and pronounced his intention of marching on the East or destroying the Niger bridge. Later in detention, on hearing of the flight of Ifeajuna he remarked that this officer ought to be shot for fleeing to Ghana. In detention he continued to write friendly letters (often in Hausa) to his old Northern friends Gowon, Hassan, M. D. Yusufu, etc.

18. General Gowon to the author (1968).

19. I first heard of the killing of Unegbe in this way from an Ibo diplomat. I had it confirmed by a Northerner, very close to the army, and finally confirmed in writing in *Nigeria 1966*. All agree that Col. Arthur Unegbe was threatened by the plotters after he had refused to open the armoury to them, and that even after he had been wounded he refused to surrender the keys, and that he was in consequence killed. "The only officer of the Eastern origin killed on January 15th was Lt. Col. Arthur Unegbe, Quarter Master General Army Headquarters Lagos. He was in charge of the armoury and refused to hand over the key of the armoury to the plotters when they woke him up in

the early hours of January 15th." *Nigeria 1966,* p. 7. This is also confirmed by Gowon himself. A police report on the January coup, however, concludes that Unegbe's murder was part of the original plan.

20. Sgt. Major Mathias was one of the N.C.O.'s involved in the rally of the Federal Guard. A Tiv soldier of this guard has told me how he was rung up on the night of January 15th by Gowon and told to keep discipline. In a British trained army a great deal of the actual running of units is the responsibility of Senior N.C.O.'s; in a situation of mutiny by officers, the Senior N.C.O.'s of Northern origin would soon show their refusal to follow. It is this sort of action which is referred to in the pamphlet, *Nigeria 1966,* as "The intervention of the bulk of the Nigerian Army" which "foiled the intentions of the plotters," p. 7.

21. Alhaji Ali Monguno, who was present at the Cabinet meeting, informed the author that Ironsi persuaded a somewhat reluctant Cabinet to hand over power by giving the impression that the hand-over would only last until he had restored order.

22. At the time of the events of August and September many stories of Ibo activities against the North were current among Northern civilians, many of them patently false and exaggerated. Belief in an "Ibo plot" aimed at the elimination of large numbers of prominent Northerners in both military and civilian circles was very widespread not only among the less educated but also among Permanent Secretaries, University Lecturers and Senior Army Officers. The investigation of the spread of this belief and of the extent to which it had any real basis will provide a task for historians of the future, with more evidence available than that possessed by scholars today. My own sources were close to the Military and it is clear that the belief in the "Ironsi Confession" and the "plot" to kill Northerners in August was general among soldiers of the 4th Btn., very soon after the event. Many explanations are possible, from an almost completely imaginary story invented by soldiers or the N.P.C. to excuse the treasonable act of the murder of an innocent Commander in Chief, to a story with a substantial basis in truth for which firm evidence is available at Federal H.Q. but is being kept secret in order not to exacerbate tribal feelings. Any sort of mid-way position is also possible; i.e. there may have been a confession but only of some very limited fore-knowledge of the January coup, and similarly the "Ibo plot" of further murders of Northerners to take place in August may have been real, but have only extended to a few hot heads, whose capacity to implement such a plot could have been gravely in doubt. For the moment we must suspend judgment, but it is to be hoped that historians will one day unravel this tangle which is so central to full understanding of these tragic events.

23. *Africa Confidential,* Jan. 30th.

24. c.f. *Africa and the World*, May, 1967, p. 15. Interview of Ejindu, correspondent of *Africa and the World,* with Nzeogwu after his release from detention. Ejindu: "But how tribalistic was it really in conception and execution?"

Nzeogwu: "In the North no." "In the South yes." "We were five in number and initially we knew quite clearly what we wanted to do". "We had a short list of people who were either undesirable for the future progress of the country or by their position at the time had to be sacrificed for peace and stability." "Tribal considerations were out of our minds AT THIS STAGE (my capitals) but we had our set back in execution . . . but the other three failed because of incompetence and misguided considerations in the eleventh hour!" Nzeogwu has always been the most outspoken and frank of the officers involved in either of the coups. One may perhaps doubt, however, how far the Northern coup which involved the murder of the two Yoruba Senior Officers as well as the Northern Premier was entirely non-tribal in execution. It is also surprising that a man as intelligent as Nzeogwu should not have realised that to entrust five majors all of one tribe with the task of carrying out so bloody a coup in a non-tribal manner was to invite a tribal twist in the actual execution of the design.

25. The reason for his disillusionment with Nkrumah remains doubtful. Ifeajuna was detained in the East until the Civil War. In October 1967 he planned to murder Ojukwu and was shot on Ojukwu's orders.

26. I have this from a reliable source. But the British Government was extremely cautious and refused to consider any application for armed assistance that did not come through the High Commissioner.

27. Northern sources, of a reasonable degree of reliability.

28. Diplomatic sources—high degree of reliability.

29. St. Augustine, *City of God.*

30. c.f. Eastern Regional Release, *Nigeria 1966.*

31. The date of the trial was finally fixed in July at a meeting of the Supreme Military Council. It was agreed that it should take place in August, but Gowon informs the author that in the minutes the date was put off to October. Gowon and other officers regarded this matter as a very serious one involving the integrity of Ironsi.

32. This attracted great attention in the North. It is also mentioned in *Nigeria 1966* (p. 7).

33. Tiv civilian sources very close to the army, high degree of reliability.

34. Interview with H. E. Lt. Col. Gowon, September 1966. He did not refer to there having been any planning of the July coup nor indicated what connection if any he had with it himself, but laid very strong emphasis on the sense of justice of the Northern rank and file outraged by the midnight murders of January and the unpunished act of treachery and indiscipline. It was this feeling that had forced certain Northern Officers to take action. The most general view among Northerners is that Gowon was NOT informed by those who planned the July coup, though he was, no doubt, aware of the general level of discontent. His choice as leader, after the coup, was due to two factors, his position as the most senior Northern Officer and the great respect commanded by his integrity and military reputation.

35. Comment made to the author in June 1965 at Legon, Ghana. Other sources confirm the existence of this sort of milieu of violent thought in some radical Ibadan circles. It was from this Ibadan environment, that quite a number of Southern Officers including Ifeajuna came to the army.

36. Letter seen by myself.

37. Mephistopheles comment to Faust. Goethe, *Faust,* Part I. "Blood is a quite unusual liquid."

38. Letters from Tiv at the time of the coup of January indicated an attitude of neutrality or of support for the coup. The Tor Tiv had been rescued from probable dismissal following his public reconciliation with Tarka on 31st December, 1965, by the coup of January 14th, 1966. Within four months, however, a strong anti-Ironsi and anti-Ibo feeling had sprung up at the grass roots.

Among Tiv Officers it is noteworthy that Lieutenant A. who had written to a friend in England in February stating that Nzeogwu and the other detained plotters had done what they all knew needed doing, had by July come out openly on the side of the rebels and is reported to have given the orders for the opening of fire on the Lagos troops during the ambush prepared by the 2nd Battalion. Exactly what had happened to crystalise opinion so clearly against Ironsi, is still not quite clear. Ironsi's failure to give amnesty to those imprisoned during the Tiv riot was particularly unfortunate.

39. I am indebted to Alhaji Akilu, head of the Northern Civil Service for this direct evidence.

40. Information from former Permanent Secretary, Ministry of Defence.

41. The influence of Francis Nwokedi appears to have been particularly unfortunate. He had already resigned from the Foreign Service before January 1966, and was refused permission to withdraw his resignation. He was however recalled by Ironsi as Commissioner to investigate the best means of unifying the Nigerian public services. He was warned by many advisers of the violent opposition that his unification decree was likely to provoke but paid no attention. Although very able, and often charming, he was the victim of a peculiar kind of over-confidence.

42. This complaint is repeated by Northerners again and again both from their own experience and from what they had heard from others. It may be hard for Europeans to understand how, to Northerners, certain sorts of abuse are more provocative and wounding than a blow. This kind of abuse is described in Hausa by the powerful word "cin mutumci" (literally to eat someone's humanity).

43. During the Ironsi period a person masquerading as a private soldier successfully ordered the arrest of the Alkali in a large Northern Emirate, claiming no other mandate than his uniform, and kept him arrested for several days. After the July coup a man masquerading as a Colonel from Katsina successfully fleeced Inuwa Wada, and other Kano businessmen of over £100 so great was the prestige of his uniform.

44. *Aburi Conversations* (page 4).

45. Evidence as to the planning of the July coup is far less extensive than that of the planning of the January coup. In July a coup and a mutiny coincided. Ejoor at Aburi suggested that in July "what began as a mutiny ended in a coup". It might be more true to say that what began as a coup ended as a mutiny. All the evidence points to there having been some planning by some Northern Officers (although the date when the coup actually occurred may not have been the date when it was originally planned to occur). But these Officers may well not have included either Gowon or Hassan. As part of the machinery of the Ironsi regime, the plotters may well have declined to take them into their confidence.

46. Evidence from a variety of Northern sources, especially of Tiv civilian sources very close to the army and of a high degree of reliability on these points.

47. General Gowon has a very high opinion of Ogunewe and remarked to the author "how loyal that Officer was to me".

48. Nigerian diplomatic sources. High degree of reliability.

49. There is a very great deal of corroborating evidence for the importance of this advice.

50. The Army Middle Belt Pressure Group was important both in keeping Nigeria together in August against Murtala's original plan to evacuate Lagos and retire to the North, and in countering the Confederal stance of the Northern delegation at the opening of the Constitutional Conference. In this task Middle Belt Officers like Colonel Akaahan and Lieutenant Ichovol, Middle Belt soldiers, and political leaders of Middle Belt origin like J. S. Tarka, worked very closely together indeed.

51. Independent and reliable evidence to author from Alhaji Sule Katagum and Colonel Hassan.

52. The author was present in Kaduna shortly after the broadcast.

53. The author was present in Gboko and Makurdi shortly after the killings and tried to make the soldiers stop the looting. Clearly many of them were more interested in encouraging it. The Tiv civilians in Gboko on the other hand, for the most part, risked their lives to hide their Ibo fellow citizens and to smuggle them out to the East. Mrs. Tarka for instance was sheltering the six members of the Ibo Post Office staff in her house, while the soldiers were looking for them outside to shoot them. All but one was successfully evacuated to the Eastern region.

54. Andrew Marvell—An Horatian Ode upon Cromwell's return from Ireland.

CHAPTER 14

Education and Integration

DAVID B. ABERNETHY

Conflict is the very stuff of politics; in every age men have competed more or less violently with each other for power to shape their own destiny and the destiny of society as a whole. Conflict is particularly evident in the early stages of modernization, when traditional ways of life and thought are upset, new patterns of dominance and dependence are forged, and politics may become a matter literally of life and death. This being so, it would be unrealistic to define an integrated society as one in which political conflict has been eliminated; there is no such society outside Utopia. Rather, we should recognize that the integrative forces in a particular society are closely bound up with the conflicts affecting it. Three questions arise in this connection. First, are there cultural and structural mechanisms for transcending conflict—that is, for focusing attention on those things that unite the members of a political unit in spite of their differences? Second, are there mechanisms for limiting conflict, so that it may be channeled

Excerpted from David B. Abernethy, *The Political Dilemma of Popular Education. An African Case* (Stanford: Stanford University Press, 1969), pp. 253–277. Copyright © 1969 by Stanford University Press. Reprinted by permission of the publisher and David B. Abernethy. The notes are presented in slightly revised form.Research in Nigeria was sponsored by the Foreign Area Fellowship Program 1963–64.

through existing political institutions with a minimum of disruptive violence? Third, is it possible to manage conflict creatively, so that in the very process of competing with each other people contribute, almost by accident, to holding their society together? According to our usage, a polity is integrated to the extent that it is able to transcend domestic conflict, limits conflict to a certain level of intensity while providing political channels for its expression, and has cleavages that cut across rather than reinforce each other.

Before considering the integrative and disintegrative consequences of rapid educational expansion in Southern Nigeria, we must choose a suitable unit of analysis. Should we discuss the individual region, the South, or the whole of Nigeria? The choice is important, since what is integrative for one part of a country may well be disintegrative for the country as a whole, and vice versa. The region might at first seem best, for in the 1960–65 period each region had recognizable institutions of government, and the elites in Ibadan and Enugu who had initiated universal primary education were eager to unify and strengthen their respective regions in response to the mounting influence of the federal and Northern regional governments. But precisely because each region was part of a larger federation that in 1960 became an "emerging nation," and because events in the federation as a whole increasingly affected political life within its constituent parts, Nigeria might be a more appropriate unit of analysis. That the educational system in the South supposedly emphasized loyalty to Nigeria as a nation reinforces this point. As for Southern Nigeria, it has the obvious drawback of being not a distinct political entity but simply a geographical designation referring to Nigeria minus its Northern Region. During the 1950's it was possible to consider the South one political system, in the sense that NCNC and Action Group leaders were principally competing with each other over the distribution of power in the Eastern and Western regions. But by the 1960's the North was far more visibly involved in Nigerian politics, and the differences between North and South overshadowed those between East and West. The ability of Nigeria to handle North-South conflict and to remain a single political system became the crucial issue following Independence. For these reasons Nigeria has been selected as the unit of analysis, even though this study deals in depth with the educational history of the Southern regions only.

It is rarely easy for scholars to determine whether integrative tendencies in a given country have outweighed disintegrative ones over a short period of time. In Nigeria, however, there is no room for doubt; the evidence for disintegration, even in the short run, is all too compelling. The military coup of January 1966 marked the first use of extralegal violence to overthrow existing political elites in the federal and regional governments; partly by accident and partly by design, the coup also marked the end of Northern dominance and an increase in the power of Southern military men and civilians. The massacre of Ibos living in the North, which began in May 1966 and continued intermittently throughout the year, demonstrated the extent of ethnic tension in the country and convinced many Ibos that their only hope was to break away from Nigeria entirely. The counter-coup of July 1966 marked another resort to violence, this time by Northern elements in the army; one result was the virtual disintegration along regional lines of the Nigerian army, the one institution that had held the country together following the events of January. With Northerners in control of Lagos, it was only a matter of months before the Eastern Region seceded, declaring itself the independent Republic of Biafra in May 1967. There followed a costly and bloody civil war, which was still taking its toll of both sides two years after Biafra's secession. Given this tragic series of events, one must necessarily emphasize those factors that have led to the disintegration of Nigeria, rather than those that kept the country together for the first five years of independence.

Many factors were at work in transforming what appeared to outsiders as the "bright hope of Africa" into one of the continent's most intractable problem areas. A federal structure in which one region was more populous than all the others combined, different rates of regional economic development, religious tensions, personality conflicts among leaders, the assassination of some leaders and not others—all these played an important part. Not least was the attainment of independence itself, for as Clifford Geertz has noted, "It is the very process of the formation of a sovereign civil state that . . . stimulates sentiments of parochialism, communalism, racialism, and so on, because it introduces into society a valuable new prize over which to fight and a frightening new force with which to contend."[1] In what follows, however, we shall concentrate on the role played by rapid educational expansion in the Southern regions, while freely granting that only for analytical purposes may education be separated from other aspects of Nigerian life.

National Integration

One criterion for integration is whether the citizens of a country possess certain things in common and believe these common possessions to be important. If people feel that they belong to a "terminal community"[2] whose values and institutions are worth preserving, they are unlikely to permit conflicts among them to reach the point where they threaten the continued existence of the community. The view that unity can exist in spite of diversity is well expressed in the American motto, "E Pluribus Unum," and in the Nigerian national anthem:

> Though tribe and tongue may differ,
> In Brotherhood we stand,
> Nigerians all, and proud to serve
> Our sovereign Motherland.

A successful emphasis on unity that transcends conflict—without necessarily eliminating it—will be termed national integration.[3]

One of the major contributions to national integration made by educational expansion in the South has been the introduction of a common language, English, to an entire younger generation. As a result of their schooling, Ibos and Yorubas can talk with each other and with Northerners who have attended European-type schools. English is not only a common language among the educated but also the official language of the country. In this respect Nigeria, along with virtually all sub-Sahara African countries, is fortunate in not possessing indigenous written languages of long standing, whose claim to official status might pit various linguistic groups against each other. The language controversy that has bedeviled the politics of India, Ceylon, Malaysia, and other Asian countries has been averted in Africa precisely because African vernaculars were not vehicles for the written transmission of culture before the coming of the European. Where, as in India or Ceylon, educational expansion has strengthened various vernaculars, it has failed to break down the communication barriers of pre-modern times; in Nigeria, by contrast, universal primary education and related programs have made possible communication among all moderately educated persons.[4]

In addition to teaching a common language, the schools have provided a common cultural experience for millions of young Nigerians. One dilemma faced by African nation builders is that the culture of their people either is rooted in a subnational entity, like a tribe, or shares with all African cultures those features attributed to "negritude" or "the African personality"; there is little in the cultural realm that is the common—and at the same time exclusive—property of the citizens of a given state. When young Nigerians attending school learn to reach the classroom on time, to stand up when reciting their lessons, to tend the school grounds, and so forth, they are building up a common store of experiences. And to the extent that the Nigerian educational system differs from that of neighboring countries—in the language used, and in the content and quality of instruction—the common educational experiences of Nigerians are also exclusive ones. From the point of view of integration, it matters little that the education is often of dubious quality, for even if, as some educators contend, the next generation of Nigerians will be intelligible only to each other, the atrocious English taught in primary schools could be the foundation for a distinctly Nigerian dialect!

If educational expansion in the South has been integrative in these respects, in other ways it has probably had the opposite effect. One important task for curriculum reformers in a new state is to write history texts emphasizing the unity of their country and minimizing its internal conflicts.[5] In fact, little has been done to revise Nigerian history texts, and British authors continue to dominate the history and civics fields.[6] But even if new texts are written by Nigerians, a serious question remains:

how much can one truthfully write about Nigerian unity? When school books discuss the enormous ethnic and linguistic diversity of the country, the separate administration of North and South in the formative early years of the twentieth century, and the predominantly Southern origins of nationalism, they cannot but make explicit how few past experiences have affected all Nigerians equally. And since education has made young Nigerians acutely aware of their country's troubles following Independence, increased knowledge of their fellow countrymen cannot be expected, by itself, to create good feelings among the educated members of contending groups. When students in the author's survey did express a commitment to national unity, their views were based less on knowledge than on the hope that an unhappy state of affairs would one day right itself.

A school can, however, provide more than academic knowledge about a country. Through its recruitment policies it can bring together members of many different groups, and the school can become a miniature nation by instilling cooperative habits among a diverse student body. This integrative function is particularly important when one considers that grammar school and university graduates constitute a substantial portion of the elite whose decisions will affect a country's destiny. If leaders of competing groups have in common an "old school tie" and the memory of eccentric teachers, mutual friends, and devilish pranks that binds Old Boys everywhere together, it is more likely that their political differences can be mediated than if their educational experiences are quite dissimilar. In the early years of a country's educational history, when few schools are operating, each school tends to recruit from a wide geographical area; the best early schools may have a national or even international clientele. This was true, for example, of Achimota College in Ghana, the Ecole Ponty in Senegal, Munali Secondary School in Northern Rhodesia, and Gordon College in the Anglo-Egyptian Sudan. In Southern Nigeria, St. Andrew's College, Oyo, in its first years recruited from as far away as the Niger Delta; Table 1 shows that in 1902 Hope Waddell Training Institute drew more than one-third of its students from areas outside the Eastern Region, including several West African countries.

TABLE 1

Matriculation by Ethnic Group in Boarding Section, Hope Waddell Training Institute, Calabar, 1902–63

Ethnic group and area of origin	1902 (N=59)	1910 (N=65)	1920 (N=97)	1930 (N=106)	1940 (N=86)	1945 (N=87)	1950 (N=59)	1955 (N=98)	1960 (N=79)	1963 (N=90)
Eastern Region:										
Lower Cross River groups[a]	38.9%	30.7%	40.2%	23.5%	19.7%	11.4%	13.5%	10.2%	12.6%	20.0%
Upper Cross River groups	5.0	4.6	10.3	4.7	3.4	5.7	3.3	3.0	1.2	5.5
Ibibio	5.0	26.1	15.4	18.8	24.4	34.4	13.5	30.6	16.4	22.2
Eastern Ibo	10.1	27.6	23.7	30.1	37.2	36.7	55.9	50.0	64.5	45.5
Ijaw	3.3	3.0	1.0	3.7	1.1	2.2	1.6	0	2.5	2.2
Others; unknown	1.6	0	0	6.6	0	1.1	3.3	1.0	2.5	1.1
Western Region:										
Bini	3.3	0	1.0	2.8	1.1	0	0	0	0	0
Western Ibo	3.3	1.5	0	3.7	3.4	0	3.3	1.0	0	1.1
Yoruba	15.2	1.5	3.0	2.8	2.3	3.4	3.3	2.0	0	1.1
Other West African countries[b]	13.5	4.6	5.1	2.8	6.9	4.5	1.6	2.0	0	1.1

Source: Principal's Roll Book, 1900–1963.

[a] The Lower Cross River category includes Efiks, Quas, Efuts, and Efik-speakers up to Ikorofiong, a town about twenty miles northwest of Calabar. The Upper Cross River category includes non-Ibos north of Ikorofiong.

[b] Includes British Cameroons, Gold Coast, Togo, Sierra Leone, and Liberia (Kru).

With educational expansion the recruitment radius for the older schools tends to contract, since new schools enroll local young people who in earlier days would have traveled much greater distances to obtain a good education. At Hope Waddell, for example, fewer students from outside the Eastern Region were enrolled as the twentieth century advanced, although within the region itself a certain leveling process occurred; by the 1930's the numerically dominant Ibos and Ibibios had surpassed the Efiks and other Lower Cross River peoples living in the immediate vicinity of Calabar. As for the new schools, their initial recruitment radius is limited not only by their lack of reputation but also by the need to enroll "sons of the soil" to attract local financial support. Table 2, based on the author's survey, shows that secondary schools founded before 1950 recruited from a wider area than schools founded between 1956 and 1964; a similar phenomenon has been noted in Ghana, Indonesia, and India.[7] One consequence of educational expansion, therefore, is that schools become progressively less capable of giving their students the kind of personal contact with different groups that can give rise to truly national sentiments. What little instruction there was in the early 1960's concerning Nigeria was not reinforced outside the classroom by inter-ethnic contacts, which were much more frequent thirty years earlier, when the elite that brought Nigeria to independence was attending grammar school.[8] Hence the nationalism of the post-Independence generation of secondary students, such as it was, remained an abstract sentiment that could not readily be translated into concrete action.

TABLE 2

RECRUITMENT RADIUS OF SECONDARY SCHOOLS, 1964

Parental residence	Schools founded before 1950 (Enrollment: 140)	Schools founded 1956–64 (Enrollment: 400)
Within 10 miles of school	31%	37%
10–50 miles from school	27	32
Over 50 miles from school	42	31

Source: Survey made by the author in 1964 of Southern Nigerian schoolchildren.

Government secondary schools can recruit their students from many different parts of Nigeria as a matter of policy. With the regionalization of education, however, pressures were exerted on such schools to admit only children born in their own region. Edo College, Benin, for example, admitted more Eastern Ibos than Binis in 1949–51; in 1952 its examination center east of the Niger was closed down and a verbal arrangement was made with the Western Region Director of Education to exclude Eastern Ibos except those whose parents were working in the West. Within the West, moreover, government schools during the 1950's tended to recruit locally: Edo College concentrated on Benin Province, Government College Ughelli on Delta Province, and Government College Ibadan on the Yoruba-speaking areas.[9] With Independence the federal government proposed a large National High School for each region that would draw students from all the regions. The idea found its way into the Six-Year Plan but was never implemented. In general, political pressures prevented government schools from realizing their integrative potential.

Thus far we have considered the mixed effects of educational expansion on young Southern Nigerians attending school. We consider next its effect on the central institutions that should be the most effective expressions of Nigerian unity. It should be said at the outset that the federal government has always lacked those features one associates with an actively centralizing regime: a powerful single party, a centralized civil service, charismatic leadership, and a coherent ideology. Of all the world's countries Nigeria is perhaps second only to India in the diversity of its peoples, and the kind of regime best able to accommodate this diversity has been not a mobilization system but a reconciliation system, to use David Apter's terms.* When Southern Nigerians looked to Lagos, therefore, they found little to elicit their active loyalty. It may be argued—although this is

*See Apter's *Politics of Modernization* (Chicago, 1965), pp. 397–402. "The role of government in a reconciliation system is not organizational; rather, it works to reconcile diverse interests; it mediates, integrates, and above all coordinates, rather than organizes and mobilizes. In contrast to the mobilization system, which 'fights' society, the reconciliation system is often a prisoner of society." *Ibid.,* pp. 398–99.

difficult to document—that rapid educational expansion has further reduced the integrative capacity of the federal government in two respects. First, the educational programs of the Southern regions, which initially reflected the decentralization taking place in the early 1950's, in turn strengthened the influence of the regional governments; the ministries of education responsible to Ibadan and Enugu were enlarged, and it was to the politicians in the regional capitals that people attributed both the successes and failures of universal primary education. When in the 1960's the Southern regions looked to the federal government for assistance in meeting their educational obligations, the unwillingness of federal officials to help out probably increased tensions between the two levels of government. Many Southern Nigerians felt that at least in the educational field the federal government had done little for them in the past and had no interest in improving its record.

Second, the fact of an increasingly educated populace in the South may have encouraged Southern politicians to enflame ethnic and regional tensions. The security dilemma confronting federal politicians in the 1960's was if anything more acute than that confronting regional leaders a decade earlier: how could each leader maintain influence within his own party and within a federal coalition of parties that threatened at any moment to collapse? The power base of each politician lay within his own region and ethnic group, and it was tempting for him to protect his position by posing as the champion of his constituents against real or imagined threats from other groups. This temptation increased as the politician realized that his words and deeds were being given careful attention by increasing numbers of voters. Politicians typically responded to this interest by phrasing their ideas simply, directly, and dramatically, and more often than not in the language of what is commonly termed tribalism. For their purposes it was irrelevant that tribal tensions were not an important feature of traditional Nigerian life and still mattered little in the daily life of the average farmer. As we have argued, . . . seeing the world in terms of Ibo, Yoruba, Hausa, and so forth requires a fundamental break with a traditional outlook based on face-to-face and kinship relationships. Mass education enabled large numbers of people to expand their horizons from the parochial to the ethnic level, and federal politicians intuitively realized that the language of tribalism would strike a responsive chord among such people, who probably felt more comfortable with an ethnic identity than with any alternative identity open to them. In a word, politicians said what the voters wanted to hear, until a time came when neither leaders nor followers could prevent the tensions within Nigeria from shattering the fragile institutions of unity.

Horizontal Integration: North Versus South

If a polity lacks a sense of unity-in-diversity, it may still be considered integrated if its domestic conflicts do not become so intense that extralegal methods must be used to resolve them. A polity may also be considered integrated if the lines of conflict cut across rather than reinforce each other, and if this cross-cutting pattern leads not to a stalemate of hostile forces but to a dynamic process of mutual interaction that strengthens the institutions through which contending groups struggle for power.[10] Many of the new states are beset by conflict among ethnic, racial, religious, and linguistic groups that may be equal or unequal to each other in power, wealth, or status (the vertical dimension of society) but are different from each other in certain other objective respects (the horizontal dimension). Conflict among these groups is particularly threatening when, as often happens, each one occupies a fairly well-defined piece of land and can use this territory as a base for launching a civil war or establishing an independent government. The most serious horizontal cleavage in Nigeria, one that eventually took on aspects of vertical cleavage as the parties contended for political dominance, was between the Northern Region and the rest of the country. By the early 1960's it was clear to Nigerians that the North-South conflict overshadowed the conflict between Ibos and Yorubas and the conflict between dominant ethnic groups and minorities, although to be sure ethnic rivalries remained an important part of Nigerian politics following Independence. We shall now consider whether educational expansion in the South contributed to the "horizontal integration" of Nigeria by moderating North-South conflict and by fostering new cleavages that cut across North-South lines.

Differences between Southern Nigeria and the North—particularly the far North with its powerful emirates—may be discussed from several points of view: traditional factors, the British impact, response to the forces of change, and the drive for independence. The people of the South are primarily forest dwellers growing root and tree crops, whereas Northerners live in the drier Sudanic belt and have a grain-oriented subsistence economy. Traditional political structures are less centralized in the South than in the far North, and prior to this century most Southerners were pagan whereas the Northern Emirates were officially, and aggressively, Islamic. With the coming of the British, the impact of modernization in its many forms—education, health facilities, cash economy, roads, ports, and so on—was more direct and persistent along the coast than in the Northern hinterland. British efforts at indirect rule proved fruitless in the East and only moderately successful in the West; in the North, on the other hand, the British strengthened in many respects the existing native authority system. The North was separately administered by the British from 1900 to 1914, and not until 1946 were Northerners and Southerners permitted to meet together in the Legislative Council. In general, Southerners responded quickly to the forces of change in their midst; moreover, as we have seen, their acceptance of Christian missionaries meant that educational opportunities were widely diffused. Northerners, on the other hand, responded more cautiously and selectively to change;[11] in at least the Muslim areas Christian missionaries were discouraged from operating schools, and officially sponsored schools like Katsina Training College tended to reinforce the existing indigenous power structure by recruiting heavily from leading families within the emirates. The significant Southern lead in primary education from the early years of the twentieth century is shown in Figure 1.

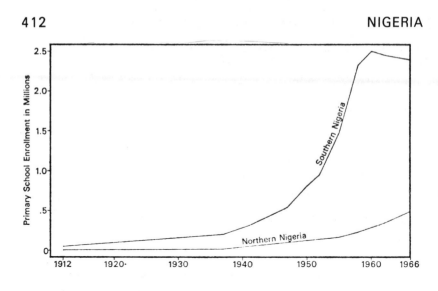

Fig. 1. Primary School Enrollment, 1912–65 (from annual reports of the education departments of the federal and regional Nigerian governments).

The drive for independence helped to call attention to these traditional differences between North and South, and also created new grounds for conflict. The nationalist movement was led predominantly by Southerners, but the very success of Southerners in pressing for Nigerian self-determination and democracy meant that the real holders of political power after Independence would be Northerners, whose region contained 55 per cent of the country's population. Thus, the North stood to gain many of the benefits of an independence that its leaders had not particularly sought. Indeed, the man who subsequently became Nigeria's first Prime Minister, Alhaji Abubakar Tafawa Balewa, earned his reputation as an orator by stressing the artificiality of Nigeria and the North's unreadiness for self-government.[12] Most articulate Southerners deeply resented the dominant role of the Northern People's Congress in national life; to them the very name of the party betrayed an unseemly preoccupation with its own region that was confirmed when the Sardauna of Sokoto, party president and "eminence noire" behind Prime Minister Balewa, chose to remain Premier of the North rather than assume national office.

But if the North had sufficient voting strength to dominate Nigerian political life, why should its leaders have been reticent about attaining independence and generally defensive toward Southerners? The answer lies in Northern fears that administrative power would be monopolized by the Southerners because of their long-standing educational lead. The Sardauna made this point quite explicit in his autobiography:

> As things were at that time [the early 1950's], if the gates to the departments were to be opened, the Southern Regions had a huge pool from which they could find suitable people, while we had hardly anyone. In the resulting scramble it would, we were convinced, be inevitable that the Southern applicants would get almost all the posts available. Once you get a Government post you are hard indeed to shift. . . . [This] was a matter of life and death to us. . . . If the British Administration had failed to give us the even development that we deserved and for which we craved so much—and they were on the whole a very fair administration—what had we to hope from an African Administration, probably in the hands of a hostile party. The answer to our minds was, quite simply, just nothing, beyond a little window dressing.[13]

Were a Southerner to reply that administrators simply carry out the orders of political leaders, the Sardauna might well have asked why, if that were so, Southern politicians were so concerned about the reliability of their British civil servants.

Perhaps even more disturbing to Northerners were the possible effects of independence on their own region. For to a greater degree than any other political party in Africa, the Northern People's Congress recruited its leadership from and based its political power on a powerful administrative apparatus, the native authority system.[14] If educated Southerners were to replace the British in key positions in the Northern civil service, they might not only sabotage their ministers' programs but undermine the very structure of traditional authority on which the ministers relied for their political power. For understandable reasons, therefore, an explicit policy of Northernization was followed when the Nigerian civil service was regionalized in 1954: British civil servants would remain in office until they could be replaced by Northerners with the proper qualifications. As might be expected, Southerners, especially those qualified in administration, interpreted the Northernization policy as a calculated insult, a denial of the common nationality of Nigerians, and further evidence that "feudal" Northern leaders were closely collaborating with the colonial regime.

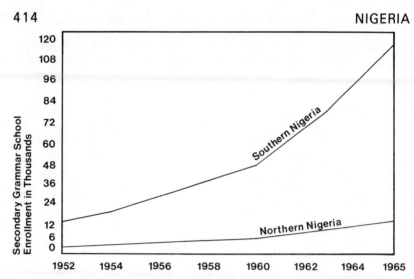

Fig. 2. Secondary Grammar School Enrollment, 1952–65 (Archibald Callaway and A. Musone, *Financing of Education in Nigeria* [Paris, 1968], Table 8, p. 115; Education and World Affairs, *Nigerian Human Resource Development and Utilization* [New York, 1967], p. 43.

Thus the different rate of educational expansion between South and North, dating back over a century, contributed significantly to tension between these two areas of Nigeria. The events of the 1950's described in Part II simply widened the educational gap: the South concentrated its energies on a crash program in primary education, whereas the North worked on a more balanced and less spectacular program of regional development. As Figure 1 shows, the absolute gap in primary enrollment levels was far greater in 1960 than ten years earlier; in fact, the Northern figure as a proportion of the Southern fell during the decade from 20 per cent to slightly above 10 per cent. Following Independence the North's position rapidly improved, its growth curve approaching that of the South during the 1940's while enrollment levels in the South declined somewhat. But even if these enrollment trends were to continue, the North would not approach parity with the less populous Southern regions until about 1980. At the highly important grammar school level, Figure 2 suggests that the North's chances of catching up to the South following Independence were slim, and were, in fact, growing slimmer with every passing year. Thus the drive for equality in the South, expressed in the rapid expansion of primary and secondary school enrollments, accentuated educational inequalities in Nigeria as a whole.

Of course, the education explosion in the South doubtless stimulated expansion in the North,[15] much as the initial Yoruba lead acted as an incentive for Ibos from the 1930's onward. But the North–South gap was too large to be rapidly closed, and its effects were far more damaging politically after Independence than when Ibos and Yorubas were both under British control. On the one hand, educated Southerners in the 1960's, faced with unemployment in their own regions, grew increasingly bitter at being denied jobs in the North. On the other hand, Northerners grew increasingly worried over the prospect of being "swamped" by educated Southerners, in private business if not in the civil service. Northern resentment of Ibos was particularly intense, for educated Ibos were quick to move North in search of commercial opportunities.[16] The very ethnic group whose traditional way of life Northerners respected least—the Ibos were not Muslim and lacked hierarchical patterns of government—seemed to be benefiting disproportionately from the modernization of the North. The stage was set for the pogroms of 1966.

Although this study does not extend to the events of 1966, a word may be in order on their relationship to educational expansion in the South. For the first few years of independence, Southerners were willing to permit Northern domination of politics in the hope that eventually the South would come into its own: a new census might shift the balance of power, for example, or the Northern populace might rise up against the feudal system on which the Northern People's Congress was built. But the results of two national censuses (1962 and 1963), of the federal election of 1964, and of an obviously rigged Western Region election of 1965 that retained the NPC's ally, Chief Akintola, as Premier, made it clear that the North would continue to dominate Nigerian politics, perhaps even more openly and ruthlessly than in the past. The only tactic open to those who found this situation unacceptable was to overthrow the democratic process itself; this the military coup of January 1966 accomplished by eliminating key political leaders and outlawing all political parties.

In certain respects the January coup represented a triumph

not simply for the South, but for Nigerian nationalism. Both Colonel Nzeogwu, who initiated the assassination plot, and General J. T. U. Aguiyi Ironsi, who became first Head of the Military Government, were genuinely bent on saving the nation as a whole from civil disorder. But the tragedy was that nationalist policies, in a situation where conventional politics had been suspended, inevitably favored the South. The old political class, dominated at the federal level by Northerners, was gone; in its place, elevated to unprecedented power and status as advisers to the military rulers, were the nation's higher civil servants, who because of the country's educational history happened to be predominantly Southern. General Ironsi probably believed that delegating greater authority to the civil servants was an eminently nonpolitical act, and his May 1966 announcement of the unification of the country's regional civil services seems to have been an honest expression of nationalist sentiment. Influential Northerners, however, saw the first move as highly political, given the number of Southerners in administrative positions, and the second as a thinly disguised plot to flood the North with Southern civil servants. Significantly, it was the unification announcement that triggered protests by leading Northern emirs, as well as the first large-scale massacres of Ibos living in the North.[17] General Ironsi's well-meaning efforts to change the status and organization of the civil service probably contributed more than any other factor to his demise. The counter-coup of July 1966 replaced him with a Northerner, Lieutenant Colonel Yakubu Gowon, and put an end to all talk of a unified civil service. This counter-coup in turn led to the secession of the Eastern Region, whose predominantly Ibo population was more directly affected than Westerners by events in the North.

The effect of rapid educational expansion in the South, therefore, was to increase the South's already substantial lead over the North at a time when educational inequalities had become a source of bitter political conflict. This conflict was merely intensified by the attempt to replace democratic politics with the rule of "neutral" civil servants, for the close link between the educational system and civil service recruitment meant that any upgrading of the administrative apparatus was also an upgrading of the most educationally advanced groups in the country.*

To what extent did educational expansion foster cleavages that cut across North–South lines? The question is not easily answered, but certainly there were conflicts within Southern Nigeria prior to 1966 that diverted attention from the basic division in the country at large, conflicts in which education played a part. For one thing, tension between Yoruba and Ibo members of the elite remained high following Independence. Matters were hardly helped by a public dispute between the Yoruba Federal Minister of Communications and the Ibo Chairman of the Nigerian Railways Corporation in which each charged the other's agency with tribal favoritism, or by the unexplained replacement of an Ibo by a Yoruba educator as Vice-Chancellor of the University of Lagos.[18] A prominent Yoruba once known for his nationalist sentiments told the author in 1964 of his bitterness at the Ibos' aggressiveness and duplicity, and concluded, "My heart is filled with tribalism." This cleavage, which as we have seen is based in part on patterns of educational expansion dating back several decades, helps to explain the Yorubas' cool response to the news that Ibos had been massacred in the North and the isolation of Ibo military leaders in the delicate negotiations following the July coup—an isolation that led eventually to the East's secession.

A second set of cleavages was between minority and dominant ethnic groups within each Southern region. Resentment of Yoruba hegemony over the people of Benin and Delta provinces was the prime motive behind the creation of the Mid-West State in 1963; here the accidents of missionary history played a rather ironic part, for non-Yorubas ascribed the small number of secondary grammar schools in their area to Yoruba discrimination rather than to missionary settlement patterns.[19]

---

*There is an interesting parallel between recent developments in Nigeria and the Muslim-Hindu tensions that eventually led to the partition of India. As Bruce McCully noted in 1940, "English education failed to bridge the gap permanently between the two great communities. Indeed, by qualifying disproportionate numbers of Hindus for Government service and professional employment, it probably accentuated inter-communal rivalry." *English Education and the Origins of Indian Nationalism* (New York, 1940), p. 395.

Third, the denominational tensions that were so important an aspect of educational expansion in the South may have served a useful cross-cutting function. Loyalty to particular voluntary agencies created conflicts within a given ethnic group or region—the 1961 Eastern Region election was if anything more openly a Protestant-Catholic struggle than the election of 1957—while at the same time it fostered links across ethnic and regional lines.[20] The very fact that denominational tensions were imported from abroad and hence had little in common with other cleavages in Nigerian society may be a compelling argument not for their divisiveness but for their integrative potential. Unfortunately, however, none of the cleavages within Southern Nigeria was sufficient in magnitude to offset the major cleavage between the North and the South.

Vertical Integration: The Role of Teachers

. . . we saw how the elite-mass gap became a politically explosive issue in Nigeria. Here we are concerned with ways of bridging this gap, of getting rulers and ruled to see themselves as belonging to the same society. Vertical integration, as we shall use the term, is a two-way communications process by which elite attitudes and values are transmitted to the populace and popular demands and grievances are transmitted to the elite. Successful vertical integration does not necessarily mean that the elite loses power relative to the populace; it means only that each listens to the other and gains some comprehension of what the other is trying to say. Meaningful communication will not automatically lead to a sense of community, but it is almost a prerequisite.[21]

In practice top politicians and administrators have little occasion to meet any of the poor farmers who constitute most of Southern Nigeria's population. Direct contact is made possible by the mass media, but the integrative potential of radios and newspapers is limited by their unavailability in many rural areas, their impersonality, and the one-sided nature of the announcements they carry. In Nigeria, at least, a steady two-way flow of ideas depends heavily on the existence of intermediaries who can serve as brokers and even, quite literally, as translators between the elite and the masses. As we have seen, teachers were ideally suited for this role in Southern Nigeria; it was for precisely this reason that so many of them were elected to federal and regional office in the early 1950's, when the British were still the ruling elite. As the politicians themselves became an elite, teachers continued to perform an intermediary role; indeed, in some ways the teacher's potential as a vertical integrator increased. Teachers were responsible for disseminating the language of the elite—English—to an entire generation, and for conveying, through their own behavior as well as through classroom instruction, the rudiments of good citizenship. They were also in a good position to transmit messages from students and their parents upward to the new elite, particularly in rural areas, where there were few educated adults. Furthermore, as the size of the teaching force grew, teachers were increasingly able to command the respectful attention of the government by well-organized pressure tactics.

The realization of a teacher's potential as an intermediary depended in large measure on his status in the community; generally speaking, the higher and more secure his status, the more likely he was to play a constructive role as an interpreter of ideas. The net effect of rapid educational expansion, however, was to erode the teacher's standing seriously, and to give at least the primary teacher a general feeling of insecurity. For as he taught children to read and write, the teacher was imparting to others the very knowledge that had formerly raised him above the illiterate populace. Recruitment standards inevitably declined with the onset of universal primary education, and as thousands of untrained teachers were hired to staff the new classes of the mid-1950's, the public image of the profession suffered. Indeed, the early years of universal primary education made a mockery of the idea that teaching was a profession requiring prolonged and rigorous training; the proliferation of untrained teachers had a greater effect on the public than the continued presence of grammar school principals and other educators who were professionals in every sense of the word. The teacher's status was further lowered by the public's tendency to attribute rising unemployment among school leavers to a decline in educational standards—that is, to the failure of the teacher to get his material across to the students. Finally, his status was probably lowered by the shift in primary school proprietorship toward the local authorities. Voluntary agency teachers enjoyed a certain reputation for probity and benevolence by virtue of their links to the missionary past; local authority teachers had no such legacy to protect them, and were widely regarded as little more than the hired men of the local council.

Untrained and poorly trained primary teachers faced an additional problem: the very real prospect that they would soon be in the same position as the students they were preparing for the "unemployment market." Teacher training colleges, enlarged in the late 1950's in a belated effort to improve the quality of the primary school teaching force, were by the mid-1960's producing a large number of well-trained teachers. Enrollment in Southern Nigerian Grade II colleges, many of whose students had earned the West African School Certificate, was over 18,000 in 1965;[22] of these, about one-third were in their final year and ready to assume classroom duties. It was assumed by the government that trained teachers would replace the untrained, and this process occurred so rapidly that by 1965 some 75 per cent of the primary teachers in the East and 55 per cent in the old West had at least Grade III qualifications. Many untrained or uncertificated teachers enrolled in a teacher training college, thus temporarily securing their positions against the claims of the better-qualified. But thousands of others—the very ones without whom universal primary education would have been impossible—found themselves jobless, or about to become so. They had been drafted in an emergency, and once the emergency was over they found they were no longer needed. Like the Nigerian ex-serviceman of the 1940's returning to civilian life, the untrained teacher of the 1960's returned to his home and small farm, the embittered veteran of years of thankless service.

The declining status of the teacher, combined with insecurity of tenure at the lower end of the scale, had a profoundly demoralizing effect on Southern Nigeria's teaching force at the secondary as well as the primary level. Morale has deteriorated further in recent years because thousands of primary school teachers, particularly in the East, have had to wait months before their salaries were paid. Under the circumstances, far from continuing to serve as a vertical integrator of his society, the teacher became preoccupied with his own problems; in search of his own scapegoat, he tended to blame the government for his plight. Discouraged over their prospects, many teachers left the classroom to seek more lucrative and secure jobs elsewhere. But those who remained inevitably communicated their discontent to those around them—their students, neighbors, and employers, as well as the regional and federal governments.

The institution through which Nigeria's teachers have normally channeled their demands for better salaries and service conditions is the Nigeria Union of Teachers. The educational expansion of the 1950's vastly increased the union's membership—from 22,000 in 1950 to 57,000 in 1962—but this very increase brought problems. Among the new members were thousands of young, poorly educated teachers who increasingly came to favor union action—including strikes—as a way of protecting their jobs and of increasing the income and prestige of their profession. The union's leaders, however, remained essentially unchanged from the 1940's, and the philosophy of close collaboration with the British that had won them the gratitude of the colonial regime* continued to guide their relationships with the federal, the Western, and to a lesser extent the Eastern government. Many teachers resented this collaboration, which they saw as a preference for mediating between the teachers and the government rather than for presenting the teachers' case as forcefully as possible. Indeed, it was widely believed that the N.U.T., by virtually refusing to strike against the regional and federal governments, had confined itself to presenting humble petitions that could be ignored with impunity.

Teachers with little or no training were further disturbed by the union's apparent lack of concern for their welfare. The N.U.T. carefully nurtured an image of itself as a professional organization with high recruitment standards that had been only temporarily lowered. Thus although the union did sponsor some quite successful vacation courses for its untrained members to improve their qualifications, its annual conferences did

*The key leaders of the union possessed British "titles" as of 1964: E. E. Esua (C.B.E.), Alvan Ikoku (O.B.E.), Bishop Seth Kale (M.B.E.), and Canon E. O. Alayande (M.B.E.).

little more than express regret when thousands of teachers, including many who had served long before universal primary education, were sacked to make way for a new, more academically qualified generation. The resulting bitterness felt by dismissed teachers against the N.U.T. as well as the regional governments is well expressed in this poignant letter from the president of a breakaway group, the Nigerian Association of C/S [uncertificated] Teachers, to the N.U.T. Executive Working Committee:

> We C/S teachers view it with great concern that we are the pioneers and the stepping stone and the runnersup of civil, political, religious and educational advancement of this growing National.
>
> Now that we should reap the fruits of our strenuous labour, now that we should be raised shoulder high, now that we should be proud because we have moulded you up as useful Nigerians: —the Graduates, Premiers, Prime Ministers, Ministers with or without Port-folios, other Parliamentarians, Professors, Lecturers, doctors and Magistrates, judges, and Lawyers, engineers, all certified teachers, School Certificate holders and all educated elements of varying educational outlook, you form the vile brooms by which we are swept away because of non-certification which is not an evidence of inefficiency or old age.[23]

To disaffection among the lower ranks of the teaching force should be added restlessness among recent university graduates teaching in the secondary schools. These graduates felt that the N.U.T. represented the interests of an older group of men who had not obtained university degrees and who were in fact threatened by the new intelligentsia. A Graduate Teachers Association was formed in the late 1950's with the aim of bypassing the N.U.T. and negotiating directly with the government for better salaries and working conditions. Thus as the teaching force became more differentiated, cleavages developed within its ranks, and the N.U.T. found it increasingly difficult to speak convincingly for all members of the profession.

A turning point in the history of the union came in May 1964 with E. E. Esua's retirement from the post of General Secretary, which he had held since 1941. He was thereupon appointed

Chairman of the Federal Electoral Commission, a move that merely confirmed the widespread suspicion that he was more a member of the ruling elite than a representative of the "sub-elite"[24] of teachers. With Esua's departure from the union, pressures for more radical tactics built up. This change in the internal dynamics of the N.U.T. coincided with a general increase in labor-government tension that finally resulted in the General Strike. Teachers in Lagos and a few other parts of the country joined in the strike, but it was not supported by the N.U.T. National Executive, which at that time placed its hopes on the Morgan Commission's proposal (in line with a long-standing union demand) of a National Joint Negotiating Council for Teachers that would set salaries and working conditions on a national rather than a regional basis. It soon became clear, however, that the regional and federal governments were not going to participate voluntarily in such a body. The regional governments were particularly uneasy because the establishment of national scales would reduce their policy-making power in the educational field. In the Western and Eastern regions, where salary scales were below those in Lagos and the North, authorities feared the financial implications of revising their scales upward. The authorities in Kaduna for their part feared the implications of a unified teaching service, which might bring Southern teachers to the North.

Faced with stalling tactics by the bureaucrats, the N.U.T. National Executive took the unprecedented step of calling a nationwide teacher strike beginning on the fourth anniversary of Independence, October 1, 1964. The selection of this date was quite significant, for on previous Independence Day celebrations teachers had shown their commitment to the nation-building effort by organizing public parades of their students, raising the Nigerian flag in ceremonies on the school grounds, and the like. The strike went ahead as planned, and for a week virtually the entire Nigerian teaching force of 100,000 failed to show up in school. The teachers did finally win their point, and a National Joint Negotiating Council was established. But the victory was a Pyrrhic one, for the council turned out to be another stalling device, and the various governments refused to regard its recommendations as anything more than advisory. Threats of strike action again grew loud in late 1965, and only the military coup halted what would probably have been an even more decisive confrontation between the country's teachers and its rulers.

The teachers' changing role illustrates the rather complex effect of rapid educational expansion on vertical integration at both the regional and the federal level. As the teaching force grew, so did its potential for bridging the elite-mass gap by transmitting messages between the elite and the populace. But the very increase in the size and competence of the teaching force lowered the teacher's effectiveness as a vertical integrator, for in the face of greater job competition he became increasingly preoccupied with defending his status and security and began to give top priority to expressing his own viewpoint. Since, as we have seen, this viewpoint was likely to be in conflict with the government's, and since the teacher was the most important live source of political information for his students, his expressions of discontent were likely to play a significant part in alienating the younger generation from political authority.

Integrative Behavior

A fourth and for our purposes final aspect of integration is "the readiness of individuals to work together in an organized fashion for common purposes and to behave in a fashion conducive to the achievement of these common purposes."[25] Integrative behavior, in this broad sense, depends on a minimal level of interpersonal trust and a belief that cooperation with others is both possible and worthwhile for all concerned.[26] The importance of what Lucian Pye calls "associational sentiments"[27] lies in their effect not only on a society's capacity to get things done but also on the way things get done; a society is in our view more truly integrated if people cooperate willingly than if they do so out of suspicion or fear. In this sense, integrative behavior is relevant in all kinds of organizations, nonpolitical as well as political, small as well as large and complex.

Spokesmen for the new states, anxious to attribute to their societies virtues believed to be lacking in the West, often describe their people as skilled in the arts of cooperation. Certainly this is the dominant theme of the doctrine of African socialism. Sekou Touré insists that solidarity is the richest resource of the black race; Julius Nyerere that *ujamaa,* or familyhood, is a traditional resource that can be used in nation-building; Léopold Senghor that the African is not an individual so much as a member of a collectivity.[28] However correctly these views apply to traditional society—and there is an almost irresistible temptation for intellectuals in the new states to idealize the pre-colonial era—there is some reason to believe that in the early transition to modernity the willingness of people to cooperate with each other actually decreases. Modernization creates value conflicts within and between individuals, puts them in unfamiliar situations, whets the appetites of the ambitious, and produces a general atmosphere of uncertainty about the future that increases the risk of trusting others. To be sure, new and often quite powerful organizations are formed in the modernization process, but it is by no means certain that the rise of a powerful single party, for example, automatically increases the total organizational capacity of a society.

One of the striking features of Southern Nigerian life in 1960–65 was the extent to which people complained about the absence of trust. Another was the large number of organizations—from tribal unions to divisional councils to political parties—that appeared to the outside observer less effective after Independence than in earlier years. Remarks on this score are necessarily impressionistic, but it is surely significant that Nigerians themselves made so much of the decline in associational sentiments. One primary school student described the situation succinctly on the author's questionnaire: "The Nigeria greatest problem is that we don't like ourselves."

Difficult as it is to measure changes in integrative behavior over time, let alone to isolate the effect of particular events on these changes, we may speculate on the role played in Nigeria by educational expansion. It seems reasonable to assert that universal primary education and related schemes at the post-primary level increased the cooperative capacity of Southern Nigerians, in the sense that a common language and the tools of literacy widened the possibilities for communication. At the same time, however, educational expansion may have had a negative effect on people's incentive to cooperate with each other. We have already noted the decline in the spirit of voluntarism that occurred when the regional governments took over educational responsibilities formerly borne by tribal unions, progress associations, and voluntary agencies; an increase in governmental capacity was offset to some extent by the decreased capacity of the private sector. Moreover, rapid educational expansion produced generational tensions between young literates and older illiterates that weakened many different kinds of organizations. For example, the Ibibio and Ibo national high schools were both plagued in the 1950's and 1960's by conflict between well-educated principals—normally young men who had received scholarship aid from their tribal union —and the older, more traditional members of the school's Board of Managers. A third factor conducive to mistrust, at least between the people and their rulers, was the increasing awareness of educated people that resources were being wasted by those rulers, often on luxuries for themselves and their families.* When government officials invoked the need for austerity as a reason for rejecting the salary scales recommended by the Morgan Commission, they sounded insincere. Why should people cooperate with the government when the government was not cooperating with them?

Charges of corruption in awarding jobs and contracts assumed the proportions of a favorite national pastime in post-Independence Nigeria. As some political scientists have recently pointed out, corruption can have an important integrative effect on a society in that the expectation of money or other favors binds people to each other and facilitates action that might never occur in a society that relied solely on legal procedures and formal institutions; certainly the overall impact of corrupt practices need not be as harmful to political development as moralists might imagine.[29] In Nigeria, however, the widespread belief that other people were making money and getting ahead by corrupt means probably had an important disintegrative effect, for it reduced public trust in the integrity of officials at all organizational levels and caused deep resent-

---

*Archibald Callaway observed of unemployed school leavers he met in the Enugu slums that in 1960 they complained in a vague way about the wealth of politicians, whereas in 1963 they frequently knew government officials' precise incomes, car allowances, and so on. Interview, Dec. 15, 1963.

ment among those who lacked "long leg," the West African term for influence or "pull." As one secondary student wrote in response to a question about his problems in finding a job, "My parents are illiterates, and if no 'long leg' no work in Nigeria."

It may be that rapid educational expansion contributed to the belief that corruption was widespread—leaving aside the imponderable question of the actual incidence of bribery and nepotism. Prior to the education explosion, when a primary or secondary school certificate was an automatic passport to salaried employment, it could be reasonably argued that a person obtained a particular job by his academic achievements; the certificate, as a kind of personal merit badge, legitimated the officeholder in the eyes of the public. Once the link between certificate and job was broken, the lucky recipient of a job could no longer credibly explain his good fortune solely in terms of educational achievement, since large numbers of school leavers with similar or even better qualifications were going jobless. An inevitable result was the charge of corruption, which seriously affected the performance and morale of the civil service when directed against its members. It would be a mistake to take all allegations of corruption in a developing country at face value; one should appreciate the function such allegations perform for those who fail in the competition for scarce resources, as well as the function corruption itself may serve for those who succeed.

Summary

It must be concluded that the educational developments of the 1950's and early 1960's in Southern Nigeria had, on balance, a disintegrative effect on the country as a whole. Their most important consequence was to widen the already substantial educational disparity between North and South, thus intensifying the potential conflict between the two areas. Since any effort to reduce political tension by strengthening and unifying the civil service was bound to arouse Northern opposition, the Nigerian political system had no way of transcending or reducing the North–South conflict, or of coming to grips with it in a creative manner.

But apart from the North–South cleavage, even if we take the

South alone as our unit of analysis, the disintegrative effects of educational expansion seem to outweigh the integrative ones. To be sure, a general consequence of universal primary education was to raise the integrative potential of the Nigerian political system by spreading literacy in a common language and increasing the size of the teaching force—by widening and deepening, in short, the communications network. But far more important for integration than the sheer amount of communication within a system is the content of that communication,[30] and here the signs were not favorable. Teachers ceased to be effective vertical integrators and concentrated on venting their own grievances against the government; charges of tribalism and corruption filled the communications channels. These things happened in part because of the very spread of literacy among the populace. That educational expansion increased Nigeria's potential for integration is theoretically interesting; that it also contributed despite itself to the underutilization and distortion of that potential is of greater practical relevance.

NOTES

1. Clifford Geertz, "The Integrative Revolution," in Clifford Geertz (ed.), *Old Societies and New States: The Quest for Modernity in Asia and Africa* (New York: Free Press, 1963), p. 120.

2. Rupert Emerson, *From Empire to Nation* (Cambridge, Mass.: Harvard University Press, 1960), p. 96.

3. "National integration . . . refers specifically to the problem of creating a sense of territorial nationality which overshadows—or eliminates—subordinate parochial loyalties." Myron Weiner, "Political Integration and Political Development," *Annals of the American Academy of Political and Social Science*, CCCLVIII (March 1965), p. 53. Rupert Emerson (pp. 95–96) makes a similar point when he defines a nation as "the largest community which, when the chips are down, effectively commands men's loyalties, overriding the claims both of lesser communities within it and those which cut across or potentially enfold it." Other relevant literature on integration includes Philip E. Jacob and James C. Toscano (eds.), *The Integration of Political Communities* (Philadelphia: Lippincott, 1964); Karl Deutsch, *Nationalism and Social Communication* (Cambridge, Mass.: M.I.T. Press, 1966);

Claude Ake, *A Theory of Political Integration* (Homewood, Ill.: Dorsey Press, 1967); and James S. Coleman and Carl G. Rosberg, Jr. (eds.), *Political Parties and National Integration in Tropical Africa* (Berkeley: University of California Press, 1964).

4. See John Spencer, ed., *Language in Africa* (Cambridge, Eng., 1963). Relevant sources on Asia include R. B. LePage, *The National Language Question* (London: Institute of Race Relations, Oxford University Press, 1964); Selig Harrison, *India: The Most Dangerous Decades* (Princeton: Princeton University Press, 1960), pp. 55–95; W. Howard Wriggins, *Ceylon: Dilemmas of a New Nation* (Princeton: Princeton University Press, 1960), pp. 241–270. As Dankwart Rustow, *A World of Nations* (Washington: Brookings Institute, 1967), p. 56, has observed, "In a country where only a small elite can read and write, it makes little difference in what language the vast majority are illiterate. Concerted drives for literacy and mass education, by contrast, emphasize the importance of the linguistic alternatives."

5. McKim Marriott, "Cultural Policy in the New States," in Clifford Geertz, *op. cit.,* pp. 27–56; Immanuel Wallerstein (ed.), *Social Change: The Colonial Situation* (New York: Wiley & Sons, 1966), pp. 592–674. For a revisionist effort in the field of African history, see Cheick Anta Diop, *L'Unité culturelle de l'Afrique noire* (Paris, 1959).

6. Timidity in curriculum reform is not confined to "moderate" states like Nigeria. As Philip Foster notes of Ghanaian education, "the startling thing . . . is not the Radical break with the colonial past but the persistence of neo-colonial values and practices among a political elite which ostensibly rejects them." *Education and Social Change,* p. 299. See also Coleman, *Education and Political Development,* pp. 43–48.

7. Joseph Fischer, "Indonesia," in Coleman, *ibid.,* pp. 102–107; Joseph DiBona, "Indiscipline and Student Leadership in an Indian University," *Comparative Education Review,* X, 2 (June 1966), p. 309; Foster, *op. cit.,* pp. 238–39.

8. It would be most unlikely for a young Ibo in the 1950's or 1960's to have matched the educational mobility, in a geographical sense, of Nnamdi Azikiwe; birth and early childhood in the North; primary education in Onitsha and Lagos; secondary education in Calabar (Hope Waddell) and Lagos (Methodist Boys High School); higher education in the United States. K. A. B. Jones-Quartney, *A Life of Azikiwe* (Baltimore: Penguin, 1965), p. 49.

9. Interview with the Principal of Edo College, Jan. 28, 1964. The rolls of the Benin and Ughelli schools confirm these statements. In both

schools roughly 70 per cent of the students from 1950 on were recruited from the province where the school was located.

10. An integrated polity, in this formulation, is similar to David Easton's "political community," in which people may or may not be culturally unified but in which they at least agree to struggle with each other through common institutions. David Easton, *A Systems Analysis of Political Life* (New York: Wiley & Sons, 1965), esp. p. 177. The functions of cross-cutting cleavages are discussed in Georg Simmel, *Conflict and the Web of Group-Affiliations* (Glencoe: The Free Press, 1955); in Lewis A. Coser, *The Functions of Social Conflict* (Glencoe: The Fress Press, 1956); and in S. M. Lipset, *Political Man* (Garden City: Doubleday, 1959), pp. 88–90.

11. C. S. Whitaker, "A Dysrhythmic Process of Political Change," *World Politics*, XIX, 2 (Jan. 1967), pp. 190–217.

12. James S. Coleman, *Nigeria: Background to Nationalism* (Berkeley and Los Angeles: University of California Press, 1958), p. 361.

13. Alhaji Sir Ahmadu Bello, *My Life* (Cambridge, Eng.: Cambridge University Press, 1962), pp. 110–11. Similar remarks are to be found in Coleman, *Nigeria: Background to Nationalism*, p. 362.

14. "The party acts in defense of traditional authority, and traditional authority sustains the party." Richard L. Sklar and C. S. Whitaker, "Nigeria," in James S. Coleman and Carl G. Rosberg, Jr. (eds.), *Political Parties and National Integration in Tropical Africa* (Berkeley: University of California Press, 1964), p. 625. Detailed confirmation is given in Richard L. Sklar, *Nigerian Political Parties: Power in an Emergent African Nation* (Princeton: Princeton University Press, 1963), pp. 323–338, 365–371.

15. Recent educational developments in the North are described by J. F. Thornley, *The Planning of Primary Education in Northern Nigeria* (Paris: UNESCO, International Institute of Educational Planning, 1966).

16. Robert A. LeVine, *Dreams and Deeds* (Chicago: University of Chicago Press, 1966), pp. 69–71, gives striking evidence that achievement motivation among the Ibos is far higher than among the Hausa-Fulani.

17. *West Africa*, May 28, June 4 and 11, 1966.

18. *West African Pilot*, April 6 and 8, 1964; "The Chronicle," *Minerva*, III, 3 (Spring 1965), p. 415, and III, 4 (Summer 1965), p. 592.

19. Great Britain, *Nigeria: Report of the Commission Appointed to Enquire into the Fears of Minorities and the Means of Allaying Them.* Cmnd. 505 (London: HMSO, July, 1958), p. 19.

20. The leadership of the First Conference of the Methodist Church of Nigeria, which met in Lagos in 1962, reflected the inter-ethnic appeal of many religious bodies. The President-Designate was Rev. J. O. B. Soremekun, a Yoruba; the Vice-President Designate was E. Eyo Moma, an Efik; and the Secretary-Designate was Rev. George Egemba Igwe, an Ibo. See Methodist Church, Nigeria, *Foundation Conference, Lagos: 28–9–62* (Yaba: Pacific Printers, 1962), pp. 72–74.

21. The concept used here is similar to Weiner's "elite-mass integration" and to Coleman and Rosberg's "political integration." See Weiner, *op. cit.,* pp. 60–62; and Coleman and Rosberg, *op. cit.,* p. 9. The importance of communications in all aspects of integration is stressed in the writings of Karl Deutsch; see Deutsch, *op. cit.,* and his contributions to Jacob and Toscano, *op. cit.,* pp. 46–97.

22. Education and World Affairs, Nigeria Project Task Force, Committee on Education and Human Resource Development, *Nigerian Human Resource Development and Utilization* (New York: Education and World Affairs, December 1967), p. 80.

23. Letter from F. M. Obasi to N. U. T. Executive Working Committee, Oct. 16, 1964. I am indebted to Dr. Dennis Storer, who has conducted a detailed study of the N. U. T., for making available a copy of Mr. Obasi's letter.

24. Peter C. Lloyd (ed.), *The New Elites of Tropical Africa* (London: Oxford University Press, 1966), p. 13

25. Weiner, *op. cit.,* p. 62.

26. The importance of trust for effective political action is emphasized in Lucian Pye, *Politics, Personality, and Nation-Building: Burma's Search for Identity* (New Haven: Yale University Press, 1962); and in Edward C. and L. F. Banfield, *The Moral Basis of a Backward Society* (Glencoe: The Free Press, 1958). The related notion of empathy is discussed in Daniel Lerner, *The Passing of Traditional Society: Modernizing the Middle East* (New York: The Free Press, 1958), pp. 49–50.

27. Lucian Pye, *Aspects of Political Development* (Boston: Little, Brown & Co., 1966), p. 100.

28. For exposition and analysis of the African socialist doctrine, see William H. Friedland and Carl G. Rosberg, Jr. (eds.), *African Socialism* (Stanford: Stanford University Press, 1964); and "Special Issue on African Socialism," *Africa Report,* May 1963.

29. J. S. Nye, Jr., "Corruption and Political Development: A Cost-Benefit Analysis," *American Political Science Review,* LXI, 2 (June 1967), pp. 417–427; Colin Leys, "What Is the Problem about Corruption?" *Journal of Modern African Studies,* III, 2 (August 1965), pp. 215–230. Both Nye and Leys attack the moralism of Ronald Wraith and Edgar Simkins' *Corruption in Developing Countries* (London, 1963).

30. Even the volume of domestic communications can be a misleading index of transactions within a country. Karl Deutsch infers from increases in the domestic flow of Nigerian mail from 1929 to 1948 that conditions grew more favorable over time for independence demands; see Jacob and Toscano, *op. cit.,* pp. 76–77. Given the different literacy rates of the North and South, it is probable that greater mail flow over this period simply reflected the increasing solidarity of the South rather than of Nigeria as a whole. For a discussion of the dangers of using national statistics without breaking them down by regions, see Charles Nash Myers, *Education and National Development in Mexico* (Princeton: Princeton University Press, Industrial Relations Section, 1965).

CHAPTER 15

Education and National Integration in Nigeria*

ALAN PESHKIN

Introduction

The new nations of the world hold many expectations for their education systems. They expect that schools will produce the labor force for their manpower requirements, the leadership for their bureaucracies and the citizenry for an enlightened social order. In pluralistic countries, governments expect also that schools will assist in integrating sub-populations fragmented by religious, linguistic, or ethnic differences. This article will examine the theme, "education and national integration," in Nigeria, whose federation was formed in recognition of profound cultural disparities.

Contemporary independent Nigeria was shaped by colonial conquest rather than by indigenous historical and traditional factors. For example, a relationship of rivalry and hostility existed among many of the tribes included within the borders of Nigeria. In the face of this divisiveness, colonial military force created a semblance of peace and unity over formerly

Reprinted, in slightly revised form, from Alan Peshkin, "Education and National Integration in Nigeria," *The Journal of Modern African Studies,* 5, 3 (1967), pp. 323–34. Copyright © 1967 by *The Journal of Modern African Studies.* Reprinted by permission of the publisher and Alan Peshkin.

distinct polities. The use of a common language in government and business, the development of trade and transport and the creation of trans-tribal administrative units tended further to expand political identifications. However, other features of colonial rule limited the development of a national consciousness as broad as the political boundaries of the country. First, regardless of the over-all administrative form adopted by Britain, there were separate government structures for the Northern and the Southern Provinces from 1900 to 1922, and for the Northern, Eastern, and Western Regions from 1922 until the present. Second, traditional tribal cultures were perpetuated by the effects of indirect rule, especially in the North.

In keeping with both official and missionary expectations, schooling in most of the colonial period was meant to serve rather limited economic and political purposes. The extent to which education in the independence period has been used for the purpose of national integration is an important indicator of the governments' desire to create a united Nigeria and, therefore, we will focus on this point. Since the 1960 constitution placed all pre-university education under regional authority, judgments regarding the roule of the schools in developing national unity will be based on an examination of regional Ministry of Education documents. It is assumed that such documents are adequate indicators of official intent in educational policy, although it must be acknowledged, at the same time, that what individual teachers do in their own classrooms may vary significantly from Ministry policy. This investigation is confined to three of the nations' four Regions: the Northern, the Western, and the Eastern. The Mid-West is excluded because of a paucity of relevant data. However, since that Region was part of the Western Region until 1963, observations of the latter should apply equally well to the Mid-West until that time.

The Northern Region

For reasons considered elsewhere, the British colonial administration restricted missionary activities in the dominant Muslim areas of the North.[1] The first official departures from traditional education were taken under Hanns Vischer who was Director of the Education Department in the Northern

Provinces from 1910 to 1919, when these Provinces for purposes of education were still administratively separate from the rest of Nigeria. He established schools for the sons of Chiefs and for the training of artisans, taking care to ensure that tradition was not disrupted. These first schools, built in Kano with the support of the Native Administration,

> in matters of dress, correct practice in the form of saluta-
> tion and courtesies to chiefs and those in authority, and in
> general behaviour and mode of life . . . were required to
> conform to the best traditions of local society.[2]

Graduates of mission schools in the more educationally-advanced Southern Provinces were considered by Lugard, Governor-General of the Colony and Protectorate of Nigeria, to be disrespectful of authority and to have lost touch with their own people; he hoped such results could be avoided in the North. Acknowledging that education inevitably "produces a ferment of new and progressive ideas," he advocated the training of character as the best antidote to the effects of this ferment and specified the components of a character-building education:

> (1) residential schools; (2) a more adequate British staff;
> (3) the delegation of responsibility for discipline to school
> monitors; (4) encouragement of field sports; (5) the classi-
> cation of the order of merit of schools, and the grant to
> aided schools, to be partly dependent on tone and disci-
> pline; (6) religious and moral instruction to be recog-
> nized.[3]

Interestingly, these ideas are still advocated in the schools and training colleges of the Region, no longer as an antidote to progressive notions, but, rather, as a means of training good citizens.

Education in the then Northern and Southern Provinces of Nigeria was separately administered until 1928 when a single Director of Education was appointed for both areas. Despite the now national scope of education, the post-1928 syllabi for history and geography (two subjects likely to reflect a desire to promote national integration) emphasize more the cognitive components of instruction and those relating to citizenship than concern for supra-tribal identification. For example, the

1931 history syllabus for primary schools provided that "indigenous life in Nigeria" be studied in class three, including an
explanation of how the country is governed. In class four, there
was to be an Introduction to other societies and to Nigerian
history during the British period. In 1932, the syllabus for history and geography in the middle schools emphasized Nigerian
geography in class two, world history in classes two and three,
and the history of Nigeria and the British Empire in classes
four, five and six, with special concern for developing "respect
for authority and good citizenship."[4]

In 1951 education again became a regional subject and by
1952 an autonomous Northern Ministry of Education was operative. A new set of syllabi for the Region's primary schools was
prepared; they were complete by 1956 and with few modifications remained as the syllabi in use during the independence
period. Looking again at history and geography, we see that the
courses of study indicate a general attempt to move from the
culturally known to the unknown and from the geographically
near to the remote, with the exception that classes five and six
focus on the history of Nigeria and class seven emphasizes
contemporary Nigeria. The most nationalistic statement in
these syllabi is found under the outline for geography. Students
are to learn about "Goods from other parts of Nigeria: where
and how they are produced or grown, the life of the people who
grow or make them, leading the class to an appreciation of the
main tribes of Nigeria and how they live."[5]

Following the announcement in 1959 of self-government for
Northern Nigeria, we would expect to find in educational documents more nationalistic statements reflecting a genuine concern for unity, but this is not the case.[6] For example, D. H.
Williams, an Englishman in the Ministry of Education, prepared a history of education in Northern Nigeria in honor of
the self-government celebrations. The major problems he identified were purely regional: correcting the imbalance (1) between educational opportunities in the riverain area, where
missionaries had been operative, and in the far north, where
they had been largely prohibited and (2) between levels of education, so that an adequate supply of high-level manpower
could be prepared to take over from expatriates in government
and business.[7] Similarly, the *White Paper on Educational De-*

velopment in Northern Nigeria (Kaduna, 1961) examined the quantitative problems of development with no reference to political issues. H. Oldman, an English school administrator, was invited by the Northern Government to survey the financial and administrative problems of the Region in its move towards universal primary education. In his lengthy report there is only a single statement acknowledging the need for unifying different tribes and it is confined to the Region.[8] In 1963 some English educators prepared a guide for primary school inspectors,[9] specifying that history teaching should be Nigeria-centered and referred to the importance of using Hausa as a lingua franca where books in other vernaculars were not available.

Clearly, the quantitative needs identified in the White Paper prevailed in deliberations of education. The teaching of history did not become "Nigeria-centered"; the 1956 syllabus remained in use. To be sure, the syllabus for 1956, or even the one from 1931, could be used to stress broad national ends or narrow tribal, provincial, or regional ones. Since there were, and are, no external examinations in any primary-school subject except English and arithmetic, teachers were more or less free to shape other subjects as they pleased. In fact, after 1956, judging from my recent experience working in primary and teacher education in Northern Nigeria, primary school social studies were neglected, as were most subjects in the curriculum, in favor of English and arithmetic; when taught, they were most often presented uninspiringly from notes dictated by expatriates to the teachers when they were in a training college. It is doubtful whether most school children had ever heard, let alone knew, their national anthem.[10] They were not provided with politically integrative experiences.

At the post-primary level, we get the same picture in the North's teacher training colleges, both from their syllabi and from their actual instruction. The 1964 syllabi do not include content relative to political loyalty, historical heroes and the like.* Moreover, most teachers both in the teacher's colleges

*Not that there is any certainty that reading laudatory tales of folk heroes, writing essays on "fighters for independence," or singing about past glories and dreams of the future measurably increases one's feeling for the object of devotion or for the political unit with which it is associated. However, we expect that in nations concerned with establishing affiliation to a new polity schoolchildren will have these experiences—when they do not, we conclude that such concern probably does not exist or is not widespread.

and the secondary schools were expatriates who were devoted enough to Nigeria but hardly the bearers of nationalistic qualities.

We see, then, that in the post-independence period there has been little stated intent to promote national unity through the schools of Northern Nigeria. Some documents written by Englishmen embody desires to foster integration via education, but such desires are not reflected either in government documents, in school textbooks or in the emphases of classroom teachers.

The Western Region

An examination of the Western Region's education documents reveals, with one exception discussed below, a neglect similar to that of the North. The *Proposals for an Education Policy for the Western Region* (Ibadan, 1952), a white paper written after the Region's new political party, the Action Group, won the 1951 elections, essentially reflected economic needs. Universal primary education was to be introduced, technical and scientific education was to be developed, and manpower was to be trained to "man the machinery of state."[11] Interest in national unity is not manifest in any of the annual reports of the Ministry of Education, or in the *White Paper on the Establishment of a University in Western Nigeria* (Ibadan, 1960), the *Report of the [Banjo] Commission Appointed to Review the Educational System of Western Nigeria* (Ibadan, 1961), or the *Western Nigerian Development Plan for 1962–1968* (Ibadan, 1962).

Contrasting with the silence of these documents is the April, 1964 motion brought before the House of Assembly by a member of the Nigerian National Democratic Party, then the Region's majority party, that called for the introduction of Ibo, Hausa, and French in all the schools of the Region. A choice of any two of these three languages was to be compulsory. Support for the motion was urged on the grounds of combating tribalism and promoting national unity. Chief Sogbein, leader of the opposition, rose to support the motion, saying, "We, members of the opposition, are lovers of Nigeria—one Nigeria." After further debate, in which aspersions were cast on the "true" motives of both sides of the House and the Minister of Education explained the practical difficulties of implementing such a motion, the question was put and agreed to.[12] Because of a lack of textbooks and qualified teachers, the motion did not materially affect the teaching of languages in the Western Region's schools.

The Eastern Region

The Eastern Region's intention to use schools to promote national integration distinguishes them from the other Regions. There is no reason to believe that daily teaching in the schools of this Region conveyed a more nationalistic spirit. Yet, judging from the documents promulgated by the respective Ministries of Education, Eastern Nigeria was manifestly the most responsive to ideological considerations and all-Nigeria interests. Note the following statement for example:

> Any educational system—new or mature—constantly faces the question of its role, its appropriate sphere of action . . . One way of getting at its function . . . is first to describe a . . . model . . . community. . . . A . . . characteristic of a desirable community is social stability and continuing progress in handling complex inter-relationships among people. It is one which is free from untoward social tensions, whether they arise from political, economic, religious, racial or ideological causes.[13]

Although supportive details are not specified in the latter sections of the Report where the more practical matters of curricula in the primary and secondary schools are discussed, two years later, at a major educational conference, there were indications of a desire to implement these and other integrative ideas. The recommended syllabus for primary social studies required class five to study the country as it evolved into an independent and industrial nation, emphasizing the "struggle towards independence"—such phrasing is not found in the official literature of the other Regions. Class six was to focus on the political history of Nigeria with particular attention given to the "development of democracy." The targets for the secondary school were even more explicit:

This is the level of education where we deal with adolescents and the most fertile field for giving a nationalistic slant to our teaching of such subjects as History, Civics, Biography, Art, Music, Cookery, Needlework and Drama. The overall aim should be to develop a love of our own background and culture, a veneration of our elders and eminent men and women, past and present, and an appreciation of what is best in our own way of life. This should lead progressively to examination of peoples and ways of other lands and an appreciation of the unity of mankind in this mosaic of diversity.[14]

Though it is not perfectly clear from the context whether or not "love for our own background and culture" refers to Nigeria as a whole, the conference's recommendations for the teaching of geography, history and civics clarify the application of the "overall aim" referred to above.

We recommend that in every Secondary School, History should be taught by a qualified, preferably Nigerian, teacher. Both in this subject and in Geography emphasis should be placed on the detailed study of the History and Geography of Nigeria before anything else . . . Civics also should be given a prominent place on the Time Table and conscious effort made by secondary school teachers to instill in our youth the right attitude to and respect for our culture, our eminent men and women and our National Anthem and Flag.[15]

The Federal Government

The Federal Government is involved in education through its control of schooling in Lagos, its joint administration with the regional governments of higher education, and its capacity to allocate educational funds to the Regions (note below the large grant for primary education to Northern Nigeria). Thus, it can make an impact on educational development broader than its authority might indicate.

At the federal level, the Ashby Report while directed essentially to education for manpower needs, at least in one instance acknowledged the school's role in promoting national unity. "All universities," the Report stated, "should admit, without discrimination and on the criterion of merit alone, students from any Region or Tribe."[16] However, to ascertain the scope of the Federal Government's interest in national integration we must examine its *National Development Plan 1962–1968* (Apapa, 1962). The Plan outlines the projected expenditure of federal funds for a six-year period. To be sure, its primary concern was to provide for future manpower needs, but the Plan displayed an awareness of problems that was not merely economic.

The 26 projects listed under the education sector were separated into four categories: essential projects, and priorities A, B and C. Topping the list was the provision of £1.8 million to build a national high school in each Region capable of enrolling 570 students. These schools would provide hostel facilities for students from *all* the Regions.

Under priority A, listed sixth, was £150,000 to support the Citizenship and Leadership Centres which offered short-term courses to various groups, such as promising young men holding senior appointments in government and to students in teacher training colleges. Among the problems given special attention by the Centres was the need "to break down the barriers of fear and suspicion which reflect the intertribal antagonisms of the past; and . . . to develop a strong sense of social obligation in the minds of those people fortunate enough to rise to posts of authority and responsibility in the community."[17]

One may question the appropriateness of viewing as an integrative expenditure the £3.1 million designated for primary education in the Northern Region. This grant, pertaining only to the North, probably reflected the strength of Northern influence in the Federal Government. It is interpretable as a contribution to national unity in the sense that it tended to correct the educational imbalance between the North and the other Regions which was a constant source of insecurity among Northerners and, therefore, a perpetually antagonising and disruptive factor in public affairs. Further, in some respects the universities, with their open admission policies and hoped-for national outlook, served integrative ends despite disputes among students and teachers fostered by tribal animosities. Thus, the £9.5 million allocated for university development also may be included in the "national" column. In all, approximately £14.6 million, or 44 per cent of the federal allocation for education, was designated for projects with potentially integrative effects.

In light of the immensity of the problem and the imminence of political strife, one would have expected to see in the *National Development Plan* the quality of language used by Pakistan in her first five-year plan.

> The first of the needed changes (in secondary education) is to enrich the programme by putting emphasis, in the humanities and social sciences, on the great principles of our culture in order to develop individual character, righteous living, dignity among our youth, and to strengthen and purify the base of patriotism founded on the historic role of their nation in the marching life of mankind.[18]

That such language was nowhere used in the documents of the Federal Government is suggestive of Nigeria's political dilemma. Nigeria was nominally one nation, but the fragile foundations of her federal union had been besieged since independence by internecine political hostilities of an inter- and intra-regional and tribal nature. A vicious cycle was created in that these hostilities threatened national union and, at the same time, precluded using the rhetoric of nationalism to support national union.

Conclusions

During the colonial period it is not surprising to find that the schools did not foster broad national sentiments. Coleman accounts for this "disinclination of the (then) Nigerian government to adapt the content of education to the country's changing needs" with three reasons. First, British interests were primarily economic. Second, their political concerns were directed to the "maintenance of law and order and the gradual development of native administration." Third, a major portion of the education system was in the hands of missionaries whose avowed purpose, evangelization, was satisfied by emphasizing reading, writing and religion.[19]

After independence in 1960, the three original Regions displayed special interest in the expansion of education, the training of teachers, the development of higher education, and the introduction of specialized programs to train the manpower requisite for economic development. Based on their respective Ministry of Education documents, the schools of Northern and Western Nigeria were minimally responsive to aims of national unity. In contrast, Eastern Nigerian documents devoted considerable attention to the problem of integration; whether or not the schools also reflected this concern cannot be ascertained from available reports. The plans of the Federal Ministry of Education reveal a fairly marked interest in integration, if certain interpretations are justified for some of its proposed expenditures. To summarize, during the first six years of independence Nigeria's large and growing network of schools was not put to work in behalf of national political goals; intentions stated on paper remained largely unrealized.

In explanation of this fact we suggest that the schools cannot reflect a nationalism which does not exist. Schools do not usually create beliefs, attitudes or values de novo; they communicate them from sources outside the school. The absence of activities oriented to unification in Northern Nigerian schools is commensurate with the outlook of the North's dominant political figure, the late Prime Minister of the Region, Alhaji Ahmadu Bello. Since Ahmadu Bello's Northern Peoples Congress was the majority party in the legislatures of the Federal and Northern Region Governments, his view of the Federation is relevant to understanding the course of Nigerian history since independence. After returning home from a conference in Lagos in 1953, at which the question of unity was raised, he recalled:

> We had no sentimental illusion about leaving the others [the Southerners]: they had acted in such a way that it was abundantly clear to us that they would sooner see the back of us; but what about this transport difficulty? [He refers here to the fact that Northern Nigeria has no access to the sea.] ... We therefore had to take a modified line. We must aim at a looser structure for Nigeria while preserving its general pattern—a structure which would reduce the powers of the Centre to the absolute minimum and yet retain sufficient national unity for practical and international purposes.[20]

This perception of Southerners colored his thinking until his assassination in 1966.

Differences found in the documents of the Regions may reflect different experiences in the independence movement. For example, there was a trans-national character to the first nationalist movements in West Africa. Thus, when Ibo tribesman Nnamdi Azikiwe (later President of the Federal Republic of Nigeria) became prominent in the nationalist movement of Nigeria, his interests followed the pan-African themes of earlier Afro-American writers, such as Marcus Garvey and W.E.B. DuBois, and of the London-based West African Students' Union. Azikiwe was a leader of the National Council of Nigeria and the Cameroons, the group that occupied the centre of nationalist politics and was "the leading all-Nigerian nationalist organization."[21] The policy makers of Eastern Nigeria, accordingly, have been able to identify with a political leadership that had larger than regional pretensions. In addition, it is likely that the "struggle for independence" was a more palpable event for Eastern Nigerians than for Nigerians of other regions and this may have helped to foster their stronger sense of Nigerian nationality.

This explanation is admittedly too simple to account for the position of the Eastern Region. One finds in the debates of the Regional Houses of Assembly statements advocating unity made by important members of all political parties. And in the election of 1959, the Action Group, primarily a Western Region party, won more seats outside its Region than any other party, thereby establishing its claim to supra-regional orientation. Finally, for all its stress on national unity, no Region has been as ready as the East to use the threat of secession as a political weapon, not without cause after the devastating massacres and mass migrations of 1966. Nevertheless, there has been a climate of opinion in that Region, possibly engendered by political tradition and sustained by the considerable number of Easterners formerly employed in other regions, that led it to extol the virtues of national unity more than the North and the West.

It should be noted that even if the schools were directed toward integrative ends, they were not well suited to serve such ends. The Northern Region was unusually dependent on expatriate teachers to staff its post-primary schools; almost 60 per cent of the 1,300 teachers in its craft, commercial, technical, secondary, and teacher-training institutions were non-Nigerians. At the same level, non-Nigerians in the East composed approximately 22 per cent of 3,100 teachers, and in the West, less than 10 per cent of 8,000 teachers.[22] Such teachers are not likely to enhance what for them is a foreign nationalism. Furthermore, most Northern students were in schools controlled by the Christian missions at least until 1966, when regional and local government bodies assumed control of many mission schools.[23] As of 1962, 75 per cent of all schools (but not universities) were owned by the missions in the East and 73 per cent in the West.[24]

Admittedly there is a certain intractable quality to the problem of staffing such that a dependency upon expatriates is readily understood. There may be less justification for continued dependence upon textbooks written by expatriates. A majority of the books used in both primary and secondary-level schools were written by non-Nigerians. This is of particular importance in literature, civics, geography and history, the subjects most likely to be shaped by political needs. It is not that the books available do not provide a complete treatment of Nigeria; it is, rather, that they are too bland to make a major contribution to Nigerian political integration. An exception to the once exclusive domination of the textbook field by foreigners was the publication of Wale Ademoyega's *The Federation of Nigeria* (London, 1962). Easterners might object to this book's reference to Azikiwe as "opportunistic" and "calculating," and Northerners might be justifiably unhappy with the judgment that Islam "inculcated rigid social caste, and militated against any social mobility," but it is one of the few books available which rings with feeling for Nigeria.

Finally, the quiet civic style of Britain's educational legacy to Nigeria militated against a notably overt response to fostering national integration through the schools. Lugard's advice about establishing residential schools, encouraging sports, having student monitors, and the like, characterizes the British tradition and more or less adequately describes the response of Nigerian schools to political socialization, "that process by which individuals acquire attitudes and feelings toward the political system and toward their role in it."[25] This tradition may be effective in the English public school, but it is not sufficiently dynamic to meet the demands of Nigerian pluralism.

The threat of political fragmentation in Nigeria is distressing in view of that country's aspiration, strongly encouraged by the western powers, to be an African colossus, rich, democratic, peace-loving and a model to her neighbors. However, Nigerian unity, western support notwithstanding, appears at best to be a dormant seed. The upheavals of 1965–67 suggest the seed was born a-dying. National leaders willing and able to provide the mandate for its survival appear absent and without such leadership the schools are mostly impotent in promoting goals of national unity.

NOTES

1. See James S. Coleman, *Nigeria: Background to Nationalism* (Berkeley, 1958).

2. D. W. Bittinger, "An Education Experiment in Northern Nigeria in its Cultural Setting" (unpublished doctoral dissertation, University of Pennsylvania, 1941), p. 214.

3. F. D. Lugard, *The Dual Mandate in British Tropical Africa* (London, 1922, reprinted Connecticut, 1965), pp. 432–3.

4. Bittinger, *op. cit.* pp. 242–6.

5. Northern Ministry of Education, *Geography and History Syllabus* (Kaduna, 1956), p. 10.

6. Only in a theoretical sense would we expect this to be true. The reluctance of the Northern leadership in regard to an independent Nigeria is well known.

7. D. H. Williams, *A Short Survey of Education in Northern Nigeria* (Kaduna, 1960), pp. 56–60.

8. Northern Ministry of Education, *The Administration of Primary Education* (Kaduna, n.d.), p. 41.

9. Northern Ministry of Education, *A Handbook for Inspectors* (Kaduna, 1963).

10. See J. S. Coleman, (ed.), *Education and Political Development* (Princeton, 1965), *passim*.

11. H. Weiler, *Education and Politics in Nigeria* (Breisgau, Verlag Rombach Freiburg, 1964), p. 119.

12. *Western Nigeria House of Assembly Debates,* 14th Session 1965 (Ibadan, 1965), cols. 349–59.

13. Eastern Ministry of Education, *Report on the Review of the Educational System in Eastern Nigeria* (Enugu, 1962), p. 23.

14. Eastern Ministry of Education, *Report of the Conference on the Review of the Education System in Eastern Nigeria* (Enugu, 1964), pp. 16 and 21.

15. *Ibid.,* p. 21.

16. Federal Ministry of Education, *Investment in Education* (Lagos, 1960), p. 44.

17. L. J. Lewis, *Schools and Progress in Nigeria* (Oxford, 1965), pp. 119–21.

18. Government of Pakistan, *The First Five Year Plan (1955-1960): Education and Training* (Karachi, 1955–1960) p. 31.

19. Coleman, *Nigeria: Background to Nationalism,* pp. 129–31.

20. Ahmadu Bello, *My Life* (Cambridge, 1962), p. 136.

21. Coleman, *op. cit.* p. 265.

22. Federal Ministry of Education, *Statistics of Education in Nigeria in 1963* (Apapa, 1963), p. 49.

23. Northern Ministry of Education, *Classes, Enrollments and Teachers in the Primary Schools of Northern Nigeria in 1966* (Kaduna, 1966), p. 24.

24. Weiler, *op. cit.,* p. 272.

25. Coleman, *Education and Political Development,* p. 18.

CHAPTER 16

Tarka and the Tiv:
A Perspective on Nigerian Federation

M. J. DENT

To write academically about the role of one's close personal
friends, for whom one has great admiration, is difficult. But the
role of Tarka in Nigerian leadership is of the utmost interest
to the political scientist, and one can learn many lessons from
it of the way that particular backgrounds affect the style and
values of leaders and condition the way they act in a national
situation.

Tarka is not, and never has been, a "Tiv leader." For a time
during his rise from the tribal to national level of leadership he
was in a sense a Tiv champion, but not a Tiv leader. Even at
that time, however, he was seeking to express his political
ideas in more general "Middle Belt" terms and to avoid a purely
tribal orientation although, in practice, this was the orientation
given to the propaganda of his party at this time by its propagandists at the grass roots. Now he regards his function as a
Nigerian one, and strives to resist the tribal pressures for jobs
and patronage which come upon him as upon every Nigerian
leader.

Tarka is one of the group of three or four modern political
leaders, mostly of radical provenance, who are dominant in the
Nigerian political scene at the moment. With Enahoro and
Arikpo, he shares the advantage of coming from a smallish

tribe (by Nigerian standards). It is characteristic of such leaders that they are under less temptation than those from larger tribes to confuse tribe and nation, to practise what Sklar has called "big tribe chauvinism." Chief Awolowo was unwisely persuaded at a crucial moment in his career to assume the title of "leader of the Yorubas". There is some reason to seek one's destiny as the leader of a people stretching from Dahomey to Ibadan, to Ondo and up to Illorin, with a history of empires and states. For Tarka to have sought to call himself "Leader of the Tiv" would have been ludicrous as well as being unacceptable to a people as egalitarian as the Tiv. In any case, the Tiv already had a Tor Tiv, and Tarka, from the time of his dramatic reconciliation with the Tor Tiv at the end of 1965, has been on good terms with him and would not have thought of trying to replace him. He would be at once too proud and too humble. Too proud because he sees himself as a Nigerian in a Nigerian role (even in the political days he tended to leave Tiv political matters to be dealt with by his lieutenant while he dealt with national or regional ones), and too humble because he continued to treat chiefs and elders with the humility which they expected as a matter of courtesy from a younger person.

Azikiwe could speak of the "Ibo nation created by God to lead the people of Africa from darkness to light," for the size and importance of the Ibo people in terms of jobs occupied and collective self-confidence made such *hubris* comprehensible; Sardauna could speak of his inheritance as "my grandfather's empire." But the Tiv, though proud of their traditions—the "Shagbaondo i Tiv" (the way the Tiv were created)—have no history as an empire or a state, and are under no temptation to put the clock back. Nor has Tarka had the doubtful advantage of sitting, like Kenyatta, at the feet of the anthropologists. He is not torn between the old and the new: he can be at the same time a Tiv man and a modernist.

It is from the Tiv background that he draws the model for that function which is of the greatest importance in Nigeria at the moment, the function which he is in one sense ideally placed to fulfil—the function of reconciliation, which in Tiv is referred to by the potent name of "Soron Tar" or land mending. This function in Tiv society is known to be separate from the function of coercion and to involve a specific skill in the setting right of relationships, usually by prolonged consultation. The Tiv are ideally placed by geography as a bridge between North and South, and Tarka himself is perhaps the only figure with a past record of support from West and East, from the minorities and from the North. These qualities can be of vital importance now that the task of peace making begins, and the issue of the war is settled.

Tarka's position now is a national one, but his origin as a political figure was from within the milieu of Tiv and Middle Belt politics. He was born in 1930 in the Mbakor clan of the Pusus half of the Tiv lineage. He is descended from Kibo and from Wannune, important figures in Mbakor history, and his own father, after many years as an N. A. elementary schoolteacher, was chosen as chief of Mbakor. This was a mark of the respect in which he was held personally rather than of any hereditary title. To be a member of a "good" family conveys some slight advantage in Tiv society, but Tiv know nothing of hereditary lines, since all are sons of Tiv. Tarka went to the Katsina Ala provincial middle school and on to teacher training and higher teacher training at the Rural Education Centre before returning to Katsina Ala secondary school to teach. He was a good teacher, respected but not an outstanding figure and was one of many men of the younger generation interested in radical politics of a not very clearly defined type. At this time Tarka was still immature in his political judgments and somewhat pugnacious; it has been his strength to learn from experience and grow continually in stature and in balance. He stood for the federal election of 1954 in his own constitutency of Jengbar, and was elected by the electoral college on the principle of "eat and give to your brother"; the previous member had come from the other half of the intermediate area and it was his turn. As yet, he had no political reputation and did not win the election on a political platform. In the first elections of 1951 Tiv had swept the board in Benue province but the members elected had gravitated towards the N.P.C., if they were satisfied with the establishment, or towards the N.C.N.C., if they were not. But in neither case had they politicised the people as a whole; the N.P.C. was yet not so much a political party as a group of notables satisfied with the establishment, of which they mostly formed a part at the local level, while the N.C.N.C.

attracted the radically minded without forming any deep roots or mass base. Awolowo's brief effort to enter Tiv by direct Action Group invasion with Isaac Kpum as his agent had likewise failed to strike root. From 1953 onwards, however, precise political ideas began to have influence with the masses. The N.P.C. had demonstrated by its adoption of the eight points plan in 1952 that it felt threatened by Southern domination and wanted to awaken the Northern people to the need to express their separate identity in political terms. This awoke in the peoples of the non-Hausa-Fulani parts of the North a similar desire to express their own identity separate not only from the South but from the far North as well. To most of them this implied a separate Region, but the early attempts to form Middle Belt parties proved hopelessly fissiparous, chiefly because of the split between those who allied with the N.P.C. and those who did not.

In this general climate of striving towards a separate political identity for the Middle Belt, Tarka seized his chance. Soon after his election he went to seek alliance in the South, failed to find it from Azikiwe, and went on to Awolowo who agreed to supply funds for the organization of the Middle Belt party and to Action Group support for the creation of a Middle Belt State. It was at this time that Awolowo was seeking to expand his party from the narrow confines of the Western Region, which it had run fairly efficiently for the last four years, to an all-Nigerian party. To do this Awolowo relied upon a carefully thought out programme of welfare politics to appeal to the elite, and the tribal appeal to minorities to win the masses. Awolowo's basic doctrine of ethnic Federalism was calculated to encourage tribalism. Tarka used the funds obtained from Awolowo to set up a thorough organization to propagate the cause of the United Middle Belt Party into the thirty thousand or so compounds in which the million population of Tiv lived. The message of the party propagandists was openly tribal. "Are you Tiv or Uke (descended from Uke, the father of all non-Tiv and especially of Hausa, according to Tiv mythology)?", they would ask. To the reply "We are Tiv," the propagandist would answer: "Then you must vote for our party, not the party of the Hausa, the N.P.C." The name "Damkor" or "Dankaro" was resurrected from past history and used to refer to the whole

N.P.C. party—Dankaro was a Fulani warrior who had made unsuccessful slave raids on Tiv in the nineteenth century. The latent Tiv persecution complex was fanned by the singing of old war songs—"Today if another nation attacks us we shall die, we shall never submit," etc.—while a religious turn was given to the politics by the suggestion that the N.P.C. was a Muslim party and would seek to make Tiv become Muslim and give up eating pork. At the grass roots level, a great hatred was built up for the idea of N.P.C. Sometimes the hostility splayed out to involve Hausas resident in Tiv, while Tiv who supported the N.P.C. were described as "Hausa men". The deliberate evocation of tribal prejudice by the U.M.B.C. party apparatus was in marked contrast to Tarka's own personal freedom from tribal prejudice. At present, for instance, he is not only on the best of terms with very many Northerners but has as one of his closest friends, personal and political, Ibrahim Immam, a person from a completely different background who combines radical politics with a pride in the traditions of Bornu and a deep Arabic scholarship. The very difference of background cements the fellowship in an attraction of opposites. Tarka allowed the tribalism in the party apparatus for two reasons: first, because the party, although well organized, was not well disciplined, and it would have been difficult for him to have prevented this sort of talk; and, second, because in the medium of Tiv politics, in the first introduction of politics to the masses, the medium itself dictated the style. If Tarka wished to build up a following, these were the sentiments to which he had to appeal. An exactly similar line was being followed by the N.P.C. in the rest of the North, except that whereas the hostility of the U.M.B.C. was being directed to the Hausa, that of the N.P.C. was being directed to Southerners. "We had to teach the people to hate Southerners; to look on them as people depriving them of their rights, in order to win them over", Alhaji Ladan Baki, Provincial Commissioner, Zaria, explained it to Dr. Dudley.[1] It is the tragedy of the first introduction of democratic politics to the masses that it forces the elite to reduce themselves to the level of their prejudices. This may well explain why Tarka, like Aminu Kano, does not wish to see the return of the old politics of mass mobilization, in terms of slogans, processions and activity under the old divisive party labels.

In building up the U.M.B.C. Tarka was assisted by the alliance of Ugoor Iwoo, the President of the T.P.U. (Tiv Progressive Union), who was in some financial difficulty at this time and welcomed financial help along with U.M.B.C. alliance. The T.P.U. had been formed some ten years earlier to represent the collective interests of the tribe, especially among the educated and the traders, and to act as a mutual benefit society. It had considerable support and collected a considerable amount of money but was in no sense as well organized as the Ibo State Union, nor did it achieve any useful works of improvement with its funds.

Tarka's own position in the party was rapidly built up. The propagandists used his name frequently, portraying him as the local David fighting for the rights of Tiv against the Goliath of Sokoto, and as "Ozhemen wase" (our leader)—the leader, that is, not of the Tiv people but of the Middle Belt movement. He had the qualities necessary to appeal to an egalitarian people like the Tiv. He received the ordinary farmer in his house with honour. He did not assume the pompous airs of the N.P.C. but treated ordinary people as equals. He had very great charm and a quality in mass appeal which approximates to what political sociologists refer to as charisma. "He has a sweet tongue," some Tiv would say. In a society which admires oratory and gives it its due honour, this is a high compliment. Tarka's appeal to the Tiv was as a courageous person who would fight for their rights and as a prophet of the Middle Belt State which, when created, would bring them "life more abundant," even though some sacrifices would be demanded. Within three years of the launching of the campaign Tarka's name had penetrated to the farthest corners of Tiv, and the majority of the people had been worked up to a great enthusiasm for Tarka and his party. Meanwhile, in 1957, at the Regional level he had become President of the U.M.B.C., being chosen in perference to Abuul, an elderly leader of the Tiv Progressive Union, who did not have Tarka's educational qualifications and command of English.

The authorities at the local level were originally quite favourable to the U.M.B.C. When the Minorities Commission visited Makurdi in 1957, the Tor Tiv refused the invitation of the other chiefs of Benue to join them in testifying against the creation of the Middle Belt State, saying that the chief should be neutral in these matters. But two years later, when regional self-government was obtained without the creation of the state, and when the actual power of the Sardauna and the N.P.C. was apparent in Kaduna, the Tor Tiv was induced to use his coercive authority and that of the Native Authority on behalf of the N.P.C. to coerce the people back from their allegiance to the U.M.B.C./A.G. alliance and to make them join the party in power in the North. Tarka and the Tor Tiv had been on good terms in the past. The Tor Tiv, Gondo Aluor, had been instrumental in helping the choice of Tarka's father as chief of Mbakor. But now they quarrelled with extreme violence.* For six and a half years, from 1959 until their dramatic and public reconciliation at the end of 1965, the Tor Tiv and Tarka remained on the worst of terms. Tarka's supporters abused the Tor Tiv (often, for safety's sake, by analogy, under the pseudonym of "the man Nebuchadnezzar who had an 'upstairs' (a two-storey house)," and the Tor Tiv and his councillors sought to imprison Tarka and his supporters. Within three months of self-government he was framed and imprisoned for six months but released by the D.O. (myself) and the case was reviewed as a "grave miscarriage of justice". Some eight other efforts to imprison Tarka also failed, chiefly through the intervention of the administration, and it was not until 1964 that Tarka was finally convicted and sentenced to four months in prison. The bad relation between Tarka and Tor Tiv at this period was in sharp contrast to that between the other radical leader Aminu Kano and the Emir of Kano. The N.E.P.U., unlike the U.M.B.C., were regarded by the Sardauna as "prodigals," while the U.M.B.C. were hated for being in alliance with Awolowo, who was at this time the number one enemy of the N.P.C. Aminu Kano never underwent this sort of persecution, although his followers did.

In Tiv the persecution of the U.M.B.C. by the N.A. grew more and more intense. Its followers lost their jobs, were removed from their chieftainships, failed to obtain licenses to trade or to brew beer, lost their scholarships and went to prison on flimsy evidence or for "holding illegal meetings." In the last

*There was between them a generation as well as a political gap.

stages the local court came to be known as "Ambe Loko" (the Loko Crocodile).[2] Whether you were guilty or innocent, so long as you were U.M.B.C. it would get you. Party allegiance was often referred to specifically in cases. The U.M.B.C. struck back by abuse of chiefs, by ignoring summonses, and by shouting Tarka's name at all passing cars and lorries. In the Federal Election the utmost efforts of the N.A. on behalf of the N.P.C. failed even to save their deposits, all seven seats in Tiv being won by U.M.B.C./A.G. with over 85% of the votes. Finally, further persecution produced the Tiv riots of 1960 and 1964, which I have described in my chapter in *Nigerian Government and Politics*.[3] It is noteworthy that the pressures of the N.P.C., which proved so successful through most of the North in forcing or persuading the opposition to join the Government party, failed to prevent Tarka from winning his own constituency of Jengbar by the same colossal majority (35,000 to less than 1,500) in 1964 as he had won it in 1959. The Tiv are not a people who quickly change their minds, or take away from a person the trust which they have once given, nor are they the kind of people who can be coerced *en masse*. Those dependent upon government mostly joined the N.P.C., but the masses refused to follow them. Only in the Chongo half of Tiv was the N.P.C. able to appeal to some extent to the sense of loyalty to the Tor Tiv, who came from this side of Tiv, and to hostility to Pusu, Tarka's side. In the 1964 election the N.P.C. won the three seats with a Chongo or partly Chongo electorate, although it is not clear if the counting was fully fair, since the U.M.B.C. counting agents had apparently boycotted the count.

Towards the latter part of the political period Tarka began to find help from Northern administrators and police officers who, although loyal to the north, had radical sympathies and distrusted the ways of the Kaduna establishment. M.D. Yusufu, the Commissioner of Police, and Abdul Karim Lafiene, the Senior District Officer, refused to allow the persecution of the U.M.B.C. and of Tarka to proceed, when they were able to stop it. Tarka was respected by this kind of elite and quickly made close friends among it. After the appointment of the Kumasi Commission into the affairs of Tiv in 1965, his relations with the Northern authorities began to improve. Finally, at the end of 1965, fourteen days before the coup, preliminary work of a land mending kind by intermediaries of N.P.C. and U.M.B.C. resulted in a dramatic reconciliation between Tor Tiv and Tarka. The Tor Tiv, partly on the advice of a Tiv pastor, called a great meeting of his people, apologised to them for taking sides in a political battle, when all were his children, and declared that in future he would treat them all alike. Tarka replied "Aondo ver Tor Tiv" (God bless the Tor Tiv) "we can all now go to your palace because from now on it belongs to us all and not only to one political group". The Tor Tiv was about to be dismissed by the Sardauna for this initiative, when the coup of January 14th occurred and saved him, now restored to his people's respect. The effect of the reconciliation was quite dramatic. After it Tarka went out of his way to heal old quarrels. When he became a Commissioner he deliberately found jobs for old N.P.C. opponents, even those who had assisted in his prosecution, and helped them in other ways. Tarka realizes the wisdom of trying to unite the people in his home political base and of not allowing the sort of bitter and continuing quarrels which still divide the West. If one goes to Tiv today, there is, at least on the surface, hardly a trace of the old animosities which once so divided the people as to cause 2,000 deaths. As long as this sort of political wisdom is practised by the leadership the old animosities will not revive.

The coup of January was initially welcomed in Tiv, for it relieved them of the burden of the government of Sardauna. Tarka respected the person and aims of Nzeogwu, but like other radicals was bitterly antagonised by the one-sidedness and treachery of the killings in Lagos and by the interpretations subsequently put upon the coup by certain Ibo officers and by certain Ibos at the local level. Particularly was he alienated by Ironsi's refusal to create a Middle Belt. He went twice to Lagos to meet Ironsi, and on the second visit was apparently offered some sort of financial grant to set up as a businessman; he refused to be bought out of politics in this way.

Ironsi lost the opportunity of winning Tiv alliance; he declined to release the thousand or so Tiv prisoners still detained from the riots of 1964 and allowed a map to be circulated showing the frontiers of the Eastern Region advanced to the Benue river. When Professor James O'Connell warned him of the dangers of discontent among the Tiv soldiers he changed the subject to the problem of the Tijaniyya in Kano!

Within a few months of the coup, considerable anti-Ironsi sentiment grew up in most parts of Nigeria including Tiv. Tarka and Aminu Kano had both been in alliance with Okpara and the U.P.G.A. and had derived substantial support from Enugu during their persecution in the North. Tarka still considered himself indebted to the Ibo lawyers who defended him in his second treason trial, but in the sharp polarity produced by the killings of January and the coerciveness of military government, it was no longer possible to make alliances over the Regional boundaries. Tarka, Aminu Kano and Maitama Sule of the old N.P.C. met in Kano in April considering that they faced a common threat of tribal domination over Nigeria. After the May riots Ironsi thought of detaining Tarka, on the mistaken information that he was in some way responsible. In fact, the killings of Ibos were confined to the far North. The Tor Tiv and Tarka kept the peace in Gboko and Makurdi.

From June onwards the army faced a situation of lawless confrontation with soldiers from East and North living in perpetual fear of a coup from the opposite faction. Finally the Northerners struck first in a coup, which they considered preemptive. In this coup officers (and men) from Tiv and neighbouring areas played a leading part. Whether Tarka had any previous information of the planning of the coup is not clear, but after the coup the Tiv, who comprised some 20% of the riflemen of the Nigerian army, emerged as a most important element in the political process.

Tarka was called to the "leaders of thought" conference at Kaduna, and there soon found support from his former opponents and persecutors from Middle Belt areas. Both Orodi (Tarka's brother-in-law and a former N.P.C. Minister) and Tanko Yusufu (the former N.P.C. Provincial Commissioner for Benue) supported him in asking for the creation of states in the North. The proposal was accepted by the conference, and Tarka was chosen as one of the three Northern delegates to go to the *Ad Hoc* Constitutional Conference in Lagos, his selection being due to military as well as civilian support.

At the conference a strange volte-face occurred. Ojukwu had apparently telephoned Hassan to ask him to keep the states issue out of the conference. The Northern delegation brought forward a confederal proposal based on the East African Common Services Organization. Tarka's personal views were hostile to this proposal, yet he seems to have subscribed to it initially. The reason is not clear. Very soon a military pressure group of Middle Belt officers and men, led by such formidable figures as the Tiv lieutenant, Ichovol, expressed their dissatisfaction with the Northern position, sponsored the production of a new document and forced the Northern delegation to change its position to one of maintenance of federal power and creation of states. Colonel Mohammed Murtala, who had been the advocate of the breaking away of the North in July, was instructed to tell the Northern delegation that the army would not accept confederalism. The Northern delegation changed its view and submitted another memorandum. The massacres of September/October followed. Tarka was at this time the only figure I met in Lagos who seemed to be really roused to fury by these massacres, and kept asking why the Military Government had not shot some of the soldiers responsible in order to nip the trouble in the bud. In Gboko, Mrs. Tarka sheltered the Ibo staff of the Post Office in her house while the thugs and soldiers went around outside seeking to kill them. As a respected personage in Gboko, and as a courageous woman, she was able to ignore their threats and get the Ibos away home, except for one who went the wrong way, met a soldier and was shot.

After the failure of the constitutional conference, further Northern conferences occurred, and at one of these Tarka, Aminu Kano and the old man Makaman Bida were asked to tour the North together to demonstrate their unity as the representatives of the three political forces previously in conflict—U.M.B.C., N.E.P.U. and N.P.C. Tarka became a very close friend of the Makama, a situation which makes the previous hatred of Tarka by the Kaduna establishment of the N.P.C. seem all the more gratuitous.

It had been the intention of Gowon to bring in political figures to Government at an early date, but the hostility of the Officer corps to this prevented him from doing so. For six months events drifted. It appeared possible that the country would disintegrate by easy stages, with the secession of the East and of the West, and that the creation of states, agreed to in principle, would be nullified by failure to carry out the creation in practice. Several of the old establishment of Kaduna hoped that this would be the case. At this time Tarka's informal contacts with Gowon, with civil servants and important police figures who made Federal policy, were very close. He had, after July, twice braved the dangers of a visit to the East but had been rebuffed, and feared that to go again would expose him to danger from both sides. As Nigeria itself became threatened and as the propaganda of the Eastern Regional Broadcasting Service became more abusive and indiscriminate, suggesting that all Tiv had participated in the killings when the vast majority had hidden Ibos, often at the risk of their lives, Tiv feelings hardened against Ojukwu and sought a military solution, if no other was available.

Tarka and Enahoro emerged as the two leading proponents of the Federal cause, advising Gowon to take a firm line over the defence of the powers of the Federal Government; both were critical of the Aburi document. It is a Tiv characteristic to be blunt and down right. Tarka was in no sense anti-Ibo, but on the issue of the maintenance of the Federation he was not prepared to allow any shuffling. Meanwhile, behind the scenes a bloodless battle was going on about the creation of states. The assistance of Middle Belt officers, Ichovol and others, was sufficient to persuade Kaduna that the creation had to take place and to be made effective by the announcement of the names of the State Governors and the State capitals. At the same time Gowon assumed emergency powers personally and brought in eleven civilian commissioners to join the Executive Council and to head all the ministries except Defence and Internal Affairs. Tarka was offered one of the three most important Ministries—Transport—the Ministry which Abubakar had held before his elevation to the Premiership and which Dipcharima, the senior N.P.C. Minister, had held under the Abubakar Government. As a commissioner, Tarka was for the first time in a position of executive power and proved a good administrator, firm and decisive yet listening to the advice of his officials and resisting tribal pressures. He carried the Tiv egalitarian ethos into easy relations with those in the Ministry and close contacts with as many of its employees as possible. In the Ministry of Transport Headquarters there are at present three Tiv only,

Tarka and two messengers. It is hard to imagine a similar restraint from Commissioners from larger tribes, who are more dependent upon a tribal base.

Tarka, on the other hand, does become involved in state affairs, his advice being sought on appointments in Benue Plateau and neighbouring states. A kind of tacit alliance grows up between soldiers, civil servants and even academics from the same area, and they discuss matters of common concern. Tarka is particularly aware of the dangers of tribal splits within the Benue Plateau State or of divisions between the State Governor and the Commissioner in Lagos from that state. He has, therefore, to resist very strongly the pressure that comes on him from various Tiv to intervene on their behalf in their complaints against their superiors. In state matters he and the Governor have to strive to preserve a situation of balance, while the commissioner, although he exercises a kind of "elder statesman influence" in the background, has to resist the temptation to try to run the State from Lagos.

The political figures under the military regime are in a curious quasi-political role. Tarka regards himself as an appointee of Gowon, for whom he has a personal affection as well as respect, yet insists that the military are a temporary expedient until the country can be returned to fully civilian rule. Tarka, like Aminu Kano, is glad not to be worried with party affairs, since party activity is banned, yet he still regards himself as a "politician" and is not ashamed of the title. A great deal of his time is taken up with alliance building, a most necessary function if Nigeria is to be knit together, after the end of military rule.

Tarka's relations with his old protege, Awolowo, are personally friendly but politically competitive. The ethos of the old Action Group was personalist and leader-orientated. For a time this unfortunate ethos also penetrated into Tarka's own position vis-à-vis his followers, people referring to him (as to Awolowo) as "the leader". This has, however, now disappeared, one hopes, never to return.

Tarka found the leadership claims of Awolowo difficult to accept; as a Nigerian figure he could be no one's lieutenant, and soon after his release Awolowo began to adopt policies with which Tarka was bound to come into conflict. He abandoned the cause of the immediate creation of states, of which he had so long been the proponent, giving the impression that he would be ready to allow the East to secede and take the reluctant minorities with them while the West would likewise secede. Perhaps Awolowo's was only a tactical position, but to his old lieutenants it looked like a betrayal of principle.

The danger of the return of the old ethos of the Ministers, the ostentation, the corruption, the "insufferable arrogance of elected persons" is always present. The Commissioners have been told to regard themselves in a different role; they have submitted lists of assets, and live in a style in contrast with that of the old Ministers. In Lagos, Tarka keeps open house to an endless stream of visitors, who come in and out as they choose and preserve the invaluable friendly and egalitarian ethos of a Tiv household.

In matters ideological Tarka is pragmatic. During his days in opposition he visited the Soviet Union and Ghana, but he regards the jargon of the professional left with some contempt, while he is equally hostile to the far right. In Tiv norms and values, the socialism of "eat and give to your brother," he finds an adequate model to ensure social equality without the need for any violent revolution in economic relationships. As regards the organization of the Nigerian state, he is equally pragmatic. Realizing that effective federal power must be maintained at all costs he is also shrewd enough to realize that there must be a real state sphere in which individual states can work without federal interference, filling certain sensitive jobs in administration and other sectors with their own men and running their own state affairs.

As regards the Ibos, Tarka combines a rooted hostility to the idea of Biafra with a firm desire to bring them back into the Federation as equals, and a feeling that whoever seeks to rule in Nigeria will find it essential to have the support of the Ibo people as of the other important groups. The ties that used to bind Tarka to many important Ibo figures were loosened by the war, but with the return of peace will again be of use in easing the Ibos' return to the Federation.

What Tarka's position in the future civilian government of Nigeria will be is not clear, but whether in the first position or in an ancillary one, as part of a general alliance of pragmatic federal leaders who know the value of the specifically political as well as of the administrative functions, he has a large part to play for he has qualities of true statesmanship.

NOTES

1. B. Dudley, *Parties and Politics in Northern Nigeria,* (London: Frank Cass and Co., 1968), p. 181.

2. From an old myth of a man who turned himself into a crocodile in the Loko River to kill his enemy, and pursued him when he climbed a tree!

3. M. J. Dent, "A Minority Party—the U.M.B.C.," in J. Mackintosh (ed.), *Nigerian Government and Politics* (Evanston: Northwestern University Press, 1966), pp. 461–507.

CHAPTER 17

The Contribution of Tribalism to Nationalism in Western Nigeria

RICHARD L. SKLAR

Tribalism is the red devil of contemporary Africa. It was condemned by nationalists at the first All-African Peoples Conference as "an evil practice" and "a serious obstacle" to "the unity
. . . the political evolution . . . (and) the rapid liberation of
Africa."[1] The case against tribalism rests mainly on the premise that tribal movements thrive on ethnic group loyalties
which undermine wider loyalties to emerging national states.
Moreover, tribal loyalties are supposed to entail implicit attachments to traditional values and institutions which are
thought to be incompatible with the requirements of social
reconstruction.

These assumptions are questioned in this article which is
limited to the discussion of two manifestations of tribalism in
southwestern Nigeria. The first, pantribalism, is a vigorous offspring of modern urbanization and the distinctive expression
of ethnic group activity for the most politically conscious members of a new and rising class. The second, communal partisanship, is endemic to rural areas and old towns where traditional
values are paramount and the socially cohesive ties of tradi-

Reprinted from *Journal of Human Relations,* Vol. 8 (1960), pp. 407–418.
Copyright © by *Journal of Human Relations.* Reprinted by permission of the
publisher and Richard L. Sklar.

tional authority are binding upon the people. Both manifestations of tribalism have given impetus to the growth of mass political parties and the movement for national independence.

It will suffice as background to outline briefly the political setting of Nigeria, a nation of some 35 million people (according to a dated census), and to identify the main tribal groups and the major political parties. Nigeria is a Federation of three political Regions, each of which has a Legislature and an Executive Council headed by a Premier. In every Region a single "nationality" group of culturally related tribes[2] is numerically preponderant: The Yoruba in the Western Region, the Ibo in the Eastern Region and the Hausa in the Northern Region. There are three major political parties: the Action Group, the National Council of Nigeria and the Cameroons (N.C.N.C.), and the Northern Peoples Congress; they control the Governments of the Western, Eastern, and Northern Regions respectively. The Action Group is the official Opposition in the East and in the North; the N.C.N.C. is the official Opposition in the West and operates through an ally in the North; the Northern Peoples Congress is restricted to persons of Northern origin. The Northern Region, however, contains about 54 per cent of the population of Nigeria, and the Northern Peoples Congress emerged from the federal election of December, 1959 with 142 of the 312 seats in the Federal House of Representatives, followed by the N.C.N.C. with 89, the Action Group with 73, and 8 members who are independent of the major parties. Presently the Federal Government consists of an N.P.C.-N.C.N.C. coalition with an N.P.C. Prime Minister, while the Action Group forms the Federal Opposition. Nigeria is destined to achieve independence within the British Commonwealth on October 1, 1960.

Pantribalism

The Yoruba people, or "nationality," of Western Nigeria comprise a number of tribal sections that have a long history of conflict with one another attributable largely to precolonial effects of the slave trade. Pan-Yoruba unity was an ideal fostered by a twentieth century elite of educated men and women who followed entrepreneurial, professional, managerial, and clerical vocations in new urban areas, principally in the commercial centers of Lagos and Ibadan. In 1944 a group of Yoruba students and professional men in London organized a Pan-Yoruba cultural society called *Egbe Omo Oduduwa* (Society of the Descendants of Oduduwa).[3] Four years later the society was inaugurated in Western Nigeria at a conference attended by illustrious Yoruba personalities who claimed to follow the example of pantribal organization set by other tribes and nationalities, in particular the Ibo people of Eastern Nigeria. It is not improbable that the founders of the *Egbe Omo Oduduwa* were motivated by interests that were political as well as cultural. Most of them were politically-oriented men of the new and rising class—lawyers, doctors, businessmen, civil servants, and certain far-sighted chiefs—who perceived that the locus of economic and political power was not local but Regional and national. In 1950, leaders of the *Egbe Omo Oduduwa* were among the principal organizers of a new political party called the Action Group, which came to power in the Western Region as a result of a general election held the following year. It was the chief aim of the founders of the Action Group to overcome the ingrained particularism of the Yoruba tribes and weld them together behind a political party that would serve their common interests. In the rural areas and in traditional towns of Western Nigeria, chiefs are among the most influential leaders of opinion, and the fate of a political party may hinge on the extension of their support. The Action Group applied that principle and reared its mass organization largely upon the foundation of support by traditional authorities. Two powerful inducements attracted various chiefs into the fold of the Action Group: some of the chiefs were nonparochial in outlook and responded to the cultural appeal of Pan-Yoruba unity; others were impressed by the political and economic power of the pantribal elite and embraced the new party with enthusiasm or with resignation to the new facts of political life.

The rise of the Action Group in the city of Lagos attested to the efficacy of collaboration between a traditional authority and the pantribal elite. Lagos, the capital of the Federation, is a Yoruba town that burgeoned into the principal port and main commercial center of Nigeria. Prior to 1954 it was administered under the Western Regional Government. The population of

Lagos may be said to comprise three main ethnic categories: the indigenous Yorubas, the nonindigenous Yoruba settlers, and other settlers who are non-Yoruba. Traditional values weigh heavily upon the indigenous community while the values and social perspectives of the settler groups are primarily nontraditional. For about 25 years prior to 1950, Lagos local politics pivoted on the rivalry between a majority of the Yoruba indigenous community and the main body of Yoruba settlers. When the Action Group was organized in 1950, it derived its following in Lagos mainly from the Yoruba elite, most of whom were settlers. The vast majority of indigenous Yorubas and most of the non-Yoruba settlers favored an older party, the National Council of Nigeria and the Cameroons (N.C.N.C.). Within a few years of the inauguration of its Lagos branch, the Action Group managed to obtain the support of a majority of the Yoruba indigenes, an achievement that was due largely to the efforts of the *Oba* (Paramount Chief) of Lagos. The latter was an enthusiastic proponent of pan-Yoruba unity and he applied his influence among the indigenes effectively in behalf of the Action Group.

Everywhere in the Western Region, leaders of the Action Group solicited the active co-operation of traditional chiefs. Those few chiefs who were hostile to the party or obstructed the implementation of its policies courted jeopardy. A celebrated case of opposition by one paramount chief, the ex-*Alafin* (king) of Oyo, created a general impression throughout the Western Region that no chief could stand against the Government Party and survive. Oyo was once the capital of an extensive Yoruba empire, and the *Alafin* is one of the most exalted of the Yoruba chiefs. However, the ex-*Alafin* was a conservative chief of the old order whose relationship with the Action Group deteriorated rapidly soon after that party came to power. Supporters of the *Alafin,* including nontraditionalists who opposed the Action Group for political reasons, formed an Oyo Peoples Party and decided to affiliate with the N.C.N.C. In September, 1954, there was an outbreak of partisan violence at Oyo in the course of which several people were killed. The Regional Government held the *Alafin* to blame and suspended him from office; eventually he was deposed. In this context the substance of the issue at Oyo is irrelevant. What matters to us is the fact that a powerful chief was suspended by the Government and banished from his domain upon the recommendation of a committee of *Obas* (Paramount Chiefs) at a joint meeting with the leaders of the *Egbe Omo Oduduwa.* The Action Group may have resolved to banish the *Alafin* in any case, but the *Egbe,* technically a pantribal cultural organization, supplied a moral sanction from the most respectable elements in Yoruba-land, including the *Alafin's* traditional peers.

It must be emphasized that the Action Group as a political party, and the *Egbe Omo Oduduwa,* as a cultural organization, are technically distinct organizations. In theory the *Egbe* is nonpartisan and its relationship to the Action Group is wholly unofficial; in practice its service to the Action Group is beyond compare. The two associations are virtually inseparable in certain rural areas where the traditional chiefs bless them both in the name of the cultural and political interests of the people. Frequently, the pantribal organization is employed to settle disputes between Yoruba personalities, in particular among chiefs, that might otherwise embarrass the Action Group. Occasionally, it has been utilized by the pantribal elite, as in the extreme case of the ex-*Alafin* of Oyo, to coerce a recalcitrant chief. In general, the *Egbe Omo Oduduwa* functions as a crucial link between the Action Group, the chiefs, and other men of influence to facilitate the implementation of party policies (including policies affecting the position of chiefs), with a minimum of difficulty or resistance.

Communal Partisanship

Communal partisanship, unlike pantribalism, implies the affirmation of traditional value. Yet the nationalistic parties have relied upon it for mass support in areas of traditional habitation. The Government Party of the Western Region has enlisted communal partisanship by means of a systematic program involving the co-operation of chiefs. However, there are examples of communal partisanship emerging in opposition to the Government Party and persisting in defiance of the communal chief. Two such cases, at Benin and Ibadan, are examined here.

Benin, the capital city of the Edo people, provides an example of conflict between a traditional community and a rising class. The Edo are a minority group in the predominantly Yoruba Western Region. Some years ago, Edo men of wealth and high social status formed a Benin branch of the Reformed *Ogboni* Fraternity,[4] an exclusive society founded at Lagos by rising class Yorubas who were inspired by the example of European freemasonry. At first, membership in the Lodge was restricted to the town elite, i.e., professionals, businessmen, employees of firms, and leading chiefs. Subsequently, the Lodge was transformed by its leadership into a political machine and opened to all administrative and business officials, both high and petty. From 1948 to 1951 the *Ogbonis,* under a dynamic leader, dominated the administration of the Benin Division to the chagrin of its traditional ruler, the *Oba* of Benin, and the distress of the people. *Ogbonis* are reported to have controlled the tax system, the markets, the police, the courts, access to the firms, etc. It is said that the members of the Lodge could violate the law with impunity, and that they enjoyed special privileges in most spheres of political and economic activity. By 1950 *Ogbonism* had become synonymous with oppression. Moreover, the people of Benin identified it with the bugbear of Yoruba domination, and their anxieties mounted in 1951 when the principal *Ogboni* leaders affiliated with the Action Group, a new political party under Yoruba control. Meanwhile, non-*Ogbonis* formed a popular party, known as the *Otu Edo* (Benin Community), dedicated to defend tradition and the sacred institution of *Oba-ship* against the alleged encroachments of usurpers. In 1951 the popular party swept the *Ogbonis* from office in local government elections and defeated them soundly in contests for the Regional Legislature.

However, the vindication of traditional value by the electorate did not restore the political supremacy of the *Oba.* His attempts to control the *Otu Edo* were frustrated by progressive leaders of that party for whom the cause of tradition had been an expedient means to further nationalistic and other political ends. Since the *Ogbonis* were partisan to the Action Group, the leaders of the *Otu Edo* resolved to affiliate with the N.C.N.C. The *Oba* spurned the thought of affiliation with either national party. His primary interest was the creation of a new state in the non-Yoruba provinces of the Western Region where *Edo* influence would be dominant, and he organized an independent party to attain that objective. But it is perilous for any chief to stand against the party in power. In the words of an official report, commenting on the case of the ex-*Alafin* of Oyo, to which we have referred: "The shadow of one great Chief, now desposed and in exile, lies across the foreground of every Chief's outlook today."[5] In 1955 the *Oba* made his peace with the Western Regional Government; the Government endorsed the idea of a non-Yoruba state in principle, and the *Oba,* in turn, agreed to join the Government as a Minister without portfolio. A small minority of the Benin people who supported him against the *Ogboni* menace to his authority now followed him into the Action Group; but the vast majority remained loyal to their communal party, the *Otu Edo.* Their reverence for Benin tradition and the institution of *Oba*-ship (Chieftaincy) persisted, but they condemned the incumbent *Oba* (Paramount Chief) for his switch to the party that was associated in Benin with *Ogbonism* and class interest.

Our second case of communal partisanship, at Ibadan, capital of the Western Region, reflects an underlying conflict between urban settlers and sons of the soil. Ibadan, with a population of nearly 500,000, is the largest African city on the African continent. Urbanization at Ibadan exemplifies the two sector pattern of development that is typical of traditional towns. A vast majority of the people dwell in the teeming indigenous sector; they live in family "compounds" of more than one hundred people in most cases, subject to the traditional authority of a family head. An average Ibadan man divides his time between the town and the rural districts, where he cultivates cocoa on family land. Men of initiative from other towns and villages have settled in the new sectors of Ibadan for commercial and occupational reasons. Among them, the Ijebu people are the most numerous. The Ibadan and the Ijebu are neighboring Yoruba tribes; traditionally they were rivals and in recent years the historic antipathy between them has been revived by economic competition. In 1950 the indigene-settler conflict reached a climax over issues involving land ownership and local representation. The non-Ibadan group formed a Native Settlers Union to press for the rights of settlers both to acquire landed property in Ibadan on a freehold basis and to stand for election to the Ibadan local government. These demands were supported by the pan-Yoruba tribal association.

We have observed that in 1951 the Action Group triumphed in the Western election and became the Regional Government Party. It is pertinent to this discussion of Ibadan politics that the Action Group leader, an Ijebu Yoruba, was the General Secretary of the pan-Yoruba tribal union and a highly successful barrister, resident at Ibadan, where he was a legal adviser to the Native Settlers Union. Six Ibadan indigenes were elected to the Western House of Assembly on the platform of an Ibadan Peoples Party. Following the election, five of them declared for the Action Group and one was appointed as a Minister in the new Western Regional Government. The Ibadan chiefs and people reacted sharply. For several years the trend of events had run against their perceived interests; Ibadan chiefs had been shorn of their traditional prerogatives by a number of administrative reforms; acres of cocoa plants belonging to Ibadan farmers had been destroyed by the Government in a well-intentioned but costly, and unpopular attempt to check the spread of a contagious blight; Ibadan lands were acquired by settlers who supported various objectionable reforms; and a settler personality had suddenly become the leader of the Government. In 1954 the single elected member who did not join the Action Group organized an Ibadan tribal party with the support of the chiefs and the leaders of an Ibadan farmers' movement. The new party, called the *Mabolaje,* which means in Yoruba, "[Do] not reduce the dignity of Chiefs," affiliated with the National Council of Nigeria and the Cameroons. Swiftly the *Mabolaje* established its supremacy in Ibadan; eventually its leader became the First Vice President of the N.C.N.C. and Leader of the Opposition in the Western House of Assembly. Only a small minority of the indigenous rising class embraced the populist *Mabolaje.* The great majority of entrepreneurial, professional, and educated men of Ibadan gravitated to the Government Party. Furthermore, in 1955, an Action Group supporter was elevated to the head chiefship of Ibadan, whereupon most of the chiefs and aspirants to chieftaincy, who require the endorsement of the Head Chief for promotion or recognition by the Government, transferred their support from the party named in their honor to the party in power. As at

Benin, the loss of the citadel of chieftaincy did not weaken the party of traditional value, and the dominance of the *Mabolaje* at Ibadan has been evinced at every election of recent years.

At Benin and Ibadan, communal partisanship emerged as a reaction to the political drives of a rising class. In Benin the new class was wholly indigenous; in Ibadan it was mainly a settler class with an indigenous component. In both cases the outlook of the indigenous rising class was supratribal, which led it to embrace a political party that the people at large identified with interests which they regarded as being inimical to the values of their communal traditions. The tribal parties affiliated with a rival national party, in both cases the National Council of Nigeria and the Cameroons. They are properly termed tribal party affiliates because their respective memberships are confined to the indigenous communal groups of Benin and Ibadan. Nonindigenous supporters are considered to be partisans of the N.C.N.C. at Benin or the N.C.N.C.-*Mabolaje* Grand Alliance at Ibadan, but not of the *Otu Edo* or the *Mabolaje* per se.

The ordinary follower or member of a tribal party in an area of traditional habitation is likely to regard it as an extension of the social order to which he is spiritually, sentimentally, and spontaneously attached. In his mind, and in the minds of others with whom he habitually associates, the party is endowed with the values of the traditional order. Partisanship of this nature is communal in the classical sense.[6] It implies the ideal of an integrated system of values involving the combination or synthesis of political, spiritual, and cultural values into a unified moral universe similar to the symbolic universe of traditional society.[7] Consequently, supporters of a communal membership party are apt to view opposition to that party by a member of the community with moral indignation and to punish it as antisocial conduct. Of course, the concept of communal partisanship does not correspond exactly to the psychology of any particular individual. It does not apply at all to the leadership of the tribal parties of Benin or Ibadan which was drawn primarily from the rising class, mainly from those populist and radically disposed individuals who rallied to the popular cause in principle or in consequence of a perceived advantage. The nature of their partisanship is properly termed associational rather than communal; it implies rational, deliberate affiliation without ritual significance in affirmation of a political belief or in pursuit of a personal goal.[8] Owing to the influence of radical leaders, communal participation parties have assimilated nationalistic principles within their codes of traditional values. A prime example is the *Mabolaje* of Ibadan, which was conservative with respect to administrative reform but radical with respect to political nationalism, i.e., the movement for independence.

Conclusion

In Western Nigeria most rising class elements in every tribal and nationality group are drawn by their interests into the fold of the party in power. By and large, ethnic affinities are outweighed by class interests, as at Ibadan where most of the indigenous rising class joined their social peers among the settlers within the Government Party. Prudent chiefs normally go along, since the Government Party controls the system of appointment and deposition. In 1958 only one member in 51 of the Western House Chiefs (a co-ordinate chamber of the Regional Legislature) was identified as a supporter of the Opposition Party, while 31 elected members out of 80 in the House of Assembly belonged to the Opposition.[9] Furthermore, Nigerian chiefs in general are associated with the economic as well as the political interests of the rising class, and the number of chiefs in business is legion. Progressive chiefs and other culturally conscious members of the enlightened minority required an ideological nexus of their ethnic and class values that would supply a rationale for their nontraditional and supratribal interests. That need was admirably satisfied by the theory of pantribalism.

Within its defined cultural sphere, pantribalism is cosmopolitan and consistent with the affirmation of nontraditional interests or the negation of traditional interests that obstruct the policies of the pantribal elite. Pantribalism like Jewish Zionism, is innately secular, and produces a sense of "national" identity among peoples who are ethnically or tribally diverse but culturally related. The pantribal spirit was ardent in the breasts of those who felt the most urgent need for unity beyond the parochial confines of their tribes. These were typically men of the rising class to whom the conditions of colonial rule were least tolerable. When their perspectives rise above the stage of ethnic "nationality," pantribalism may be expected to lose its class distinction and the magic of its political appeal.

Communal partisanship is a social and psychological form of party-type tribal movement in areas of traditional habitation where the integral values of traditional society have not been transformed by the process of social change. In many cases local parties based on communal partisanship have been brought into existence deliberately by nationalists and rising class elements with the co-operation of chiefs. Occasionally, as at Benin and Ibadan, the emergence of communal partisanship has reflected the repudiation of a rising class by the people of a traditional community in transition where class structure is incipient and a lower class psychology has not evolved. Most chiefs have a leading foot in the rising class, especially if it supports a governing party, and they are likely to disavow communal parties that are associated with the Opposition. At Benin and Ibadan, the nature of conflict was class versus community, rather than modern elements versus traditional elements or higher class against lower class.[10] However, rising classes herald the decline of old orders, and the transformation of classless communities into class societies is perceptible in the tendency of communal partisans to shed their traditional values and to adopt lower class perspectives.[11]

Throughout Nigeria, millions of tradition-bound people were drawn through the medium of communal partisanship into the mainstream of political activity where they accepted the leadership of progressive nationalists. Therein lies its historic significance. No nationalist movement or political party could have achieved independence for Nigeria without the massive support of the people, especially the rural masses and those millions who live in traditional urban communities. The British Government would not, in principle, have agreed to transfer power to a leadership group that was not broadly based. On the other hand, Britain could not, in principle or in fact, deny independence to popularly elected leaders who enjoy the confidence of a decisive majority of the people and insisted upon the termination of colonial rule. Communal partisanship, based on psychological commitments to the traditional values of tribal groups, was utilized by nationalist leaders to mobilize mass support in rural areas and old towns.

These observations will not restore tribalism to grace in Africa. But the devil deserves his due; and in Nigeria, at least, the contribution of tribalism to nationalism has been crucial.

NOTES

1. These strictures were applied to religious separatism as well as to tribalism. See the Resolution on Tribalism, Religious Separatism, and Traditional Institutions, adopted by the All-African Peoples Conference held at Accra, Ghana, December 5–13, 1958.

2. James S. Coleman has defined the concepts of "tribe" and "nationality" as follows: A tribe is "a relatively small group of people who share a common culture and who are descended from a common ancestor. The tribe is the largest social group defined primarily in terms of kinship, and is normally an aggregation of clans." "A nationality is the largest traditional African group above a tribe which can be distinguished from other groups by one or more objective criteria (normally language)." *Nigeria: Background in Nationalism* (Berkeley and Los Angeles: University of California Press, 1958), pp. 423–24.

3. *Oduduwa* is a culture hero and mythical progenitor of the Yoruba people. The principal founder of the society, who later became Premier of the Western Region and is now Leader of the Opposition in the Federal Government, expounded a theory of nationalism based on pantribal integration under the auspices of educated elites. See Obafemi Awolowo, *Path to Nigerian Freedom,* (London: Faber & Faber, Ltd., 1947).

4. The traditional *Ogboni* was a politico-religious institution in certain historic Yoruba states. See W. R. Bascom, "The Sociological Role of the Yoruba Cult Group," *American Anthropologist,* 56, No. 1, Part 2, Memoir 63. (January, 1944), pp. 64–73; and Saburi O. Biobaku, *The Egba and Their Neighbors,* 1842–1872, (Oxford: Clarendon Press, 1957), p. 6.

5. Colonial Office, *Report of the Commission appointed to enquire into the fears of Minorities and the means of allaying them.* (London: H.M.S.O., 1958), p. 11.

6. Ferdinand Tonnies, *Fundamental Concepts of Sociology (Gemein-schaft and Gesellschaft)*, translated and supplemented by Charles P. Loomis (New York: American Book Company, 1940), pp. 37–39; 67–70.

7. Cf. M. Fortes and E. E. Evans-Pritchard, *African Political Systems* (London: Oxford University Press, 1940), pp. 16–18. S. F. Nadel drew attention to the cohesive value systems of subtribal groups that we find operative in the case of tribal parties. *A Black Byzantium* (London: Oxford University Press, 1942), pp. 22–26.

8. Maurice Duverger utilized the concepts of Community and Association to distinguish between ideal types of participation. He observed "... the nature of participation can be very different according to the categories of members: especially does it seem probable that electors and members are not joined to the party by links of the same nature and that it is the Community type party that is predominant among electors, even in parties where members and militants belong rather to the Association type." *Political Parties* (London: Methuen & Co., 1954), pp. 128–29. Duverger's analysis of participation goes beyond the purpose of this paper to general theory of party classification.

9. Most chiefs are supporters and patrons of the Government Party rather than members in the technical sense. The fiction of their non-partisanship in theory is still respected on occasion by party leaders and chiefs alike.

10. Needless to say, party division never corresponds exactly to sociological differentiation, but it is significant if most of the rising class and most chiefs affiliate with a particular party in areas where popular sentiment is to the contrary. In this paper competition between rising class and communal membership parties is not regarded as a manifestation of class conflict inasmuch as the tribal societies involved are not structured in terms of class. Anthropological studies of them generally describe communal societies of a corporate nature, segmented vertically by lineages and stratified by age grades and title associations. Chieftaincies may be vested in particular families; but the families of kings, chiefs, elders and titled men have not been differentiated in terms of social class.

11. This kind of change in perspective is evident at Ibadan and elsewhere, as at Enugu in the Eastern Region, where many of the communal partisans are employed as industrial laborers. In the Emirate states of Northern Nigeria, class structures are traditional and the

class factor is fundamental to the analysis of competiton between parties in that section. Rising classes in Northern Nigeria emerge within an existing class structure which they alter; rising classes in the part of Nigeria with which this paper is concerned emerge from classless communities which they transform into class societies. Since the new classes do not rise relative to other classes it might be preferable to term them emerging or emergent classes.

Part III

COMMUNAL TRANSFORMATION AND COMPARTMENTALIZATION

Communal Transformation and Compartmentalization

Editorial Introduction

It has been noted that social mobilization creates conditions for the emergence of entirely new communal formations (Proposition 9, Chapter 1). In his study of Ibo politics in Port Harcourt, Howard Wolpe found that immigrants to the city related to each other politically on the basis of communities which were not traditional (pre-colonial), but instead were formed during the colonial period. These "geo-ethnicities," which divided the Ibo-speaking population into "Onitsha" and "Owerri" Ibos, had been formed by administrative fiat in the 1920's. Nevertheless, it was around these new identities that most political competition in Port Harcourt revolved. Like the identities of nationality which emerged in the course of the colonial occupation, the geo-ethnic formations were products of communal fusion and expansion.

A second aspect of the relationship between social mobilization and communalism pertains to the internal differentiation of communal groups along socio-economic and ideological lines (Proposition 10). Here the papers by Sklar, Whitaker and Melson are particularly relevant.

In his essay on "Contradictions in the Nigerian Political System," Sklar describes the class and ideological cleavages which developed within the communally-based nationalist parties of southern Nigeria both during and following the struggle for independence. He suggests that regionalism was the natural ideological posture of Nigeria's "political class," while anti-regionalism was the logical position of those out of power. This important class-ideological cleavage is illustrated by the internal struggle within the Yoruba-dominated Action Group between Awolowo's "federal faction" and Akintola's "regional faction." Whereas the struggle for control of the Federal government, to which Awolowo was primarily committed, dictated an anti-regional strategy, those who were in power at the regional level in Western Nigeria preferred a strategy of "regional security."

Sklar's analysis indicates clearly that the process of inter-communal conflict need not entail complete intra-communal solidarity. In this regard, his paper converges with the earlier papers of Magid on the Idoma (Chapter 12), and Dent on the Tiv (Chapter 15), and with the papers in this section by Whitaker on the Hausa-Fulani (Chapter 19), and by Cohen on the Kanuri (Chapter 20). These writers point to a recurrent pattern: the socio-economic, ideological and generational differentiation of communal groups in the process of communal conflict. This theme is especially pronounced in the essay by Whitaker on "Three Perspectives on Hierarchy," which argues that the divergent ideological positions of three of Northern Nigeria's most eminent political figures were congruent with the respective positions each occupied in the hierarchical structure of Hausa-Fulani society. The point is not simply that the Northern traditional system is highly complicated and contains a variety of social divisions and perspectives, but rather that the inherent tensions of the traditional order *in conjunction with* external cultural contact yield new divisions and conflicts. Consequently, men of differing traditional backgrounds— though they be of the same general cultural milieu—may well respond differently to the opportunities and values accompanying Western contact. The tragedy of Nigeria lay in the failure of this process of internal differentiation of communal groups to work its way in such a manner as to allow for cross-cutting alliances across communal boundaries. Indeed, the failure of the UPGA coalition (the last such cross-cutting alliance) to win the Federal election of 1964 tolled the end of the precarious communal equilibrium that characterized the Nigerian federation.

The paper by Ronald Cohen on "Bornu and Nigeria" focuses on the third major dimension of communal transformation, that of deparochialization (Proposition 11). The ancient kingdom of Bornu (which dates back to the 10th century A.D.) was allowed considerable autonomy during the colonial period—thereby perpetuating the Kanuri sense of independence vis-à-vis their neighbors. This meant that during the nationalist and post-independence phases of Nigerian development, the rate of communal transformation was slower than that of the rapidly mobilizing southern peoples. However, after the events leading up to and following upon the Nigerian/Biafran civil war, the degree of interdependence between Bornu and the rest of Nigeria greatly increased. This has, in turn, led to a bureaucratization and diminution in the power of traditional authorities—or, in the language of our theoretical formulation, to "deparochialization." The case of Bornu as contrasted, for example, to that of Port Harcourt suggests that the rate of communal transformation is related to the rate of intensity of interaction among communal groups.

The last two papers in this section relate to the process of communal compartmentalization (Propositions 13, 14). In his study of the "cross-pressured" Nigerian worker, Robert Melson illustrates the extent to which Nigerian trade unionists "compartmentalized" their communal and class identities—with the consequence that when labor leaders tried to translate a trade union movement based on class-interest into support for an electorally-oriented political party they failed to carry the rank-and-file of the trade unionists with them. Melson's observations, together with those made by Wolpe in connection with the labor movement in Port Harcourt, suggest that there is no necessary developmental trend leading to a politics of class displacing a politics of communalism. These papers suggest that individuals and groups are capable of maintaining both communal and class loyalties, and that these loyalties become politically significant in different kinds of situations. This is what leads Wolpe to suggest that communal loyalties are "situationally specific" and cannot simply be derived from the history or psychology of individuals and groups. This view is supported by Leonard Plotnicov's analysis of the biographies of several Jos respondents. Plotnicov suggests that an aspect of the socialization or acculturation experience of persons living within both tradition and modernity, community and class, is the learning of multiple frames of reference which are each applicable to different situations:

> Complex as the Jos plurality might be, the participating actors knew the boundaries which defined appropriate institutional behavior. These boundaries contained different social and cultural fields, but the individuals, in most cases, knew that the different situations were to be understood by different frames of reference.

CHAPTER 18

Port Harcourt: Ibo Politics in Microcosm[1]

HOWARD WOLPE

To the political scientist concerned with the relationship between social and economic modernisation, on the one hand, and
political change and integration, on the other, the Ibo experience has long held particular interest. In his pioneering study
of Nigerian nationalism, James Coleman observed that Ibos
had played a singular role in the post-war political era: "Ibos
overwhelmingly predominated in both the leadership and the
mass membership of the N.C.N.C., the Zikist Movement, and
the National Church. Postwar radical and militant nationalism, which emphasized the national unity of Nigeria as a transcendent imperative, was largely, but not exclusively, an Ibo
endeavor."[2] But radical and militant pan-Nigerian nationalism
was only one part of the Ibo political posture. No less noteworthy was the parallel development of a highly cohesive and
organisationally sophisticated pan-Ibo movement, the very
success of which ultimately undermined the pan-Nigerian aspirations of the Ibo-led N.C.N.C. and, subsequently, was one of
several factors operating to impair the national legitimacy of

Reprinted from *The Journal of Modern African Studies,* 7, 3 (1969), pp.
469–93. Copyright © 1969 by *The Journal of Modern African Studies.* Reprinted
by permission of the publisher. The notes are presented in slightly revised
form.

an Ibo-led military regime. It is this paradoxical blending of "civic" and "primordial" sentiments which, perhaps, best defines the modern Ibo political experience.[3]

The aim of this article is to explore the bases of Ibo organisational adaptability and internal political cohesiveness through an analysis of the changing patterns of power within the predominantly Ibo-speaking urban metropolis of Port Harcourt. This analysis has relevance not only for our understanding of Ibo political dynamics, but also for our understanding of the relationship between communalism ("tribalism") and modernisation. More specifically, this study calls into question the widely held view that, as economic development accelerates, the creation of new, functionally specific, social identities will eventually undermine the organisational bases upon which a politics of communalism rests.

Port Harcourt is an especially appropriate arena for the study of integrative processes in general, and Ibo political behaviour in particular. First, Port Harcourt is in many respects the prototype of the non-traditional, communally heterogeneous African cities which emerged as a result of the western impact upon African society. Established in 1913 as a sea outlet for newly discovered coal deposits to the north, Port Harcourt was organised and administered according to European models and by European personnel, and was populated primarily by culturally diverse rural immigrants.[4] And, like so many new cities, Port Harcourt's industrial and commercial expansion—by 1965 the municipality had become the site of Nigeria's second largest harbour, the centre of the country's petroleum industry, and the nation's second largest industrial centre—has not been able to match an extraordinary rate of immigrant-based population growth. Between 1953 and 1963 alone, the urban population expanded by nearly 2½ times (see Table 1), and an estimated 11 per cent of Port Harcourt's 180,000 residents were unemployed in 1963.[5]

A second factor which lends particular interest to the Port Harcourt experience is that in the early 1960's Port Harcourt mirrored more accurately than any other urban community the ethnic and religious make-up of the wider, regional society from which most of the city's immigrants were drawn. Port Harcourt, like Eastern Nigeria, was composed of a large Ibo-

TABLE 1[6]

PORT HARCOURT POPULATION GROWTH

	Port Harcourt proper[7]	Mile 2 Diobu[8]	Municipal totals
1921	7,185	—	—
1931	27,000	—	—
1953	59,512	12,788	73,300
1963	95,768	83,795	179,563

speaking majority, with the Ijaws, Ibibios, and Efiks constituting the principal linguistic minorities.[9] Moreover, all the various sub-cultural Ibo groups around which most Eastern political competition revolved were well represented. Likewise, both the Protestant and the Catholic religious camps, which constantly warred on the regional level, were present in significant numbers in the Delta city. Thus, in both culture and religion, Port Harcourt offered a microcosm of the regional system in which the municipality was embedded.

Thirdly, Port Harcourt has had a role of special significance in the movement towards pan-Ibo social and political integration. The city's importance for Ibo-speaking elements elsewhere derives from the community's distinctive social and economic characteristics. On the one hand, Port Harcourt is the only important Ibo-speaking urban centre situated on land identified with neither of the major Onitsha and Owerri Ibo blocs. The indigenous owners of Port Harcourt land, the Diobu-Ikwerres, are part of an Ibo-speaking clan possessing cultural and historical ties with Ijaw-speaking communities to the south. Though the Ikwerres are in fact more culturally related to the Owerri Ibos, they have tended to deny any significant community of interest with their northern neighbours, who formerly served as their casual labourers. Port Harcourt, consequently, has long been considered 'neutral ground' by most Ibos and, as such, an appropriate site for the headquarters of the pan-Ibo movement. As a result, Port Harcourt in 1948 replaced Lagos as the administrative headquarters of the premier Ibo organisation, the Ibo State Union.

On the other hand, Port Harcourt's importance as a commercial, industrial, and administrative centre yielded an extremely high concentration of Ibo wealth and entrepreneurial and professional skills. Consequently, Port Harcourt residents, who lived in much closer proximity to their communities of origin than their equally advantaged Lagos-based kinsmen, exercised exceptional influence in the rural hinterland. For this reason, Eastern Nigerian leaders attributed extreme political importance to Port Harcourt affairs. As a leading N.C.N.C. official pointedly observed in 1964, 'Port Harcourt has very little direct influence on decisions which are made in Enugu, but elections and politics in Port Harcourt are important because they can affect outlying areas.' It should be added that Enugu's attentiveness to Port Harcourt developments stemmed also from the N.C.N.C.'s long-term financial dependence upon the township's African (and, more recently, European) business establishment.

Finally, Port Harcourt politics are immediately relevant to the present crisis, inasmuch as the city has long figured prominently in both the intra-regional and the interregional forms of political competition which have characterised Nigeria's postwar era. Ijaw and Ibibio-Efik separate state proposals are invariably inclusive of Port Harcourt, and the city's Ibo majority and non-Ibo minority elements have been centrally involved in these separatist debates. At the national level, Port Harcourt's considerable economic potential, represented as much by the city's harbour and industrial facilities as by the adjacent oilfields and petroleum refinery, has made control of the city a crucial objective—perhaps *the* crucial objective—of the federal forces.

This, then, is the setting of our study: between 1963 and 1965, a rapidly growing, crowded, culturally heterogeneous community of 'strangers', mostly Ibo rural immigrants who had been drawn to the city by the prospects of trade or by the hopes of wage employment, and who confronted the same kind of social, economic, and political complexities as face new urban dwellers throughout the developing world. But similar complexities do not always yield similar responses. It is true that urban life carries with it certain kinds of organisational imperatives which inevitably transform traditional patterns of behaviour. But, at least in the Nigerian context, the urban immigrant's response to the new urban environment, and to other persons within this cosmopolitan setting, can be understood only in terms of his rural origins and his continuing associations with rural life. Consequently, the rural heritage of the township's population is the starting point of our analysis of Port Harcourt political life. Following a brief sketch of this rural heritage, we attempt to trace the changing patterns of power within the city from 1913 to 1965, and to identify the major social bases of political cleavage within the community. The last two sections of the article consider the relationship between communalism and social change and assess the theoretical significance of the Ibo experience.

THE REGIONAL BACKDROP

Three elements of the rural heritage of Port Harcourt's citizens are crucial to an understanding of contemporary political life: (1) the pre-colonial inter-group relationships, (2) the traditional Ibo political institutions, and (3) the western impact upon these relationships and institutions.

Pre-colonial relationships

It is true that, as Kenneth Dike has observed, 'beneath the apparent fragmentation of authority [in pre-colonial Eastern Nigeria] lay deep fundamental unities not only in the religious and cultural spheres, but also . . . in matters of politics and economics.'[10] But the dominant political characteristic of the Eastern Nigerian traditional order was the fragmentation of the countryside. Before 1900 each of the Region's major nationalities was divided into small independent political units.[11] The most conservative ethnographic estimates place the number of autonomous Ibo-speaking communities at over 200. The Ijaws, Efiks, and Ibibios were similarly divided, though the structure of the local political unit varied across nationalities and even between different cultural sections of the same nationality. The important point is that an Ijaw man identified with his 'house' in much the same way as an Ibo-speaker identified with his village-group and an Ibibio-speaker with his village. Seldom did ongoing political organisations extend beyond the level of the local community, and in no instance was there an awareness of 'nationality'. 'Ibo-ness' and 'Ijaw-ness' were as yet unknown qualities. As Simon Ottenberg has observed with respect to the Ibos:

> No political superstructure, such as a federation, a confederacy, or a state existed. The Ibo units remained a relatively balanced grouping of independent political structures which never developed into a large formal organization, though some units absorbed or conquered others, some died out, some fragmented, and some changed their characteristics through immigration and emigration.[12]

The Ibo political system

The traditional Ibo political system can perhaps be best described in terms of the structural principle of segmentation. Each level of the Ibo social structure constituted an implicitly unstable federation of segments: village-groups (the largest traditional political units) were divided into villages, villages into extended families, extended families into still smaller segments. As in the case of the segmentary Nuer society of the Southern Sudan, the 'affect' associated with each segment was inversely related to its size.[13] The feeling of unity in a village tended to be stronger than that within a village-group; the social cohesion of a village-group, similarly, was stronger than that of allied or ancestrally related village groups. At each level, 'government' consisted of the collective rule of representatives of each segment, and not in the imposition of a central authority standing above the federated units.

Every individual, it should be noted, was at one and the same time a member of several segments and, consequently, shared several socio-political identities. The relative salience of these different identities (or, in the vernacular of role theory, reference groups) was variable, a function of the individual's perception of the always changing social situation. In this respect, too, Ibo society closely resembled Nuer society:

> a man counts as a member of a political group in one situation and not as a member of it in a different situation, e.g., he is a member of a tribe in relation to other tribes and he is not a member of it in so far as his segment of the tribe

is opposed to other segments. In studying the Nuer political constitution, it is therefore essential that we view it together with those of their enemies as a single political system, for the outstanding structural characteristic of Nuer political groups is their relativity . . .

. . . fission and fusion are two aspects of the same segmentary principle and the Nuer tribe and its divisions are to be understood as a relation between two contradictory yet complementary tendencies . . . the tendency towards segmentation seems to be inherent in political structure itself.[14]

In short, the stability of the Ibo political system lay in 'ad hoc, ever-shifting alignments at different levels of the society rather than in hierarchical, continuously functioning structures and institutions.'[15]

Effective internal power rested with the community's 'natural leaders', who had attained their positions through their personal qualities of leadership and their financial prominence. As G. I. Jones has noted, the Ibo leader functioned in a manner not unlike that of the American political boss: 'Ibo leaders were not war leaders, but rather first class negotiators, judges and party organizers.'[16] Rule by fiat played no part in the Ibo system of government by consensus. Ultimately, all decisions had to be approved by a meeting of the entire adult male community. As in the urban communities of Boston, New Haven, and New York, political survival in an Ibo community hinged, fundamentally, on the leader's ability to mould and to maintain a cohesive personal following by using the political system to the advantage of his constituents. In the Ibo context, as in the American, the politician acted as a broker of conflicting interests and personalities and as a provider of personal favours. His political success, in short, was a function both of his ability to resolve disputes and of his generosity.

The western impact

While a detailed analysis of the western impact lies beyond the scope of this article, it is necessary to consider, briefly, the changing patterns of social and political cleavage induced by western contact. In particular, two points require emphasis.

First, variations in the timing, intensity, and character of the western impact heightened the previously latent socio-political cleavage between the landlocked Ibo interior, on the one hand, and the marginal Ibo riverain groups and non-Ibo coastal communities, on the other. This differentiation occurred because those communities which were so situated as to control access to the interior, or which were at the centre of the developing trade routes, were in a better position to take advantage of the new commercial and educational opportunities brought by the European traders and missionaries. Not infrequently, the new commercial prosperity of the riverain and coastal communities was directly attributable to the exploitation of the more isolated hinterland.

Within Iboland, it was Aro Chuku and Onitsha Town which assumed positions of commercial—and hence political—pre-eminence with respect to their Ibo-speaking neighbours. The Aros were a distinctively aggressive and shrewd people, who were feared and respected throughout Iboland as agents of their oracle. The awe and esteem in which the 'Long Juju' was held enabled Aros who were identified with the oracle to travel along a number of trade routes freely and without fear of attack. This freedom of movement, in turn, enabled the Aros to dominate many of Iboland's major markets and, more especially, to control the profitable interior trade in slaves.[17]

The commercial significance of Onitsha Town, by contrast, stemmed from its location on the trade routes linking the Northern, Central, and Southern Ibos with the Niger and, by extension, with Northern and Western Nigeria. As G. I. Jones has commented, 'Onitsha was in the right geographical position to become the focus for the political, economic, and cultural development of the Ibo'.[18] By the end of World War I, Onitsha Town was established as the headquarters for one of Iboland's two main provinces, and had become a major educational centre. Culturally distinct from the main body of Ibos, the Onitsha townspeople and those from adjacent and related communities are considered by many non-Onitsha people to be marginally Ibo, despite the fact that the symbols of modern-day Ibo unity, Dr Nnamdi Azikiwe and Colonel Ojukwu, are from

Onitsha Town. Nevertheless, the Onitshans have long occupied prominent positions within the Region's economic, social, and political life. Largely as a consequence of their educational and commercial pre-eminence, the most fundamental communal cleavage within Iboland, as within the city of Port Harcourt, is between those of 'Onitsha' (variously defined, depending upon the social context, as Onitsha Town, Onitsha Division, or Onitsha Province) and those of non-Onitsha or 'Owerri' (also variously defined as Owerri Town, Owerri Division, or Owerri Province).

Outside Iboland, it was the Ijaw- and Ibibio-speaking peoples on the coast who prospered as a result of their control of the riverain ports. Ibo slaves, predominantly of Owerri provincial origin, were carried by the Aro traders to the coast, where they were placed in the custody of the Ijaws, Ibibios, and Efiks who handled the final transactions with European merchants. These middlemen thus acquired a substantial interest in the maintenance of the slave trade and, as Coleman has pointed out, 'were as much aggrieved by its cessation and their consequent displacement as were the white slave dealers. The first Nigerian middle class was liquidated by the abolition of the external slave trade.'[19] With westernisation and the introduction of the franchise, the historical tables were suddenly turned: the formerly disadvantaged but always numerically superior Ibos emerged as Eastern Nigeria's dominant group. Significantly, 'It was among the Ibos, formerly despised by the people of Calabar as a source of slaves and as a backward people of the interior, now feared and disliked as energetic and well-educated, that the first political party was formed.'[20]

The second aspect of the western impact requiring mention is the stimulus given by western contact to the creation of new social, economic, and religious bases of political alignment. In some instances, as in the emergence of new occupational and 'class' identities and in the adoption of Christian sectarian labels (e.g. Catholic and Anglican), the new bases of alignment cut across existing communal partitions. In other instances, however, the new bases of alignment perpetuated communal modes of organisation. Sectarian religious boundaries, for example, generally coincided with communal frontiers. Similarly, new administrative boundaries, rather than undermining the organisational bases of the communal order, had the effect of providing a foundation for broader-based and more politically effective communal units. The new administrative units of Native Court Area, Division, and Province, for example, incorporated traditionally autonomous communities within a common structural framework and, in the process, generated new political interests and identities which were related to, but transcended, the village and village-group boundaries of the traditional system.

It should be stressed that the new administrative units were essentially artificial entities representing additions to, rather than substitutions for, traditional social units. New and wider concentric circles of authority were simply superimposed upon the traditional circles of village and village-group. Moreover, though the British administrative partitions were often arbitrarily placed, at the widest, 'provincial' level, the boundaries did correspond with the Region's major linguistic divisions, thus making Eastern Nigeria's five provinces politically critical rallying points for the cultural-linguistic political movements of a later era. In 1959, these five provinces—Ogoja (linguistically mixed), Calabar (Efik-speaking), Rivers (Ijaw-speaking primarily), Owerri, and Onitsha (both Ibo-speaking) —were divided into 12 smaller and more culturally homogeneous provincial units. Nevertheless, Port Harcourt's Eastern Nigerian inhabitants still identified themselves (in 1963–5), socially and politically, by reference to the older provincial and divisional boundaries. Even the especially artificial partition between Ibo-speaking Owerri and Onitsha provinces had retained its political significance.

PORT HARCOURT COMMUNITY POWER

Having sketched the 'regional backdrop', we are now in a position to examine the processes of change and conflict in Port Harcourt. This analysis falls into two parts. The first traces the changing patterns of power within the town from 1913 to 1965, focusing primarily upon the social characteristics of Port Harcourt's political leaders, while the second explores the major social bases of political cleavage within the community.

Community power: the historical view

Over the 50-year span of the municipality's history, Port Harcourt has passed through four distinct historical periods, each characterised by a structurally distinctive political system and the political ascendancy of a different segment of the growing immigrant population. This historical pattern is strikingly similar to that of the immigrant community of New Haven, as described by Robert Dahl,[21] and a comparison with the New Haven experience illuminates the dynamics of political change in Port Harcourt. In both cases, the changing social characteristics of public officials—with leadership passing, to use Dahl's terminology, from the 'patricians' to the 'entrepreneurs' and thence to the 'ex-plebes'—reflected profound alterations in the structures and criteria of political recruitment. In Port Harcourt, the sequence of immigrant-group ascendancy corresponded roughly to the sequence in which the rural home communities of the urban immigrants were exposed to the western educational and acculturative impact.

During Port Harcourt's first historical period (1913–20), the available political resources were monopolised by the local European minority. Port Harcourt from its earliest days was, in many respects, as much a European as an African town. Ultimate power resided in the hands of the British 'Local Authority', and his Township Advisory Board was comprised entirely of European officials and representatives of European mercantile firms. Like New Haven's patricians, the members of Port Harcourt's first colonial élite 'had all the political resources they needed: wealth, social position, education, and a monopoly of public office; everything, in fact, except numbers—and popularity with the rank and file'.[22] And, as in New Haven, what these men lacked in popularity was more than compensated by the sense of legitimacy with which their claim to govern was endowed, not only by themselves but by their African subjects.

Port Harcourt's second period (1920–43) was really an extension of the first, 'patrician' phase. Important changes occurred within the African community as the related processes of social differentiation and political integration gathered momentum, but the effective political resources remained concentrated in the local European 'establishment'. It is this which explains the political ascendancy *within* the African community of a non-Ibo patrician élite—that element of the African population which was most closely identified with, and had access to, local colonial officialdom. Thus, of the 12 Africans who served on the Advisory Board between 1926 (the date of the first African appointment) and the Board's demise in 1949, only four were Ibo. Of the eight non-Ibo members, only three were of Eastern Nigerian origin (Ijaws); the remainder included two Yorubas, two Sierra Leoneans, and one Gambian. No Ibo was appointed to the Board until 1937, almost 20 years after the Board's inception and 11 years after the appointment of the first African members. Non-Ibo dominance manifested itself also in the origins and control of the local press,[23] and in the leadership of the African Community League, a federation of urban improvement unions which led the struggle for local self-government.[24]

The members of this ascendant group—the non-Ibo patricians—controlled within the African community what were the vital political resources of the era: education, occupational position, social status, and, because of their possession of these, access to the world of the Europeans. Of the four League presidents between 1935 and 1951, for example, one was a retired supervisor of customs and a well-to-do building contractor; two were Methodist pastors, one of whom had established a secondary school and the community's first newspaper; and one was Port Harcourt's first African private medical practitioner, a man who had spent many years overseas studying and then practising medicine.

In addition to their control of crucial political resources, the ethnic minority status of Port Harcourt's non-Ibos placed them in an advantageous position to lead the movement towards local self-government, a movement which in the colonial context placed a premium upon racial unity. On the one hand, non-Ibos were neutral vis-à-vis the principal Ibo factions, factions which were defined primarily in terms of the administrative boundaries of the rural hinterland. On the other, they did not pose the same political threat to non-Ibo groups that might have been the result of Ibo majority leadership. In this respect, the ethnic identity of Port Harcourt's 'patricians' was inseparable from their other social characteristics, and their political position derived, in large measure, from the very ethnicity of the urban political milieu. Communal identities comprised the most convenient mode of social and political categorisation in the new urban community, and the primary points of social and political reference for the newly urban citizens. From this perspective, Port Harcourt politics were from the outset "ethnic" politics; and Port Harcourt's non-Ibo patricians, no less than their Onitsha Ibo and Owerri Ibo successors, were 'ethnic' political actors.

These years, 1920 to 1943, were a period of political coalescence for Port Harcourt's African population. By far the most critical political cleavage in the town was that which divided the European governors from the African governed. The token representation of Africans on the Township Advisory Board did not alter the essential fact of a European monopoly of governmental power. Both the white and the black worlds were divided internally: a division within the European population between official, mercantile, and mission elements was paralleled in the African community by the broad social cleavage between the Diobu indigenes and the predominantly Ibo-speaking strangers, and by cultural and occupational divisions. But as against the racial partition imposed by the colonial system these internal sub-divisions paled into insignificance. Indeed, it was the salience of the racial distinction which provided the catalyst for the movement towards African political unity and, indirectly, for the political ascendancy of the non-Ibo patricians.

But the confrontation between Port Harcourt's black population and the town's white officials was still muted. Through the early 1940's the African community was turned in upon itself, its attention concentrated upon the tasks of internal integration and organisation. Port Harcourt was a new township possessed of young and transient urban immigrants. Most carried with them to the city a tradition of popular participation in the affairs of the community, and the urban improvement unions which proliferated during these years served as an invaluable training ground in the skills and norms of western-style democratic participation. But time was still required to develop the organisational sophistication and political self-confidence necessary for a direct confrontation with the colonial system.

That confrontation was initiated as Port Harcourt entered its third political phase (1944–54). In this third period, the nationalist challenge to the legitimacy of the colonial system, the devolution of local governmental power to the African community, the introduction of the franchise in 1949, and the post-war financial boom, all combined to alter the distribution of local political influence in two ways: first, by making numerical strength and wealth independently important political resources; and, second, by increasing the sharpness of intra-African political divisions. The end-product of these alterations was the political exclusion of the non-Ibo 'patricians' and the rise of a new class of Ibo entrepreneurs and young professionals. Most of the 'new men' were from the more educationally and occupationally advantaged sections of Iboland—Onitsha Province and culturally related areas in Mid-Western Nigeria. In strictly numerical terms, the Owerri Ibos achieved parity with Onitsha and Mid-Western Ibos on such local institutions as the town council; but Owerri Ibos seldom controlled the crucial offices until 1954. The Onitsha official pre-eminence, it should be noted, was simply the political counterpart of Onitsha superiority within both the educational and occupational hierarchies of the local Ibo community. The Onitsha Ibos lacked the numbers of the always more numerous Owerri Ibos, but they had the skills and the organisational expertise which the Owerris lacked.[25]

As the democratisation of local government institutions proceeded, the local branch of the N.C.N.C.—the eastern-based and Ibo-dominated political party—and the new town council succeeded the patrician-dominated African Community League and Township Advisory Board as the focal points of African political power. At the same time, the leadership of the African community was bifurcated, the 'locals' on one side, the Zikists and other nationalist 'cosmopolitans' on the other.[26] Whereas the former tended to focus on strictly local affairs, especially as they related to the town council, the nationalists tended to look beyond the city to the broader confrontation between the colonialists and the Azikiwe-led N.C.N.C. The council-oriented politicians and the nationalists were in no sense opposed groupings; they simply operated in different political spheres and symbolised different political issues. Thus, town council elections were essentially of local concern, while elections of members of the regional and the central Government were of national import. The criteria of political recruitment varied accordingly: non-Ibos could be excluded from the town council at the same time as the Mid-Westerner, non-Ibo (but nationalist hero), John Umolu, could be elected to the regional House of Assembly.[27] However, as the transfer of power accelerated at both the national and local levels, the nationalist confrontation with the colonial establishment was increasingly subordinated in Port Harcourt to the local struggle for political position, and Port Harcourt politics came increasingly to focus upon the sub-cultural competition between Owerri and Onitsha Ibos—a competition in which the better-educated and better-organised Onitshas had the initial, though short-lived, advantage.

In Port Harcourt's fourth historical period (1955–64), numbers (to use Dahl's phrase) were 'split off' from wealth and social standing, and the always more numerous Owerri Ibos displaced the Onitsha Ibos. The Onitshas no longer held an Ibo monopoly on the necessary skills, and Owerri politicians acted on a new awareness of the political potential of their numerical superiority. Thus, the percentage of Owerri seats on the town council climbed from 46.8 per cent and 35.3 per cent in 1949 and 1952 to 56.5, 62.0, and 65.2 per cent respectively in 1955, 1958, and 1961, while the total number of seats rose by stages from 15 to 46. Simultaneously, Onitsha strength declined from 40.0 per cent and 35.3 per cent of total council membership in 1949 and 1952 to 13.0, 9.5, and 19.6 respectively in the subsequent years. The Owerri advance was made possible by the fact that wealth and numbers became significant political resources: men who lacked occupational and social standing but were in a position to assist the party financially, or were simply members of large and well-organised immigrant groups, were permitted entry to the political arena. The wealthy businessmen and traders became party 'patrons', the petty traders and contractors, party workers (and town councillors). Thus, the proportion of N.C.N.C. executive members engaged in private enterprise rose from 40 per cent in 1951 to 75.1 per cent in

1962–4 (total membership rising from 30 to 90 in the same period). Simultaneously, the proportion of administrators and clerical functionaries, on the one hand, and of professionals, educators, and journalists, on the other, declined.

During this fourth period, the approach of independence further diminished the relative importance of Nigerian political unity and the few non-Ibo nationalists who had survived the tide of 'Ibo-isation' in the post-franchise years, such as John Umolu, were unceremoniously discarded. Until the confrontation with Northern Nigeria loomed into the political foreground, the divisions *within* the Ibo community were similarly permitted more open expression. After the 1959 federal elections, the division between the Owerris and the Onitshas became an increasingly salient point of political reference and appeal within the 'main township'. In the Mile 2 Diobu slum, where Onitshas were even fewer relative to the Owerris, political competition centred on the rivalry between different subgroups of Owerri immigrants. In Mile 2, as in the main township, these groupings corresponded to the pattern of administrative segmentation in the rural hinterland. Thus, Ibos from Owerri Division tended to be allied against a coalition of Ibos from Okigwi and Orlu Divisions, which at one time had been administered as a single unit.

It would be well to note here, in qualification of the preceding analysis and in anticipation of the theoretical material which follows, that there were some significant exceptions to the generalisation of 'Owerri ascendancy' during these years, in the form of a few minority figures who prevailed simply by virtue of their personalities and abilities. Perhaps the most notable example was an Ijaw-speaking businessman, Councillor A. D. W. Jumbo, who had access to the upper echelons of both party and government. A personal friend and long-time political associate of the regional Prime Minister and of the chairman of the party's eastern working committee, Jumbo in 1964 was serving simultaneously as deputy chairman of the Eastern Nigerian Development Corporation, member of the board of directors of the African Continental Bank, member of the national executive committee of the N.C.N.C., and regional chairman of the reorganised Zikist Movement. Locally, he was one of the most popular and influential members of the municipal council. He had previously served one year as deputy mayor and, in 1964, was serving as chairman of the council's education, library, and welfare committee. Significantly, however, notwithstanding his personal popularity, his participation in high-level party deliberations, and his prominence within the municipal council, Jumbo was repeatedly denied the local party's nomination for office as mayor. In this respect, Jumbo was the exception that proved the rule of the 'communalisation' of Port Harcourt's party machinery.[28]

The apparent incongruity between Jumbo's prominence within the walls of the council chamber, on the one hand, and his political impotence within the local party executive, on the other, sheds light on a significant dualism inherent in Port Harcourt political life. For 'communalism' in Port Harcourt impinged only upon issues of political *recruitment* and *patronage*—issues upon which the prestige and recognition of immigrant groups depended—and did not affect routine council deliberations on such matters as finance, road and market maintenance, school construction, and the like. These latter subjects did not involve the communal interests of Port Harcourt's citizens. On these and related matters, councillors and party members either divided themselves according to their *residential* interests (as when amenities, such as paved roads and electric lighting, were to be allocated among Port Harcourt's communally heterogeneous neighbourhoods) or followed the direction of the council's informal leaders.[29] Within the council, at least when the distribution of contracts and jobs was not at issue, an individual's soundness of judgment, reputation for personal integrity, and oratorical skills were the principal requisites of political leadership, and his communal origins were irrelevant. Thus, Jumbo could be immensely influential in local affairs and still not be able to translate this influence into the kind of communal backing required in contests for higher office. There was, then, no contradiction between Jumbo's commanding position within the council, a body which did not usually involve itself with matters affecting the communal interest of its membership, and his failure to capture his party's nomination as mayor.

In closing this historical survey of Port Harcourt's political development, one final point must be made. The increasing political diversification of the African community manifested itself not only in the open communal competition for position and recognition, but also in the emergence of class and religious conflict, which cut across—but did not materially alter— the underlying communal divisions. Class conflict was revealed in the two-week general strike of June 1964 which virtually paralysed not only Port Harcourt but the entire nation; religious conflict, in Catholic agitation throughout Eastern Nigeria directed at certain of the Government's educational policies. Significantly, in Port Harcourt both the trade union and the Catholic protest leaders were drawn almost exclusively from persons who were working outside the dominant N.C.N.C. party establishment. For example, six of the ten leaders who organised the local strike action were non-Ibos who had previously broken with the N.C.N.C. Similarly, several of the local Catholic leaders who helped to organise anti-government demonstrations in 1963–4 were at odds with the local party establishment. However, the Ibo rank-and-file, both of the trade union movement and of the Catholic protest group, were firmly tied to their respective communal organisations ('improvement unions'), which, in turn, were closely integrated with the fused institutions of party and government. Consequently, neither the successful 1964 general strike nor the militant Catholic opposition to government educational policy threatened the communal foundations or stability of the urban political system.

The social bases of political cleavage

The lines of political cleavage in Port Harcourt were constantly shifting in response to an always changing social milieu. Immigrants to the city carried diverse social allegiances —to their traditional communities of origin, their religious denominations, and the administrative units of their rural homeland. The urban situation created yet further (often crosscutting) roles and social identities, based on class, occupation, and political party. As a result, the lines of political opposition were never rigid in the municipality. In some situations, as in the Catholic protest movement, men joined together in defence of their common religious commitment. In others, as in the general strike, they organised to protect their economic interests or, at election time, to promote the interests and prestige of their communities of origin. As in the immigrant communities of America's eastern seaboard, so in Port Harcourt it was these latter communal identities which were at the centre of the urban political process. Even within this limited sphere of ethnicity, however, politically salient identities had no fixed reference point, but were in a constant state of flux.

A typical Port Harcourt resident (like the typical Eastern Nigerian villager) belonged not to one but to several communities of origin. He was, at one and the same time, a member of a family, a village, a village-group, a division, a province, and a linguistically defined nationality; and the relative political salience of each communal reference point shifted according to the changing political situation. A stranger in one situation could well be a political ally in another.[30]

Broadly speaking, communalism in Port Harcourt manifested itself on four structural levels. First, the narrrow ethnic loyalties of the highly fragmented Eastern Nigerian traditional order were carried into the urban setting and played an important role in structuring social relationships and shaping political affiliations. The immigrant's loyalties to his family, village, and village-group were constant, and were invariably given priority in any ordering of social relationships. Moreover, it was these primary groups that served as the principal channels of recruitment into wider socio-political systems.

Secondly, in most situations the politically critical communal identities were those grounded in what might be termed 'geo-ethnicity', the feeling of loyalty to the rural administrative units in which the immigrant's traditional communities of origin were located.[31] Port Harcourt residents typically identified themselves to new acquaintances by reference neither to their village-group nor to their (usually Ibo) nationality, but rather to the intermediate communities of administrative division and province. It was around these geo-ethnic identities that the urban political process normally revolved, for it was only at these wide, non-traditional levels of social grouping that Port Harcourt's Ibo-speaking immigrants were sufficiently numerous to make a political impact upon the urban community as a whole.

It is significant that these geo-ethnic units were essentially artificial entities, commanding relatively little affect on the part of their members. As a consequence, electoral competition in Port Harcourt had a distinctively pragmatic and opportunistic character. Geo-ethnic blocs were extremely unstable, and the successful politician was one who, by a skilful trading of promises and favours, could forge an alliance of geo-ethnic community leaders. The successful politician was, in short, the ethnic ward-healer of American renown. This analysis, it should be noted, applies with equal force to regional and to urban politics. No traditional Eastern Nigerian village or village-group was sufficiently large to 'go it alone' at the regional level. Regional electoral constituencies incorporated numerous traditional communities, and regional politicians depended upon communal alliances to ensure their political survival. This suggests that the 'secret' of Ibo organisational adaptability is to be found, at least in part, in the political realities of a highly fragmented social order.

Thirdly, communalism manifested itself in the emergence of new, affectually laden, identities of 'nationality', identities which reflected a modern consciousness of cultural and linguistic unities of which traditional man was largely unaware. In Port Harcourt, a city in which Ibos comprised 80 per cent or more of the total population and held a virtual monopoly of political power, local political conflict usually centred on intra-Ibo cleavages, and the wider identities of nationality were generally of less significance. Even in Ibo-dominated Port Harcourt, however, the always latent conflict between Eastern Nigeria's Ibo and non-Ibo nationalities frequently became manifest, forcing at least a temporary closing-of-ranks at lower levels of the city's communal structure and transforming identities of nationality into viable instruments of political action.

The protracted conflict between Port Harcourt's Ibo majority and Ijaw minority over the creation of a separate Ijaw-dominated Rivers State (in which Port Harcourt was to be included) best illustrates the political mobilisation of identities of nationality. This conflict first came to a head in 1958, when the Ijaw demands for a separate state were pressed before the touring Minorities Commission. The political and economic stakes of this confrontation were high, both for the Ijaws and for the main Owerri-Onitsha body of Eastern Nigeria's Ibo population, to which belonged all but a fraction of Port Harcourt's politically dominant Ibo immigrants. On the one hand, Ibos had no desire to be the members of a communal minority in an Ijaw-dominated region. On the other, the projected Rivers State implied the excision from Ibo-controlled territory of much of Eastern Nigeria's economic potential, as represented by the expanding harbour and industrial facilities of Port Harcourt and by the rich oil-palm plantations of the Ibo-speaking (but politically ambivalent) Ikwerre people in Ahoada and Port Harcourt divisions. In 1958, before the full extent and significance of the petroleum deposits within the Ijaw-speaking Niger Delta were recognised, Ijaw separation *per se,* however politically distasteful, did not appear to threaten any vital interest of the Ibo people. Ijaw separatism involving a claim to Port Harcourt and Ahoada did.[32]

Locally in Port Harcourt, the conflict of nationalities expressed itself in a bitterly fought contest between the city's 'stranger-Ibo' majority and Ijaw minority for the allegiance and support of the small indigenous Diobu-Ikwerre community. Diobu support was solicited by both sides because it was believed the Minorities Commission would give special weight to the wishes of the indigenous population. For their part, the Diobus had long been hostile to the economically dominant strangers in their midst and were sympathetic to the Ijaw separatist movement. At the same time, Diobu leaders were confronted by the political reality that the Rivers State was unlikely of realisation and that open advocacy consequently entailed considerable political risk. Moreover, not a few Diobus feared that their inclusion in a new Ijaw-dominated Rivers State would simply perpetuate the Ikwerre minority status and subordinate position. In the end, the Diobus divided into two camps, one contending that the Ikwerres were not Ibos and should join with the Ijaws in a new state, the other insisting that the Ikwerre and Ibo peoples were one and that Diobus were therefore opposed to their inclusion within a separate Rivers State.

During this period, when the Ijaw demands for a separate state were being pressed with particular urgency, the fulcrum of the political process in Port Harcourt temporarily shifted from the town and divisional unions of the Ibos to the all-embracing nationality structures, the Ibo State Union and the Rivers Chiefs and People Congress. The moment the conflict of nationalities was concluded, however, by the Minorities Commission denial of the Ijaw demands, the narrower identities reasserted their political primacy: the Onitshas and Owerris renewed their political feud, and the Ijaws divided into rival factions. In 1964, there were no less than three different Rivers State organisations operating in Port Harcourt, each attempting to maximise the political strength of a different cultural sub-group by drawing the boundaries of the proposed Rivers State in such a way as to give that sub-group a numerical advantage.

Finally, as implied in the above analysis of nationality conflict, communalism in Port Harcourt also manifested itself in the intermittently marked cleavage between the township's small 'native' community and its numerically preponderant 'stranger' population. This division between the indigenes and the strangers did not have the same political significance as in many other African urban centres, in as much as the indigenous population was too small to compete on equal terms with the immigrants. Moreover, an important source of indigenous political and economic power was destroyed when the Diobus lost control of their valuable urban lands—first to the colonial government, and later to Ibo land speculators. The Diobus, however, still wielded considerable political influence at times, and their interaction with the Ibo strangers comprised an important part of the urban political scene.

COMMUNALISM AND SOCIAL CHANGE

Perhaps the most striking characteristics of Port Harcourt politics in the early 1960's were the flexibility and effectiveness of a variety of modes of political organisation, through which the municipality's residents related themselves to the rapidly changing exigencies of urban life. Four illustrations of organisational variability in Port Harcourt have been cited—the organisation of Ibos *qua* Ibos when their political position was threatened by the creation of a separate Rivers State, the activation of socio-economic identities and institutions during the general strike, the mobilisation of a religious protest which cut across both communal and socio-economic lines of cleavage, and the geo-ethnic structure of urban political recruitment.

These organisational examples testify to the capacity of Port Harcourt's residents to move between different institutional structures without materially altering their fundamental communal commitments. A Catholic and a trade union member and a market trader remained, politically, an Ibo and an Onitsha and an Oba man; and it was at election time or, more generally, when issues of political recognition and formal political position were at stake, that the individual's basic ethnicity was most sharply manifested. Thus, the same non-Ibo trade unionists who had enjoyed the complete support of Port Harcourt's predominantly Ibo rank-and-file during the general strike in 1964 were deserted when they subsequently tranformed themselves from leaders of a protest movement into parliamentary candidates of political parties which were in opposition to the communally oriented N.C.N.C. The moment the strike was concluded, the lines of political cleavage within the urban community were redrawn. The socio-economic identities which Port Harcourt's Ibo workers shared with workers in all Nigeria's urban centres and which for two weeks had shaped the political life of a nation were once again subordinated to the communal identities of region and nationality. Concurrently, the alternative fused leadership structure of regional party (N.C.N.C.) and ethnic community (Ibo), a structure quite distinct from that which had guided Nigeria's politics of socio-economic protest, was reactivated.[33] In short, the general strike had left undisturbed the communal foundations of the urban political system.

This study, then, calls into question the widely held view that, as economic development accelerates, the creation of new, functionally specific social identities will eventually undermine the organisational bases upon which a politics of communalism rests. Viewed over time, communal structures and sentiments in Port Harcourt not only have persisted but appear to have been increasingly diversified and politicised. The formation of new identities of nationality and the emergence of the intermediate geo-ethnic points of social and political reference are illustrative of these developments. It would seem, therefore, that the assumption of incompatibility between intersecting communal and noncommunal (e.g. 'class') identities and institutions requires re-examination. A Port Harcourt resident, to rephrase an earlier argument, held multiple group affiliations and social identities, whose relative prominence varied from situation to situation. His fundamental communal loyalties did not preclude his participation in non-communal modes of political organisation, for these latter were operative in situations in which his communal identities were relatively less salient. Conversely, his involvement in trade union or church activities did not imply the lessened significance of his 'communal organisation' as a social and political point of reference at other times. He was, in effect, able to compartmentalise his various urban identities and thereby to respond flexibly to changing social and political circumstances. In so doing he had the best of two worlds—the collectivism inherent in the functionally diffuse ties of language and community of origin, and the individuation requisite to his effective performance in the modern commercial and industrial milieu.

We must pause at this point to consider two objections which might be raised to this interpretation of Port Harcourt political development. The first objection is that the municipality's historical experience spans too short a period of time to permit any meaningful assessments as to the future of a politics of urban communalism: that, with the passage of years and generations, socio-economic identities will become of more general significance and eventually provide an organisational framework for the urban political system. The tenability of this point is self-evident. It might be well, however, to recall the persistence of ethnic sentiments even in the comparably tradition-free United States. In point is Robert Dahl's reference to 'the independent force of ethnic feelings' in New Haven:

An awareness of ethnic identification is not something created by politicians; it is created by the whole social system. Ethnic similarities are a palpable reality, built into the everyday awareness of the ethnic from early childhood into old age. Nor are they always subordinate to socio-economic factors; if they were, it would be difficult to account for certain aspects of the political behavior of the New Haven electorate.[34]

The force of this comparison becomes more evident when it is noted that Port Harcourt's immigrants, unlike New Haven's, remained tied to their communities of origin physically as well as psychologically. The institution of the extended family, the pattern of home-town visiting, the involvement of urban improvement unions in the formulation and execution of rural development schemes—all emphasised the concreteness and immediacy of an individual's ties with his homeland. Fifty years after Port Harcourt's inception, there appeared to be few second-generation Port Harcourt residents.

The second objection to consider is that the cultural uniqueness of Eastern Nigerians generally, and of the Ibos particularly, limits the general application of Port Harcourt's political experience. The important point, in this regard, is that certain of the structural variables considered in the analysis of Port Harcourt politics—such as the relationship of politically important identities to an always changing social context—would seem to relate to general characteristics of urban life.[35] Objectively, a trade union refers to an individual's relationship to his employer; a religious interest group refers to his concern for the education of his children; a community association refers to his requirements for companionship and social and economic assistance. Our argument is not that all urban dwellers possess the same organisational flexibility as the Ibos, but that, in structural terms, the Port Harcourt experience suggests that there is no *a priori* reason to assume that the emergence of new, functionally specific, urban identities will eliminate the political tenacity of the communal order. Indeed, it may well be argued that economic modernisation in a communal milieu expands the scope and intensity of communal conflict by widening the scale of communal organisation and by generating new kinds of competition for the scarce goods of wealth, status, and power. Ultimately, of course, comparative urban research will be necessary to differentiate that which is peculiar to the Ibo experience in Port Harcourt from that which is common to the urbanisation process.

Conclusion

The Ibo experience calls into question many of the conventional constructs which have tended to guide our study of social and political change in the developing areas. In particular, the Ibo case runs counter to the view that communal 'particularism' is essentially an historical anachronism, ultimately destined to be submerged by the 'universalistic' tidal wave of modernity. Yet the theoretical alternative, that communal particularism may well be a persistent and eurhythmic feature of modernity, is obscured by the conventional formulation.[36] The analysis of Ibo political dynamics presented in this article suggests, further, that models which dichotomise 'tradition' and 'modernity'—even for the limited purpose of establishing 'ideal types'—do little to further our understanding of the processes of change in any particular society.[37] Not only do such models presuppose an inherent incompatibility between 'traditional' and 'modern' values, institutions, and behaviour—a presupposition which the Ibo experience directly challenges—but they imply a unilinear view of development which is empirically unsound and theoretically limiting. The recent recognition that 'traditional' elements are to be found in 'modern' political systems led to queries concerning the appropriateness of the conventional dichotomous framework as a tool for the analysis of social and political change.[38] The conclusion reached then was that it was not the theory which was at fault, but rather its application. The case of the Ibos appears to indicate a need for theoretical revision, as well.

NOTES

1. An earlier version of this paper was read at the 1968 annual meeting of the (American) African Studies Association in Los Angeles. The Center for International Studies of the Massachusetts Institute of

Technology and the Institute of African Studies of the University of Ife provided field support, 1963–5. The article employs the administrative names in force prior to the Biafran secession.

2. James S. Coleman, *Nigeria: background to nationalism* (Los Angeles, 1958), p. 335.

3. The terminology is Clifford Geertz's. See his "The Integrative Revolution", in C. Geertz (ed.), *Old Societies and New States* (Glencoe, Ill., 1963), pp. 105–57.

4. It is estimated that in 1963 less than 7 per cent of Port Harcourt's population was indigenous to the area.

5. The unemployment figure is derived from data supplied by Dr. Archibald Callaway.

6. Sources: the 1921 Census, reported by P. Amaury Talbot, *Peoples of Southern Nigeria* (London, 1926), vol. IV, p. 22; *Population Census of Eastern Region of Nigeria, 1953* (Lagos, 1953), pp. 42–7; 1963 Census Reports for Census Districts Nos. 309301 and 309302 (Lagos, mimeo); and *Annual Report for Port Harcourt District, 1943* (National Archives File OW 5389/7; Riv Prof; 1/29/1101).

7. Inasmuch as some of the larger industrial establishments lie outside the municipal boundaries, the Port Harcourt urban area is technically larger than the municipality. However, most of those employed even in the outlying industrial plants reside within the municipal boundaries.

8. Mile 2 Diobu, deriving its name from its location two miles to the north of the main township, contains the city's slum. In 1963 over 80,000 were crowded into a space of less than one square mile, and newly arrived immigrants moved into Mile 2 and the surrounding area every day in search of cheap land and accommodation. Mile 2 Diobu was administratively joined with the municipality in 1960.

9. In 1953, Ibos constituted 68.1 per cent of the regional population and 77.3 per cent of Port Harcourt's population. The controversial 1963 census reported a somewhat lower Ibo percentage at the regional level; in Port Harcourt no comparable figures are obtainable, but Ibos appeared to have slightly increased their proportion of the total urban population.

10. K. Onwuka Dike, *Trade and Politics in the Niger Delta, 1830–1885* (London, 1959), pp. 43–4.

11. Following Coleman, *op. cit.,* p. 423, a "nationality" is defined as "the largest traditional African group above a tribe which can be distinguished from other groups by one or more objective criteria (normally language)". Thus, the Ibos (taken as a whole to mean all Ibo-speaking tribes), the Efiks, the Ibibios, and the Ijaws are all termed "nationalities".

12. Simon Ottenberg, "Ibo Oracles and Intergroup Relations", in *Southwestern Journal of Anthropology* (Albuquerque), XIV, 3, Autumn 1958, p. 296.

13. See E. E. Evans-Pritchard, "The Nuer of the Southern Sudan", in M. Fortes and E. E. Evans-Pritchard (eds.), *African Political Systems* (London, 1940), p. 13.

14. *Ibid.,* pp. 282 and 284.

15. James S. Coleman, "The Politics of Sub-Saharan Africa", in Gabriel A. Almond and J. S. Coleman (eds.), *The Politics of the Developing Areas* (Princeton, 1960), p. 256.

16. G. I. Jones, "From Direct to Indirect Rule in Eastern Nigeria", paper presented to the Institute of African Studies, University of Ife (mimeo, 1964). The term, "natural leaders", is borrowed from Jones.

17. Ottenberg, *op. cit.,* pp. 299 and 304.

18. G. I. Jones, *Report of the Position, Status, and Influence of Chiefs and Natural Rulers in the Eastern Region of Nigeria* (Enugu, 1956), p. v.

19. Coleman, *Nigeria,* p. 40.

20. Colonial Office, *Commission Appointed to Enquire into the Fears of Minorities and Means of Allaying Them* (London, 1958), p. 36.

21. Robert A. Dahl, *Who Governs* (New Haven, 1960).

22. *Ibid.,* p. 15.

23. L. R. Potts-Johnson, a Sierra Leonean Methodist pastor and secondary school proprietor, founded *The Nigerian Observer* in 1930, the town's only newspaper until 1940, when an Ibo, Nnamdi Azikiwe, introduced the nationalist *Eastern Nigerian Guardian* to Port Harcourt.

24. Despite the fact that the Ibos constituted the largest single nationality group within the town and, after 1943, within the League as well,

no Ibo ever held the critical post of the League presidency. Between the League's inauguration in 1935 and its end in 1951, the presidency was held by two Sierra Leoneans, one Yoruba, and one Ijaw. Non-Ibos were also disproportionately represented among other important official posts during most of the League's existence, through the position of secretary was often filled by prominent Ibo leaders.

25. Some indication of the social differentiation of Ibo sub-communities is given by a comparison of the executive bodies of Port Harcourt's Onitsha Divisional Union (Onitsha Province), and Orlu Divisional Union (Owerri Province). In 1964, for example, the Onitsha executive body was composed of a smaller proportion of persons who had received no schooling (9.8 per cent of the total of 41, as contrasted with 26.3 per cent of the 19 Orlu executive members) and a higher proportion who had studied beyond the primary school certificate (26.8 per cent as compared with 15.8 per cent). Occupationally, 36.6 per cent of the Onitshas occupied clerical posts, compared with 10.5 per cent of the Orlus; on the other hand, 73.7 per cent of the Orlu executive members were either businessmen or petty traders and contractors, as compared with 36.6 per cent of the Onitsha members. In short, while immigrants from Onitsha Province came to occupy the prestigious African posts within the local civil service and European mercantile firms, it was the relatively less educated Orlu and other Owerri Provincial Ibos who assumed the leadership of Port Harcourt's African commercial sector.

26. This terminology is borrowed from Robert K. Merton, *Social Theory and Social Structure* (Glencoe, Ill., 1957), pp. 387–420.

27. John Umolu was a trade unionist who came to public attention through his activities in the famous 1950 strike of the United Africa Company African Workers. He was elected to the Regional House of Assembly in 1953; upon his re-election he was appointed parliamentary secretary to the Premier. Umolu was subsequently to become the first Minister of Establishments in Mid-Western Nigeria.

28. The concepts of "communalism" and "communalisation" in this article refer to the grouping of urban residents according to the ascriptive characteristics of community of origin and native dialect. The ubiquitous Ibo "improvement union" exemplifies this mode of communal grouping. It is to be noted that the communal associations operative in the city did not always correspond to traditional groupings and that their goals were almost invariably secular and change-oriented. Moreover, membership and participation were normally voluntary.

29. The other side of the "communal coin" is that the *absence* of ethnically defined and segregated residential areas in Port Harcourt

limited the extent to which residentially defined electoral wards developed meaningful political identities. A significant neighbourhood stimulus to community development was therefore lacking.

30. This phenomenon of "shifting salience" is not unlike that of the American citizen identifying himself as a Worcester resident while in Massachusetts, as a native of Massachusetts while visiting California, and as an American when travelling in Europe. Ibos, however, especially compared with the members of other Nigerian nationalities, seemed particularly adept at closing ranks and combining against outsiders.

31. The concept of "geo-ethnicity" has much the same meaning as that of "ethnicity", as used by Immanuel Wallerstein, "Ethnicity and National Integration in West Africa", in *Cahiers d'etudes africaines* (Paris), VII, 3, October 1960, pp. 129–39. The former term is preferred here for two reasons. First, it offers a sharper conceptual tool than does "ethnicity" to describe the new kinds of urban groupings which are based upon non-traditional or neo-traditional communities of origin. The differences between Orlu Division and Okigwi Division (two Ibo-speaking administrative units around which socio-political groupings in Port Harcourt have formed), for example, are no more "ethnic" in character than are the differences between Kansas and Nebraska. The new administrative units are differentiated primarily by the arbitrary placement of colonial boundaries and only secondarily by cultural variations. Second, the use of the "geo-ethnicity" concept to describe urban groupings based upon new, artificial entities enables us to reserve the concept of "ethnicity" for urban groupings based more strictly on kinship, cultural, and linguistic ties.

32. This historical point acquires added significance in the light of recent events. For the new state boundaries of Federal Nigeria, created in 1967, separate both Ahoada and Port Harcourt divisions from the Ibo-speaking East Central State. The recent discovery of petroleum and natural gas resources in the Ikwerre area—reportedly between one-third and one-half of Eastern Nigeria's oil resources are centred in the Ikwerre Ibo hinterland—very likely guided the federal map-makers.

33. With respect to the fusion between ethnic structures, on the one hand, and those of party and government, on the other, it is interesting to note that in 1964 virtually all the members of the N.C.N.C.-controlled municipal council and (though this point was not investigated directly) probably a like number of N.C.N.C. executive members held high offices within their respective improvement unions. In many instances, the highest-ranking politicians were also the highest-ranking union officers.

34. Dahl, *op. cit.,* p. 54.

35. The theoretical perspective outlined here parallels the "situational analysis" approach taken by M. Gluckman, J. C. Mitchell, A. L. Epstein, and, more recently, by Leonard Plotnicov, *Strangers to the City: urban man in Jos, Nigeria* (Pittsburgh, 1967).

36. For similar critiques, see C. S. Whitaker Jr., "A Dysrhythmic Process of Political Change", in *World Politics* (Princeton), XIX, 2, January 1967, pp. 190–217; and Lloyd and Susanne Rudolph, *The Modernity of Tradition* (Chicago, 1967).

37. The failure of dichotomous models to correspond to empirical reality has led recently to the introduction of a number of caveats qualifying the asserted polarities. But, as Whitaker cogently observes (*op. cit.,* p. 190), these caveats do not avoid the central theoretical dilemma: "To claim that qualities associated with the terms 'traditional' and 'modern' do not diverge significantly would be to nullify the supposed significance of the terms, namely, that they identify distinguishable classes of societies."

38. See Gabriel A. Almond, "Introduction: a functional approach to comparative politics", in G. A. Almond and James S. Coleman (eds.), *The Politics of the Developing Areas* (Princeton, 1960), p. 22.

CHAPTER 19

Contradictions in the Nigerian Political System[1]

RICHARD L. SKLAR

There are three basic contradictions in the Nigerian political system. They may be stated briefly at the outset. First, the machinery of government is basically regionalised, but the party machinery—the organisation of the masses—retains a strong trans-regional and anti-regional tendency. Secondly, the main opposition party has relied upon the support of a class-conscious regional power group in its drive against the system of regional power. Depending upon a regional section of the political class to effect a shift in the class content of power, it was really asking that section to commit suicide. This contradiction produced a crisis in the Western Region which might easily be repeated elsewhere. Thirdly, the constitutional allocation of power is inconsistent with the real distribution of power in society. The constitution gives dominant power to the numerical majority—i.e., under existing conditions, to the north—but the real distribution of power is determined by technological development, in which respect the south is superior.

Reprinted from *The Journal of Modern African Studies,* 3, 2 (1965), pp. 201–213. Copyright © 1965 by *The Journal of Modern African Studies.* Reprinted by permission of the publisher and Richard L. Sklar. The notes are presented in slightly revised form.

Introduction

On 27 March 1951 a meeting composed of representatives of rival factions of the Nigerian nationalist movement was held in Lagos under the auspices of an *ad hoc* Committee of National Rebirth. The principal conveners were associated wtih Dr. Nnamdi Azikiwe and his party, the National Council of Nigeria and the Cameroons (N.C.N.C.). No one as yet has provided a full account of this somewhat obscure but highly significant event in Nigerian party history. We do know that the committee failed in its attempt to unify the divided nationalist movement of southern Nigeria. Its critics said that it was little more than a devious design to inveigle opponents of the N.C.N.C.—including members of the Nigerian Youth Movement and its offshoot, the recently surfaced Action Group—into a united front that would be dominated by Azikiwe and his political friends. To be sure, the committee did at length 'summon' the N.C.N.C. to implement its programme for 'national rebirth'.

At the committee's first meeting, the aims of the conveners were criticised trenchantly by a highly influential member of the Action Group, namely the late Chief Bode Thomas of Oyo, who is reported to have spoken forcefully in favour of the organisation of regionalised political parties.[2] However, his colleague and leader, Obafemi Awolowo, is said to have given serious and sympathetic consideration to the committee's proposal of political unity. In retrospect, Thomas and Awolowo appeared to have represented rival schools of thought which were never fully reconciled within the Action Group.

Cultural Nationalism and Regional Power

Dr Azikiwe has observed that among the founders of the Action Group, Chief Thomas was the leading exponent of a 'theory of regionalism'.[3] Of course, Chief Awolowo's contribution to regionalist thought is better known; strictly speaking, however, he was never an ardent regionalist, certainly not in the Thomastic sense in which regionalism is meaningful in Nigeria. His early book, *Path to Nigerian Freedom,* defends a principle that tends to undermine the Nigerian system of regional power, namely the right of every cultural nationality group to autonomy and self-determination.[4]

Basically, Awolowo was concerned to demonstrate that Nigeria is and should be regarded by nationalists and colonial officials alike as being a multi-national state. The various Nigerian nationalities, he observed, have their own indigenous constitutions. These African 'constitutions', he argued, have been perverted by alien rule to the detriment of public welfare and social progress. In particular, the traditionally 'limited' or 'constitutional' governments of his own nationality group, the Yoruba, were despotised by the colonial rulers. Reform was overdue, but, he insisted, it should be accepted that the constitution of each cultural nationality is its own 'domestic concern'. Every such nationality is entitled and should be encouraged to develop its own political institutions within a federal framework. Furthermore, he asserted, it is the 'natural right' of the educated minority of each cultural group 'to lead their fellow nationals into higher political development'.

These ideas, namely political reform at the local level, unity at the cultural nationality level, federalism at the national level, and the assumption of leadership by a broadly based educated élite, were incorporated in a programme for political action by opponents of the N.C.N.C. in Western Nigeria. Their first step was to organise an all-purpose association for persons of Yoruba nationality, named, after their legendary ancestor, the Society of the Descendants of *Oduduwa*. Later, the most militant among them organised a political vanguard which they called the Action Group.

In principle, Awolowo's doctrine holds that every cultural nationality, irrespective of size, is entitled to separate statehood within the Nigerian federation. In practice, however, the members of a major cultural nationality group, such as the Yoruba in Western Nigeria, were easily reconciled to the existence of big and culturally diverse regions within which their group would be dominant. This was equally true for members of the Ibo nationality in Eastern Nigeria, and the Hausa nationality in Northern Nigeria. In their respective regions, the leaders of these dominant nationality groups controlled the means of access to power and wealth. Naturally, and justifiably to a degree, they tend to equate their private interests with the objective interests of their nationality groups; conversely, they exploited the sentiments of their groups to promote their private interests. Political parties which were identified with the interests of particular nationality groups tended to reflect the class structures of those groups. Inevitably, such parties were used to promote class interests in the acquisition and retention of regional power.

Party and Class

For a decade prior to independence, the nationalist movement in Nigeria was headed by three political parties, each being rooted primarily in the predominant nationality group of a governmental region. In every region, the party waxed fat in its house of patronage. It had money, favours, jobs, and honours to distribute among those who would support it. To a large extent, these regional patronage systems were based on regional marketing boards, which had been set up to purchase export crops from farmers at stabilised prices for sale abroad. Concretely, the marketing boards have accumulated trading profits which have been used by the regional governments to promote economic development. Specifically, they supply capital to regional development corporations, which undertake agricultural and industrial projects independently and in partnership with other governments or with private interests. In all regions, these corporations and their related loan agencies are managed by politically reliable administrators. The same is true of those commercial banks which are owned and operated by regional governments.

Invariably, the vast majority of those who receive or hope to receive loans from the boards or the banks are attracted by powerful inducements to join or support the regional government party; in so far as they prosper, they may be expected to support the party financially. The same may be said of commercial contractors who work for the regional governments and their statutory corporations. Furthermore, the marketing boards are required to license qualified firms and individuals as certified agents to purchase specified crops from the primary producers. While such licences are granted on the basis of commercial criteria, political considerations are not always negligible, and it is not unknown for the whip of commercial patronage to crack over the head of a politically obtuse businessman.

Who are the masters of the regional governments? High ranking politicians, senior administrators, major chiefs, lords of the economy, distinguished members of the learned professions—in short, members of the emergent and dominant class. This class is an actual social aggregate, engaged in class action and characterised by the growing sense of class consciousness. It may be termed the "political class", as defined by Gaetano Mosca,[5] in that its members have controlling positions in the dominant institutions of society. The value of this term is magnified in the analysis of a developing country, like Nigeria, where it may serve to suggest that political power is the primary force that creates economic opportunity and determines the pattern of social stratification. This is not to say that all members of the political class have been associated with or dependent upon a governing party; nor, obviously, is every militant (active and dedicated) party member also a member of the dominant class. But the well-entrenched regional government party has been a veritable engine of class formation. We may say, with Milovan Djilas, that the leaders of the ruling parties constitute the core of the political class.[6]

Within the major parties, especially the old nationalist parties of southern Nigeria, cleavages have developed between the 'haves' and the 'have nots'. While regionalism is a characteristic attitude of the political class, anti-regionalism is the logical posture of the ideological opponents of that class. Here we perceive a contradiction in the political system. The 'machinery of government'—the system of governmental power, including the power of patronage—is largely and basically regionalised, but the 'machinery of politics'—the party system, i.e. the organisation of the masses—continues to exhibit a strong trans-regional and anti-regional tendency. This contradiction is related to another involving the ideology and tactics of opposition to the Federal Government.

The Ideology and Tactics of Opposition

Few developments of recent Nigerian history have excited more wonderment than the transformation of Chief Awolowo from a moderate "Fabian" socialist into a fervent opponent of neo-imperialistic capitalism and domestic class privilege. Various explanations come to mind. In psychological/ideological terms it might be suggested that Awolowo never became a typically class-conscious politician, i.e. he never developed strong loyalties to his class. As we have noted above, his distinctive contribution to the Action Group's theory of regionalism was a doctrine of self-determination for cultural nationalities rather than a doctrine of regional power. He was always more of a 'federalist' than a 'regionalist', although this distinction may have been too subtle to grasp during most of the 1950's. A person of deep conviction and pragmatic temperament, he could and did develop ideologically to meet the challenges of post-colonial society.

Another explanation is couched in terms of political opportunism, i.e. the logic of his position as Leader of the Opposition. It may have appeared politically necessary to champion the cause of radical anti-regionalism—the viewpoint of social and political protest—if ever he hoped to lead the Action Group to power. In any case, the Action Group rapidly developed a flagrantly split personality. As the Federal Opposition, it tried to be the chief spokesman for opponents of the political class. As a governing party in the Western Region, it was identified with indulgence toward the social and political status quo. The "federal" faction, led by Awolowo, wanted the Action Group to intensify its opposition to the regional power groups that controlled the Federal Government. The 'regional' faction, led by the Premier, S. L. Akintola, favoured a general settlement with the other regional power groups and the formation of a national government at the federal level that would include all the regionally-dominant parties. This rupture was exposed at the Action Group congress of February 1962. In his presidential address Awolowo admitted, 'openly for once', the existence of 'real and dangerous contradictions' within the party.

The basic contradiction was manifest in Awolowo's own tactical position: he relied upon a class-conscious regional power group to support a nation-wide movement of the 'have-nots'. Previously, there had been a real basis for class collaboration within the party. It was money: members of the political class generally wanted to make it, while the party militants wanted to spend it. But the costs of competition were not in fact, being defrayed by philanthropic members of the party. For the most part, they were being borne indirectly by the people of the Western Region. The £4 million or so diverted from the Western Region Marketing Board to the Action Group via the National Investment and Properties Company represents a fraction of what went down the political drain between 1959–62.

A comprehensive statement of the political account would require a study of the operations of various governmental agencies in order to calculate the hidden political costs of commercial loans, contracts, personal allowances, and so on.[7] Awolowo testified in court that his party spent about £300,000 per annum for organisational purposes. In addition, large sums were expended on elections: the Action Group was reported to have spent about £1 million on the federal election of 1959; it fought three costly regional elections in 1960–1 and numerous local elections. Can a developing country which depends heavily on public capital formation afford to foot the bill of modern party competition? The Coker Commission found that the Western Region Marketing Board had transferred so much money to the Regional Government for various purposes, including politically-tinged objects of dubious economic value, that it had to borrow in order to perform its own routine operations.[8]

If the public had to pay such a price, it seemed only logical for a socialist party to insist upon a reciprocal sacrifice by members of the political class. On ideological grounds, therefore, Awolowo demanded austerity measures in respect of the emoluments and allowances of politicians. Small wonder if his more conservative colleagues said that he had fallen into the hands of 'communists'. Akintola merely expressed a widespread doubt among members of the political class of Western Nigeria when he questioned the widsom of spending so freely to dislodge the political classes of the other regions.

Now we have identified a second contradiction in the political system of post-colonial Nigeria, to wit, that the opposition party depended upon a section of the political class to effect a shift in the class content of power. As a tactical matter, therefore, Awolowo had to protect his own regional base while he undertook to assault the regional bases of the Federal Government parties. In September 1960, he obtained permission from the federal executive council of the Action Group to set up a secret committee on tactics to cope with anticipated moves by the Federal Government which might menace the Action Group's base of power in the Western Region.[9] Some 30 months later, during his trial for the commission of a treasonable felony, Awolowo described the work of this committee as being strictly legal and largely precautionary rather than retaliatory in nature.[10] The prosecution alleged to the contrary that the committee had been set up by Awolowo specifically to engineer a *coup d'état.* Ultimately, this contention was accepted by the courts.[11]

It would not be surprising if some leaders of the Action Group had thought that a *coup d'état* was the most logical alternative to positive co-operation with the Federal Government parties.[12] They may have despaired of ever coming to power by means of the ballot box, especially after the disheartening performances of their party in the Northern and Eastern regional elections of 1961. (In May 1961, the Action Group obtained nine seats in the Northern House of Assembly to 156 won by the Northern Peoples' Congress; in November the Action Group won a mere 15 seats in the Eastern House of Assembly to 106 by the renamed National Convention of Nigerian Citizens and 25 won by other parties.) In the light of previous declarations by spokesmen for the Federal Government coalition, to the effect that the Federal Government could, in the event of emergency, dissolve a regional legislature and appoint a caretaker administration,[13] members of the Action Group may have discerned the choice before them in a nutshell: 'join' 'em or fight 'em.' Even Awolowo no longer expected the Action Group to win a Federal election on its own. He counted on the formation of a 'progressive alliance' that would include the main body of the N.C.N.C. in addition to opposition elements in the Northern Region. But the issue between Awolowo and his critics within the party was not simply tactical in nature, and it could not be resolved by a tactical compromise. The Action Group had come to an ideological breaking point, with the class content of power in question. From the standpoint of the political class, Awolowo had become 'irresponsible'; in *its* court of political judgment he was guilty of 'constructive treason' (or action that was certain to injure it), for which the classic penalty is anticipatory retaliation (or preventive defence).

The Resurgence of Regionalism

While many members of the political class of Western Nigeria questioned the wisdom of Awolowo's determination to keep up his good fight, they could not calculate its worth simply in material or class value-laden terms. They were, after all, intensely proud of their party and its leader; they wanted him to become Prime Minister and they were deeply pained by their own disaffection from him. They could not betray him without destroying a part of themselves. Until the crisis of May 1962, most of the party 'elders'—the old guard—stood behind Awolowo while they counselled moderation and restraint. Eventually, they made their peace with the triumphant regional Premier. Typically, they dropped out of the Action Group and affiliated with a new and technically nonpartisan Yoruba cultural organisation, called the Society of the Descendants of *Olofin* (said to be the proper name of the legendary *Oduduwa*). If they did not actually join Akintola's new party (the United People's Party), at least they accepted the essence of his theory of regionalised political organisation.

While the Action Group was reduced to a hard core of loyalists, the N.C.N.C. joined with the U.P.P. to form a coalition government in the Western Region. Nonetheless, a substantial part of the N.C.N.C. had been won over to Awolowo's proposal of a 'progressive' alliance and they urged their party to reassert its traditional identity as the major party of radical, equalitarian democracy. In the Western Region, however, and in the newly created Midwestern Region—an N.C.N.C. stronghold—old-line N.C.N.C. leaders were hostile to the idea of an alliance with their old enemy, the Action Group. But pressure for a realignment of the parties mounted as tension increased between the N.C.N.C. and its northern partner in the Federal Government coalition. That coalition was strained to near breaking point when the N.C.N.C.-controlled governments of the Eastern and Midwestern Regions challenged the accuracy of the 1963 census results which preserved the Northern

Region's population edge over the rest of the country and, consequently, its numerical supremacy in the House of Representatives.[14]

At this point, we encounter a third, possibly the most acute, contradiction in the Nigerian political system. Constitutionally, Parliament is supreme; and Parliament is controlled by the dominant party of the Northern Region. But in terms of its educational and technological development, Northern Nigeria is retarded in comparison with the south.[15] The Northern Region still relies heavily upon expatriates for administrative assistance, and persons of northern origin constitute a very small minority in the higher civil service of the Federal Government, which is now overwhelmingly Nigerian. Therefore, northern control of the Federal Government, based on the population principle, is difficult for many southern Nigerians to accept, especially in the light of their misgivings about the accuracy of the population count in the Northern Region, not to mention their general lack of confidence in the fairness of elections in that region.

While the Northern Peoples' Congress is dominant in all provinces of Northern Nigeria, the political structure of that region is far from being monolithic. On the contrary, the northern political class is highly vulnerable to political attack at various points,[16] and northern leaders, who are traditionally sensitive to the threat (or bugbear) of 'southern domination', have resented the continuous efforts by southern-based parties to exploit their political weaknesses. Logically, the northern leaders, notably Premier Ahmadu Bello, the Sardauna of Sokoto, supported Akintola, who promised to respect the principle of regional security, in the crisis that convulsed the Action Group in 1962. Naturally, Akintola reciprocated by supporting the northern position in the census controversy.

At this juncture, all but two of the eleven N.C.N.C. Western Regional Ministers bolted from their party and rallied to Premier Akintola's standard in the formation of a new regional party, named the Nigerian National Democratic Party, to which their supporters in Lagos also adhered. Thereupon, N.C.N.C. loyalists in the Western Region formed an alliance with the Action Group, which still appeared to be the most popular party in the Region, despite the decline of its contingent in the House of Assembly to a doughty band of 27 (out of a total membership of 90). Meanwhile, opposition parties in the Northern Region, principally the Nigerian Elements Progressive Union (an ally of the N.C.N.C.) and the United Middle Belt Congress (formerly an ally of the Action Group), combined to form a Northern Progressive Front. Only die-hard opponents of the Action Group, mainly in the Midwestern Region, still held out against the formation of a nation-wide 'progressive' alliance.

As a result of the disputed census (challenged unsuccessfully in the Supreme Court by the Eastern Regional Government), the Northern Region was allotted 167 parliamentary seats (a reduction of 7) out of a total of 312, the Eastern was alloted 70 (a reduction of 3), the Western received 57 (an increase of 10), the Midwestern 14 (a reduction of 1), and Lagos 4 (an increase of 1). In August 1964, the N.P.C. in alliance with the N.N.D.P., the regionalist Midwestern Democratic Front, and the separatist Niger Delta Congress of Eastern Nigeria, inaugurated the Nigerian National Alliance (N.N.A.), to which other small parties in the Eastern Region also adhered. In accordance with the terms of this alliance, the Prime Minister invited two N.N.D.P. members of Parliament to join the Federal Cabinet. Soon thereafter, the N.C.N.C.-Action Group-Northern Progressive Front alliance was launched formally as the United Progressive Grand Alliance (U.P.G.A.). Now the stage was set for a two-party battle on election day.

We need not recapitulate subsequent events, including a bitter election campaign and its dramatic conclusion: U.P.G.A.'s allegation that the election had been maladministered, its decision to boycott the polls, the harrowing six-day crisis, and the makeshift settlement.[17] In the end, U.P.G.A. agreed to accept the election results in those constituencies where polling had taken place, however lightly, subject to the proviso that particular results could be challenged in the courts. All told, the N.N.A. won 198 seats to the U.P.G.A.'s 55. Subsequently, the U.P.G.A. total was boosted over the 100 mark by supplementary elections; their leaders also salvaged a promise of early arrangements to review the constitution and the machinery for elections.

In this analysis, it suffices to observe that the two nation-wide alliances stand for rival conceptions of the Nigerian political system, which resemble the ideas of Awolowo and Akintola respectively. U.P.G.A.'s conception is that of a relatively centralised federal system based on truly national, i.e. transregional, political parties. By contrast the N.N.A. conception accepts the existing regional power system and favours the regionalisation of political parties to safeguard regional security. To the leaders of Northern Nigeria, however, regional security implies something more than regionalised political organisations; it also means preservation of the unity of the existing Northern Region, so that it will continue to contain a broad belt of cultural minorities, thereby enabling the N.P.C. to control the Federal Government by virtue of its hold on a single region. At this point, the line between Northern Regional 'security' and 'northern domination' may be difficult to distinguish.

It may be expected that the N.N.A., in substantial control of the Federal Government, will seek to reorder Nigeria's political system in accordance with its theory of regional security. A step in that direction has already been taken with the inclusion of N.C.N.C. ministers from the Eastern and Midwestern Regions, in addition to N.N.D.P. ministers from the Western Region, in the Federal Cabinet. Eventually, N.C.N.C. leaders in the Eastern and Midwestern Regions might be persuaded to cut their losses in the Northern and Western Regions and work within the National Alliance. Such terms, if accepted (and it will be difficult to refuse them if the N.N.D.P. wins the forthcoming Western Regional electon), would probably spell the end of radicalism as a potent force inside the N.C.N.C. Radical elements, including Marxian socialists and left-wing trade unionists who supported the U.P.G.A. in the election crisis, would regroup outside the major parties. Nigeria would continue to develop as a capitalist state, and political competition would tend increasingly to coincide with class conflict.[18]

*   *   *

Undoubtedly, the northern leaders intend to exploit their constitutional power to promote social and economic development in the north and thereby to increase the Northern Region's real power *vis-à-vis* the south. In the meantime, southerners are prone to regard the powerful northern presence in Lagos with some disdain and resentment. The upshot is a climate of discontent that detracts gravely from the legitimacy (acceptance by the people) and, perforce, the viability of the Nigerian Federal Government. To remedy this potentially dangerous situation, various changes in the structure of government have been proposed.

One approach contemplates a division of the north into two or more regions so as to diminish the political power of the northern political class. This was Awolowo's objective; it is now a plank in the U.P.G.A. platform. It would almost certainly lead to a redistribution of federal seats among the parties. It would also entail a decisive shift of power to the Federal Government. Recently, the Eastern Regional Premier and National President of the N.C.N.C., Dr M. I. Okpara, has advocated a reorganisation of Nigeria into as many as 25 states, in which case the constitution would doubtless be revised to assume a more unitary aspect.

Another approach, also favoured by leaders of the U.P.G.A., seems to face in the opposite direction. It would involve a diminution of the power of the Federal House of Representatives; correspondingly, the status of the Senate, which gives equality of regional representation, would be raised to that of a co-ordinate legislative chamber. U.P.G.A. leaders in southern Nigeria want a strong Senate to countervail northern dominance in the House of Representatives. However, this 'reform' would also have another effect; it would enhance regional security in the south. U.P.G.A.'s current espousal of this proposal would seem to constitute an acceptance, perhaps inadvertently, of the regionalist logic of the political class. A really radical and popular party might be well advised to remember that strong Senates are usually inimical to the democratic principle of majority rule.

NOTES

1. An earlier version of this article was presented at the first West African Political Science Conference held at Ibadan, 4–6 March 1965.

2. *Daily Service* (Lagos), 29 March 1951. There is a brief account of the Committee of National Rebirth in my *Nigerian Political Parties* (Princeton, 1963), pp. 112–14.

3. Nnamdi Azikiwe, *The Development of Political Parties in Nigeria* (London, 1957), pp. 15–17.

4. Obafemi Awolowo, *Path to Nigerian Freedom* (London, 1947).

5. Gaetano Mosca, *The Ruling Class* (1896; republished New York, 1939).

6. Milovan Djilas, *The New Class* (New York, 1957). Eme O. Awa has observed that it is the intention of "some politicians" to form the core of a dominant social class. They "believe", he wrote, "that in a modern society there must be a bourgeois class and they should therefore use their political influence to establish themselves as the nucleus of that bourgeoisie." "Roads to Socialism in Nigeria", in *Nigerian Institute of Social and Economic Research. Conference Proceedings, March 1962* (Ibadan, 1963), p. 20.

7. Cf. Sayre P. Schatz, "The Repayment Problems of the Regional Loans Boards", paper prepared for the annual conference of the Nigerian Economic Society at the University of Ife, February 1965.

8. Federation of Nigeria, *Report of (Coker) Commission of Inquiry into the Affairs of Certain Statutory Corporations in Western Nigeria* (Lagos, 1962), vol. I, pp. 28 and 36. It should be emphasized that the Coker Commission was empowered to investigate the operations of governmental agencies in the Western Region only. Were similar investigations to be held in the other regions, disclosures of a somewhat similar nature might result. A suggestive case is mentioned by G. K. Helleiner, "The Eastern Nigerian Development Corporation: a study in sources and uses of public development funds, 1949–1962", in *The Nigerian Journal of Economic and Social Studies* (Ibadan, 1964), p. 117.

9. Minutes of a meeting of the federal executive council of the Action Group on 23 September 1960, quoted in "The Queen and Maja *in re* Omisade"; *Record of Appeal from the High Court of Lagos to the Federal Supreme Court of Nigeria* (Lagos), vol. 9, p. 13.

10. *Ibid.* vol. 7, pp. 4–6.

11. The Queen *v.* Omisade and 17 others; F. S. C. 404/63. However, one Justice of the Supreme Court demurred on the ground that the validity of this contention depended upon the uncorroborated evidence of an

accomplice, although he concurred in the conviction of Awolowo on other grounds. In fact, those few persons who were in a position to testify with any degree of certainty about the activities of the tactical committee were, in every case, deeply committed to one faction or the other.

12. An inference to this effect may be drawn from the trial record of The Queen and Maja *in re* Omisade, *op. cit.* vol. 6, p. II, and vol. 7, p. 59.

13. Federation of Nigeria, *Parliamentary Debates, First Parliament, First Session, 1960–61. House of Representatives* (Lagos), vol. I, 29 November 1960, cols. 573–86.

14. 55.7m. people were enumerated, distributed thus: Northern Nigeria, 29.8m.; Eastern Nigeria, 12.4m.; Western Nigeria, 10.3m.; Midwestern Nigeria, 2.5m.; Federal Territory of Lagos, 675,000. The announced total indicates a statistically startling population rise of 5.5 per cent per annum since the previous census.

15. In 1963 there were 2,485,676 pupils in the primary schools of southern Nigeria—i.e. the Eastern, Western, and Midwestern Regions, and the Federal Territory of Lagos—compared with 410, 706 in Northern Nigeria. At the secondary school level, including general education, technical, vocational, and teacher training schools, 231,261 pupils were enrolled in southern Nigeria compared with 20,312 in Northern Nigeria. See Federal Ministry of Education, *Statistics of Education in Nigeria, 1963* (Lagos, 1965), pp. 9–13.

A revealing index of technological development is the official report of electricity sold in Nigeria for all commercial and industrial uses. In the year ending 31 March 1964, approximately 270,000,000 kwh. were sold in the Eastern, Western, and Lagos areas, compared with 40,-000,000 in the entire Northern area. Electricity Corporation of Nigeria, *Thirteenth Annual Report and Statement of Accounts for the Year ended 31 March 1964* (Lagos, 1964), p. 56.

16. E. g. shortly after independence, the political authority of the Premier of the Northern Region was defied by the Emir of Kano, one of the most powerful of the traditional rulers. In 1963 the administration of the Kano Native Authority was investigated by the Regional Government and the Emir was compelled to abdicate. Meanwhile, it had been reported that Action Group strategies for penetration of the north had contemplated co-operation with the ex-Emir of Kano; "The Queen and Maja *in re* Omisade", *op. cit.* vol. 2, pp. 169–71, and vol. 7, pp. 49–50. In 1964 a political party loyal to the ex-Emir aligned with the opposition bloc in Kano.

17. See the account by Richard L. Harris, "Nigeria: Crisis and Compromise", in *Africa Report* (Washington), X, 3, March 1965.

18. This is not, by any means, intended to suggest that the anti-regionalist cause has been lost, certainly not before the impending Western Regional election. The two big electoral alliances may indeed be refined into permanent electoral parties. Such a development would gladden the hearts of liberal democrats who perceive in the two-party system a promise of stable democracy, especially if each party is broadly based and ideologically diffuse, so that each includes within its fold members who share fundamental beliefs with members of the other.

But the viability of a two-party system in Nigeria at the present time is open to question. First of all, it could be undermined by an excessive identification of either party with a "home" region of the country. Secondly, a competitive party system would require for its survival a greater degree of political toleration than we can take for granted in the light of recent experience. This said, a compromise alternative to the rival ideas of the U.P.G.A. and the N.N.A., involving the formation of a national front or congress of regional elements, may not be inconceivable. See my essay, "For National Reconciliation and a United National Front", in *Nigerian Opinion* (Ibadan), I, 1, January 1965, pp. 5–6.

CHAPTER 20

Three Perspectives on Hierarchy

C. S. WHITAKER, JR.

This paper has two principal objects: 1) to show that on a central issue of speculative political thought, namely the proper basis and structure of political participation, the three leading Northern Nigerian political figures take three different positions, each compatible with the practice of government within a democratic framework; 2) to contend that the ideological differences between these men may be explained, in part at least, by the fact that each occupies a different position within a common traditional political culture, the structure of which is hierarchical. The contention, in other words, is that the decisive influence on each man's view of the desirable structural implications of a modern democratic political system has been his particular relationship to, and experience of, a certain kind of traditionally stratified polity.[1] Implicitly this contention touches on a controversial theoretical issue concerning political behaviour which in this paper is not pursued as such: whether socio-cultural situations engender political ideologies.[2] It is hoped, however, that in this respect the paper will be suggestive and that it may in particular encourage considera-

Reprinted from *The Journal of Commonwealth Political Studies,* III (March 1965), pp. 1–19. Copyright © 1965 by *The Journal of Commonwealth Political Studies.* Reprinted by permission of the author, the editors and the publisher, Leicester Press.

tion of the influence of traditional society on the contemporary political thinking of other African leaders.

The paper may incidentally shed light on certain political roles which might well befuddle the casual observer. Thus, the Northern Nigerian political leader who most conspicuously identifies himself with the cause of traditional rulers is also the person most responsible for certain measures patently contrary to their own true wishes and inclinations. In this curious championship this leader's most important ally is a man who at one time held an extremely disparaging opinion of the traditional system—in which his personal status is decidedly inferior. The office he now holds in Nigeria's modern scheme of government is in principle the paramount one; yet he has shown no inclination to use his power to undermine traditional authority. The third leader was a colleague of the other two for purposes of operating the coalition of political parties that governed Nigeria in its first five years of independence, notwithstanding the fact that professedly he absolutely rejects important traditional values which the others proclaim should be upheld.

The inference that such apparently anomalous roles merely represent the sacrifice of convictions to ambition or, alternatively, the lack of any clear political conceptions in the first place, would be consistent with frequently encountered interpretations of leadership in African and other new independent states. The analysis in this paper should indicate, however, that either inference in this case would be inadequate to the reality involved. Specifically, it may help to explain, as such inferences do not, persistent interparty and intraparty cleavages in Northern Nigeria which to a large extent reflect the coherent views which separate these three leaders. Alhaji Sir Ahmadu Bello, Sardauna of Sokoto (Sardauna, like Earl, is a traditional title), is the Premier of the Northern Region of the Federal Republic of Nigeria, and President-General of Nigeria's largest single party, the Northern People's Congress (NPC). The NPC forms both the Government of Northern Nigeria and, in coalition with the National Council of Nigerian Citizens (NCNC), that of the Federal Republic (this at the time of writing—just prior to the 1964 Federal election). Alhaji Sir Abubakar Tafawa Balewa is the First Vice-President of the NPC and Prime Minister of the Federal Republic. Malam Aminu Kano is the Life-

President of the Nigerian Elements Progressive Union (NEPU) which has bitterly opposed the NPC within the Northern Region, although it has been linked to it in the Federal Government by virtue of an alliance with the NCNC, in which Aminu Kano holds the office of Vice-President. All three are natives of the distinctive political culture area made up of the thirty-odd, mostly Hausa-Fulani peopled, states or emirates which together dominate Northern Nigeria in population and territory.

These emirates are traditional political entities whose salient common characteristics are hierarchical and quasi-theocratic authority, a high degree of social stratification, well-developed bureaucratic machinery, and in several instances, extensive demographic scale. They have flourished in their present form since being conquered in a *jihad* or Islamic holy war led by a Fulani devout, Shehu Usman dan Fodio, early in the nineteenth century, although the characteristics of emirate government noted above antedate Fulani rule by centuries.[3]

The advantages of political organisation these traditional states offer were primarily responsible for their becoming the classic case of the British colonial policy of indirect rule or "native administration" in Africa.[4] This policy greatly contributed, in turn, to the survival of emirate political culture in the present era, with the result that it has profoundly influenced the course of the parliamentary system of government and politics which the British introduced into Nigeria before its independence,[5] the political outlooks of the three Northern leaders being not the least of that influence.

II. FORMATIVE EXPERIENCES

Alhaji Sir Ahmadu Bello

Ahmadu Bello might well have attained as eminent a position in a pristine traditional society as he occupies as Northern Premier. The pinnacle of traditional leadership in the emirate system—the Sultanship of Sokoto—is reserved to prominent descendants of dan Fodio, who founded the Sokoto (emirate) ruling dynasty along with the Fulani empire. Ahmadu's father, a District Head of Rabah, in Sokoto, was the son of the eighth Sokoto Sultan; the first Sultan, Muhamman Bello, son of dan Fodio, was Ahmadu's great-grandfather. He is otherwise well-connected on his maternal side, his grandmother being the daughter of the fourth Fulani Emir of Kano, most populous and wealthy of the emirates. (In *My Life,* Bello's autobiography, he asserts a claim, the merits of which need not detain us here, to descent, on both sides, from the Holy Prophet.)[6]

Such a pedigree obviously justifies regarding Bello as an exemplification of leadership continuity in modern Africa. Merely to attribute his present station and views to a silver spoon, however, would do injustice both to the political dynamics of a traditional emirate and to his pivotal role as at once modern politician and traditional ruler.

With no custom of primogeniture or any other rule determining a strict order of succession, the office of emirship (like many lesser ones in the state hierarchy) is in principle open to all male members of the royal dynasty—inevitably a large group, since the ruling stratum values maximum procreation of males, and practices both polygamy and concubinage. In practice, *isa,* the Hausa word for "influence", in this context meaning wealth and followers to sway the kingmakers, determines success. The critical units in the competition are corporate groups rather than individuals, for the dynasty of each emirate is split for these purposes into one or more lineages (a few emirates also have multiple dynasties). The collective intensity, indeed, frequent bitterness, which characterises contests for a throne is partly attributable to the fact that customarily the victorious candidate is expected eventually to bestow state offices and titles on his kinsmen and clients, which often necessitates more or less arbitrary removal of incumbents associated with a rival lineage or dynasty.

The British outlawed the practice of forcible confiscation *(wasau)* of rivals' possessions, including offices, and they also threw into the balance of rivalry the criteria of western educational qualification and administrative competence. But the very logic of British policy, which involved upholding a certain discretionary power on the part of traditional rulers, precluded elimination of that ample measure of royal patronage around which the government of an emirate largely revolves to this day. Indeed, concerning the milieu of the typical native administration in the colonial phase, Bello himself has written: "There was obviously a great deal of jealousy and intrigue—and I don't say there isn't any now".[7] He also acknowledges the impact of that milieu on his own career.[8]

Having completed primary school in Sokoto, the young Ahmadu earned distinction as a student at the famous Katsina College, the Northern secondary school the British had established with the explicit aim of equipping the emirate ruling class with western education. After graduating in 1931, he taught in the Sokoto Middle School for three years, resigning to succeed his deceased father as District Head of Rabah. The death of the Sultan in 1938 occasioned the usual struggle for the Sokoto throne, and Ahmadu, as a grandson of the eighth Sultan and by British standards one of the most promising District Heads, was one of several contestants. However, his first cousin, Abubakar, the present Sultan, won.

A common ancestor of Ahmadu and Abubakar was Muhamman Bello, whose descendants form a royal lineage group, called Bellawa. The Bellawa duly competed in 1938 with their main rivals, the Atikawa (descendants of the second Sultan). However, the energetic candidacies of the two Bellawa prospects reduced solidarity in that lineage. The new Sultan, perhaps as an outward show of reconciliation, awarded his own former title, Sardauna, to Ahmadu, who also became the first holder of that title to be appointed to the Sultan's traditional council of advisers. Simultaneously, the new Sardauna was given the novel assignment of supervising the eastern portion of the Emirate, from the important commercial town of Gusau. An interesting question is whether a premeditated motive of this assignment was to entangle the Sardauna in difficulties; the Sardauna's own account clearly implies as much.[9] Another version of the story, not necessarily in conflict with the first, is that the Sardauna's energetic and efficient administrative performance in Gusau was deemed a potential threat to the Sultan's own reputation and position. In any case, the undisputed facts are that he was tried and convicted in 1944, in the Sultan's Court, on a charge of having embezzled the *jangali* or cattle tax, with the collecting of which he was officially concerned at Gusau; yet on appeal to the British High Court he was completely exonerated. Subsequently he was reinstated as a Sultan's councillor (an office he still holds) in which capacity he is known to have served faithfully and indeed, it is said, with evident effort to cultivate the Sultan's goodwill.

The Sardauna's reaction to his ordeal seems a harbinger of his later political posture. Thus, appealing against the judgment of a judicial council of the Sultan was by customary standards an exceedingly unconventional act, more especially coming from a Sokoto subordinate official (the English translation of the Sultan's traditional title, *Sarkin Musulmi,* is "Commander of the Faithful", i.e. spiritual head of all the Muslims in Northern Nigeria). It was undoubtedly indicative of determined personal ambitioh, extending to a willingness to invoke secular authority against the highest sanctions of religion and tradition. On the other hand, the vicissitudes of traditional politics had nearly dealt the Sardauna's career a fatal blow. Similar experiences produced in other young aristocrats a disaffection with the traditional system, in some cases to the point, later on, of willingness to serve the cause of radical democratic change. The Sardauna's superior scholastic and administrative abilities set him apart from the ordinary princely title-holder. Yet, far from disaffection, his response to his experience (as suggested in his seeking reconciliation with the Sultan) was in effect to reaffirm his belief in the fundamental legitimacy of the traditional order.

Alhaji Sir Abubakar Tafawa Balewa

The Prime Minister of Nigeria's status in traditional terms is as humble as the Sardauna's is exalted. He was born in Bauchi Emirate in 1912, a son of Yakubu, whose minor traditional title (*Garkuwan Shamaki*—literally "bodyguard" or "keeper" of the horses) was at the time reserved strictly to members of slave lineages.[10] Unlike certain other slave-titles, that of his father, who was a menial of the *Ajiya* (traditional title of the usually Fulani District Heads of Lere), did not carry political power or authority. An apocryphal version that he was the District Head or *Ajiya's* son has been published in several places in Nigeria and abroad (*Who's Who in Nigeria, West Africa, Time,* Ronald Segal's *Political Africa,* etc.). That

Balewa has apparently seen fit to leave this error uncorrected may be taken as a sign of his society's profound preference for the person who retains his hereditary status over the "self-made" man whom western societies applaud.[11]

Bauchi lore relates that Abubakar, like several other now prominent Northerners, owes his start in western secular education to the fact that the Muslim emirates' ruling classes, being in those days implacably hostile to that innovation, often contrived to placate the British by sending to school the sons of their retainers in place of their own. Whatever the true facts in Balewa's particular case, it is certain that few if any of his class were, at the time, knowingly recruited for the kind of education he received: first at Bauchi, then at Katsina College, where, like Bello, he confirmed an earlier scholastic promise. A career in education, probably the only suitable one readily available to him then, followed; he first taught in 1933 at Bauchi Middle School, of which he became Headmaster less than two years later.

In keeping with post-war British policies that opened up Government education departments to Africans and native administration (emir's) councils to commoners, Balewa was, successively, one of a handful of Northern Nigerians sent abroad in 1945 to study for a diploma (Institute of Education, London University) and then, after his return in 1946, the first traditionally non-eligible person ever appointed to the venerable institution of the Emir of Bauchi's Council. Instead of directly entering Government service, Balewa accepted the option of comparable rank and salary within the native administration education department.

Educated, highly articulate in English, and familiar with British customs, Balewa was a natural choice to serve as the Bauchi Native Administration's nominee in the new Northern legislature (established initially with strictly advisory powers under the 1946 Constitution) and later to attend the series of consultative meetings that preceded promulgation of the 1951 Constitution. This instrument introduced a Northern Assembly (with legislative authority), to which Balewa was elected. That institution in turn offered Balewa a realm of leadership that transcended traditional society, in the form first of simultaneous membership in the Nigerian legislature at Lagos, then a federal (or central as it was then styled) ministry, and eventually the highest national office.

The central feature of Balewa's experience then is upward social mobility, thanks to modernity. He almost certainly would have remained fastened in obscurity were it not for the historical contingencies of western contact and Nigerian nationhood under parliamentary forms. A singularly low-born member of an emphatically ascriptive society that change has incorporated rather than displaced, Balewa's sociopolitical point of vantage is truly that of the "new man".

Malam Aminu Kano

Aminu Kano was born into the Fulani clan of Kano Emirate called Genawa. In the structure of that state, the Genawa are prominent, even patrician, but they are not royalty or ordinary nobility. Rather they are renowned for pursuing the specialised Islamic vocations: jurists, priests, and scholars. Aminu Kano was reared in this tradition. His father, Malam Yusufu, was for a time Acting Chief *Alkali,* or Muslim judge, of Kano. His grandfather, was Hassan Abdulaziz, a celebrated *malam* or religious scholar; his grandmother's reputation for religious learning earned her the respectful title, *Modibo.* Before Aminu was educated in western-type schools, his mother, who was literate in Arabic and Hausa, a rare accomplishment among women of her generation, taught him to read and write and introduced him to Koranic study.

The peculiar aspects of this heritage would seem to furnish insight into Aminu Kano, the leader of a modern, radical democratic party. *Alkalai, malamai,* and *Limani* ("Imams" or "priests") constitute the principal transmitters of the spiritual and moral values of Islamic society, and the bona fide interpreters of its laws. In theory "Islam knows only one law, the divinely revealed *Shari'a,* which holds sway over political no less than over social, economic and cultural life".[12] It follows that those officially concerned with its exposition and dissemination not only hold high and respected positions in orthodox Islamic communities like the emirates but they are also in principle the ultimate source of authoritative political judgment.

While in theory the *Shari'a* admits of no separation between temporal and spiritual authority, it of course does not prevent the emergence of purely *de facto* political power, nor guarantee that rulers' behaviour will conform to its prescriptions. If there is to be any legitimate criticism of the conduct of the state, obviously it must come from the Muslim clerics, scholars and judges, who historically have been disposed to scrutinise, evaluate and even censure the acts of rulers in the light of ideal prescriptions. Furthermore, they constitute persons to whom victims of oppression naturally look for redress of grievances, for "apart from actual rebellion, extralegal recourse against (individual acts of) the government is had only through the protests and admonitions of the religious elite".[13]

However, like their counterparts in medieval Christendom (e.g. Becket), these defenders of the faith lack both independent machinery to enforce their assessments and means of "protecting against governmental reprisal".[14] The result is a sociopolitical role which entails responsibility to a concept of higher law and its derivative standards of earthly justice and moral probity, but imposes severe limitations of action on those who assume the role. That such personal orientation towards traditional state authority tends to be either indignant hostility or abject resignation is only to be expected. The Kano Genawa, it is pertinent to note, customarily take pride in preferring service in independent or Alkali courts to subordinate membership of the Emir's Court, a custom nowadays not always individually honoured in the observance.

To be sure, influences other than those of the family were at work in Aminu Kano's earlier life: in particular western education (also partly at the Northern elite secondary school, which having been relocated at the Northern capital was accordingly renamed Kaduna College) and travel to England, where he was in touch with personalities on the left-wing of the Labour Party and exposed to the writings of Marx, Laski and Gandhi. Surely it is not without significance, however, that his earliest modern political mentor was one Malam Sa'adu Zungur. Zungur, whose great-grandfather is said to have studied under dan Fodio, was himself a noted Koranic scholar and, by the time Aminu met him, the most outspoken Northern detractor of the system of native authority and indirect rule.

In an interview with the author, Aminu Kano traced the roots of a deep enmity between himself and the Kano Native Authority to the six months when his father was Acting Chief Alkali. He related that on several occasions his father found himself at variance with the throne on questions of justice. One such incident he cited as a turning point personally: a servant of the late Emir (Bayero) had fallen out of royal favour and was to be ejected from the palace. His father insisted that justice required compensation to the servant for labour and money spent on improving his house, located within the palace walls. The Emir refused and there ensued a bitter dispute which eventually drew in the sons of the principal adversaries, Sanusi, then *Ciroma* (heir apparent) and later a powerful Emir of Kano, and Aminu. The incident illustrates the friction between traditional authority and the sort of ideals that engaged Aminu Kano's attention from his youth.

III. MODERN POLITICAL FOUNDATIONS

The three leaders' divergent backgrounds and future political views are reflected in the very manner and occasion of their entrance into the realm of modern politics. We have already noticed that Balewa began his political career in 1946 as a nominee of the Bauchi Native Authority (in effect the Emir of Bauchi) in a regional legislature then devoid of decision-making powers. In 1949 the Sokoto Sultan nominated the Sardauna to the same body in place of his deceased *Waziri* (Hausa corruption of "vizier" or prime minister). Neither Balewa nor the Sardauna associated himself openly with any overtly political organisation until late 1951, when the provisions of the new Constitution induced the NPC to convert from a self-styled "cultural society" to a political party. Elsewhere the point has been made that at this juncture the NPC virtually shed its original identity as a forum essentially for western educated, reform minded, "progressives" and became in essence a parliamentary caucus dominated by holders of traditional offices and titles in the emirates.[15]

This last development was in part a consequence of the 1951 constitutional provisions governing elections, which utilised various tiers of traditional councils as a chain of electoral colleges, and in effect helped emirs to control the results by authorising them to appoint 10 per cent of the membership of the highest level college. Modified systems of indirect election on this pattern were in force during the 1954 (federal) and 1956 (Northern region) elections: direct voting and adult male suffrage being introduced for the first time in the federal ("independence") election of 1959.

The 1955 Annual Party Convention of the NPC, of which the Sardauna had in the meantime become President-General and Balewa First Vice-President, voted to freeze its roster of officers for five years. (In the event, by the end of 1963 no further election of party officers and only a few party conventions had actually been held.)

The sum significance for our purposes of the circumstances described in the last three paragraphs is that during the whole period of Northern Nigeria's advance to self-government (1959) the Sardauna and Tafawa Balewa operated independently of direct mass political support, and of any real popular accountability. In fact they were modern politicians only in the quite limited sense that they were parliamentarians. As such they were free to formulate their own political roles—within the limits set by virtual dependence on the political sponsorship of traditionally composed native authorities.

Leading NPC members of the period state that originally the favourite candidate for the Presidency-General among the pre-1951 or "young Turk" wing of the party was Balewa, but that the party as a whole became persuaded that the Sardauna must occupy this office if the party was to enjoy the confidence of traditional rulers and their politically orthodox subjects. (Much the same line of reasoning was responsible for his selection by the British as the first Northern Minister for Local Government.) As head of the party commanding a majority in the regional legislature, the Sardauna later naturally assumed the post of Northern Premier. His attitude toward the forces mainly responsible for his position was summed up in an inimitable paraphrase of Churchill widely attributed to him: that he had not become Premier of the Northern Region in order to preside over the disintegration of his great-grandfather's empire. In a 1950 speech, otherwise famous for its incisive criticisms of the shortcomings of native administration, Balewa had already given some hint of his own inclination: "I do not wish to destroy, I call for reform"[16].

In contrast to the others, Aminu Kano did not occupy a seat in any Parliament before 1959. Along with Malam Sa'adu Zunger, he was forced out of the Executive Committee of the NPC in 1950 by the vote of a majority, who already by that date considered their radical slant inimical. To win support for his political programme, Aminu Kano was compelled to foster a mass political movement. An opportunity was presented in the form of the Northern Elements Progressive Union (NEPU), founded in August 1950; he joined and quickly thereafter assumed leadership. His newspaper article explaining the motive for this action, which entailed his resignation from a relatively secure position as a teacher in government service, made very plain the passions underlying his intention to employ NEPU as an uncompromising foe of traditionally constituted authority:

> I resigned because I refuse to believe that this country is by necessity a prisoner of the Anglo-Fulani autocracy or the unpopular indirect rule system.
> I resigned because there is no freedom to criticize this most unjust and anachronistic and un-Islamic form of hollow institutions promulgated by Lugard. I resigned because I fanatically share the view that the Native administrations, as they stand today, coupled with all their too trumpeted 'fine tradition', are woefully hopeless in solving our urgent educational, social, economic, political, and even religious problems . . .
> I cannot tolerate these institutions because of their smell. I cannot tolerate them because they do not tolerate anyone. They even go to the extent of dooming the future of their critics. I am prepared to be called by any name. Call me a dreamer or call me a revolutionary, call me a crusader or anything you will. I have seen a light on the far horizon and I intend to march into its full circle either alone or with anyone who cares to go with me.[17]

To complete this background to contemporary Northern Nigerian political controversy it is important to observe the suddenness with which the traditional society was confronted with modern western institutions of government. Indirect rule had assisted the survival into the present era of an extraordinarily resilient system of political autocracy. It was not primarily ferment from within that system but British colonial policy—revised under the pressure of African nationalism elsewhere (notably in southern Nigeria and Ghana)—that led to the introduction of democratic forms in Northern Nigeria, for the British invariably made acceptance of these forms a pre-condition to the transfer of power. The same influence determined the pace and timing of change, with the outcome that virtually within seven years (1952–59) Northern Nigeria spanned the enormous distance separating European medieval political institutions from those of modern representational government.

The democratic apparatus was introduced at the regional level of government, which did not, however, supplant local traditional systems. In fact the framework of emirate government was retained for the express purpose of a gradual transition to democratic local government. Apart from this deliberate "caution", the mere superimposition of representational forms was in itself powerless to eradicate the substance of a people's political habits, expectations, beliefs and values.

The net result has been to rule out explicit consideration, from first principles, as it were, of the merits of democratic institutions; doubtless a general desire to attract western investment capital further helps to obviate that issue still. Instead, the working ground of political contention in Northern Nigeria has been whether, or to what extent, those institutions are reconcilable with pre-established political norms, notably the traditional emirates' basis and structure of political participation. In essence, this has meant a dialogue, or rather trialogue, as we shall see, on the place, if any, of hierarchy in a putatively democratic society.

IV. THREE VIEWS

The Sardauna's roots and experience dispose him to be concerned primarily with values appropriate to the state as such, not particularly with those of the democratic variety. Thus, he is preoccupied with obedience, order, stability and discipline; and these are key words in almost all his important speeches. "Among the traditions we have inherited from our forefathers and which we intend to transmit to our descendants", he asserted in an address marking the attainment of Northern self-government, "there is none we prize more highly than respect for lawful constituted authority."[18] That the respect whereof he speaks has been inculcated by a century of rule under an autocratic regime based on conquest apparently represents in his eyes not the slightest debasement of its quality.

On the contrary, he takes enormous pride in the fact that the new democratic institutions of Northern Nigeria have so far derived their legitimacy and security from being linked, through himself and a considerable number of others in the new position of power,[19] to the Sokoto Empire. Thus he deliberately chose March 15, the date of the fall of Sokoto to British troops in 1903, to celebrate the resumption, as it were, of Northern self-government. A year later he confirmed that "to follow in the footsteps of my ancestors" was his ideal.[20]

However conspicuous is the element of sentiment in the Sardauna's visions of the past, it would be mistaken to conclude that these are devoid of political realism or resolved into indifference to modernity. He has repeatedly stressed the importance of social discipline in the task of economic development, which his government has in fact been pursuing seriously.[21] But many of the generally useful qualities for which he applauds ancient Fulani rule—the ability to command obedience, maintain order and stability, tax, administer, and even innovate[22]—plainly are also relevant to that task. Hence the Sardauna sees no good reason why the advantages of traditional hierarchy should be repudiated.

At the 1950 Ibadan Conference on the Nigerian Constitution, the fiery southern Nigerian nationalist, Mbonu Ojike, alluded to what he termed the universal decline of hereditary monarchy in this "the century of the common man". "If my friend might live for centuries," retorted the Sardauna coolly, "he might still find natural rulers in the North."[23] This remark, made in the context of negotiating the introduction of the democratic forms which, to the surprise of many observers, the Sardauna's regime increasingly welcomed, clearly did not mean espousal of the *status quo ante.* Evidently, what he meant to deny was that the right to choose representatives, or the injection of novel governmental functions, must require a wholly transformed structure of leadership.

In reckoning that a newly enfranchised people may affirm

the supremacy of its established rulers—that it may cling to belief in an innate capacity to govern—the Sardauna does not, of course, lack the comfort of historical precedent, that of the British being nearest to hand: "I am told that this belief [in continuity] has helped other nations to greatness, God willing it will do so for us".[24] With respect to the premise of Hausa-Fulani (and related) culture(s), which, as already indicated, evinces "a general preference for social continuity and for stability in the status order,"[25] he is on equally solid ground. In a mood of African self-discovery and self-affirmation, he even enjoys the grudging admiration of some of his strongest ideological assailants, who take pride in the emirate phenomenon as evidence of African ability to sustain a complex society.

But the Sardauna does not appear content to rely indefinitely on such propitious reflexes, however essential they may be to his initial opportunity to shape the future, in regard to which he approvingly cites the Hausa proverb "it is better to repair than to build afresh".[26] Rather, he seems to envisage a regime of aristocratic composition which will, like himself, accept the conditions and restraints of a framework of modernising and democratic institutions, and within it *earn,* as it were, the right to go on ruling.

An integral part of this vision is the insistent encouragement he has given the ruling classes to ensure that their offspring acquire the qualifications and skills of modern leadership. A number of emirs and hereditary nobles have responded by continuing in the practice, initiated in colonial days, of sending their sons to English public schools. The Sardauna's grasp of the long-term political significance of western education also underlies the gratitude he has often expressed to the founders of Katsina College, graduates of which, he points out with pride, "hold almost all the key positions in the administration of the Region today".[27]

The same vision has also led him to censure the behaviour of emirs far more frequently and forcefully than might otherwise be expected. His government, he warned early in 1961, "would not hesitate to remove any chief who is found guilty of oppression or of neglect of his duty".[28] Two years later came the abdication, under threat of deposition for maladministration, of the most powerful recent Northern Emir, Sanusi of Kano.[29] Such utterances and actions have naturally gone a long way towards reconciling the "young Turk" faction of the NPC to his steward-ship. Seemingly lest he create the impression of having lost faith in the traditional order, however, in the legislative com-mons he has more recently turned to expressions that leave little room for doubting his basic stand:

> Now all of us here are butterflies, we come and go but the Emirs are there. I wonder if any of those people who think that we are trying to down-grade the Chiefs or make them rubber stamps, can be called as *Sarkin Musulmi* or the Sardauna. (Applause). I am a member of the royal family and it will be a great shame and down-fall for me to see that Chieftaincy is degraded and if that should happen in this Region, I pray to God to do away with my life.[30]

The allusion to a connection between his personal destiny and that of traditional authority is more than fanciful. Indeed, cultivation of the style of ancestral figures in his role as Premier is pronounced and calculated. His dress (exquisite gowns and brocaded cloaks, the high turban—tied behind with the flourish reserved by custom to princes) and his magisterial physical bearing are only part of this. Lavish giftgiving, annual pilgrimages to Mecca accompanied in his aircraft by favoured associates, evening meals taken in his private residence with a large permanent inner circle, regularly widened by more oc-casional attenders (the scene's resemblance to that of dan Fo-dio and disciples is compelling), all help to build the image.

Opportunities for more pointed references are seldom lost. Campaigning for the first time in Bauchi Emirate, in connec-tion with the 1959 election, he gloried in the parallel that—with Tafawa Balewa acting as the Northern Premier's biggest lieu-tenant in the present day set-up of Nigeria—the relationship between Sokoto and Bauchi was as it had been "since the begin-ning of Fulani rule in the Region". (Yakubu, Bauchi Emir, was one of dan Fodio's early pupils and later a principal liegeman of the first Sokoto Sultan, Bello.)[31] When, at a post-election rally in Kaduna, the Sardauna announced a decision (since re-scinded) to retire soon from politics, he compared this to dan Fodio's action in renouncing earthly power in favour of his son Bello and brother Abdullahi. "When the current political battle is over", he stated, "I, too, will divide this country between two trustworthy lieutenants"; he then presented, in the manner of an emir conducting an investiture, an *alkyabba* (traditional cloak signifying bestowal of authority) to his "lieutenant in the South", Balewa.[32] The presentation of a horse to each of his ministers on the occasion of the first of a series of cabinet meetings at his Sokoto residence in January 1961 was in like vein.

Thus by 1963 the Premiership had already in certain quarters acquired a pseudonym (*Sarkin Arewa*—Emir of the North), although the Sardauna's ultimate personal ambition remains in Northern Nigeria a matter of some speculation, complicated by his often reiterated desire eventually to become Sultan of Sokoto. An ambition to ascend to that still lofty office is obviously inconsistent with an intention to reduce its dignity or impair its integrity. Whatever the future course of the Sardauna's role, clearly it serves at present not just to acknowledge but to reinforce his society's acceptance of the premise of hierarchy.

Succinctly put, the Sardauna's conception of democratic development is steady improvement and widening popular acceptance of governmental performance without essential damage to the elite composition of those who govern. In contrast, Aminu Kano's profound wish is to see the present basis and structure of authority, leadership and political participation transformed. His understanding of democracy extends to government "by", rather than just "for" and "of", the people. Whereas the Sardauna propounds in effect a doctrine of hierarchy based on a supposed natural harmony of interests between rulers and the ruled, Aminu Kano subscribes to the view that social hierarchy inevitably embodies conflict of divergent social class interests. Democracy to him is therefore the antithesis of hierarchy. Its development connotes a levelling process, indeed provides a necessary channel for the ultimate resolution of class conflicts.[33]

Distaste for the lordly comportment of aristocracy led Aminu Kano, as long ago as 1944, to place an advertisement in the Northern vernacular newspaper, *Gaskiya Ta Fi Kwabo,* calling on commoners *(talakawa)* to abandon such traditional habits of deference as taking off their shoes and prostrating themselves in the presence of *sarakuna* (royalty, nobility, and indeed all holders of traditional title and office). In one of his first speeches as NEPU leader, he asserted, before an astonished audience at Sokoto, that for emirs to defer to the *talakawa* whose taxes paid emirs' salaries would be more appropriate than the other way around.[34] At his insistence NEPU petitioners to emirs' judicial and executive councils nowadays usually keep their feet shod, their backs erect and withhold the traditionally prescribed praise-greetings (such as *"Zaki"* "Lion" or *"Rankya dade"* "May your life be prolonged") on the grounds that these gestures are offensive to human dignity.

One of the first and probably most successful of NEPU campaigns under Aminu Kano's leadership was directed against the practice of compulsory labour, for non-communal purposes, that in the North survived the enactment of the Nigerian Labour Code. Until the recent (1960) enactment of a new Penal Code the Northern legal setup, in which Native Authorities were in effect authorised to define and adjudicate native law and custom, protected these and other popularly detested official practices. Characteristically, Aminu Kano's response to such legal immunities to prosecution for maladministration was to try and inculcate in his followers respect for the doctrines of *satyagraha,* or non-violent civil disobedience as developed in India.[35] Although the principle of non-violence seems not to have penetrated, justifiable resort to action outside or even contrary to presently constituted authorities represents an important if unpublicised tenet of NEPU's political creed. At the same time Aminu Kano was a forceful advocate of legal limitations on government, such as prerogative writs (most of them were suspended between 1956 and 1959 in Northern courts), separation of judicial, legislative and executive authority (these still coalesce in the Native Authority system),[36] constitutional guarantees of civil liberties and due process of law. In keeping with the last principle, he was also closely identified with the successful movement to write the provisions of fundamental human rights, based on the UN Declaration, into the Nigerian Constitution. (The Sardauna not long ago expressed the view that the Fundamental Human Rights section of the Nigerian Constitution hinders "dealing with subversive elements in an emergency" and ought accordingly to be amended.)[37]

The crux of Aminu Kano's outlook is its transcendence of received sociopolitical arrangements, however viable these may now be in the circumstances of Northern Nigeria. It appears to stem, rather, from an *a priori* conception of man, in a manner consistent with a habit of deducing political institutions from religious premises and pitting their ideal sanctions against an opposing reality. Whether Islam actually endorses Aminu Kano's central political values, as he in fact contends,[38] is less important in the present context than the intellectual and moral *process* they reflect. His anti-hierarchical presuppositions apparently rest on a belief in universal perfectability—hence his abhorrence of a servile human posture. NEPU poems and songs, many of them written by Aminu Kano personally, are full of eschatological images expressing his perception of a desperate plight of the masses (e.g. "as skewered meat before the fire") and promising deliverance, a "new day", a basic reordering of the system of roles and rewards.[39]

While his party's programmes reflect the prevailing enthusiasm among contemporary African political leaders for economic development, his objective would appear to be an optimum point between material progress and active popular control; short of the ideal, might he in practice sacrifice a measure of the former goal for the sake of the latter? The possibility is suggested by the fact that, despite what has been called the African leader's belief in a divine right of the educated to lead, Aminu Kano has often said that the attraction of new leadership opportunities frequently leads the newer educated elite to compromise with political principle, hence to forfeiture of a claim to democratic leadership.[40] Ironically, this is a judgment to which his role in the Federal government has made him personally vulnerable, whether or not the role was assumed in order to combat the national political isolation and financial debility of NEPU as an organisation, as he insists.[41] However, his refusal to join other former opposition leaders in support of the NPC, or in a moratorium on criticism of Northern political life, together with his recent leadership of NEPU into a Northern Progressive Front in active opposition to the NPC, all suggest persistence of a political vision, once concisely expressed by him in these words:

We interpret democracy in its more traditional, radical sense, and that is the rule of the common people, the poor, the illiterate, while our opponents (the NPC) interpret it in its modern Tory sense, and that is the rule of the enlightened and prosperous minority in the supposed interest of the common people.[42]

Like the Sardauna, Balewa is highly conscious of the special requisites of leadership in a modernising state, and, like Aminu Kano, he clearly recognises the change in the scope of participation and source of political authority such a state may involve. Balewa's reaction to these matters differs, however, from that of either of the other two.

Thus he assumes that in the long run new conditions will give rise to a new class whose attributes and self-interests do not coincide with those of even "enlightened traditional rulers". The assumption was articulated in a now famous speech, in the Northern legislature, calling for reforms in the system of native administration:

The Natural Rulers of the North should realise that Western education and world conditions are fast creating a new class of people in the North. That this new class must exist is certain, and the Natural Rulers, whom the North must retain at all costs, should instead of suspecting it, try to find it proper accommodation.[43]

As probably the most outstanding of this "emergent" class, Balewa might have been expected to welcome the development even at the expense of "Natural Rulers". This and other speeches definitely show otherwise, however. To the remarks above he added:

I will personally prefer to see such changes coming first from the Natural Rulers rather than from the new class. Things are rapidly changing and much trouble and bitterness could be avoided if those in high positions of authority would keep their eyes open and agree to move with the times.

At the same time, his indictment, in the same speech, of a propensity on the part of native administration for "putting square pegs in round holes" revealed a disbelief in the claims to inherent superiority made by the traditional class.

The clue to this speech and to Balewa's general outlook would appear to lie in his perception of a dilemma confronting him and others like him in developing societies. In brief, the dilemma is that, while a person like Balewa is aware that objectively his talents and skills are potentially beneficial to his society in terms of economic progress, he is also aware that the overwhelming majority of his society's people are illiterate, relatively isolated from the outside world, and otherwise in no position fully to appreciate his potential contribution, or even to share his aspiration for them. He understands, in other words, that democratic control of political recruitment under these circumstances may prejudice both the progress of his society and his own chances for leadership. In the case of western societies the dilemma was obviated, or at least alleviated, by the protracted extension of the franchise and other devices that delayed exercise of popular sovereignty. Balewa appears to have sensed that the suddenness of institutional change rendered far more vulnerable the position of the "new class" in Northern Nigeria. The misgiving underlies his remarks concerning the initial proposal to install elected representatives as government ministers in the North:

> There are men, as I say, Mr. Chairman, who can shoulder these responsibilities but do we all believe that it is those type of people whom I have in mind who will be given the opportunity of shouldering those responsibilities?[44]

Active participation and control on the part of the peasant masses of Hausaland might take one of two forms, equally deplorable from Balewa's point of view: acquiescence in autocracy and despotism, or the embrace of revolutionary programmes of change and of leaders productive of chaos. Thus, distrust of politicians and anxiety about the response of the masses are the two recurrent major themes in Balewa's reflections on the coming of democracy.[45] "Even when Nigeria is ripe for responsible government," he argued, "leadership . . . should not be granted through the medium of its people who are agitating."[46] "The few of us here", he remarked on another occasion in the Legislature, "represent millions of people, the majority of whom, apart from being illiterate, is still very incapable of understanding what we are doing."[47] To the radical critics of traditional authority he remonstrated: "Now let me warn them ... that if they abuse authority, in the same way the people of whom they expect to be masters will abuse their authority in their time".[48]

For these problems, Balewa's solution has been a partnership patterned on his personal history. Traditional rulers can use their hold on popular loyalties to elevate new men of talent to responsible positions of power. In return, traditional leaders may be reassured, as he has repeatedly insisted, that modern and traditional leadership need not be antagonistic.[49]

In contrast to the Sardauna, Balewa's commitment to traditional authority is essentially instrumental or pragmatic; the partnership between the new men of talent and the knights of traditional legitimacy might in due course be happily liquidated. In keeping with his experience, Balewa's conception of the proper basis and structure of authority in the modern state is in essence bureaucratic, or, to use a more current term, meritocratic. Indeed, it may be this element in his thinking, rather than personal taste for dead ideological centre, that makes him a disappointment to the Northern Nigerian far right and far left alike.

Conclusion

The three leaders' different perspectives on hierarchy might be traced in their attitudes on other currently unresolved controversies in Northern Nigeria, such as socialism, female suffrage, constitutional reform, pan-Africanism, foreign policy and the implications of Islamic faith in the modern world. The analysis here of their positions on one central issue may at least suggest, however, their respective approaches to other matters.

The contention here has not been that the traditional culture alone has influenced them, nor that it has done so in mechanistic fashion. Islamic doctrine, western education, Katsina College, careers in teaching, European contact and travel, to mention only those factors alluded to above, are doubtless separable and important. It is worth observing, however, that each appears to have reacted selectively to his set of common experiences, seizing on different possible interpretations of it.

Thus, Aminu Kano fastened on the egalitarian implications of Islam and was drawn to the more radical strains in English politics represented by Laski and the left wing of the Labour Party, while pre-democratic aspects of Islamic doctrine and English society were perceived by Balewa and the Sardauna.[50] The essence of the argument is that traditional political culture has constituted for these leaders a special kind of "cognitive map", pointing each in a different direction of thought and action.

While the political thinking and behaviour of these men may have been oriented by the character of an indigenous African society, the substance of the issue discussed here is hardly unfamiliar to western societies. Without overstressing the parallel, one may, for instance, find in the predilections of the Sardauna, Balewa, and Aminu Kano clear echoes of Adams, Jefferson and Tom Paine. Indeed, the current Northern Nigerian scene serves to remind that, far from resolving all important issues, the formal adoption of democratic institutions leaves open to choice some of the most basic political values and objectives.

NOTES

1. Field-work in Northern Nigeria in 1959–60 and July-September 1963 was made possible through grants from the Social Science Research Council, and African Studies Center, University of California, Los Angeles, respectively. The author is also indebted for related assistance to the Center of International Studies, Princeton University. None of these organisations bears any responsibility for statements in this paper.

2. According to Professor Gabriel Almond, "political systems tend to perpetuate their structures through time, and. . . they do this mainly by means of the socializing influences of the primary and secondary structures through which they pass in the process of maturation . . . Political socialization is the process of induction into the political culture. Its end product is a set of attitudes—cognitions, value standards, and feelings—toward the political system, its various roles and role incumbents". *The Politics of the Developing Areas,* (Princeton, 1960), 27. The concepts of political socialisation and political culture,

which appear to bear resemblance to the concept of "national character" and perhaps also to the Marxian notion of a relationship between "structure" and "superstructure," are implicitly applicable in the context of this paper. It is not to be inferred, however, that the relationship of such general factors as these concepts point to in the case herein discussed is, in the view of the author, either inevitably decisive or universally operative.

3. See M. G. Smith, "The Beginnings of Hausa Society: A. D. 1000–1500" in J. Vansina *et al* (ed.), *The Historian in Tropical Africa,* (London, 1964), 339–54.

4. For recent illuminating discussions of indirect rule and its architect in Northern Nigeria, see M. Perham, *Lugard: The Years of Authority, 1898–1945,* (London, 1960), 138–73; M. Bull, "Indirect Rule in Northern Nigeria, 1906–1911" in K. Robinson and F. Madden (ed.) *Essays in Imperial Government,* (Oxford, 1963), 47–87.

5. The impact of the traditional emirate system of government and politics on the modern system is the subject of C. S. Whitaker, Jr., *The Politics of Tradition: A Study of Continuity and Change in Northern Nigeria, 1946–60* (PT) (Unpublished Ph. D. thesis, Princeton University, 1964).

6. Alhaji Sir Ahmadu Bello, *My Life,* (London, 1962), 239.

7. *Ibid.,* 102

8. *Ibid.,* 58–9.

9. *Ibid.*

10. As a legal status, slavery in Northern Nigeria was abolished in principle by Lugard's Proclamation, 1 January 1900. However, the designation of individuals as slaves or descendants of slaves is a social usage which persists in Northern Nigeria, thanks in no small measure to the fact that Lugard's Proclamation in effect allowed those slaves who failed to apply for legal manumission to continue functioning as before. The progeny of such slaves were automatically free at birth before the law, but Hausa society has emphasised slave parentage, as reflected in use of the terms *dimajo* (pl. *dimajai*) or *bacucune* (*cucunawa*—used especially in Kano). Hence, as the author has witnessed, in Bauchi Emirate the Prime Minister is sometimes referred to in these terms. In and outside Bauchi, however, most people appear to be either ignorant of the facts of Balewa's background or anxious to conceal them, perhaps particularly from foreign researchers. For fuller discussion and interesting analysis of the Hausa institution of

slavery and the British impact on it see M. G. Smith, *Government in Zazzau* (GZ) (London, 1960), 253 ff,; and "Slavery and Emancipation in Two Societies (Jamaica and Zaria)", 3 *Social and Economic Studies* (1954), 239–88.

11. See M. G. Smith, "The Hausa System of Social Status", 39 *Africa* *(1959)*, 239–52.

12. E. I. J. Rosenthal, *Political Thought in Medieval Islam* (London, 1958), 23.

13. G. E. Von Grunebaum, *Islam: Essays in the Nature and Growth of a Cultural Tradition* (Memoir No. 81) 57 pt. 2, *American Anthropologist* (1955), 133–4.

14. *Ibid.*

15. R. L. Sklar and C. S. Whitaker, Jr., "Nigeria", in J. S. Coleman and C. G. Rosberg (ed.), *Political Parties and National Integration in Tropical Africa* (Berkeley and Los Angeles, 1964), 607–9.

16. Northern Nigeria, R. C. Deb., 19.8.50,4.

17. "My Resignation," *Daily Comet* (Kano), 11.11.50, 1 and 4.

18. *Northern Nigeria's Day of History: Speeches made by H. E. the Governor, Sir Gawain W. Bell and the Hon. Premier, Alhaji Sir Ahmadu Bello, on Sunday, 15th March, 1959* (NNDH) (Kaduna, 1959), 2.

19. See Whitaker, PT, 389–90, which contains a tabulation, based on intensive interviews and surveys, showing that from 72 to 84 per cent of the emirate members of the Northern House of Assembly in 1959 belonged to the traditional ruling class. The corresponding figure for Northern Ministers is 17 out of 19.

20. Northern Nigeria, H. A. Deb, 16.4.60, 291.

21. See Ministry of Trade and Industry, Northern Nigeria, *The Industrial Potentialities of Northern Nigeria* (Kaduna, 1963), 11–14.

22. For an account of the incorporation of modern technical functions and departments of administration into the traditional bureaucracy during the colonial period see M. G. Smith, GZ, 230–4.

23. *Proceedings of the General Conference on Review of the Nigerian Constitution,* January 1950 (Lagos: 1950), 142.

24. *NNDH,* 6.

25. M. G. Smith, "The Hausa System of Social Status", *loc. cit.,* 248.

26. *NNDH,* 6.

27. *Ibid.,* 2.

28. *Daily Times* (Lagos), 30.1.61, 1

29. See the brief summation of the background to this case in B. J. Dudley, "The Nomination of Parliamentary Candidates in Northern Nigeria", 2 *Journal of Commonwealth Political Studies* (1963), 58 (note 51).

30. Northern Nigeria, H. A. Deb., 9.9.63, 66.

31. *Nigerian Citizen* (Zaria), 11.11.59, 16.

32. *Ibid.,* 19.12.59, 1.

33. *NEPU/SAWABA Declaration of Principles* (Jos, 1950), articles 2 and 3.

34. First-hand account of speech in possession of the author.

35. *Daily Comet* (Kano), 2.10.51, 1.

36. *Native Authority Law, 1954* (as amended) (Kaduna, n.d.), Part III and, for a discussion of its provisions, Whitaker, PT, 234 ff.

37. Northern Nigeria, H. A. Deb., 9.8.63, 46.

38. A persistent theme in mass-rally political speeches of Aminu Kano and other NEPU religious "specialists" is, in essence, that the modern ideals of political accountability and popular participation are implicit in the Islamic concept of *"ijma"* (consensus of the community in being) as a source of law and legitimacy. Interviews in Kano, Zaria, and Kaduna, May and October 1959; Tunis, January 1960; New York, November 1961; Kano and Kaduna, August 1963.

39. The name of a NEPU ancillary organisation, inaugurated by Aminu Kano, is *Nujumu Zaman* ("start of a new day"); others include *Zaharal Haq* ("truth is revealed"), and *Tab'iunal Haq* ("the masses will rule those now ruling").

40. The verse of one NEPU song-poem about the educated elite reads:

> You through hankering for a salaried job
> your attitude has made a volte-face,
> so that continually you take the way of corruption.
> On the day of resurrection, the day of settlement,
> you will be cast into the fire.

Alba Maikwaru, "The song: we recognize those who have wronged us", pamphlet (Kano, n. d.).

41. Interview in Tunis, January 1960, Kaduna, August 1963.

42. "Presidential Address to the Fifth Annual Conference of the Northern Elements Progressive Union", quoted in R. L. Sklar, *Nigerian Political Parties: Power in an Emergent African Nation* (Princeton, 1963), 372.

43. Northern Nigeria, H. C. Deb., 19.8.50,4.

44. *Proceedings, 1950, loc. cit.,* 68; c. f. Nigeria, L. C. Deb., 16.3.49, 47.

45. Nigeria, L. C. Deb., 24.3.47, 212; 21.8.48, 193; 16.3.49, 474; 30.3.49, 723-4; Northern Nigeria, R. C. Deb., 21.1.47, 17–18; Northern Peoples' Congress, *Minutes: Emergency Convention,* 1953 (mimeographed, n. d.), 1.

46. Nigeria, L. C. Deb., 24.3.47, 212; c.f. Northern Nigeria, H. A. Deb., 20.2.54, 242–4.

47. Nigeria, H. R. Deb., 20.3.52, 325.

48. Nigeria, L. C. Deb., 30.3.49, 724.

49. Northern Nigeria, R. C. Deb., 11.12.50, 105, see also note 45 above.

50. Upon the occasion of British Prime Minister Macmillan's visit to Northern Nigeria, just after the British and Nigerian Federal elections of 1959, the Sardauna remarked that "the conservatives had won in England and the conservatives also won in Nigeria." *Northern Nigeria Daily Press Service,* No. 87, 16.1.60. Most likely the Sardauna had in mind a parallel in sociopolitical history, not a comparison of party manifestoes!

CHAPTER 21

Bornu and Nigeria: "Political Kingdom" in a Troubled Nation[1]

RONALD COHEN

The Theoretical Problem

All societies exist in an inter-societal environment and always have, even if such societies are simply series of widely separated families wandering across an unfriendly landscape hunting and gathering for food. This means that relations between groups are as old and as widespread as man himself, even though anthropologists have concentrated more often upon the social interaction of persons at the intra-societal level. With the disappearance of isolated or semi-isolated autonomous non-Western societies, it now becomes essential to look at ethnic groups with a new perspective. Instead of viewing them as if they were whole and independent units, it becomes important to see them as part of some larger system of interaction.[2] Applying this approach to the particular case under investigation, we can explore the Bornu kingdom's pattern of interaction with other societies in the past and the present.

At a more abstract level, such a probe into one case can pose some fundamental questions about the nature of persistence—a basic quality in both functional analysis and systems theory.[3] In classic functional analysis in anthropology, the ultimate reason given for the existence of a particular behavior is the contribution such an activity makes to the continuity or persistence of the system. If this is a basic weakness in functional theory, then the crucial way to break through this criticism is to compare interaction systems that do persist through time with those that do not. Such phenomena as, for example, marriage and divorce, international relations (especially (a) war and peace and (b) the creation and atrophy of international organizations), revolutions, or solvency and bankruptcy—all represent systems that exist along a continuum from persistence to non-persistence. Such investigations can thus produce more than sterile imputations of functionality, since the "more than - less than" variation in persistence is available for empirical study. Research and theory which pays just as much attention to the "death" of the system as it does to its continued existence must be designed.

In summary, I wish to ask two rather broad questions. First —what has been the nature of Bornu relations to other societies, and second—what factors have contributed to the persistence and lack of persistence of these relations as the conditions of inter-societal relations have changed?

The Pre-Colonial Independence

Before the days of Nigeria, Bornu was an old empire and a great power of the Sudan. Founded in the fifteenth century as a successor state to Kanem, she has survived upheavals, wars, economic recessions, conquest, colonialism and Nigerian independence.[4] This long period involved great power relations with other Sudanic empires—Songhai, Wadai, Sokoto—and the states of North Africa as well. Such relations were characterized by diplomacy, trade, the exchange of Islamic scholars and the see-saw ups and downs of power politics in which each state acted as a nucleus of power surrounded by its tributary states and wider area of hegemony.

What distinguishes Bornu from almost all of the other Sudanic kingdoms is the sheer longevity of its national status. The dynasty was founded, as far as we can tell, some time in the first millenium A.D. in the kingdom of Kanem, to the northeast of Lake Chad. After this earlier kingdom was taken over by a rebel group in the 14th century, the members of the royal clan, their friends, followers, and slaves fled to present-day Bornu and ultimately set up a new state—Bornu, with a great capital, Birni Gazargamo or "walled fortress"—on the Yo River. Ghana, Mali, Songhai and Darfur rose and fell, coming at last to be part of the archaeological record. But Bornu, along with Sokoto—which was founded in the nineteenth century (the recent past in Bornu terms)—continued on to the present day as the two great emirate kingdoms of what is now the northern part of modern Nigeria.

This longevity is an important quality in the cultural birthright of every Kanuri. If a culture is, among other things, a system of values, then the Kanuri culture of Bornu has always been dominant and independent in its part of the world. A separate language—the only central Saharan language presently spoken in Nigeria—and distinctive tribal markings and women's hair styles, as well as other distinctive Kanuri cultural modes are highly valued, as such things are within all cultures. But to the Kanuri their cultural idiosyncracies are also a part of the historic uniqueness, independence and greatness of their society in its relation to others.

Again, such pride is not unique, but in relation to most of the other peoples in this area it rests not only on past glory but on the fact that they survived while others did not. Songhai was overthrown by the Morroccans; the Hausa states and Nupe were conquered by the Fulani; the Jukun kingdom disappeared. But Bornu survived, or as one old and learned Kanuri friend put it, "Kanuri have always been strong."

The reaons for this exceptional adaptive capacity are complex and I have dealt with them in greater detail elsewhere.[5] Suffice it to say here that the Kanuri developed a highly centralized and flexible form of government in the Chad basin in which outlying territories could be added or lost, without destroying the continuity of the centuries-old administration. The system of open recruitment to office, in which eligibles for places in the administration were chosen either from among the entire lineage of the previous incumbent or transferred to a loyal follower of the monarch or superior lord in a feudal hierarchy, ensured that no entrenched patrimonies developed as they did in Europe. This was strengthened by the use of eunuchs and slaves for many important offices in government whose entire social position was a function of their loyalty and obedience to the monarch. Thus power and authority constantly gravitated towards the center rather than away from it, as it did in classical European feudalism of the 12th and 13th centuries. In Europe the dispersion of centralized power eventually meant the destruction of royal prerogatives which could only be resuscitated many years later under new kinds of governments and social systems. By contrast, the lack of tendencies towards decentralization of power in Bornu meant that the state—or at least its central government—could persist and thrive over a very long period.

As I have already noted, such survival also brings with it an ideology of longevity and an identity that has become part of the political culture of the people. Cultural values emphasize this persistence and the Kanuri use these beliefs as a rationale for the fostering of Bornu autonomy and Bornu interests in their relations with other ethnic groups and polities. In other words, to be a Kanuri living in Bornu is to be part of an ancient and living tradition that claims Bornu as a political system whose interests are to be fostered and whose local autonomy is to be protected.

The Colonial Period: Autonomy Within Conquest

Bornu was widely known throughout Europe long before the colonial period. Mentioned in European maps of the 15th century and in Barth's famous history of the area in the 1850's, it was first visited by English explorers in the early 19th century.[6] Thus when the British first arrived as colonial masters in the early 20th century, they were prepared to take over an ancient kingdom rather than just another unknown African tribe. Old "Bornu hands" in the colonial service such as McLintock, Palmer, Niven, Letchworth and many others who served in Bornu, developed a reverence, loyalty and respect for the emirate and its traditions that parallels that of the Kanuri themselves. Several of them, such as Palmer, Benton and Ellison came to be accomplished scholars of Bornu history and culture. In other words, here was a people with a culture and a history that made sense to the English, many of whom had sentimental feelings about the feudal roots of their own society.

Even Lugard, who rarely ever visited Bornu, was convinced by what he and his wife knew of Bornu that he should protect the Kanuri language. He therefore did not insist that Hausa be taught in Western schools when such schools were opened in the emirate early in this century.[7] As a result, Kanuri continued to be the recognized language of the emirate government—a language not closely related to other Nigerian tongues. The uniqueness and separate identity given to the area by its possession of a different language was thereby preserved by an official decision.

This does not mean that colonialism did not bring change to Bornu. But just as Lugard had helped to create Buganda as a political kingdom in Uganda, so did his overlordship and those who followed his policies create, allow, or adjust to the inevitability of a similar phenomenon in Northern Nigeria.[8] By 1914 the outlines of the present political system had emerged from a decade of experimentation and mutual adaptation in which the Kanuri and British argued politely over the emerging structure of the twentieth century emirate government. In general, Kanuri leaders tried to maintain existing offices and to create as many new offices as possible so that government patronage could be expanded downwards from the throne to every sector of society. On their side, the British felt that restricting the number of office-holders would increase efficiency and decrease the possibilities of "corruption." In the end, hundreds of nineteenth century fiefs were consolidated into approximately twenty districts under a district head. This official was moved from the capital to the districts and served locally as a direct representative of the central emirate government. At the center a Shehu's Council—under the chairmanship of the Waziri or chief minister—served as an appointed cabinet with each councillor taking over the duties of an evolving emirate or Native Authority (N.A.) department.

The emirate was, however, only one, albeit by far the largest portion of Bornu Province. At the head of the province was a Resident Officer responsible for the various emirates and divisions of the province. Under him were the district and technical officers. The former dealt with the administrative hierarchy and the courts, while the technical officers dealt with the various departments in each emirate and division of the province. As it finally evolved, the provincial government—staffed almost entirely by colonial officials—was in turn responsible to the Northern Regional administration in Kaduna, and from there to the federal government of Nigeria.[9] If this were put in American terms, it would be similar to making Texas into a major county of the state or province of New Mexico, while New Mexico would be under the jurisdiction of the regional government of the southwestern states, which in turn would be responsible to Washington. In other words, there would be four levels of hierarchy from Texas to Washington, as there were from the Bornu kingdom to Federal Nigeria until 1968. In such situations, local autonomy flourishes and federal power is weakened by its lack of direct authority at the local level.

Not only were the administrative levels numerous and complex between the emirate government and the federal capital at Lagos, but the enforcement of policy was extremely difficult. A small handful of colonial officials at the provincial level and possibly three to six administrative officers at the emirate level were responsible for carrying out regional and federal policies. No wonder then that officially banned practices—such as slave raiding—were carried on for several decades. Important administrative policies, such as that in which district heads were enjoined to act through the local village area heads rather than their own followers, took many years to implement. Although the system of taxation was reformed and a modern treasury set up, feudal tributes continued to be delivered and collected as well. This helped to maintain a political system that remained in many respects very similar to its pre-colonial progenitor in form and function. Thus chiefs still adjudicated disputes, and still had to use their own clients and unsalaried retainers to collect tax revenues. To maintain their tax collecting organization, district chiefs had to obtain larger revenues than they were allowed as salaries under the colonial system. Their answer was to continue many of the feudal practices of their pre-colonial chiefly antecedents, while at the same time acknowledging the new demands of office fostered by the colonial regime.[10] Not to do so would have meant inability to round up cattle nomads, leading to a drop in revenue collections and a drop in their reputation as efficient chiefs.

However, autonomy was by no means total. Over and over again, ordinary peasants have told me that the one great gift of colonialism was the protection it afforded them against the excesses of the few unwise and despotic chiefs. Where previously they could only run away from over-tax-conscious fief holders, they could—under the British—complain to a touring British officer. In other words, colonialism did offer the peasant a way out of the tightly organized polity of Bornu—and everyone seems to have known this from early in the present century onwards. At the center of the emirate, the administration was ultimately responsible to higher provincial authorities, and through them to Kaduna (regional) and Lagos (federal) levels of administration. Indeed, in the middle 1950's a treasury scandal brought these higher levels to bear on the local scene; many of the Bornu officials were forced to resign, while some were successfully prosecuted for embezzling emirate funds.

Up until the end of World War II, as I have reported elsewhere, a see-saw balance developed in which the British kept thrusting gently in the direction of western bureaucratic norms while the Kanuri parried to preserve their own autonomy.[11] After the war, increased tax revenues and the development of Nigerian nationalism brought new influences into the emirate which required a response. However, the end result was—not surprisingly—the maintenance of Bornu control over its own affairs and the achievement of a recognized place in the nationalist movement. Increased revenues produced more complex development schemes and programs for the emirate government. However, the N.A. Council, especially under the very able leadership of Sir Kashim Ibrahim (as Waziri 1956–60)—a former federal minister of education—was perfectly capable of using the new funds for locally productive purposes. New schools, roads, wells, market places and modern office buildings for the emirate government were planned and developed along with programs for the encouragement of local entrepreneurial activity. There was, and is, nothing necessarily anti-progressive in emirate government structure or ideology. Indeed, I have never met a Bornu official who is not convincingly committed to the modern development of the emirate in the social and economic spheres. As long as their hallowed traditions and the essentials of their present political system remain unthreatened, Kanuri officials have always been devoted to progress in the emirate.

In the realm of trade, national and local policies dovetailed to reinforce each other. The national marketing boards—set up during the war to ensure price stabilization and crop delivery to the metropole country—encouraged local entrepreneurship by limiting the buying operations of the large expatriate companies so that Africans could enter the export trade. Local, regional, and national loans stimulated the development of local traders and curtailed the older oligopolistic control of larger-scaled trade by non-Nigerians. One sombre forecast was sounded, however. In the early to mid-nineteen-fifties, pressures built up locally in Bornu to limit the commercial access of Ibos to trade and transport in ground-nuts, whether they were resident in Bornu or not. In general, though, post-war economic growth stimulated local development and this was regarded favorably at all levels of government. Except for this limiting of expatriate commercial enterprise and various local attempts to limit Ibo competition, there was little difficulty in both developing economically and maintaining previous levels of autonomy. Indeed, these limitations were themselves signs of the clarity of Bornu's policies—development, yes; but by and for non-Bornuans, no!

In the political realm, Bornu had few if any really significant relations outside the province until after the second world war. Until that time, basic contacts went in and out of the emirate through the provincial government—i.e. through the local colonial officials. These officials spoke and acted for what they believed to be the best interests of the emirate throughout most of this century. It is the very essence of a master-servant relationship that the master take seriously his responsibilities for the welfare of his charge. Most British officials whom I knew in pre-independence Bornu were men who rationalized their superior social and political positions with a Schweitzer-like paternalism. But certainly in order to do so, they had to feel they were acting in the best interests of the "native population". Thus these men pressured for more funds, more local health programs, more development schemes for "their" territory. They thus acted not only as administrative agents who had to initiate and enforce regional and national policies locally, but they represented Bornu to the outside world.

However, that outside world began to change with accelerating swiftness from the 1940's onwards. Nationalist agitation in the 1940's led to various constitutional conferences in the late 1940's and 1950's. Participation in these conferences stimulated a growing northern awareness that Nigeria was moving towards independence. Within this overall development, Bornu experienced quite suddenly in terms of what had gone on before, the thrusting on to the local scene of a number of phenomena that permeated her protective shield of local autonomy and created a demand for new adaptations—some of which were easy, others of which brought deep travail.

The easiest adaptation to make was to the Nigerianization of the federal and regional civil service, the army, and the incipient diplomatic corps. As one of the "great powers" in the federation, Bornu demanded her place at conference tables, in Commonwealth high commissions around the world, and in the rapidly expanding agencies at all levels of regional and federal governments. As one Kanuri put it to me, "We may not have as many technically trained people, but we are natural rulers and administrators." The implication here is simply that Kanuri have natural talents which are useful for governing at all levels. Although exact data are lacking, there is no question that Kanuri began showing up in appointment lists at all levels, and that almost without exception there has always been at least one Kanuri of cabinet-level rank in the Nigerian federal government. This does not mean that such appointees were men of inferior talents foisted on a weak central government by the strength of an ethnic pressure group. Men like Sir Kashim Ibrahim, Zana Bukar Dipcharima and Shettima Ali Monguno, are government servants of exceptional talents and would honor any administration by the contributions they made and are making to the Nigerian federal government.

Reconciliation politics requires some form of significant representation at the center by the major polities within the system. In the country as a whole each region came to have two vital interests which it wished to have represented in the federal government—namely regional autonomy and access to power and privilege at the center. During the 1950's furthering these interests came to be the function of political parties each of which represented a different area of the country. Although efforts were made to widen Southern bases of support, in the North very little ever came of them. Instead Northern interests were articulated by the N.P.C. (Northern Peoples Congress) which came to dominate representative government in the North and carry Northern interests onto the national scene. The reasons for this are complex and beyond the scope of this paper;[12] suffice it to say here that the nationalist and Nigerianization thrust began in the South and was soon articulated through the programs of southern-based political parties and the speeches of their leaders. When the competitive stimulus provided by federal elections and appointments to high office hit the North, the traditional leaders responded with their own national party (N.P.C.) in order to meet this competition.

During the 1950's the N.P.C. was the means by which the Bornu government joined onto emerging Nigerian politics while the nation took on the superficial shape of representative institutions. Locally, an opposition party developed, known as the Bornu Youth Movement (B.Y.M.). It allied itself ultimately with N.E.P.U. (Northern Elements Progressive Union) which was in turn linked loosely to the Ibo-dominated N.C.N.C. in southern Nigeria. Led by a well-intentioned reform-minded Kanuri, the party gathered to itself a mixed following of the disenchanted elements of Bornu. These ranged from small traders who felt left out of an authority system to junior civil servants who resented traditional recruitment practices and promotional criteria. Many well-qualified persons felt disappointed that the mere accidents of age and recruitment timing had put them into subordinate positions.

B.Y.M. political meetings emphasized these grievances and proposed more rationalized bureaucratic procedures using a merit system plus more elective positions open to all within the emirate, and most importantly—according to leaders whom I interviewed in 1957—the establishment of an independent judiciary. This last point was important because they felt that with no independent rule of law they would be unable to operate without continual harassment from those in power who supported the dominant N.P.C.

It is important to note in this regard that no unified system of law has existed in Bornu throughout the twentieth century.

Non-Muslims, such as Ibos, some Yorubas and others who had civil disputes involving Muslims could go before a Muslim judge or a magistrate. In such situations one of the persons involved was on extremely foreign soil in which legal rulings, rules of evidence, indeed the entire corpus of conflict resolution was something very different from anything the person might be used to in the past. Thus there was no commonly agreed upon technique for resolving disputes between persons living in Bornu who might represent Muslim and non-Muslim elements in Nigeria as a whole.

In such a situation the British were caught in the chain of their own prejudices without the standards of procedure for which their own democratic political traditions should have prepared them. Thus in 1957 when B.Y.M. night meetings were being heavily attended in Maiduguri, the emirate authorities withdrew permission for such meetings and issued permits for daylight gatherings only. The reason given by emirate authorities to the British for such a restriction was fear of night-time disorders—which the British believed and which may have been true. However, the change from night to daytime meetings cut attendance drastically and embittered the B.Y.M. leadership. The British felt the opposition to be a group of rowdies who threatened law and order. On the other hand, if party politics was to upset the grandeur of Bornu, then the colonial officials believed that it was much the wiser course to leave the direction of such activities to those with political experience and sagacity—namely, the traditional leaders of the emirate whom they knew and whose behavior was predictable.

On their side, the dominant party also organized meetings. At such gatherings, local headmen, district heads, emirate government senior officials, including leading alkali (judges) would attend and be given special seats of honor. Speakers, who were invariably not candidates but specialists at political harangue, would describe the evils of the opposition party, not in political but in moral terms. The B.Y.M. was accused of making sons disobey their fathers, of enticing wives to leave their husbands, and of preaching disrespect for traditional chiefs and ultimately for Islam itself. On this latter note it was pointed out that the opposition party had ties to the N.C.N.C. (Ibo-dominated) party and could not therefore be considered pro-

Islamic, meaning therefore that it was against Islam—indeed, against everything dear, proper and holy.

In such an atmosphere it is not surprising that ultimately violence broke out. A number of clashes occurred between followers of the two parties, or rather between B.Y.M. supporters and the combined forces of N.P.C. followers and followers of the traditional authorities. These climaxed in riots during 1958 —when many on both sides were killed. The B.Y.M. broke up and its leaders fled to other parts of Nigeria and to neighboring Chad.

Thus several years before Nigerian independence, multi-party politics was a dead issue in Bornu. The N.P.C. gave the emirate access to positions in Nigeria outside the emirate and was controlled locally by the emirate government itself. Nigerian party politics had come and gone—not without strife— but leaving the emirate again in control. Party conflict and competition was to be something that occurred elsewhere—at a different level. This was the level of national politics; and here Bornu joined forces with those of similar interests in the N.P.C. in competition and sometimes cooperation with the southern regions of Nigeria, in order to maintain a dominant position in the federal government.

Paper Independence: 1960–1964

Compared to many countries in Africa and throughout the colonial world, Nigeria's struggle for independence was minimal, more similar to Canada than Kenya in the type of efforts needed to obtain international recognition as a nation state. In providing the federal, regional, provincial and sub-provincial structures through negotiation and consultation with Nigerian leaders the British believed a lasting viable democracy had been successfully planted in Africa. And for a while, at least, the system seemed to operate as intended. But just under the surface, forces were gathering which would threaten and ultimately destroy the federal structure of 1960.

The most potent of these forces was what came to be called "tribalism" in Nigerian English. This is the use of ethnic constituencies as interest groups whose leaders compete for power and control in the national government. Whether or not the ethnic group was united before "tribalism" is of little importance since ethnic politics produces the unity, once leaders propagandize the point that the "tribe" is being treated as a unit in the federal and regional system.

In Bornu the politics of the northern region was seen in precolonial terms. In the nineteenth century the two great powers of the Nigerian Sudan had been Sokoto and Bornu. After 1960, the Sardauna of Sokoto was head of the N.P.C. and Premier of Northern Nigeria. To balance this leading position by Sokoto, Bornu was given the Governorship and Sir Kashim Ibrahim resigned as Waziri or chief minister of Bornu to become the first Nigerian governor of the North. Thus the two most senior political posts were shared between Sokoto and Bornu, reflecting the importance paid to such traditional ethnic distinctions.

However, back in Bornu little was changed. The structure of Nigerian government which had evolved before independence gave the emirate as much autonomy as before. More positions were made available regionally and federally for Kanuri, and local leaders saw the need for more education so that Kanuri would continue to qualify for their ethnic share of the national patronage pie. Relations to the outside still went through provincial officials—who were now Northern Nigerians. The party also served this purpose and in some few cases, such as elections and the 1962–3 census, Bornu was expected to act in union with the North in competition with the South. These few occasions were always in her best interests and even ordinary people on the streets knew the basic issue involved—viz. that of continued N.P.C. dominance of the federal government.

In terms of development, local autonomy interacted with regional membership. Leaders from Bornu fought for the inception of a ground-nut oil mill in Maiduguri and ultimately won the day. On the other hand, when funds for a drainage ditch— necessary to further industrialization of Maiduguri—were refused by the region, the federal government, and even outside agencies like A.I.D., Bornu simply scrimped and used local tax receipts. This has meant major financing problems, dealing with foreign companies and well-coordinated planning—all of which were accomplished by this "tribal" government. Obviously local autonomy has not meant inhibition of local initiative or non-dedication to modern developments.

On the other hand, the continuity of local autonomy and its expression on the national scene as ethnic politics meant that a serious sense of Nigerian nationalism was simply not present in Bornu in the first few years after independence. Peasants in rural areas had only vague ideas of what the identity meant and little or no nationalistic propaganda was taught in the schools.[13] However, primary school texts on Kanuri history, its past glories and the greatness of its people were ubiquitous. Bornu was a part of Nigeria in a formal sense, because that membership required very little sacrifice or change of identity. To generalize from this relationship to the nation as a whole means that national unity was simply a complex resultant of a loosely-knit set of alliances between semi-independent peoples. This lack of cohesion had not appeared so clearly before independence because the British served as an authoritative and binding force whose contribution to national unity, unfortunately, could not be understood or gauged clearly until it was removed.

The Troubled Path to Nigerianism: 1964–1968

In 1964 Nigeria was shaken by its first general strike. On the national level, the strike frightened those in power because it indicated a strength in the union movement that very few people could have predicted. Inflationary price tendencies, along with slow wage rises, and most importantly—the filling up of the wage labor economy which dried up the post-independence boom in promotions, all combined to create common grievances and a basis for organized effort.

The strike came to Bornu as a shock. A nation-wide organization demonstrated its capacity to upset the calm hierarchial autonomy of Bornu. Extra police patrolled the streets, and officials were mistrustful of strangers—especially of itinerant social scientists like myself. Slowly during the year, however, things settled back to normal even though the strike was in fact a symptom of much more serious storms that would ultimately engulf the entire country.

These grievances against corrupton, "tribalism," favoritism in civil service appointments and promotions, Northern dominance of the central government, and the political chaos that developed in the Western region, led finally to the first military coup of January 1966. At first the Ironsi military government was not considered a necessarily bad thing in Bornu. People there, as everywhere, said that perhaps there would be less corruption in the federal government. Again, as elsewhere, federal civil servants came home, some to be absorbed into the emirate government, others to wait on the side for some trends to develop.

But this wait-and-see attitude on the part of Bornu and other Northern groups meant that Ironsi could not obtain ethnically representative administrators and as a consequence had to employ more and more members of his own group—the Ibos. This was what many non-Ibos had feared, and their fears and initial desires not to cooperate produced a self-fulfilling prophecy— namely an Ibo-controlled military dictatorship. This is contrary to the widely held view that Ironsi simply moved directly towards Ibo-izing the Federal government. Ironsi, albeit a generally poor administrator and politician was not so politically naive as not to know that his government would be more stable if he could obtain some northern cooperation. But why should Northerners participate in a government whose future seemed so insecure? And one in which they had a minority position— something they had never experienced at the Federal level. So when approached by the new regime to remain at their posts or take other jobs the Northerners refused and returned instead to their own areas.

These problems over forming an administration, plus the difficulties concerning the fate of the Ibo officers—who had led the coup, and were heroes in their own region but traitors in the North—led to an initial period of inaction. Ultimately this inaction itself produced a tension in the country and to meet the demand for action, Ironsi proclaimed his famous decree unifying Nigeria. It is difficult to over-estimate the panic that Ironsi created with his decree—and it led directly to the riots of May 1966 in which Northerners attacked Ibos living in the North in all of the major urban centers. During those months of May, June and July 1966, young elites spoke of a new country in Africa to be called "Hausa". This reflected their fear and disillusionment with the Ironsi regime. I do not know whether actual plans for Northern secession were being made, but it is clear that Ironsi set the stage for the support of such a move by his maladroit and undiplomatic handling of an extremely delicate situation.

In Bornu there were no riots or massacres, even though everyone knew that Ibos were being molested elsewhere in the North. Formally, it is reported that the Shehu (emir) called in all local leaders of wards of the city, and ex-N.P.C. ward organizers. They were told that riots were taking place elsewhere in the North but that Bornu was to remain peaceful. If not, then these local leaders would be held responsible and punished severely. Whether or not this was the reason that Bornu remained peaceful, is open to question, but the outcome is important. Maiduguri was the only city of its size with a large minority of Ibos in which there were no riots. Indeed, no disturbances of any kind occurred in Bornu during the May outbreaks in Northern Nigeria.

It is interesting to speculate about this seeming anomaly. The first thing to notice is that Bornu again went its own way. No matter that northern Muslims were reacting against southern Ibos in their midst. The maintenance of law and order by the emirate was more important (at least in May-June 1966) than participating in a program against a common enemy. One other point should be made. Memories of violence in Bornu streets were very fresh. The political party strife of 1958 was spoken of as if it had occurred very recently. Leaders in the area therefore had clear memories of what such violence involved and how difficult it was to control once an outbreak occurred. I believe that this latter factor acted as a strong restraining force on the leadership and helped them to make a very independent decision in favor of law and order.

Whatever the exact reasons for the lack of violence in May 1966, Kanuri informants remarked that this showed how different they were as a people and how powerful their Shehu was as a monarch. They also mentioned ominously that the lack of massacres in Bornu did not mean that the Kanuri were not ready to move against Ibos. Not only could they do so if they wished—said informants—but the slaughter when it came would be awesome.

Such comments were not lost on local Ibos—who began leaving Bornu during the summer of 1966, accelerating their movement rapidly after the counter-coup of mid-summer. However, several thousands remained when the massacres and rioting of late September finally occurred. This time the Shehu did not order people to leave Ibos alone; possibly there was not enough time or Bornu was now allied more closely to other Northern groups—it is impossible at present to know the exact reason. Whatever the reason in a matter of days there were no Ibos left in Bornu. Many fled, many were killed and some were rounded up by the N.A. and placed under protective custody away from rampaging mobs. Later this latter group was helped to leave for Iboland.

Throughout that appalling summer, however, I was struck most by Bornu autonomy. This could be seen mainly in the widespread resentment when federal troops arrived on the scene in July. The thought that Bornu could not handle its own affairs and internal security was galling to ordinary people on the street. Two military coups, anti-Ibo riots, an uncertain future for Nigeria as a nation—in the fall of 1966 none of this seemed to me to have really brought significant changes to the essential quality of Bornu's relationship to Nigeria. But such change was to come, partly because of the civil war and partly as a result of an internal event which was unrelated at first to the outside world.

The civil war began in earnest during the summer of 1967. Troops were engaged in actual fighting, and recruiting was being carried on throughout the country. In Bornu all leaders and mass communication media emphasized over and over again the inviolability of "one Nigeria". To be right thinking and supportive of the society as it was duly—and ultimately as it was morally—constituted, was to be pro-Nigerian. Just as it was right and proper to be pro-N.P.C. in the 1950's and anti-B.Y.M., so now it was proper, indeed necessary, to be pro-Nigerian. Now—as then—the opposition was linked to the Ibo, and the concept was persistence. But before, where it had been Bornu, Muslim and local, the theater of action was now national—and good men had to volunteer to die for this idea in a far away part of the land. Thus, after sixty years, the notion of Nigeria suddenly meant something very real because it was put in terms that were part of local political experience and involved life and death participation.

One of the reasons historians can still explain much that is left unexplained by other social scientists, is the constant muddying up of correlative tendencies by accidental events. Such happenings provide much of what is unique and surprising in the human condition, and therefore they account for some causal forces—which may prove very significant when we try to understand a local situation.

Such an approach is vital to the understanding of Bornu's relations to itself and Nigeria. In the midst of all these crises-ridden changes, the venerable and widely respected Shehu of Bornu died (December 29, 1967). I have dealt at length with the nature of the Shehu's office and the effects of this particular succession, and wish to make only a summary evaluation here.[14] The emirate had not witnessed a change in the person of the royal office since 1937. Thus all of the major modern changes in Bornu had occurred during this one royal incumbency. For purposes of this present analysis, however, two extremely significant things occurred during and just after the royal succession in 1968. First, as reported in the newspapers, levels of government over and above those within the emirate were closely involved in the choice of a successor. My own interpretation of their interference is that it went well beyond the gentle give and take that characterized such appointments under the colonial regime. Thus, the choice was not finally agreed upon until the early spring of 1968, several months after the death of the previous monarch. I know of no other succession in Bornu history that took so long, and the royal genealogy runs back nearly one thousand years.

The reason why successions have always been carried out rapidly, of course, is the so-called inter-regnum chaos which is considered inevitable. All order is ultimately dependent upon the king and with his death legitimacy itself is suspended. In Bornu the people were obviously frightened of such an eventuality. Everyone went to his own household, shops were closed up, so was the market and a tense fright seized the capital city during December 29 and 30, 1967. But disorders did not break out and property was safe; by Sunday, December 31 (after the royal burial on Saturday) the market re-opened. Nigerian police and the army had maintained order. It is suggested by one observer who witnessed this entire period, that more than anything else this event made the Kanuri as a people realize their Nigerian as opposed to Bornu citizenship.[15] It is therefore this second event that prepared the support for the first. Nigeria not Bornu, was in control of law and order and therefore it was possible to wait an unheard of length of time before appointing a new Shehu.

A third event—not as striking in its effects as the two already mentioned, but still of major importance—was the assassination attempt on the new Shehu's life soon after his appointment. The details of this event are not known, but one of its effects was to replace many of the traditional palace clients and servants with emirate police, thus bureaucratizing and in effect modernizing the palace staff. In so doing, the Shehu was also signaling his move into a more active role as a *constitutional* monarch of Bornu. His officiating at a football match the day after his formal installation (on October 24, 1968) and his touring of the emirate districts are also signs of a more civil service approach to the office than has been the case up to now. By civil service, I mean a recognition of official duties in a bureaucratic organization in which he is a participating member with a hierarchy above and below him—and the one above him is the government of Nigeria. It is not insignificant that not only Northern, but Southern Yoruba leaders from all over the country attended the installation, signalling a new kind of unity between the emirates and the rest of Nigeria.

The final change to be considered is that of the new states. As of May 1967, General Gowon announced the formation of the new states, and abolition of regional government. These states came into existence in the spring of 1968. At first Bornu was to be part of the Northeast state, whose capital would be Bauchi. After much negotiation and Bornu pressure, the capital was switched to Bornu's central city—Maiduguri. The emirate government argued that their native authority buildings were by far the most developed in the new state; and they offered to give these up to the new state government, if the capital were to be re-located to Maiduguri, which finally it was.

Today, Bornu is for the first time a minority group in the next highest tier of government. Bauchi, Adamawa, and other emirates could, if they band together, outnumber the Kanuri. Whether Bornu achieves a working integration with these peoples within the Northeast state remains to be seen. If so, their integration into a wider socio-political sphere will have been completed. If not, then they may choose to carry through their Nigerian integration as a more separate unit. Only time can tell.

Conclusions

I. *Historical*

    A.   Bornu was an autonomous independent state prior to the colonial experience, and its policy under colonialism was to maximize its autonomy in order to maintain its traditional political system as unchanged as possible.

    B.   The advent of a nationalist movement in Nigeria brought political parties into existence on a nation-wide level and allied Bornu to the Muslim north in national affairs. In return for this support, Bornu was assured of local autonomy and a share in appointments at regional and federal levels of government.

    C.   Political opposition in the form of party organization disappeared for all practical purposes in Bornu in 1958, two years before the advent of independence, maintaining the internal unity of the emirate.

    D.   Minorities, such as Ibos, from other parts of Nigeria were really strangers in a semi-autonomous state without any effective political representation or legitimacy on the local scene.

    E.   Only the civil war and the death of the Shehu (emir) in the period from 1968 forward has brought to Bornu any widespread sense of national membership in the political culture of Nigeria.

II. *Systemic*

    A.   In any new wider-scaled political entity, such polities with well-defined boundaries cannot automatically expand loyalties outwards to the boundaries of the new system unless:

        1.   Special institutions of mass education, policies of recruitment for rewarding jobs in the

new larger entity, and a common set of obligations are equally recognized by all sub-polities in the new system.

2. The autonomy of sub-polities is significantly limited by agreement, or force, or both.

B. The persistence of autonomy by a polity after conquest and formal subordination in a larger system is dependent upon a belief by those in authority that the stability of the larger system requires the internal autonomy of some or all of the incorporated sub-polities. This belief is dependent upon a number of factors such as the relative weakness of the larger unit vis-à-vis the sub-parts, the values placed on cultural differences by those practicing these distinctions and the nature of alliances among sub-polities who favor more and less local autonomy.

Discussion

These few generalizations above are an attempt to create some order out of the plethora of events and crises that have occurred in such rapid succession in Nigeria. The tragedy of Nigeria is that the British, in creating such a disparate nation, had every confidence in it as long as they were retained as the superior authority to mediate disputes and hold the pieces together. But they did not reckon on the short-lived mortality of colonialism. Left to themselves, the Nigerians were soon in a serious struggle over control of the federation. At stake was the hard-won autonomy of emirates like Bornu as compared to more radical unitary principles of national mobilization as preached by African socialists at home and abroad. The Ironsi decree of May 1966 was proof positive that such fears of loss of autonomy were realistic and Bornu, as did the other Northern emirates, resented such policies bitterly and feared the outcome. The result was a counter-coup and enflamed anti-Ibo sentiments that had violent results.

The paradox in all this is that up until very recently Bornu, and possibly other emirates as well, were pursuing their goals at the national level in order to maintain local control and not for any reason of long-run ideological or development goals at the national level. Again, up until very recently in Nigerian history, the Ibo have been the most clearly outspoken Nigerian nationalists. However, from 1968 forward, Bornu has become genuinely interested in, and a meaningful component of, Nigeria—while the Ibos have given up that loyalty for a more limited ethnic and regional one. Nigerian nationalism is now a firmly established part of Bornu's political culture and, ironic or not, this is an important factor in the support the federal government can expect for its policy of continuing with the present war. There was no question in the minds of young Bornu friends with whom I spoke in the fall of 1968. Certainly they still feel strongly about Bornu and its interests—but Nigeria as a concept and an identity has achieved a totally new and very much stronger place in their feelings of membership. Somehow the idea has caught on that Biafran secession if successful will be demeaning to them and what they hope for, for themselves and Bornu. Furthermore close relatives are dying for this cause—and to make these deaths meaningful it is necessary to believe in the reasons given by government—i.e. the protection of the national integrity.

From the point of view of Bornu as well as Nigeria, it is tragic yet true that it has taken this present crisis and its effects to finally bring the emirate into a meaningful membership in the Nigerian nation. Independence dates from 1960, but Nigeria's real birth pangs as a nation, facing the realities of its own nature as they have come into being in the contemporary world, are more recent. And out of this travail, it is my hope that there will come a Nigeria tempered by the realization that a nation must limit local autonomy if all its peoples are to have any lasting faith in their citizenship.

NOTES

1. This essay was written during a leave of absence from Northwestern University. The writer wishes to acknowledge his appreciation to the Program of African Studies and the Council for Intersocietal Studies at Northwestern for making this free time possible through their financial support.

2. This approach has been taken by F. C. Bailey, *Politics and Social Change* (Berkeley: University of California Press, 1963), and more recently by M. Swartz (ed.), *Local-Level Politics* (Chicago: Aldine, 1968), and R. Cohen and John Middleton (eds.), *From Tribe to Nation in Africa* (San Francisco: Aldine, 1969).

3. See D. Easton, *A Framework of Political Analysis* (Englewood Cliffs, N. J.: Prentice-Hall, 1965), p. 82.

4. For a summary of this history see R. Cohen, *The Kanuri of Bornu* (New York: Holt, Rinehart and Winston, 1967) and the relevant chapters in J. F. A. Ajayi and M. Crowder, *The History of West Africa* (Cambridge: Clarendon, 1969 (2 Vols.)).

5. See R. Cohen, "The Dynamics of Feudalism in Bornu," in J. Butler (ed.), *Boston University Publications in African History,* Vol. 2 (Boston: Boston University Press, 1966); R. Cohen, *The Kanuri of Bornu;* R. Cohen, "Incorporation in Bornu," in R. Cohen and J. Middleton (eds.), *From Tribe to Nation in Africa (Scranton: Chandler, 1970), pp. 150–174.*

6. *See D. Denham and (Captain) Clapperton, Travels and Discoveries in Northern and Central Africa* (London: Murray (2 Vols.), 1826); H. Barth, *Travels and Discoveries in North and Central Africa* (London: Longmans (5 Vols.), 1857).

7. See *Bornu Annual Reports,* 1905–7.

8. See D. E. Apter, *The Political Kingdom in Uganda: A Study in Bureaucratic Nationalism* (Princeton: Princeton University Press, 1961). The title of this article is taken from Professor Apter's book because the situation being described here is structurally as well as historically similar in many important respects, although there are significant differences in the relative sizes of units concerned.

9. See K. Ezera, *Constitutional Developments in Nigeria* (Cambridge: Cambridge University Press, 1964).

10. See R. Cohen, "Conflict and Change in a Northern Nigerian Emirate." in G. Zollschan and D. Hirsch (eds.), *Explorations in Social Change* (Boston: Houghton, Mifflin & Co., 1964), pp.495–521.

11. R. Cohen, "Conflict and Change in a Northern Nigerian Emirate," and "From Empire to Colony: Bornu in the 19th and 20th Centuries."- Cambridge series on colonialism, Vol. III; V. W. Turner (ed.). *The Impact of Colonialism* (Cambridge: Cambridge University Press, 1971).

12. For an extended discussion of this point, see R. L. Sklar, *Nigerian Political Parties: Power in an Emergent African Nation* (Princeton: Princeton University Press, 1963). B. J. Dudley, *Parties and Politics in Northern Nigeria* (London: Frank Cass, 1968).

13. A. Peshkin, "The Influence of Education on Pluralist Loyalties." in O. Olankanpo, R. Cohen, and J. Paden (eds.), *Problems of Integration and Disintegration in Nigeria* (Proceedings of a conference held at Northwestern University, March 1967).

14. R. Cohen, "The Kingship in Bornu," Michael Crowder and Obaro Ikime (eds.), *West African Chiefs* (New York: Africana Publishing, 1971).

15. Personal communication from Bornu.

CHAPTER 22

Ideology and Inconsistency: The "Cross-Pressured" Nigerian Worker[1]

ROBERT MELSON

After the nationwide general strike of June 1964, Nigerian workers gained unprecedented political prominence. The timing of the strike had much to do with this, for only five months hence the Federal Elections of December 1964 were to be held and Nigerian politicians had become keenly aware of the labor movement. Two kinds of politicians began to compete for the labor vote. On the one hand, there were politically oriented labor leaders who wanted to take the opportunity of the strike and of the elections to form a Nigerian Labor party. They made their appeals to the class-consciousness and self-interest of Nigerian workers defined as workers, not as members of this or that ethnic group. On the other hand there were the politicians of the major political parties who made their appeals to the ethnic loyalties of the workers.[2] Thus between June and December 1964, and for some months after, workers were cross-pressured between their labor and their ethnic loyalties.[3] Working against the effect of the cross-pressures were first, the appeal to class-consciousness and labor interest of the ethnic parties themselves, and second, the climate of ethnic and national insecurity which raised the saliency of one's ethnic

Reprinted in slightly revised form with the permission of the publisher from *The American Political Science Review,* Vol. 65, No. 1 (March, 1971), pp. 167–171. Copyright © 1971 *The American Political Science Review.*

membership over one's membership in the working class.

What we shall try to show in this analysis is that the Nigerian worker, like the worker in other countries, tends to support his ethnic group when that group is threatened. This is not surprising and was not surprising to Nigerian labor leaders. What was surprising was the fraction of workers who claimed to support a labor party while *at the same time* supporting ethnic parties. This fraction which we have called "inconsistent respondents" or for short, the "inconsistents," played an important role in allowing Nigerian labor leaders to count on more support than they actually had.[4] Beyond that, it would seem to us, that inconsistent respondents in transitional societies such as Nigeria, make political predictions difficult and in that sense, they contribute to the felt unpredicability of such societies. Focusing more closely on the Inconsistents we make a distinction between descriptive and prescriptive inconsistency.

The cross-pressured Nigerian worker was likely to be inconsistent in either of two ways. On the one hand, he was likely to describe himself as supporting *both* an ethnic and a labor party. On the other hand, he was likely to prescribe support for a labor party while actually supporting an ethnic party. It may be useful to diagram the hypothesized relationships among the cross-pressured and inconsistent voters, as in Figure 1 below:

FIGURE I

THE RELATIONSHIP AMONG CROSS-PRESSURED AND INCONSISTENTS

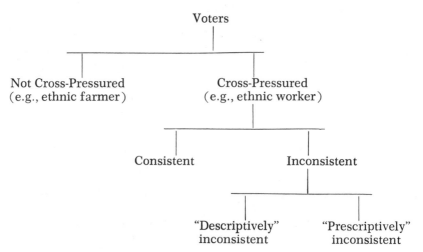

We shall show that the first kind of inconsistency (descriptive) may be due to the voter having too little information to distinguish between ethnic and labor parties and that the second kind of inconsistency (prescriptive) may be due to the unwillingness of the voter to do what he feels he "should" do, that is, support labor against ethnic parties. Both kinds of inconsistency, we shall suggest, tend to confound the predictions of politicians like labor leaders who count on the consistent and stable support of their followers.

In what follows we briefly discuss, first, the data upon which this analysis is based. We then describe the population of Nigerian workers with which this study is concerned, and analyze the impact of labor and ethnic cross-pressures upon their political behavior.

Data and Assumptions

All findings in the present study are based on five non-probabilistic sample surveys. These were (1) a group of 58 trade unionists attending a meeting sponsored by the University of Ibadan in July 1964; (2) a group of 29 workers who attended a training program for trade unionists at the United Labour Congress in Lagos in October 1964; (3) a mail questionnaire (response rate 43 out of 300) sent out in October and analyzed in December 1964; (4) a group of 89 trade unionists attending two trade union conferences in Lagos in April 1965; and (5) a group of 574 railway workers in the Lagos yards of the Nigerian Railway Corporation in May 1965. For further discussion of the data see footnotes 10, 13, and 14.

In all cases the data on which the results of this study are based were drawn from non-probabilistic samples. However, this should not prevent us from suggesting the presence of inconsistent respondents in a theoretical sense and from building a case for their existence in the wider society. Our methodological argument rests on a suggestion made by Zettenberg:

> The relationships expressed in theoretical propositions are presumed to be universally present. They are accordingly, present both in representative and non-representative samples. To disprove or demonstrate their existence is hence possible in any kind of sample—biased or unbiased.[5]

We suggest, moreover, that in most cases the data *under-estimated* the frequency of cross-pressured and "logically" inconsistent respondents in the Nigerian labor force as a whole. This assumption is based on the characteristics of the samples drawn. In all cases, our respondents were better educated, better payed, longer in the trade union movement and more likely to be trade union officers than was the labor population as a whole. Consequently, if the results of Tables 4 and 5 are to be believed (where we show that descriptive inconsistency declines with education and length of exposure to the trade union movement), we would expect that the Nigerian working class population as a whole would tend to be *more* logically inconsistent than our results indicate. As for the results of Tables 6, 7 and 9, the high rate of prescriptive inconsistency may be *exaggerated* if one agrees with the argument that prescriptive inconsistency is more likely the *higher* the level of education of the respondent.

The Workers

In this paper, by "workers," we mean wage-earners. As of 1963 about 800,000 to 1,000,000 Nigerians were wage-earners; they and their families constituted the majority of Nigeria's urban population.[6] On the eve of the general strike of 1964, the governments—federal, regional, and local—employed 54 per cent and European-owned private firms another 38 per cent, of the wage-earning population. Any widespread unrest in the labor force would necessarily involve some level of government.[7]

In 1964, there were approximately 300,000 trade union members organized into about 300 ongoing unions. Unions were organized into four superordinate central labor body organizations. These were the United Labour Congress (ULC), the Nigerian Workers Council (NWC), the Nigerian Trades Union Congress (NTUC), and the Labour Unity Front (LUF). The leadership of the labor movement during and after the strike consisted largely of the leaders of these four central labor bodies.

Cross-cutting the four central labor bodies were two major factions. One was Marxist, anti-federalist, admiring of Ghana under Nkrumah, and determined to launch a labor party.[8] The other was, on the whole, not explicitly Marxist. It had made its peace with the federalist system and tried strenuously to keep labor out of politics. Although it is an oversimplification, one can identify the Nigerian Trades Union Congress and the Labour Unity Front with the Marxist faction; the United Labour Congress and the Nigerian Workers Council with the non-political faction.

Simple numbers tell a great deal about the political significance of workers. From the perspective of the political elites who needed numbers to win elections, it was clear that workers were an insignificant segment of the population. It comes as no surprise, therefore, that in the full bloom of ethnic politics, workers and their leadership carried little weight compared with peasants in the deliberations of the major parties. To those politicians who had a long-range view of Nigerian development, however, workers were somewhat more important.

To Marxist labor leaders especially, it was clear that, in time, the ratio between peasants and workers would shift in favor of workers. For the Marxists, Lagos with its urban working population was a future Nigeria writ small. If they could capture the wage-earning vote in Lagos, they argued, then economic interest, and not the tribalism of the peasant would be "the coming thing." The strike of 1964 seemed to give the Marxist labor leaders an opportunity to prove their point.

The Cross-Pressured are the Changers

Like the wealthy American of Irish descent or the poor American of Yankee descent, the Nigerian worker of whatever nationality was cross-pressured between his loyalty to his ethnic group and loyalty to his economic interest group.[9] Applying this cross-pressure model to the period between the strike of June and the election of December 1964, one would expect that as the election neared, it would make the workers' ethnic groups more salient. Their support for their economic interest group, the labor party, would decline and support for the ethnic parties would increase. One would also expect that the number of cross-pressured would decline with the coming of the election. In fact, this is just what happened, as can be seen from Tables 1 and 2.

TABLE 1

DROP IN LABOR PARTY SUPPORT BETWEEN JULY AND DECEMBER 1964*

Percentage Who:	July	October–December
Indicate some Labor Party support	88%	41%
Indicate ethnic Party support only:	5%	41%
Other:	7%	17%
Total	100%	99%
	(N = 58)	(N = 72)

TABLE 2

CROSS-PRESSURED VOTERS BETWEEN JULY AND DECEMBER 1964*

Percentages who are:	July	October–December
Not cross-pressured (choose only one party):	24%	63%
Cross-pressured (choose at least two competing parties):	69%	19%
Other:	7%	17%
Total	100%	99%
	(N = 58)	(N = 72)

* The July responses were based on the following two questions: (1) "Which party do you think behaved with most friendliness toward the workers during the strike?" (2) "Would you support a labor party?" The October–December responses were based on the following two questions: (1) "Which parties are most helpful to workers in 1964?" (2) "Do you think Mr. Imoudu's labor party is useful for workers?" Note: Imoudu was a popular trade union leader who had been a founder of the Nigerian Labour Party.

Thus in July, right after the strike, 88 per cent of our sample of workers indicated support for a labor party and 5 per cent indicated support for an ethnic party.[10] By December, on the eve of the election, in a similarly constituted sample 41 per cent indicated support for a labor party and 41 per cent indicated unambiguous support for an ethnic party.

Turning to the question of the cross-pressured, one notes

from Table 2 that in July, 69 per cent of our respondents indicated, by their choice of competing parties, that they were
cross-pressured; by December, only 19 per cent of our respondents indicated that they were cross-pressured. This was clearly
a significant shift of 50 per cent. In effect, this meant that in a
four month period, the labor party lost up to half of its support.

Consider the political market place from the point of view of
the labor party boosters. In July, nine out of ten workers would
say that they support a labor party, by December only four out
of ten workers indicated such support, and out of those four,
two would also say that they supported an ethnic party. Thus,
what seemed like victory in Lagos in July turned into a rout by
December. This result was due in part to the changeability of
the cross-pressured and in part to the expectations of the labor
leaders.

Descriptive Inconsistency

It has been found in the United States and elsewhere, that
cross-pressures lead to a delay in the voting decision and to a
higher probability of the voter changing his mind. In this sense,
then, the cross-pressured voter infuses any election with an
element of unpredictability; consequently, the cross-pressured
vote can often change victory into defeat.[11] As insightful as the
literature on cross-pressures has been, however, it has not distinguished between at least two types of reactions to cross-
pressures. The first type, which can be termed the "consistent"
reaction, is one in which a person recognizes that he has contradictory loyalties and tries to deal with the contradiction as best
he can. For example, he can delay the choice. He can choose
among two options. He can compartmentalize the choice by
claiming that one option fits one situation and the second fits
other situations.[12] Lastly he can refuse to choose.

A second reaction to cross-pressures, the "inconsistent" reaction, one not reported in the literature on American elections,
is the reaction in which the person either does not recognize the
contradiction or can live with it easily. In either case, he does
not necessarily delay his decision, he does not indicate strong
support for one or the other choice, he does not compartmentalize and he does not refuse to choose. Instead, to everyone's

confusion, he verbalizes both options at the same time.

For example, workers were asked: "Should trade unionists support a political party?" Responses were distributed as indicated in Table 3.[13] From Table 3 it is seen that, in addition to the respondents who make a party choice, the cross-pressured can be divided into two groups: those who indicated that they "do not mix" their political and workers' roles (option 3) without, however, indicating how they will vote or what party they support, and the inconsistents (option 4) who indicate possibly contradictory opinions. We call the reader's attention to option 4, the "inconsistent" responses.

TABLE 3
LABOR SUPPORT FOR A POLITICAL PARTY*

Option	Per cent
1. Trade unionists should form a labor party.	30%
2. Yes, trade unionists should support one of the existing political parties (ethnic)	6%
3. Trade unionists as trade unionists should not mix in politics although they may do so as private citizens.	39%
4. Inconsistent responses: (a) trade unionists should not mix in politics *and* they should support a labor party; (b) they should not mix in politics *and* they should support an existing party; or (c) they should support a labor party *and* they should support an ethnic party.	19%
5. N.A.	6%
Total	100%
	(N=89)

* Respondents were given the first three options to choose from in this closed item. However, respondents were not asked to choose only one of the three options given, and since this was a self-administered questionnaire, one would expect that some respondents would check more than one item. It turned out that 19 per cent of them did.

The frequency varies somewhat, but the pattern remains the same. Ask workers if they support a labor party and a sizeable proportion of those who say "yes" report support for an ethnic party. The relevance of the inconsistents to labor party people lay in their representing a sizeable fraction (19 per cent) of the total distribution. Given the relative division between the respondents who consistently voiced support for the labor party

(30 per cent) and those who consistently chose to say that they would not mix in politics as workers (39 per cent), the inconsistents played the role of a potential swing vote in an American election. This changeability of the inconsistents need not have interested the labor politician had the 19 per cent swung ultimately in favor of a labor party, but they did not. As we have seen above, by December 1964, the swing was in the direction of ethnic parties.

One would imagine that awareness of the issues and, therefore, consistency would vary with accessibility to information and that such accessibility would be a function of education and English language competency on the one hand, and duration in the labor movement, on the other. Consider the results of Tables 4 and 5. Note that the rate of inconsistents is significantly greater among those with only primary education than it is among those with some secondary education. In Table 5, note that the rate of inconsistents is more than three times as great among those with less than five years experience in the labor movement as it is among those with more than five years experience.

TABLE 4

CONSISTENCY OF POLITICAL ATTITUDES BY EDUCATION*

	Per cent primary only	*Per cent some secondary*
Inconsistent	28%	18%
Consistent	72%	87%
Total	100%	100%
	(N=36)	(N=46)

$x^2=2.2$
$p<.08$

* The group of workers on which Table 4 is based is the same as that on which Table 3 is based. The inconsistent and consistent respondents were derived as in Table 3. The education of the respondent was derived from his response to the question: "What was the last class you attended in school?"

It should be added that although we did not test for it, language competency or rather the lack of it in English may have been an important factor in eliciting the pattern of inconsistent responses. This leads up to the suggestion, that what we have called "descriptive inconsistency," might have been due to the respondents not having enough information at his command (lack of education, lack of acquaintance with the labor movement) on the one hand, or to his not having recognized the meaning of the questions posed in English on the other hand. Nevertheless to a labor movement which conducted most of its business in English (the common language among the many ethnic groups comprising the movement) it was really of no consequence *why* there existed a pattern of inconsistent support. For whatever reason, lack of information, lack of education, lack of English-language-competency, the inconsistent respondent made reliable estimates of political support difficult to make. As a rule his responses were to make labor leaders (and the author) *overestimate* labor party support.

TABLE 5

CONSISTENCY OF POLITICAL ATTITUDES BY DURATION
IN A TRADE UNION*

| | Duration in a Trade Union | |
	Per cent Under five years	Per cent Five years and over
Inconsistent	36%	10%
Consistent	64%	90%
Total	100% (N=30)	100% (N=52)

$$x^2 = 7.2$$
$$p < .01$$

* The group of workers on which Table 5 is based is the same as that on which Tables 3 and 4 are based. The inconsistent and consistent respondents were derived as in Table 3. Duration in a trade union was measured from responses to the question: "How long have you been a member of your trade union?"

It comes as no great surprise that an ordinary worker who is not familiar with the ideological position of the labor party is inconsistent. But what is of interest is that some workers and especially some labor leaders who were well aware of such quarrels and who ostensibly belonged to one or the other side were also inconsistent.

Prescriptive Inconsistency

Having discussed results which seem to show that a sizeable fraction of our respondents were "descriptively" inconsistent in reporting support for mutually exclusive options, we can now turn to results which seem to show that an even greater fraction were "prescriptively" inconsistent. This second group of respondents seemed to prescribe one kind of party while actually supporting another kind. Consider Tables 6 and 7 below.[14]

TABLE 6

PRESCRIBED PARTY SUPPORT AND ACTUAL PARTY SUPPORT*

	Prescribed support	*Actual support*
	Per cent who indicate that workers should	*Per cent who indicate that they actually*
1. Support a labor party	43.2%	8.9%
2. Support an ethnic party	9.6%	49.1%
3. Not mix in politics	35.9%	—
4. Support no party ("none")	—	35.0%
5. Other	11.2%	6.9%
Total	99.9% (N=574)	99.9% (N=574)

* The data for the "Prescribed Support" column were derived from the responses to the closed question: "What parties should *trade-unionists* support?" The data to the "Actual Support" column were derived from the open question: "What parties do *you* find most helpful?" The options given to respondents in the closed question were: (1) "Workers should form a labor party." (2) "Yes, workers should support one of the existing political parties." (3) "Workers as workers, should not mix in politics although they may do so as private citizens." Note that this was not a self-administered question and interviewers were instructed to take down only one choice per question. This means that we were *not* able to gauge the frequency of *logically inconsistent* respondents in this group. It should be noted that logical and prescriptive inconsistency are not mutually exclusive categories and may be present in the same respondent.

We suggest that the magnitude of the differences between prescribed and actual support as reported in Table 6 are due to the wording of the questions on the one hand, and to their closedness (openness), on the other hand. Thus, the first question makes salient the occupational identity of the respondent because it asks him to respond in his role as a "trade unionist," or as a worker (e.g., "As a trade unionist, I should support a labor party, but as a member of my community, I support my ethnic party.") The second question, on the other hand does not specify the respondents identity (it asks him to respond as a global, "you"). It is contended that in the second question the respondent is freer to express his real feelings, and consequently his *actual* support. This effect is heightened by making the first question closed (thus giving the respondent the clear choice between labor and ethnic parties), whereas in the open question, the respondent need not *explicitly reject* a labor party as he indicates his choice for an ethnic party.

In Table 6, we note immediately that 43.2 per cent (248) respondents prescribed support for a labor party, while only 8.9 per cent (51) actually supported an existing labor party. By the same token, only 9.6 per cent (55) prescribed support for an ethnic party, while 49.1 per cent actually supported such a party.

TABLE 7

ACTUAL PARTY SUPPORT BY PRESCRIBED PARTY SUPPORT
(in per cent)

Actual party support	Prescribed Party Support			
	Labor Party	Ethnic Party	"Not Mix"	Other
Labor Party	11.7%	5.5%	7.8%	4.6%
Ethnic Party	51.6%	56.4%	44.6%	47.6%
"None"	30.6%	25.5%	43.2%	33.8%
Other	6.0%	12.7%	4.4%	13.8%
Total	99.9%	100.1%	100.0%	99.8%
	(N=248)	(N=55)	(N=206)	(N=65)

Cross-tabulating actual by prescribed support (Table 7) and looking more closely at the group prescribing support for a labor party, one notes that of the 248 respondents only 29 or 11.7 per cent actually supported such a party, while 128 or 51.6 per cent actually supported ethnic parties. In this example can be seen the difference between the "should" and "do" of labor party support: One prescribes support for labor, but one doesn't actually support it. One prescribes opposition to ethnic parties, but actually supports them.

We would like to suggest that "prescriptive" inconsistency may be due to little opportunity for consistency, a lack of commitment to the issues and a lack of social support for consistency. Before turning to the survey data, a short case study may be illuminating.

Consider the case of Peter A., a labor leader. During the elections of 1964, Peter A., who calls himself a "communist," in turn supported the following political parties: the Nigerian Labour Party, the "capitalist" NCNC and the "feudalist" Northern Peoples Congress (NPC). First consider how A. became a communist.

A. was born in 1935 in the Midwest region, not far from the

home of the great Nigerian labor leader Michael Imoudu. He attended secondary school in Warri where he graduated in 1949. In 1951 he came to Lagos where he worked as a journalist for the *Nigerian Daily Times.* In 1953, he went to Ghana where he worked as a full time organizer for the TUC.

Upon his return to Lagos, A., looking for a job, approached Lawrence Borha, General Secretary of the United Labour Congress.[15] Because Borha was also a Bini speaker from the Midwest and because of his long experience with the TUC in Ghana, A. felt sure that Borha would give him a job. But Borha refused, calling him a communist and an agent of Nkrumah. Rejected by Borha, he went to see Imoudu, also a Bini speaker. Imoudu was glad to see him. With Imoudu and the more militant trade unionists A.'s Ghana experience gave him prestige. People called him "comrade" and assumed that he was a Marxist. "That's when I became a Marxist," says A.

Peter A.'s philosophy is a blend of Marxist rhetoric and mildly humanist values.[16] He is strongly egalitarian and supports higher wages for workers. Yet he is not "ready to sacrifice my generation for the future. We must all live well." Although he contends that Marxism can predict the future, he doesn't insist that he or anyone else has the only "correct" philosophy. "Since I do not know all the philosophies in the world how can I tell that there is one which is correct?"

We can assume that Peter A. is not a fanatical Marxist and like other inconsistents, he does not demand ideological congruence from his friends. Asked, "Is it your view that the best way to live is to pick friends and associates whose tastes and beliefs are the same as one's own?" A. answered "Not at all. What does friendship have to do with politics? As a matter of fact, I am now staying with my best friend (a townsman). He does not believe as I do. Of course I might persuade him that my views are right." Unlike those of true believers, A.'s easy attitude toward ideology is shared by other inconsistents within the ranks of the labor movement.

Friendship and Ideology

We asked the same questions of a group of workers: "Is it your view that the best way to live is to pick friends and associates whose political beliefs are the same as one's own?" Respondents were given the following options:

1. I always choose friends whose political beliefs are the same as my own_____
2. Although I prefer people who share my beliefs, most of my friends need not hold the political beliefs that I do_____
3. My friendship with a man is not at all dependent on his political beliefs_____

In asking this question, we had in mind the following proposition. In general, we assumed that a person who tries to homogenize his political environment is more committed to his political beliefs than a person who does not.[17] Being more committed to his political beliefs a person who chooses friends whose political beliefs are the same as his own would be less likely to be changeable in his political allegiances. Consider the results of Table 8.

TABLE 8*

IDEOLOGICAL FRIENDSHIP BY INCONSISTENT AND CONSISTENT
PARTY COMMITMENT

| | Party commitment | |
Friendship (per cent who)	Inconsistent	Consistent
Choose ideological friends, or prefer ideological friends	11%	38%
Think friendship independent of politics	48%	54%
Contradictory: Always choose ideological friends but think that friendship independent of ideology	41%	8%
Total	100% (N=17)	100% (N=65)

* Note that this table is based on the same group of respondents discussed in Table 3.

The results are in the expected direction. One notes that consistents on party choice are three times (38 per cent) as likely to choose ideological friends as are the inconsistents (11 per cent) but the inconsistents are five times as likely (41 per cent to 8 per cent) to be in contradiction not only with respect to party choice but with respect to friendship. That is, inconsistents on party choice tend also to say (1) "I always choose friends whose political beliefs are the same as my own" *together with* (3) "My friendship with a man is not at all dependent on his political beliefs." In passing, one should observe that both inconsistents and consistents most frequently indicated that friendship and ideology were *independent.* Both groups chose with greatest frequency option (3) "My friendship with a man is not at all dependent on his political beliefs." This last result dovetails with the result of Table 3 in which it was indicated that persons most frequently prefer to compartmentalize ("not mix") their workers' roles from their political roles.

These results further confirm our belief that the inconsistents, like the cross-pressured, are the changers, because if they do not make friendships based on a firm commitment to ideology they are free to change from political opinion to opinion, from supporting a labor party to saying that they are opposed to workers mixing in politics.

But friendship is only one way that the inconsistents differ from the consistents. We would expect that if the inconsistents do not have a firm commitment to their beliefs they would be less likely to have a strong commitment to norms of behavior. One is reminded of the warning against "opportunism" in the labor movement issued by Eskor Toyo, a committed Marxist labor leader who had stayed in the movement despite great personal and financial loss. For example, the same Peter A. who answered that his friendship with a man was not dependent on his friend's beliefs, told the following story:

A. tried to contest in the last Federal election. He went to his home town where he addressed a meeting of his clan. He would be a great help, he explained, in getting amenities for the town. He distributed £500 in gifts and since no one in the clan challenged him, he expected to get the NCNC nomination. All his adult life he had been a member of the party. He was chagrined, therefore, when he discovered that the local NCNC refused to endorse him. When A. heard that someone else had been endorsed, he hurried to get the endorsement of the opposition party, an ally of the Northern Peoples Congress. The point of the story is how irrelevant ideology or loyalty to the party was to A. He switched to the opposition as soon as it became clear to him that he would not win the NCNC nomination. He did this during an election which was said to pit "socialism" and "capitalism" against the "feudal" North.

One suspects that for Peter A. inconsistency was based on a lack of commitment to the issues and to a lack of social support for consistency. There were others in the labor movement, however, who may have been inconsistent in prescribing support for a labor party on the one hand, while actually supporting ethnic parties, on the other, because they found no viable alternatives for such support. This may explain the striking differences in prescribed and actual support for labor and ethnic parties found in Tables 6 and 7.

Turning to Table 9 below, one notes that prescriptive inconsistency, whatever its underlying causes, is common to all ethnic groups, levels of education, ages, incomes, expected incomes, and levels of seniority in the labor movement. Indeed, unlike descriptive inconsistency, prescriptive inconsistency is *higher* for persons with secondary education than it is for persons with primary education. (For those with primary education, the percentage difference between prescribed and actual labor party support is $32\% - 11\% = 21\%$. The same difference for those with secondary education is $46\% - 8\% = 38\%$.)

The results of Table 9 help to clarify the difference between descriptive and prescriptive inconsistency. As has been noted above, a person may describe his position in an inconsistent manner because he is not aware of the issues. On the other hand, a person may be inconsistent between his prescription and his actual choice because he is aware of a norm (support for a labor party), but unwilling to act on that norm. This may explain why better informed workers (those with secondary education) who, one would expect, are aware of the norm to support a labor party, were more likely to prescribe support for such a party than were less well informed workers (those with primary education only). The better informed workers were not, however, necessarily any more predisposed actually to support such a party than were the less informed workers. This would explain why the difference, or the inconsistency, between prescription and actual support was *higher* for the *better* informed workers.

The Political Consequences of the Inconsistents

The political importance of the inconsistent supporter derives from his making practical (i.e. stable and predictable) politics difficult. Indeed, the more a politician expects commitment and consistency the more likely he is to become confused by the information given him about the support of the inconsistent follower. This was especially true for mature Marxist labor leaders in Nigeria who had staked their careers on the long-range predictability of the Nigerian worker.

From the point of view of committed Marxist labor leaders who opposed the ethnic parties, to support the Labor Party and to support the ethnic parties was not consistent and therefore not possible. During the period of the Federal Election, a leader of a Marxist labor party contrasted the "ruling circles," that is, the ethnic party elites, to the "workers."[18] The "ruling circles" were corrupt and tribalist. Each political party represented the tribal and economic interests of its group. Thus the Northern Peoples Congress (NPC) represented the Northern "Feudalist Emirs." The National Convention of Nigerian Citizens (NCNC) and the Action Group (AG) represented the interests of the Ibo and Yoruba and the business classes:

> The Emirs and their immediate relations control the Native Administrations and the law courts . . . These things confirm the NPC as a party of Feudal nobility . . . The NCNC formerly a mass movement has degenerated into an instrument of unbridled capitalism.[19]

These groups were strongly contrasted to the "working classes." In Nigeria and in Africa as a whole,

> The working class is the most rapidly developing class. The historic mission of this class is to become the leading force in the struggle for socialism.[20]

It was the task of socialists to abolish all "class distinctions" and all social inequalities. The workers were progressive because in this view their rise to power was inevitable and because they believed in progressive programs. This dual capacity of the working classes stemmed from their work expe-

TABLE 9

PER CENT PRESCRIBED PARTY SUPPORT AND ACTUAL PARTY SUPPORT
BY ETHNIC GROUP, EDUCATION, AGE, INCOME, EXPECTED
INCOME AND TIME IN THE LABOR MOVEMENT

Ethnic group

	Yoruba (N=277)		Ibo (N=186)		Midwest (N=74)		Northerners (N=14)		Eastern Minorities (N=12)	
	P.*	A.**	P.	A.	P.	A.	P.	A.	P.	A.
Labor	40%	8%	43%	9%	55%	11%	43%	7%	33%	8%
Ethnic	9%	50%	11%	55%	5%	43%	0%	29%	33%	25%

Education

	Primary (0–3 yrs.) (N=91)		Primary (3–6 yrs.) (N=338)		Some secondary (N=141)	
	P.	A.	P.	A.	P.	A.
Labor	32%	11%	46%	9%	46%	8%
Ethnic	15%	43%	9%	52%	8%	50%

Age

	Under 30 yrs. (N=176)		30–50 yrs. (N=324)		Over 50 yrs. (N=70)	
	P.	A.	P.	A.	P.	A.
Labor	43%	11%	46%	7%	34%	11%
Ethnic	9%	47%	9%	53%	16%	48%

Yearly income

	100–199 (N=139)		200–299 (N=197)		Over 300 (N=243)	
	P.	A.	P.	A.	P.	A.
Labor	44%	12%	43%	8%	43%	7%
Ethnic	9%	43%	8%	47%	11%	50%

Yearly income expected in five years

	100–199 (N=56)		200–299 (N=108)		Over 300 (N=280)	
	P.	A.	P.	A.	P.	A.
Labor	48%	14%	44%	10%	45%	8%
Ethnic	9%	43%	3%	43%	10%	52%

Length of trade union membership

	1–7 yrs. (N=134)		8–10 yrs. (N=73)		Over 10 yrs. (N=354)	
	P.	A.	P.	A.	P.	A.
Labor	40%	11%	34%	3%	46%	9%
Ethnic	10%	45%	7%	56%	11%	50%

* P.=Prescribed Party Support. ** A.=Actual Party Support.

Note: Because of the elimination of categories like "Other" and "None,"
percentages do not necessarily total 100 per cent.

rience during which they become "skilled and educated as they become acquainted with the technology of modern production."[21] Most importantly, unlike the "feudal" and "Capitalist" classes who have created tribal discord in order to further their ends, *The sentiments of tribal discord are alien to the working class.*"[22]

It was conceivable in this system to be a duped worker and to support the ethnic parties, but once one gained class-consciousness and supported a labor party, one was then opposed to ethnic parties. This did not mean that one could not enter into temporary alliances with such parties—it did mean that one knew his friends and his enemies. There was no room for being *both* class conscious *and* supporting "ruling circles." For ideological Marxists who were caught up in the political struggle, the hardness and validity of support was often not questioned. If a worker said he supported a labor party, that was enough. That a worker would be both in support of a labor party and of an ethnic—that was clearly out of the question.

The inconsistents were unpredictable in two ways. First, as individuals they were more likely to change their minds about their party support. Second, as a group they gave the impression of more support and more solid support than actually existed for a labor party. By oscillating in their private views, they made the political market oscillate between seeming to indicate that a labor party could succeed and that a labor party would fail.

We should like to call the reader's attention again to an important distinction between the inconsistents and those who compartmentalize their roles. The inconsistents say that they would support a labor party but they don't deliver; those who compartmentalize their roles do not say they would support a labor party. This does not mean that the compartmentalizers are more politically predictable than the inconsistents. It does mean that they do not give out information that can be falsely perceived by political actors. The inconsistents, perhaps because they do not perceive inconsistency the same way as committed Marxists do, communicate false information.

In conclusion we would like to suggest that false predictions are based not only on faulty ideology, but also on the information available to those who make predictions. In a period of rapid change where interests and identities have not as yet crystallized, and where information is scarce one would expect a high rate of "inconsistents." The importance of the inconsistents is that they confused politicians, Marxist as well as non-Marxist, whose predictions of political support assumed logical and prescriptive consistency. Though in the short run the inconsistents make politics unpredictable, and in some ways opportunistic, in the long run they may serve as an important counterweight to those who would squeeze transitional societies into rigid ideological compartments. Precisely because they are inconsistent, our respondents may be more humane (feeling friendship is more important than ideology) and more open to the possibilities of change.

NOTES

1. I have benefited from suggestions made by Paul Abramson, Rufus Browning, Frederick W. Frey, Paul Hinker, Willard Johnson, John Kramer, Norman Miller, Lucian W. Pye, Richard L. Sklar, and Howard Wolpe. As research assistants, Platon Rigos and Ronald Stockton were most helpful. I wish to acknowledge also the assistance of the Department of Political Science and the African Studies Center at Michigan State University. Data collection in Nigeria was financed by grants from the Carnegie and Ford Foundations.

2. For a discussion of Nigerian politics in the post-independence period, see the following studies: James S. Coleman, *Nigeria: Background to Nationalism* (Berkeley and Los Angeles: University of California Press, 1958); Richard L. Sklar, *Nigerian Political Parties: Power in an Emergent African Nation* (Princeton: Princeton University Press, 1963); Kenneth W. Post, *The Nigerian Federal Election of 1959* (London: Oxford University Press, 1963) and John P. Mackintosh, *Nigerian Government and Politics* (Evanston: Northwestern University Press, 1966).

For a discussion of the problem of ethnic and class-based orientations in Africa, see Max Gluckman, "Tribalism in Modern British Central Africa," in *Cahiers D'Etudes Africaines,* 1 (January, 1960), pp. 55–70. Also, A. L. Epstein, *Politics in an Urban African Community* (Manchester: Manchester University Press, 1958), and Clyde Mitchell, *The Kalela Dance* (Manchester: Manchester University Press, 1956).

For a recent application of the situational mode of analysis developed by the Rhodes-Livingstone group to the Nigerian scene, see Leonard Plotnicov, *Strangers to the City: Urban Man in Jos, Nigeria* (Pittsburgh: University of Pittsburgh Press, 1967).

3. "Cross Pressures" are "combinations of characteristics which in a given context would tend to lead the individual to vote on both sides of a contest." Bernard Berelson, Paul F. Lazarsfeld, *et. al., Voting* (Chicago: University of Chicago Press, 1954), p. 283.

4. In the literature on attitudes and attitude change, two major types of inconsistency may be distinguished. These are the psychological inconsistency between two attitudes, and the psychological inconsistency between an attitude and an action. In each case, the subject of the inconsistency is presumed to be aware or cognizant of the two or more attitudes at variance. In this paper, we draw attention to two kinds of inconsistency, "descriptive" and "prescriptive," in which the subject may or may not be aware of maintaining two inconsistent attitudes at the same time. See Leon Festinger, *A Theory of Cognitive Dissonance* (Palo Alto: Stanford University Press, 1957). Also see Daniel Lerner's discussion of transitional Turks. "They are persons marked by aspirations for a future which will be better than the past, but they have not yet acquired a comprehensive set of new values to replace the old. Hence they exhibit *ambivalent* feelings about the choices between the old and the new which must be made along the way. . . . Ambivalence also takes the form of self-contradictory preferences. . . . Ambivalence often shows itself in incompleteness and inconsistency of attitudinal structures." *The Passing of Traditional Society* (Glencoe: The Free Press, 1958), pp. 160–161.

5. Zettenberg immediately qualifies this assertion by noting that

> When using a biased sampling for a verification, we must have assurance that the relationship we want to prove is not introduced into our data by selective sampling . . . Also, when using a biased sample for verification, we should realize that we have no knowledge of the population to which the result can be safely generalized.

See Hans L. Zettenberg, *On Theory and Verification in Sociology* (The Bedminster Press, 1965), pp. 128–129.

6. The 800,000 to 1,000,000 figure is reported by the National Manpower Board, *Manpower Situation in Nigeria, 1963* (Lagos, 1963). According to the *Annual Abstract of Statistics 1963* (Lagos, 1964), approximately 4,000,000 Nigerians lived in towns of 20,000 or more

inhabitants. Thus, one concludes that wage earners constituted at least one-fourth of the urban population, and that wage earners plus their families constituted at least half of the urban population.

7. See Table 3.6 of the *Annual Abstract of Statistics 1964* (Lagos, 1965).

8. See Robert Melson, "Marxists in the Nigerian Labor Movement" (unpublished Ph. D. dissertation, Massachusetts Institute of Technology, 1967), p. 57.

9. Berelson estimates that a "quarter to a third" of the electorate is cross-pressured. See Berelson, *et. al., op. cit.,* p. 320.

10. The data from which Tables 1 and 2 are derived are based on: 1) a non-probabilistic survey of 58 trade unionists who attended a meeting sponsored by the University of Ibadan in July 1964; 2) a non-probabilistic survey of 29 workers who attended a training program for trade unionists, sponsored by the United Labour Congress (one of three central labor bodies of the time) in October 1964; and 3) a mail questionnaire whose response rate was 43 out of 300 possible responses. (The figure 300 is based on the estimated number of extant Nigerian trade unions which were listed by the Federal Ministry of Labour.) The mail questionnaire was sent out in October and the responses were analyzed in December 1964. In all three surveys, the questionnaires were self-administered.

It should be noted that what is called the "October-December" column in Tables 1 and 2 is based on the aggregation of responses from the second and third surveys above (N=72). In all three surveys, the characteristics of the respondents did not differ significantly from those listed under Table 3 below. In terms of validity, we might expect that our respondents overly represented the better educated leadership of the Southern Nigerian trade union movement, and by the same token, under-represented the uneducated rank-and-file, especially of Northern origin. Since it is estimated that over 90 per cent of the rank-and-file both in the South and North were of Southern ethnic origin, the small number of Northern respondents reflects the national makeup of the labor force at the time.

11. For a discussion of the effects of cross-pressures, see Robert Lane, *Political Life* (Glencoe: Free Press, 1959).

12. As the Rudolphs note, "Compartmentalization not only physically separates . . . home and family from work place and colleagues, but also prevents the different norms of behavior and belief appropriate to modernity and tradition from colliding and causing conflict in the lives of those who live by both." Lloyd I. and Susanne Hoeber Rudolph,

The Modernity of Tradition: Political Development in India (Chicago: University of Chicago Press, 1967), pp. 121–122. Also see Howard Wolpe, "Port Harcourt: Ibo Politics in Microcosm," *Journal of Modern African Studies,* Vol. VIII, No. 3, (September 1969), pp. 469–494.

13. The data on which Table 3 is based are derived from a nonprobabilistic survey of trade unionists attending two national conferences in Lagos in April 1965. Below we indicate a number of characteristics of the sample: Position of respondent in branch trade union, ethnic background, religion, occupation, education, and age.

TABLE 3.1

POSITION OF RESPONDENTS IN BRANCH UNION IN PER CENT

Position	Per cent
General secretary	43
President or chairman	30
Treasurer	2
Vice-president	2
Other executive	16
Non-executive	4
N.A.	3
Total	100
	(N=89)

TABLE 3.2

ETHNIC BACKGROUND OF RESPONDENTS IN PER CENT*

Ethnic group	Per cent
Yoruba	33
Ibo	31
Mid-western	13
Eastern minority	15
Northern	1
N.A.	6
Total	100
	(N=89)

* Note that we had too few respondents to break down the Mid-Western and Eastern minority categories into tribal sub-categories. Note also that only 1 out of 89 trade union leaders attending the conference was of Northern ethnic background. This corresponds to the observation that most wage earners and trade unionists working in the North were of Southern (Ibo, Yoruba, Mid-West) origin.

TABLE 3.3
RELIGION OF RESPONDENTS IN PER CENT

Religion	Per cent
Muslim	10
Catholic	21
Protestant	60
Other	7
N.A.	2
Total	100
	(N=89)

TABLE 3.4
OCCUPATION OF RESPONDENTS IN PER CENT

Occupation	Per cent
Full-time trade unionist	7
White collar	22
Skilled	30
Unskilled	9
Farmer, trader, craftsman, or artisan	12
N.A.	20
Total	100
	(N=89)

TABLE 3.5
EDUCATION OF RESPONDENTS IN PER CENT

Education	Per cent
Primary only	30
Some secondary	66
N.A.	4
Total	100
	(N=89)

TABLE 3.6
AGE OF RESPONDENTS IN PER CENT

Age	Per cent
Below 20	0
20–29	36
30–39	42
40–49	16
50–59	2
60 or over	0
N.A.	3
Total	100
	(N=89)

14. The last set of data presented in this paper (see Tables 6, 7 and 9) is derived from a survey of 574 railway workers in the Lagos yards of the Nigerian Railway Corporation. The workers were interviewed in May 1965 by a team of twelve interviewers, including the author. Interviews were recorded in English only. The survey was conducted every working day for six days. For a composition of the sample, the reader is directed to Table 9.

15. In 1965, the time of the study, Nigerian labor was divided among four organizations: The United Labour Congress, the Nigerian Trades Union Congress, the Nigerian Workers Council, and the Labour Unity Front.

16. Questions were based on the "Dogmatism scale" of Milton Rokeach. See his *The Open and Closed Mind* (New York: Basic Books, 1960), pp. 71–80.

17. See Berelson, *et. al., op. cit.,* "The political conviction of the individual is closely bound to the political character of his personal relations—or at least his perception of their political complexion." p. 98.

18. Dr. Tunji Otegbeye, *Ideological Conflicts in Nigerian Politics,* (Published by Socialist Workers and Farmers Party (SWAFP), Lagos, 1964), pp. 20–21.

19. *Ibid.,* p. 21.

20. *Ibid.*

21. *Ibid.*

22. *Ibid.,* my underline.

CHAPTER 23

Situational Ethnicity in Jos, Nigeria

LEONARD PLOTNICOV

This chapter reviews the lives of the principal informants . . . and attempts to place them analytically within the fabric of modern urban life in Jos, relating their different patterns of adjustment to historical, social, and cultural determinants. The fact that an individual was born at a particular time and place, into a certain family and community, influences his life chances, his career, occupation, religious and political affiliations, etc. Discussion of each informant's prior personal experiences, whether unique to himself or shared with other members of his culture, should lead to an understanding of the significant influences on his manner of adjustment to urban life.

Because of its cool climate, extensive mining activities, and large population of relatively permanent European residents, Jos contrasts with most West African urban centers and is reminiscent of modern cities in East, Central, and South Africa. The number of Europeans, who were first attracted to the area by the prospect of tin ore mining, swelled when Jos became an

Reprinted from Leonard Plotnicov, *Strangers to the City: Urban Man in Jos, Nigeria* (Pittsburgh: University of Pittsburgh Press, 1967), pp. 268–289. Copyright © 1967 by the University of Pittsburgh Press. Reprinted by permission of the publisher and Leonard Plotnicov. The notes are presented in slightly revised form.

administrative center and a transportation and communications hub. The African population reflects the great ethnic diversity of Nigeria in rough approximation to their national proportions.

Although the large European population encouraged an early and generous development of social services and amenities, the colonial government's segregation policy based on race in the use of these facilities rankled Nigerian nationalists. The European bias in favor of Muslim northern Nigerians further aggravated the sensitivity of southerners, who formed the core of the educated, modern Nigerian elite, oriented toward Western culture, and did little to alleviate the traditional animosity between southerners and northerners. In 1945 these ethnic and religious antagonisms resulted in a riot in Jos; however, most often they found expression in local and national political activities. Economic competition formed part of the undercurrent of hostility, and political activities in turn had economic consequences. Southerners, who held favorable positions in the past because of the skills they obtained through Western education received earlier than northerners, were being effectively displaced by northerners, due to the Northernization Policy of the Northern Regional Government.

In Jos, as well as in other cities of the Northern Region, the southern "aliens" who were initially attracted to the area by its economic opportunities have become rooted over the years and now bitterly resent the current pressures placed upon them. While they frequently assert the wish to leave Jos, where they are not welcome, and to return to their tribal homelands, they sometimes also verbalize a reluctance to do so. The fact is that most cannot return to their tribal areas and expect to resume their economic or occupational pursuits easily, for economic developments in their home areas have not kept pace with the technical skills which many educated individuals now possess. But their investments in Jos are not merely economic, for it is here that they experience a rewarding social life which they do not want to interrupt.

To many southerners, Jos represented an advance toward the ideal of modernization and the bright future projected for an ethnically integrated Nigeria. The discrimination based on tribal origin and a forced return to the tribal area carry the implications of traditional parochialism and a reversion to the past. These polar ideas—modern versus traditional—do not serve as foci sharply dividing the population, but are attributes held by everyone to varying degrees. The most ardent conservatives to some extent value the modernization of Nigeria, often expressed in the wish to have their children or grandchildren receive a substantial formal education. And Nigerians who are modern-oriented hold nostalgic sentiments for tribal traditions.

Just as past colonial policy and expatriate attitudes toward blacks heightened African nationalism and helped submerge tribal differences, so have such features as the Northernization Policy worked in the reverse by inhibiting the decline of ethnic loyalties and even encouraging the resumption of very parochial allegiances. Thus it is not surprising that individuals in Jos may hold office or be prominent members of modern Western institutions—school boards, traders associations, church congregations, political parties, trade unions, social clubs, and international fraternal orders—in which they interact with members of other tribes, while at the same time participating in tradition-oriented institutions such as tribal unions.

Isaac Olu Oyewumi

Isaac Olu Oyewumi, the 60-year-old Yoruba informant, was born in the old Yoruba city of Ogbomosho, and was raised there in the tradition of the Yoruba people. He came to Jos in his early twenties to seek his fortune, following a pattern typical of Ogbomosho men who traditionally traded far afield and who, just after the founding of Jos, became a part of the initial core of its African mercantile element. Olu's lack of formal education and his inability to speak English were no more of a handicap to him in achieving great wealth through trading than they had been to many of his illiterate Yoruba contemporaries and forefathers.

Olu considered his marriages and family life successful and emotionally rewarding, except his third marriage which produced no living children and ended in an early divorce. His other two marriages were stable and notably fruitful. Many of his children were married, had children of their own, and had been, on the whole, successful in their own careers.

That Olu chose a Baptist Christian religious affiliation is not remarkable when we realize that the vast majority of Christians in Ogbomosho are Baptists, constituting almost half the city's total population. Olu delayed making this personal decision until he had lived in Jos for a while, but he could have just as well still been living in Ogbomosho as far as conditioning influences are concerned, for the Ogbomosho community in Jos is large, localized, and has a stronger sense of corporate identity than do other ethnic groups in Jos. It is a tightly-knit community wherein one would expect that the applied social pressures designed to influence decisions of political and religious affiliations would be the same as those in Ogbomosho.

A core value held by Olu was maintaining the dignity and good reputation of his immediate lineage. This traditional Yoruba ideal, which he verbalized as keeping the family name spotless, could be upheld only by constant unreproachable conduct. This was a difficult burden, for a single thoughtless act by himself or any person under his charge could undo the results of generations of self-control and create a blemish that would be remembered and recalled in the future. Nor could he, as he put it, rest on his laurels. Therefore, Olu was civic-minded, participating actively in many community organizations, and at one time even serving as a Jos Town Council member. He was a prominent member of his traders' organization and the Baptist Church and a leader of various Yoruba tribal voluntary associations.

Elements in Olu's account suggest that he valued Yoruba tradition all the more because of his lack of a Western education and command of English, a lack which denied him a wider range of opportunities to exploit for the enhancement of his prestige. He could not direct more of his energies into Western-type or national institutions, such as assuming political party leadership, toward which, I suspect, his intelligence and drive inclined him.

Sensitive to his public image, he constantly validated his earned prestige by doing good works and maintaining the deportment of a socially prestigious figure. He was equally committed to his own integrity and ethic, so that he readily assumed the roles of mediator in the family disputes of friends, neighbors, and relatives, and of guardian of the welfare of other people's children. In brief, he tried to be, and to a large extent was, the traditionally good Yoruba man with overlays of Western culture and Christian morality.

Isaac Cookey-Jaja

The 43-year-old Ijaw informant Isaac, was born and raised in the Niger Delta area where the Anglican Church and its influence were established early in colonialization. He attended mission-sponsored schools, eventually becoming a civil engineer and beginning his own contracting business in the Northern Region. He held Anglican Church membership and was an active member of a congregation in Jos. Most Opobo Ijaw men of Isaac's generation have similar life histories; if they are not engineers, they very likely have a professional or white-collar job.

Outwardly, Isaac Cookey-Jaja appeared highly Europeanized, but a closer inspection revealed his strong adherence to traditional Opobo Ijaw culture. For a better understanding of this and some of Isaac's other characteristics, it is necessary to understand something of Ijaw culture and history. Prior to European administration, the Ijaw lacked an integrated polity of the scope and complexity of the Yoruba or Edo, with whom they had cultural and economic contacts. Ijaw political, social, and economic organization somewhat resembled the Greek maritime city-states, each polity being independent of the other, and the traditional autonomy and mutual hostility of traditional Ijaw polities such as Brass, Bonny, and Opobo are reflected today in their inability to achieve a pan-Ijaw integration. Historically, the Ijaw were imperialistic, economically and politically, and dominated the Nigerian peoples in and around the Niger Delta area. Their slaves came from such groups as the Ibo and the Ibibio, but the Ijaw society did not have a caste rigidity; men of proven ability could rise to high political office and achieve great wealth, and even slaves of foreign birth could become Ijaw chiefs. The Ijaw selected only those items of the European cultural inventory which suited them: bronze cannons for their large war canoes, tailored clothing, prefabricated houses, European furniture, and Western education and training. They were practiced international diplomats, pragmatic and skilled military strategists, and clever businessmen. The traditional Ijaw man has been described as proud, confident, and aggressive, his haughtiness extending even over Europeans. Extremely ethnocentric, the Ijaw traditionally held himself superior to all other peoples.[1]

Like other Opobo men, Isaac's sense of superiority and confidence and his entrepreneurial spirit contributed to his pioneering sense of enterprise and his choice of a professional occupation. His confidence left him convinced that he could achieve whatever he set out to do. When the evidence of reality contradicted his self-assurance, he attributed his failures to mystical causes, thereby maintaining confidence in his own technical abilities. He showed an orientation toward innovation and experimentation, and boasted of his avant-garde engineering practices. Perhaps more than other Africans, because he was an Ijaw, he bitterly resented European attitudes of superiority toward himself and other Africans. Much of his energy was therefore directed toward demonstrating his equality with, if not superiority to, Englishmen, who symbolized the European for him.

His anger at being rebuffed by Europeans who did not welcome him as an equal was chauvinistically channeled into the idealization of African cultural elements, such as traditional forms of divination and the glories of Opobo's past. This reaction was also expressed in his militant Nigerian nationalism. With regard to these polar cultural elements, European as against African, he was oscillating rather than ambivalent in belief and behavior, syncretic rather than synthetic. The diverse cultural elements were not merged but remained distinct, so that it was possible for Isaac to shift back and forth between traditional Westernized and African behavior. In public he always wore Western clothing in good taste, spoke English flawlessly, and took pride in these accomplishments. He was equally proud of his skills as an architect, engineer, and mechanic. In private he consulted native diviners, following their prescriptions in such details as propitiating spirits and having his children's faces scarred to "disguise" them from the malevolent supernatural being who sought their souls. Isaac's supernatural beliefs may be generally considered as an example of his traditional orientation, but the particular form these beliefs took was somewhat idiosyncratic.

His American car, trucks, and heavy construction equipment belied his actual near-bankruptcy. His loss of prosperity, occasioned by a combination of personal circumstances and the northern government's discrimination against southerners, Isaac partly attributed to supernatural sanctions, which he had incurred through neglect of his personal spiritual mentors. After residing in Jos for fifteen years, Isaac began making efforts to remove the remains of his business to the Eastern Region, where he felt conditions would be more favorable for its revival and success. If he could successfully accomplish this transfer and rehabilitation, he thought he would go into semi-retirement and, because he was close to his natal home, assume more responsibilities in traditional activities. This incorporation of Western and traditional native goals and forms of behavior, each held as distinct and appropriate for specific times and places, is perhaps the most significant aspect of modern African urbanization at the individual level.

Isaac, like his ancestors, had a good deal of the cosmopolite about him. In spite of the Ijaw sense of superiority as a people, he was not bound by particularistic and parochial attitudes in his personal relationships. He could appreciate valued qualities in persons not of his tribe, as indicated by the fact that all but one of his closest friends were not Ijaw. Along with a cosmopolitan outlook he could also be parochial, but it was not always clear under what conditions one principle superseded another. He avoided the exclusively Ibo congregation of the Anglican Church, while the members of his own congregation were of many backgrounds. In acquiring a lawyer, his first choice was an Ijaw, but when he sought the services of native magicians, he readily expressed appreciation for the mystical reputations of various tribes. His father's two wives (including Isaac's own mother) were Ibo (as was his best friend), but Isaac insisted that his children follow his own example in marrying only Opobo Ijaw. While he felt an affinity toward Ibo, especially those of the Niger Delta area, whence came his servant girls with whom he and his family established fictive kinship relations, he could also express contrasting hostility toward them, especially in his national political views. In his alternating praise and deprecation of national political figures, he again demonstrated the pervasive Ijaw qualities of flexibility and opportunism.

Isaac felt that his marriage had been blessed. He admired, respected, and loved his wife, whom he considered as perfectly suited to him, especially because she combined traditional with modern elite orientations. Both were leaders in the activities of the Anglican Church and their tribal unions. His children were developing according to his ideals and ambitions for them, which included the realistic possibility that they might be educated at overseas universities.

Like the Yoruba informant, Isaac was a leader within his tribal community in Jos and was often called upon to mediate in disputes between spouses, kinsmen, or unrelated persons. He was eminently eligible for membership in the modern Nigerian elite, where his propensity for civic prominence could have been implemented, but his precarious financial situation forced him to decline reluctantly the repeated invitations to membership. He maintained friendships with individual members of the modern elite, thereby keeping open the opportunity for his future full entrance to their group, but he concentrated his community voluntary activities within his church and the tribal organizations of his fellow countrymen.

Gande Ikowe

The Tiv informant was born at the turn of the century and reared according to custom at his lineage home in a small hamlet. Gande Ikowe and his brothers were forbidden by their father to attend the Protestant mission school which had been started during his early childhood. In his boyhood he witnessed the first appearance of Europeans in his area, but Western cultural influences remained negligible there for a long time. In his own estimation he was in his youth a progressive, in his old age a conservative. As a boy he played truant from his father's farm and surreptitiously attended the mission school, as an old man he regretted that he had not acquired more of the traditional native lore that his father had been willing to give him. As a youth he left home (against his deceased parents' wishes) and joined the army, whereas his contemporaries chose to remain home and farm. At the time of the study he most fervently wished to return home and live out his life on his farm in a traditional Tiv manner; in contrast, a younger generation of his tribesmen at home held aspirations of experiencing modern city life.

Whatever initially impelled Gande to act contrary to the pattern of his peers, little could be ascertained, but it is clear that he was premature and ill-prepared for entry into modern urban Nigerian life. Although his army experience gave him an understanding of the discipline desired by European employers and a rare command (when compared with other Tiv of his generation) of the Hausa lingua franca, these initial occupational advantages did not serve him for long, especially in Jos, and he eventually decided that life away from his homeland was unrewarding and unsatisfactory. As both his age and the labor force in Jos increased, his work continuum retrogressed from semi-skilled to unskilled and then from unemployed to a depressing dependence on the charity of friends and relatives.

Gande married five times. His first wife, now dead, left him an unmarried son and a married daughter living in Lagos. His second wife was living at his lineage home with married and unmarried sons. The third wife died without issue, and the fourth, also barren, deserted Gande after much marital difficulty. He considered his youthful fifth mate to be a good wife and mother by traditional standards. She had given him two daughters in quick succession. But by Tiv native law and custom his last wife and her offspring were not fully legally his for he had not paid the full bridewealth for her. In addition, since it was not entirely seemly for himself to have two wives while his mature son had none, he was under some parental obligation to acquire a wife for one of his sons at home, for which money was needed. Two of his sons-in-law were tardy in fulfilling their bridewealth obligations to him, and the money he had looked forward to upon the marriage of his older daughter was not forthcoming for she ran away from her husband soon after the marriage.

Gande's evaluation of himself as a prominent member of the Tiv community in Jos was based on traditional Tiv criteria that equated advanced age with power. During the period of study, a series of events made him aware that in the changing Nigerian world his age no longer assured him automatically an influential role in the community. He tried to assume the responsibility toward the Tiv community in Jos which he felt was incumbent upon him because of his age and knowledge of tradition. He was an elder in the main Tiv tribal union and had taken the initiative to found one of its segments. People had sometimes come to him with their disputes or problems or to seek native medical attention. But when he was drawn into a quarrel between his brother-in-law and a younger man, who was the son of the leader of another and larger Tiv segment in Jos, he found himself lacking support from the Tiv community. The situation forced Gande to question the reality of his presumed leadership. Because of his economic and social disappointments in Jos, he increasingly looked forward to returning to Tivland and to the traditional life he idealized.

From Gande's account we see that, while cultural changes had taken place, he and other Tiv living in Jos still viewed their intra-tribal relations on the model of their traditional localized segmentary lineage system. Alliances and factions were determined on this basis, as was expressed in the support withheld at his daughter's naming ceremony. Indeed, the traditional segmentary structure that provided for such segmentary fission and factionalism caused serious concern to those modern-oriented leaders of the Tiv community in Jos who sought to develop and maintain a sense of pan-Tiv solidarity and a strong Tiv tribal union.

In national politics, the same sort of parochial allegiances exhibited by the Yoruba informant (but not by the cosmopolitan Ijaw) were demonstrated by Gande. His party allegiance and ethnic allegiance were one and the same. In religious affiliation he claimed Christianity and saw little distinction between the different Protestant sects. Following his initial mission introduction to Christianity, he was disinclined toward Catholicism, and his peripheral position in the congregations which he sometimes attended may be related to the rather shallow religious impact the Protestant missions in his area made on him when he was a boy. It is interesting that Gande, unlike the other informants, verbalized conflicts in syncretizing traditional cutoms and religious beliefs with his adopted Christianity. He saw a conflict or contradiction in "having two Gods."

Many other good African Christians, including the Yoruba informant, were able to resolve what appears to Westerners as a conflict between traditional practices and Christian teachings. Many times I was asked where in the Bible it was stated that a man may not have more than one wife. Since a good many "*Christian* fathers of the Old Testament" were polygynists, many Africans found it reasonable to observe this precedent in spite of criticism from European missionaries. The Ijaw informant went so far as to insist that the traditional African spirits were manifestations of the one, true Christian God.

The contrast between Gande and other informants at first seemed anomalous, for the latter were far better versed in Christian knowledge and should, presumably, be more sensitive to Christian teachings and thus more aware of conflicts between Christianity and traditional beliefs and behavior. It occurred to me, however, that if I stood this conclusion on its head, the relationships might fall properly into place. It was because Gande lacked adequate knowledge of Christianity that he was thus unable to resolve a satisfactory synthesis. Although he could read a little Tiv, it was a struggle for him to do so, and the tracts on Christianity which he sometimes perused were of the simplest sort. He lacked the sophistication in Christian theology with which other Africans could make personal interpretations of dogma that were suitable to avoid conflicts with their cherished traditional beliefs.

Peter Ekong

The Efik informant, Peter Ekong, aged 55, was born and reared under Roman Catholic influence at his lineage home in the city of Calabar, and he remained Catholic in adulthood. Like most other Efik, Peter received sufficient formal education to assure him, until a brief period prior to my contact with him, of an income that provided a fair amount of comfort. Skilled mechanics were so rare in Nigeria during most of his adult life that even during the depression of the thirties he remained regularly employed at relatively high wages. After his formal retirement from the United Africa Company in 1954, he continued to work as a free lance mechanic and thereby earned enough to continue financing his children's education. Peter was not thrifty, however, and in 1961, when his major contract was not renewed, he was forced to seek steady employment. The only available job paying respectable wages was physically exhausting for a man of his age, and insecure because of the Northernization Policy.

Calabar's historic position as a trading port shows certain economic, cultural, and political parallels with Opobo and, thus, the Efik informant manifests certain characteristics shared with the Ijaw. These, however, must not be overstressed. The people of Calabar kept aloof from their neighbors, over whom they claimed a measure of superiority, and maintained distinction from their Ibibio cousins by calling themselves "Efik." They are indeed much more cosmopolitan than other Ibibio, and they also show greater Anglophilia than most Nigerians. Peter, in fact, signified his allegiance to European culture by claiming superiority for Efik because they were more acculturated than other Nigerians through longer European contact. This attraction to Western culture, coupled with the Efik sense of superiority over neighboring and related Nigerian peoples, may partially account for the Efik's lack of success in combining with Ibibio and other peoples from Calabar Province to form a strong tribal union in Jos (and other urban areas).[2] By themselves the Efik were too few in Jos to create a viable union. Characteristically, Peter expressed the attitude of being above political involvement, as if it were tainted because of party association with tribe, and hence uncivilized.

Peter's attempt to integrate his desire to be cosmopolitan and modern and his pride in traditional Efik culture appears to have been unsuccessful. The cosmopolitan and Western orientation impels Efik to associate with modern elite Nigerians, West Africans, and Europeans, and when they speak of the achievements of Efik men, it is usually within a Western institutional framework, so that examples often include outstanding doctors or athletes. Ambivalently, they sometimes express pride in the achievements of their native magicians but counter this by deprecating such "uncivilized" customs of their forefathers as human sacrifice. The informant typically expressed these ambivalent sentiments and had difficulty in relating to traditional type institutions. His sense of Efik superiority would not allow him to accept a position of less than full leadership in the integrated tribal unions of his region.

Peter had once been a leader of his tribal organization in Jos, but a factional dispute split the Calabar Community, and Peter was disinclined to join the new or other tribal unions for which he was an eligible member. At one time he had also been a member of a modern elite social club in Jos, but he had allowed his membership to lapse because of his financial difficulties, and since then he had received no encouragement to revive it. Nonetheless, his orientation to Western culture was so strong that he felt his life would not be satisfactorily complete without membership in the Royal Freemasons. Despite the Catholic Church's traditional opposition to it, he fixed his attention on this particular order because his father had belonged to it.

This informant's orientation to European culture was strengthened by his slight incorporation in his tribal group and its network of social relations in Jos. In the terminology of reference group theory, Peter may be described as the "non-member type" of person who is "dependently hostile" toward the group of his former membership—national, tribal, and kinship. These became for him negative reference groups when he, to varying degrees, alienated himself from them. He then sought closer affiliation with Westernized institutions (although he was uncertain of his eligibility for membership in some), and tried to adopt their associated norms and values.[3]

On the whole, Peter seemed pleased enough with his wife, but the fruits of their marriage were largely disappointing. He was accustomed to her constant complaints of illness—he himself often did not feel well—and the death of a child, such as that of his grandson which occurred during the course of study, was also familiar to him; three of his own children died in infancy. These family troubles seemed not to concern him as much as those he experienced with his children in Jos and Kaduna, who had socially disappointed him, and with his kinsmen at Calabar. Only one of his children still seemed to hold a realistic possibility of living up to the goals he had established for them; the others had in one way or another behaved to his discredit. Peter's shame over their failures and his own financial plight he correctly viewed as severely limiting his prestige and his chances of being accepted as an equal by the modern Nigerian elite. These circumstances caused him to withdraw still further from community social life.

A good measure of his family problems originated in Calabar, where his eldest half-brother had squandered the father's wealth, where his full-brothers had exploited his properties to their own advantage, and where relatives had continually tapped him for money. The profits he had derived from the properties given him by his mother, and supervised by a brother, had been used to further his children's education, had helped start the building of his retirement house in Calabar, and, had they still been forthcoming, could have been used to help him out of his dire economic circumstances. Instead of aiding him, his brothers at home pocketed the money Peter regarded as rightfully intended for him. Under these circumstances he found it difficult to reconcile his declaration that Calabar, not Jos, was his true home, and his professed wish to live out his years of occupational retirement there. Ultimately, he had to admit that conditions at Calabar prevented him from returning there; he was stuck in Jos.

For all the informants, living in Jos meant living away from home—home being defined as that area of their tribal territory specifically associated with their ancestors. In Jos, each informant felt he was a member of an ethnic immigrant group where the dominant group (usually, but not always, subjectively ascribed to the Hausa-Fulani) was actively or potentially hostile. The Opobo Ijaw informant, Isaac Cookey-Jaja, felt himself especially persecuted in this respect. Each said he would rather live in his tribal homeland, with the exception of the Efik (Peter Ekong), who altered his initial expression of preference for Calabar over Jos. None was actually committed to living in Jos permanently. Nonetheless, all but the Tiv, Gande Ikowe, were able to make a suitable, if not totally successful, adaptation to urban living. He was the only one prone to complain about urban life—its unsatisfactory social nature, deceptive economic advantages, immorality, etc. While the others did so on occasion, he consistently compared the disadvantages of residence in Jos with the economic and social benefits available to those living and farming in his homeland. In this respect Gande was not necessarily typical of other Tiv living in Jos, most of whom were very much younger than himself. His initially poor orientation toward western, urban culture was undermined further by his history of tenuous employment.

The three southerners, in marked contrast to the Tiv, had been accustomed early to urban life and were quite prepared to accept the necessity of spending most of their lives in cities. They had been raised in urban environments, and their cultures shared ideas of accommodation to life away from home. All four informants looked upon the economic advantages of living in an alien community as a means of gaining subsequent prestige at home. But while return to the homeland was an actual or ideal goal, living in Jos gave these immigrants positive satisfactions and moral and economic support from the company of their fellow tribesmen, with whom they shared similar circumstances and familiar traditions. The differences in their cultural backgrounds and in their emerging tribal communities in Jos had important consequences for their urban adjustments.

In addition to the traditional Ogbomosho Yoruba orientation to trade far afield, the Ogbomosho community in Jos was large, long-established, and its members were long accustomed to life in a large community. These factors served to facilitate the Ogbomosho immigrants' adjustment to Jos. On the other hand, the Opobo Ijaw and Calabar Efik had very small and highly transient ethnic populations in Jos, although the cosmopolitan ethos of their cultures permitted these immigrants to rely less on their own tribesmen for their social networks. That the Efik informant was not successful in his own adjustment was due to conditions peculiar to himself. Compared to the Calabar and Ijaw populations in Jos, the Tiv population was relatively large. Almost all of its members, however, had only recently arrived, and they had not yet developed into a community; they may more accurately be considered as a Tiv population rather than as a community. In the strange surroundings, Tiv traditional institutions had not adapted sufficiently to alien and urban conditions. Therefore, their tribal unions were not as yet able to serve as continuity bridges with the homeland. Lacking a traditional cosmopolitan ethos was an added disadvantage to Tiv immigrants, who tended to rely heavily on their tribesmen. This was even more true for older, less acculturated men, such as Gande.

Each informant believed that the ideal conclusion to life was retirement to the homeland. Although they all planned for this goal, each of them was obliged to modify his plans. Thus, because his wives wished to remain in Jos, Olu, the Yoruba, planned to marry again so that he might be surrounded by the proper entourage when he returned to Ogbomosho. Isaac, the Ijaw, shared with other southerners the increasingly uncertain business prospects in the Northern Region, and he considered relocating to the Eastern Region. Aba was Isaac's choice for relocating his business in preparation for his eventual retirement or semi-retirement for reasons of its advantageous location for business purposes, proximity to his hometown of Opobo, and its desirable modern amenities, which were lacking in his hometown. However, the undesirable political and economic developments in the Northern Region caused him to alter his original plans of remaining longer in the North and to advance the date of his resettlement. Gande, the Tiv informant, stayed on in Jos because he was unable to save enough money for even the semblance of an honorable return home. Peter, the Efik, was ambivalent about returning home. He lacked the armor of wealth and success with which he could combat his full brothers who had defrauded him, and against whom he was uncertain of finding allies of sufficient strength among his other relatives.

The Tiv and Efik men provide examples of immigrants who may not easily return to their native land when economic opportunities in the employment centers cease to exist for them. Even when they were still committed to their eventual return home, the informants were also intensely concerned with gaining and holding a position of prestige in Jos, albeit within different evaluative criteria. Only the Yoruba could be said to have assuredly achieved his goals, and he alone among the informants was not faced with immediate problems of economic survival.

Forde . . . has noted that a lack of clear-cut class divisions among Africans in urban settings is reflected in multiple and cross-cutting criteria for prestige. To enhance his social status, a person is not necessarily restricted to operating within a modern framework to the exclusion of a traditional one. The Ijaw informant, for example, was almost equally oriented to both types. Nonetheless, a person's chances of attaining recognition in one of the systems may be limited because he lacks the requisite qualifications, as with a person ignorant of the finer points of tribal custom, lore, and religion. For the Tiv informant, a knowledge of native cures was advantageous, but he realistically appraised his deficiencies with regard to Western institutions and oriented himself exclusively to traditional avenues of gaining prestige. Finally, we must not fail to realize that some individuals may be so disadvantageously situated that we could not realistically expect them to achieve or maintain leadership in either traditional or Western institutions. Peter, the Efik, had come to such a position.

Plural Reference Groups

From the extended description of the lives of the principal informants and the urban social setting in which they operate, it should be clear that these people recognized the plurality of the social and cultural worlds which Jos contains. Complex as Jos plurality might be, the participating actors knew the boundaries which defined appropriate institutional behavior. These boundaries contain different social and cultural fields, but the individuals, in most cases, knew that the different situations were to be understood by different frames of reference. When the informants did not understand all the norms for the institutions they participated in, they were sometimes troubled. If an individual is unaware of the characteristics that define culturally different institutions, and if he has not learned the full set of appropriate behaviors, he is either not fully enculturated, acculturated, educated, or socialized. But this is a condition common to all men, whether it is part of the socialization experience of the child or the learning of new and appropriate cultural habits of an adult immigrant to any alien area.

The following examples, taken from the accounts of the informants, illustrate the degree to which they were aware of what behaviors were appropriate within culturally different frames of reference and to what extent they were aware that their behaviors could be considered inconsistent.

For the Tiv informant, Gande, the social community forming his frame of reference in Jos was almost entirely that of his fellow tribesmen. Of all the informants, he was the most un-comfortable when it came to behaving outside his familiar and traditional cultural context. Insofar as he was able, he avoided contact or participation in non-Tiv institutions, and the main area of his outside participation was in the unavoidable eco-nomic and occupational institutions. Overly conscious as he was about his lack of sophistication in modern institutions, it was always clear to him where the boundaries lay. He knew what qualities employers desired, and he could behave accord-ingly when he worked for them. He could present rent receipts, the testimonials of former employers, and other documents that protected him in a culturally alien world; and, although he was functionally illiterate, he knew precisely what each docu-ment contained. He knew it was illegal for him to practice his native medicine, but (perhaps due to an excess of faith in the licensing powers of government) he falsely believed that one could obtain administrative permission to practice native magic. When he worked for the railways he knew what the penalty was for overstaying his leave, and thus anticipated a defense against this charge.

The Yoruba, Olu, like the Tiv, was most comfortable in famil-iar cultural surroundings. Yoruba music was sweetest to his ears, and he described his favorite Yoruba dishes with great relish. However, he also displayed some pride in his familiarity with the alien plural worlds of Jos. If we compare him with the Tiv, we may surmise that his greater confidence in relating to these plural conditions was based on a longer experience and a knowledgeability that the Tiv lacked. Olu claimed a modest acquaintance with Arabic, the Koran, and Islamic ritual, and he knew when to distribute gifts of food among his Muslim friends and neighbors. He was equally familiar with non-traditional institutions. Despite his illiteracy, when called on to make a civic donation, he knew how much to give and he knew how to write the check for the money. Perhaps the designation entre-preneur is not, strictly speaking, applicable to Olu, but he cer-tainly possessed the qualities of adaptibility and flexibility associated with that term. When dealing with clerks in a Ni-gerian bureaucratic setting, he knew how to gain sympathy, and thereby preferred attention; he knew whom to bribe for what purpose, when to receive bribes, and what amounts were customary for particular circumstances. He entertained old Yoruba men in one fashion, and young Yoruba men, and sometimes Europeans, in another, in each case in accordance with the guests' respective standards of hospitality. His description of his hospitality stressed the necessity of relating behavior appropriately to varying social and cultural contexts. As if in anticipation of the present theoretical discussion, he pointed out to me incidents which would seem contradictory to the ideal of rational economic action held by both Europeans and Yoruba—his support of relatives and his charity to non-kinsmen, none of which would bring him any economic return. With a similar awareness of plural social conditions that are concomitant with rapid cultural change and divergent views between different generations of the same society, he commented that a traditional Yoruba man would not have been able to understand why he did not give his daughter in marriage to an old and wealthy friend, and that a European observer might have been dismayed when he refused to allow his son to help him carry a heavy load of cloths.

In addition to conducting his business and running his family successfully, Olu participated vigorously in the plural cultural worlds of which he felt a part. These worlds included his home town, his ethnic community in Jos, his church, his neighbors and his friends (who were not necessarily of his tribe, religion, or town) in and outside of Jos. In these areas of his life he was acting within institutional frameworks that existed either exclusively for his own ethnic group or that provided extra-tribal participation and interaction.

Peter, the Efik, was ingenious in making inconsistent statements, largely because of his attempt to live the life of a more socially prestigious man than he actually was. In some areas he was quite aware of contradictions in his behavior. He admitted that becoming a Freemason was not condoned by his religion, but he had calculated the advantages and disadvantages and deliberately chose to live with the discrepancy; his conscience was large enough to accommodate the ego-satisfaction of belonging to an elite social organization that went contrary to his religious tenets. It was this same quest for favorable community recognition that elicited from him a conservative Catholic viewpoint of his son's polygynous union with a Muslim girl.

Earlier I have discussed and analyzed the nature of Isaac's (the Ijaw informant) apparently contradictory and inconsistent behavior. It is sufficient to note here that for him, also, Jos presented plural communities to which he oriented his behavior. His world consisted of his own ethnic group and the inter-tribal modern Nigerian elite, within which he had achieved and maintained a small measure of recognition.

The Yoruba informant chose to acquire an elite status primarily by traditional criteria, to be climaxed by a successful retirement at home. The Ijaw, on the other hand, expressed his hope for inclusion in the modern elite by wishing for a house fine enough to entertain prominent national figures. Both men made use of existing institutions in Jos, creating a viable dual allegiance to Jos and to their tribal homes. The Tiv informant was totally committed to home, a man entirely alienated in the non-traditional arena of Jos. The Efik man, uncertain where his commitments should lie, was a misfit unable to operate effectively within any framework.

NOTES

1. See K. Onwuka Dike, *Trade and Politics in the Niger Delta: 1830–1885* (Oxford: Clarendon Press, 1956), p. 17.

2. For an extended discussion and analysis of historical influences on Calabar Efik social characteristics and contemporary values, see W. T. Morrill, "Immigrants and Associations: The Ibo in Twentieth Century Calabar," *Comparative Studies in Society and History,* 5 (1913), pp. 424–48. For a contrasting interpretation of the same phenomena, see Richard Henderson, " 'Generalized Cultures' and 'Evolutionary Adaptability': The Comparison of Urban Efik and Ibo in Nigeria," *Ethnology,* Vol. 5, No. 4. (October 1966), pp. 365–391.

3. See Robert K. Merton, *Social Theory and Social Structure* (Glencoe: The Free Press, 1957), p. 270.

Conclusions:

PERSPECTIVES ON HISTORY
AND POLICY

CHAPTER 24

Authority and Community in Nigeria

JAMES O'CONNELL

INTRODUCTION

Continuing the autocratic and modernising initiatives of the colonial era, government in developing countries plays a greater role in determining the social status of persons and classes, in allocating roles and income and in distributing welfare benefits and amenities than it does in developed countries. Nigeria was no exception. But authority or the lawful possession of political power is considered to be legitimate within a political community when the possessors are thought to be the right persons to rule and persons who are ruling rightly. In a multi-ethnic and developing country legitimacy faces two dangers that are embedded in its own requirements of the acceptance and achievement of rulers. First, each ethnic group that has been joined politically to other groups only in the colonial period is uneasy about the power that with independence other groups may come to exercise over it. Second, in many developing countries aspirations rise faster than the rate of economic growth which the government can foster or the society achieve. In Nigeria these two dangers were to coincide: degenerating relations between ethnic groups and increasingly frustrated social aspirations combined to threaten the two-fold basis of the legitimacy of authority. And once a struggle broke out to challenge and control authority, an attempt also got under way to break the political community.

This paper attempts to explain how the challenges to political authority and community came about in Nigeria. The first part of the paper analyses how the political and social changes that worked on tradition during the colonial period contained seeds of division. Divisions became acute in the last stages of colonization and worsened still further with the coming of independence. In the process constitutionalism eroded and the way was open to the use of violence against authority. The second part discusses how this violence built up and government was overthrown. Although some blame for further breakdown attaches to the first military regime which failed to seize its opportunities imaginatively, revolt and the actual pattern of the first coup provided the precedent and provocation that led to the second coup. The third part discusses the struggle to control political authority in the context of the complex relations existing between the socially mobilised ethnic groups of the Nigerian political community. The issue of constitutional relations between the peoples which had apparently been settled before independence had now to be resolved anew. One ethnic group or nation that controlled a federal region decided to break from the unity of the Nigerian state. That decision served to precipitate the outbreak of a civil war and to polarize the other peoples of the country against the Ibo. The final part of the paper does no more than try to draw some simple conclusions—which may have comparative implications—on the role of authority and the nature of political community in Nigeria.

TRADITION, MODERNIZATION AND DIVISION

Competitive Modernisation and the Roots of Division

Much of the Nigerian political development after 1950 cannot be understood without taking into account the growth of ethnic sentiment. The basic units of social identity in Nigeria are the traditional communities—villages, groupings of lineages, towns, districts, emirates—which vary in size and shape with the social structures of the individual peoples. Within these communities an individual inherits his traditions, shares most deeply his fellowship, and seeks the esteem of his peers. But once politics began, these communities combined for the most part along ethnic lines. The elite members of the communities were their opinion leaders and guided their political decisions. These men—civil servants, local government officials, teachers, clerks, produce buyers, traders, building contractors, small industrialists, traditional title-holders—formed the bulk of the participants in and the audience for politics. Since these elite members functioned mostly in the modernising sectors of society where they had to cope with members of other ethnic groups and where community differentiation and representation was less important—if only for the reason that the number of educated persons from any single community tended to be small—they combined most easily among themselves along ethnic lines to protect and to advance their interests. Hence, both the struggle for political power and the competition for jobs and contracts evoked ethnic alignments. The resulting inter-ethnic hostility tends to be called "tribalism" in Nigeria.

Tribalism is the competitive struggle of the elite members of ethnic groups for the rewards of the modernizing sectors of society. All the strains of social change—and they are considerable—have served to embitter this competitive ethnic modernization. Only within their own ethnic groups did individuals reckon that they could safely predict the actions of others and find the co-operation with which to protect and promote their interests in an environment to some extent alien. One of the worst features of tribalism was that it led members of competing groups to see one another through unfavourable stereotypes, and so to dislike and distrust one another. Hard-line tribalists constantly urged that decent conduct towards members of ther groups was a form of weakness because the others who acted badly as a matter of course only took advantage of fair behaviour. Under these conditions a two-fold social morality developed: law held only for relations within the group; outside the group only power relations existed. Inevitably ethnic lines hardened and lack of communication intensified ethnocentricity and deepened distrust.

The main tribalist conflict was carried on between the two large and rapidly modernizing Southern peoples, the Yoruba and the Ibo. The Yoruba had early taken to Western-style education and had for long held most of the administrative and commercial posts open to Nigerians. The most developed of the Nigerian towns and the administrative and commercial capital, Lagos, was in Yoruba territory. The Ibo challenged the Yoruba quasi-monopoly of posts from 1940 on. They displayed considerable energy; they gave every proof of understanding the role of formal education; and they adapted their traditions quickly and subtly to the requirements of a money economy. The Yoruba disliked the arrival of their Ibo competitors, resented their presence on Yoruba soil, and condemned them as alien and backward. The Ibo remained sensitive to this hostility of the people of the land. Attached to land even more than the Yoruba, they remained uneasily present on what for all their nationalist logic they kept on considering to be alien soil. And they could only hope to compensate for this hatred of the people of the land by making their gains in status and wealth.

The two worst periods of tribalist conflict between Ibo and Yoruba were the years between 1948 and 1952 and the years after 1964. In the first period with the advent of elections the political activists in the nationalist cause split largely along ethnic lines. The Western-based Action Group party explicitly sought Yoruba backing and campaigned on an anti-Ibo platform. At the same time with the effective opening up of the senior ranks of the public service to Nigerians the educated elites battled to get in on the ground floor of an expanding service that expatriates were beginning to leave. After this unpleasant encounter there was a lull. In politics the parties set about consolidating their hold on the regions they had taken over after the 1951 elections. Moreover, the emergence of the Northern People's Congress whose leaders were allied to the emirs and who were committed to the protection of Hausa-Fulani and Kanuri traditional social structures led the Southern-based party leaders to realize belatedly that Northern traditionalists might benefit most from the gains of the nationalist movement. But wounds left by the 1950 clashes between the Yoruba and Ibo leaders kept on festering and were a decisive factor in preventing a Southern alliance to form a federal cabinet after the 1959 federal election. Instead the Ibo-led NCNC joined with the NPC to form a federal coalition government. The two parties co-operated to dislodge the Action Group-controlled Western Region government in 1962. And during the suspension of the Western government they pushed through constitutional measures to enable the non-Yoruba minorities of the West to set up their own Mid-Western Region.

The second tribalist flare up began in 1964 once the Southern elite groups had divined that opportunities were closing up in the federal administration and public corporations and a scramble began for the last top posts. The same phenomenon occurred in the federal universities. Antagonism broke out openly to the point of student riots and staff manifestoes and counter-manifestoes when in 1965 a Lagos University board of trustees with a Yoruba majority arbitrarily replaced an Ibo Vice Chancellor with a Yoruba. The conflict over this post was particularly intense because more than other posts the few university Vice Chancellorships revealed how quickly top posts were being taken up and were about to be filled for a long time by comparatively young men.[1] The general struggle between Yoruba and Ibo elite groups whose numbers were increasing rapidly from the growth of schools and universities was exacerbated by the arrival on the scene of Northern contenders whose entry to the public service and promotion were being facilitated by the Northern control of the federal government. Moreover, the NPC politicians had few scruples in advancing elite members of Northern minority peoples who were proportionately and in absolute numbers more advanced in education than the Muslim peoples of the emirates. In this way a certain solidarity was created among the Northern elite in spite of political hostility between the Hausa-Fulani and Kanuri-controlled regional government and most of the Middle Belt peoples.

The significance of these tribalist struggles was that they extended conflict far beyond the political realm and into spheres which made the inter-ethnic struggles tangible in the loss and gain of status, roles and money to the different elites. In that sense the general Nigerian belief that tribalism was a phenomenon generated by politicians was a misleading simplification. The first military regime which succeeded the civilian politicians tended to accept this simplification and paid dearly for it. Political tribalism was only—the climatically inappropriate metaphor will be forgiven—the top of the tribal-ist iceberg. The struggles, too, were taking a psychological toll of their participants. Individuals were growing weary of forms of competition whose rewards were considerable but whose cost in insecurity and bitterness was high. Yet the various elite groups might have gone on paying the price asked for their achievements but for the hazards of political change which caused the strains imposed on the Ibo elites to pass beyond what they reckoned to be the bounds of physical security and psycho-logical endurance. When this happened after the second mili-tary coup, it became perfectly clear that Ibo bureaucrats who were lobbying for secession were at least as much socially marked by their conflict with the Yoruba as they were politi-cally influenced by their hostility to the Hausa-Fulani. In a sense they were more deeply alienated from Lagos, though they stated more openly their aversion to Kaduna.

International Relations Without Safeguards

Were one to try and sum up the situation existing between the ethnic groups—and to some extent the communities—in Ni-geria by the 1960's one might say that it came close to being a state of international relations between them. But the situation was without the safeguards of genuine international situations because they lived within one state. G. I. Jones described the peoples and communities of one part of the country before colonisation and his description would equally well fit other parts:

> The whole (Eastern) region was, and to a large extent still is, divided up between a very large number of small local communities each virtually independent and autonomous. You can call these communities "villages" in the case of the Ijo and Ibibio, village-groups, in the case of Ibo. . . . The Ibibio villages were joined together into larger groups which you can call "tribes" (government reports refer to them as "clans"), so were Ibo villages in some areas— notably in the East. But except in the case of the smaller ones these tribes were held together by ritual and cultural ties rather than by any unifying political system. Each of these villages or towns was in a state of opposition to, if not of armed neutrality with, its neighbours and unless

you were related to neighbouring towns or had a guide who was, it was extremely hazardous to travel any distance from your home. You risked losing your head or falling into an ambush. But this was not a condition of ordered anarchy or anything like it. It was more like the relationship between European nations in the eighteenth and nineteenth centuries but on a smaller scale. There was a system of law which covered relations between different communities and it was supported by economic sanctions. As in the European case a community had the choice of enforcing its rights by resort either to law, or by the use of force (war). It usually preferred the former because, unlike Western Nigeria, a war was hardly ever decisive, the communities (except in the Ogoja Province) were too evenly matched.

The British forcibly united different nations and communities within the colonial boundaries. These groups were thus drawn together by a common administration, a shared set of laws and a single currency; they expanded their economic relations with one another; and in the later stages of colonial rule they built up a certain unity as they collaborated against the colonial administrators to hasten the advent of independence. But they did not have time enough nor were communications between them good enough for the different groups to become integrated into a political system of strong common identity and trust. While the British stayed, there was an arbiter who, partial though he might be on occasion, was accepted as ready to prevent extreme exploitation of any people or community. After independence the communities had to live together alone and accept a federal logic in which the central and regional government could to some extent act on each community in determining roles, deciding facilities and allocating rewards. The federal system was designed to offer political safeguards to the three largest peoples. But developments subsequent to independence—in particular the suppression of the Western government—led all groups to doubt the efficacy of those safeguards. And the federal system left unconciliated minority peoples in each region who considered themselves discriminated against by the regional government and who were substantial enough in numbers not to have their claims to regional self-determination entirely disregarded.

The communal approach of the political elites did little to redeem the distrust of the communities for one another. Those who formed the governments derived their authority from a political system that transcended the former autonomy of the ethnic groups and communities. Yet hardly any of the politicians thought of their communities as being in other than an extrinsic relationship with other communities. The inevitable result was an increasingly muddled logic of political behaviour. When it suited their desire to maintain their authority, enhance their status or increase their wealth, the politicians accepted the logic of a single Nigerian constitutional system. When it threatened their interests, they rejected the implications of a single system and fell back on traditional claims to communal autonomy. Sometimes it was impossible to work out which system of political logic they were acting on.[3] Given this situation, it was impossible to have anything other than inadequate political integration, unpredictable modes of action, and inter-communal distrust. Few communities felt secure.

Since such considerable tensions existed between the communities, it is in some ways surprising that the unity of Nigeria went unchallenged—or relatively unchallenged—as long as it did. Various reasons explain this lack of challenge: the remnant of nationalist ideology remained from the independence movement; the ruling groups were willing to employ the coercive power of the state against any single group that sought to break away from the political community; and no substantial set of elite groups had yet concluded that it had become impossible for them to achieve their particular interests within the Nigerian state. Understandably in those circumstances the first violent challenge to the political system was made to political authority and not to political community. But once the first break took place, Pandora's box was open. Before long worsening relations between the peoples led to political community being challenged as well as authority. The violent break in constitutional development, the fear of an international system without safeguards, and the socio-psychological traumas of modernising change combined to worsen relations between different peoples and to shake the unity of the country.

In other words, if the central government (and to a lesser extent the regional governments) could maintain stability and unity by conciliating elites and communities through its allocation of roles and rewards and preserve order under certain circumstances through its control of coercive power, it could also provoke dissent among those groups who considered that they had not been conciliated. In post-independence Nigeria each group that was dissatisfied with its access to central and/ or regional power felt alienated. Also, there was no group that did not think it was being dominated at one time or another by another group and did not seethe with consequent resentment. In the alienation there were sentiments of hurt pride, concern for the integrity of local traditions, fear of utilitarian interests being harmed, and resentment of real or imaginary injustice. But more corrosive than anything else was the distrust of the intentions of other groups. The post-coup developments bring out with great clarity the correlation of dissent and distrust.

The Vicissitudes of Constitutionalism

Built into their tribalist struggles after 1960 was the growing realisation among Nigerians in the modernizing sectors that the economy was no longer growing at a pace sufficient to permit it to absorb all the products of the expanding educational system at a level to which these graduates aspired—or even to absorb some of them. Moreover, general standards of living had either stopped rising or were rising more slowly than before. A symptom of the growing frustrations was the general strike of intermediate and lower salaried workers in 1964. This strike which was fully effective only in the South combined elements of contempt for the political elites of all parties, envy of the higher standard of living of the senior public servants and hostility towards Northern control of the federal government. It was a prelude to a Southern alliance for the 1964 federal election—the United Progressive Grand Alliance which linked the Action Group and the NCNC and which argued that a more progressive approach to government depended on removing Northern traditionalist elements from the control of the federal government.

The Northern political class after some initial resistance and hesitation bowed before the general strike. But they were unwilling to conciliate in the political sphere. They had already used their federal powers to manipulate population censuses to retain a majority of parliamentary seats in the North. They employed every means at their disposal to win nearly all those seats in the regional and federal elections. But they were dangerously wielding political and administrative power to hold a position against the weight of Southern skills and economic development and were discounting the corroding constitutional effects of Southern alienation.

The Northern political control depended on a continuing constitutionalism that accepted that power could be won by appealing to votes. But constitutionalism itself depends on the existence of a mixture of just or acceptable law and the contained use of political power which is often called "the rules of the game." The Northern leaders were beginning to observe law only when it suited their own interests and they became increasingly intolerant of groups who resisted their use of power. The first real break with constitutional order in the post-independence era came in 1961 when the Northern government employed its control of electoral machinery to eliminate, for practical purposes, their regional opposition. In that act they also showed to the rest of the country that they could from then on win enough federal seats in the North to indefinitely maintain a Northern majority at the centre.[4] In a second move the federal opposition was utterly reduced in power as the NPC and the NCNC coalition government seized on a squabble in the Western lower chamber as a pretext to suspend the regional government and to break the Action Group's political base. Subsequent influencing of court decisions, the falsification of censuses and the rigging of elections let the Southern elites and communities see that the constitutional possibilities for a change in the location of power were minimal in the foreseeable future.

Political opposition continued. A hard core of the Yoruba political elite who gave their allegiance to the Action Group leader, Obafemi Awolowo, refused all blandishments to join the Northern-aligned Nigerian National Democratic Party (NNDP), composed of break-away members of the Action Group and Yoruba members of the National Council of Nigerian Citizens (NCNC), which formed the regional government in the West after parliamentary rule had been restored.

At the same time the NPC-NCNC coalition at the centre was crumbling under various stresses: the NPC resented the continuing alliance of the NCNC with Northern opposition groups; the NCNC considered that the NPC had by backing a new party in the Mid-West broken a tacit agreement to leave that region to the NCNC; the Ibo elites were dissatisfied with two abortive and falsified censuses and were beginning to move against their own political leaders for not taking a stronger stand against the Northerners; statements by the Northern Premier, Ahmadu Bello, and other Northern leaders against the presence of Ibo workers and traders in the North were upsetting the Ibo generally; and NPC tactics in the 1964 election and the constitutional stalemate after the election angered the militant NCNC party members and convinced them that they had now little or nothing to gain from the coalition government.

Early in 1965 there was talk of Southern secession. This might have proved a practicable proposition except for the tribalist conflicts that split the Yoruba and Ibo bureaucratic, academic and commercial elites in spite of the growing rapprochement between the political elites of the two peoples. The Mid-Western political leaders formed a wing of the NCNC and shared the general Southern sentiments. But they were still too concerned with their newly found regional autonomy and with compensating themselves politically and financially for years spent in the wilderness of regional opposition to play more than a verbally soothing role in the national dissensions. Though the Action Group militants had suffered most from the hazards of political change and the use of federal power, the Yoruba elites outside active politics had to some extent been conciliated by the influence and posts that the NNDP won for them through that party's alliance with the NPC. The most alienated Nigerian group at this stage was a hawkish set of Ibo politicians who included the Eastern Premier, Michael Okpara. After the loss of the 1964 federal election they seriously considered Eastern secession. But the Ibo elites, even in the East, were not yet ready mentally to challenge the existing legitimacy. They were also not sure that their area would be economically viable on its own. And, not least, they were not certain that they could successfully carry the non-Ibo minority peoples of the East with them into secession. Resistance by these groups would weaken secession efforts morally and threaten them militarily were the federal government to deploy force against the secessionists.

If the Southern political class who were under pressure from their own elites and communities were faced with a situation of *compelled* modernization, the Northern political class which was under much less pressure hoped to carry through a policy of *controlled* modernization. They had entered politics under the sponsorship of the Northern traditional rulers. But while wanting to retain the continuity of Northern secular and religious traditions and social structures, they had also gradually asserted the supremacy of the party over the emirs and made that supremacy perfectly clear by deposing the powerful Emir of Kano when he broke with the party leaders. In the years immediately after 1960 they had seen their policy principally in the shape of the defence of the North. But as they gained experience of federal politics and decision making possibilities, they realised that there were rich pickings available to themselves at the center and that they could channel various forms of economic development towards the North. To achieve their objectives they were determined at all costs to hang on to Federal and Northern power. The attitude of the Northern bureaucratic elite was divided. Those who came from the Middle Belt communities would have preferred to have a state or states of their own. But since they saw little or no political opportunity of achieving such a result, they preferred to take the opportunities that were open to them to rise in the ranks of the Northern public service or to make use of Northern backing to obtain advancement at the centre. The bureaucrats from the Hausa-Fulani and Kanuri communities were more ambivalent. In many respects these elites and the emirates from which they came were more mobilised within than integrated into the Nigerian state. They were intelligent enough to know that their political elite controlled federal power only precariously. They feared the implications of the educational and economic disparity between the North and the rest of the country. They knew that they provided only a tiny section of the federal public service and that they were provoking fierce Southern reactions in trying to remedy the imbalance. They knew that similar reactions were likely as the Northern politicians strove to increase the number and improve the placing of Northerners in the officer corps of the army. Paradoxically many members of the Northern elite groups were as ready as Southern secessionist-minded individuals to move out of the Nigerian political community should they no longer be able to control the impact of its authority and influence on their communities or should they be unable to use central and regional authority to make themselves competitive with educated Southerners.

CHALLENGE TO AUTHORITY

The Move to Resist

Surprisingly enough, the first overt moves against the Nigerian political system came from traditional communities rather than from elite groups. These communities in the late 1950's and early 1960's were disappointed by a rate of economic growth that did not match their expectations; and they shared the general contempt for and anger against the all-too-visible corruption of the politicians. But they could be moved into violent opposition only by issues that touched directly on traditional and local values: issues of inherited status, community pride, justice and customary courts, reasonable rates of taxation and a just incidence of taxes within the community, adequate prices for their crops, and access to governmentally distributed amenities. Alienation from governments deriving from these latter issues spurred two sets of communities into revolt: the notoriously turbulent Tiv of the Northern Middle Belt and the resilient and prosperous cocoa farmers, the Ekiti Yoruba.

The Tiv rioted first in 1960 and then again in 1964. They were protesting against an imposed local government system, the arrogance of the local NPC supporters and their disrespect for the Tiv system of segmented authority, the dearth of justice in the customary courts, the brutal unfairness of the native authority police and the lack of proportion between the taxes they had to pay and the amenities they were receiving from the regional government. The Tiv were somewhat conciliated by late 1964 by sensible army action that (unlike federal police riot squad action) showed force without using it and by serious proposals made by the government to reform the local government system.[5] The significance of the Tiv revolts lay in the notice that they served on the Nigerian rulers that there was a point beyond which social discontent among their peoples would not confine itself to constitutional action. In a lesser way in 1961 the Ishan communities of the Mid-West had served the same notice on the Western government when they drove many Action Group supporters from their towns and villages.

The Ekiti Yoruba revolt broke out in 1965 after a flagrantly rigged regional election had returned the N.N.D.P. party to power. The revolt quickly spread to other parts of Yorubaland. The NNDP politicians had banked on the assumption that Yoruba communities bowed before the possession of power. But the communities were hurt in their pride and incensed by the assumption. They refused a minimal political consent to the rule of a government that they had rejected at the polls. These communities and their opinion leaders disliked and despised the venal petit bourgeois individuals who seized power within their areas by having themselves appointed members of caretaker local government councils and by appropriating customary court judgeships; they blamed Premier Akintola and his government for an economic recession that stemmed from a fall in cocoa prices and the exhaustion of the region's financial reserves; and they detested the NNDP alliance with the Hausa-Fulani-led NPC—the conquering pride of the Fulani had been feared in Yorubaland since the 19th century war. This Yoruba revolt was more serious than the Tiv revolt, if only because it occurred when constitutionalism had eroded a good deal further in the country and when Southern feeling against a Northern-led government had mounted considerably. Moreover, while the Tiv revolt remained isolated, the Ibo politicians contributed financially and organisationally to support the Yoruba revolt. And there was little possibility of insulating the rest of the country from the effects of violence that spread in a bloody manner into the suburbs of the federal capital.

The chief significance of the revolt of the Yoruba communities was that it created an atmosphere of violence in which other tensions converged. Before this revolt the more obvious prediction for the Nigerian political future was a crisis in which a general strike, sparked off by economic frustration and poor labour relations, would be successful in the South, and, mismanaged by Northern rulers, would make government impossible and prompt the army to take over power. But the labour trouble occurred rather within the army itself where the young Southern officers reacted against Northern politicians who were hastening Northern promotions and blocking their prospects. With the atmosphere of violence induced by the Yoruba revolt that crowned a period in which constitutionalism had decayed, tribalist distrust had been exacerbated by the closing up of opportunities in the public service, and contempt for inmcompetent and corrupt politicians had grown, it was easy for a set of young Southern, mainly Ibo officers, to decide to use the arms they possessed in the national cause by getting rid of worthless governments. At the same time they were not altogether (or, at least, not all of them) unaware that they were promoting their own utilitarian interests.

Remnants of Legitimacy and Relations of Power

The first military coup in dissolving constitutional authority threw the communities into a dominant power relationship with one another. But it took some time for it to become clear that constitutional relationships had not, however, lost all value. The remnants of the continuing legitimacy of the federal centre and its concomitant international recognition enabled those who held the centre to use federal organizing structures and financial resources to support Nigerian unity and to impede or ward off certain forms of outside help to a secession movement. But it was also the regional legitimacy (or quasi-legitimacy) that it held which offered a secessionist leadership the opportunity to challenge the state. Two accidental factors exercised considerable influence on subsequent decisions and events. First, there was the historical factor that the rank and file of the Nigerian army had been recruited mainly among the Middle Belt minority peoples of the Northern Region. These peoples—like the other minority groups—thought that they could escape domination of larger peoples only by retaining the federation. The soldiers recruited from among them were willing to fight to preserve the federation. And so the federal centre after the second military coup by Northern

soldiers continued to be in the hands of men who were able to
use coercive power to preserve the unity of the state. Second,
there was the geographical factor that oil in great quantities
had been discovered in the Eastern Region. The income possibilities from oil convinced the Ibo leadership of the East that
they could cope with the economic hazards of secession. But the
oil lay mainly in the land of the non-Ibo peoples of the Rivers.
Hence, the Ibo could not secede alone as a people but were
obliged to carry with them unwilling peoples who saw their
own safeguards against the more numerous Ibo in the continuation of the federation. So, if the oil permitted the Ibo to
risk seceding, its location ranged peoples against the Ibo who
posited a threat to them from within and whose plight persuaded many outside the region to stand against the secession
who might otherwise have accepted that the Ibo with their
grievances could secede alone. The two factors—possession of
military skills by minority peoples and location of petroleum
deposits—became part of the general interplay of legitimacy
and power that ranged around the role of political authority
and the nature of the political community.

But before the threat to unity arose there was a period after
the fall of the civilian governments when a first army regime
seemed to be presented with the opportunity of making a fresh
governmental start. The young officers who toppled the Nigerian authority structures had not succeeded in taking over
power. Other officers contained the coup and the army commander, Major General Johnson Aguiyi-Ironsi, took over power
himself in a military regime. The semblance of legality was
maintained by the rump of the federal cabinet delegating its
powers on the day of the coup to the army commander. But in
spite of the partial failure of the rebellion there was general
rejoicing, particularly in the South but even to some extent in
the North, that corrupt politicians had been eliminated. People
dared to hope for a new era.

General Ironsi began his military regime with a built-in problem. The young rebel officers had ruthlessly shot a number of
top Northern officers in an army that was predominantly
Northern in rank and file. Though the private soldiers remained largely passive in the shock of the revolt, they also
remained sullen and unreconciled to the loss of men they had

liked and respected. Ironsi's dilemma was that if he punished the rebels, he would alienate the Southern, and particularly the Ibo, intelligentsia. If he did not, he left his own soldiers embittered. His only hope was to carry through reforms that would conciliate all parts of the country and in the process heal the rift in the army. But he never could make up his mind whether he was continuing the legitimacy of the previous federal government or whether he was carrying on the revolt of the majors and implementing wide constitutional and social reforms. He had early on appointed four army officers to the different regions to exercise the powers of the regional governments. Part of his general ambiguity of purpose was that he did not decide initially whether he alone exercised full power or whether he exercised power in conjunction with regional governors and accepted federal limitations on his power. In practice he allowed time and opportunity for regional sentiment and interests to reassert themselves. When belatedly in May—five months after his takeover—he tried to unify the country by decree, he found that the bureaucrats, particulary in the North and the West, resisted his efforts and aroused opinion against him. They put word around that the Ibo East (from which the majority of the rebel officers, Ironsi himself, and most—though not all—of his advisers came) was planning to dominate the rest of the country through the discarding of the federal constitution.

It is worth emphasising that had Ironsi handled the army more perceptively, the second coup might not have taken place and subsequent events might have been different. In spite of the problems that Ironsi faced there was nothing inevitable about his failure: Pascal's remark about Cleopatra's nose must restrain the social scientist in interpreting Nigerian developments as well as other historical developments. Ironsi managed his communications badly not only with the country but within the army. In May he explained his unification proposals poorly to the country. Then in July without any attempt to prepare his political audience for sensitive changes he proposed to shuffle the regional military governors between the regions and to introduce a system of provincial military governorships. The North particularly was made nervous by the proposals. An element of fear sparked off the second coup.

Word spread among Northern soldiers that their Ibo officers were going to reshape the army, disarm all Northerners and eliminate them from the army one way or another. Moreover, Ironsi had scattered too many of his officers in civilian tasks. Flushed with their sense of importance in ruling the country, the officers neglected to concentrate on restoring the army discipline broken in the January coup. Finally, arrogant attitudes among young officers, their lack of a military tradition and the lack of respect among Northern soldiers for Ibo fighting qualities deepened the divisions that ethnic differences brought with them into the army and which had already been worsened by the pattern of the January killing of officers. These different factors culminated in a revolt among the Northern rank and file that had populist overtones as well as ethnic feeling. Ironsi was killed in the revolt. The Chief of Staff, Colonel Yakubu Gowon, a Christian Angas from the Jos Plateau, replaced him as army commander. Gowon was put into power by the Middle Belt N.C.O.'s and soldiers.

In response to the second coup the military governor of the East, Colonel Odumegwu Ojukwu, put his region as best he could on a footing of military defense. Except for the purposes of revenue allocation and common services the Eastern Region went into a state of *de facto* secession. It was to resolve this situation and to try to work out the general framework of a constitutional settlement that Gowon called a constitutional conference for the middle of September. Between the beginning of August and the middle of September confederal proposals were being bandied about among Northern, Western and Eastern bureaucrats and among many other politically articulate elite groups. But the conference itself was to allow for the emergence of new groups that were seeking to transcend the structures of the past rather than to permit them to grow more rigid in a confederalism that turned the regions into countries.

THREAT TO COMMUNITY

Caution and Reaction

Many educated Northerners had heaved a sigh of relief when the army first took over. They admitted among themselves that their political leaders had squandered through incompetence and corruption opportunities to promote Northern political and economic interests within the federation; they were relieved that the North was no longer obliged to hold down a more socially mobilised South by dubious electoral methods and coercive intimidation; and they did not much mourn the loss of the Premier, Ahmadu Bello, who for all his embodiment of Hausa-Fulani tradition, his possession of charismatic authority and his administrative capacity had grown more and more arbitrary and tyrannical over the years. But the Northern bureaucratic elites and educated Northerners wanted an assurance that the North would be conciliated politically. They wanted consideration given to their region's economic development and its educational lag. They wanted an assurance, too, that they themselves would not be discriminated against in any administrative changes. So they waited cautiously to see how an Ibo-led army command and an almost completely Southern federal administration would govern. But a few top Northern bureaucrats and almost all the NPC politicians—the latter after their first fright had worn off—remained bitter and hostile to the new regime.

Most Northern elite groups were alienated within a few months. Ironsi and those advising him vacillated over policy and reforms; they went only sluggishly into action against corrupt politicians; and they made little attempt to communicate on important matters of decision with the regional administrations. Lack of communication with Lagos upset the Kaduna administration deeply and gave them the impression that they had no hope of influencing whatever future political and administrative structures would be worked out. In May when the unification decree that abrogated the regions seemed to them to take away Northern safeguards, they were also upset by concomitant plans to unify the country's public services. They considered that these plans had not been adequately discussed with them and that they contained conditions of service unfavourable to them. By this time Ironsi had allowed the impression to grow up in many parts of the country that he was in the hands of an Ibo clique whose members were furthering their own interests and those of their own ethnic group.

The Northern bureaucrats began to think of ways of resisting the unification of the country. Influential ones among them propounded the doctrine that the "region had unified the peoples" and the North should remain a political and administrative entity. This beginning of resistance coincided with social developments that had been coming to a head in the North for a long time and that led to upheavals that nobody initially could easily have foreseen. The upheavals took the form of riots in which several thousand Ibo were killed. The organisers involved helped to unleash them first at the end of May as part of a protest against the unification decree. Later they set off a second series of riots at the end of September to try to wreck the proceedings of the constitutional conference at Lagos in which the Northern delegation had come to accept the division of the North into states and the maintenance of the federation. But though the organisational group behind the pogrom had immediate political objectives, the pogrom was more than anything else a sympton of a crisis of change and authority in Hausa-Fulani and Kanuri society.[6]

The British colonial administration in its policy of indirect rule had conserved and reformed the Hausa-Fulani and Kanuri hierarchical structures. In the process these structures had ceased to adapt in a continuing way to social change and had become rigid. Yet their system of sanctions was being undermined because the ultimate location of power was outside the emirates. When politics began after 1950, it soon became clear that in spite of the alliance between the traditional rulers and the leaders of the NPC, the latter were carrying further the undermining of traditional authority by new secular forces. The situation was complicated by the failure of the emirates and the British administration to establish an adequate system of modern-type education. Southerners, and particularly Ibo, had to be accepted as immigrants to undertake clerical and technical work in the civil service, the railway, other public services and the commercial firms. In this way Ibo took over control of a good part of the modernizing sectors of Northern society. And Northern society lost the advantages it would have derived from a modernizing elite of its own who could have mediated social change by spreading more effectively among Northerners new ideas and skills, bringing many communities more effectively into a money economy, and offering the example and the stimulus of local achievement.

In a traditionalist society it was almost inevitable that bureaucrats and traders who were involved in new (and colonial) authority forms and who were engaged in peddling goods in new areas of trade should be disliked and the dependence of the Hausa-Fulani on outside skills thus confirmed should be resented. Northern dislike of the Ibo was reinforced by the British colonial officers who did not generally take well to Southern auxiliaries who talked to them in their own language, imitated their ways and stood up for rights and privileges. Moreover, the British officers in the North took a strong stand against the Southern nationalists as these officers set out to protect the political interests of Northerners—a stand that further reinforced among the British and the Hausa-Fulani a dislike of the Ibo who were among the most vocal nationalists. Not least as a factor of cleavage between Northerners and Ibo was the fact that the Ibo were a people whose social structure was governed by the principle of lineage segmentation and who consequently tended to maintain closer bonds with their kinsmen and members of their own ethnic group than peoples governed by other principles of social structure. Official policy (which in certain towns enforced segregation in the *sabon gari* —ethnic ghettoes) and Ibo social structure combined to keep them apart from Northern groups, not to mention the religious and other barriers against their being accepted into the Hausa-Fulani social system.

There was little friction between the local people and the Ibo while Northern society stayed resolutely traditional. But once political development brought accepted authority into question and once awareness of the value of modernizing benefits was coupled with the realization that they were linked with a system of formal training that took a long time to acquire, frustration began to grow among Northerners. It was easy to project this frustration on to the highly visible privileged-pariah group that the Ibo were in the interstices of Northern society. They were the intermediaries in an administrative and modernizing process and could easily be represented as embodying all the facets of it—from police control through bribe-taking to the high cost of imported goods—that the common people resented. By May 1966 many factors were accumulating to explode the existing ill will into a series of massacres: the crisis of traditional authority coincided with a delayed reaction of fear over the loss of Northern power at the centre in the January coup; the politicians were seeking to find a way back to power; bureaucrats were embittered over the administrative implications of unification; Northern merchants and job seekers resented Ibo competition and thought that in the new political scheme of things this competition would grow more intense; a poor harvest had sent food prices rocketing; and there was bitterness against minor expressions of arrogance among some Ibo since the January coup.

The organisation and funds for the massacres were provided by a combination of politicians and traditionalists. The neutrality or the connivance of Northern administrators and the weakness of the Lagos authorities prevented security measures being put into effect that might have saved many lives. Some eight hundred Ibo perished in the first round of killings and six to eight thousand in the second.[7] A drop in the Northern standard of living from the exodus of Ibo skills after the first pogrom almost certainly contributed to the social malaise that made possible the second. An unexpected feature of the September killings was the participation of Middle Belt groups. But they were upset because they were themselves competing economically with Ibo, were stirred up by Hausa-Fulani *provocateurs,* and were uneasy and angry over Ibo resistance to the creation of states in the North.[8] In short, a group of determined and unscrupulous men used the insecurity and frustrations of social change to turn members of their own society against a privileged-pariah group whose members were hated because they benefited from the modernizing process and who could be killed because they were outside the rank system of society and so were less than human. The pogrom succeeded in alienating the Ibo from Nigerian society. But it did not succeed in enabling the North to secede in its old regional form. If anything, like most atavistic movements, it made sensible men look to the future. And its horror consolidated the determination of the Northern minorities to unloose themselves from the Hausa-Fulani.

The Ibo East: Retying the Umbilical Cord

The Ibo East, in spite of the spread of its emigrants through-out the country, through its segmentary social structures and its geographical separateness and compactness, was a more psychologically self-contained area than most other parts of the country. Several Ibo political leaders and members of the Eastern public services had not been reconciled to staying in the Nigerian federation after the census and election debacles of 1962–65, and their hand was strengthened by the growing awareness that the oil deposits of the region were considerable. Secessionist ideas were however set aside in the great welter of Ibo enthusiasm that greeted the results of the army revolt. The middle and lower members of the intelligentsia had dis-liked and despised the political class. They saw in the new era an opportunity to introduce more honest procedures, to get rid of a divisive and unbalanced constitutional structure, and to renew the situation under colonial rule in which Ibo were able to seek jobs in every part of the country. And they were proud that most of the coup leaders were Ibo.

When the Ironsi regime failed to maintain its initial popularity and when the first killings of Ibo took place in the North in May, the Ibo elites and people were taken aback. Yet for all their disappointment with Ironsi himself, the Ibo con-sented to Nigerian political authority and accepted the politi-cal community while its head was Ibo. The later fall of the Ironsi government and the flight of Ibo soldiers from the Ni-gerian army changed the attitude of many educated Ibo. From the beginning of August leading members of the federal public service and academics followed the soldiers back to the East. Members of the professional and commercial classes also (though to a lesser degree) took part in the exodus. Most of them swore that they would never return.

Into that exodus crowded all the strains of competitive mod-ernization that had rendered men insecure, weary and es-tranged. These men wanted to go back to their own people and their land; they wanted to live where they were able to hold and to shape more surely their social identity; they wanted to get away from Yoruba competition, hostility and vindictiveness; and they felt that the physical dangers that emerged after the

July coup were unbearable. Hurt pride, realisation that Ibo influence at the centre was going to be reduced, and bitter anger at the killing of Ibo officers combined with the existing strains to cause these men to abandon gains that had taken them many years to make. They rationalized their return home in saying that they had spent their talents in building up the whole country, had been ill thanked for it, and were now going to invest in their homeland. But with many, if not most, the decision to go home was beyond rationalization. They were retying the umbilical cord with their local communities and were moving away from storms that had been blowing a long time with strong and unpredictable force. The kind of alienation that grew up among these men drew on deep roots of sentiment and was initially more a psychological reaction than a political decision.

The bureaucratic and academic elites who returned to the East were given places in the public service and at the Eastern university; they became known later as "returnees" to distinguish them from the jobless "refugees". They were able to bring home their assets in the form of money and skills. The fact of unity touched this group lightly, if at all. On the reverse side of their flight some of them quickly glimpsed possibilities of promotion to permanent secretaryships, ambassadorships and professorships. Many among them joined with influential separatists already in the region and became a most powerful lobby for secession. This combined group gained control of the radio and government press. They set off a propaganda barrage that preached Ibo solidarity (thinly disguised as Eastern solidarity), urged the return of Ibo emigrants from all other parts of the country and promised revenge on the North. They began this barrage in August and ignored what effects it might have on the precarious safety of the thousands of Ibo who remained in the North and in other parts of the country. Yet it was significant that a large part of their more sophisticated argument was directed against federal public servants and the Yoruba-controlled and Lagos-based national press. The second round of killings in the North strengthened the position of these separatists. They then began to formulate clearly the argument that the massacres of Ibo prevented them from ever again trusting themselves to a political system over whose allocation functions and security system they did not exercise either positive control or negative veto. Their will to secede and its plans had preceded the second massacres. But their argument that the Ibo should seek the safety of a proper system of international relations—whether it was called "confederation" or "loose association" or whatever else—inevitably drew strength from the reaction to the massacres and fitted in with many aspects of the evolution of inter-ethnic relations after independence.

The common Ibo people were not separatist until the September killings. In that tragedy there was hardly an Ibo lineage without members who were killed, wounded or forced to flee or who had property stolen or destroyed. During the months after September more than a million persons poured back into the small area of Iboland. They were absorbed by the segmentary lineage system that coped flexibly with the influx and prevented a disaster of homeless and unprovided-for refugees that might have been greater than the disaster of the killings. The refugees who made up a sixth of the Ibo population were a burden on many incomes and they stretched housing and welfare services beyond normal capacity. But there was some compensation in that most of the more well-to-do had repatriated their savings and by turning their money into buildings and by other forms of spending produced a temporary boom in certain sectors of the economy. By and large, however, living conditions in the region were deteriorating and there might easily have been social disturbances as people grew more and more dissatisfied with their lack of prospects. Before that could happen large middle sections of the population had worked themselves into a sociopsychological condition that absorbed the emotional energies of the Ibo and led them inexorably towards secession.

Those groups among the Ibo who formed the link between secessionist top bureaucrats and academics and the mass of people and who furnished the die hard determination and grass roots social organisation to carry the East into secession came from the middle ranks of the socially mobilised classes. These middle cadres—intermediate grade civil servants, clerks in commercial companies, artisans, newspaper and radio reporters, elementary school teachers, university students and their likes—were worked on by many sentiments. They were closely attached to their communities and were terribly affected by the massacres; they were ashamed that their kinsmen in the North had had to flee like stricken animals and they wanted to vindicate Ibo honour in blood; and not far removed from traditional village attitudes where in small communities a man or family could demand to be conciliated, they refused to co-habit in a political community where they had not been given redress for their wrongs and they were willing to remain obdurate until conciliated, even if Samson-like they were bringing the walls of the house down on themselves and everyone else. As well as being hurt by the massacres, these men were disillusioned by the result of the 1960 independence. They were further disillusioned by the hopes that were dashed in the faltering Federation and then in the fall of the Ironsi regime. They saw that opportunities for posts and promotions were closing up or had closed up. They felt that they were excluded from the advantages that a few years earlier easy social mobility had brought to others like themselves who had had either qualifications such as degrees or the timing of opportunities on their side—earlier graduates and even non-graduate clerical workers had won rapid promotions in the expanding civil services. So, cherishing few prospects in the existing political situation, they were ready to gamble on the radical possibilities offered by secession as a second independence.

In a sense what frustrated and yet ambitious members of the middle ranks of society were seeking was a magic opportunity to better themselves in one swoop. By a kind of social osmosis the same attitudes spread among the whole Ibo people. Traumatically damaged by the experiences of their kin, they turned in on themselves as a people and spurned the outside gains in posts, property and commerce that had enabled a dynamic people to profit from education and to improve poor and overcrowded areas. They proclaimed the stay-at-home man as king, propounded a *Sinn Fein* or "ourselves alone" doctrine, and raced back against the current of their own expanding history. There were many elements of a cargo cult in their reaction: they wanted to do without the laboured and insecure efforts of measured time; they called their people together on their ancestral lands; they wanted a return to the trustworthy solidarity and the pristine ways of their ancestors, and yet mixed up with this return were contemporary and imported notions of achievement; they wanted to destroy, and did destroy not only their incorporation into the federation but consumed savings by turning them into buildings that consolidated their hold on ancestral land but that had little meaning as a profitable investment. No matter what the outcome of a civil war might be, the hopes of these men were bound to be challenged again. The transformation they sought was beyond immediate possibilities.

In short, various factors and groups co-operated to cause the Eastern secession. By and large the Ibo people as a whole came to believe that they were not wanted in other parts of the federation, not least because they thought that the other peoples envied their ability and resented their competitiveness. They carried the mental wound of the September holocaust in their bones and feared that their lives were not secure in many parts of the federation. They convinced themselves that they could construct a new prosperity by seceding from Nigeria; they were going to rely on their new efforts in farming, on their growing industries and on the massive revenue predicted from petroleum to make themselves economically viable; and they believed that they possessed the solidarity and determination to bear the sacrifices that the first years of independence would exact. The one significant foreign element in the secession appears to have been the substantial support given and promised by oil interests to Ojukwu's government at a crucial stage of the discussion of secession and which encouraged the Ibo leaders to run the military and other risks that faced them.

The pressures that were built up had to come to bear on one man, flanked mainly but not exclusively by secessionist advisers, in whose hand the decision making was concentrated. The military governor of the East, Colonel Ojukwu, was a moderate in the sense that he understood the military and economic problems of secession and preferred to negotiate a confederal solution in which his region retained various common services with the other regions but was free to make its own political decisions and to control its own economic resources (the oil revenue not least). But he was also determined to retain power personally; and he was anxious that no one should be able to appeal to the people against him. If he had been a leader of great calibre, aware of demographic pressures on his people, able to estimate the long term advantages to be derived from the vast Nigerian resources and market, and sensitive to the likelihood of an interminable struggle with the minority ethnic groups who formed about two-fifths of the region's population,[9] he might have tried to help heal his people's wounds and utilized the tremendous bargaining position they held (it was most substantial by December, 1966) and might have won favourable agreements on constitutional safeguards and revenue allocation. But he refused to try to heal, harped on the sufferings of his people to promote their solidarity, and rejected every offer to negotiate a federal settlement. By May, 1967 feeling had so built up in the region that Ojukwu could no longer have hesitated even if he had wanted to. And so on the 30th May he declared the independence of his area as the Republic of Biafra. Its symbol was a rising sun.

The West: The Spoiling of Joy and the Enduring of Hope

Except for the NNDP party members and regional bureaucrats compromised by their co-operation with them, the Yoruba West rejoiced over the fall of the Balewa government and was proud of its own role in bringing the country's political crisis to a head. With the fall of the government they would have liked to have seen Obafemi Awolowo, the imprisoned Action Group leader, set free: he had become a martyr-symbol of the Yoruba and his premiership was looked back to nostalgically as a time of peace and plenty. But they accepted to begin with that Ironsi could not immediately release him lest he offend further a North which had been most hit by the coup.

The Western bureaucrats reacted cautiously to the advent of the military regime. Like other members of the Southern intelligentsia they took for granted that the former federal system which had failed was finished. But as they refurbished their administrative apparatus under a shrewd and genial military governor, Colonel Adekunle Fajuyi, they began to think again in terms of consolidating their own region. By May they were bitterly opposed to the unification decree. They were allied also in friendship and sentiment with the Yoruba public servants in

Lagos whose struggle with Ibo colleagues had begun to pass the previous bounds of competitiveness. Though in absolute numbers in the upper ranks of the federal public service and universities the Yoruba dominated, they believed that their position was threatened by the Ibo access to Ironsi and influence on his policy. So the Yoruba federal and regional elites began to seize on and carefully leak or communicate every weakness of the regime. And by these means they played no small role in creating the mental climate in which the Northern soldiers overthrew Ironsi.

Ironically, it was the Northern military leader, Colonel Gowon, who finally released Awolowo and gave the Yoruba a political leader as constitutional debate reopened. Ironically again, Awolowo, who had gone to jail for insisting on a national policy for his party and refusing one of regional security, joined with the Northern and Eastern delegates in the September conference in putting forward confederal proposals. The Western delegation stuck to those proposals even when the Northern delegation had changed its stand to supporting the federation.

Awolowo's change to a regional policy underlined the stresses of Yoruba political experience. He and his associates wanted to take hold of power soon and thought that a confederation easily agreed on would hasten civilian government; they had little heart left for the uncertainties of federal politics and preferred to consolidate power at home; and as time went on, they began to fear federal support for Yoruba groups who had begun to advocate dividing the Western state along the lines of its sub-ethnic units. The top bureaucrats supported Awolowo's stand. They saw that not only would it prevent the division of their administrative domain but it would free them from a federal supervision that they much resented. Finally, both politicians and administrators realised that the continuation of a federation in which the North had been divided into states would imply a stronger centre and a reduction in the power of all the states.[10]

By taking the stand they did at the constitutional conference the Yoruba leaders opted out of the real debate over the future of the country. Thoughtful observers had early on in the conference pointed out that confederation meant the virtual break up of the country. Public opinion could understand why the Ibo leaders whose people had suffered should take up a confederal position. The Yoruba leaders could put forward no equivalent sense of wrong to justify an extreme stand. Neither did they possess an armed force nor did they completely control a regional administrative apparatus to back their case. Finally, they proved unable to rally their own people. Throughout the discussion the Action Group leaders themselves were not united—some of them disagreed with Awolowo, and others simply argued that their confederalism was a tactical manoeuvre to bolster their bargaining power and was not their true objective.

The strength of the existing federation was shown in the failure of Awolowo to rally his people behind him—except in his demand that Northern troops be removed from the West. Within the traditional communities people wanted mainly to consolidate the law and order restored after the fall of Akintola; they scarcely understood the federal-confederal problematic; and they could not easily be aroused against a Nigerian state that they still took for granted from the colonial experience. The elite groups retained by and large from their educational formation and the nationalist days an attachment of sentiment to the concept of Nigeria and latter-day vicissitudes had not been enough to break their attachment; many realised the advantages that accrued to the Yoruba from the jobs, market and mineral resources that the federation made available; some sophisticated Yoruba believed that only competitive co-existence with other ethnic groups prevented internal Yoruba divisions from becoming excessively disruptive; educated individuals from the eastern and central parts of Yorubaland were afraid that in a quasi-sovereign state the Ijebu and Egba civil servants would consolidate their hold on civil service jobs; and many disliked Awolowo's autocratic and unforgiving ways and were uneasy over his rash promises to make schooling free on all levels and to provide full employment within five years.

Though Ibo secessionists were heartened by the brave references of Yoruba politicians to "complementary secession", the latter never dared to specify whether their own secession was to take place when the Ibo secession was announced or when the Ibo secession had been made to stick. In the event Awolowo, who sponsored peace moves in May which were spurned by Ojukwu, joined the civilian executive council established by the federal military government. When Biafra was declared, the Yoruba West stayed in the federal camp. But neither the Yoruba themselves nor anybody else reckoned that they were going to fight to preserve the federation.

The Emergence of the Minorities

Had the Nigerian crisis been resolved by representatives of the three main peoples only, a confederation would almost certainly have been the result. What prevented this result was the intervention of the minorities. Minority groups wielded control over one region, the Mid-West. This control gave them institutionalised access to the September conference that Colonel Gowon called to try to resolve the constitutional stalemate after the second army coup. At that conference representation was by region. Conscious that on the dissolution of the federation their region would be torn by internal dissension—the Mid-Western Ibo were strengthening their ties with their linguistic kin across the Niger—and would be threatened by external takeovers from the East and the West, the Mid-Western delegation proposed that the federation should continue. But they argued that a necessary condition of federal survival was the division of the North. And they showed their willingness to follow a federal logic by accepting to forego certain regional revenues.

The Eastern minorities originally hesitated to put their views strongly to the conference. To take a stand in Lagos might damage them at Enugu. They were not sure that they would be able to rely on support from outside the Eastern Region to enable them to detach themselves juridically from the region. They took heart at the Mid-Western stand. Though their official representation at the conference table had been controlled by the Ibo leaders, they used unofficial spokesman to proclaim that they wanted the federation to continue and that the East should be divided as well as the North. The circumstances of the conference focused attention on their stand and they made good use of the publicity possibilities.

But the decisive move at the conference came from the

Northern minorities, represented now by the Middle Belt soldiers, the Tiv in particular. The soldiers threatened the Northern delegation and obliged them to change their confederal proposals for federal ones. Influential Hausa-Fulani public servants who wanted the federation to continue backed the Middle Belt initiative and federally-minded Yoruba public servants, academics and businessmen moved at the same time to counter the stand of the Western delegation. The Ibo-controlled Eastern delegation was increasingly isolated. Its members bargained to obtain a mitigated federal solution. Then the bargaining was overtaken by events. Once the Northern delegation had made its *volte face,* the second round of killings began in the North. After that the Ibo leaders retreated into an obdurate refusal to negotiate any settlement that might permit other Nigerian peoples to exercise power over them.

The conference itself symbolised the new opportunities that had become available to the minorities with the breakdown of the independence settlement. They seized their opportunities with a vehemence that was proportionate to their long frustrations. Scattered among the regions, each of which had been controlled by representatives of a majority people, they had been unable to organise politically to secure a measure of self-determination and to reverse the discrimination against them in the location of amenities and the distribution of rewards. The Lagos conference gave them the chance to assemble and to pool their strength. They were not without some disagreements among themselves but they were willing to set these aside while they worked out their relations with the main peoples. They did not want to allow the worst features of the previous political system to be perpetuated in a confederation whose units were the former regions. They discovered that they had an important common language—English—that they used between them in their cause. And they had the guns that for the time being counted for more than the numbers of the larger peoples.

The core of the federal leadership was composed of Northern and Eastern minority army officers, minority public servants from all the regions, and a few military officers and public servants from the majority peoples. Various groups of educated minority persons formed a wider caucus of advisers and lobby-ists. A great deal had depended on the army commander, Yakubu Gowon, who had to crystallise in his decisions the various forms of willingness to support the federation. He was personally most reluctant to use force to hold the country together. But as he found it impossible to work out a negotiated solution, he gradually organised his own forces for war. Once by the end of May it was clear that the East was about to secede, Gowon acted first. Unilaterally by decree he broke the North into six States, the West into two, and the East into three. He personally had wanted to rely on economic sanctions to bring the secessionist leadership to heel. He resorted to force only when his advisers insisted that the Eastern regime had been, and still was, importing arms, hiring mercenaries, had been given substantial sums of money by oil interests, and was likely to be recognised by more than one country should it make its independence stick for a relatively short time. Soon after the beginning of July the Federal forces were sent across the Eastern boundary.

Those who took up arms against the secessionist move of the Ibo leadership were impelled by a variety of reasons: the Northern groups generally were given a new unity by Ojukwu's refusal to raise his blockade of the North which convinced the most secessionist minded among the Hausa-Fulani that in the event of the breakup of Nigeria the access of the North to the sea would be precarious and costly; opinion leaders from the minority peoples of the East, North and Mid-West believed that only the continuation of the federation and its new system of states could enable them to escape from future domination by larger neighbouring peoples—the Tiv from the Hausa-Fulani, the Ibibio and the Ijo from the Ibo, and the Edo from the Yoruba; the Yoruba elites had come to realise that their path to jobs and their economic security depended on the size of the Nigerian market; federal civil servants knew that their own professional future was linked with maintaining the federation; and sensible men from all peoples foresaw that once the principles of separation were accepted a fission logic was most likely to set in and the country would split along the seams of ethnic, and even sub-ethnic, differences.

The Biafran moral case lay principally in the massacres of the Ibo in 1966 and the lack of effective redress for the "wrong doings". Yet it seems fair to say that whatever redress was likely—though the federal authorities handled the whole matter with consistent ineptness—was made impossible by the refusal of the Ibo leadership to be conciliated after August or to accept any agreement that kept the federation in being. The federal protagonists drew their moral strength from the conviction that the Ibo had no right to carry the Eastern minorities with them into an unwilling captivity. Biafran apologists argued that the Ibo could not be kept in Nigeria—where they form one-sixth of the population—by *force majeure*. But the same case could be made more conclusively against Ibo attempts to keep two-fifths of a population against their will in a country fashioned from a federal region.

The one aspect of the war that strongly influenced the political situation was the invasion of the Mid-West with the connivance of Mid-Western Ibo officers and soldiers—although the Mid-Western Governor, Ejoor, had persuaded the federal authorities to keep troops of non-Mid-Western origin out of the region so as to conciliate his Ibo officers whose fidelity he relied on. The Biafran army installed a puppet regime in Benin under a Mid-Western Ibo, Major Albert Okonkwo, that declared itself independent of Nigeria. The invasion embittered the Edo-speaking and the other non-Ibo Mid-Westerners and worsened considerably their relations with the Mid-Western Ibo. While the Mid-West stayed a buffer zone between the opposing forces, it had been a symbol of a contained war. Once it was invaded, the war moved much more towards a total form. And as federal forces retook the Mid-West (and later as they moved into the Eastern minority areas), massacre and countermassacre by both sides deepened insecurity and hatred.

Westerners were shaken by the Ibo advance into the Mid-West. They saw their own security threatened for the first time. Their pride also was hurt as they heard the Enugu radio station promise that the West would be liberated as the Mid-West had been. They rejected the crude tactic that the Biafrans had employed in putting a Yoruba officer in the Biafran army in charge of the military operation in the Mid-West so as to solicit their support for a front against the North. The Yoruba leader, Chief Obafemi Awolowo, who had in June accepted the top civilian post in the federal government, came to Ibadan, the Western capital, to meet Yoruba leaders and to state his stand in favour of the federation. He rallied all but a few diehard Yoruba secessionists and removed a certain ambiguity that had up to then plagued the Western stand. After the Yoruba rallying all the Nigerian peoples were ranged against the Ibo.

CONCILIATION AND DISSENT

The following paragraphs do no more than draw out conclusions from the two previous parts of the paper. They make some tentative predictions about the Nigerian situation and they suggest some political adaptations that might reduce the level of dissent once representative government begins again. And they try to work out some comparative implications of the Nigerian data.

Nationalism and the Multi-National State

The Nigerian experience underlines conclusions that studies of post-independence happenings in other developing countries have also begun to emphasise. The anti-colonial movements were too hastily equated both by their own participants and by foreign scholars with old-fashioned European nationalist movements—the Irish and Polish are examples—in which a sense of cultural individuality and a drive for political freedom coincided. In multi-national, colonial quasi-states it makes more sense to speak of independence movements than nationalist movements. Yet it would be a mistake to fail to recognise the beginnings of national sentiment that identifies with the new state. And this sentiment can exercise more influence than its inchoate nature might suggest because it tends to be possessed by members of small elite groups who are more upright and politically committed than are those individuals who belong to the divisively-minded or apathetic majority.

However in spite of the beginnings of national sentiment on the level of the state it is often the case that the generation of elite groups which comes after the nationalist generation is less committed to the political system than the latter. These groups have been less formed in their experience and less welded together by conflict with the colonial authorities. And they are marked by the trauma of competing with one another under conditions of insecurity and bitterness for the gains won by the independence leaders.

If in the colonial period it is more accurate to speak of independence movements than nationalist movements, what are the prospects for a nationalism of the state after independence —at least once the conflicts that rearrange power after independence are over? It is little likely—and even less desirable— that an exclusivist nationalism of the former European kind is going to develop: it is too soon for the different nations to merge into one. It is also too late because no country now is going to be permitted the separate experience that made for unity in the past. What can be hoped for is a sense of distinctiveness that grows out of the common experience of nations which co-operate with one another in the one state. In this sense Nigerian development can be built into the utilitarian interests of peoples who possess deep cultural affinities with one another. It should resemble the development that is taking place within the European Economic Community where gradually in a consciousness of a common Western tradition peoples are drawing together and emphasising more their distinctiveness from other parts of the world than from one another.

One of the few positive gains from the Nigerian civil war may be the common experiences and sacrifices of peoples who have fought alongside one another to defend the unity of the political community. It is true that this may still leave the Ibo alienated. But it is worth remarking that the poorer Ibo who were outside the Eastern Region either did not leave or did so at the last moment before secession. No people more than the Ibo will need the Nigerian state once they cease to control the administration and economy of their former region. There is no reason why they should forego the proud memory of having imposed on the other peoples a hard-fought war at a time in which they considered themselves unconciliated. In the American South the confederal flag is more a cultural than a political symbol and yet it recalls one of the bloodiest wars fought up to that time.

International Relations with Safeguards

Those elite groups in Nigeria who thought that they could afford to be divisive and even secessionist came from the so-called majority peoples. They believed that their peoples were large enough to be self-sufficient. They pointed out that their peoples were greater in numbers than the populations of most African countries. But apologists of confederation or secession had to take history and economics into account more than they originally thought. Administrative structures and economic links were not easy to unscramble. The advocates of secession among the Hausa-Fulani began to realise this as they thought out the problem of access to the sea. The Yoruba secessionists failed to carry their elite with them as the latter became more conscious than before of the advantages that accrued to them from the federation. Only the Ibo finally reckoned that they could make their way alone. And their concept of making their way alone included the attempt to carry an unwilling and potentially rebellious minority population about half their own size with them.

The minority peoples were obliged by their smaller numbers, resources and geographical dispersion to recognise the international character of their political existence. So they remained staunchly federal. But they wanted to establish new safeguards for themselves by redrawing the federal structures. The political upheavals of 1966 gave them an opportunity which up to that time the majority peoples in defending their own vested interests had denied them. It was this steadfastness of the minorities that held the Nigerian federation together while two majority peoples belatedly came to accept that the alternative to federation and its quasi-international exigencies was economic loss and interminable strife. It may still be necessary to modify aspects of the recent twelve-region decree. But its main outlines offer much better prospects for a political balance in the country than did the old regional system.

Uniforms and Filing Cabinets

Those scholars who described the independence movements and thought that the future belonged to the political and other elites of the period by and large did not foresee the role of the military after independence. Later writers more easily grasped their importance but some of the predictions they began to make have not been fulfilled. The military in most African countries have not been able to restrain through their common formation and discipline the ethnic antagonisms that divide other elite groups. In Nigeria local loyalties and sentiments split the army and served to lead the country directly towards civil war. Moreover, there is little evidence that military formation, discipline and experience tend to modernize its recipient faster than formation for, and service in, other parts of the public service or even private sectors of the economy.

But the military officers are not a Latin American style wing of an established oligarchy. They are best understood as the "intelligentsia in uniform"[11] (Seton-Watson). They share the general attitudes of the other modernizing elite groups and differ from them mainly in possessing access to instruments of violence. In Nigeria and elsewhere they come from all sectors of society and form part of the educated oligarchy that wields power in the state. Up to the present that oligarchy remains open. And the spread of schools, elementary and secondary, will make it most difficult for an oligarchy that contains so many divisions within itself to close its ranks and to form an establishment. But for some time to come Nigerian civil rulers must reckon with the possibility of military intervention whenever serious dissent besets the state.

Economic Growth and Ideology

In African countries there is little likelihood of economic take-off in the present generation. That failure carries its frustrations with it. Moreover, even the growth that takes place and the education that underpins it exacerbate discontent. Some writers who prize stability highly argue that economic growth as a political target in developing countries should be de-emphasised. But in the global village that our world is this is hardly possible, even were it desirable. What might be done, however, is for government to communicate better with its people to explain what the realistic possibilities of growth are. But for government to do this it has itself to convince those to whom it counsels patience that it has a radical program that respects justice and equality among individuals and groups, that it is implementing this program with a sense of social urgency and administrative efficiency, and that its members are upright men who share to some proportionate extent the privations of their people. Countries like Nigeria may in spite of appearances to the contrary be presently reaching a certain equilibrium in aspirations and consequently in the prevailing sense of relative deprivation. The period of rapid promotions has almost come to an end and with it the "large and rapid increments in the quality of rewards received (which) disrupt the participation of the gainers in the hitherto dominant consensus" (Shils). But only able rulers will be able to seize the opportunity to make use of this relative equilibrium so as to win time and beget patience.

The Inevitability of Instability

Disruptive as political instability in Nigeria and other African countries has been, it is important to recognise that in post-colonial developing countries there is a certain inevitability of instability. Nigeria developments in their complexity offer a case study from which variables can be gleaned for the study of the other countries. The factors leading towards instability can be grouped into three main categories: constitutional development, economic growth and leadership calibre.

(i) The presence of a colonial referee falsifies the power struggle before independence. Not only may the colonial power and its officials be an interest group in the pre-independence settlement but their very presence, no matter how fairly they act, has the effect of a referee who artificially determines the rules of the game and backs them with his power. Often the nationalist leaders add to the artificiality of the independence settlement by being more bent on hastening independence than on settling the location of power before independence. This restricted form of political process may produce not only a constitutional framework that does not reflect the relative strength of the various power groups within a state but it tends to impede politicians from gaining the kind of experience which teaches them that power must normally be limited in its use (the rules of the game) to prevent politics from being destructive for all those who take part in it. This experience is all the more important for men accustomed only to the autocracy of a colonial government which combined in its functioning the exercise of executive, legislative and judicial powers. The trouble is that new leaders with this inheritance often underestimate the need to soften conflict and to bargain politically.

(ii) The failure of economic growth to meet expectations creates frustrations that explode more easily against government than against other institutions. Moreover, as growth takes place it not only leads to a scramble for its benefits but it seldom fails to increase tensions between ethnic and other groups as previous relations between them change. Nigeria offers illustrations of this revolt against authority as well as the bitterness of the competitive modernization of the elite groups of the most socially and economically advanced of the peoples.

(iii) Political skills are no more abundant than any other set of skills in a developing country. Political leaders whose own background is traditional do not easily acquire attitudes that enable them to correlate financial expenditure and economic development, to understand the potentialities and exigencies of machine technology, and to cope with highly structured and relatively impersonal bureaucratic procedures that are required for decision-making in societies that are striving to modernize rapidly.

Any one of these three factors is capable of threatening the stability of political authority in a developing country. But in several countries, as in Nigeria, they have converged in varying forms.

Conclusion: The Primacy of Conciliation

The central political conclusion that I want to draw from the Nigerian situation is the primacy of conciliation. Political authority whose function is to lead and to co-ordinate (and where need be, to coerce) the actions of members of the political community as they seek collectively goals that include an ideal of welfare, the maintenance of law and order and the carrying on of external relations with similarly organised groups conciliates when "sociologically and ethically" it respects the fact that "civilized communities are internally diverse" (Crick). But if those who govern are those who most actively need to conciliate, groups who compete for the possession of power must also accept restraints on their competition that prevent those who do less well from being driven into the alienation of complete dissent. It is in relation both to government and to politically organized groups that Crick writes: "Politics can . . . be defined as the activity by which differing interests within a territory are conciliated".[12] This contention puts the emphasis on conciliation rather than on consensus, especially in relation to the activity of government. Consensus which relates to representatives, institutions and the allocations of rewards made through these institutions keeps shifting. It is the actively conciliatory role of government that prevents the shifts of consensus from breaking down in active dissent.

The case is constantly made in developing countries for autocratic government. In point of fact governments seldom need to be urged to act autocratically when it is the only mode of government they saw at work in ruling the peoples of the colonial quasi-state. Yet autocracy usually demands skilled, upright and ideologically committed leaders, a well-organized political following or party, the relative dominance of a single ethnic group, and an efficient and pervasive bureaucracy. These factors were available in Russia in the early Stalinist period. They are not available in Nigeria nor are they available in most other developing countries.

The case that needs to be made in a politics of conciliation approach is that government should be representative in its composition, *flexible* and *open* in dealing with changing consensuses, and *fast* and *firm* in its decisions. (1) Given a situation of inadequate trust between communities, it is better that these communities should as far as possible be represented in government. The easiest way to achieve this end is for government to contain representatives of a state's important groups. Hence, political institutions and the ethos that animates them must permit and encourage broad-based representation in government. Future Nigerian leaders may profit from the past to learn that no considerable group can be left unconciliated without undue strain being placed on the whole political system. Moreover, Nigerian experience suggests how little validity there was in the contention that ethnicity—which in this context might better be called "aggressive ethnicity" or "tribalism"—would lead groups to compete for power without challenging the political system or without trying to break the political community.

(2) Government needs to be flexible in responding to demographic, economic, technological and occupational factors that cause a shift in the existing consensus. For that reason it needs communication channels that carry and receive messages. Free criticism whose measure it belongs to the art rather than the science of politics to determine is an essential part of such communication. Tyrants notoriously perish for want of hearing the truth. But not only must government be flexible in changing policies in reaction to a changing consensus and ahead of a changing consensus, but it must also be open to accepting new recruits and to eliminating those in whom the political audience has lost confidence.

(3) In developing countries governments are constantly more in danger of making decisions too slowly in order to embody a quasi-traditional consensus among the rulers than in making rapid decisions that alienate subject groups. This understanding of consensus derives from pre-technological conditions in which rulers were under little pressure to make rapid decisions and in which a consensus could be arrived at eventually out of interminable discussions. While keeping in mind the primacy of conciliation those who govern in a country where machines have begun to roll have no option but to respect their speed. Moreover, in elaborating representative institutions it is important to establish the possibility of firm decision-making to avoid institutions that weaken and slow up decisions by allowing veto power to small groupings whose composition may change from one issue to another or who may hold up indefinitely decisions that benefit society generally but conflict with their particular interests. Government needs to be representative but it also has to govern.

To conclude: The future never repeats the past, even if it makes no clean break with the past and if it must learn from the past. Should Nigeria emerge as one country from the present civil war, the politics of competitive ethnic modernization are not likely to cease overnight. Yet if the struggles of the recent past have been predominantly ethnic struggles exacerbated by competing elite interests, there is greater likelihood that the struggles of the immediate future will be predominantly class struggles modified by ethnic interests. Already the output of the schools threatens to engender competition for scarce resources within communities as much as between them. In the event of social strife in the form of class struggles the state may be spared the danger to political community that it is now threatened with. But it may make no gain whatsoever in the stability of political authority.

NOTES

1. This dispute left great bitterness behind it. Nearly all the Ibo teachers at the University of Lagos quit and went to the Eastern university, the University of Nigeria, Nuskka. Inevitably they formed a powerful lobby for secession when the 1966–67 crisis took shape. Some of the bitterness of the Lagos dispute can be gauged from publications put out by each side—e.g., *The Crisis Over the Appointment of Vice-Chancellor of University of Lagos by the Senior Members of the Staff* (Lagos, 19 March, 1965); *Appointment of a Vice-Chancellor,* University of Lagos Official Publication (Lagos, 16 June, 1965).

2. *Odu,* January, 1966, p. 83.

3. On this point see B. J. Dudley's acute comments in "Traditionalism and Politics: A Case Study of Northern Nigeria," *Government and Opposition,* July, 1967.

4. See J. O'Connell, "The Northern 1961 Election," *Nigerian Journal of Economic and Social Studies,* July, 1962.

5. On the Tiv disturbances see M. J. Dent, "A Minority Party—The United Middle Belt Congress," in J. P. Mackintosh, *Nigerian Government and Politics* (Evanston: Northwestern University Press, 1966), pp. 493–507; also *A White Paper on the Government's Policy for the Rehabilitation on the Tiv Native Authority,* Kaduna, 1965.

6. A slightly fuller consideration of the move against the Ibo in the North can be found in J. O'Connell, "The Anatomy of a Pogrom: An Outline Model with Special Reference to the Ibo in Northern Nigeria," *Race,* July, 1967.

7. These casualty figures have been put together from careful inter-
viewing and from some knowledge of the police reports. Colonel
Ojukwu himself accepted a figure of 10,000 dead at the Aburi talks.
Secessionist propaganda later raised the figures. But they are bad
enough already without being inflated.

8. The Ibo insistence that the North had 'a common determination'
and that states in the North would 'only be on paper' can be seen in
Ojukwu's speech to the Eastern Consultative Body at Enugu on the
31st August, 1966. The text of this speech is reproduced in *Crisis 1966:
Eastern Nigerian Viewpoint* (Enugu: Ministry of Information, 1967),
pp. 33–37. At the September constitutional conference when the
Northern delegation opted for the creation of more states in the country, the Eastern delegation declared that it did "not believe that the
splitting of the country into more states at this stage" was needed and
that "immediate constitutional arrangements for the country as a
whole should be made on the basis of the existing Regions". *Crisis
1966,* p. 61.

9. I am not holding that all the non-Ibo communities were opposed to
secession. Undoubtedly some Ijaw groups and many Efik (though
hardly any Ibibio) preferred to stand with the Ibo. But these groups
were small alongside the massive opposition. The indications of this
opposition seem to me clear from several factors (apart from personal
acquaintance with many individuals from the Eastern minority
areas): the patterns of electoral voting in the earlier and relatively
free Eastern elections were anti-Ibo in the minority communities;
abundant evidence was put before the Minorities Commission to show
that these groups wanted a state or states of their own; Ojukwu himself conceded that their areas had been neglected and that their peoples were alienated from the Enugu government; very few non-Ibo
Easterners responded to the call to return home during 1966–67; the Ibo
leaders placed Ibo officers effectively in charge of the security forces
in minority areas once the crisis became acute; Ibo security officers
employed considerable brutality against the minority groups; and the
federal troops had little trouble in re-taking these areas compared to
the difficulties they faced in taking over Ibo areas.

10. The documents submitted to the September constitutional conference can be found in *Memoranda submitted by the delegations to the
Ad Hoc Conference on constitutional proposals for Nigeria.* Government Printer, Lagos, 1966.

11. H. Seton-Watson, *Neither Peace Nor War* (New York: Praeger,
1960), p. 182.

12. B. Crick, *In Defence of Politics* (Chicago: University of Chicago
Press, 1962), p. 167.

CHAPTER 25

Conclusion: Communal Conflict and Communal War

Earlier it was suggested that as modernization transforms the nature of communal groups it creates imbalances in wealth, status and power among them. The effects of modernization, linked to those of political regionalism, promoted communal conflict in Nigeria. But communal conflict need not mean coup d'etat, coup d'etat need not mean secession, and secession need not mean civil war. In this concluding section we would like to touch on some factors which seem to transmute communal conflict into communal war in societies such as Nigeria.

In tracing the proximate causes of the civil war, Sklar and O'Connell take to task the political ineptitude of the leadership of the first coup (January 1966). This regime, it is suggested, tried to substitute administrative fiat for politics and in this it failed. Its attempt to abolish the Regions without creating new states was seen in the North as an attempt at domination by the South. For in a unified Nigeria with a unified civil service would it not be the better educated and hence more qualified Southerners who would ultimately wield power? Similarly, Major General Aguiyi-Ironsi's failure immediately to release Chief Awolowo from jail, and his failure to prosecute the Ibo officers who were responsible for the assassination of senior military officers of Yoruba lineage, in time compromised the regime as being "Ibo dominated." It is not surprising, therefore, that when the second coup occurred (July 1966), it was resisted by few non-Ibo Nigerians. Yet, it was the events which followed upon the second coup which were the primary precipitants of secession and civil war.

O'Connell and Sklar both argue convincingly that the pattern of political violence, whereby Ibos in the North were set upon first in May and then in September of 1966 played into the hands of separatists in the Eastern Region and undercut any possibilities for compromise. In that sense, events which were not necessarily predictable from the structure of regionalism and communalism had decisive effects on subsequent developments. Who could have predicted the extent and ferocity of the pogroms which saw thousands of Ibo civilians killed in the North? This question calls our attention to the fact that while social scientists may have some notion as to the roots of communal antagonisms we as yet know very little about those factors which transform pacific competition into violent conflict. It might be noted, however, that in the Nigerian case a pattern of intergroup relations which has been seen to operate in Europe and in Asia repeated itself with deadly consequences. This pattern seems to involve ten variables at the following settings 1) Competition—Extensive; 2) Insecurity—High; 3) Dehumanization—Widely accepted; 4) Inter-Communal Communication—Broken; 5) Information—Low; 6) Rumors—Widely Diffused and Extensively Accepted; 7) Authority—Absent or Tacitly Approving of Violence; 8) Instruments of Violence—Readily Available; 9) Institutions of Control and Retribution—Distant and Ineffective; 10) Instruments of Self-Defense—Not Available to Attacked Group.

Sklar, R. Cohen, O'Connell and Paden all testify as to the extensive competition in the North which preceded the first coup and the high level of insecurity which followed it. With regard to "dehumanization," O'Connell states that the Ibos were perceived as "a privileged pariah group whose members were hated because they benefited from the modernizing process and who could be killed because they were outside the rank system of society and so were less-than-human." As to a pattern of broken communication and low information, Paden, Dent and Plotnicov have alerted us to the low level of inter-communal tolerance and understanding present in the North as between the Ibos and the Northern peoples. As to authority being distant or tacitly approving, we have the testimony of Paden, Dent and R. Cohen, who indicate that even where the Northern leadership was not actively encouraging of violence it did very little to stop it. It is significant that when the first killings took place in the North in May, the leadership of Bornu made clear that it disapproved of violence, with the consequence that there were no killings in Bornu. Finally, O'Connell and others indicate that many of the killings were perpetrated by armed Northern soldiers, with the Federal government too distant and ineffective to intervene.

Though the pogroms of May and September were terrible in terms of the human costs, they had political consequences which at the time were probably unintended. It was not only the extent of the riots, it was also their timing which proved so crucial for the political disintegration of the Federation. Coming at a time when Nigerians were attempting to reconstitute their commonwealth, they played into the hands of separatists who could argue with some credibility that the life and property of their communal groups could not be protected in one Nigeria. The Eastern fears of discrimination and victimization were very keenly felt. One suspects that it was these fears, together with a genuine national identity carved out of violent conflict, which kept the Biafrans fighting so valiantly for so long.

On the Nigerian side, political motivations were similarly mixed. On the one hand, many federal leaders were genuinely committed to the ideal of one Nigeria. On the other hand, there were the more pragmatic considerations that the internal stability of Federal Nigeria and the new found power of the minorities within Federal Nigeria were both gravely threatened by the Biafran secession. Indeed, one of the truly extraordinary results of the second coup was the emergence of the previously suppressed minorities into positions of control within the army and within the federal government. To the leaders of such minorities it had been clear for a long time that their fortunes and the fortunes of their communal groups depended greatly on an equilibrium provided by competition of many groups in a large federation. As suggested earlier, it was better to be a minority in a large federation inclusive of Biafrans than to be a minority in a small state of few competing groups. It is one of the many ironies of the Nigerian tragedy that as soon as competitive politics is reintroduced into Nigeria, the peoples of the former breakaway region will likely find ready allies among some of their most bitter critics.

To the extent that governments and international organizations, such as the Organization of African Unity, are in the business of preventing tragedies on the Nigerian scale, they might take heed of O'Connell's suggestion that the politics of culturally plural developing areas must become the politics of active conciliation. Organizations responsible for the well being of communal societies must intervene firmly and rapidly to break the vicious cycle of communal conflict which ultimately can lead to communal violence. Efforts must be made by such agencies to defuse communal insecurities; to counteract the spread of dehumanizing stereotypes; to encourage the extension, fidelity, and sensitivity of inter-communal communications; and to prevent the distribution of instruments of violence among communal antagonists. Finally, there must be a clear recognition that the gravest danger to communal peace are governments which use their instruments of rule, violence and communication to pit one communal group against another in a too often successful attempt to perpetuate and extend their power.

CONTRIBUTORS

DAVID B. ABERNETHY is Associate Professor of Political Science and University Fellow at Stanford University. He recently completed a year as Visiting Lecturer at University College, Dar es Salaam. He is the author of *The Political Dilemma of Popular Education: An African Case*, and is currently focusing on the political and administrative aspects of development planning in Africa.

ABNER COHEN is Lecturer in African Sociology at the School of Oriental and African Studies, University of London. He is the author of *Custom and Politics in Urban Africa: A Study of Hausa Migrants in Yoruba Towns.*

RONALD COHEN is Professor of Anthropology and Political Science at Northwestern University. He is the co-editor of *From Tribe to Nation in Africa* and is the author of a forthcoming book on Kanuri marriage and divorce, *Dominance and Defiance.*

JAMES S. COLEMAN is Director of the Institute for Development Studies, University College, Kenya. He is the author of *Nigeria: Background to Nationalism*, the co-editor of *The Politics of the Developing Areas* and *Political Parties and National Integration in Tropical Africa*, and has published several articles within the fields of African politics and political development.

MARTIN J. DENT is Lecturer in the Department of Politics at Keele University. He served as an Assistant District Officer and as District Officer in Tiv, Kano and Bauchi Divisions within Northern Nigeria from 1952 to 1961. He is presently writing a book for the Royal Institute of International affairs on *The Military and the Political Process. Nigeria 1966–1967.*

JOHN R. HARRIS is Associate Professor of Economics and Urban Studies at the Massachusetts Institute of Technology and is Associate Director of the Institute's Special Program for Urban and Regional Studies in Developing Areas. He was an Associate Research Fellow of the Nigerian Institute for Social and Economic Research, 1965 and a Visiting Research Fellow at the Institute for Development Studies, University College, Nairobi, 1968–69. He has published widely on the subjects of entrepreneurship and urbanization in developing countries.

RICHARD N. HENDERSON is Associate Professor of Anthropology at Yale University. He is the author of the forthcoming *Every Man A King: Evolutionary Trends in Onitsha Ibo Society and Culture.*

ULF HIMMELSTRAND is Professor of Sociology at the University of Uppsala. Between 1964 and 1967 he was Professor of Sociology at the University of Ibadan.

ROBERT A. LEVINE is Professor of Human Development and Anthropology at the University of Chicago. He is the author of *Dreams and Deeds: Achievement Motivation in Nigeria* and *Nyansongo: A Gusi Community in Kenya.*

ALVIN MAGID is Associate Professorof Political Science at the State Univeristy of New York at Albany. He is co-editor of *Poverty: New Interdisciplinary Perspectives* and the author of a forthcoming book, *Men in the Middle: Leadership and Conflict in a Nigerian Society,* and of numerous articles within the fields of African politics and political development.

ROBERT MELSON is Associate Professor of Political Science at Purdue University and a former member of the Political Science Department and African Studies Center at Michigan State University. His most recent work on communalism and ideology has been published in the *American Political Science Review.*

JAMES O'CONNELL is Chairman of the Department of Government at Ahmadu Bello Univeristy, Zaria, and a former member of the faculty of the University College, Ibadan. He has written extensively on politics and social change in Africa.

JOHN N. PADEN is Associate Professor of Political Science at Northwestern University. He is a co-author and co-editor of the four volume work, *The African Experience,* and the author of the forthcoming *Religion and Political Culture in Kano.*

ALAN PESHKIN is Professor of Comparative Education at the University of Illinois. His particular research interest concerns the contribution of schooling to modern value-orientations, and he has recently completed the forthcoming book, *The Kanuri Schoolchildren: Education and Social Mobilization in Nigeria.*

LEONARD PLOTNICOV is Professor and Chairman of the Department of Anthropology at the University of Pittsburgh. He is co-editor of *Social Stratification in Africa,* co-editor of *Comparative Social Stratification,* and author of *Strangers to the City: Jos, Nigeria.*

MARY P. ROWE is a consulting economist on two Office of Economic Opportunity projects in the Cambridge, Massachusetts area, and is the co-author of a forthcoming volume on the economics of child care. She has published several ariticles on the subject of Nigerian entrepreneurship.

RICHARD L. SKLAR is Professor of Political Science at the University of California, Los Angeles. His publications include *Nigerian Political Parties: Power in an Emergent African Nation,* and numerous contributions to scholarly books and journals. He has taught at the University of Ibadan and the University of Zambia.

AUDREY CHAPMAN SMOCK, formerly Assistant Professor of Government at Barnard College, is Research Associate of the Institute of African Studies at Columbia University. She has done field work in Nigeria and Ghana and is the author of *Ibo Politics* (Harvard University Press, forthcoming), and editor of *Institutionalization and Mobilization.*

C. S. WHITAKER is Professor in the Politics Department, on the faculty of the Woodrow Wilson School, and head of the Afro-American Studies Program at Princeton University. His most recent book is *The Politics of Tradition: Continuity and Change in Northern Nigeria 1964–1966.*

HOWARD WOLPE is Associate Professor of Political Science at Western Michigan University. His articles on communalism and African urbanization appear in the *Journal of Modern African Studies* and the *American Political Science Review.*